Reduce your buildings and contents insurance

At BURKE FINE ART & JEWELLERY LIMITED we can now offer a *specialised* insurance policy which is only available for home owners with a required sum insured between £150,000 and £10,000,000 covering your home, contents, fine art and jewellery. In return for accepting a small deductible (minimum of £250), and providing a reasonable level of security in your home, our policy will offer you the *broadest coverage available*, and give you substantial premium *reductions* – in some cases 40% or more. In addition to this special policy we also offer a range of policies catering for personal fine art and jewellery, art galleries, museums and exhibitions.

BURKE FINE ART & JEWELLERY LIMITED is a specialist insurance broker insuring risks in the Lloyd's and London insurance markets. Our team of *experts* dealing in the fine art and personal insurance sector are well aware of the fact that prompt, *personal service* still has a major part to play in the field of insurance. Many of our competitors have lost this edge in the days of major insurance institutions.

We are here to *help and advise,* and through our extensive network of contacts are able to offer the *highest* standard of guidance with relation to such matters as security, valuations and risk assessment. Continuity of service is ensured as each account is the responsibility of a specialist team led by one of our senior account managers. We fully understand the need for *confidentiality* in respect of all your insurance needs.

We also firmly believe that claims settlement is equally as important as placing the original insurance policy, and we will ensure a *speedy and professional* settlement in each case.

Our Home and Contents policy is fully underwritten by certain Underwriters at Lloyd's of London.

Compare our policy with your existing policy.

Our Policy offers:

Accidental Damage Coverage:
for Buildings and Contents, Fine Art, Personal Jewellery and Possessions is automatically included at no additional premium.

Worldwide Coverage:
for Contents, Fine Art, Personal Jewellery and Possessions is automatically included.

Contents and Fine Art:
Only items in excess of £15,000 need to be listed separately.

Personal Possessions/Jewellery:
Only items in excess of £5,000 need to be listed separately.

Excess or Deductible:
Your chosen excess, or deductible *only applies* to section A) Buildings, and section B)(i) General Contents, and not to any other section except losses due to subsidence. In addition you should note that the excess or deductible does not apply to claims settled for more than £10,000 except for subsidence claims, where the excess of £1,000 each and every loss will always apply.

The role of an Insurance Broker

As your broker, we are your agent, and as such are duty bound to ensure that we provide you with the *broadest coverage* at the most *competitive premium* available whilst using only those insurers with the highest financial standing and reputation for settling claims. You can be sure that by contacting us, we will give you *independent advice* and our *full support* in ensuring that in the unfortunate event of a claim, we will obtain a quick and satisfactory settlement.

For further information on our complete range of services please contact:

Gary Burke,
Jonathan Merritt,
Quentin Holland
or John Callant

136 Sloane Street, London SW1X 9AY
Telephone 071 824 8224 Facsimile 071 730 0466.

BURKE FINE ART
& JEWELLERY LIMITED

MILLER'S
Picture
PRICE GUIDE

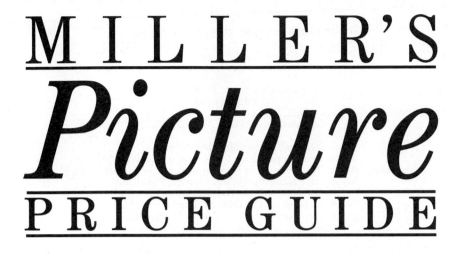

MILLER'S *Picture* PRICE GUIDE

Consultants
Judith and Martin Miller

General Editor
Madeleine Marsh

1995
Volume III

MILLER'S PICTURE PRICE GUIDE 1995

Created and designed by
Miller's Publications
The Cellars, High Street,
Tenterden, Kent, TN30 6BN
Tel: 0580 766411

Consultants: Judith & Martin Miller

General Editor: Madeleine Marsh
Editorial and Production Co-ordinator: Sue Boyd
Editorial Assistants: Gail Jessel, Sue Montgomery, Marion Rickman, Jo Wood
Production Assistants: Gillian Charles, Helen Burt
Advertising Executive: Liz Warwick
Index compiled by: DD Editorial Services, Beccles
Design: Stephen Parry, Jody Taylor, Darren Manser
Photographers: Ian Booth, Robin Saker

First published in Great Britain in 1994
by Miller's, an imprint of
Reed Consumer Books Limited,
Michelin House, 81 Fulham Road,
London SW3 6RB
and Auckland, Melbourne, Singapore and Toronto

© 1994 Reed International Books Limited

A CIP catalogue record for this book is
available from the British Library

ISBN 1-85732-342-4

Bromide output by Perfect Image, Hurst Green, E. Sussex
Illustrations by G.H. Graphics, St. Leonards-on-Sea
Colour origination by Scantrans, Singapore
Printed and bound in England by William Clowes Ltd.,
Beccles and London

Front Cover Illustrations:
Top. *John William Godward (1861–1922) – A Souvenir.* **£85,000–95,000** *S*
Bottom left: *Thomas Moran (1837–1926) – The Grand Canal, Venice.* **£32,000–35,000** *S(NY)*
Bottom right: *Gail Lilley (20thC) – The Blue Jug.* **£300–500** *RMG*

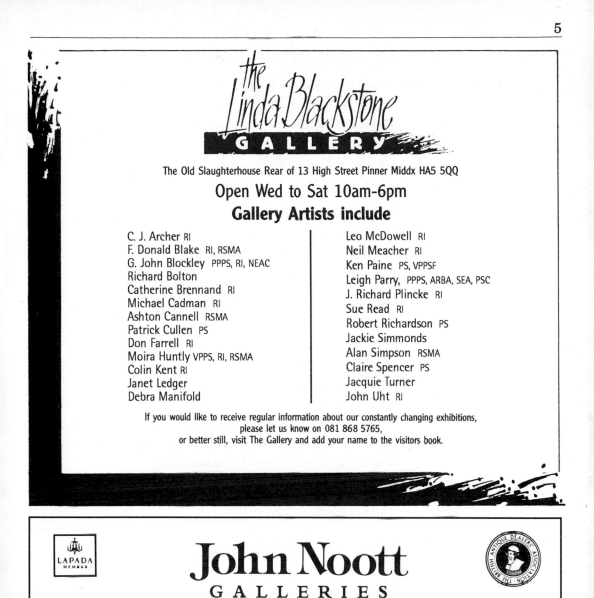

6

ACKNOWLEDGEMENTS

**The publishers would like to acknowledge the great assistance
given by our consultants:**

John Brandler	Brandler Galleries, 1 Coptfold Road, Brentwood, Essex.
Gary Burke	Burke Fine Art & Jewellery Ltd., 136 Sloane Street, London SW1.
Alistair Laird	Bonham's, Montpelier Street, Knightsbridge, London SW7.
Michael Leslie, A.B.P.R.	The Garden Studio, Denniker Cottage, Fletching, Uckfield, Sussex.
James Lloyd	Burlington Paintings, 12 Burlington Gardens, London W1.
Susan May	Arnold Wiggins & Sons, 4 Bury Street, London SW1.
Paul Mitchell	Paul Mitchell Ltd., 99 New Bond Street, London W1.
John Morton Lee	John Morton Lee Fine Watercolours, Cedar House, Bacon Lane, Hayling Island, Hants.
David Moore-Gwynne	Sotheby's, 34–35 New Bond Street, London W1.
John Noott	John Noott Galleries, 14 Cotswold Court, Broadway, Worcs.
Caroline Oliphant	Bonham's, Montpelier Street, Knightsbridge, London SW7.
Nick Potter	Burlington Gallery, 10 Burlington Gardens, London W1.
Bernard Reed	Marine Watercolours. Tel: 0372 272374.
Crispian Riley-Smith	Phillips, Blenstock House, 101 New Bond Street, London W1.
John Stainton	Christie Manson & Wood, 8 King Street, St. James's, London SW1.
Dr. Robert Travers	Piano Nobile Fine Paintings, 26 Richmond Hill, Richmond, Surrey.
Eugene Traynor	Bonham's, 65–69 Lots Road, London SW10.
Christopher Wood	Christopher Wood Gallery, 141 New Bond Street, London W1.

KEY TO ILLUSTRATIONS

Each illustration and descriptive caption is accompanied by a letter code. By reference to the following list of Auctioneers (denoted by *) and Dealers (•) the source of any item may be immediately determined. In no way does this constitute or imply a contract or binding offer on the part of any of our contributors to supply or sell the goods illustrated, or similar articles, at the prices stated. Advertisers in this year's directory are denoted by †.

A • Alma Gallery, 31a Rivers Street, Bath. Tel: 01225 317060

AAV * Academy Auctioneers & Valuers, Northcote House, Northcote Avenue, Ealing, London W5. Tel: 0181-579 7466

ABA • Anna Bornholt Associates, 3-5 Weighhouse Street, London W1. Tel: 0171-499 6114

AdG • Adam Gallery, 13 John Street, Bath.

AG * Anderson & Garland (Auctioneers), Marlborough House, Marlborough Crescent, Newcastle-upon-Tyne. Tel: 0191-232 6278

AH *† Andrew Hartley, Victoria Hall, Little Lane, Ilkley, W. Yorks. Tel: 01943 816363

ALG • Alberti Gallery, 114 Albert Street, London NW1. Tel: 0171-485 8976

AMC • Anna-Mei Chadwick, 64 New Kings Road, London SW6. Tel: 0171-736 1928

BCG •† Betley Court Gallery, Betley, Nr. Crewe, Cheshire. Tel: 01270 820652

Bea * Bearnes, Rainbow, Avenue Road, Torquay, Devon. Tel: 01803 296277

BIR • Birchall's, Cotebrook, Tarporley, Cheshire. Tel: 01829 760754

BLD • Unit 10, Canalside Studios, 2 Orsman Road, London N1. Tel: 0171-739 4383

Bne •† Bourne Gallery Ltd., 31/33 Lesbourne Road, Reigate, Surrey. Tel: 01737 241614

Bon * Bonhams, Montpelier Galleries, Montpelier Street, London SW7. Tel: 0171-584 9161

BOU • Boundary Gallery, 98 Boundary Road, London NW8. Tel: 0171-624 1126

BRG •† Brandler Galleries, 1 Coptfold Road, Brentwood, Essex. Tel: 01277 222269

Bri * Bristol Auction Rooms, St John's Place, Apsley Road, Clifton, Bristol. Tel: 0117 973 7201

BuP •† Burlington Fine Paintings Ltd., 12 Burlington Gardens, London W1. Tel: 0171-734 9984

Bur •† Burlington Gallery, 10 Burlington Gardens, London W1. Tel: 0171-734 9228/9984

BWe * Biddle and Webb, Ladywood Middleway, Birmingham. Tel: 0121-455 8042

C * Christie, Manson & Woods Ltd., 8 King Street, St James's, London SW1. Tel: 0171-839 9060

C(S) * Christie's Scotland Ltd., 164-166 Bath Street, Glasgow. Tel: 0141-332 8134

CAG *† Canterbury Auction Galleries, 40 Station Road West, Canterbury, Kent. Tel: 01227 763337

CAS • Castle Gallery. Tel: 01926 58727

CAT •† Catto Animation, 41 Heath Street, London NW3. Tel: 0171-431 2892

CBL • Chris Beetles Ltd, 8 & 10 Ryder Street, St James's, London SW1. Tel: 0171-839 7551

CCA • CCA Galleries, 8 Dover Street, London W1. Tel: 0171-499 6701

CCG • Cynthia O'Connor Gallery, 17 Duke Street, Dublin 2 Tel: 00353-1-6792177/6792198

CDC * Capes Dunn & Co., The Auction Galleries, 38 Charles Street, off Princess Street, Manchester. Tel: 0161-273 6060

CE • Century Gallery, 100/102 Fulham Road, London SW3. Tel: 0171-581 1589

CFA • Cooper Fine Arts, 768 Fulham Road, London SW6. Tel: 0171-731 3421

CG •† Coltsfoot Gallery, Hatfield, Leominster, Herefordshire. Tel: 01568 82277

CGa •† Cobham Galleries, 65 Portsmouth Road, Cobham, Surrey. Tel: 01932 867909

Ch • Churzee Studio Gallery, 17 Bellevue Road, London SW17. Tel: 0181-767 8113

ChG • Charterhouse Gallery Ltd., 14 Birds Heath, Leighton Buzzard, Beds. Tel: 01522 523 379

CNY * Christie, Manson & Woods International Inc., 502 Park Avenue, New York, NY 10022, USA. Tel: (212) 546 1000 (including Christie's East)

CON •† The Contemporary Fine Art Gallery, 31 High Street, Eton, Windsor, Berkshire. Tel: 01753 854315

CSG • Church Street Gallery, Stow-on-the-Wold, Glos. Tel: 01451 831698

CSK * Christie's South Kensington Ltd., 85 Old Brompton Road, London SW7. Tel: 0171-581 7611

CSKe • Corrigan, Sandby and Kerraiduti, 55 Eton High Street, Eton, Berks.

CW • Christopher Wood Gallery, 141 New Bond Street, London W1. Tel: 0171-499 7411

DA * Dee Atkinson & Harrison, The Exchange Saleroom, Driffield, East Yorks. Tel: 01377 253151

DN * Dreweatt Neate, Donnington Priory, Donnington, Newbury, Berks. Tel: 01635 31234

Dr •† Driffold Gallery, 78 Birmingham Road, Sutton Coldfield, West Midlands. Tel: 0121-355 5433

DrG • Drew Gallery, 16 Best Lane, Canterbury, Kent. Tel: 01227 458759

EAG • Equus Art Gallery, Sun Lane, Newmarket. Tel: 01638 560445

EG •† Ealing Gallery, 78 St. Mary's Road, London W5. Tel: 0181-840 7883

ELR * Eadon Lockwood & Riddle, 411 Petre Street, Sheffield Tel: 0114 261 8000

F * Francis Fine Art Auctioneers, The Tristar Business Centre, Star Industrial Estate, Partridge Green, Horsham, Sussex. Tel: 01403 710567

FCG • Flying Colours Gallery, 35 William Street, Edinburgh. Tel: 0131-225 6776

FdeL •† Fleur de Lys Gallery, 227a Westbourne Grove, London W11. Tel: 0171-727 8595

FGL • Frinton Gallery Ltd., 145 Connaught Avenue, Frinton-on-Sea, Essex. Tel: 01255 673707

FL • Fine Lines Fine Art Ltd., The Old Rectory, 31 Sheep Street, Shipston-on-Stour, Warwickshire. Tel: 01608 662323

FT • The Florence Trust, St. Saviour's Church, Aberdeen Park, Highbury, London N5. Tel: 0171-354 0460

FWA * F. W. Allen & Son, Central Salerooms, 15 Station Road, Cheadle Hulme, Cheshire. Tel: 0161-485 4121

G •† Gavels, 3 Station Road, Long Preston, N. Yorks. Tel: 01729 840384

GAK *† G. A. Key, 8 Market Place, Aylsham, Norwich, Norfolk. Tel: 01263 733195

Gan • Gandolfi House, 211-213 Wells Road, Malvern Wells, Hereford & Worcs. Tel: 01684 569747

GCP • Graham Clarke (Prints) Ltd., White Cottage, Green Lane, Boughton Monchelsea, Maidstone, Kent. Tel: 01622 743938

GG •† Graham Gallery, 1 Castle Street, Tunbridge Wells, Kent. Tel: 01892 526695

GH * Giles Haywood, The Auction House, St. Johns Road, Stourbridge, W. Midlands. Tel: 01384 370891

GK • Gallery Kaleidoscope, 64/66 Willesden Lane, London NW6. Tel: 0171-328 5833

GL • George Large Gallery, 13/14 Margaret Place, Woburn, Beds. Tel: 01525 290658

GPS • Glasgow Print Studio, 22 King St., Glasgow. Tel: 0141 552 0704

Gra • Graham Gallery, Highwoods, Burghfield, Nr Reading, Berkshire. Tel: 01734 832320

GRO •† Grosvenor Gallery, 18 Albemarle Street, London W1. Tel: 0171-629 0891

HaG • The Hart Gallery, 23 Main Street, Linby, Nottingham. Tel: 0115 963 8707

HALC• Halton Court, Alkham, Nr. Dover, Kent.

HC • Heritage Classics, Heritage Cottage, London Road, Marks Tey, Colchester, Essex. Tel: 01206 211954

HFA •† Haynes Fine Art, The Bindery Gallery, 69 High Street, Broadway, Worcester. Tel: 01386 852649

HFFA• Hamilton Forbes Fine Art, The Garden Market, Chelsea Harbour, London SW10. Tel: 0171-352 8181

HI •† Hicks Gallery, 2 Leopold Road, Wimbledon, London SW19. Tel: 0181-944 7171

HLG •† Hayloft Gallery, Berry Wormington, Broadway, Worcs. Tel: 01242 621202

HO •† Angela Hone, The Garth, Mill Road, Marlow, Buckinghamshire. Tel: 01628 484170

HOLL* Holloways, 49 Parsons Street, Banbury, Oxon. Tel: 01295 253197

HSS * Henry Spencer and Sons, 20 The Square, Retford, Notts. Tel: 01777 708633

IM *† Ibbett Mosely, 125 High Street, Sevenoaks, Kent. Tel: 01732 452246

JA • Jenny Asplund Fine Art. Tel: 01372 464960 (By Appointment)

JAR • Jarrotts, Hales Place, Woodchurch Road, High Halden, Kent. Tel: 01233 850037

JBA • John Bonham, Murray Feely Fine Art, 46 Porchester Road, London W2. Tel: 0171-221 7208

JC • J Collins & Son, The Studio, 63 & 28 High Street, Bideford, Devon. Tel: 01237 473103

JD *† Julian Dawson. Lewes Auction Rooms, 56 High Street, Lewes, Sussex. Tel: 01237 478221

JDG • John Denham Gallery, 50 Mill Lane, London NW6. Tel: 0171-794 2635

JG •† Jerram Gallery, 7 St John Street, Salisbury, Wilts. Tel: 01722 412310

JGA • Jigger (Golf Art), 3 Sunny Hill, Kirton-in-Lindsey, Gainsborough, Lincs. Tel: 01652 640118

JJ • Janet Judge, 24a Argyle Avenue, Hounslow, Middlesex. Tel: 0181-898 8939

JML • J. Morton Lee, Cedar House, Bacon Lane, Hayling Island, Hants. Tel: 01705 464444. (By appointment)

JN •† John Noott Fine Paintings, 14 Cotswold Court, Broadway, Worcester. Tel: 01386 852787

JNic *† John Nicholson, The Auction Rooms, Longfield, Midhurst Road, Fernhurst, Haslemere, Surrey. Tel: 01428 653727

JS • James Starkey Fine Art International, Highgate, Beverley, North Yorks. Tel: 01482 881179

KHG • Kentmere House Gallery, 53 Scarcroft Hill, York. Tel: 01904 656507

L * Lawrence Fine Art Auctioneers, South Street, Crewkerne, Somerset. Tel: 01460 73041

L&E * Locke & England, Black Horse Agencies, 18 Guy Street, Leamington Spa, Warwicks. Tel: 01926 889100

LA • Llewellyn Alexander (Fine Paintings) Ltd., 124-126 The Cut, Waterloo, London SE1. Tel: 0171-620 1322

Lan • Lantern Gallery, 27 Holland Street, London W8. Tel: 0171-937 8649

LANG* Langlois, Westaway Chambers, Don Street, St Helier, Jersey. Tel: 01534 22441

LF * Lambert & Foster, 102 High Street, Tenterden, Kent. Tel: 01580 763233

LFA • Lincoln Fine Art, 33 The Strait, Lincoln. Tel: 01522 533029

LH • †Laurence Hallett Tel: 0171-798 8977

LIO • Lions Den, 11 St. Mary's Crescent, Leamington Spa, Warks. Tel: 01926 339498

LRG * Lots Road Chelsea Auction Galleries, 71 Lots Road, London SW10. Tel: 0171-351 7771

LS • Lotus House Studios, 25 Station Road, Lydd, Romney Marsh, Kent. Tel: 01797 320585

LT * Louis Taylor Auctioneers & Valuers, Britannia House, 10 Town Road, Hanley, Stoke-on-Trent. Tel: 01782 214111

LW • Lawrences Auctioneers, Norfolk House, 80 High Street, Bletchingley, Surrey. Tel: 01883 743323

LyB Lynne Broberg. Tel: 01889 270234

Mar •† Marine Watercolours. Tel: 01372 272374

MBA • 4 Miles Buildings Fine Art & Antiques, 4 Miles Buildings, (off George St), Bath.

MCA * Mervyn Carey, Twysden Cottage, Benenden, Cranbrook, Kent. Tel: 01580 240283

MEA * Mealy's, Chatsworth Street, Castle Comer, Co. Kilkenny, S. Ireland. Tel: 0035356 41229

Mer • Merz Contemporary Art, 62 Kenway Rd., London SW5. Tel: 0171-244 6008

MGK • M. Gauss Keown. Tel: 01303 248694

MI • Manya Igel Fine Arts Ltd., 21-22 Peters Court, Porchester Rd, London W2. Tel: 0171-229 1669

Mit * Mitchells, Fairfield House, Station Road, Cockermouth, Cumbria. Tel: 01900 827800

Mon • Montpelier Studio, 4 Montpelier St., London SW7.

MSh • Manfred Schotten, The Crypt Antiques, 109 High Street, Burford, Oxon. Tel: 01993 822302

MSW *† Marilyn Swain, The Old Barracks, Sandon Road, Grantham. Tel: 01476 68861

MT • Martin Tinney Gallery, 6 Windsor Place, Cardiff. Tel: 01222 641411

MTG • Music Theatre Gallery, 1 Elystan Place, London SW3. Tel: 0171-823 9880

MWe • Michael Webb Fine Art, Cefn-Llwyn, Bodorgan, Anglesey, Gwynedd. Tel: 01407 840336

NAG • New Apollo Gallery, 17/18 Duke Street, Dublin 2, Ireland. Tel: 00353-1- 6712609

NBO • Nicholas Bowlby, 9 Castle Street, Tunbridge Wells, Kent. Tel: 01892 510880

NZ •† Nina Zborowska, Damsels Mill, Paradise, Painswick, Glos. Tel: 01452 812460

OLG • On Line Gallery, 76 Bedford Place, Southampton, Hants. Tel: 01703 330660

Om • Omell Galleries, Goswell Hill, 134 Peascod Street, Windsor, Berks. Tel: 01753 852271

OSG • Oliver Swann Gallery, 170 Walton Street, London SW3. Tel: 0171-581 4229

P * Phillips, Blenstock House, 101 New Bond Street, London W1. Tel: 0171-629 6602

P(S) * Phillips, 49 London Road, Sevenoaks, Kent. Tel: 01732 740310

PBG • Penn Barn Gallery, By The Pond, Elm Road, Penn, Bucks. Tel: 01494 815691

PCA • Peter Cardiff Fine Art Tel: 0171-736 5916

PCh * Peter Cheney, Western Road Auction Rooms, Western Road, Littlehampton, Sussex. Tel: 01903 722264/713418

PG • Portland Gallery, 9 Bury Street, St James's, London SW1. Tel: 0171-321 0422

PHG •† Peter Hedley Gallery, 10 South Street, Wareham, Dorset. Tel: 01929 551777

PN • Piano Nobile Fine Paintings, 26 Richmond Hill, Richmond-upon-Thames, Surrey. Tel/fax: 0181-940 2435

RA • Roberts Antiques. Tel: 01253 827794

RB •† Roger Billcliffe Fine Art, 134 Blythswood Street, Glasgow. Tel: 0141-332 4027

RBB * Russell, Baldwin & Bright, Fine Art Salerooms, Rylands Road, Leominster, Hereford. Tel: 01568-611166

RGFA •† Roger Green Fine Art, Hales Place Studio, High Halden, Ashford, Kent. Tel: 01233 850794

RMG • Roy Miles Gallery, 29 Bruton Street, London W1. Tel: 0171-495 4747

RS Richardson & Smith, 8 Victoria Square, Whitby. Tel: 01947 602298

S * Sotheby's, 34-35 New Bond Street, London W1. Tel: 0171-493 8080

S(Am) * Sotheby's Amsterdam, Rokin 102, 1012 KZ Amsterdam. Tel: 31 (20) 627 5656

S(NY) * Sotheby's, 1334 York Avenue, New York NY 10021, USA. Tel: 212 606 7000

S(S) * Sotheby's Sussex, Summers Place, Billingshurst, Sussex. Tel: 01403-783933

SAV •† The Saville Row Gallery, 1 Saville Row, Alfred Street, Bath. Tel: 01225 334595

SBG • Stephen Bartley Gallery, 62 Old Church Street, London SW3. Tel: 0171-352 8686

SG • Savannah Gallery, 45 Derbyshire Street, London E2. Tel: 0171 613 0474

SHF • Sally Hunter Fine Art. Tel: 0171-235 0934

SJG • St. James's Gallery, 9 Margaret Buildings, Brock Street, Bath. Tel: 01225-319197

SK * Skinner Inc, The Heritage On The Garden, 63 Park Plaza, Boston, MA 02116 USA. Tel: 617 350 5400

SLN * Sloan's, C.G. Sloan & Company Inc., 4920 Wyaconda Road, North Bethesda, MD 20852, USA. Tel: 301 468 4911/669 5066

SMi • Sally Mitchell Fine Arts, Thornlea, Askham, Newark, Notts. Tel: 01777 838234

SOL •† The Solomon Gallery, Powerscourt Townhouse Centre, South William Street, Dublin 2. Tel: 00353-1-6794237

SRAB • Sarah Russell Antiquarian Books & Prints, 11 Oxford Row, Lansdown Road, Bath. Tel: 01225 427594

SRB • Susan and Robert Botting, Rosedene, 38 Firs Avenue, Felpham, Sussex. Tel: 01243 584515

STA • Michelina & George Stacpoole, Main St. Adare, Co. Limerick, Ireland. Tel: 00353-61-396409

STD • Stern Art Dealers, 49 Ledbury Road, London W11. Tel: 0171-229 6184

TAB • Tabor Gallery, The Barn, All Saints Lane, Canterbury.

TAG • Taylor Galleries, 34 Kildare Street, Dublin 2. Tel: 00353-1-6766055

TAY * Taylors, Honiton Galleries, 205 High Street, Honiton, Devon.

TER • Terrace Antiques, 10 & 12 South Ealing Road, London W5. Tel: 0181-557 5194/567 1223

TFA • Turtle Fine Art, 30 Suffolk Parade, Cheltenham, Glos. Tel: 01242 241646

THG •† The Hunt Gallery, 33 The Strand, Sandwich, Kent. Tel: 01304 612792

Tho • Thompson Gallery, 38 Albemarle Street, London W1. Tel: 0171-499 1314

TLB • †The Linda Blackstone Gallery, The Old Slaughterhouse, Rear of 13 High Street, Pinner, Middlesex. Tel: 0181-868 5765

TOT • The Totteridge Gallery, 61 Totteridge Lane, London N20. Tel: 0181-446 7896

Tr • Treadwell's, Upper Park Gate, Bradford. Tel: 01274 306065/306064

TRG • Thackeray Rankin Gallery, 18 Thackeray Street, London W8. Tel: 0171-937 5883

ULG • Upton Lodge Galleries, 6 Long Street, Tetbury, Glos. Tel: 01666 503416. Also at Avening House, Avening, Tetbury.

VCG •† Vicarage Cottage Gallery, Preston Road, Northshields. Tel: 0191-257 0935

WFA •† Wimbledon Fine Art, 41 Church Road, Wimbledon Village, London SW19. Tel: 0181-944 6593

WG • Walker Galleries, 6 Montpelier Gardens, Harrogate, Yorks. Tel: 01423 567933

WH •* William Hardie Ltd, 114 West Regent St., Glasgow. Tel: 0141-221 6780

WHL * W. H. Lane & Son, 65 Morrab Road, Penzance, Cornwall. Tel: 01736 61447

WHP • W. H. Patterson, 19 Albemarle St, London W1. Tel: 0171-629 4119

WIL * Peter Wilson, Victoria Gallery, Market Street, Nantwich, Cheshire. Tel: 01270-623878

WL * Wintertons Ltd., Lichfield Auction Centre, Wood End Lane, Fradley, Lichfield, Staffs Tel: 01543-263256

WO •† Wiseman Originals Ltd., 34 West Square, London SE11. Tel: 0171-587 0747

WOT The World Of Transport, 37 Heath Road, Twickenham, Middx. Tel: 0181-891 3169

WrG •† Wren Gallery, 4 Bear Court, High Street, Burford, Oxon. Tel: 01993 823495

WT • William Thuiller, 180 New Bond Street, London W1. Tel: 0171-499 0106

WWG • Wilkins and Wilkins Gallery, 1 Barrett Street, London W1. Tel: 0171-935 9613

CONTENTS

HOW TO USE THIS BOOK

Miller's Picture Price Guide provides an illustrated reference to pictures available at auction and through dealers over the past year. The Guide covers pictures of every style, medium and value, ranging from Old Master paintings worth millions of pounds to contemporary prints for less than £100.

For easy reference, pictures have been classified by subject matter. If all you know about your picture is that it portrays a ship, turn to the Marine section, where you can compare and contrast your work with the examples illustrated. Each section is arranged chronologically, so that you can see how a particular subject has been treated over the centuries, how styles have changed and how prices compare. Where possible, each individual entry includes the name, dates and nationality of the artist, the title, medium and measurements of the picture, the price range and finally, the source code. The full Key to Illustrations can be found on page 7.

Price ranges have been carefully worked out to reflect the current state of the market-place. While Miller's offers a carefully considered GUIDE to prices, no publication could attempt to provide a definitive price list. As with any other business, the art market changes and prices fluctuate depending on both internal and external factors. The generally high prices across the board in the 1980s have, in many instances, been replaced by considerably more modest ones in the recession-hit 1990s.

No two pictures are ever identical. Each work has its own individual value depending on artist, subject, rarity, quality and condition. Other important considerations include whether a picture is fresh to the market, where it is being sold, how many people want to buy it, and what they are prepared to spend. Buying from a dealer often might appear more expensive than buying at auction, but in real terms this is not necessarily the case. Unless you know what you are doing when buying at auction, you are taking a risk.

Auction catalogues warn that information about items offered for sale is a statement of opinion rather than fact, and the underlying principle is 'buyer beware'. A good dealer provides you with knowledge, experience and security as well as a picture. It is their job to guarantee the authenticity, quality and condition of a work. 'We do the selection, put our name behind a picture and our money,' explains James Lloyd of Burlington Paintings. 'It has got to be a very saleable work and the best example of its kind for us to buy it.' Most, if not all, of the world's great art collections have been built up with the help of dealers and a reputable dealer will not only sell you a picture but advise you how to hang and look after it and can help you develop a fine collection of your own.

Many sections come complete with a helpful introduction and in addition details about individual pictures. Also provided are reports on the state of the marketplace, information about specific artists and movements and general advice about pictures.

The aim of all our publications is to be as comprehensive as possible. With each edition of the *Miller's Picture Price Guide*, new sections are included and different areas covered. If you, the reader, have any information to add or suggestions for topics that we might use in future editions, please let us know. We rely on feedback from the people who use the Guide to help us to make it as useful and interesting as possible.

LOOKING AFTER YOUR PICTURES

A thing of beauty is a joy forever, but only if it is properly looked after. Like people, pictures benefit from sensitive handling and a good home. As prices of pictures and antiques have escalated, so has our awareness of the importance of conserving them in the best possible state – but what qualifies as good care?

Anyone who has ever watched the *BBC Antiques Roadshow* will have seen experts tut-tutting sadly over objects that have been over-restored, over-cleaned and otherwise loved to death by owners convinced that they were doing the best for their cherished possessions. As in every other aspect of life, fashions in conservation change. What one generation regarded as necessary restoration, the next will see as vandalism. An old painting that has been relined, repainted, reframed and made to look 'as good as new' can easily be worth far less than a picture which has never been touched. To the untrained eye, the latter might look a complete wreck – dirty, dingy and torn. A dealer or expert will recognise the value of its unadulterated state and its potential for proper restoration. Paradoxically, it is often such apparently sad-looking works that are described as being 'in perfect saleroom condition' and fetch correspondingly high prices at auction.

Too much messing about with an object can compromise its historical integrity and ruin its financial value. Conversely, total neglect can be equally damaging, and a sensible compromise must be found. Caring for a collection begins at home and should start the very moment a picture enters your possession.

The first step in caring for a work of art is to preserve all known information about it. When buying a picture keep any accompanying records and paperwork – bill of sale, auction or gallery catalogue, the artist's biography (if available), provenance details, any newspaper clippings or reviews relating to the exhibition or artist. Write down when, where, and how much you paid for it and any verbal information given to you by the vendor. Also keep a photograph of the picture, inscribed with basic details.

Forget any ideas about DIY when it comes to restoring pictures. Serious cleaning and restoration are best left to the experts. 'Caring for pictures is a bit like looking after your teeth,' one dealer told Miller's. 'Although you can keep them clean and do your best to avoid damaging substances and situations, only an idiot would carry out his own dental work.' Day-to-day care is a matter of common sense, rather than expertise.

Hang pictures out of direct light, especially sunlight. Watercolours, and to a lesser extent oils, are affected by exposure to light which can alter the pigment of the paint, changing its colour. Watercolours and drawings which have been kept in folios and albums, protected from natural light, will often be in pristine condition and command high premiums at auction. It is always important to display them in a sympathetic environment.

Damp can rot both paper and canvas, encouraging fungus and mould. With panel paintings, seasonal variations in humidity can alter the moisture content of the wood, leading to drastic consequences. Central heating can be extremely drying and damaging to a picture and where possible avoid hanging pictures over radiators.

A smoky atmosphere can discolour the varnish of an oil painting and is best avoided but, warns restorer Michael Leslie, 'no matter what preventative measures you take, varnish itself will eventually turn yellow in daylight.'

Good professional framing is a must. Frames protect a picture and a mount will prevent watercolours, drawings and prints from touching the glass. Poor mounting, however, and the wrong adhesives can lead to the deterioration of works on paper. 'If you are having a work re-mounted,' advises watercolour expert Huon Mallalieu, 'you should insist on either conservation or museum board,' both of which are acid free.

Dust pictures gently, using a wad of cotton wool for the surface of oil paintings. Frames should also be cleaned with great care. Antique frames are now valuable in their own right, and a gilded surface can easily be ruined. Susan May, Workshop Director of the renowned framers, Arnold Wiggins, told Millers. 'We very often find that the bottom edges of frames have been worn out because of regular dusting. The most one should do is use a very soft brush to dislodge dust. Whatever else, never apply too much friction to a gilt frame and do not rub a damp cloth around it.'

In recent years there has been much debate and some confusion about the respective merits of 'conservation' and 'restoration'. Both conservators and restorers share the same goal of preserving the object and are often undertaken by the same person. There are, however, some important differences between the two terms.

As the Conservation Unit of the Museums and Galleries Commission explain, the aim of conservation is to establish the cause of an object's deterioration. In addition, conservation will reveal what has become hidden over the years – perhaps uncovering an area of a picture that has been overpainted or exposing any previous restoration work. 'On the whole, 'restoration means restoring something back to how we think it looked at some time,'claims the Conservation Unit. This could include repainting any lost areas of a picture so that the whole thing looks homogenous.

How much or how little restoration is carried out depends largely on the individual owner. For museums, whose interest in a work is primarily academic, conservation is all important – for a private owner, who wants an attractive picture to hang on the wall, more restoration might seem necessary. Michael Leslie stresses emphatically, 'restorers should go to the utmost trouble to keep a picture in its original condition.' The Conservation Unit recommend that when restoring an object or a picture one should always do as little as possible to it, and that any changes made should be discernible to the trained eye.

Organisations such as the Conservation Unit of the Museums and Galleries Commission and the Association of British Picture Restorers will be able to offer conservation advice and put you in touch with restorers who will best suit your needs. Always ensure that the restorer you choose is a member of an accredited body or association.

'Picture restoration is a very skilful service,' advises restorer Paul Mitchell. 'People should never try to clean or restore their own pictures and it is vital to find a reputable restorer.' Pick a restorer who has specialist training and experience in your field and ask for and take up references from previous clients.

Conservation is a labour-intensive and time-consuming business and is costed accordingly. Ask for a written estimate, check whether the quotation is fixed price and whether expenses and VAT are included in the price. As far as possible, be precise about how much work you want done and discuss it with the restorer. 'It is vital that people should not be frightened to ask advice of their restorers,' Paul Mitchell emphasises. 'Any reputable restorer will always provide a condition report of a picture before work is undertaken and this is free of charge.' Listen to your conservator and be prepared to be consulted during the course of the work about any discoveries which could change the cost or direction of the project.

If your work is valuable, ask about the security of the premises. Check the firm's insurance arrangements as it may be necessary to extend your own policy to cover transport and conservation.

Finally, if you have several works that require attention and are using a restorer for the first time, have the least valuable item treated first to see if you are happy with the results. Keep all documentation connected with the restoration work and ask your restoration company for their advice on preserving the, hopefully, fine condition of your newly-restored picture.

INSURING PICTURES

Little in life is more distressing than a burglary in your home. With house break-ins on the increase, police strongly advise certain precautions. All external doors should be fitted with five-lever mortice deadlocks and all ground floor windows, fanlights, skylights and patio doors should, ideally, have key operated locks. Bars and security grilles on basement and ground floor windows might not look very attractive, but they do provide both protection and are an obvious deterrent to the more casual thief. Should you have possessions in excess of, say, £50,000, an alarm system may be a sensible option.

Insurance companies have been much in the news recently, and although premiums are an added financial burden, the cover they provide is essential. Should you have an art or antiques collection, you should check whether your policy only covers individual items up to a certain value, as many insurance companies specify separate cover for the loss of any one item up to the value of £500.

If you have several valuable items it may be a better option to take out separate cover for your fine art or antiques which may not prove as expensive as you think. Such insurance can also offer a reduction in premiums if you accept an excess, install a safe for valuable items, or keep objects in the bank. Specialist brokers can also provide policies which will cover home and contents as well as art and antiques collections.

Taking photographs of your possessions is one of the best means of recording them. In the event of a burglery, the police and insurance companies will be greatly assisted if you can provide them with photographs and cataloguing details. *Trace*, a monthly theft alerting publication, founded in 1988, has a wide readership in both the art market and the police force. For a small fee they will publish photographs and cataloguing details of stolen artefacts, mainly in the U.K., but some Interpol reports are also included. The *Antiques Trade Gazette*, also features pictures and details of stolen works of art. Another alternative being adopted by some insurance companies and private collectors is use of the *Art Loss Register*, founded three years ago. This private company provides a database recording items and artefacts thought to have been stolen or destroyed by fire. Each entry is matched with auction house catalogues, and so far £13.5 million of art, antiques and jewellery have been recovered.

One bright note on which to conclude is that Parliament have approved a bill to abolish 'Market Overt'. This ancient law enables buyers to acquire legitimate title to any goods offered at Bermondsey and other traditional markets between the hours of sunrise and sunset, even if they have been stolen. Market Overt, known as the thieves charter, has been a major stumbling block to those trying to recover stolen works of art.

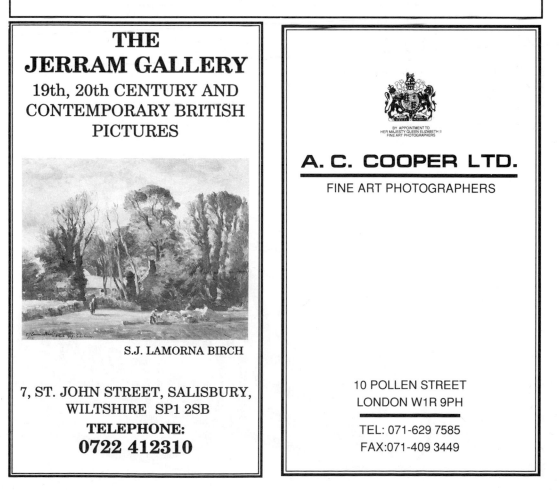

LANDSCAPES

'Back to basics' is a cry that has resounded in the art market as well as in Parliament. The past year has seen a healthy demand for traditionalist Victorian and Edwardian pictures, particularly landscapes.

As many of the following works suggest, the more decorative the scene, the more desirable the picture. Highland lochs bathed in the light of the setting sun, English country gardens in perpetual flower, happy harvesting scenes, portrayals of Venice, Naples and other Continental beauty spots are always popular.

'Ideally, a landscape should reflect the best and most well known aspects of a specific artist,' states James Lloyd of Burlington Paintings. 'Take the example of Alfred de Breanski, one of the biggest and most commercial names in 19thC landscape painting. He is best known for his Scottish loch scenes, particularly at sunset, and it is these typical Breanski views that tend to be the best sellers.'

Buyers know what they want, and like their expectations fulfilled. For example, the Scottish 19thC landscape painter Joseph Farquharson is particularly noted for his winter scenes and snowy views. However, a large picture of sheep wandering around in the mist, (est. £16,000–20,000) failed to sell at Sotheby's Glasgow in February 1994, largely because of the absence of snow – mist seemed to be no substitute.

There are signs of renewed interest in 20thC pictures which are both decorative and representational. 'Figurative art is back on the agenda,' agrees Dr. Robert Travers of Piano Nobile, a gallery specialising in pictures from 1860 to the present day. At Art '94, the showcase of contemporary art in Britain, Piano Nobile achieved a considerable success, with the landscapes of Paul Kenny (see p90). 'His work is always hugely popular,' stated Dr. Travers. 'People want good quality pictures, fine technique and attractive, recognisable images – an artist can be modern without sacrificing the traditional values of painting.'

The traditionalists, both in terms of dealers and collectors, were certainly out in force at the World of Watercolours Show in London in January, which this year attracted more visitors than ever before. The show has become the highlight of the year for water-colour collectors and certainly a place to view the art of landscape painting at its best and most varied. Works on offer ranged from the 16thC to the present day, with prices ranging from under £50 to an impressive £420,000 for a watercolour of Conway Castle by J. M. W. Turner. Whilst few of us can ever hope to possess a Turner, one of the great joys of the fair and the watercolour market in general is that there are plenty of good quality and reasonably priced works on offer. 'The crazy days of the speculators have largely evaporated,' claimed Chairman of the Show, William Drummond, welcoming visitors back to 'a more sober world where one can enjoy finding desirable items even for the most modest purse.' You don't have to chase big names to catch good pictures. 'For every fifty well-known watercolour artists, there are five hundred more who are not and not nearly as expensive,' dealer and Victorian expert Christopher Wood told Miller's. 'Good drawings are still far too little appreciated, and you can begin a serious collection with hundreds rather than thousands of pounds.'

16th–17th Century

Jan Brueghel the Elder
Flemish (1568–1625)
A Rocky Landscape with the Flight into Egypt
Signed and dated 'Brueghel/1600'
Oil on oak panel
7¼in (18.4cm) diam.
£90,000–110,000 *S(NY)*

Landscapes of this period often included religious or mythological scenes portrayed in miniature, as though to justify the choice of a secular and naturalistic theme. This characteristic landscape by Jan Brueghel the Elder depicts Mary on a donkey holding the Christ child, with Joseph leading them over the rocks.

Attributed to Dirck van Bergen
Dutch (c1640–90)
Italianate Landscape
Oil on canvas
34¼ x 39¼in (87 x 99.5cm)
£5,000–6,000 *S*

Domenico Campagnola
Italian (active 1517–62)
Landscape with a Fortified Town
Pen and brown ink, laid down
14 x 9½in (35.5 x 23.5cm)
£16,500–20,000 *P*

Claude Gellée, called Le Lorrain
French (1600–82)
Le Chèvrier
Etching
7 x 9¼in (17.5 x 23cm)
£6,500–7,500 *S*

Philippe van Dapels
Flemish (1654–after 1659)
Wooded Landscape with Figures on a Path
Signed with initials, oil on canvas
25¼ x 28¾in (64 x 73cm)
£6,000–7,000 *S*

Manner of Claude Lorrain
French (1600–82)
Classical River Landscape with a Traveller
and his Dog resting in the foreground
Oil on canvas
28 x 37¾in (71 x 96cm)
£2,250–2,750 *S(S)*

Manner of Cornelis Decker
Dutch (1625–78)
A River Landscape with Figures
beside Cottages
Oil on canvas
28½ x 41½in (72.5 x 105.5cm)
£1,200–1,500 *S(S)*

Dirk van Dalens
Dutch (c1600–76)
Landscape with Latona and her Children and
the Lycian Peasants being turned into Frogs
Oil on panel
23 x 27in (58.5 x 68.5cm)
£10,500–12,000 *S(NY)*

*According to Ovid, Latona was the mother of
Apollo and Diana who, being thirsty, stopped
at a lake in Lycia to drink. The local peasants
there prevented her and her two children from
quenching their thirst and she punished them
by turning the peasants into frogs.*

Manner of Allaert van Everdingen
Dutch (1621–75)
A Scandinavian Landscape with Loggers
Oil on panel
16 x 20¾in (40.5 x 53cm)
£1,250–1,500 *S*

Gillis Claesz. d'Hondecoeter
Dutch (c1575–1638)
Extensive Landscape with Elijah and the
Widow of Zarepath
Signed with initials, oil on panel
14 x 25¾in (35.5 x 65.5cm)
£9,500–12,000 *S*

Laurent de la Hyre
French (1606–56)
Landscape with Two Women at a Fountain
Signed and dated '1653', oil on canvas
25 by 34¾in (63.5 x 88.5cm)
£285,000–310,000 *S(NY)*

**Circle of Alessandro Magnasco,
il Lissandrino**
Italian (1667–1749)
A Valley with Washerwomen in
the Foreground
Oil on canvas
32¾ x 44¼in (83.5 x 112.5cm)
£22,000–25,000 *C*

Flemish School (17thC)
Winter Landscape with the Flight into Egypt
Oil on panel
9½ x 13½in (24 x 34cm)
£5,250–6,000 *S*

Jan van Goyen
Dutch (1593–1656)
A Winter Landscape with Skaters on a
Frozen River near a Windmill
Signed and dated '1630', oil on panel
19½ x 25¼in (49 x 64cm)
£180,000–200,000 *S*

Italo–Dutch School (late 17thC)
Southern Landscape with Travellers
Oil on canvas
38½ x 41in (97.5 x 104cm)
£1,500–2,000 *S(S)*

Hendrick van Minderhout
Dutch (1632–96)
A Rhenish Landscape
Signed and dated '1653', oil on canvas
62 x 81in (157.5 x 206cm)
£80,000–100,000 *S*

Attributed to Klaes Molenaer
Dutch (c1630–76)
Fisherfolk on the Beach at Scheveningen
Signed (?), oil on panel
22¾ x 29in (58 x 73.5cm)
£6,000–7,000 *C*

Pieter de Molyn
Dutch (1595–1661)
Wooded Landscape with Peasants on a Road
by a Village
Signed, oil on panel
15½ x 23⅜in (39.5 x 60.5cm)
£8,250–10,000 *S*

**Follower of Joos de Momper and Jan
Brueghel the Younger**
Flemish (17thC)
Rocky Landscape with Riders Approaching
Peasants on a Path
Oil on panel
9 x 12in (22.5 x 30.5cm)
£8,500–10,000 *S*

Isaac van Oosten
Flemish (1613–61)
Landscape with a Stag Hunt
Signed, oil on panel
10½ x 16¾in (26.5 x 42.5cm)
£9,500–10,500 *S*

Rembrandt Harmensz. van Rijn
Dutch (1606–69)
The Windmill
Etching, 1641
5¾ x 8¼in (14.5 x 20.5cm)
£90,000–100,000 *S(NY)*

Rembrandt Harmensz. van Rijn
Dutch (1606–69)
Landscape with a Square Tower
Etching and drypoint, 1650
3½ x 6in (8.8 x 15cm)
£55,000–60,000 *S(NY)*

Follower of Johann Heinrich Roos
German (1631–85)
Italianate Landscape with Drovers beside Ruins
Oil on canvas
42 x 56¾in (107 x 144cm)
£4,250–5,000 *S*

Follower of Mathijs Schoevaerdts
Flemish (1665–94)
Peasants and Cattle by the Banks of a River
Oil on panel
8½ x 11in (21.5 x 28cm)
£1,600–2,000 *S(S)*

Attributed to Reyer Claesz. Suycker
Dutch (17thC)
A Valley with a Horseman and Traveller
Indistinctly signed 'E. van der Velde', oil
on panel
12½in x 18½in (31.5 x 47cm)
£8,000–10,000 *P*

Attributed to David Teniers II
Flemish (1610–90)
Fishermen at a Stream, a Castle beyond
Monogram 'DTF', oil on panel
8 x 11in (20 x 28cm)
£5,000–6,000 *C*

Esaias van de Velde
Dutch (1587–1630)
Peasants on a Hill with a Chapel and a
Village beyond
Signed and dated '1630', oil on canvas
11½ x 16¼in (29 x 41.5cm)
£7,500–8,000 *S*

Circle of Lucas van Uden
Flemish (1595–1672)
An Extensive River Landscape with Herders
and Animals in the foreground
Oil on canvas
22½ x 30½in (57 x 77.5cm)
£4,500–5,000 *S*

David Vinckeboons
Flemish (1576–1629)
An Alpine Valley with Gypsies and a Monk
Signed (?) with monogram 'DVB', oil on panel
17¼ x 32in (43.5 x 81cm)
£32,000–40,000 *C*

David Vinckeboons
Flemish (1576–1629)
Peasants on a Hillside with Goats
Oil on panel
4½ x 6¾in (11 x 17cm)
£1,500–2,000 *JNic*

Roelof Jansz. van Vries
Dutch (1631–81)
Travellers and Anglers by a Lake
Signed, oil on canvas
32½ x 42½in (82.5 x 108.5cm)
£17,000–20,000 *S(Am)*

Follower of Jan Wyck
Dutch (1640–1702)
Landscape with a Nobleman and his
Entourage beside an Encampment
Oil on canvas
37 x 50in (94 x 127cm)
£3,000–3,500 *S(S)*

John White Abbott
British (1764–1851)
Ugbrooke, Devon
Pen and grey ink and washes, 1816
14½ x 20½in (37 x 52cm)
£4,750–6,000 *S*

18th Century

John Henry Campbell
Irish (1757–1828)
The Liffey, Palmerstown in the distance
Signed with initials and inscribed verso,
oil on canvas
15¼ x 20⅛in (38.5 x 51cm)
£7,200–7,800 *CCG*

*Regarded as one of the leading Irish
watercolourists of his day, Campbell also
worked in oils. His views were almost entirely
painted in Ireland, in particular around
Dublin and Wicklow.*

John Constable, R.A.
British (1776–1837)
Borrowdale by Moonlight
Watercolour over traces of pencil, recto;
The Bridge at Watendlath
Grey washes over pencil, verso
4¼ x 9½in (10.5 x 24cm)
£35,000–45,000 *S*

John Constable, R.A.
British (1776–1837)
Dedham Vale from the Lane between East
Bergholt and Flatford
Watercolour over pencil on laid paper,
with a Britannia watermark
7¾ x 12in (19.5 x 31cm)
£55,000–65,000 *S*

John Constable, R.A.
British (1776–1837)
A Ploughman near East Bergholt
Overlooking the Stour Estuary
Watercolour over pencil on laid paper
7¾ x 12in (19.5 x 31cm)
£100,000–125,000 *S*

As the Antiques Trade Gazette *reported,
these two previously unrecorded watercolours
by John Constable were brought in to
Sotheby's in a shopping bag by an Essex
vendor who was oblivious to their value. Both
were dated to 1805, and only three other
Constable watercolours are known to exist
from this period. Bidding was fierce and
furious, resulting in prices that far exceeded
the top estimates suggested by Sotheby's of
£18,000–£20,000. They were both sold to a
British collector.*

John Robert Cozens
British (1752–97)
An Extensive River Landscape
Signed, pencil and watercolour heightened
with touches of white
19½ x 27in (49 x 69cm)
£19,000–25,000 *C*

Attributed to John Crome
British (1768–1821)
A Riverside Workshop
Grey wash over traces of pencil on paper
watermarked 'J. Whatman 1801'
5¼ x 10¼in (13.5 x 26cm)
£750–900 *S*

English School (c1720)
A View of Walgrave Hall, Northamptonshire,
the seat of Sir William Langham, Bt.
Inscribed and dated '1690' on reverse,
oil on panel
17¼ x 35½in (43.5 x 90cm)
£5,000–6,000 *C*

Edward Dayes
British (1763–1804)
Pembroke Castle from the South West
Signed and dated '1789/London',
pencil and watercolour
14 x 23½in (35.5 x 59.5cm)
£2,500–3,500 *C*

Thomas Jones
British (1742–1803)
Villa of Maecenas and the Villa d'Este, Tivoli
Signed, inscribed and numbered '2',
watercolour over pencil on laid paper
11 x 16½in (28 x 42cm)
£7,500–8,000 *S*

Circle of Alexander Nasmyth
British (1758–1840)
Loch Katrine
Oil on canvas, framed
35½ x 44½in (90 x 113cm)
£11,000–12,500 *S*

*The frame originally came from Lawers Castle
in Perthshire, the seat of the Hon. Brigadier
General James Campbell (c1680–1745), son of
James, 2nd Earl of Loudoun.*

Locatelli
Italian (18thC)
Classical landscape with Figures
and Animals
Oil on canvas
34 x 32in (81.5 x 86cm)
£3,500–4,000 *MEA*

Attributed to Alexander Nasmyth
British (1758–1840)
Castle overlooking a wooded Valley,
with Figures
Oil on canvas
14 x 21in (35.5 x 53cm)
£1,550–1,650 *LH*

*Alexander Nasmyth 'was the founder
of the landscape painting school of
Scotland, and by his taste and talents
took the lead for many years in the
patriotic aim of enriching his native
land with the representations of
romantic scenery,' recalled his pupil,
the painter David Wilkie. As well as
influencing the next generation of
Scottish landscape painters, Nasmyth
also helped to swell their numbers. He
had eleven children, several of whom
became artists. The most celebrated,
and possibly the most unfortunate, was
Patrick, his eldest son. As a youth, an
injury to his right hand forced him to
learn to paint with his left hand, and at
seventeen an infection resulted in total
deafness. Understandably, he sought
some consolation and became, according
to the Redgrave brothers (see
Bibliography), addicted to 'habits of
excess' and 'low company', which
further weakened his already fragile
constitution, and Patrick died before
his father. Nevertheless,the artist had
a successful career and his works were
extremely popular, particularly
landscapes painted in the countryside
surrounding London, influenced in style
by 17thC Dutch painting.*

Alexander Nasmyth
British (1758–1840)
A View of Drumtochty Castle on Luther
Water, Kincardineshire
Oil on canvas
25¼ x 37¼in (64 x 94.5cm)
£17,500–22,000 *C*

Patrick Nasmyth, R.A.
British (1787–1831)
Surrey Landscape
Signed and dated '1830', oil on panel
13½ x 18in (34 x 45.5cm)
£2,000–2,500 *WH*

Jean-Baptiste Le Prince
French (1734–81)
An Imaginary Russian Landscape
Signed and dated '1763', oil on canvas
10¾ x 15⅛in (27 x 38.5cm)
£5,500–6,000 *S*

Paul Sandby, R.A.
British (1725–1809)
A Quiet English Hamlet
Signed and dated '1770',
watercolour
12¼ x 19in (31 x 48.5cm)
£6,750–7,750 *P*

Christian Georg Shütz the Younger
German (1758–1823)
A Summer Landscape
Oil on canvas
9 x 11¾in (22.5 x 30cm)
£3,250–3,750 *S*

John Skelton
British (1735–59)
A Bridge over a Continental River
Watercolour
10¼ x 14½in (25.5 x 36.5cm)
£1,250–1,750 *P*

Francis Towne
British (1739–1816)
Dunsmoor: a rocky wooded Landscape
Pen and grey ink and watercolour on
joined paper, 1790
7 x 15½in (17.5 x 39.5cm)
£5,000–5,500 *C*

Johann Christian Vollerdt
German (1708–69)
A Winter Landscape with Figures
Oil on canvas
24¼ x 30¾in (62 x 78cm)
£5,500–7,000 *P*

Attributed to Raphael Lamar West
British (1769–1850)
Trees in a Rocky Landscape
Watercolour and bodycolour
18½ x 24in (47 x 61cm)
£400–500 *S*

19th Century

Charles Partridge Adams
American (1858–1942)
Mountainous Landscape
Signed, oil on canvas
14 x 18in (35.5 x 45.5cm)
£1,600–2,400 *CNY*

Guido Agostini
Italian (19thC)
A distant view of an Italian Hilltop Town
Signed and dated '1885', oil on board
12½ x 10in (32 x 25cm)
£550–700 *Bea*

Johannes Evert Akkeringa
Dutch (1861–1942)
Children in the Woods
Signed, oil on canvas
15 x 19½in (38.5 x 49cm)
£4,000–5,000 *S(Am)*

Ernest Albert
American (1857–1946)
Golden Day
Signed and inscribed, oil on canvas
25 x 30in (64 x 76cm)
£3,500–4,000 *CNY*

George Ames Aldrich
American (1872–1941)
A Castle on a Hillside
Signed, oil on canvas
30 x 28in (76 x 71cm)
£880–1,200 *CNY*

David Bates
British (1840–1921)
On Pen-Craig Moor, Bettws-y-Coed
Signed and dated '1905', inscribed
verso, watercolour
13 x 17in (33 x 43cm)
£2,800–3,000 *WrG*

William Ayrton
British (active 1889–1904)
Boathouses at Hickling, Norfolk
Signed and dated '1911', watercolour
12¾ x 20½in (32.5 x 52cm)
£500–550 *JC*

John James Bannatyne
British (1835–1911)
Highland Scene with Sheep Grazing
Signed, oil on canvas
35 x 27in (89 x 69cm)
£450–550 *GAK*

Follower of Thomas Barker of Bath
British (1769–1847)
Landscape with a Mill, Figures and a Bridge
Oil on canvas
17½ x 23½in (44.5 x 59.7cm)
£700–800 *L*

David Bates
British (1840–1921)
A River Scene
Signed, watercolour
14 x 20in (35.5 x 50.5cm)
£1,500–1,800 *BWe*

François-Simon Bidau
Swiss (19thC)
A Mountainous Lake Landscape
Signed, oil on canvas
27½ x 35½in (70 x 90cm)
£1,000–1,500 *CSK*

A. Birbeck
British (active 1880–1920)
The Kyles of Bute, Scotland
Signed and titled on original
backboard, watercolour
13½ x 20in (34.5 x 50.5cm)
£250–350 *JC*

Edwin Henry Boddington (1836–1905)
and Charles Jones (1836–92)
British
Sheep on a Country Lane
Signed and dated 'Edwin Boddington 1862',
and monogrammed, oil on canvas
24½ x 36¼in (62 x 92.5cm)
£5,500–6,000 *C*

Samuel Bough, R.S.A., R.S.W.
British (1822–78)
Near Bergen, Norway, with the
Artist sketching
Signed and dated '1858', inscribed verso,
oil on panel
9¾ x 14in (24 x 35.5cm)
£2,500–3,000 *C(S)*

Albert Edward Bowers
British (active 1875–93)
An English Summer
Signed, watercolour
5¼ x 13¼in (13.5 x 33.5cm)
£300–350 *JC*

Creswick Boydell
British (active 1889–1916)
On the Avon
Signed, oil on board
10½ x 18in (26 x 46cm)
£240–340 *BCG*

Charles Branwhite
British (1817–80)
Figure approaching a Windmill on
Felton Common
Watercolour with bodycolour
8½ x 12½in (21.5 x 31.5cm)
£800–900 *PCA*

Charles Branwhite
British (1817–80)
Winter's Morning
Signed, dated and inscribed '53', pencil and
watercolour with bodycolour
26 x 39½in (66 x 99.5cm)
£4,500–5,500 *C*

Attributed to Maurice Braun
American (1877–1941)
A Quiet Pool
Signed, oil on canvas
25 x 19in (63.5 x 48.3cm)
£780–880 *CNY*

Alfred de Breanski, Snr.
British (1852–1928)
The Stepping Stones, Keston, Kent
Signed and dated '1873', oil on canvas
26 x 44in (66 x 111.5cm)
£14,000–16,000 *HFA*

*'Alfred de Breanski was a distinguished
landscape painter who became famous for his
breathtaking views of Wales and Scotland,'
writes Haynes Fine Art Gallery in Worcester.
At his best, Breanski was capable of
producing excellent effects, often bathing his
landscapes with a flood of golden light. Born
in London, Alfred was the eldest son of
Leopold Breanski. In 1873 Breanski married
Annie Roberts. They had seven children, two
of whom, Alfred Fontville and Arthur, were
to become painters. He exhibited at the Royal
Academy between 1872 and 1890 and also at
Suffolk Street. His work is represented in
several public collections including the
Southampton Art Gallery and the Laing Art
Gallery, Newcastle-upon-Tyne.*

Alfred de Breanski, Snr.
British (1852–1928)
Lochearn-Head N.B.
Signed and inscribed with title on reverse,
oil on canvas
16 x 24in (41 x 61cm)
£14,500–15,000 *S*

Alfred de Breanski, Snr.
British (1852–1928)
Tarbet and the Cobbler
Signed, oil on canvas
16 x 22in (41 x 56cm)
£5,000–6,000 *C*

Alfred de Breanski
British (19thC)
The Western Highlands
Signed and inscribed on reverse,
oil on canvas
23½ x 35½in (59.5 x 90cm)
£14,000–15,000 *Bea*

*This present work was found by Torquay
auctioneers, Bearne's, under a blanket in
the garage of a local house. Paradoxically,
neglect can sometimes be more beneficial to
a picture than excessive over cleaning. The
picture was under glass, in its original frame
and in unrestored condition - just what the
trade likes to see, and it almost doubled its
upper estimate at auction. Bearne's did not
specify whether it was painted by Breanski
Senior or Junior, but the price would lead
one to assume the former.*

Alfred Fontville de Breanski
British (1877–1945)
Ullswater
Signed, oil on canvas
16 x 24in (40.5 x 61cm)
£2,500–2,750 *FdeL*

John Brett
British (1830–1902)
Cligga Pools
Indistinctly inscribed and
dated 'June 26, 81' on reverse,
oil on canvas
7 x 14in (17.8 x 35.5cm)
£2,500–3,500 *C*

Taylor Brown
British (19th/20thC)
Ayrshire Landscape with a Figure
Signed, oil on panel
6½ x 8½in (16 x 21cm)
£200–300 *WH*

British School (early 19thC)
Bay Horse in a Provincial Landscape
Oil on canvas
21 x 28¼in (53 x 71.5cm)
£1,250–1,750 *S(NY)*

Joseph Burgaritski
Austrian (1836–90)
A River Landscape
Signed, oil on canvas
18½ x 36¼in (47 x 93cm)
£900–1,000 *CSK*

Vincenzo Cabianca
Italian (1827–1902)
Cottages by the Sea in La Spezia
Signed and inscribed, oil on panel
12¼ x 23½in (31 x 60cm)
£60,000–70,000 *S*

*Cabianca worked in Florence from 1853
becoming closely associated with the
Macchiaioli, a group of young artists reacting
against the Academy and frequenting the
Caffé Michelangelo, an international meeting
point. This painting belongs to the artist's
Macchiaioli period (1858–75), during which
time he executed his most popular works.*

Jacques Carabain
Belgian (1834–92)
A Village Scene
Signed, oil on panel
15 x 11¾in (38 x 30cm)
£5,000–6,000 *S*

Jean-Charles Cazin
French (1841–1901)
A Wooded Landscape with Farm Buildings
Signed, oil on panel
12½ x 15¾in (32 x 40cm)
£2,500–3,500 *C*

Johan-Herman Carmiencke
Danish (1810–67)
A View of Castello Malcesine,
Lake Garda, Italy
Signed and dated 'New York 1857',
oil on canvas
48 x 62in (122 x 157cm)
£13,000–14,000 *S*

*Decorative Italianate landscapes are always
popular in the salerooms. Estimated at a
modest £2,000–3,000 at Sotheby's, this view
of Lake Garda, a favourite beauty spot,
comfortably exceeded expectations.*

Carlton Theodore Chapman
American (1860–1926)
A Snowy Winter Stream
Signed, oil on canvas
14 x 20in (35.5 x 50.5cm)
£1,500–2,000 *CNY*

Harry Harvey Clarke
British (b1869)
Haywagon in Country Lane
Signed, oil on canvas
15½ x 19½in (39 x 49cm)
£900–1,000 *LH*

George Cole
British (1810-83)
Cattle and Figures in a River Landscape
Signed and dated '1880', oil on canvas
18 x 24in (46 x 61cm)
£2,500–3,500 *P*

F. G. Coleridge
British (active 1866–1914)
On the Thames with Figures and Dogs
Signed, watercolour
6 x 9in (15 x 22.5cm)
£500–600 *TAY*

Chinese Artist
(unknown) (18th/19thC)
Man with Cow in Extensive Landscape
Watercolour on silk, mounted on scroll
62 x 20½in (157 x 52cm)
£350–450 *SLN*

F. G. Coleridge
British (active 1866–1914)
Grenada
Signed and dated on back of mount 'May
1862', watercolour heightened with white
13½ x 22½in (34 x 57cm)
£1,500–2,000 *P*

F. G. Coleridge
British (active 1866–1914)
Trinidad
Signed and dated '1861', watercolour
and bodycolour
14 x 23½in (36 x 59.5cm)
£1,900–2,300 *P*

Samuel David Colkett
British (1800–63)
Figures by a Cottage
Oil on canvas
10 x 13¾in (25 x 35cm)
£2,800–3,800 *PCA*

Jean-Baptiste Camille Corot
French (1796–1875)
Le Batelier au bord de l'étang
Signed, oil on canvas
18 x 22in (45.7 x 55.5cm)
£100,000–120,000 *S(NY)*

*'In front of any site or object, abandon
yourself to your first impression,' advised
Corot in his notebooks, c1856. 'If you have
been truly moved, you will communicate to
others the sincerity of your emotion.'*

Hermann David Salomon Corrodi
Italian (1844–1905)
Italian Fisherfolk by the Sea, Southern Italy
Signed and inscribed, oil on canvas
27½ x 15¾in (70 x 40cm)
£7,750–8,750 *S*

Gustave Courbet (1819–77) and
Cherubino Pata
French
Le Val aux Biches
Signed, oil on canvas, c1877
38½ x 51in (98 x 130cm)
£16,000–18,000 *C*

David Cox
British (1783-1859)
The Old Bridge, Bridgnorth, Shropshire
Watercolour over pencil with scratching out
and touches of bodycolour
8½ x 24¾in (21 x 63cm)
£9,000–12,000 *S*

David Cox
British (1783–1859)
A Beck in the Welsh Mountains
Signed and dated '1854', watercolour
over pencil
7 x 9½in (17.5 x 22.5cm)
£800–1,200 *P*

David Cox
British (1783–1859)
Asking the way - 'Take the Left Road'
Signed '1853', watercolour over pencil
14 x 20½in (35.5 x 52cm)
£12,000–13,500 *S*

Attributed to David Cox
British (1783–1859)
A Huntsman with his Horse and Dog
looking towards Powys Castle on the edge
of a Deer Park
Pencil and watercolour heightened with white
22¾ x 33in (58 x 84cm)
£1,200–1,400 *CSK*

*In 1836, Cox discovered an ordinary
wrapping paper, produced in Scotland, which
he was to use consistently for his drawings.
Its firm surface was a perfect medium for
watercolour and its rough texture suited his
rapid and instinctive painting style. Off-white
in colour, the paper's only disadvantage was
a scattering of small dark flecks. These were
concealed in the landscape parts of a picture
but showed up in the sky. When Cox was
asked how he dealt with this problem, his
answer was simple - 'Oh, I just put wings to
them and they fly away as birds!'*

Bruce Crane
American (1857–1934)
Grey October
Signed, oil on canvas
14 x 20in (35.5 x 50.8cm)
£2,800–3,800 *CNY*

T. Crawshaw
British (19thC)
An Italianate Lake Landscape, with
Peasants resting by the Ruins
Signed and dated '1862', oil on canvas
16in (40.7cm) diam.
£550–650 *C*

G. Norman Crosse
British (active 1890–1900)
The Primrose Wood
Signed, watercolour
9¾ x 16in (24.5 x 40.5cm)
£250–350 *JC*

Arthur Croft
British (b1828)
Airolo, near St. Gothard, Switzerland
Signed and dated 1891, oil on canvas
14 x 24in (35.5 x 61.5cm)
£650–750 *HSS*

Alexandre Joseph Daiwaille
Dutch (1818–88)
A Drover with Cattle on a Woodland Track
Signed and dated 'A.J. Daiwaille ff50',
oil on canvas
28¾ x 36in (73 x 91.5cm)
£7,000–8,000 *CSK*

Attributed to Francis Danby, R.A.
British (1793–1861)
Clovelly, Devon
Signed, pen and black ink and wash
on grey paper
13½ x 16¾in (34 x 42cm)
£600–700 *S*

Diezler
German (19thC)
The Rhine at Honneff and Rolandseck
Signed and dated 'Diezler 1829', oil on panel
14½ x 22in (86.8 x 55.8cm)
£6,000–7,000 *CSK*

Charles Davidson
British (1824–1902)
Sheep on a Country Road by a Tinker's Camp
Signed, watercolour
11¾ x 18¾in (30 x 47.5cm)
£600–650 *Bea*

Thomas Dingle
British (19thC)
Harvesting at Sundown
Signed, oil on board
8½ x 13in (21.5 x 33.5cm)
£450–650 *S(S)*

Charles François Daubigny
French (1817–78)
A Cloudy Riverscene
Signed and dated '1871', oil on panel
10 x 18½in (25 x 47cm)
£5,000–6,000 *S*

George Haycock Dodgson
British (1811–80)
The Ferry Crossing
Pencil and watercolour
12 x 25in (31 x 64cm)
£850–1,000 *CSK*

Victor Dupré
French (1816–79)
A Wooded River Landscape with
Anglers on a Bank
Signed, oil on panel
12½ x 20½in (32 x 52cm)
£4,500–5,500 *CSK*

Mark Edwin Dockree
British (active 1856–90)
Banks of the Dee between Llangollen
and Berwyn
Signed, inscribed and dated '68',
oil on millboard
9 x 13in (23 x 33cm)
£1,450–1,650 *JG*

Edwin Earp
British (active c1900)
Lakes, Boats and Mountains
A pair, both signed, watercolours
9½ x 22½in (24 x 57cm)
£900–1,000 *LH*

Edwin Ellis
British (1841–95)
Autumnal Landscape with Sheep
Signed, watercolour
17 x 32in (43 x 81cm)
£450–550 *HSS*

David Farquharson, A.R.A., A.R.S.A., R.S.W.
British (1839–1907)
On the Banks of the Allan Water
Signed and dated '87', oil on canvas
12 x 20in (31 x 51cm)
£3,000–4,000 *WH*

John Faulkner
British (c1830–87)
Near Warwick
Signed, watercolour
heightened with bodycolour
17¾ x 30in (45 x 76cm)
£2,000–3,000 *C*

Thomas Fearnley
Norwegian (1802–42)
Farmhouses in a Mountainous Landscape
Signed and dated '1830', oil on canvas
11¾ x 15⅝in (30 x 40cm)
£4,500–6,000 *S*

Anthony Vandyke Copley Fielding
British (1787–1855)
Rustics and Cows on the Shores of Loch Tay
Signed, watercolour over traces of pencil with
scratching out and gum arabic
7 x 10¼in (18 x 26cm)
£4,000–4,500 *S*

Anthony Vandyke Copley Fielding
British (1787–1855)
Near Capel Curig, North Wales
Signed and dated '1811', watercolour
18 x 26in (45.5 x 66cm)
£1,000–1,200 *TAY*

Mario Moretti Fogia
Italian (b1882)
Chalets near Mont Blanc
Signed, oil on panel
20 x 15¾in (51 x 40cm)
£2,000–2,500 *CSK*

Baron Joseph James Forrester
British (1809–61)
A View of Douro with Figures overlooking
the River Tagus; and a Portuguese River
Landscape with a Ferry crossing by an
Island verso
Oil on zinc
16¾ x 23½in (43 x 60cm)
£10,000–12,000 *C*

*Forrester was born in Kingston-upon-Hull,
the son of a jeweller, but achieved fame and
wealth as a Port Shipper in Portugal and
eventual head of Offley Forrester and Co.
In addition to this he was a cartographer,
photographer, award-winning writer,
agriculturist and an accomplished amateur
artist who worked mainly in watercolour.
Clearly a man of tremendous energy,
Forrester was enormously popular in his
adopted land, where he was known as
'protector of the Douro', the wine-producing
district of Portugal. The calm and happy
river scene that he portrays here is, in one
sense, ironic. In 1861, while descending the
Douro by boat, Forrester's craft was sunk in
the rapids and his body was never recovered
from its waters.*

Myles Birket Foster
British (1825–99)
Dutch Coastal Scene
Signed with monogram, watercolour
4¾ x 5½in (12 x 14cm)
£1,650–1,850 *WrG*

Henry Charles Fox
British (b1860)
Springtime on the Farm
Signed and dated '1912', watercolour
15 x 22in (38 x 56cm)
£1,400–1,650 *CG*

Jacobus Freudenberg
Dutch (1818–73)
Frozen River Landscape with Figure Skating
Oil on canvas
22 x 31in (56 x 79cm)
£20,000–22,000 *WHP*

George Arthur Fripp, R.W.S.
British (1813–96)
A Traveller and his Dog by a Lake at Sunset
Signed, watercolour over pencil with
scratching out
10 x 14in (25 x 36cm)
£1,200–1,700 *S*

Robert Gallon
British (1845–1925)
Reflections of Autumn
Oil on canvas
24 x 40in (61 x 101.5cm)
£18,000–19,000 *HFA*

William Fraser Garden
British (1856–1921)
An Angler on the River Ouse, Bedfordshire
Signed and dated '88', pencil and watercolour
7½ x 11in (19 x 28cm)
£3,500–4,000 *C*

Edward Gay
American (1837–1928)
Resting by a Brook
Signed, oil on canvas
15 x 21in (38 x 53.4cm)
£750–850 *CNY*

Giacinto Gigante
Italian (1806–76)
A view of Arlamato Caserlano, Sorrento
Signed and indistinctly dated, watercolour
13 x 18in (33 x 46cm)
£6,000–6,500 *S*

Baldomero Galofre y Gimenez
Spanish (1849–1902)
A View of Aifi with Horses in the Foreground
Signed and inscribed 'Aifi', watercolour
25½ x 38in (65 x 96.5cm)
£6,500–7,000 *P(S)*

Francois Régis Gignoux
American/French (1816–82)
Winter Landscape with Hunter and Dog
Signed, watercolour and gouache on paper
4¾ x 6¾in (12 x 17cm)
£1,500–1,800 *S(NY)*

William Alfred Gibson
British (1866–1931)
The Ferry
Signed, oil on canvas
23½ x 28½in (59.6 x 72.3cm)
£5,500–6,000 *C(S)*

John Hamilton Glass, A.R.S.A.
British (1820–85)
St Monans, Fife
Signed, watercolour
12½ x 19½in (32 x 49cm)
£350–450 *S(S)*

Arthur Gilbert
British (1819–95)
Estuary Scenes
A pair, oil on canvas
7 x 10in (17.5 x 25cm)
£4,500–5,500 *HFA*

Alfred Augustus Glendening, Snr.
British (19thC)
Tending the Flock, Arundel
Signed, oil on canvas
16 x 26in (41 x 66cm)
£4,750–5,750 *Dr*

Vincent van Gogh
Dutch (1853–90)
Paysage de Brabant
Oil on canvas, painted in 1885
9 x 14¾in (23 x 38cm)
£190,000–220,000 *S(NY)*

C. Goddard
British (active 1870–90)
Down from the Hills
Signed, watercolour
7 x 14¾in (17.5 x 38cm)
£300–350 *JC*

Albert Goodwin, R.W.S.
British (1845–1932)
Port Antonio, Jamaica
Signed, watercolour heightened with
bodycolour and scratching out
7½ x 10in (18.7 x 25cm)
£8,500–9,500 *C*

*Christie's sale devoted to the works of Albert
Godwi, was a huge success. Pictures went
considerably over estimate, with only one of
the 51 lots failing to sell, and that found a
buyer immediately after the sale. The
selection of West Indian scenes, all dated
from 1902, were of particular interest.
On arriving in Barbados the artist wrote:
'It is singular how often one paints a so-
called imaginative picture to find the actual
place in nature soon after, only nature
making one's imagination to be entirely poor
and common. Here was the background of
Ali Baba all waiting to be done.'*

Albert Goodwin, R.W.S.
British (1845–1932)
The Gorge of the Teign, Dartmoor
Signed and inscribed, pencil and watercolour
heightened with touches of bodycolour and
scratching out
7¼ x 9½in (18.4 x 24.5cm)
£1,400–1,800 *C*

Albert Goodwin, R.W.S.
British (1845–1932)
Port Antonio, Jamaica
Signed and inscribed with colour notes,
pencil and watercolour heightened with
touches of bodycolour
4¾ x 10¼in (12 x 26cm)
£2,500–3,000 *C*

James Edward Grace
British (1851–1908)
Haymaking at Sunset
Watercolour
15 x 21in (38 x 53cm)
£780–1,000 *LH*

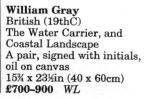

William Gray
British (19thC)
The Water Carrier, and
Coastal Landscape
A pair, signed with initials,
oil on canvas
15¾ x 23½in (40 x 60cm)
£700–900 *WL*

Ferdinand Joseph Gueldry
French (b1858)
Fishing on a Summer's Day
Signed, oil on board
9¼ x 13½in (23.5 x 34.3cm)
£2,500–3,000 *Bon*

H. J. van Hardevelt
Dutch (19thC)
Elegant Figures on a River Bank
Signed, oil on canvas
24 x 32in (61 x 81.3cm)
£1,500–2,000 *CSK*

James MacDougal Hart
American (1828–1901)
Landscape
Signed, oil on canvas
12¼ x 10¼in (31 x 26cm)
£2,500–3,000 *CNY*

Henri-Joseph Harpignies
French (1819–1916)
A view of the Château de Beauvoir
Signed, inscribed and dated
'août 84', watercolour
10½ x 15in (26.7 x 38cm)
£2,500–3,000 *C*

Thomas Alexander Harrison
British (1833–1930)
Falls at Montigny, France
Signed and dated '1901', oil on canvas
28 x 39½in (71 x 100.5cm)
£2,500–3,000 *CNY*

Sydney D. Hart
British (19th/20thC)
Lizard Point, Cornwall
Signed, watercolour
10½ x 14in (27 x 36cm)
£280–320 *LH*

Claude Hayes, R.I.
British (1852–1922)
Extensive landscape with a
Windmill and grazing Sheep
Signed, watercolour
13 x 20in (33 x 51cm)
£600–650 *HSS*

William M. Hart
American (1823–94)
In the Berkshires
Signed and dated '1873', oil on canvas
18 x 13¾in (45.7 x 35cm)
£7,000–8,000 *CNY*

Claude Hayes, R.I., R.O.I.
British (1852–1922)
Crossing the Moor
Watercolour
13½ x 20in (34 x 51cm)
£700–750 *Gan*

*Son of marine painter Edwin Hayes, Claude
ran away to sea when his father tried to
persuade him to follow a business career.
Having spent a year in America he returned
to England, where his father relented and
allowed him to enter the Royal Academy
Schools. Hayes became a popular landscape
painter, working in the loose and atmospheric
style of David Cox. He clearly delighted in his
commercial success and according to one
contemporary, whenever he was invited out,
he would always bring the conversation to a
point where he could proudly declare: 'For
many years I have never made less than £700
a year by my painting.'*

Joseph Henderson, R.S.W.
British (1832–1908)
The Swimming Race
Signed, oil on canvas
18 x 24in (45.7 x 61cm)
£2,500–3,000 *C(S)*

Joseph Morris Henderson, R.S.A.
British (1863–1936)
Gathering Hay in a sunlit River Landscape
Signed, oil on canvas
43¼ x 60½in (109.8 x 153.6cm)
£4,500–5,000 *C(S)*

Geradus Hendriks
Dutch (active 1850–80)
Winter Landscape with Skaters
and Woodcutters
Signed and dated '1862', oil on canvas
32 x 40in (81 x 101.5cm)
£12,000–15,000 *WG*

Harold Hill
British (19thC)
Powick Weir
Watercolour
10 x 15in (25 x 38cm)
£1,100–1,400 *HFA*

Theodore Hines
British (active 1876–90)
The Silver Strand, Loch Katrine
Signed on reverse, oil on canvas
10 x 7in (25 x 17.5cm)
£300–400 *BCG*

Arthur Hopkins, R.W.S.
British (1848–1930)
An Orchard by the Sea
Signed, indistinctly inscribed and
dated '12 Aug 1914, 13th, 14th, 16th, 18th',
overmounted, pencil and watercolour with
touches of white heightening
11¼ x 15¼in (28.5 x 38.8cm)
£3,000–4,000 *C*

Thomas Huson
British (1844–1920)
A River Landscape
Signed and dated '1877', oil on canvas
38½ x 59½in (97.5 x 151cm)
£3,000–3,500 *Bea*

George W. Horlor
British (active 1849–91)
Rosslyn Castle
Oil on canvas
11½ x 19½in (29 x 49cm)
£1,500–1,750 *Gan*

Thomas Swift Hutton
British (c1875–1935)
An Incoming Tide
Signed and indistinctly dated, watercolour
23½ x 35½in (60 x 90cm)
£1,000–1,200 *AG*

Andrew Jameson
British (19thC)
View near Alloa, Stirling in the Distance
Oil on canvas
20 x 30in (51 x 76cm)
£1,600–1,800 *MEA*

Japanese School (19thC)
Mount Fuji
Signed and sealed illegibly, ink wash on silk,
mounted on a scroll
18 x 29¼in (46 x 74cm)
£350–450 *SLN*

George Henry Jenkins
British (late 19thC)
Rocky Coastal Views at Sunset
A pair, signed, oil on canvas
10½ x 16½in (27 x 42cm)
£700–900 *LH*

Johann Jungblut
German (1860–1912)
Winter Sunset
Signed, oil on canvas
30 x 47in (76 x 119cm)
£15,000–16,000 *WHP*

Barend Cornelis Koekkoek
Dutch (1803–62)
A Cart on a Country Road in Summertime
Signed, oil on canvas, c1830
17¼ x 21½in (44 x 55cm)
£35,000–40,000 *S*

Frank Tenney Johnson
American (1874–1939)
Canyon Creek
Signed, dated and inscribed '1931',
oil on canvasboard
20 x 15¾in (50.8 x 40cm)
£4,800–5,800 *CNY*

Antonie Lodewijk Koster
Dutch (1859–1937)
In the Bulb Field
Signed, oil on canvas laid down on board
15¼ x 10¾in (39 x 27.5cm)
£4,000–5,000 *S(Am)*

Hendrik Barend Koekkoek
Dutch (1849–1909)
Summer and Winter
A pair, signed, oil on canvas
14 x 11½in (35.6 x 29.3cm)
£900–1,200 *CSK*

Vilhelm Kyhn
Danish (1819–1903)
A View of Himmelbjerget, Jutland
Signed and dated '1896', oil on canvas
48½ x 74in (123 x 188cm)
£4,500–6,000 *S*

F. Mortimer Lamb
American (1861–1936)
The Old Apple Tree
Signed, oil on canvas
18¾ x 24in (47.5 x 61cm)
£800–900 *CNY*

E. Lambert
British (late 19thC)
A Rocky Coastline with Figures on a Shoreline
Signed and dated '88', oil on panel
12½ x 23½in (30.5 x 59.7cm)
£750–900 *CSK*

Jonas Joseph Lavalley
American (1858–1930)
An Autumn Stream
Signed, oil on canvas
20¼ x 14in (51.4 x 35.6cm)
£850–1,000 *CNY*

Attributed to Charles B. Lawrence
American (1790–1864)
An Extensive River Landscape
Oil on canvas
24 x 32in (61 x 81.5cm)
£3,000–4,000 *CNY*

Benjamin Williams Leader, R.A.
British (1831–1923)
On the River Severn
Signed and dated '1902', oil on canvas
12 x 18in (30.5 x 45.7cm)
£3,000–4,000 *C*

Benjamin Williams Leader, R.A.
British (1831–1923)
Punting Day
Signed and dated '1886', oil on canvas
18 x 30½in (45.7 x 77.5cm)
£7,500–8,500 *C*

Benjamin Williams Leader, R.A.
British (1831–1923)
Near Capel Curig, North Wales
Signed and dated '1885', oil on canvas
19½ x 29½in (49.5 x 75cm)
£15,500–17,000   *S(S)*

*With conservative taste and decorative
Victorian landscapes performing well in the
salerooms, the works of Benjamin Leader
have been enjoying considerable success.
The present work doubled its auction
estimate at Sotheby's Billingshurst and a
few months previously, a large and sunny
harvesting scene, sold by Bonham's, set an
auction record for the artist of £60,000.
Immensely popular in his own period,
Leader's naturalistic landscapes are certainly
providing what the market wants today.*

Edward Lear
British (1812–88)
A North Italian Lake
Watercolour heightened with touches
of bodycolour
6¾ x 14¾in (17 x 38cm)
£2,500–3,000   *S*

Edward Lear
British (1812–88)
Monkeys on a Crag in the Western
Himalayas from Simla
Signed with monogram, dated '1875',
watercolour over traces of pencil
9¾ x 15½in (24.5 x 39cm)
£10,500–12,500   *S*

Stanislas Lepine
French (1835–92)
Cattle and Figures in a River Landscape
Signed and dated '58', oil on canvas
8 x 12½in (20.3 x 31.7cm)
£2,300–2,600   *CSK*

Jonas Lie
American (1880–1940)
Winter Stream
Signed, oil on canvas
43 x 50½in (109 x 128.2cm)
£2,600–2,800   *CNY*

Auguste Xavier Leprince
French (1799–1826)
Soldiers outside a Chateau; Figures and
Animals in a Farmyard
A pair, one signed and dated 1820, the other
indistinctly signed, oil on panel
12½ x 15½in (31.5 x 39cm)
£35,000–45,000   *S*

John Linnell
British (1792–1882)
Figures and a Cottage in a Hilly Landscape
Signed, oil on board
9 x 12in (23 x 31cm)
£1,400–1,600 *P*

Edgar Longstaff
British (active 1885–89)
Wagners Wells
Oil on canvas
10 x 8in (25 x 20cm)
£2,300–2,500 *HFA*

Thomas Lound
British (1802–61)
A distant view of Ely with Windmills
at Sunset
Signed and dated '1856', pencil and
watercolour heightened with white and
scratching out
13 x 19½in (32.5 x 49.2cm)
£4,500–5,000 *C*

Max Ludby, R.I., R.B.A.
British (1858–1943)
Lush Pastures
Signed and dated '1887', watercolour
13 x 20in (33 x 51cm)
£600–800 *JC*

Andrew McCallum
British (1821–1902)
Spring
Signed and dated '1862', oil on canvas
28 x 37in (71 x 94cm)
£9,000–9,500 *HFA*

William Henry Mander
British (active 1880–1992)
On the Lledyr, North Wales
Signed, oil on canvas
20 x 30in (51 x 76cm)
£5,600–5,800 *HFA*

William Manners
British (active 1885–1910)
Sherwood Forest
Signed, watercolour
14 x 10in (35.5 x 25cm)
£550–600 *G*

Robert Angelo Kittermaster Marshall
British (1849–1923)
The Vale of Evesham
Signed, watercolour
18 x 27in (45.5 x 68.5cm)
£5,000–5,500 *WG*

John Martin
British (1789–1854)
Figure with a Harp on the Shore
Signed and dated '1843', watercolour
and bodycolour
10½ x 27½in (26.5 x 70cm)
£5,500–6,500 *P*

Paul Mathieu
Belgian (1872–1932)
Une Journée d'Eté
Signed, oil on board
15¾ x 22in (40 x 55.5cm)
£10,000–11,000 *HFFA*

Maxime Maufra
French (1861–1918)
La Grand-Route
Signed and dated '1909', watercolour
and crayon
12 x 17½in (31 x 44cm)
£2,400–2,800 *C*

Edwin L. Meadows
British (active 1854–72)
The Farmstead
Signed and dated '1867',
oil on canvas
24 x 42in (61.5 x 106.5cm)
£12,500–13,000 *HFA*

William Mellor
British (1851–1931)
Pont-y-Pant, North Wales
Signed, oil on canvas
20 x 30in (51 x 76cm)
£1,700–1,900 *Dr*

William Mellor
British (1851–1931)
Bolton Abbey from the Wharfe, Yorkshire
Signed, inscribed on reverse, oil on canvas
19½ x 29½in (50 x 75cm)
£3,500–4,000 *AG*

William Mellor
British (1851–1931)
Cattle watering on the Glaslynn
Oil on canvas
20 x 24in (51 x 61.5cm)
£4,800–5,200 *HFA*

Antonij Andreas de Meyer
Dutch (b1806)
Figures on a Frozen Lake
Signed and dated '1841', oil on panel
19½ x 25½in (50 x 65cm)
£12,000–12,500 *S*

William Watt Milne
British (19thC)
Punting
Signed, oil on canvas
36in (91.5cm) square
£10,000–11,000 *S*

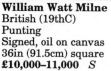

William Snell Morrish
British (1844–1917)
A Moorland Stream
Signed, watercolour
10¼ x 29in (26 x 74cm)
£450–550 *JC*

Philip Mitchell, R.I.
British (1814–86)
The Lobster Boat
Signed, watercolour
9¾ x 15in (25 x 38cm)
£250–350 *JC*

Henry Moret
French (1856–1913)
Bord de Mer, Bretagne
Signed, oil on canvas
13 x 16in (33 x 40.6cm)
£6,000–7,000 *C*

William James Muller
British (1812–45)
Two Children on a road at Whitchurch,
near Bristol
Watercolour over traces of pencil
9¾ x 14½in (25 x 36cm)
£1,400–1,800 *S*

George William Mote
British (1832–1909)
Fine Weather for Ducks
Signed and dated '1869', oil on canvas
28 x 36in (71 x 91.5cm)
£6,500–7,000 *WG*

Rosa Muller
British (active 1836–71)
At Hay Hill, Sherbourne, Dorset
Signed and dated '1860', oil on canvas
22 x 40in (55.5 x 101.5cm)
£10,500–11,000 *HFA*

William James Muller
British (1812–45)
Rocky Stream and Ravine, Lynmouth (1844)
Oil on canvas
34 x 25¾in (86 x 66cm)
£1,800–2,200 *S*

Laszlo Neogrady
Hungarian (b1900)
Winter Landscape
Signed, oil on canvas
24 x 30in (61 x 76cm)
£1,800–2,500 *S(NY)*

E. H. Niemann
British (active 1863–67)
Rural Landscape
Signed, oil on canvas
20 x 30in (51 x 76cm)
£2,250–2,500 *FdeL*

Edmund John Niemann
British (19thC)
A Fisherman by a Quiet Stream
Signed, oil on canvas
34 x 44in (86 x 112cm)
£1,200–1,600 *Bea*

T. Noelsmith
British (active 1889–1900)
Spetsbury, near Blandford, Dorset
Signed, pencil and watercolour
17¾ x 30in (45 x 76cm)
£550–650 *CSK*

Richard Pratchett Noble
British (active 1830–61)
Guildford Castle
Signed, inscribed and dated '1844',
watercolour heightened with white
11½ x 8½in (29 x 21.5cm)
£1,000–1,500 *P*

Robert Noble, R.S.A.
British (1857–1917)
Shaded by Trees
Signed, oil on board
9 x 12in (22.5 x 31cm)
£800–1,000 *WH*

Adelsteen Normann
Norwegian (1848–1918)
A Norwegian Fjord
Signed, oil on canvas
39 x 62in (99 x 157cm)
£8,000–9,000 *WH*

John William North, A.R.A., R.W.S.
British (1842–1924)
A Quiet Home: 'See where my blooming/pear
tree in the hedge hangs over'
Signed with initials and dated 'JWN/RWS
April' and inscribed, pencil and watercolour
with scratching out
12 x 17½in (30.5 x 44.5cm)
£4,000–5,000 *C*

George O'Brien
New Zealander (active 1860-80)
Woodhaugh, Nr Dunedin, New Zealand
Signed and dated '1865', watercolour
heightened with white
18 x 24½in (46 x 62.5cm)
£3,300–3,800 *P*

*George O'Brien, having worked for ten
years as a civil engineer, was appointed in
1872 as Dunedin's Assistant Surveyor. He
was an enthusiastic artist and recorder of
local views.*

Harry Sutton Palmer
British (1854–1933)
The River Ure, Hackfall
Signed and dated '1881'
13 x 20in (33 x 51cm)
£1,600–1,800 *AH*

Samuel Palmer, R.W.S.
British (1805–81)
The Silver City: Morning on the Jura
Mountains looking towards the Alps
Signed and dated '1844', watercolour
heightened with bodycolour, gum arabic and
scratching out
7¼ x 16in (18.5 x 40.5cm)
£20,500–25,000 *S*

Samuel Palmer, R.W.S.
British (1805–81)
The Cascades at Tivoli
Watercolour over pencil heightened with
bodycolour and gum arabic
10½ x 14¾in (27 x 37.5cm)
£20,000–25,000 *S*

Samuel Palmer, R.W.S.
British (1805–81)
Landscape with Cottage Roof
Black chalk, pen and ink and
watercolour heightened with white,
pencil and watercolour with touches
of white heightening
6 x 10½in (15.4 x 26.6cm)
£12,000–15,000 *C*

Henry H. Parker
British (1858–1930)
Harvest Time on the South Coast -
Littlehampton, Sussex
Signed and inscribed verso
12 x 18in (30.5 x 45.5cm)
£6,500–7,500   *LW*

Orrin Sheldon Parsons
American (1866–1943)
Adobe Houses, outside Sante Fe, New Mexico
Signed, oil on board
16 x 20in (40.6 x 51cm)
£3,000–3,500   *CNY*

James Peel
British (1811–1906)
A North Wales Landscape
Monogrammed and dated '1867', oil on canvas
14 x 23½in (35.5 x 60cm)
£700–1,000   *JNic*

Charles Henry Passey
British (active 1870–85)
Meeting on a Country Lane
Signed, oil on canvas
35½ x 27¼in (90 x 69.5cm)
£400–600   *S(S)*

Samuel John Peploe, R.S.A.
British (1871–1935)
Haystacks, Comrie
Signed, oil on panel
5 x 8½in (12.5 x 21cm)
£3,800–4,200   *C(S)*

Edward D. Percival
British (active 1877–1905)
Ilfracombe, North Devon
Signed and inscribed,
watercolour
11½ x 27¼in (29 x 69cm)
£350–450   *JC*

Sidney Richard Percy, R.A.
British (1821–86)
Sunshine and Shadow in the Welsh Highlands
Signed and dated '1850', oil on canvas
14 x 21in (35.6 x 53.4cm)
£5,000–6,000 *C*

Sidney Richard Percy, R.A.
British (1821–86)
Loch Katrine
Signed and dated '1865'
24 x 35in (61 x 89cm)
£10,750–15,000 *WH*

Sidney Richard Percy was a member of the almost unbelievably prolific Williams family of painters, who infiltrated 19thC landscape painting like a benign but all-pervasive mafia. His father, landscape painter Edward Williams (1782–1855), was descended from a line of artists. He had six sons, all of whom became painters and who, in turn, produced numerous artist children. Percy was Edward's fifth son and like two of his brothers he understandably changed his last name in order to distinguish himself from the ever-expanding Williams clan. Percy was perhaps the most successful artist in the family, his competent and pleasing pictures were highly popular, and he repeated the same formulae again and again for an appreciative clientele. According to his great-granddaughter, compiler of the family biography, one of Percy's most distinguishing features is his strong sense of design. She recommends turning his pictures upside down or looking at them in a mirror, as 'a reliable test of accuracy and balance'.
The Williams Family of Painters, by Jan Reynolds, Antique Collectors' Club, Woodbridge, 1975.

Percy's five artist brothers were: Edward Charles Williams (1807–81), Henry John Williams, called Boddington (1811–65), George Augustus Williams (1814–1901), Arthur Gilbert Williams, called Gilbert (1819–95), and Alfred Walter Williams (1824–1905).

Sidney Richard Percy, R.A.
British (1821–86)
The Falls of Dochart, Killin, Perthshire
Signed and dated '81', oil on canvas
24 x 38in (61 x 96.5cm)
£14,000–18,000 *C(S)*

Sidney Richard Percy, R.A.
British (1821–86)
A Landscape in the Lake District with Cattle at a Ford
Signed and dated '1893'
24 x 30in (61 x 76cm)
£45,000–50,000 *WH*

Locate the Source
The source of each illustration in Miller's can be found by checking the code letters below each caption with the list of contributors.

Attributed to Henry Pether
British (1828–65)
A Moonlight River Scene
Oil on board
8½ x 10½in (21 x 27cm)
£180–200 *FWA*

Reginald P. Phillimore
British (b1855)
Firth of Forth Coastal Scene, with Bass Rock
Signed and dated 'May 1929', watercolour
10 x 13½in (25 x 34.5cm)
£180–200 *LH*

Anton Pick
Austrian (b1840)
An Italianate Lake Landscape
Signed, oil on canvas
21½ x 29in (54.6 x 73.8cm)
£650–750 *CSK*

W. H. Pigott
British (c1810–1901)
Haddon Hall and the River Derwent
Signed, watercolour
9 x 13in (22.5 x 33cm)
£600–800 *ELR*

W. H. Pigott
British (c1810–1901)
Barnard Castle
Signed and dated '99'
17 x 26in (43 x 66cm)
£1,200–1,600 *ELR*

Camille Pissarro
French (1830–1903)
Paysage Tropical avec Masures et Palmiers
Signed and dated 'Paris 1856', oil on panel
9½ x 12¾in (24 x 32.5cm)
£140,000–150,000 *C*

*In 1883, an exhibition of Impressionist pictures, including eleven
works by Pissarro, was held by Durand-Ruel in London. None of the
exhibits were sold and, although the press was a little less hostile
than had been expected, reviews were decidedly mixed. 'My best
works ... were regarded as uncouth in London,' wrote Pissarro to his
son. '...my work offends English taste. Remember that I have the
temperament of a peasant, I am melancholy, harsh and savage in my
works, it is only in the long run that I can expect to please, and then
only those who have a grain of indulgence... But no more of that,'
Pissarro concluded confidently. 'Painting, art in general, delights me.
It is my life. What else matters?'*

Camille Pissarro
French (1830–1903)
La Sente du Chou, Pontoise
Signed and dated '76', oil on canvas
18 x 15in (46 x 38cm)
£375,000–450,000 *S(NY)*

Attributed to Rufus Porter
American (1792–1884)
A decorated pine fireboard, composed of
five planks with applied breadboard ends,
painted with a genre landscape, fully rigged
sailing ship and feathery trees, in tones
of green, yellow, orange and blue, New
England, early 19thC.
35 x 46in (89 x 117cm)
£16,000–18,000   *S(NY)*

*Rufus Porter was a portrait and mural
painter, as well as a silhouettist and
scientific inventor. He was born in West
Boxford, Massachusetts but was brought
up in Maine, and began his career there
as a house and sign painter. From 1824–45,
he worked primarily as an itinerant painter
of mural decoration in New England where
he became the most prolific practitioner of
this art form. He ended his career in art in
1845 to devote himself to editing the
Scientific American, which he founded in
New York City.*

George Frederick Prosser
British (active 1826–71)
On the Thames near Eton
Signed and dated '1871', watercolour over
traces of pencil heightened with touches of
white and scratching out
8¾ x 14½in (22 x 37cm)
£1,900–2,400   *S*

Karl Rettich
German (1841–1904)
Palermo
Signed, oil on canvas
46 x 69in (116.5 x 175.2cm)
£3,250–4,000   *CSK*

William Trost Richards
American (1833–1905)
Seascape at Sunset
Signed and dated '1870', oil on canvas
14½ x 26in (36.8 x 66cm)
£35,000–45,000   *S(NY)*

Thomas Miles Richardson, Jnr., R.W.S.
British (1813–90)
Latimer, Hertfordshire
Signed with initials, dated '1847',
watercolour
8 x 13in (20 x 33cm)
£650–800   *AG*

Thomas Miles Richardson, Jnr., R.W.S.
British (1813–90)
Taormina, Sicily
Signed with initials, dated '1875',
watercolour
4½ x 8in (11.5 x 20cm)
£1,300–1,500   *WrG*

Thomas Miles Richardson, Jnr., R.W.S.
British (1813–90)
Near Positano
Signed, inscribed and dated '1886',
watercolour
7½ x 18in (19 x 46cm)
£1,500–2,000 *WrG*

Thomas Miles Richardson, Jnr., R.W.S.
British (1813–90)
Dumbarton Castle, Clyde
Inscribed on mount, watercolour over traces
of pencil with scratching out
4 x 6in (10 x 15cm)
£3,750–4,500 *S*

Thomas Miles Richardson, Jnr., R.W.S.
British (1813–90)
Near Amalfi
Signed and dated '1858', watercolour and
gum arabic heightened with bodycolour
26 x 39½in (66 x 101cm)
£8,000–9,000 *C(S)*

After William Roberts
British (early 19thC)
The Natural Bridge, County of
Rockbridge, Virginia
Aquatint, 1808, printed in blue and
black, with hand colouring, engraved
by J. C. Stadler
30½ x 20¾in (77.5 x 52.5cm)
£4,250–5,000 *P*

Leopold Rivers, R.B.A.
British (1850–1905)
Near Milford Heath, Surrey
Signed and inscribed
verso, watercolour
15 x 26in (38 x 66cm)
£1,750–1,950 *WrG*

Willem Roelofs
Dutch (1882–97)
Cattle in a Meadow
Signed, oil on panel
8 x 12in (20 x 30.5cm)
£6,500–7,500 *C*

Federico Rossano
Italian (1835–1912)
The Hunters
Signed, pastel
17¼ x 23¼in (44 x 59cm)
£5,250–6,000 *S*

Auguste Roux
French (19thC)
A Rural Village
Signed, oil on canvas
26 x 36¼in (66 x 93cm)
£5,000–6,000 *S*

Etienne Pierre Théodore Rousseau
French (1812–67)
Pont dans le Jura
Signed with initials, oil on paper laid
down on canvas
8¾ x 12½in (22 x 31.4cm)
£20,000–25,000 *S(NY)*

Thomas Rowden
British (1842–1926)
The Pathfields at Woodbury
Signed, titled on backboard, watercolour
12¾ x 8½in (32.5 x 21.5cm)
£350–450 *JC*

Charles Rowbotham
British (active 1877–94)
Above San Gevanni
Signed, inscribed on mount, watercolour
6 x 11in (15 x 28cm)
£600–800 *HSS*

Herbert Royle
British (1870–1958)
Landscape with Cattle Watering
Signed, watercolour and gouache
21¼ x 16¾in (54 x 43cm)
£1,600–2,000 *AH*

John Ruskin
British (1819–1900)
The Thames from Richmond Hill
Watercolour over pencil, with pen and brown
ink and touches of white on grey paper
10¼ x 14¼in (26 x 36.5cm)
£17,500–20,000 *S*

*Although Ruskin's fame as a writer has
somewhat eclipsed his work as an artist, he
drew and painted voraciously from childhood
onwards. 'There is a strong instinct in me
which I cannot analyse to draw and describe
the things I love,' he wrote to his father in
1852, 'not for reputation, nor for the good of
others, nor for my own advantage, but a sort
of instinct like that for eating or drinking.'*

Gaudenz von Rustige
German (1810–1900)
Figures Skating
Signed and dated '1857', oil on canvas
23½ x 31in (60 x 78cm)
£3,750–4,500 *S*

George Sheffield
British (1839–92)
Donegal Cliff
Signed and dated '1874', watercolour
10 x 13½in (25 x 34cm)
£325–425 *BCG*

George Shalders
British (1826–73)
Children Blackberrying, with a Shepherd
and his Flock
Signed, bodycolour
11¼ x 19¼in (29.2 x 49cm)
£4,500–5,000 *C*

Daniel Sherrin
British (active 1895–1915)
Landscape with a Farmstead and Figures
Signed, oil on canvas
14 x 23in (35.5 x 59cm)
£600–700 *AH*

Daniel Sherrin
British (active 1895–1915)
Landscape at Sunset
Signed, oil on canvas
20 x 30in (51 x 76cm)
£1,200–1,500 *JNic*

Thomas Sidney
British (active c1900)
Low Tide, near Paignton, South Devon
Signed and inscribed, watercolour
6 x 19¼in (15 x 49cm)
£250–300 *JC*

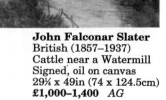

Peter Christian Skovgaard
Danish (1817–75)
The Cliff of Møen, Denmark
Signed and dated '1852', oil on canvas
49½ x 73in (126 x 185cm)
£5,500–6,000 *S*

John Falconar Slater
British (1857–1937)
Cattle near a Watermill
Signed, oil on canvas
29¼ x 49in (74 x 124.5cm)
£1,000–1,400 *AG*

William Harding Smith
British (1848–1922)
Lyme Bay, Dorset
Signed, watercolour
7 x 14in (17.5 x 35.5cm)
£180–250 *TAY*

Charles J. Smart
British (active 1867–91)
The Shark's Tooth Rocks, Hartland,
North Devon
Signed, inscribed and dated '85', watercolour
9¾ x 13¼in (25 x 34cm)
£200-250 *JC*

William Louis Sonntag
American (1822–1900)
Adirondak Landscape
Signed and dated '1868', oil on canvas
20¼ x 36in (51.4 x 91.5cm)
£4,300–5,300 *CNY*

Henry Sylvester Stannard
British (1870–1951)
Haymaking, Bedfordshire
Signed, watercolour
10 x 14in (25 x 35.5cm)
£4,500–4,800 *Dr*

Henry Sylvester Stannard
British (1870–1951)
Landscape with Shepherd and Sheep
Signed, watercolour
12 x 21in (30.5 x 53cm)
£1,000–1,400 *BWe*

James Stark
British (1794–1859)
Wooded Landscape with Figures
Oil on canvas
17¾ x 24¾in (45 x 63cm)
£3,200–4,000 *HOLL*

James Stark
British (1794–1859)
Near Trowse, Norwich
Oil on panel
22 x 30½in (55.5 x 77.5cm)
£20,000–25,000 *C*

E. Steinbach
German (19thC)
Dutch Winter Landscape at Sunset
Signed, oil on canvas
17 x 22½in (43.2 x 57.3cm)
£400–500 *CSK*

Arthur Suker
British (b1857)
The Approaching Mist
Signed, pencil and watercolour
23 x 36½in (59 x 93cm)
£600–800 *CSK*

August Strindberg
Swedish (1849–1912)
Fyrtornet II
Oil on canvas, painted in 1901
39 x 27¼in (99 x 69cm)
£320,000–360,000 *S*

*August Strindberg is best known as a
pioneer of modern drama, but was also
an important and influential artist. He
was a forerunner of abstract expressionist
painting in Northern Europe.*

Thomas Thomas
British (active 1882–92)
Herding the Sheep
Signed, oil on canvas
20 x 30in (51 x 76cm)
£4,600–5,200 *HFA*

Willem Bastiaan Tholen
Dutch (1860–1931)
Children and Chickens
in the Woods
Signed, oil on canvas
14 x 42in (36 x 106cm)
£11,500–12,500 *S(Am)*

Edward H. Thompson
British (19thC)
An Autumn Morning, Derwentwater and
Bassenthwaite Lake with Skiddaw from
above Lodore
Signed, watercolour
10 x 15in (25 x 38cm)
£950–1,100 *Mit*

Edward H. Thompson
British (19thC)
The Mountain Stream with Sheep and Fells
in the background
Signed, watercolour
7 x 10in (17.5 x 25cm)
£850–950 *Mit*

Joseph Thors
British (active 1863–1900)
Fishing in the River
Oil on canvas
22 x 31in (55.5 x 79cm)
£4,400–4,800 *HFA*

Joseph Thors
British (active 1863–1900)
An Oak-lined Woodland Path
Oil on canvas
19½ x 23½in (49 x 60cm)
£1,000–1,400 *DA*

Charles Towne
British (1781–1854)
Travellers in an extensive Landscape
Signed, oil on canvas
9 x 14in (22.5 x 36cm)
£1,000–1,200 *Dr*

Francis William Topham
British (1808–77)
Figures by a Cottage
Watercolour
9½ x 13½in (24 x 34cm)
£900–1,100 *PCA*

George Turner
British (1843–1910)
A Brook near Barrow, Derbyshire
Signed and inscribed with title verso,
dated '1873', oil on canvas
10 x 14in (25 x 36cm)
£3,000–3,650 *WG*

Circle of Alfred Vickers
British (19thC)
A Wooded Landscape with Figures in a
Meadow by a River
Oil on canvas, c1880
12 x 16in (30.5 x 40.6cm)
£1,500–1,700 *CGa*

A. H. Vickers
British (active 1853–1907)
River Landscape
Signed, oil on canvas
12⅛ x 24in (30.7 x 61cm)
£1,750–1,950 *FdeL*

George Vincent
British (1796–1831)
Cattle, Pigs, Ducks and Chickens before
a Barn and a Cottage
Monogrammed, oil on panel
8½ x 7¼in (21 x 18cm)
£1,600–2,000 *JNic*

Richard Whateley West
Irish (1848–1905)
Homeward Bound
Oil on canvas
8 x 10½in (20 x 27cm)
£550–600 *Gan*

Bryan Whitmore
British (active 1871–97)
Chertsey Meadows on the River Thames
Signed, watercolour over traces of pencil
9¾ x 30in (24 x 76cm)
£1,600–1,800 *JG*

Frederick John Widgery
British (1861–1942)
Barnstaple Bridge and the River Taw
Signed, watercolour
6¼ x 10in (16 x 25cm)
£1,500–2,000 *JC*

Alfred Walter Williams
British (1824–1905)
Estuary Scene with Figures and
a Horsedrawn Cart
Monogrammed, oil on canvas
14 x 22½in (35.5 x 57cm)
£800–900 *JNic*

William Tatton Winter, R.B.A.
British (1855–1928)
Path by the Somme
Watercolour
13½ x 15in (34.5 x 38cm)
£1,600–1,800 *CGa*

Edmund Morison Wimperis
British (1835–1900)
The Coastal Path
Signed with initials, watercolour
13½ x 20½in (34 x 52cm)
£600–700 *BCG*

Francesco Foschi
Italian (d1805)
Winter Landscape with a Sportsman Shooting Duck,
beside a Stream
Oil on canvas laid down on panel
18¼ x 29¼in (47.2 x 74.3cm)
£9,500–12,000 *S*

Isaak van Oosten
Flemish (1613–61)
Peasants and a Cart on a Path by a Stream
Signed, oil on panel
10¾ x 14½in (27.2 x 37cm)
£17,500–20,000 *C*

Attributed to Richard Wilson
British (1714–82)
Classical Landscape with Figures
Oil on canvas
17½ x 21¼in (44 x 54cm)
£5,500–6,500 *WT*

Robert Ladbrooke
British (1770–1842)
The Cottage in the Wood
Oil on Canvas
18 x 22in (46 x 56cm)
£2,000–3,000 *HOLL*

George Cuitt
British (1743–1818)
Langton Hall, Northallerton, North Yorkshire
Bodycolour
19 x 26in (48 x 66cm)
£7,000–9,000 *C*

Egbert Lievensz. van der Poel Dutch (1621–64)
A Winter Landscape with Peasants
Signed, oil on panel
9½ x 13¼in (24 x 34cm)
£50,000–60,000 *C*

l. **Filippo Angeli, called Filippo Napoletano**
Italian (c1587–1627)
A River Landscape, with a Hamlet and a Tower
Oil on canvas, 30½ x 47in (77.5 x 119.3cm)
£35,000–45,000 *C*

Henry Bright
British (1810–73)
Mont Blanc
Signed, coloured chalks
24¼ x 33¼in (62 x 84.5cm)
£4,200–5,000 *C*

Alfred de Breanski, Snr.
British (1852–1928)
Loch Ness and Ben Lomond
A pair, both signed, oil on canvas
20 x 30in (50.5 x 76.5cm)
£22,000–25,000 *S*

John Anderson
British (active 1858–86)
Still Waters
Signed with monogram, dated '1886', oil on canvas
18 x 30in (45.5 x 76cm)
£6,000–7,000 *HFA*

Alfred Fonteville de Breanski
British (1877–1945)
Loch Katrine at Sunrise
Oil on canvas
20 x 30in (50.5 x 76.5cm)
£5,000–6,000 *HFA*

Thomas Baker
British (1809–69)
Cattle by a Churchyard
Signed and dated '1860', watercolour
8 x 11in (20 x 28cm)
£800–1,000 *Dr*

Jean-Baptiste Camille Corot
French (1796–1875)
Les Ramasseuses de Pissenlits
Signed, oil on canvas
18½ x 22in (47 x 55.5cm)
£250,000–300,000 *S(NY)*

l. **G. Hamilton Constantine**
British (b1878)
Sheep in a wooded Derbyshire Landscape
Signed, watercolour
13½ x 20in (34.5 x 50.5cm)
£800–1,000 *ELR*

English School (19thC)
View of Warwick Castle with moored
Rowing Boat, Riverside Houses and Trees
Oil on canvas
36 x 51in (92 x 129.5cm)
£3,200–4,000 *RBB*

David Cox
British (1783–1859)
A Windy Day
Signed, watercolour
10¾ x 14¾in (27 x 37cm)
£3,500–4,500 *HOLL*

Myles Birket Foster, R.W.S.
British (1825–99)
Watering the Cattle
Signed with monogram, watercolour
13 x 19in (33 x 48cm)
£16,000–17,000 *HFA*

Albert Dunington
British (1860–c1928)
The Ferry, Overton on Dee
A pair, signed, oil on canvas
24 x 16½in (61.5 x 42cm)
£2,000–2,300 *CGa*

Edward Duncan
British (1803–82)
Coastal Scene
Signed and dated '1849', oil on canvas
15½ x 21½ in (39 x 54.5cm)
£2,000–2,500 *HOLL*

Robert Winter Fraser
British (active 1870–99)
On the Ouse
Signed and dated '1893', watercolour
14 x 20 (35.5 x 51cm)
£800–900 *EG*

Arthur Anderson Fraser
British (1861–1904)
A Grey Day in August
Signed with initials, dated '1895' and
inscribed verso, watercolour
9½ x 17in (24 x 43cm)
£900–975 *WrG*

Above and left
Robert Gallon
British (1845–1925)
Fishing on the Lledyr and
A Mountain River
A pair, oil on canvas
20 x 30in (51 x 76cm)
£14,000–14,800 *HFA*

*Robert Gallon specialised in British
landscapes, painted in a realistic style
similar to B. W. Leader and Vicat Cole.*

*These works are typical of the decorative
landscapes that have been performing well
in the currect market.*

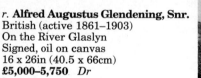

r. **Alfred Augustus Glendening, Snr.**
British (active 1861–1903)
On the River Glaslyn
Signed, oil on canvas
16 x 26in (40.5 x 66cm)
£5,000–5,750 *Dr*

l. **Albert Goodwin, R.W.S.**
British (1845–1932)
The Avon, Salisbury
Signed and inscribed, pencil
and watercolour
10 x 14in (25 x 36cm)
£4,500–5,500 *C*

John Henderson
British (1860–1924)
Children playing in a Sunlit Landscape
Signed, oil on canvas
20 x 36in (50.5 x 91.5cm)
£5,500–7,000 *C(S)*

David James
British (active 1881–98)
Seagirt Cliffs
Signed, oil on canvas
40 x 30in (101.5 x 76cm)
£2,000–2,500 *WH*

l. **William Havell**
British (1782–1857)
Classical Landscape
Oil on millboard
11¼ x 15½in (29 x 39.5cm)
£3,000–3,500 *BuP*

r. **William E. Harris**
British (active 1883–91)
Road at Broadway
Signed and dated '1888',
oil on canvas
18 x 34in (45.5 x 86cm)
£6,000–7,000 *HFA*

l. **Benjamin Williams Leader, R.A.**
British (1831–1923)
Driving Cattle through
the Valley
Signed and dated 1871,
oil on canvas
23 x 36in (58.5 x 91.5cm)
£16,500–17,500 *HFA*

*Born as Benjamin Williams, he
added the surname Leader, his
father's middle name, to
distinguish himself from the
Williams family, of which he was
no relation. He became a pupil at
the Royal Academy in 1853.*

William Mellor
British (1851–1931)
Woodland Brook, Wharfedale
Oil on canvas
11½ x 17in (29 x 43cm)
£3,000–3,500 *LT*

Adelsteen Normann
Norwegian (1848–1918)
Norwegian Fjord
Signed, oil on canvas
32 x 43¾in (81 x 110cm)
£18,500–19,500 *BuP*

James Peel
British (1881–1906)
Rural Landscape
Signed, oil on canvas
20 x 30in (50.5 x 76cm)
£2,000–3,000 *FdeL*

Henry H. Parker
British (1858–1930)
The Stort, Harlow, Essex
Signed, oil on canvas
14 x 22in (35.5 x 55.5cm)
£4,000–5,000 *WG*

r. **Samuel Palmer, O.W.S.**
British (1805–81)
Evening: A Cottager
returning Home greeted by
his Children
Pencil and watercolour
heightened with bodycolour
7½ x 16in (19 x 40.5cm)
£30,000–40,000 *C*

l. **Sidney Richard Percy**
British (1821–86)
The Wayside Path
Signed, oil on canvas
16 x 24in (40.5 x 61.5cm)
£8,000–9,000 *HFA*

Leopold Rivers
British (1852–1905)
Witley Common, Surrey
Signed and dated '1881', oil on canvas
16 x 24in (40.5 x 61cm)
£1,750–2,250 *Dr*

W. H. Pigott
British (1810–1901)
Conisborough Castle, with River and Barge
Signed and dated '1876', watercolour
14 x 20in (35.5 x 50.5cm)
£1,500–2,000 *ELR*

Frank Corbyn Price
British (b1862)
Village Green, Pulborough
Signed, watercolour
15 x 23in (38 x 58.5cm)
£1,250–1,450 *WrG*

Joseph Paul Pettitt
British (active 1845–80)
The New Pony
Signed and dated '1868',
oil on canvas
24 x 42in (61.5 x 106.5cm)
£11,000–12,000 *HFA*

Charles Frederick Robinson
British (active 1874–1915)
Hurley Lock, Nr. Marlow
Signed, watercolour
13 x 19in (33 x 48cm)
£1,200–1,500 *HO*

Camille Pissarro
French (1830–1903)
Vue de Bazincourt
Signed and dated lower right '84',
oil on canvas
21½ x 25½in (54.5 x 65cm)
£360,000–450,000 *C*

*In April 1884 Pissarro settled in Eragny-Bazincourt,
near Gisors. With some financial help from Monet,
Pissarro was able to buy his house. It had a huge
garden with an orchard and he converted a
substantial barn into his studio. This painting may
well have been executed from his studio looking
across the fields.*

John Brandon Smith
British (1848–84)
Waterfall near Dolgelley
Signed and dated '1874',
oil on canvas
18 x 14in (45.5 x 35.5cm)
£4,000–5,000 *BuP*

Jesse Talbot
American (1806–79)
Landscape by a River with Mountains in the Distance
Oil on canvas
36 x 56in (91.5 x 142cm)
£8,000–9,000 *S(NY)*

Thomas Charles Leeson Rowbotham
British (1823–75)
An Italian Coastal Scene
Watercolour with white heightening
6¾ x 12½in (17 x 32cm)
£500–600 *PCA*

Arthur Sorer
British (active 1882–1902)
Fisherman on the Moors
Watercolour
15½ x 23¼in (39 x 59cm)
£1,000–1,200 *CGa*

Charles Rowbotham
British (1858–1921)
Mondola, near Palermo, Sicily
Watercolour
6½ x 11½in (16 x 29cm)
£1,200–1,300 *AdG*

l. **Henry John Sylvester Stannard**
British (1870–1951)
Going to Pasture
Signed, watercolour
14 x 21in (35.5 x 53cm)
£3,000–3,600 *Dr*

Joseph Thors
British (active 1863–1900)
Rural Landscape
Signed, oil on canvas
10 x 14in (25 x 35.5cm)
£2,500–2,800 *CGa*

Edward Wilkins Waite
British (active 1878–1927)
Picking Poppies in the Cornfield
Signed, oil on canvas
32 x 47in (81.5 x 119cm)
£35,000–40,000 *HFA*

l. **Charles Watson**
British (19thC)
Highland Cattle in a
Winter Landscape
Signed, oil on canvas
40 x 30in
(101.5 x 76cm)
£2,000–2,500 *FdeL*

Peter de Wint, O.W.S.,
British (1784–1849)
A Farm near Spalding, Lincolnshire
Pencil and watercolour with scratching out
10¾ x 17½in (27 x 44.5cm)
£3,500–4,000 *C*

Alfred O. Townsend
British (1846–1917)
Abergavenny Castle
Signed, watercolour
14 x 25in (35.5 x 63.5cm)
£500–600 *TFA*

William Williams
British (1808–95)
On the Exminster Marshes
Signed, inscribed on reverse, oil on
canvas laid on board
8½ x 12¾in (21 x 32.5cm)
£1,200–1,500 *CGa*

r. **Edmund Morison Wimperis**
British (1835–1900)
Harvest Time
Signed and dated '1892',
oil on canvas
19½ x 29½in (49.5 x 75cm)
£1,900–2,500 *AH*

Jacqueline Black
British (20thC)
April Field
Oil on canvas
22 x 32in (55.5 x 81cm)
£600–700 *AMC*

Sergei Chepik
Russian (20thC)
Christmas Day
Oil on canvas, 1987
20in (50.5cm) square
£4,500–5,500 *RMG*

Gordon Bryce, A.R.S.A.
British (b1943)
Sea Surf
Oil on canvas, 1993
44 x 69in (111.5 x 175cm)
£7,500–8,500 *TRG*

James Humbert Craig
British (1878–1944)
Sunday Morning - A Summer Landscape
Signed, oil on canvas
36 x 44in (91.5 x 111.5cm)
£16,000–17,000 *CCG*

John Denahy
British (b1922)
Darenth Trees, Winter
Oil on canvas
24in (61.5cm) square
£1,200–1,400 *AMC*

Francis Campbell Boileau Cadell, R.S.A., R.S.W.
Scottish (1883–1937)
The White Villa, Cassis
Signed and inscribed, oil on panel
17¾ x 14¾in (45 x 37.5cm)
£29,000–35,000 *C(S)*

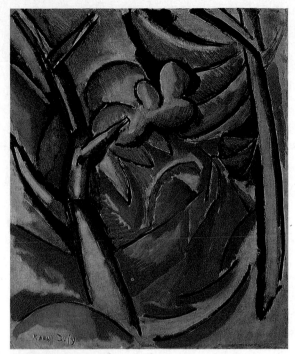

Raoul Dufy
French (1877–1953)
Les Arbres verts à l'Estaque
Signed, titled and dated '1909', oil on canvas
21¾ x 18¼in (55 x 46.5cm)
£70,000–80,000 *C*

Clara Gangutia
Spanish (b1952)
Madrid
Etching, 1990
15 x 19½in (38 x 49.5cm)
£150–200 *GPS*

Frederick Gore, R.A.
British (b1913)
Bales of Corn on the Plateau d'Albion
Oil on canvas
28 x 36in (71 x 91.5cm)
£4,500–5,500 *ULG*

James Fullarton
British (20thC)
Skye from Arisaig
Signed, oil on canvas, 1993
20 x 30in (51 x 76cm)
£2,000–2,500 *VCG*

Daniel Garber
American (1880–1958)
April 30th
Signed and dated '1952', oil on board
18 x 24in (45.5 x 61cm)
£17,000–19,000 *S(NY)*

l. **Stan Egerton**
British (20thC)
Beekeepers, Beijing
Oil on canvas
7 x 9in (17.5 x 23cm)
£700–750 *CW*

Michael Honnor
British (b1944)
Rain Passing, Isles of Scilly
Oil on canvas, 1992
38½ x 40½in (97 x 102cm)
£1,300–1,500 *TRG*

Paul Kenny
British (20thC)
Nymphéas II Giverny
Oil on canvas
36 x 40in (91.5 x 101.5cm)
£5,000–5,500 *PN*

Jean Kévorkian
French (b1933)
Meilars enneigé
Signed, oil on canvas
15 x 18in (38 x 46cm)
£1,650–1,850 *Om*

Sir Roger de Grey, P.R.A.
British (b1918)
Canal Marennes
Oil on canvas
36in (91.5cm) square
£6,500–7,000 *WHP*

l. **Robert Kelsey**
Scottish (b1949)
Farm Lane, Ayrshire
Oil on canvas
22 x 32in (56 x 81cm)
£1,000–1,200 *Tho*

Mary Lloyd Jones
British (b1934)
Cynefin
Oil on canvas
24 x 48in (61 x 122cm)
£1,300–1,500 *MT*

David Kirk British (20thC)
Watch My Finger
Acrylic
21 x 26in (53 x 66cm)
£650–850 *SJG*

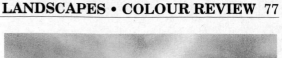

Percy Lancaster
British (1878–1951)
The Gorge
Signed, oil on canvas
28 x 36in (71 x 91.5cm)
£1,500–1,700 *Dr*

Peter Knuttel
Irish (20thC)
Connemara Light
Signed, watercolour
22 x 30in (55.5 x 76cm)
£750–1,000 *NAG*

Gustave Loiseau
French (1865–1935)
Etretat, la Pointe de la Batterie
Signed and dated '1902', oil on canvas
25½ x 36¼in (65 x 93cm)
£37,000–42,000 *S(NY)*

Norman Lloyd
Australian (b1895)
Summer Orchard
Signed, oil on canvas
18 x 22in (45 x 56cm)
£1,800–2,000 *EG*

Brett McEntagart, R.H.A
Irish (20thC)
Farm with Tobacco Barn
Oil on canvas
18 x 24in (45.5 x 61.5cm)
£1,200–1,600 *SOL*

James Longueville, R.B.S.A.
British (b1942)
Cloud over Adrigole, Beara
Oil on canvas
24 x 36in (61.5 x 91.5cm)
£1,500–2,000 *SOL*

Martin Mooney
Irish (b1960)
Besalu, near Gerona showing the
Fortified Bridge
Oil on board
18 x 57½in (45.5 x 146cm)
£3,000–4,000 *SOL*

Jean McNeil
British (20thC)
Edge of Wood
Oil on paper
16¼ x 23¼in (41 x 59cm)
£400–600 *FT*

Edward Noott
British (b1965)
Sunflowers II
Oil on canvas
25 x 30in (64 x 76cm)
£1,200–1,400 *JN*

Hamish Murray
British (20thC)
Peregrine, Winter Morning, Ballard Point
Watercolour
10½ x 7in (26.5 x 17.5cm)
£400–500 *PHG*

Ann Oram, R.S.W.
British (b1956)
Ghar Ghur Village
Signed, oil on canvas
24 x 36in (61.5 x 91.5cm)
£2,500–3,000 *TRG*

Christine McKechnie
British (20thC)
Seatoller Stream
Collage
25½ x 31¾in (65 x 81cm)
£900–1,000 *AMC*

Edgar Alwyn Payne
American (1882–1947)
Sycamore Canyon
Signed, oil on canvas
24 x 28in (61.5 x 71cm)
£12,500–13,500 *S(NY)*

Francis Picabia
French (1879–1953)
L'église de Montigny, Effet d'automne
Stamped signature on stretcher, oil on
canvas, 1908
25½ x 31¾in (65 x 80cm)
£75,000–90,000 *S(NY)*

Maria Pinschof
British (20thC)
Roof in Lot Valley, France
Signed, oil on canvas
18 x 24in (45.5 x 61.5cm)
£700–900 *FT*

Christopher Wood
British (20thC)
Red Cottages
Signed, oil on canvas, 1993
24in (61.5cm) square
£800–900 *VCG*

Joseph Henry Sharp
American (1859–1953)
Spring, The Desert and Mt. San Jacinto at Palm Springs
Signed, inscribed and dated '1938' on the reverse,
oil on masonite
15¾ x 20in (40 x 50.5cm)
£20,000–25,000 *S(NY)*

Gordon H. Wyllie
British (b1930)
Morning, Kintyre
Mixed media
14 x 15in (35.5 x 38cm)
£700–800 *RB*

Maurice de Vlaminck
French (1876–1958)
La Meule
Signed, oil on canvas
23½ x 28¾in (60 x 73cm)
£40,000–50,000 *P*

Frank Dillon
British (1823–1909)
The Pyramids from the Island of Roda
Signed, oil canvas
26 x 46½in (66 x 118cm)
£14,000–16,000 *C*

Teng-Hiok Chiu
Chinese (20thC)
North African Landscape
Oil on canvas, 1934
22 x 18in (56 x 45.5cm)
£400–475 *JDG*

Etienne Raffort
French (1802–95)
The Mihrimah Sultan Mosque
Signed and dated '1850', oil on canvas
24¾ x 38¼in (63 x 97cm)
£35,000–40,000 *S*

Jacob Jacobs
Belgian (1812–79)
Merchant Vessels off the Turkish Coast
Signed and dated '1849', oil on panel
24¾ x 38¼in (63 x 97cm)
£40,000–50,000 *P*

Peder Mønsted
Danish (1859–1941)
The Great Wall of China
Signed with initials and dated '76',
oil on canvas
12¼ x 19in (32 x 48.5cm)
£4,000–4,500 *BuP*

Joseph Warnia-Zarzecki
Polish (b1850)
A View of Istanbul, looking towards Usküdar
Signed twice, oil on canvas
27 x 39in (69 x 99cm)
£37,000–40,000 *S*

l. **Noel Harry Leaver, A.R.C.A.**
British (1889–1951)
Algerian Town Scene
Watercolour
11 x 15in (28 x 38cm)
£2,500–2,800 *HFA*

20th Century

W. J. Alberts
British (early 20thC)
The Heart of the Country
Signed, oil on canvas
24 x 39½in (61 x 100cm)
£400–500 *JDG*

Harry Epworth Allen
British (1894–1958)
Landscape with Houses
Signed, pastel
15¼ x 18¼in (39 x 46.5cm)
£1,500–2,000 *C*

Samuel John Lamorna Birch, R.A.
British (1869–55)
From the Light of Cara Dhu
Signed and inscribed, pencil and watercolour
19 x 23½in (48 x 60cm)
£2,000–2,500 *C*

Sidney James Beer
British (1874–1953)
Mullion Cove
Signed, watercolour
10¼ x 14⅜in (26 x 37.5cm)
£200–250 *JC*

Xavier J. Barile
American (b1891)
Beyond Artist Drive, Death Valley
Signed, oil on masonite
20 x 24in (51 x 61cm)
£700–800 *CNY*

Theresa F. Bernstein
American (b1895)
Folley Cove Point
Signed and dated 'T. Bernstein/16',
oil on board
12 x 16in (30.5 x 40.5cm)
£950–1,050 *CNY*

Samuel John Lamorna Birch, R.A.
British (1869–1955)
Carn Dhu and The Lizard
Signed, oil on canvas
40 x 50in (101.5 x 127cm)
£20,000–25,000 *WHL*

Samuel John Lamorna Birch, R.A.
British (1869–1955)
Hillside above Lamorna Cove
Signed, oil on canvas
12 x 18in (30.5 x 45.5cm)
£1,400–1,800 *C*

George Cyril Branscombe
British (1886–1962)
The Breakwater, Bude, Cornwall
Signed and dated '1912', watercolour
12½ x 22½in (32 x 57cm)
£250–350 *JC*

Hugh Boycott Brown
British (b1909)
Suffolk Sea
Signed with initials, oil on board
6 x 8in (15 x 20cm)
£400–500 *BRG*

James Brown
British (20thC)
The Walker
Oil on board
24in (61cm) square
£1,000–1,200 *BRG*

William Bowyer, R.A.
British (b1926)
View from Richmond Hill
Signed, oil on canvas
28 x 36in (71 x 91.5cm)
£4,500–5,000 *WHP*

John Brunsdon
British (20thC)
The Devil's Punchbowl
Etching
17¾ x 23½in (45 x 60.5cm)
£100–125 *CCA*

Charles Ephraim Burchfield
American (1893–1967)
Old Cottage in May
Signed and dated '1933', watercolour
and charcoal
18 x 27in (45.8 x 68.6cm)
£5,000–6,000 *CNY*

Francis Campbell Boileau Cadell, R.S.A., R.S.W.
British (1883–1937)
Pink Rocks, Iona
Signed and inscribed, oil on panel
14½ x 17½in (37 x 44.5cm)
£17,000–18,000   *C(S)*

*During the 1980s, works by the Scottish colourists
(Peploe, Cadell, Hunter and Fergusson) attracted
huge international interest and correspondingly
large sums of money. Values plummeted in the
recession, when demand for these and other modern
British works nose-dived and Christie's abandoned
their specific colourist sales in Scotland. Although
the prices of colourist pictures have not returned
to the 1980s level, they certainly seem to be
strengthening. This painting by Cadell more than
doubled its lower estimate at Christie's, Glasgow,
in November 1993, and the same sale saw four
Cadell's exceed the £10,000 mark.*

Francis Campbell Boileau Cadell, R.S.A., R.S.W.
British (1883–1937)
North Sands, Iona
Signed and inscribed, oil on canvas laid
down on board
14½ x 17¾in (36.5 x 45cm)
£6,500–8,000   *C(S)*

Sir David Young Cameron, R.A., R.S.A.
British (1865–1945)
Misty Mountain Tops
Signed, oil on canvas
25 x 30in (63.5 x 76.2cm)
£6,000–6,500   *C(S)*

Sir Winston Churchill, O.M., Hon R.A.
British (1874–1965)
The Atlas Mountains from Marrakesh
Signed with initials, oil on canvas, c1949
22¼ x 26¾in (56 x 68cm)
£35,000–45,000   *C*

*Churchill first visited Marrakesh in 1935,
which became a great source of inspiration to
the artist. The only painting he executed during
WWII was a view of Marrakesh with the tower
of the Katoubia Mosque. Churchill wrote to
President Roosevelt in 1943, 'You cannot go all
this way to North Africa without seeing
Marrakesh. Let us spend two days there. I
must be with you when you see the sunset on
the snows of the Atlas Mountains.'*

Eliot Clark
American (1883–1980)
A Creek in a Spring Landscape
Signed, oil on canvas
16 x 20in (40.7 x 50.8cm)
£800–1,000   *CNY*

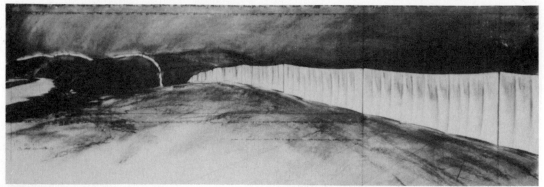

Christo
Rumanian (b1935)
Running Fence (Project for Sonoma County
and Marin County, State of California)
Signed, titled and dated '1974', charcoal
36 x 96in (91.4 x 243.8cm)
£26,000–32,000 *S(NY)*

Peter Coker, R.A.
British (b1926)
La Roche Guyon
Oil on canvas
27½ x 48in (70 x 122cm)
£3,500–4,000 *FCG*

James Humbert Craig, R.H.A., R.V.A.
Irish (1878–1944)
Irish Landscape
Signed, oil on panel
9 x 11in (22.5 x 28cm)
£1,000–1,100 *STA*

Sir Noël Coward
British (1900–1973)
Jamaican Road
Signed, oil on canvas
10 x 14in (25 x 35.5cm)
£3,000–3,500 *MTG*

*It was in 1948 that Noël Coward first visited
Jamaica. He fell in love with the island and
returned to it constantly until the very end of
his life. Coward built a house by the sea
called Blue Harbour, and a small retreat on
the land above it, Firefly Hill, where he died
in March 1973 and is buried.*

Fred Cuming
British (b1930)
Summer Landscape
Signed, oil on board
18 x 24in (46 x 61cm)
£2,500–2,800 *BRG*

John Gardiner Crawford
Scottish (b1941)
The Old Kingdom
Signed, acrylic on masonite, 1991
30in (76cm) square
£12,000–12,500 *WH*

André Derain
French (1880–1954)
Bords de Seine à Chatou
Signed, oil on canvas
23½ x 29in (60 x 74cm)
£45,000–50,000 *C*

Gabriel Deschamps
French (b1919)
Como Isola Comacina
Signed, oil on canvas
23¾ x 32in (60.4 x 81cm)
£3,500–4,000 *C*

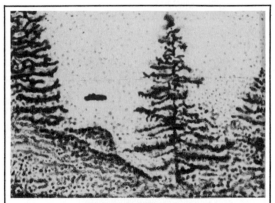

Ronald Ossory Dunlop, R.A., R.B.A., N.E.A.C.
Irish (1894–1973)
Irish Landscape with Cottages
Signed, oil on canvas
13 x 15in (33 x 38cm)
£900–1,000 *LH*

Jiri Georg Dokoupil
Czechoslovakian (b1954)
Ovni con abetos
Candle soot on canvas
28¾ x 39½in (73 x 100cm)
£2,800–3,200 *C*

Ronald Ossory Dunlop, R.A., R.B.A., N.E.A.C.
Irish (1894–1973)
Burnham Mill, Sussex
Signed, oil on canvas
15 x 19½in (38 x 50cm)
£900–975 *Gan*

Eloise Egan
American (1874–1967)
Slave Quarters, Charleston, South Carolina
Signed, oil on canvas
25¼ x 30in (64 x 76.3cm)
£650–750 *CNY*

Shan Egerton
British (20thC)
Prayer Flags
Signed with initials, pastel
11 x 15in (28 x 38cm)
£850–950 *CW*

John Duncan Fergusson, R.B.A.
British (1874–1961)
Fields, Peebles
Oil on board, c1900
4½ x 5½in (11.2 x 14cm)
£3,250–3,750   *C(S)*

John Duncan Fergusson, R.B.A.
British (1874–1961)
Beeches near Aberdour
Indistinctly signed and inscribed, oil on board
4½ x 5½in (11.2 x 13.7cm)
£2,250–2,750   *C(S)*

John Duncan Fergusson, R.B.A.
British (1874–1961)
Tweed Bridge, Peebles
Signed and inscribed, oil on panel, c1902
7½ x 9¼in (19 x 23.5cm)
£8,750–9,750   *C(S)*

Jules Flandrin
French (1871–1947)
Eglise de Cozène
Signed, oil on canvas
25½ x 31¾in (65 x 80.5cm)
£2,800–3,200   *C*

Locate the Source

The source of each illustration in Miller's can be found by checking the code letters below each caption with the list of contributors.

Sir William Russell Flint, R.A., P.R.W.S.
British (1880–1969)
Calm Spring Morning, Sutherland
Signed, watercolour
9¾ x 13in (24.5 x 33.5cm)
£3,500–4,500 *Bea*

Stanhope Alexander Forbes, R.A.
British (1857–1947)
The Village Stream
Signed, oil on canvas
20 x 25in (50.5 x 63.5cm)
£17,000–18,000 *CSG*

William Miller Frazer
British (1864–1961)
Cattle Grazing near a Farm
Signed, oil on board
10 x 13in (25.5 x 33cm)
£1,300–1,400 *LT*

Trevor Geoghegan
British (b1946)
The Terrace
Acrylic on canvas
36 x 40in (91.5 x 101.5cm)
£2,000–3,000 *SOL*

Wilfrid Gabriel de Glehn, R.A.
British (1870–1951)
St. Cassien, Cannes
Pencil and watercolour
16 x 20in (40.5 x 51cm)
£550–700 *C*

Frederick Gore, R.A.
British (b1913)
Evening, Looking Towards the Crau from
Les Baux de Provence
Signed, oil on canvas
30 x 36in (76 x 91.5cm)
£6,500–7,000 *WHP*

Paul Grimm
American (1892–1974)
Desert Colours
Signed, oil on board
18 x 24in (46 x 61cm)
£1,250–1,750 *SLN*

Paul Hawdon
British (b1953)
Police Poles
Oil on canvas
46 x 60in (117 x 152cm)
£1,750–2,000 *Mer*

Phil Greenwood
British (20thC)
Pine Light
Etching
16 x 18½in (41 x 47cm)
£200–225 *CCA*

Jack Hellewell
British (20thC)
Ilkley Moor Forms
Acrylic on paper
18 x 24in (46 x 61cm)
£300–400 *KHG*

Paul Henry, R.H.A.
Irish (1876–1958)
The Bog-Cutting, Connemara
Signed, oil on board
20 x 21¾in (51 x 55.5cm)
£8,000–9,000 *P*

*Born in Belfast, Paul Henry is celebrated for
his Irish landscapes. In the 1920s, he
designed posters for the railways and a
picture entitled 'A Connemara Landscape'
was one of the best selling railway posters of
all time. Over the past couple of years,
Henry's bleak west of Ireland landscapes
have been difficult to sell at auction, but
recently the trend seems to have reversed. At
Christie's sale of Irish pictures in County
Antrim in December 1993, three oils by Paul
Henry provided the highlight of the sale, and
all made strong prices.*

Paul Henry, R.H.A.
Irish (1876–1958)
Turf Stacks, West of Ireland
Signed, oil on canvas
13¾ x 16in (35 x 41cm)
£11,000–12,000 *CCG*

Aldro Thompson Hibbard
American (1886–1972)
A Winter Brook
Signed, oil on canvas
16½ x 21in (42 x 53.3cm)
£2,000–3,000 *CNY*

Rowland Henry Hill
British (1873–1952)
Yorkshire Landscape
Signed, watercolour
10 x 14in (25 x 35.5cm)
£450–500 *G*

Rowland Hilder
British (b1905)
Landscape with a tree-lined track
Signed, watercolour
14 x 21in (35.5 x 53.2cm)
£750–850 *CSK*

Ferdinand Hodler
Swiss (1853–1918)
Der Genfersee mit Mont Blanc
bei Sonnenaufgang
Signed and dated '1918', oil on canvas
23½ x 31½in (60 x 80cm)
£280,000–350,000 *C*

Carl Hofer
German (1878–1955)
Tessiner Landschaft I
Signed with monogram and dated '35',
oil on canvas
24¼ x 31¼in (62 x 79cm)
£50,000–60,000 *C*

John Hope Falkner
British (b1947)
The Field
Signed and dated, oil on canvas
24 x 36in (61.5 x 91.5cm)
£700–800 *SBG*

John Houston
Scottish (b1930)
Sunset, Gullane Bay II
Woodcut, 1989
16¼ x 23in (41.5 x 58.5cm)
£150–175 *GPS*

John Houston
Scottish (b1930)
Temple Garden with Waterfall and Pagoda
Lithograph
22 x 30¼in (56 x 77cm)
£175–200 *GPS*

John Houston
Scottish (b1930)
Cornfields and Sunset
Signed, watercolour
14 x 15¾in (35.5 x 40cm)
£800–1,000 *OLG*

George Leslie Hunter
British (1877–1931)
The Mill Dam, Fife
Signed, oil on canvas
20 x 27in (50.8 x 68.5cm)
£17,000–22,000 *C(S)*

Alexander Jamieson
British (1873–1937)
Summer River Bank with Trees
Oil on panel
9 x 11in (23 x 38cm)
£550–700 *C*

Colin Kent, R.I.
British (20thC)
Coastal Village
Mixed media
10½ x 16in (26.5 x 40.5cm)
£350–400 *AdG*

Jean Kévorkian
French (b1933)
Le Loing à Moret
Signed, oil on canvas
15 x 18in (38 x 45.5cm)
£1,650–1,850 *Om*

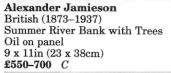

Paul Kenny
British (20thC)
Morning Scene, Dordogne
Watercolour
28 x 36in (71 x 91.5cm)
£3,000–4,000 *PN*

'Paul Kenny is one of the leading British landscape painters', enthuses Dr. Robert Travers of Piano Nobile. Recent shows of Kenny's work have been highly successful, underlining the current demand for appealing and representational contemporary works. 'Light and water' are the two constants in Kenny's work, notes critic Mary Rose Beaumont. The search for both has taken Kenny around Britain, to the Loire, to Venice, to the Nile, and to the Lake Palace at Udaipur in India. Kenny begins with watercolour sketches on the spot, which he then uses as reference material for his luminous and intensely personal pictures. 'Whilst still retaining an atmosphere of naturalism' concludes Beaumont, 'they become almost landscapes of the mind' a vision both real and poetic, that has certainly proved popular in today's market.

> **Miller's is a price GUIDE
> not a price LIST**

Ernst Ludwig Kirchner
German (1880–1938)
Berg-Vorfrühling mit Lärchen
Signed, oil on canvas
27¾ x 19¾in (70.5 x 50.2cm)
£110,000–130,000 *C*

Dame Laura Knight, R.A., R.W.S., R.E.
British (1877–1970)
Lamorna Cove
Signed, watercolour
14 x 18in (35.5 x 45.5cm)
£2,500–2,750 *JN*

Arthur Henry Knighton-Hammond
British (1875–1970)
Cyprus and Olive - Garavan
Signed, watercolour
16 x 24in (41 x 61cm)
£2,500–3,000 *NZ*

Paul Lauritz
American (b1889)
Morain Mountain
Signed, oil on canvas
19½ x 23½in (49.5 x 59.7cm)
£1,400–1,800 *CNY*

Sir John Lavery, R.A., R.S.A., R.H.A.
British (1856–1941)
The Southern Sea
Signed and inscribed, oil on canvas
25¼ x 30¼in (64 x 77cm)
£10,000–12,000 *P*

Maurice Levis
French (1860–1940)
A Mill with Willow and Poplar trees
Signed, oil on panel
5¼ x 8¾in (13.3 x 22.2cm)
£750–900 *L*

James Longueville
British (b1942)
Shadow on Worcester Cathedral
Signed, oil on panel
10 x 14in (25 x 35.5cm)
£450–550 *Om*

Laurence Stephen Lowry, R.A., R.B.A.
British (1887–1976)
Lonely House
Signed with initials, dated '1926', pencil
9¾ x 13¾in (24.5 x 35cm)
£1,350–1,600 *S(S)*

Maximilien Luce
French (1858–1941)
Chemin en Bordure de Mer
Signed and dated '1914', oil on paper laid
down on canvas
12¼ x 18½in (31.2 x 47cm)
£10,000–11,000   *C*

Brett McEntagart, R.H.A.
Irish (20thC)
Paysage des Champs
Oil on canvas
16 x 24in (40.5 x 61cm)
£1,200–1,600   *SOL*

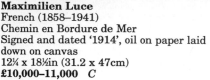

Jean Lurçat
French (1892–1966)
Le Sable
Signed and dated '33', oil on canvas
14½ x 21½in (36.8 x 54.6cm)
£3,000–3,500   *C*

John Marin
American (1870–1953)
Landscape, Castorland, New York
Signed, inscribed and dated '13', watercolour
on paper
16 x 18¾in (40.5 x 47.5cm)
£10,000–12,000   *S(NY)*

Jean McNeil
British (20thC)
Winter Trees II
Charcoal on paper, 1981
22 x 30in (55.5 x 76cm)
£300–400   *FT*

Campbell Mellon
British (1876–1955)
On the Cliffs, late August
Inscribed on reverse, oil on panel
9¼ x 12in (23.5 x 30.5cm)
£1,200–1,400   *C*

Tom Mackenzie
Scottish (b1947)
Neist Point
Etching, 1990
22 x 32in (55.5 x 81cm)
£100–125   *GPS*

John Maclauchlan Milne, R.S.A.
British (1885–1957)
North Sannox Croft
Signed, oil on canvasboard
15 x 17¾in (38 x 45cm)
£5,000–6,000 *S*

John Maclauchlan Milne, R.S.A.
British (1885–1957)
In the South of France
Signed and dated '30', oil on canvas
21¾ x 15in (55 x 38cm)
£4,500–6,000 *S*

John Minton
British (1917–57)
The Orchard
Signed and dated '1945', pen and ink
and wash
10¾ x 15in (27 x 38cm)
£1,600–1,800 *CSK*

A recent exhibition of John Minton's work in London stimulated considerable interest in his life and work. He was one of the leading figures of the Neo-Romantic movement and although he never perhaps fulfilled his early promise as a painter, he was a remarkably gifted draughtsman and illustrator. He provided illustrations for a large number of books and magazines, amongst the most notable being Alain Fournier's Le Grand Meaulnes *(1947) and Elizabeth David's* French Provincial Cooking *(1951).*

Edvard Munch
Norwegian (1863–1944)
The Red House
Signed, oil on card laid down on canvas
31½ x 26in (80 x 65.5cm)
£160,000–175,000 *C*

Robert E. Motley
American? (20thC)
Evening
Signed and dated '1932' verso, oil on canvas
24 x 30in (61.5 x 76cm)
£600–650 *LW*

Hamish Murray
British (20thC)
Buzzards, Summer Evening, Corfe Castle
Signed, watercolour
9 x 12in (22.5 x 30.5cm)
£370–430 *PHG*

*'Hamish Murray was born in Inverness and
spent his early life in Scotland, Lancashire
and Yorkshire,' writes Peter Hedley. 'His
lifelong interest in the countryside
culminated in his qualifying as a landscape
architect in 1975. He worked with several
conservation bodies until, in 1978, he settled
in Dorset where he is now head warden of
a number of projects including Durlston
Country Park and the award winning
Purbeck Heritage Coast. Hamish's
watercolour painting is a natural
development from the many hours spent
observing and sketching birds in their
natural habitat. He has illustrated many
books and magazines including a monthly
sketch book feature for* Bird Watching
Magazine *and a forthcoming* Collectors'
Guide to British Birds. *Public interest in his
paintings has grown enormously through
his extensive travels leading bird watching
tours and lecturing on wildlife.' Like many
other regional gallery owners, Peter Hedley
has noted the return to popularity of more
traditionalist artists. 'There seems to be a
turning away from shock art with horrific
subject matter and colour factor,' he notes
with obvious relief. 'It's back to good drawing,
good painting, quality and reason.'*

Edward Mossforth Neatby, R.M.S., A.R.C.A.
British (1888–1949)
An Afternoon at Fingle Bridge
Signed, watercolour
10 x 14½in (25.5 x 37cm)
£350–450 *JC*

Dale Nichols
American (b1904)
The Last Log
Signed, oil on canvas
30 x 40in (76 x 101.5cm)
£2,500–3,000 *CNY*

Walter Osborne, R.H.A.
British (1859–1903)
Shannon Floods
Signed, oil on canvas laid down on board
13¾ x 18½in (35 x 47cm)
£4,500–5,000 *P*

John Anthony Park
British (1880–1962)
Rocky Outcrop I
Oil on canvas
11½ x 15in (29.5 x 38cm)
£1,000–1,250 *Mon*

Philip Hugh Padwick
British (1876–1958)
Near Bury Hill
Oil on canvas
16½ x 23½in (42 x 60cm)
£400–450 *MBA*

James McIntosh Patrick, R.S.A., R.O.I.
British (b1907)
The Thames at Cookham, Spring
Signed and dated '47', oil on canvas
20 x 24in (50.5 x 61cm)
£8,500–10,000 *C(S)*

Tony Peart
British (b1961)
Remembered Landscape
Signed verso, dated '1992', oil on canvas
28 x 23in (71 x 58.5cm)
£2,000–2,250 *VCG*

Maria Pinschof
British (20thC)
St Martin le Redon, France
Signed, oil on canvas
16 x 15in (40.5 x 38cm)
£600–850 *FT*

John Piper
British (1903–92)
Locmariaquer, Brittany
Etching and aquatint, signed in pencil
16¼ x 24¼in (41 x 61.5cm)
£900–950 *WO*

Anthony Procter
British (1913–93)
The Swan Pool
Signed and dated '1982', oil on board
16 x 18in (40.5 x 45.5cm)
£350–400 *VCG*

Ernest Procter, A.R.A.
British (1886–1935)
The Newlyn to Mousehole Road
Signed, oil on canvas
20 x 24in (50.8 x 61cm)
£3,000–3,500 *C*

David Ralph-Simpson
British (20thC)
Maiden Castle from the South
Oil on canvas
16 x 29in (42 x 73.5cm)
£750–850 *OLG*

R. C. E. Rene-His
French (1877–1960)
Landscape
Signed, oil on canvas
13 x 18in (33 x 46cm)
£2,000–2,500 *BuP*

Alan Reynolds
British (b1926)
Study for Autumn
Signed and dated '56', wash, ink and gouache
8¼ x 13in (21 x 33.5cm)
£1,250–1,500 *P*

Elsie H. Rose
British (20thC)
Girls in a Windy Meadow
Pastel, c1910
8 x 14in (20 x 35.5cm)
£500–600 *MBA*

Herbert Royle
British (1870–58)
Snowscene, Scarr Farm, Nessfield
Signed and inscribed, oil on board
19½ x 23½in (49.5 x 60cm)
£3,800–4,500 *AH*

Richard Scholz
German (20thC)
High Summer in Montafoy
Signed and dated '1925', oil on canvas
44 x 66in (112 x 168cm)
£4,000–4,500 *CSK*

Carel Weight, R.A.
British (b1908)
A Winter Walk
Signed, oil on board
21 x 24in (51 x 61cm)
£3,800–4,200 *P*

Edward Seago
British (1910–74)
Evening Blakeney
Signed, pencil and watercolour
10½ x 14½in (26.5 x 37cm)
£2,400–2,800 *C*

*'The work of Edward Seago, an artist
considered by many critics and collectors to
be amongst the greatest landscape painters
of the century, continues to inspire interest
and acclaim whenever it is mentioned,'
claims gallery owner John Noott, who hosted
an exhibition of Seago's work on behalf of the
Seago Trust in November 1993. Seago is
certainly a regular favourite in the salerooms
and, adds Noott reassuringly, 'his prices
have remained firm throughout the recent
recession'. Although in his own day Seago
was largely ignored by the critics, his work
was enormously popular with the public. At
his annual exhibitions at Colnaghi's in the
1940s and 1950s, queues formed outside the
gallery long before the doors opened and
almost every show sold out on the first day.
Many of Seago's pictures are in the Royal
collection, and other friends and patrons
included Noël Coward, Benjamin Britten
and Henry Williamson.*

Jonathan Trowell
British (20thC)
Morston Marshes, Norfolk
Oil on canvas
12 x 14in (30.5 x 35.5cm)
£1,000–1,200 *WHP*

Louis Vivin
French (1861–1936)
Paysage et Etang
Signed, oil on canvas board
5¼ x 9in (13.4 x 23cm)
£850–1,000 *C*

*This French naïve painter was a Post Office
worker until his retirement at the age of 62.
He lived and worked in tiny lodgings in
Paris, painting his rural landscapes entirely
from postcards and engravings.*

> **Miller's is a price GUIDE
> not a price LIST**

Orrin A. White
American (1883–1969)
Brown Hillside
Signed, oil on canvas
25 x 30in (63.5 x 76.2cm)
£3,250–3,500 *CNY*

Maurice Canning Wilks, R.U.A., A.R.H.A.
British (1911–83)
Culdaff Strand, Co. Donegal
Signed and inscribed, oil on canvas
19¾ x 26¾in (50 x 68cm)
£3,250–3,750 *S(S)*

CITIES, TOWNS & STREET SCENES

The following section is devoted to cities, towns and topographical views. Artists have always travelled both in search of subject matter and patronage. A number of the works illustrated date from the 18thC when the Grand Tour brought a steady stream of painters and their wealthy patrons to Europe, most notably to Italy and the great artistic centres of Venice and Rome. With the end of the Napoleonic wars and the expansion of travel in the 19thC, the Continent was opened up to the middle classes. Both for the professional artist and the amateur painter, watercolour offered a rapid and easily portable means of recording their travels, the sketchbook providing the Victorian equivalent of the camera.

Marine painters sailed the ports of Europe, and many artists travelled further afield, painting portraits and views in the far-flung corners of the great European empires, unveiling the mysteries of the East to a Victorian public eager for Oriental glamour. The great capitals that attracted artists in the 18thC and 19thC, continue to inspire the painters of the 20thC: London, Paris and, perhaps above all, Venice. For the third year running, we have received more pictures of Venice than any other single location. Although the Grand Tour might have been replaced by the package tour, Venice remains a favourite destination and an ever popular subject in the salerooms.

General

Follower of Samuel Scott
British (1703–72)
View of a City
Inscribed, oil on panel
8 x 12½in (20.5 x 31.5cm)
£2,000–2,500 *S(NY)*

Léon Gaspard
French (1882–1964)
Russian Snow Scene
Signed and dated '1914', oil on canvas
26½ x 24in (67.3 x 61cm)
£175,000–200,000 *S(NY)*

Johann Philipp Eduard Gaertner
German (1801–77)
Schlossfreiheit von der Schlossbrücke, Berlin
Signed and dated '1855', oil on canvas
22 x 37¾in (56 x 96cm)
£950,000–1,000,000 *C*

Ernst Juch
German (1838–1909)
A Street Scene in Vienna
Oil on panel
15½ x 23½in (39.5 x 60cm)
£3,500–4,000 *S*

Hermann Neuber
German (active 1891–95)
Der Münchner Odeonsplatz im Winter
Signed and dated '92', oil on canvas
32 x 46in (81.3 x 116.5cm)
£15,000–20,000 *S(NY)*

Charles P. Pitt
British (19th/20thC)
A busy Continental street scene
Signed, oil on canvas
21 x 17in (53 x 43cm)
£675–725 *GH*

John Bratby, R.A.
British (1928–92)
Christian Snow Palaces, Russia
Signed, oil on canvas
48 x 36in (122 x 91.5cm)
£2,000–2,500 *GG*

Walter G. Schröder
German (active 1885–1932)
The Old Quay
Signed, oil on board
13 x 17in (33 x 43cm)
£700–750 *Gan*

Edward Tucker
British (c1825–1909)
The Castle of Ehrenbreistein, near
Coblenz, Germany
Signed, watercolour over pencil with
scratching out and touches of gum arabic
6 x 10in (15.5 x 25.5cm)
£1,400–1,600 *S*

Walter Nessler
British (b1912)
Urban landscape, 1939
Oil on wooden panel
16 x 20½in (40.5 x 52cm)
£1,800–2,000 *JDG*

Ferdinand Michl
Czechoslovakian (b1877)
Czechoslovakian Town
Signed, oil on canvas
11¾ x 23½in (30 x 60cm)
£350–400 *SLN*

American Towns

In Britain, 20thC architecture is often decried, most famously by Prince Charles, an amateur painter himself. In America, artists and film makers have celebrated the city in all its modernity.

M. C. Horton
American (19thC)
View of Hebron, Connecticut
Signed, oil on canvas
22 x 26in (55.5 x 66cm)
£1,300–1,400 *SK*

Colin Campbell Cooper
American (1856–1937)
Southwest Corner of Madison Square
Signed, oil on canvas
22 x 30in (56 x 76.2cm)
£26,000–36,000 *S(NY)*

Harry Humphrey Moore
American (1844–1926)
A New Orleans Street Scene
Signed, oil on panel
8½ x 6in (21.5 x 15.3cm)
£950–1,100 *CNY*

William J. Glackens
American (1870–1938)
Washington Square and Afternoon
in the Park
Signed, c1905–07, double sided pastel
17 x 21in (43.2 x 53.3cm)
£17,000–18,000 *S(NY)*

John Whorf
American (1903–59)
Spring Comes to Parnal Street
Signed, watercolour
14½ x 21¼in (37 x 54cm)
£2,250–2,750 *CNY*

British Towns

Coastal and cathedral towns predominate in the following views of Britain. The British Isles have over 7,000 miles of coastline and its ports and seaside towns have attracted generations of artists. In the 19thC, as the new middle class began to take seaside holidays, there was a growing demand for pictures of the resorts, as well as for portrayals of more inland beauty spots. 'The regional capital which is also the seat of a bishop is the grandest kind of English town,' claimed the architectural historian John Summerson. Cathedral cities, such as Durham, Exeter, and Salisbury, were favourite spots with Victorian painters, and remain so with their 20thC purchasers.

Paul Sandby, R.A.
British (1730–1809)
A View of Rooftops showing a Bookseller
Inscribed, pen and grey ink and watercolour
7 x 8¼in (17.5 x 21cm)
£5,600–6,000 *S*

Lieutenant Colonel Robert Batty
British (1789–1848)
Calton Hill, Edinburgh
Oil on board
9¾ x 13¾in (24.5 x 34cm)
£880–1,200 *S*

Samuel Bough, R.S.A., R.S.W.
British (1822–72)
View of Edinburgh from Stockbridge
Signed, watercolour
9½ x 13½in (24 x 34cm)
£1,500–1,800 *WH*

George Fall
British (1848–1925)
York Minster from outside the Walls
Signed, watercolour
9¾ x 13¾in (24.5 x 35cm)
£250–275 *DA*

A. H. Findley
British (19thC)
Durham Cathedral
Signed, watercolour
16 x 10½in (40.6 x 27cm)
£450–550 *L*

Frederick E. J. Goff
British (1855–1931)
Windsor Castle and River Thames
Signed, watercolour
7 x 9½in (17.5 x 24cm)
£850–900 *LH*

Albert Goodwin, R.W.S.
British (1845–1932)
Whitby
Signed, pencil and watercolour heightened
with white
5½ x 8¾in (14 x 22cm)
£950–1,250 *CSK*

Albert Goodwin, R.W.S.
British (1845–1932)
Edinburgh from Calton Hill at Sunset
Signed and inscribed, pencil, pen and black
ink and watercolour with scratching out
5½ x 9in (14 x 23cm)
£3,250–4,000 *C*

Joseph Murray Ince
British (1806–59)
The High Street looking towards
Carfax, Oxford
Signed and dated '1834', watercolour over
traces of pencil with scratching out
8 x 11½in (20.5 x 29cm)
£1,600–1,800 *S*

John Atkinson Grimshaw
British (1836–93)
Glasgow - After Rain
Signed and dated '1887', oil on canvas
24 x 36¼in (61 x 92cm)
£95,000–110,000 *Bon*

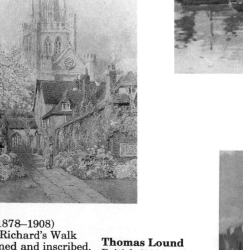

Frank Kelsey
British (active 1887–1930)
A Cornish Harbour
Signed, watercolour
9½ x 13½in (24 x 34.5cm)
£600–700 *JC*

Thomas Hunn
British (active 1878–1908)
Canterbury; St Richard's Walk
A pair, both signed and inscribed,
watercolour over pencil
14½ x 10½in (37 x 26.5cm)
£750–800 *S(S)*

Thomas Lound
British (1802–61)
Southwark
Oil on canvas
19 x 25in (48 x 63.5cm)
£3,800–4,600 *HOLL*

James Orrock R.I.
British (1829–1919)
Lincoln Cathedral
Signed and inscribed, watercolour
8¾ x 12in (22 x 30.5cm)
£250–350 *JC*

Henry Perlee Parker
British (1795–1873)
The Old Quayside, Newcastle
Signed and dated '1838', oil on canvas
29½ x 39½in (75 x 100.5cm)
£18,000–25,000 *S*

Louise Rayner
British (1832–1924)
Tewkesbury
Watercolour
19 x 11in (48 x 28cm)
£13,000–14,000 *HFA*

Louise Rayner
British (1832–1924)
Ludlow - Market Day
Signed, watercolour heightened with white
6 x 10½in (15.5 x 26.5cm)
£3,500–4,500 *P*

Claude H. Rowbotham
British (1823–75)
Wallingford, Oxford; and A Castle on a River
A pair, both signed and dated '1892' and
'1891', pencil and watercolour heightened
with bodycolour
8 x 18in (20 x 45.5cm)
£850–1,000 *CSK*

Daniel Sherrin
British (active 1895–1915)
Gloucester Cathedral
Signed, watercolour
19 x 35in (48 x 89cm)
£1,400–1,600 *GAK*

James Whittet Smith
British (active 1859–86)
Durham Castle and the Cathedral at Dusk
Signed with initials and dated '1870', pencil
and watercolour heightened with white
9 x 12¼in (23 x 31cm)
£300–400 *CSK*

John Syer
British (1815–85)
The Old Harbour, Staithes
Signed, watercolour
12¼ x 18½in (31 x 47cm)
£300–400 *RS*

William Thornley
British (active 1858–98)
Rye Harbour
Signed, oil on canvas
15½ x 23½in (39.5 x 60cm)
£3,500–4,000 *CGa*

George Stanfield Walters, R.B.A.
British (1838–1924)
Views of Whitby
A pair, both signed, watercolour
5½ x 9in (14 x 22.5cm)
£2,500–3,000 *JML*

Frederick Williamson
British (d1900)
Whitby looking to Larpool
Signed and inscribed, watercolour and gum
arabic heightened with white
18¾ x 29½in (47.6 x 75cm)
£2,500–3,000 *C(S)*

*Whitby was one of the towns most frequently
portrayed by Victorian watercolourists.
An old whaling port and home of the great
seaman and explorer Captain James Cook,
Whitby attracted scores of artists in the
19thC. The coastal landscape was not its
only appeal, nor shipping its only industry.
More jet is found in Whitby than anywhere
else in Britain. Jet, used for mourning
jewellery, was particularly popular with the
Victorians and in 1873 the town boasted
200 jet workshops.*

Edith Isabel Barrow
British (active 1887–1926)
St Ives Harbour
Signed, oil on canvas
17 x 24in (43 x 61cm)
£1,550–1,750 *CGa*

Clarence Blackburn
British (b1914)
Knaresborough
Oil on canvas
55 x 40in (139.5 x 101.5cm)
£1,300–1,500 *JDG*

Norman Cornish
British (20thC)
A Northern Pit Village
Signed, oil on board
13¼ x 21in (33.5 x 53cm)
£1,000–1,200 *AG*

Helen Bradley
British (1900–79)
Going Home through the Park we were
caught in the first Snow of Winter
Signed with the artist's fly monogram, dated
'1969', oil on canvas board
24 x 32in (61 x 81cm)
£12,000–13,000 *P*

*Helen Bradley did not begin to paint until the
age of 65 when she began to produce pictures
of her childhood to show her grandchildren
what life was like then. She shot to fame
through television shows in the 1970s, and
her paintings became familiar through her
books and greetings cards. Today, these
nostalgic visions of an Edwardian childhood
command four-figure prices, or more, at
auction, and are regarded by some as a
cheaper and softer alternative to a Lowry.*

Fred Cuming, R.A.
British (b1930)
Swanage in the Sunshine
Signed, oil on canvas
23½in (60cm) square
£2,500–3,000 *WHP*

Tom Coates
British (b1941)
Gardens at Southend
Oil on canvas
20 x 24in (51 x 61cm)
£1,000–1,200 *LA*

Klim Forster
British (20thC)
The Pantiles, Tunbridge Wells
Watercolour
9½ x 11in (24 x 28cm)
£150–200 *RGFA*

Mervyn Goode
British (b1948)
Evening Reflections in the Harbour, Bosham
Signed, oil on canvas
16 x 22in (40.5 x 55.5cm)
£950–1,200 *Bne*

Laurence Stephen Lowry, R.A.
British (1887–1976)
A Lancashire Street
Signed and dated '1960', pencil
9½ x 14⅓in (24 x 37cm)
£3,500–4,000 *C*

James Kay, R.S.A., R.S.W.
British (1858–1942)
John Knox's House, Royal Mile, Edinburgh
Signed, oil on board
19¼ x 22¾in (49 x 58cm)
£7,500–8,000 *S*

Laurence Stephen Lowry, R.A.
British (1887–1976)
Edward Henry Street, Rhyl
Signed and dated '1933', oil on panel
12½ x 17½in (32 x 44.5cm)
£45,000–55,000 *C*

In 1910 Lowry became a rent collector and clerk with the Pall Mall Property Co. in Manchester and remained with the firm until his retirement in 1952. The fact that for over 50 years he had been employed in a 9am-5pm job was the most closely guarded secret of his life, notes the Dictionary of National Biography. Lowry had a horror of being regarded as an amateur painter, and details of his work were only made public after his death. 'Well, I am a Sunday painter. It's just that I paint every other day of the week as well,' he commented defiantly. Lowry painted daily, or rather nightly, between the hours of 10.00pm and 2.00am. Perhaps significantly, one of his more notable eccentricities was that his front room was filled with clocks, all of which told a different time. When once asked why this was he replied simply: 'Because I don't want to know the real time.'

John Neale
British (20thC)
Salcombe
Signed, oil on board
18 x 12in (45.5 x 30.5cm)
£400–475 *JN*

Leonard Richmond
British (d1965)
St. Ives Harbour
Signed, oil on board
20 x 24in (51 x 61cm)
£1,250–1,400 *C*

John Yardley
British (b1936)
Fishing Boats, Whitby
Signed, watercolour
8 x 11½in (20 x 29cm)
£500–550 *Bne*

London

'When a man is tired of London, he is tired of life,' claimed Dr. Johnson in 1777, 'for there is in London all that life can afford.' What is true for the writer is also true for the painter. London has always acted as a magnet for artists, and over the centuries its landscape has provided subject matter of infinite variety. For the marine painter there was the Pool of London and the once great dockyards along the Thames Estuary, and for the landscape painter the Royal parks and the romantic riparian views of Richmond, Chiswick and Barnes. London's famous landmarks have drawn such celebrated international artists as Canaletto and Monet to the city. Less glamorous districts such as Camden Town, Soho, or in our own times the East End, have served as both home and inspiration to major groups of British painters. It is not only the surface of the city that has inspired great works of art. Harry C. Beck's design for the London Underground map of 1931 has been compared to a work by Mondrian, and has itself become a symbol of the city, famous as any monument.

English School (c1660)
A Capriccio View of the City of London with Old St. Paul's and Old London Bridge
Inscribed on stretcher, oil on canvas
24¾ x 39in (62.6 x 99cm)
£14,000–15,000 C

This picture, previously unrecorded, is unusual in that the viewpoint of London before the Great Fire of 1666 is from an imaginary hill in the location of the London Playhouses of the Swan, the Hope, the Rose, and Shakespeare's Globe.

Attributed to Samuel Wale
British (1721–86)
View of the Horse Guards with the Admiralty and Downing Street
Oil on canvas
35½ x 53in (89 x 135cm)
£38,000–48,000 S

Antonio Joli
Italian (c1700–77)
A panoramic view of the City of London from the Thames near the Water Gate of Somerset House
Oil on canvas
33¾ x 50½in (86 x 128.3cm)
£385,000–425,000 C

John Day
British (19thC)
A view of St. Mary's Church, Paddington
Signed and dated '1858', oil on canvas
20 x 24in (50.5 x 61cm)
£2,500–3,000 C

Emile Claus
Belgian (1849–1924)
Waterloo Bridge and Hungerford Bridge with the Houses of Parliament beyond
Signed and dated '16', oil on canvas
27½in (70cm) square
£50,000–55,000 C

Charles Edward Dixon
British (1872–1934)
Shipping on the Thames
Signed and dated '1889', pencil
and watercolour
8¼ x 14½in (21 x 37cm)
£900–1,200 *C*

Sir Ernest George, R.A.
British (1839–1922)
St. Paul's
Watercolour
7½ x 5½in (18.5 x 14cm)
£240–280 *TFA*

Axel Herman Haig, R.P.E.
Active in Britain (19thC)
New Law Courts
Signed and inscribed, watercolour over pencil
heightened with bodycolour
25½ x 18in (65 x 45.5cm)
£8,000–9,000 *S(S)*

Haig's architectural studies normally only sell for a few hundred pounds, and this picture was estimated at £800–1,200 when auctioned at Sotheby's Sussex in February 1994. What caused this work to sell for ten times its lower estimate? The picture was an artist's impression of William Burges's unbuilt project for the New Law Courts in London's Strand. Burges was one of the greatest and most fantastical of the Victorian Gothic architects. This design, which reputedly hung in his house in Melbury Road, Kensington, for many years, shows the architect at his most flamboyant, incorporating elements from sources as rich and varied as Salisbury Cathedral, the chateaux of the Loire and the Bridge of Sighs. Interest at this sale was expressed by private bidders and academic institutions and bidding shot way over estimate.

Frederick E. J. Goff
British (1855–1931)
Westminster Abbey
Signed and inscribed, watercolour
4 x 6in (10 x 15cm)
£1,200–1,600 *HO*

Robert Charles Goff
British (1837–1922)
Rotten Row, Hyde P0ark
Signed with initials, watercolour
6¾ x 10in (17 x 25cm)
£1,300–1,600 *GG*

Rowland Holyoake
British (active 1880–1907)
Strand On The Green
Signed and dated '1906', oil on board
9¼ x 13in (23 x 33cm)
£1,250–1,450 *BuP*

Herbert Menzies Marshall, R.W.S.
British (1841–1913)
London Bridge
Signed, pencil and watercolour
8½ x 12½in (21.4 x 31.5cm)
£1,200–1,500 *C*

John Paul
British (1802–68)
Leicester Square, London
Oil on canvas
25 x 30in (63.5 x 76cm)
£1,300–1,500 *CSK*

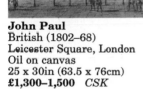

Alfred H. Vickers
British (1853–1907)
Westminster; and
On the River Thames
A pair, both signed,
oil on canvas
8 x 16in (20.3 x 40.7cm)
£1,100–1,400 *CSK*

Rubens Arthur Moore
British (active 1881–1920)
The Pool of London, Tower Bridge and the
Tower of London
A pair, signed and dated '1920', oil on canvas
15 x 20in (38 x 50.5cm)
£2,750–3,000 *P(S)*

Antoine Blanchard
French (1910–1988)
The Empire Theatre,
Leicester Square
Signed, oil on canvas
13 x 18in (33 x 45.5cm)
£5,000–6,000 *BuP*

William Bowyer, R.A.
British (b1926)
Strand On The Green
Signed, oil on canvas
40 x 48in (101.5 x 122cm)
£3,500–4,500 *BRG*

William Bowyer, R.A.
British (b1926)
Richmond Terrace
Signed, oil on canvas
36in (91.5cm) square
£4,200–4,800 *WHP*

Roberto Ferruzzi
Italian (b1927)
Early Morning, Portobello Road
Signed, oil on panel
8 x 9½in (20 x 24cm)
£1,000–1,500 *WFA*

Spencer Frederick Gore
British (1878–1914)
Mornington Crescent
Oil on canvas
16 x 20¼in (40.7 x 51.5cm)
£35,000–45,000 *C*

Anthony Gross
British (b1905)
The Old Royal Observatory, Greenwich
Signed, inscribed and numbered '17/75'
10¾ x 13½in (27 x 34.5cm)
£300–350 *BLD*

James Le Jeune, R.H.A.
British (1910–83)
The West Front of Westminster Abbey
Signed, oil on canvas
25 x 30in (63.5 x 76cm)
£1,700–2,000 *P*

John Piper
British (1903–92)
The Bells Go Down
Signed and inscribed, pen and black ink,
watercolour heightened with white, original
poster artwork
17 x 25in (43 x 63.5cm)
£5,000–6,000 *CSK*

This was a poster for The Bells Go Down,
*Ealing, 1943, directed by Basil Dearden,
starred Tommy Trinder, James Mason,
Finlay Currie, Mervyn Johns and others -
a tragicomedy which gave a good record of
the historical background of the blitz.*

Anthony Procter
British (1913–93)
The City from Waterloo Bridge
Signed and dated '1988', oil on board
21 x 27in (53 x 68.5cm)
£500–550 *VCG*

Russell Sydney Reeve, R.E., R.B.A.
British (1895–1970)
Boadicea and Big Ben, 1925
Signed and dated '1925', copperplate etching
10 x 10½in (25 x 26.5cm)
£650–850 *PN*

Russell Sydney Reeve, R.E., R.B.A.
British (1895–1970)
Roadworks London, 1927
Signed and dated '1927', pencil
and watercolour
14in (35.5cm) square
£1,500–1,750 *PN*

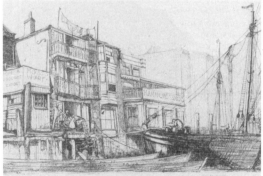

Graham Sutherland
British (1903–80)
Greenwich (Moss's Wharf)
Signed and dated in pencil '1923', etching
8¼ x 13¼in (21 x 33.7cm)
£600–700 *S*

Fred Yates
British (b1922)
London Scene
Oil on canvas
18 x 24in (45.5 x 61cm)
£550–650 *Tho*

Dutch & Flemish Towns

Dutch pictures have been performing well in the current market. Many of the following works sold for over their estimate at auction, perhaps most notably Cornelis Springer's 'A Dutch Street Scene'. Offered by Sotheby's in late 1993, the picture attracted huge interest making an eventual hammer price of £84,000.

Thomas Heeremans
Dutch (1640–97)
A Winter Landscape with Frozen River
Signed, oil on canvas
22½ x 33in (57 x 84cm)
£13,000–15,000 *P*

Wouter Knyff
Dutch (c1607–83)
River Landscape with Boats and Figures
Oil on canvas
41½ x 51¾in (105 x 131.5cm)
£6,500–7,000 *S*

George Keate
British (1729–97)
The Port of Antwerp
Signed on mount, watercolour
9½ x 13½in (23.5 x 34cm)
£4,000–4,500 *JML*

Jan Hendrik Verheyen
Dutch (1778–1846)
A Capriccio View of a Town with Figures on a Frozen Canal
Indistinctly signed, oil on canvas
25¾ x 34in (65.5 x 86cm)
£38,000–48,000 *C*

Andries Vermeulen
Dutch (1763–1814)
Figures gathered around a Bonfire on the Bank of a Frozen River
Signed, oil on panel
28 x 32½in (71 x 82cm)
£400–450 *P*

Pieter Christian Dommersen
Dutch (1834–1908)
Amsterdam - The Old Mint House
Signed and dated 1892, oil on panel
20½ x 16in (52 x 41cm)
£9,500–10,500 *Bon*

Joseph F. Ellis
British (1783–1848)
Antwerp Harbour
Signed, oil on canvas
25¼ x 30in (64 x 76.5cm)
£5,000–6,000 *S*

Johannes Frederik Hulk, Snr.
Dutch (1829–1911)
A View of a Harbour of a Dutch Town
Signed and dated '1863', oil on canvas
24½ x 33¾in (63 x 85.5cm)
£5,000–6,000 *S(Am)*

Kasparus Karssen
Dutch (1810–96)
A Village Scene, Scheveningen
Signed and dated '1872', oil on canvas
16 x 22¾in (41 x 58cm)
£10,500–12,000 *S(Am)*

Claude Monet
French (1840–1926)
Neige à Amsterdam
Signed, oil on canvas, painted in 1874
22 x 29in (55.5 x 73.5cm)
£300,000–350,000 *S(NY)*

*The scene depicted is in the north west
of Amsterdam, showing the church
of Haarlemmerstraat seen from the
Westerdoksdijk.*

Cornelis Springer
Dutch (1817–91)
A Dutch Street Scene
Signed and dated '1863', oil on canvas
22½ x 18½in (57 x 47cm)
£95,000–115,000 *S*

Cornelis Peter Hoen
Dutch (1814–80)
Dutch Winter Scene
Signed and dated '1843', oil on board
14¼ x 18½in (36.5 x 47cm)
£2,000–2,500 *AH*

Ambros Vermerrsch
Dutch (1810–52)
The Market Square in Brunswick
Signed and dated '1845', oil on canvas
22 x 26in (56 x 66cm)
£11,500–12,500 *S*

Cornelis Vreedenburgh
Dutch (1880–1946)
Barges moored on a Canal
Signed, oil on canvas
15¼ x 19in (39 x 48cm)
£700–900 *CSK*

Jan Van Couver
Dutch (active c1900–25)
On the Spaarn, Holland
Signed, watercolour
14 x 20¾in (35.5 x 52.5cm)
£750–850 *JC*

Michael John Hunt
British (b1941)
Oude Schans, Amsterdam
Acrylic on canvas
30 x 46in (76 x 116.5cm)
£5,000–6,000 *THG*

Fernand Khnopff
Belgian (1858–1921)
Le Lac d'Amour, Bruges
Signed, black crayon and pastel, c1905
18½ x 39¾in (47 x 101cm)
£215,000–225,000 *S*

John B. Marshall, R.S.A., R.S.W.
British (active 1905–40)
Dutch Harbour
Signed, watercolour
11¼ x 16¾in (28.5 x 42.5cm)
£350–400 *Gan*

Edward Seago
British (1910–74)
Summer Evening, Haarlem
Signed, oil on canvas
12 x 16in (30.5 x 40.5cm)
£7,000–8,000 *JN*

French Towns

Henri Alphonse Barnoin
French (1882–1935)
Marché de Quimperlé, Bretagne
Signed, oil on canvas
29 x 36½in (73.7 x 92.5cm)
£8,500–10,000 *S(NY)*

William Marlow
British (1740–1813)
Lyon from the Saône
Signed, watercolour over pencil on laid paper
watermarked with the Strasbourg Lily
11¼ x 20½in (29 x 51.5cm)
£2,000–2,500 *S*

William Lee-Hankey, R.A., R.W.S., R.I.
British (1869–1952)
Market Day, Dieppe
Signed and inscribed, oil on canvas
25 x 30in (63.5 x 76cm)
£8,500–10,000 *CSK*

C. J. Keats
British (19thC)
Ghent
Signed, oil on canvas
22 x 12in (56 x 30.5cm)
£1,000–1,500 *HLG*

Paul Marny
British (1829–1914)
Rouen
Signed, watercolour
17 x 11in (43 x 28cm)
£1,000–1,400 *HO*

Edward Lear
British (1812–88)
Olmeto, Corsica
Signed with monogram and inscribed,
watercolour heightened with touches
of white
11½ x 18in (29 x 46.5cm)
£4,000–4,500 *S*

Fernand Toussaint
French (19thC)
La Rochelle, and another by the same artist
Signed, stamped by studio, watercolour
on paper
8½ x 11in (21 x 28cm)
£400–500 *C*

Samuel Prout
British (1783–1852)
A Street in Normandy
Watercolour
20 x 13in (51 x 33cm)
£1,400–1,600 *AH*

John Donaldson
British (20thC)
Aix-en-Provence, Midi
Signed, watercolour
15½ x 22in (39 x 55.5cm)
£900–1,000 *Om*

Jean Kévorkian
French (b1933)
Camaret
Signed, oil on canvas
25½ x 31½in (65 x 80cm)
£3,500–4,000 *Om*

James Longueville
British (b1942)
The Harbour, Dieppe
Signed, oil on panel
20 x 30in (50.5 x 76cm)
£1,400–1,700 *Om*

Albert Marquet
French (1875–1947)
Vue de Boulogne
Signed and dated '1930',
watercolour and pencil
4¾ x 5¼in (10.5 x 13cm)
£4,000–5,000 *S*

Edward Seago, R.W.S.
British (1910–74)
The Old Basin, Honfleur
Signed and inscribed,
oil on board
20 x 30in (51 x 76cm)
£21,000–25,000 *S*

Paris

If Bouvard is the name that crops up most frequently in 20thC representations of Venice, then his Parisian equivalents are the two French artists, Eugène Galien-Laloue and Edouard Cortès. Both specialised in decorative Parisian street scenes, featuring an endless stream of bourgeois shoppers and almost invariably set in the winter months - the fashionable season to be 'en ville'. Such Paris pictures are often popular with the American market, and many of the following works in this section were sold in New York.

Guiseppe Canella
Italian (1788–1847)
Le Louvre et la Seine en 1831
Signed and dated '1831', oil on canvas
16 x 22in (40.5 x 55.5cm)
£47,000–57,000 *S(NY)*

French School (c1795)
Projects for the Place de la Concorde with Obelisks and Columns
A pair, one inscribed, pen ink, grey and brown wash
5½ x 8¼in (13.5 x 21cm)
£900–1,200 *C*

Henry Darien
French (19thC)
Boulevard St. Michel, Paris
Signed and dated '95', oil on canvas
23½ x 39¼in (60 x 100cm)
£37,000–47,000 *S(NY)*

Hippolyte Lecomte
French (1781–1857)
Students from the Ecole Polytechnique, with the Crucifix rescued from the Chapel in the Tuileries Palace at the time of the 1848 Revolution
Signed and dated '1848', oil on canvas
19¼ x 25in (48.5 x 63.5cm)
£2,500–3,000 *P*

John Donaldson
British (20thC)
Morning near Notre Dame
Signed, oil on canvas
20 x 30in (50.5 x 76cm)
£3,000–3,250 *Om*

Edouard Cortès
French (1882–1969)
La Madeleine
Signed, oil on canvas
13 x 18in (33 x 45.5cm)
£10,500–12,500 *S(NY)*

Eugène Galien-Laloue
French (1854–1941)
Flower Stalls along the Seine, Winter
Signed, watercolour and gouache on paper
8 x 11¼ (20 x 28.5cm)
£5,500–6,500 *SLN*

Eugène Galien–Laloue
French (1854–1941)
Les Quais, Notre Dame, Paris
Signed, gouache
9½ x 14in (24.5 x 35.5cm)
£12,000–13,000 *S*

François Gall
French (1912–87)
Le Pont des Arts à Paris
Signed and titled, oil on canvas
20 x 24in (50.5 x 61cm)
£2,500–3,500 *S(NY)*

Armand Guerin
French (1913–83)
View of the Seine with the Eiffel Tower
Signed, oil on masonite
23¾ x 28⅜in (60.5 x 73cm)
£750–850 *S(NY)*

Elisée Maclet
French (1881–1962)
View of Paris
Signed, oil on board
18 x 24in (45.5 x 61cm)
£2,500–3,500 *S(NY)*

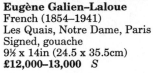

Frédéric-Louis Levé
French (b1877)
Versailles, Winter
Signed, oil on canvas
42 x 53½in (106.5 x 135cm)
£2,000–2,500 *C*

Henry Malfroy
French (1895–1944)
Champs Elysées
Signed, oil on panel
8½ x 10⅜in (21.5 x 26.5cm)
£1,000–1,500 *S(NY)*

Alphonse Quizet
French (1885–1955)
Rue à Montmartre
Signed, oil on masonite
19¾ x 25½in (50 x 65cm)
£3,500–4,000 *S(NY)*

Albert Marquet
French (1875–1947)
Quai des Grands Augustins
Signed, oil on canvas, painted 1938
25½ x 32in (65 x 81cm)
£280,000–300,000 *C*

Edward Seago
British (1910–74)
Rue de Montebello, Paris
Signed, oil on canvas
26 x 36in (66 x 91.5cm)
£20,000–22,500 *HFA*

Juan Soler
Spanish (20thC)
A busy Parisian Street
Signed, oil on panel
12½ x 15½in (31.5 x 39.5cm)
£650–750 *CSK*

Georges Stein
French (19th/20thC)
Flower Market
Signed and inscribed, oil on canvas
15 x 21½in (38 x 54.5cm)
£5,500–6,500 *S(NY)*

Maurice Utrillo
French (1883–1955)
Rue Chappe à Montmartre
Signed, oil on board, painted c1937
23½ x 28in (60 x 71cm)
£75,000–85,000 *C*

Indian Towns

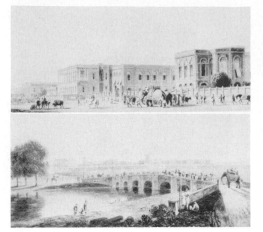

Circle of William Daniell
British (1769–1839)
Calcutta: The Approach to Fort St. George,
The Consul's House, A Procession before
a Temple, and Ram Mectus Pagoda
Four pencil and watercolours, some on
an etched outline
4½ x 7¼in (11 x 18cm)
£1,000–1,200 *CSK*

James Prinsep
British (1799–1840)
Benares from the Mundakinee Tulao
Pencil and watercolour
7 x 10¼in (17.5 x 25.5cm)
£1,000–1,500 *C*

Ludwig Hans Fischer
German (1848–1915)
The Wezir Khan Mosque, Lahore
Signed and inscribed 'Lahore', watercolour
11¼ x 16⅛in (29 x 41cm)
£6,000–6,500 *S*

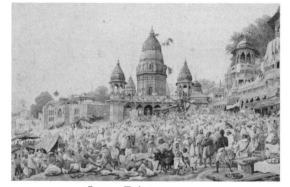

James Prinsep
British (1799–1840)
Eve of an Eclipse of the Moon,
25th November 1825
Inscribed indistinctly on reverse, pencil
and watercolour
7 x 10½in (17.5 x 26.5cm)
£4,000–4,500 *C*

Edward Lear
British (1812-88)
Kangchenjunga from Darjeeling
Monogrammed, watercolour over pencil
heightened with bodycolour
10 x 15¼in (25 x 39cm)
£18,000–20,000 *S*

Marianne L. Trench
British (b1888)
The Mosque of the Dome of
the Rock, Jerusalem
Oil on canvas
17¼ x 23½in (44 x 60cm)
£550–700 *C*

Fred Taylor
British (1875–1963)
Calcutta
Signed, gouache
19¾ x 40in (50 x 101.5cm)
£750–850 *Bri*

Italian Towns

Travelling is the ruin of all happiness!'
lamented the 18thC English novelist Fanny
Burney. 'There's no looking at a building here
after seeing Italy.' An Italian Grand Tour
was an essential part of the education of an
18thC English gentleman. 'A man who has
not been in Italy, is always conscious of an
inferiority', warned Dr. Johnson. Tourists,
whether grand or otherwise, have always
required souvenirs of their travels, and there
developed a thriving demand for pictures of
famous sights and views, which has persisted
until the present day. Italian topography has
been one of the most commercial areas of the
art market in recent times and many of the
works in the following sections have fetched
high prices. While demand for Italian views
might be healthy, the same could not be said
for the state of the Italian art market. From
1991 to 1992, reported the *Daily Telegraph*
(8.4.94), Italy spent more on pictures and
works of art than any other nation in the
world. 'Last year, with scandal, tax hunts
and a fear that communists might come into
the government, Italian buying froze.'

Only time will tell when and if the market
will re-establish itself.

Francis Towne
British (1740–1816)
The Lake of Lugano
Signed and dated '1800', watercolour over
traces of pencil
19¾ x 29⅜in (50 x 76cm)
£4,500–6,000 *S*

Antonietta Brandeis
Bohemian (b1849)
A View of the Baptistry in Florence
Signed with monogram, oil on panel
13½ x 9½in (34 x 24cm)
£4,500–5,500 *P*

William Callow, O.W.S.
British (1812–1908)
The Ponte Vecchio, Florence
Signed and dated '1877', pencil,
watercolour and bodycolour
11 x 19¾in (28 x 50cm)
£4,500–5,500 *C*

Edward Lear
British (1812–88)
Cervo, Italy
Signed, inscribed and dated '1882',
watercolour heightened with white
10¼ x 20½in (26 x 52cm)
£13,000–14,000 *S*

Consalve Carelli
Italian (1818–1900)
Figures in a Carriage passing
beneath an Arch
Signed, watercolour
12 x 10¾in (31 x 27.5cm)
£2,500–3,000 *DN*

Charles Rowbotham
British (active 1877–1914)
Genoa
Signed, inscribed with title and
dated '1902', watercolour and gouache
15¾ x 22⅜in (40 x 58cm)
£2,500–3,000 *S(S)*

Albert Trippel
German (1813–54)
Palazzo Reale, Turin
Signed, watercolour
13¼ x 16½in (33.5 x 42cm)
£3,000–4,000 *C*

Franz Richard Unterberger
Belgian (1838–1902)
Monreale, Palermo
Signed, oil on canvas
24 x 36in (61 x 92cm)
£37,000–40,000 *WH*

Franz Richard Unterberger
Belgian (1838–1902)
Capri
Signed, oil on canvas
32¾ x 27¾in (83 x 71cm)
£34,000–40,000 *C(S)*

Bernard Buffet
French (b1928)
Compo Santo, Pisa
Signed and dated '59', oil on canvas
35 x 57¾in (89 x 146cm)
£55,000–65,000 *S(NY)*

Arthur Jenkins
British (b1871)
The Road to Florence
Signed, oil on canvas
14 x 18in (35.5 x 46cm)
£500–700 *Gra*

Y. Gianni
Italian (20thC)
A Street Scene with Figures and
Flower Stalls
Signed, watercolour
24 x 18in (61 x 45.5cm)
£600–700 *GH*

Rome

Follower of Gaspar van Wittel, called Vanvitelli
Dutch (1653–1736)
Rome, The Piazza Navona
Oil on canvas
35 x 50½in (89 x 128cm)
£24,000–27,000 *S*

Bernardo Bellotto
Italian (1721–80)
The Porta Santo Spirito, with the Via dei
Penitenzieri and the Campanile of Santo
Spirito in Sassia, and The Arch of Titus, with
the Wall and Gate of the Farnese Gardens
and the Temple of Castor and Pollux beyond
A pair, oils on canvas
38¾ x 29½in (98 x 75cm)
£1,800,000–2,000,000 *C*

Carl Frederik Aagaard
Danish (1833–95)
Viale Trinità dei Monti con la
Fontana di Villa Medici da Via di
San Sebastianello, Roma
Signed and dated '1872', oil on canvas
22¾ x 33in (58 x 84cm)
£25,000–30,000 *C*

Cavaliere Ippolito Caffi
Italian (1809–66)
A Crowd gathered before St. Peter's, Rome
Oil on canvas
13½ x 22¾in (34.5 x 58cm)
£40,000–50,000 *S(NY)*

Thomas Hartley Cromek
British (1809–73)
The Forum, Rome
Signed, pencil and watercolour with
scratching out
12½ x 19in (32 x 48cm)
£3,500–4,500 *C*

Gaspar Gabrielli
Italian (19thC)
The Coliseum and Arch of Constantine,
Rome, and Part of the Roman Forum
A pair, signed and dated '1817', oil on canvas
22½ x 29in (57 x 74cm)
£25,000–30,000 *MEA*

Arthur Glennie, R.W.S.
British (1803–90)
A Deserted Town near Rome
Signed and dated '1859', watercolour
13½ x 26½in (34 x 67cm)
£1,500–2,000 *P*

A. Heinrich Hansen
Norwegian (1862–1929)
A Piazza, Rome
Signed with initials and dated '07',
oil on canvas
17½ x 24in (44.5 x 61cm)
£1,000–1,200 *CSK*

Italian School
Piazza San Pietro, Roma
Oil on canvas
32 x 56in (81 x 142cm)
£3,000–4,000 *CSK*

Italian School (19thC)
The Pantheon, Rome
Oil on canvas
8½ x 11¾in (21.5 x 30cm)
£1,800–2,200 *CSK*

Frederik Christian Lund
Danish (1826–1901)
Castel Sant' Angelo, Rome
Signed and dated '1864', watercolour
19¾ x 30½in (50 x 78cm)
£2,000–2,500 *C*

Richard Pikesley
British (20thC)
Riva degli Schiavoni
Oil on canvas
16 x 30in (41 x 76cm)
£1,400–1,600 *WHP*

François Martin
French (19thC)
St Peter's Square in Rome, and
Piazza Navona in Rome
A pair, both signed and inscribed, watercolours
19 x 28¼ and 19¾ x 27½in (48.5 x 72
and 50 x 70cm)
£7,500–8,500 *S*

John Yardley
British (b1936)
Lunch Break in Rome
Signed, watercolour
9½ x 13½in (24 x 35cm)
£850–950 *Bne*

Classical & Ancient Ruins

'Demand for classical capriccios rises from ruins' reported the *Antiques Trade Gazette*, commenting on a spate of successful results for capriccios in the provincial salerooms. Decorative old master paintings have been popular in the market place for some time, and what could be more fanciful than a capriccio? The term itself comes from the Italian for caper or caprice, and these 'ruinscapes' show landscapes or architectural scenes, combining both real and imaginary elements. The following section includes fantasy landscapes alongside faithful representations of classical ruins and monuments. A number of the following pictures sold at auction for considerably more than estimated. Nevertheless, the price range of the Buisieri sketches, £350–450 for three works, shows how old master drawings can still be picked up for very reasonable prices.

Jan Baptist Weenix
Dutch (1621-63)
A Woman, Child and Peasants resting by an
Ionic Ruin, a Harbour beyond
Oil on canvas
35 x 45½in (89 x 115cm)
£40,000–50,000 *C*

Circle of Juriaan Andriessen
Dutch (1742–1819)
A Wooded River Landscape with a
Sportsman and Peasants, and A Wooded
Landscape with Peasants
by a ruined Manor House
A pair, oils on canvas
75½ x 48in (192 x 122cm)
£20,000–25,000 *C*

George Barret
British (1767–1842)
Capriccio on Lake Nemi
Signed, watercolour
10½ x 16in (26 x 41cm)
£900–980 *LH*

Attributed to Benjamin Barker of Bath
British (1776–1838)
Peasants with Sheep and Cows by a ruined
Archway in a wooded River Landscape
Oil on canvas
39½ x 49in (100 x 124.5cm)
£3,750–4,750 *C*

Giovanni Battista Busieri
Italian (1698–1757)
The so-called 'Sepolcro degli Orazi e Curiazi'
with studies of two Figures, one on a Donkey,
on reverse
Pen and brown ink over traces of red and
black chalk
With two drawings of ruins by the same
hand, one inscribed 'the Tomb of Metellus'
6½ x 8¾in (16.5 x 22cm)
£350–450 *P*

Abraham-Louis-Rodolphe Ducros
Swiss (1748–1810)
Tivoli, Ruins in the Foreground, Figures and
Falls in the Distance
Watercolour and gouache, heightened with
white, over traces of black chalk
26½ x 39½in (67 x 99.5cm)
£15,000–20,000 *P*

Manner of Leonardo Coccorante
Italian (1680–1750)
A Capriccio of Classical Ruins with
a Gentleman and Peasants
Oil on canvas
40½ x 30¼in (103 x 77cm)
£3,500–4,000 *C*

> **Miller's is a price GUIDE
> not a price LIST**

Xaverio Della Gatta
Italian (d1829)
Palazzo Don'Anna
Signed and dated '1795', gouache
14½ x 21½in (37 x 55cm)
£7,500–8,500 *S(S)*

Jacob Philipp Hackert
German (1737–1807)
Herdsmen with Goats resting in the Temple
of Canop, Hadrian's Villa, Near Tivoli
Signed, inscribed and dated '1774', pen
and brown ink with wash
13½ x 18in (34.5 x 46cm)
£3,000–4,000 *P*

North Italian School (late 18thC)
Capriccio Street Scene
Oil on canvas
23¾ x 32½in (60.5 x 82.5cm)
£2,000–2,500 *S(S)*

North Italian School (18thC)
Capriccio of a Palace with Figures
Oil on canvas
36 x 52½in (91.5 x 133.5cm)
£3,500–4,000 *S(S)*

Franz Keiserman
Swiss (1765–1833)
The Temple at Paestum
Signed and dated '1825', watercolour and
gum arabic over pencil
25½ x 48in (65 x 122cm)
£7,500–8,500 *P*

Follower of Panini
Italian (1691–1765)
Italian Harbour, c1750
Oil on canvas
14 x 18in (36 x 46cm)
£1,300–1,600 *WIL*

Etienne Chevalier de Lorimier
French (1759–1813)
Landscape with a view of the Villa Borghese,
and Landscape with the Temple of Diana in
the Borghese Gardens
A pair, one signed '1810' the other '1811', oil
on canvas
46½ x 35¾in (118 x 91cm)
£46,000–60,000 *S(NY)*

Manner of Giovanni Paolo Panini
Italian (1691–1765)
Capriccio with Soldiers Amidst Roman Ruins
Oil on canvas
34 x 41in (86 x 104cm)
£3,000–3,500 *S(S)*

Hubert Robert
French (1733–1808)
Washerwomen at a Pool near Antique Ruins
Signed, oil on canvas
64 x 38½in (162.5 x 98cm)
£45,000–60,000 *S(NY)*

After Giovanni Paolo Panini
Italian (1691–1765)
A Capriccio of Roman Ruins with the
Coliseum and the Torre delle Milizie
Oil on canvas
24 x 48in (61.5 x 122cm)
£15,000–18,000 *C*

Circle of Antonio Visentini
Italian (1688–1782)
Two figures conversing on the Steps of
Classical Ruins observed by a Woman
A pair, both oil on canvas
17 x 12½in (43 x 32cm)
£6,000–7,000 *P*

Michael Wutky
Austrian (1739–1823)
Figures before a Capriccio View of the
Colosseum in an Italianate Landscape
Oil on canvas
39½in x 54½in (100 x 138cm)
£13,000–15,000 *C*

Walter Crane, R.W.S.
British (1845–1915)
Flora
Signed with monogram, pencil, watercolour
and bodycolour heightened with white on
oatmeal paper
9¾ x 13¾in (24.5 x 35.5cm)
£5,000–6,000 *C*

Jane Dormer
British (19thC)
Mettina and Temple Jupitor
A pair, inscribed and dated '1852',
oil on canvas
15 x 20in (38 x 50.5cm)
£1,000–2,000 *WIL*

Italian School (19thC)
A Lady spinning Wool by a Fountain
Oil on canvas
7¼ x 9¼in (18 x 23cm)
£300–500 *C*

Carl Haag
Swedish (1820–1915)
The Amphitheatre, Taormina, Sicily
Signed and dated '1870', pencil
and watercolour
12½ x 24¾in (31.5 x 63cm)
£2,000–2,500 *CSK*

Peder Mønsted
Danish (1859–1941)
Athenian Ruins
Signed and dated '1893', oil on canvas
27½ x 51in (70 x 129.5cm)
£12,000–15,000 S

This painting was executed during Mønsted's stay with King George I of Greece.

Florence Travers
British (19thC)
Greek Peasant by the Temple of Athena
Niké, Acropolis, Athens
Signed and dated '1849', oil on canvas
18 x 22in (45.5 x 56cm)
£2,500–3,500 S

Manner of Marco Ricci
Italian (20thC)
Architectural Capriccio with Christ and the
Woman of Samaria
Oil on canvas
36 x 46in (91.5 x 116.5cm)
£2,500–3,000 S(S)

Epaminondas Thomopoulos
Greek (1878–1974)
The Acropolis, and the Temple of
Herodou Atticos, Athens
A pair, both signed and dated 1933,
oil on canvas
13½ x 16in (34 x 40.5cm)
£7,000–8,000 C

Frank Taylor
British (20thC)
Ancient Stones, Selçuk
Watercolour
10 x 13in (25 x 33cm)
£350–450 PHG

Naples

Salvatore Candido
Italian (19thC)
A View of the Bay of Naples
Signed and dated '1835', oil on canvas
11½ x 15¼in (29 x 39cm)
£9,500–12,000   S

Circle of Giuseppe Carelli
Italian (1858–1921)
The Bay of Naples, and The Amalfi Coast
A pair, oil on canvas laid down on panels
£1,200–1,800   CSK

Pietro Gabrini
Italian (1865–1926)
Returning Home, Naples
Signed and dated '1907', oil on canvas
25¼ x 43¾in (64.5 x 111cm)
£6,500–8,000   CSK

Largo Cappella
Neapolitan School (19thC)
Panorama di Napoli da S. Martino,
and Continuazioni di Napoli
A pair, gouache
17½ x 36in (45 x 91.5cm)
£3,500–4,500   MEA

Thomas Dessoulavy
British (mid-19thC)
Golfo di Napoli, and Pozzuoli dal convento
dei Camaldolesi
A pair, signed and dated '1841', oil on canvas
16¼ x 24¼in (41.5 x 62cm)
£10,500–12,000   C

Carl Wilhelm Gotzloff
German (1799–1866)
A View over the Bay of Naples
Signed, oil on canvas
16¾ x 25¾in (42.5 x 65.5cm)
£7,500–8,500   P

Lamberto Lamberti
Italian (19th/20thC)
Fishermen on the shore in the Bay of Naples
Signed, oil on canvas
16 x 24in (41 x 61cm)
£3,000–4,000   S

Neapolitan School (19thC)
A View along the Waterfront at Naples
Gouache
11 x 15¾in (28 x 40cm)
£2,500–3,000 *S*

Neapolitan School (19thC)
Villa Reale
Inscribed, gouache
17¾ x 25¾in (45 x 65.5cm)
£2,000–2,500 *Bon*

Neapolitan School (19thC)
Naples from the Sea, and Vesuvius Erupting
A pair, inscribed 'Napoli da Mare' and
'Cenere del 1846', bodycolours
7½ x 10¼in (19 x 26cm)
£500–700 *CSK*

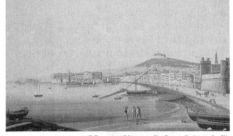

Neapolitan School (19thC)
Napoli Dal Carmine
Inscribed with title in Italian
on the border, gouache
£1,800–2,200 *S*

Attributed to La Pira
Italian (19thC)
Villa Reale, Naples
Inscribed on reverse, gouache
16 x 25in (40.5 x 63.5cm)
£2,000–3,000 *P*

Franz Richard Unterberger
Belgian (1838–1902)
Possilipo, Naples
Signed, oil on canvas
32 x 27in (81 x 69cm)
£55,000–65,000 *WH*

*Offered by Glasgow auctioneers William
Hardie, this picture more than quadrupled
its modest £8,000–12,000 estimate.
Unterburger's decorative and cheerful Italian
scenes have been making top prices in the
current market.*

Thomas Charles Leeson Rowbotham
British (1823–75)
Mount Vesuvius from across the Bay,
and Naples
A pair, both signed and dated '1874' and
'1872' respectively, pencil and watercolours
heightened with bodycolour
7¾ x 18¾in (19.5 x 48cm)
£1,500–2,000 *C*

Venice

No auction of Continental pictures is complete without some devoted to Venice, invariably one of the most sought after subjects in the saleroom. The more cynically minded might suspect that if Venice is sinking, at least some of the blame could be attached to the thousands of artists who have tramped its streets over the centuries. Some simply passed through on their European Tour, others made virtually a whole career out of portraying the city. The Bouvard family, Antoine, Colette and Noel, fall into the latter category. Antoine Bouvard, who was born in 1917, was the most famous and prolific of the clan, and his Venetian scenes are a permanent fixture in the salerooms and galleries. In spite of his popularity, very little is known about him or indeed the rest of the family. He was born Marc Aldine, and is listed in the reference books as Italian, but changed his name to Bouvard and his nationality to French. If the details of his life are confusing and sketchy, his pictures are not - they are instantly recognisable and decorative portrayals of what must surely be the most painted city in the world.

Giovanni Antonio Canal, il Canaletto
Italian (1697–1768)
The Grand Canal, Venice, looking East from the Campo S. Vio
Oil on canvas
18½ x 31in (47 x 78.5cm)
£1,300,000–1,500,000 C

This view was Canaletto's favourite Venetian scene, and the artist returned to the site repeatedly. Although a price of £1.2m might seem substantial enough to those of us without Andrew Lloyd Webber-sized cheque books, Canaletto's 'Return of the Bucentaur on Ascension Day', fetched £7.6m for Paris auctioneers Ader-Tajan in December '93, the second highest result ever achieved in France.

Giovanni Battista Cimaroli
Italian (17th/18thC)
A Town in the Veneto
Oil on canvas
17½ x 25¼in (44.5 x 64.5cm)
£58,000–70,000 C

Follower of Canaletto
Italian (18thC)
Venice, the Piazza San Marco
Oil on canvas
21 x 28in (53 x 71cm)
£9,000–10,000 S

Atributed to Johan Anton Richter
Swedish (1665–1745)
A Performance of the Commedia Dell'Arte in the North-West corner of the Piazza San Marco, Venice
Oil on canvas
20½ x 31½in (52 x 80cm)
£45,000–55,000 S(NY)

Venetian School (18thC)
Venice, the Piazzetta di San Marco
Oil on canvas
23 x 37in (59 x 94cm)
£7,500–10,000 S

Attributed to Charles-Marie Bouton
French (1781–1853)
Riva degli Schiavoni, Venice
Signed, oil on board
8 x 11in (20 x 28cm)
£2,000–2,500 *CSK*

Antonietta Brandeis
Austrian (b1849)
A Gondola by the Bridge of Sighs
Signed, oil on canvas
22½ by 13½in (57 x 34.5cm)
£6,000–8,000 *S*

William Callow
British (1812–1908)
View of Venice
Signed and dated '1868', watercolour
9¼ x 19in (23.5 x 48.5cm)
£11,000–12,000 *CAG*

*The financial troubles of the Lloyds names
have resulted in many cherished family
possessions coming on to the market. At
Canterbury Auction Galleries, one such name
and a descendant of the artist William Callow
was forced to part with Callow's 'View of
Venice, looking towards the Santa Maria
della Salute'. The picture had not been seen
in public since 1868, the year that it was
painted, and was consequently fresh to the
market, just what the trade likes best. It is
to be hoped that the vendor found some
consolation in the final price.*

Edward William Cooke, R.A., F.R.S.
British (1811–80)
The Porto, Venice
Signed, dated 'Xmas Eve 1860',
and inscribed, pencil
6¾ x 10½in (17 x 26.5cm)
£600–800 *P*

Salomon Corrodi
Italian (1810–92)
The Bacino with the Piazzetta, Venice
Signed and dated '1859', pencil
and watercolour
25½ x 39½in (65 x 101cm)
£7,000–10,000 *C*

John Robert Keitley Duff
British (1862–1936)
Piazzetta, St. Marco, Venice
Signed, pastel and crayon
10½ x 14½in (27 x 37cm)
£600–680 *LH*

Edward Angelo Goodall, R.W.S.
British (1819–1908)
The Doge's Palace, St. Mark's and the
Campanile from the Lagoon, Venice
Signed, pencil and watercolour with
scratching out
10½ x 8¼in (26.5 x 21cm)
£2,500–3,000 C

Albert Goodwin, R.W.S.
British (1845–1932)
The Cemetery, Venice
Signed and inscribed, pencil and
watercolour with scratching out
8 x 10in (20 x 25cm)
£3,500–4,000 C

Giovanni Grubacs
Italian (1829–1919)
The Grand Canal, Venice
Signed and inscribed on the reverse,
oil on canvas
21 x 29in (53 x 74cm)
£14,000–16,000 C

Pietro Gabrini
Italian (1865–1926)
Attending a Venetian Shrine
Signed and inscribed, oil on canvas
54 x 39½in (137 x 100.5cm)
£3,500–4,500 C

Pietro Gabrini
Italian (1865–1926)
Venetian Lovers in a Fishing Boat
Signed and inscribed, pencil
and watercolour
15½ x 22¼in (39.5 x 56.5cm)
£450–550 CSK

James Holland
British (1800–70)
A Canal, Venice
Watercolour over traces of pencil
scratching out and gum arabic
14 x 9¾in (36 x 24.5cm)
£2,600–3,500 S

J. Hulk
Dutch (19thC)
A Venetian Capriccio
Signed, oil on panel
11½ x 18½in (29 x 47cm)
£1,000–1,200   *CSK*

Jules Lessore
French/British (1849–92)
The Bridge of Sighs, Venice
Signed, pencil and watercolour
19½ x 13⅓in (49.5 x 34cm)
£800–1,000   *CSK*

Frederick Christian Lund
Danish (1826–1901)
Venice
Signed and dated '1880', oil on canvas
11 x 14½in (28 x 37cm)
£700–780   *LH*

Thomas Moran
American (1837–1926)
The Gate of Venice, Sunset
Signed with monogram, dated '1895',
oil on canvas
14 x 27in (36 x 69cm)
£25,000–30,000 *S(NY)*

*Born in Bolton, not a location renowned for
its romantic glamour, Moran moved to
America where he became a late exponent of
the Hudson River School of painting. This
mid-19thC American movement was
characterised by a romantic and grandiose
vision of nature that expresses itself in
Moran's luminous views of Venice. Dramatic
and decorative, Moran's landscapes can
command high prices at auction. The artist's
Venetian view illustrated on the cover of the
guide doubled its auction estimate of
$18,000–24,000 to make $48,300 (£33,000)
at Sotheby's.*

Walter Launt Palmer
American (1854–1932)
Venetian Boats
Signed, oil on canvas
21 x 28in (53 x 71cm)
£5,500–6,500 *CNY*

Henry Pether
British (1828–65)
The Grand Canal by Moonlight
Signed, oil on canvas
24 x 36in (61 x 91.5cm)
£15,000–17,000 *S*

Rubens Santoro
Italian (1859–1942)
San Geremia, with Palazzo Labia, Venice
Signed, oil on canvas
19½ x 14½in (49.5 x 37cm)
£55,000–65,000 *C*

Adolf Sukkert
German (19thC)
Procession Day in
St. Mark's Square, Venice
Signed, oil on canvas
26½ x 37¼in (67 x 94.5cm)
£17,000–21,000 *S*

J. Vivian
British (active 1869–77)
The Grand Canal, Venice
Signed, oil on canvas
18¼ x 32¼in (46.5 x 82cm)
£5,500–6,500 *C*

James Abbott McNeill Whistler
American (1834–1903)
The Rialto
Etching, 1879–80, signed in pencil
11½ x 8in (29 x 20cm)
£4,000–5,000 *S(NY)*

Marc Aldine/Antoine Bouvard
French (1917–56)
A Canal Scene, Venice
Signed, oil on canvas
21¼ x 14½in (54 x 37cm)
£3,500–4,500 *S*

*Marc Aldine was his birth name and
Bouvard his trade name.*

Antoine Bouvard
French (1917–56)
Venetian Canal Scene with a small Bridge,
and Sailing Boat
Signed, oil on canvas
20 x 24in (50.5 x 61cm)
£3,600–4,600 *JNic*

William Wyld
British (1806–89)
The Island of San Giorgio, and
Entrance to the Grand Canal, Venice
Signed and dated '1874', oil on canvas
28¼ x 43½in (72 x 110cm)
£10,000–12,000 *Bea*

Felix-François Georges Philibert Ziem
French (1821–1911)
In the Venetian Lagoon
Signed, oil on canvas
11½ x 21½in (29 x 54.5cm)
£4,500–6,000 *C*

Antoine Bouvard
French (1917–56)
Behind the Santa Maria de la Salute
Signed, oil on canvas
20 x 25in (51 x 64cm)
£7,000–8,000 *HFA*

Antoine Bouvard
French (1917–56)
The Grand Canal, with the Santa Maria
della Salute, Venice
Signed, oil on canvas
19 x 25in (48.5 x 64cm)
£13,000–13,500 *BuP*

Antoine Bouvard
French (1917–56)
A View of a Backwater Canal, Venice
Signed, oil on canvas
25 x 19in (64 x 48.5cm)
£6,000–7,000 *S*

Nicholas Briganti
American (1895–1989)
Venice
Signed, oil on canvas
20½ x 27½in (52 x 70cm)
£1,500–2,500 *CSK*

John Bratby, R.A.
British (1928–92)
Arch, Gondolas, Water Reflections and
Window Shutters
Signed and dated '87', oil on canvas
48 x 36in (122 x 91.5cm)
£1,200–1,600 *C*

Emma Ciardi
Italian (1879–1933)
A Venetian Canal
Signed and dated '1925',
oil on panel
15 x 20in (38 x 50.5cm)
£17,000–18,000 *C*

Ken Howard
British (b1932)
The Back Streets of Venice, near
Campo San Barnado, 1980
Signed, oil on canvas
24 x 20in (61.5 x 50.5cm)
£1,000–1,250 *GG*

Peter Kuhfeld, N.E.A.C.
British (b1952)
Near to Ponte Poscari, Afternoon
Oil on canvas
26 x 24in (66.5 x 61.5cm)
£5,500–6,000 *WHP*

Helen Emmeline McAlpine
British (20thC)
Three Doors on Rio S. Apostoli
Signed, watercolour
14½ x 10in (37 x 25cm)
£300–330 *LH*

Richard Pikesley
British (20thC)
Diners and Salute
Oil on canvas
12 x 20in (30.5 x 50.5cm)
£800–900 *WHP*

Edward Seago
British (1910–74)
The Red House, Venice
Signed, oil on board
26 x 20¼in (66.5 x 52cm)
£8,500–10,000 *P*

Jonathan Trowell
British (20thC)
Florians
Oil on canvas
8 x 10in (20 x 25cm)
£500–575 *WHP*

Norman Wilkinson
British (1878–1971)
Grand Canal, Venice
Signed, watercolour,
bodycolour and pencil
5 x 7in (13 x 17.5cm)
£550–700 *S*

Malta

Occupying a dominant strategic position in the middle of the Mediterranean, and with one of the finest natural harbours in the world, Malta is a major centre of maritime history. Consequently, the islands have attracted generations of marine painters. Maltese dealers and collectors are often the prominent bidders for topographical views (see also Marine section).

Luigi M. Galea
Maltese (1847–1917)
Valletta Harbour, Malta
A pair, both signed, oil on board
6 x 13½in (15 x 34cm)
£2,500–3,500 *C*

Luigi M. Galea
Maltese (1847–1917)
Valletta Harbour
Signed and dated '1912', oil on panel
19 x 32¼in (48.5 x 82cm)
£8,000–10,000 *C*

Circle of Anton Schranz the Younger
Austrian (1769–1839)
View of La Valletta from Fort Tigne, entrance of Marmuscetto, View of the Entrance of the Harbour of La Valletta from Isola Point, The Entrance of the Harbour of La Valletta, and View of La Valletta from the point at the Corradino
Set of four, watercolours, all inscribed on original washline borders
4¾ x 7in (12 x 17.5cm)
£4,500–5,500 *Bon*

Gerolamo Gianni
Italian (b1837)
The Grand Harbour, Valletta
A pair, both signed and dated '1878', oil on canvas
13¾ x 40in (35 x 101.5cm)
£10,500–12,500 *Bon*

Maltese School (late 18thC)
Vue de la Port de Marsamucetto et du Fort Manuel prise du Bastion St André, and Vue du l'Antree du Grand Port
A pair, inscribed, gouache
14½ x 25¼in (37 x 64.5cm)
£5,500–6,500 *Bon*

Oriental Views

The Orient was a favourite subject with
19thC painters. Whilst many were happy to
concoct romantic Orientalist pictures without
straying from their European studios (see
Orientalist section), other more intrepid
painters travelled the East, making informed
studies of the landscape and its inhabitants.
David Roberts visited Egypt and the Holy
Land in the 1830s, and Frederick Goodall
and the Swedish artist Carl Haag both spent
time living with the Bedouins. John
Frederick Lewis resided for ten years in
Cairo where, according to the novelist
William Thackeray who visited him in 1844,
he went 'native'. The following section is
devoted to Oriental landscapes by such
artists. Though the market for Orientalist
pictures peaked in the mid-1980s and
dropped during the recession, there are signs
of a considerable revival, the most notable
event being the sale of the Forbes collection
of Orientalist works which made £1.97million
at Christie's, New York, in Autumn 1993.

Italian School (18thC)
A Capriccio View of Constantinople
Inscribed, oil on canvas
20¼ x 28¾in (87.5 x 73cm)
£5,000–6,000 *C(S)*

Amadeo, 5th Count Preziosi
Maltese (1816–82)
A View of Istanbul looking towards Topkapi
Serai and the Blue Mosque from across the
Golden Horn
Pencil and watercolour
7 x 10¼in (17.5 x 26cm)
£2,500–3,500 *Bon*

Henrik Ankarcrona
Swedish (1831–1917)
Arabs Resting in an Oasis
Signed and dated '1894', oil on canvas
23½ x 41¼in (60 x 105cm)
£4,200–5,000 *S*

Henry Currey
British (19thC)
A Caravan, near Tunis
Signed, inscribed and dated '80', oil on card
12 x 18½in (30.5 x 47cm)
£1,500–2,000 *C*

Continental School (19thC)
Shipping off the Turkish Coast
A pair, inscribed 'Port Constantinople',
oil on panel
50½ x 26¼in (128 x 67cm)
£9,000–10,000 *P*

Charles Théodore Frère
French (1814–88)
A View of Beni Souef, Egypt
Signed, oil on panel
8¼ x 15½in (22 x 39cm)
£9,000–11,000 *S*

Johann Jakob Frey
Swiss (1813–65)
The Ruins at Philae, Egypt
Oil on canvas
29½ x 44in (75 x 111.5cm)
£10,500–12,000 *S*

Frederick Goodall, R.A.
British (1822–1904)
An Encampment in the Desert
Signed with monogram and dated '1874',
oil on canvas
11¼ x 36in (29 x 91.5cm)
£4,000–5,000 *C*

Manuel Garcia y Rodriguez
Spanish (1863–1925)
A Street Scene with a Mosque, Tangier
Signed, watercolour
12 x 7½ in (30.5 x 19cm)
£3,000–4,000 *S*

Locate the Source
*The source of each
illustration in Miller's
can be found by checking
the code letters below
each caption with the list
of contributors.*

August Johannes le Gras
Dutch (1864–1915)
Sunset Kairouan, Tunisia
Signed, oil on canvas
19 x 58½in (48.5 x 149cm)
£1,700–2,200 *S(Am)*

Edward Lear
British (1812–88)
Constantinople from the Bosphorus
Signed with monogram, watercolour over
traces pencil heightened with white
7 x 14½in (17.5 x 37cm)
£30,000–35,000 *S*

*According to expert Charles Hind, in the
1950s and 60s watercolours by Edward Lear
could be picked up for £5. Today, prices are
more likely to begin at around £500 for minor
sketches, extending well into five figure sums
for major works. As Hind notes, Lear's Greek
and Turkish views command particularly
high prices since they appeal to wealthy
collectors of both these nationalities. This
painting, estimated at £10,000–15,000,
doubled its top estimate at Sotheby's.*

John Frederick Lewis, R.A., P.O.W.S.
British (1805–76)
St. Sophia from the Great Gates of the
Great Court, Constantinople
Inscribed original label verso, watercolour
over pencil, heightened with white
13 x 19¼in (33 x 49cm)
£12,500–16,000 *P*

Auguste Meyer
French (late 19thC)
Figures embarking at the
Blue Mosque, Constantinople
Signed, oil on canvas
21 x 16¼in (53 x 41.5cm)
£20,000–25,000 C

Henry Pilleau, R.I., R.O.I.
British (1813–99)
The Sphinx and Great Pyramid of Ghizeh,
Near Cairo
Monogrammed, titled and inscribed,
watercolour
8¼ x 14½in (21 x 37cm)
£350–450 JC

Alexandre Nicolaievitch Roussoff
Russian (1844–1928)
Cairo
Signed, inscribed and dated '1891',
pencil and watercolour
16 x 10¼in (40.5 x 26cm)
£1,850–2,200 C

John Varley, Jnr.
British (d1899)
An Eastern Caravansary
Signed, pencil and watercolour
heightened with white
13 x 20in (33 x 50.5cm)
£800–1,000 CSK

Edward Bawden, R.A.
British (1903–89)
The Golden Dome of the Shrine of
Imam Reza, Mashhad
Signed, pencil, pen, black ink, watercolour
and collage
20in (50.5cm) square
£1,800–2,500 C

Albert Marquet
French (1875–1947)
Le Minaret de Sidi Bou Said
Signed, oil on canvas, 1923
19½ x 25½in (50 x 65cm)
£58,000–70,000 C

Spain

A. Moulton Foweraker
British (1873–1942)
Moonlight, Spanish Town
Signed, watercolour
20¾ x 14in (53 x 35.5cm)
£2,650–2,850 *GG*

Manuel Garcia y Rodriguez
Spanish (1863–1925)
Sevilla
Signed and dated '1912', oil on canvas
23½ x 32⅝in (60 x 83cm)
£5,800–7,000 *C*

Richard Kemp
British (20thC)
Menorca
Oil on canvas
24 x 30in (61.5 x 76.5cm)
£500–550 *TFA*

David Roberts, R.A.
British (1796–1864)
An Old Moorish Gateway at Granada
Inscribed and dated 'Feb 10th 1833', pencil
and watercolour with touches of white
heightening on grey paper
10 x 6½in (25 x 17cm)
£3,500–4,500 *C*

Felix Kelly
New Zealand (b1916)
Arco de la Sangre, Toledo, Spain
Signed and dated '49', oil on board
19¾ x 15in (50 x 38cm)
£1,650–1,800 *C*

Ignacio Zuloaga y Zabaleta
Spanish (1870–1945)
A View of La Virgen de la Peña, Graus
Signed, oil on canvas
25 x 29¾in (63 x 76cm)
£35,000–40,000 *S*

Circle of Jan Abrahamsz. Beerstraten
Dutch (1622–66)
A Winter Landscape with Figures in a
Horse-drawn Sleigh
Oil on canvas
26¾ x 41in (68 x 104cm)
£6,000–8,000 *P*

Joseph Yelverton Dawbarn
British (active 1887–1933)
Reims
Signed, inscribed and
dated '1915', watercolour
23 x 17in (59 x 43cm)
£1,500–1,750 *WrG*

Rudolf von Alt
Austrian (1812–1905)
The Theyn Church in Prague
Signed and dated '1843', pencil and watercolour
13¾ x 11in (35 x 28cm)
£37,000–45,000 *S*

Hendrick Breedveld
Dutch (b1918)
A Dutch Street Scene
Oil on canvas
24 x 36in (61 x 91.5cm)
£3,000–3,500 *SAV*

Angelo Quaglio
German (1829–90)
A View of Nürnberg
Signed, inscribed and dated '1856',
watercolour heightened with white
9½ x 11½in (24 x 29cm)
£3,200–4,000 *C*

Adrianus Eversen
Dutch (1818–97)
A Dutch Street Scene
Signed, oil on canvas
19¾ x 15¾in (50 x 40cm)
£17,000–20,000 *S*

Emily Beatrice Bland
British (1864–1951)
Menton Harbour
Oil on board, c1910–20
10 x 13in (25 x 33cm)
£1,500–2,000 *NZ*

Philip Castle
British (b1929)
The Grand Opening
Oil on canvas
39½ x 31½in (100 x 80cm)
£5,500–6,000 *SOL*

Paul Cornoyer
American (1864–1923)
Bryant Park
Signed, oil on canvas
18 x 24in (45.5 x 61cm)
£25,000–30,000 *S(NY)*

William Lee-Hankey, R.A.
British (1869–1952)
St Tropez
Signed, oil on canvas
20 x 24in (50.5 x 61.5cm)
£12,000–13,000 *BuP*

Anne Redpath, R.A., R.S.A.,
British (1895–1965)
Sospel, Alpes Maritimes
Signed, oil on panel
20¼ x 31in (51 x 78cm)
£20,000–25,000 *C(S)*

r. **Phil Kelly**
British (20thC)
Spanish Port
Oil on canvas, 1986
24½ x 29½in (62 x 75cm)
£550–600 *JDG*

Francis Towne
British (1740–1816)
Durham
Signed, inscribed, dated and numbered, pencil,
pen and grey ink and watercolour
6¾ x 20in (17 x 51cm)
£2,600–3,500 *C*

George Charlton, N.E.A.C.
British (b1899)
The Grand Parade and Beach, Eastbourne
Oil on canvas
11½ x 15½in (29 x 39.5cm)
£1,800–2,000 *JN*

Thomas Shotter Boys
British (1803–74)
Silver Street, Salisbury
Signed and inscribed, pencil and watercolour
heightened with bodycolour and scratching out
17¼ x 13in (43.5 x 33cm)
£9,000–11,000 *C*

John Yardley
British (b1936)
Queens College, Oxford
Signed, watercolour
9½ x 12½in (24 x 32cm)
£800–850 *Bne*

r. **Walter Stuart Lloyd**
British (active 1875–1929)
Ely from the River
Signed, watercolour
15 x 25in (38 x 63.5cm)
£4,000–4,500 *HFA*

Sir Hubert J. Medlycott
British (b1841)
London, 1914
Signed, inscribed, and
dated '1914', watercolour
35 x 24in (89 x 61.5cm)
£1,700–1,900 *HO*

Louis Dodd
British (20thC)
A View of St Paul's Cathedral, and the
City of London State Barge
Signed, oil on panel
16 x 24in (40.5 x 61.5cm)
£3,200–3,600 *S*

Alfons Purtscher
Austrian (1885–1962)
A London Square
Signed, oil on canvas
20 x 24in (51 x 61.5cm)
£1,800–2,000 *JDG*

Tom Coates
British (20thC)
Big Ben from Westminster Bridge
Oil on panel
10 x 12in (25.5 x 30.5cm)
£550–650 *LA*

l. **John Donaldson**
British (b1945)
Autumn afternoon in Westminster
Signed, oil on canvas
36 x 48in (92 x 122cm)
£5,000–5,500 *Om*

Edouard Leon Cortès
French (1882–1969)
Parisian Scenes
A pair, signed, oil on canvas
13 x 18in (33 x 45.5cm)
£32,000–36,000 *HFA*

Louis Marie de Schryver
French (1862–1942)
Marchande de Fleurs l'Elysée
Signed and dated '1896', oil on canvas
22 x 18½in (56 x 47cm)
£95,000–115,000 *S(NY)*

Eugène Galien-Laloue
French (1854–1941)
La Place du Châtelet
Signed, gouache
22 x 35in (55.5 x 89cm)
£17,500–20,000 *S*

Sir William Russell Flint, R.A., P.R.W.S.
British (1880–1969)
The Tuillerie Gardens, Paris
Signed, watercolour
16½ x 12½in (42 x 32)
£3,200–4,000 *Bea*

r. **Edward Seago**
British (1940–74)
Place de la Concorde, Paris
Signed, oil on canvas
30 x 40in (76 x 101.5cm)
£63,000–66,000 *C*

Arthur Glennie
British (1803–90)
Cattle grazing before a ruined Amphitheatre
Signed, pencil and watercolour
16¼ x 25¼in (41 x 64cm)
£1,500–1,800 *CSK*

Antonio Joli
Italian (1700–70)
A View of St. Peter's, Rome; and
A View on the Arno
A pair, oil on canvas
38in (96.5cm) square
£110,000–125,000 *Bon*

Ippolito Caffi
Italian (1809–66)
A View of the Pantheon, Rome
Oil on canvas
9 x 11½in (23 x 29cm)
£10,000–11,000 *S*

Frank Dillon
British (1823–1909)
The Hypaethral Temple at Philae
Signed, oil on canvas
31¼ x 53½in (79 x 136cm)
£7,000–8,000 *C*

r. **Follower of Viviano Codazzi**
Italian (17thC)
A Mediterranean Quay with
classical ruins and Renaissance-
style Buildings
Oil on canvas
50 x 60in (127 x 152cm)
£9,000–10,000 *C*

P. Schlitz
Swiss (19thC)
A View of Sorrento
Signed and dated '1863', oil on canvas
16½in x 27in (42 x 69cm)
£5,200–6,000 *S*

Johann Rudolf Buhlmann
Swiss (1802–90)
Sunset over the Bay of Naples
Signed and dated '1852', oil on canvas
28 x 38¾in (71 x 98.5cm)
£9,500–11,500 *P*

Giuseppe Carelli
Italian (1858–1921)
Naples from Meigelina, Pompei
A pair, both signed, one
inscribed, oil on panel
7¼ x 14in (18 x 35.5cm)
£3,500–4,500 *Bon*

Frans Richard Unterberger
Belgian (1838–1902)
Torre del Greco, Naples
Signed, oil on canvas
32½ x 27in (82.5 x 68.5cm)
£18,000–20,000 *CSK*

Attilio Pratella
Italian (1856–1932)
On the Neapolitan Coast
Signed, oil on canvas
12 x 19in (30.5 x 48cm)
£5,500–6,000 *C(S)*

Léon Berthoud
Swiss (1822–92)
A View from Ischia
Signed and dated 'St. Balise 1890',
oil on canvas
31½ x 53¼in (80 x 135cm)
£7,000–8,000 *S*

l. **Giovanni Antonio Canal, il Canaletto**
Italian (1697–1768)
The Church of S. Giorgio
Maggiore, Venice
Oil on canvas
18½ x 30½in (47.5 x 77.5cm)
£700,000–800,000 *C*

r. **After Michele Marieschi**
Italian (1696–1743)
Santa Maria della Salute and the
Entrance to the Grand Canal, Venice
Oil on canvas
49½ x 84¼in (125.5 x 214cm)
£50,000–60,000 *C*

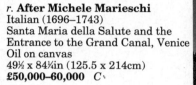

Alfred Pollentine
British (active 1861–80)
Venice
Signed, oil on canvas
20 x 31in (50.5 x 79cm)
£1,800–2,000 *SAV*

Attributed to Johann Georg Ziesenis
Danish (1681–1748)
A Carnival Scene in Piazza San Marco, Venice
Oil on canvas
25½ x 35in (65 x 89cm)
£13,000–15,000 *S*

r. **Attributed to J. Vivian**
British (late 19thC)
The Punta della Dogana with S. Maria
della Salute, Venice
Inscribed 'Clarkson Stanfield RA 1847',
oil on canvas laid down on board
32 x 57in (81 x 144.5cm)
£9,000–12,000 *C*

Peter Kuhfeld
British (20thC)
Porta della Carta, Venice, Late Afternoon
Signed, oil on canvas
23 x 17½in (59 x 44.5cm)
£6,000–7,000 *WHP*

Wilfrid Knox
British (c1889–1966)
Evening on the Lagoons, Venice
Signed and inscribed verso, watercolour
11½ x 19½in (29 x 49cm)
£1,650–1,850 *WrG*

Roberto Ferruzzi
Italian (b1927)
Burano, Venice
Signed, oil on panel
9½ x 8in (24 x 20cm)
£1,000–1,500 *WFA*

Jonathon Trowell
British (20thC)
From the Academia Bridge
Signed, oil on canvas
19 x 23in (48 x 59cm)
£2,000–2,500 *WHP*

r. **Andrew Price**
British (b1955)
The Salute, Venice
Acrylic
14½ x 10in (37 x 25cm)
£550–650 *AMC*

l. **Roy Petley**
British (b1951)
Venice
Signed, oil on panel
16 x 24in (40.5 x 61.5cm)
£5,750–6,750 *SOL*

Antoine Bouvard
French (d1956)
Bridge across a Backwater Canal
Oil on canvas
19½ x 25½in (49.5 x 65cm)
£9,000–10,000 *HFA*

John Bratby
British (1928–92)
Broken Boats Bospherous
Signed and inscribed,
oil on canvas
48 x 36in (122 x 91.5cm)
£4,500–5,000 *BRG*

Noel Bouvard
French (1912–75)
Venetian Backwater with The Doges Palace
Signed, oil on canvas
10½ x 14in (26.5 x 35.5cm)
£1,200–1,700 *JNic*

Colette Bouvard
French (19thC)
The Colours of Venice
Signed, oil on canvas
32 x 21¼in (81.5 x 54cm)
£1,800–2,200 *JNic*

Ian Armour-Chelu
British (20thC)
The Grand Canal on an Autumn Day
Watercolour
8 x 11in (20.5 x 28cm)
£500–600 *PHG*

r. **Charles Cousin**
French (19th/20thC)
Venetian Backwaters
A pair, oil on canvas
9 x 6in (23 x 15cm)
£3,000–3,850 *HFA*

Ernest Arthur Rowe
British (1863–1922)
The Gardens at Hampton Court
Signed, watercolour
9⅜ x 13¼in (24 x 34cm)
£4,000–4,500 *CW*

Frederick Samuel Beaumont
British (b1861)
In Hyde Park, 1910
Oil on board
14 x 10⅜in (35.5 x 26cm)
£400–500 *JDG*

George Samuel Elgood, R.I.
British (1851–1943)
The Cascade, Villa Cicogna
Signed and dated '1909', watercolour
14 x 10⅜in (35.5 x 26cm)
£7,000–7,500 *CW*

Lilian Stannard
British (1877–1944)
A View from the Terrace
Signed, watercolour
10 x 13in (25.5 x 33cm)
£1,650–1,850 *WrG*

John Falconar Slater
British (1857–1937)
Entrance to the Summer Garden
Signed, oil on board
20 x 25in (50.5 x 64cm)
£450–500 *MSW*

Beatrice Parsons
British (1870–1955)
Amongst the Flowers
Signed, watercolour
10 x 12in (25.5 x 30.5cm)
£3,000–3,200 *HO*

Theresa Sylvester Stannard
British (1898–1947)
Daffodil Dell
Signed and inscribed verso, watercolour
19 x 13¼in (48 x 34cm)
£2,800–3,200 *WrG*

Charles Penny
British (b1952)
Garden with Oleander
Watercolour
20 x 27in (50.5 x 68.5cm)
£800–1,000 *AMC*

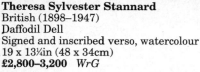

Theresa Sylvester Stannard
British (1898–1947)
The Sundial
Signed, watercolour and bodycolour
10 x 14in (25.5 x 35.5cm)
£3,000–3,500 *CW*

Jason Bowyer
British (20thC)
The Shaded Garden
Oil on canvas
24 x 18in (61.5 x 45.5cm)
£875–925 *WHP*

Mary Swanzy, H.R.H.A.
British (1822–1978)
Green Window
Oil on canvas
13 x 17in (33 x 43cm)
£4,500–5,000 *CCG*

l. **Carel Weight, R.A.**
British (b1908)
A Poet of the Western Suburbs
Signed and dated '1955', oil on canvas
28¼ x 35⅜in (72 x 91cm)
£10,500–12,500 *C*

Fortunino Matania, R.I.
Italian (b1881)
The Blackpool Palace Italian Lounge, and 5 others
Watercolour and bodycolour
19½ x 28½in (49.5 x 72.5cm)
£5,000–6,000 *C(S)*

Edouard Castres
Swiss (1838–1902)
Cataloguing the Inventory
Oil on canvas
18 x 15in (45.5 x 38cm)
£9,500–10,000 *HFA*

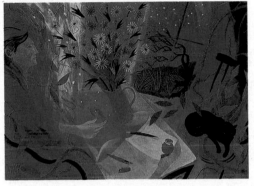

l. **Nicholas Hely Hutchinson**
British (b1955)
Celtic Night
Signed with initials, gouache and pastel
22 x 30in (55.5 x 76cm)
£1,500–1,700 *SOL*

r. **David Bates**
British (1840–1921)
Iffley Mill, Oxford
Signed and dated '1875',
oil on canvas
24 x 36in (61.5 x 91.5cm)
£11,000–13,000 *HFA*

This Midlands artist also painted in Birmingham and Worcester. His style and subjects were similar to that of other members of the Birmingham School, such as Joseph Thors and S. H. Baker. He also made small oil sketches of hedges and plants, which were usually inscribed on the reverse. David Bates exhibited at the Royal Academy from 1872.

l. **Albert Goodwin, R.W.S.**
British (1845–1932)
Durham at Sunset
Signed and inscribed, pen and black ink and watercolour with scratching out
5 x 6¾in (12.5 x 17cm)
£4,000–5,000 *C*

r. **John Atkinson Grimshaw**
British (1836–93)
Ye Ladye Bountifulle
Signed and dated '1884',
inscribed on the reverse,
oil on canvas
20 x 30¼in (50.5 x 76.5cm)
£52,000–60,000 *S*

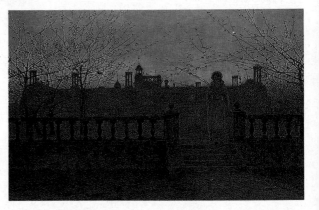

William Prinsep
British (1794–1874)
Belvedere House at Alapore
Signed, pencil and watercolour with touches of white heightening
8 x 11¾in (20 x 29.5cm)
£2,500–3,000 *C*

James Burrell Smith
British (1822–97)
A View of Windsor Castle from the Thames
Signed and dated '1884', pencil and watercolour with touches of white heightening
13¼ x 20in (34 x 50.5cm)
£3,700–4,500 *C*

Robert Bevan
British (1865–1925)
The Courtyard at Szetiewy
Oil on canvas, laid down
on board
12 x 10in (21 x 25.5cm)
£1,800–2,500 *P*

Pierre-Auguste Renoir
French (1841–1919)
La Maison de l'Artiste
Signed with initials, oil on canvas
10 x 11½in (25.5 x 29cm)
£95,000–110,000 *C*

Ian Weatherhead
British (b1932)
On the Banks of the Welland at Spalding
Signed and inscribed, watercolour
12 x 15in (30.5 x 38cm)
£250–300 *MSW*

Peter Evans
British (b1943)
Café des Sports
Signed, acrylic
24in (61.5cm) square
£3,000–3,500 *CSG*

Rockwell Kent
American (1882–1971)
Aasgard Farm
Signed, oil on panel
20 x 24in (50.5 x 61.5cm)
£12,000–15,000 *S(NY)*

Sir William Russell Flint, R.A., P.R.W.S.
British (1880–1969)
Souvenir of Barbasque
Signed, watercolour
20 x 26½in (51 x 67cm)
£5,000–7,000 *P*

Helen Allingham, R.W.S.
British (1848–1926)
East End Farm, Pinner
Signed, inscribed by a later hand on
old label, watercolour heightened with
scratching out
14½ x 21½in (37 x 54.5cm)
£13,000–15,000 *C*

Harold Lawes
British (late 19thC)
A Hampshire Cottage
Signed and inscribed, watercolour
13½ x 21½in (34.5 x 54.5cm)
£2,000–2,500 *WrG*

William Frederick Measom, R.B.A.
American (b1875, active in Britain)
Country Cottages
Watercolour
10 x 14in (25.5 x 37cm)
£1,600–1,850 *GG*

Henry John Sylvester Stannard
British (1870–1951)
The Little Tabby
Signed, watercolour
9¼ x 13¼in (24 x 34cm)
£3,000–3,500 *CGa*

Gordon Rushmer
British (20thC)
Thomas Hardy's Cottage
Watercolour
3½ x 5in (8.5 x 12.5cm)
£150–175 *PHG*

Arthur Claude Strachan
British (b1865)
Hoeing Potatoes, Surrey Cottage
Signed, numbered and inscribed, pencil
and watercolour heightened with white
12 x 18½in (30.5 x 47cm)
£1,400–1,800 *CSK*

r. Myles Birket Foster
British (1825–99)
At Sandhills, Surrey
Signed with monogram,
watercolour
10 x 14in (25 x 35.5cm)
£9,500–10,000 *L*

PARKS & GARDENS

Gardening is without question the greatest British pastime of the nineties. We spend some two billion pounds a year on our gardens and since the mid-1980s the Royal Horticultural Society has doubled its membership. Television is blooming with gardening programmes, bookshops are bursting with decorative gift books and practical guides, and galleries and salerooms are flourishing with garden pictures. Many of the following works date from the late 19th to the early 20thC, the period that saw the emergence of the English cottage garden. Initially, the main function of cottage gardens was to provide labourers with extra food. But, notes Andrew Clayton-Payne (*Victorian Flower Gardens,* Weidienfeld and Nicolson, 1988), many landowners who wanted their estate villages to reflect their taste and position, insisted on the planting of flower gardens as well. As town dwellers began to purchase weekend country cottages, so the gentrification of their gardens continued and it was these flower filled retreats that attracted most artists. Garden pictures were hugely popular with the Victorian and Edwardian middle classes, representing an idyllic vision of English country life. 'I defy any lover of an old fashioned English garden to see these drawings without real delight,' commented *The Observer* in 1906, reviewing an exhibition of garden pictures by Lilian Stannard. 'There is a peace, a repose, almost a fragrance about each and all of them ... see the foxgloves, the delphiniums, the stately hollyhocks, the tender greens, the sunny atmosphere, and then you will not wonder that men will struggle for forty years in any part of the world so as to come home at last and die in a house set in an old English garden.'

18th–19th Century

Francis Towne
British (1740–1816)
A View in Hyde Park looking towards the Serpentine River
Signed and dated '1797', pen and grey ink and grey wash
7¼ x 5¾in (18 x 14cm)
£2,000–3,000 *S*

Carl Frederic Aagaard
Danish (1833–95)
In the Garden
Signed and dated '1878', oil on canvas
26¾ x 39¾in (68 x 101cm)
£11,500–12,000 *C*

Rose Maynard Barton, R.W.S.
Irish (1856–1929)
In the Row, out of Season
Signed, pencil and watercolour with touches of white heightening
13¾ x 10¼in (35 x 26cm)
£22,000–27,000 *C*

Anglo-American School
(19thC)
Colonial Estate Scene - West Indies
Watercolour and bodycolour
12¾ x 19¼in (32.5 x 49cm)
£2,800–3,800 *P*

Rose Maynard Barton, R.W.S.
Irish (1856–1929)
The Row in the Morning
Signed and dated '1892', pencil and
watercolour heightened with bodycolour
9½ x 7¼in (23.5 x 18cm)
£10,500–12,500 *C*

Born in Dublin, Rose Barton studied abroad
before making a career as an artist. In the
early 1880s she went to study under the
Belgian artist, Henri Gervex. She exhibited
at the Royal Academy from 1884 and in
1911 was made a member of the Royal
Watercolour Society.

Mildred Ann Butler, R.W.S.
British (1858–1914)
The Garden in August
Signed, watercolour
13¾ x 20½in (35 x 52cm)
£3,800–4,800 *P*

Attributed to Mary Helen Carlisle
British (d1925)
A Flowering English Style Garden
Signed with initials, pastel on board
17½ x 20¼in (44.5 x 51.5cm)
£500–600 *CNY*

Charles Camoin
French (1879–1965)
Le Jardin aux Palmiers à St. Tropez
Signed, oil on paper laid down on canvas
41¾ x 28¼in (105 x 72cm)
£5,000–6,000 *C*

Emma Ciardi
Italian (1879–1933)
Scena Settecentesca
Signed and dated '1912', oil on board
12¼ x 10¾in (31 x 27cm)
£4,200–5,200 *C*

David Cox, O.W.S.
British (1783–1859)
In the Garden at Haddon Hall
Watercolour and bodycolour
12½ x 19in (32 x 48cm)
£800–1,000 *P*

Ella Du Cane
British (19th/20thC)
A Tower in an Ornamental Garden
Signed, pencil and watercolour
17¼ x 11½in (43.5 x 29cm)
£700–900 *CSK*

George Samuel Elgood, R.I.
British (1851–1943)
Bulwick, the Gateway
Signed, inscribed and dated '1893', watercolour
12½ x 19¾in (31.5 x 50cm)
£9,000–10,000 *CW*

George Samuel Elgood, R.I.
British (1851–1943)
Raundscliffe - Everywhere are Roses, Roses
Signed and dated '1906', pencil
and watercolour
14 x 11in (35.5 x 28cm)
£8,500–9,500 *CW*

Joseph Farquharson, R.A., R.O.I.
British (1846–1935)
The Rose Garden, Finzean, Aberdeenshire
Signed, oil on canvas
12 x 20in (30.5 x 50.5cm)
£5,000–5,500 *C(S)*

Joseph Farquharson, R.A., R.O.I.
British (1846–1935)
Flowering Herbaceous Borders
Signed, oil on canvas
20 x 24in (50.5 x 61cm)
£17,000–18,000 *S(NY)*

Leyton Forbes
British (active 1900–20)
Midsummer in a Cornish Garden
Signed, watercolour
11½ x 19½in (29 x 49cm)
£650–750 *JC*

Leslie Hervey
British (19th/20thC)
La Regate, Jardin du Luxembourg
Signed and inscribed, oil on canvas
19½ x 23½in (49 x 60cm)
£4,500–5,500 *S(S)*

A. Moulton Foweraker
British (1873–1942)
A Spanish Garden with Church in Cordoba
Signed, watercolour
13½ x 9½in (34 x 23.5cm)
£1.000–1.500 *GG*

Ernest William Haslehurst
British (1866–1949)
In a Deserted Garden, Ely
Signed, numbered 5, pencil and watercolour
20¼ x 15¼in (51 x 38.5cm)
£500–700 *CSK*

Harold Lawes
British (late 19thC)
The Dovecote, and The Rose Arch
A pair, signed, watercolours
10 x 14in (25 x 35.5cm)
£4,000–4,500 *HFA*

John Linnell
British (1792–1882)
Kensington Gardens, London
Signed and dated '1812', watercolour
over traces of pencil
4 x 5½ (10 x 13.5cm)
£36,000–46,000 *S*

Tom Lloyd, R.W.S.
British (1849–1910)
Footsteps
Signed and dated '1898', watercolour
12⅛ x 10¼in (31.5 x 25.5cm)
£900–1,000 *Bea*

Tom Lloyd, R.W.S.
British (1849–1910)
An Evening I Remember
Signed and dated '1897', watercolour
18 x 44¾in (47 x 113cm)
£3,800–4,800 *Bea*

Thomas Noelsmith
British (active 1880–1900)
Flowers for the House
Signed, watercolour
9¾ x 13¾in (24.5 x 35cm)
£1,550–1,750 *WrG*

George Marks
British (active 1876–1922)
Gorse in flower
Signed, watercolour
10 x 14½in (25 x 37cm)
£800–1,000 *Bea*

Beatrice Parsons
British (1870–1955)
A Rock Garden in August, The Pleasaunce,
Overstrand, Norfolk
Signed and inscribed, watercolour
10 x 14in (25 x 35.5cm)
£2,500–3,000 *WrG*

Beatrice Parsons
British (1870–1955)
A Cottage Garden
Signed, watercolour
12 x 16in (30.5 x 40.5cm)
£3,500–4,000 *HO*

Beatrice Parsons
British (1870–1955)
The Long Border, New College, Oxford
Signed, watercolour
10 x 14in (25 x 35.5cm)
£1,500–2,000 *DN*

*An extremely successful garden painter,
Parsons' pictures were reproduced in many
gardening books. During the 1920s her
watercolours were used by Sutton's to
decorate the covers of their seed catalogue.*

Beatrice Parsons
British (1870–1955)
Rose Gardens, The Lodge,
Bembridge, Isle of Wight
Signed, watercolour
15½ x 11½in (39 x 29cm)
£8,000–8,500 *CW*

*Left: Renoir and Monet worked together
frequently in 1872 and 1873, often painting
the same subject, and their work was more
closely aligned at this time than at any
other period in their respective careers.
Unlike Monet's paintings, however, it was
more unusual for Renoir to treat his figures
in such a secondary manner - in this work,
the two female figures are just discerned in
the centre background walking down the
path and towards the viewer. The brilliant
and spontaneous brushwork and the glories
of the garden are the true protagonist of
this picture.*

Pierre–August Renoir
French (1841–1919)
Femmes dans un Jardin
Signed, oil on canvas
21½ x 25¾in (54 x 65.5cm)
£4,500,000–5,000,000 *S(NY)*

Ernest Arthur Rowe
British (1863–1922)
The Old Yew Hedge, Speldhurst, Kent
Signed, pencil and watercolour
7 x 9½in (17.5 x 23.5cm)
£1,000–1,500 *CSK*

*Topiary was a distinctive feature of the
Renaissance garden, and became extremely
popular in the last quarter of the 19thC,
particularly in the formal gardens favoured
by such artists as Rowe and Elgood.
Peacocks, both real and sculptural, appear
frequently in their works. Decorative and
grand, in Christian symbolism the peacock
represents immortality, making it a perfect
symbol for the painted garden.*

Ernest Arthur Rowe
British (1863–1922)
A Garden on an Italian Lake
Signed, watercolour
10 x 13¾in (25 x 35cm)
£2,000–2,500 *CSK*

Leon Spilliaert
Belgian (1881–1946)
Le Parc, Bruxelles
Signed and dated '1917', watercolour
on paper
18 x 25½in (46 x 65cm)
£6,500–8,000 *CSK*

John Falconar Slater
British (1857–1937)
Pink Cyclamen in the Greenhouse
Signed, oil on cardboard
21 x 31in (53 x 78.5cm)
£700–800 *MSW*

Lilian Stannard
British (1877–1944)
A Garden Walk
Signed, watercolour heightened with white
13¼ x 9½in (33.5 x 24cm)
£3,000–3,500 *S*

Lilian Stannard
British (1877–1944)
Michaelmas Daisies
Signed, watercolour heightened
with bodycolour
13¾ x 9¾in (35 x 25cm)
£1,000–1,500 *S(S)*

*Garden painting was one of the areas where
women artists excelled, and none more so
than Lilian Stannard. Daughter of Henry
Stannard and sister of H. J. Sylvester
Stannard, by the age of 30 she was one of the
best known painters of gardens and flowers
in England, her many patrons including the
Royal Family.*

Lilian Stannard
British (1877–1944)
Gables Cottage Garden
Watercolour
10 x 14in (25 x 35.5cm)
£4,500–5,000 *HFA*

Theresa Sylvester Stannard
British (1898–1947)
A Summer Garden
Signed, pencil and watercolour
10 x 7in (25 x 17.5cm)
£1,200–1,500 *CSK*

20th Century

Stanley Roy Badmin, R.W.S., R.E.
British (1906–89)
K Shoes for the Town, St. James Park
Signed, pen, ink and watercolour
5¾ x 6¼in (14 x 15.5cm)
£2,250–2,750 *CBL*

George Gardner Symons
American (1863–1930)
Van Cortland Park, Bronx
Signed and inscribed, oil on canvas
15 x 21in (38 x 53cm)
£1,500–2,000 *CNY*

Rodolphe Wytsman
French (1860–1927)
A Small Farm
Signed, oil on canvas
19¼ x 23¼in (49 x 59cm)
£4,000–4,500 *S*

William Bowyer, R.A.
British (b1926)
Suffolk Garden
Oil on canvas
36in (91.5cm) square
£4,600–4,800 *WHP*

John Denahy
British (b1922)
Winter - Abingdon Park, Northampton
Oil on canvas
22 x 20in (55.5 x 51cm)
£700–800 *AMC*

Paul Dawson
British (b1946)
The Garden Room
Signed, watercolour
13 x 18in (33 x 45.5cm)
£550–650 *JN*

'Garden pictures are in demand at the moment,' comments John Noott, 'riding on the back of the enormous popularity of gardens and gardening.' Noott's Worcester gallery covers both 19th and 20thC painting and, like many of the dealers that we spoke to, he has noticed a distinct demand for good quality, representational work. 'People love definition and obviously well-crafted works,' he explains. 'We choose our contemporary artists very carefully - the problem with many painters today is that they simply haven't been taught how to draw.'

Annabel Gosling
British (20thC)
In the Greenhouse
Signed, oil on canvas
16 x 24in (40.5 x 61cm)
£500–560 *JN*

Peter Graham
British (b1959)
Gardens Rue Eble
Oil on canvas
20 x 16in (51 x 40.5cm)
£850–950 *Bne*

Jean Kévorkian
French (b1933)
Jardin Fleuri en Bretagne
Signed, oil on canvas
28½ x 36in (72.5 x 91.5cm)
£3,750–4,250 *Om*

John Mackie
Scottish (b1953)
Café in the Park, Montpellier
Oil on canvas
30 x 40in (76 x 101.5cm)
£1,500–2,000 *Tho*

Anthony Gross
British (b1905)
Valentine's Fortune
Signed, inscribed and numbered 20/75, print,
only edition printed in 1968
12¼ x 9½in (31.5 x 23.5cm)
£300–400 *BLD*

Christoper Miers, R.B.A.
British (b1941)
Summer Flowers in the Fulham Allotments
Signed, oil on canvas
12 x 16in (30.5 x 40.5cm)
£600–700 *JN*

John Neale
British (20thC)
Hollyhocks by a Window
Oil on canvas
10 x 18in (25 x 45.5cm)
£400–450 *JN*

Colin Newman, F.S.B.A.
British (b1923)
Summer Garden
Signed, watercolour
14 x 10in (35.5 x 25cm)
£575–675 *JN*

Edward Noott
British (b1965)
After Tennis
Signed, oil on canvas
30 x 25in (76 x 64cm)
£1,200–1,400 *JN*

Roy Petley
British (b1951)
St. Stephen's Green
Oil on panel
18 x 12in (45.5 x 30.5cm)
£5,000–6,000 *SOL*

H. Claude Pissarro
French (b1935)
Le Parc d'Urville
Signed, inscribed, oil on canvas
19½ x 24in (49.5 x 61cm)
£3,500–4,000 *S(NY)*

Joanna Price
Irish (b1956)
Garden with Primulas and Survivors
Signed and dated 1990, oil and Dutch
gold on canvas
60in (152cm) square
£2,000–2,500 *ABA*

Tessa Spencer Pryse, R.B.A.
British (b1939)
The Garden at Wivenhoe
Signed, oil on canvas
10 x 8in (25 x 20cm)
£300–350 *JN*

Norman Smith
British (b1949)
Under the Greengage Tree
Pastels
14 x 17in (35.5 x43cm)
£500–600 *JN*

Graham Sutherland
British (1903–80)
Maygreen
Etching, signed and inscribed, 1927
7½ x 8in (19 x 20cm)
£400–500 *S*

John Yardley
British (b1936)
Petunias and Garden Chair
Oil on canvas
18 x 14in (45.5 x 35.5cm)
£1,000–1,200 *Bne*

Carel Weight
British (b1908)
Two Ladies in the Garden
Oil on board
12 x 16in (30.5 x 40.5cm)
£6,000–8,000 *BRG*

ENGLISH COUNTRY COTTAGES

Although cottage pictures appealed greatly to a largely urban Victorian public, these rustic dwellings were certainly far more pleasant to look at than to live in. When Myles Birket Foster's *Pictures of English Landscape* was published in 1863, his series of engravings of country scenes was accompanied by the following warning poem by Tom Taylor:

'The cottage homes of England! Yes, I know,
How picturesque their moss and weather stain,
Their golden thatch, whose square eves shadows throw
On white-washed wall and deep sunk latticed pane...
Know too the plagues that prey
On those who dwell in these bepainted bowers:
The foul miasma of their crowded rooms,
Unaired, unlit, with green damps molded o'er,
The fever that each autumn deals its dooms
From the rank ditch that stagnates by the door;
And then I wish the picturesqueness less...'

Then, as today, however, it was the picturesque vision of the English country cottage that captured the imagination of the artist and the interest of the picture buyer.

Helen Allingham, R.W.S.
British (1848–1926)
A Berkshire Cottage
Signed with initials, inscribed and dated '1914', pencil and watercolour with scratching out
10¾ x 13in (26.5 x 33cm)
£3,000–4,000   *C*

George Samuel Elgood
British (1851–1943)
Anne Hathaway's Cottage from the Orchard
Signed, inscribed and dated '1906', watercolour
13½ x 10¼in (34 x 26cm)
£1,700–2,500   *Bon*

Helen Allingham, R.W.S.
British (1848–1926)
A Berkshire Cottage
Signed, watercolour
12 x 10in (30.5 x 25cm)
£17,500–19,500   *HFA*

Watercolour painter of rural scenes, sunny gardens and children, Helen Allingham was educated at the Birmingham School of Design and at the Royal Academy Schools. She was strongly influenced by Birket Foster and Frederick Walker. In 1874 she married William Allingham, the Irish poet, thus entering a literary circle where she met Ruskin, who became a great admirer of her work. Helen Allingham was elected an Associate of the Royal Watercolour Society in 1875 and a Member in 1890. She exhibited almost exclusively at the Old Watercolour Society, where she showed a total of 221 works. Though prices for Helen Allingham are not quite what they were in the 1980s, her decorative landscapes and above all her idyllic cottage scenes still command substantial sums.

William Banks Fortescue
British (c1855–1924)
A Village Street
Signed, oil on canvas laid on board
22 x 30in (55.5 x 76cm)
£5,800–6,800   *C*

Myles Birket Foster, R.W.S.
British (1825–99)
Cottage Near Ballater
Signed with monogram, watercolour
and bodycolour
6¾ x 10¼in (17.5 x 26cm)
£5,000–5,800 *S(S)*

Alfred Augustus Glendening, Jnr., R.B.A.
British (1861–1907)
The Cottage Garden
Signed with monogram, dated '1884', oil
on canvas
24 x 16in (61 x 40.5cm)
£13,000–14,000 *S(NY)*

Robert Gallon
British (1848–1925)
A Rural Landscape with a Thatched Cottage
Signed, oil on canvas
17 x 31in (43 x 79cm)
£5,000–6,000 *S(S)*

J. A. Lynas-Gray
British (active 1898–1928)
Near Ebenezra and Near Llanberis
A pair, signed, watercolour
11 x 8in (28 x 20cm)
£4,500–5,200 *HFA*

Caroline Lawes
British (1842–95)
Summer, Old Harpenden
Signed and dated '1870', watercolour
11½ x 16in (29 x 40.5cm)
£250–300 *JA*

Claude Hayes
British (1852–1922)
Children by a Cottage
Signed, watercolour
6¾ x 10½in (17 x 26cm)
£350–450 *Bea*

Dorothy Livermore
British (19thC)
Cottage Scene
Signed, watercolour
10 x 14in (25 x35.5cm)
£800–900 *HLG*

G. K. Mason
British (active c1890–1930)
By the Garden Gate
Signed, watercolour
6¾ x 9¾in (17 x 25cm)
£250–350 *JC*

Though the big names in cottage and garden painting now fetch four and even five figure sums, there are many less celebrated painters who worked in the same field and whose watercolours are far less expensive, as the present example shows. Judge the quality of a picture first and the name of the artist second. As with all watercolours, condition is all important and beware of faded works.

T. Noelsmith
British (active 1880–1900)
Anne Hathaway's Cottage
Signed and inscribed, watercolour
9¾ x 13¾in (24.5 x 35cm)
£500–600 *CSK*

Herbert William Piper
British (late 19thC)
Mother and Child outside thatched cottage at Uplyme, Devon
Signed, dated on backing, watercolour
13½ x 9½in (34.5 x 23.5cm)
£500–600 *LH*

Alexander Molyneux Stannard
British (1878–1975)
Figure by a Thatched Cottage
Signed, watercolour
10 x 15in (25 x 38cm)
£400–500 *TAY*

Henry John Sylvester Stannard
British (1870–1951)
Thatched Cottage before a Hayfield
Signed, watercolour
10¾ x 14¼in (27 x 36cm)
£400–450 *FWA*

Ernest Arthur Rowe
British (1863–1922)
Coddington Rectory, Worcester
Signed and inscribed, watercolour
9¾ x 7in (24 x 17.5cm)
£2,000–2,350 *WrG*

Henry John Sylvester Stannard
British (1870–1951)
Near Bromsgove, Worcestershire
Signed, pencil and watercolour
heightened with white
14 x 20¼in (35.5 x 51cm)
£4,000–6,000 *CSK*

Henry John Sylvester Stannard
British (1870–1951)
A Thatched Cottage by a Stream
Signed, watercolour heightened with
touches of bodycolour and scratching out
10½ x 14½in (26.6 x 36.5cm)
£2,000–2,500 *C*

Arthur Claude Strachan
British (c1865–1929)
At the Cottage Door
Signed, watercolour heightened with white
10¾ x 7½in (27 x 19cm)
£750–1,000 *CSK*

Arthur Claude Strachan
British (c1865–1929)
A Gardener's Cottage near Warwick
Signed, watercolour
23 x 47½in (59 x 120cm)
£4,000–4,600 *FWA*

Kate Sturgeon
British (late 19thC)
Summer, with Mother and Child
Signed, watercolour
14½ x 21in (37 x 53cm)
£1,400–1,600 *LH*

Arthur Claude Strachan
British (c1865–1929)
Feeding the Ducks, and The Village Pump
A pair, watercolour
8 x 11in (20 x 28cm)
£5,000–5,500 *HFA*

Joseph Thors
British (active 1863–1900)
Coleshill, and one untitled
A pair, oil on canvas
8 x 12in (20 x 30.5cm)
£6,500–7,500 *BuP*

Thomas Nicholson Tyndale
British (active 1900–25)
Swallowfield, Berkshire
Signed and inscribed, watercolour
9¼ x 6in (23 x 15cm)
£800–900 *S(S)*

Edward Arthur Walton, R.S.A., P.R.S.W.
British (1860–1922)
The Red Roof
Signed, watercolour
15¼ x 21½in (38.5 x 54cm)
£2,200–2,600 *Bea*

R. Hollands Walker
British (active 1892–1920)
A Warwickshire Village
Signed, watercolour
6 x 10in (15 x 25cm)
£850–950 *LH*

W. F. Witherington
British (1785–1875)
Cottage Scene
Signed, oil on canvas
12 x 16in (30.5 x 41cm)
£1,200–1,500 *HLG*

David Woodlock
British (1842–1929)
A Young Girl feeding Poultry by her Cottage
Signed, pencil and watercolour with touches
of white heightening
13½ x 9½in (34 x 23.5cm)
£500–600 *CSK*

HOUSES & BUILDINGS

The following section is devoted to houses, buildings and architectural drawings. Prices peaked for architectural drawings in the 1980s when property prices were booming, the building trade was flourishing, and the drawings were fashionable both with collectors and interior decorators. The market collapsed in 1989/1990 and has still not recovered.

Comparatively few architectural drawings come up for sale, and those which do, with some exceptions, fetch considerably lower prices than during the 1980s. Low prices and interesting subject matter make this a good area for private collectors as long as they are buying for enjoyment's sake rather than for investment.

Exteriors 17th–18th Century

English School (c1790)
A Sketchbook of Proposals, Plans and Elevations of Buildings and Docks at the Royal Dockyard, Portsmouth
Inscribed, pen, black ink and grey wash
83 leaves in all in red straight grained morocco wallet style binding
4½ x 6¾in (11 x 17cm)
£4,000–5,000 *C*

By the 1780s the Royal Dockyard at Portsmouth had become the largest naval base in England, eclipsed in the early 1800s by Plymouth. From the 1760s plans were made to develop the yard to take account of its growing operational significance. These plans were carried out under the supervision of Charles Middleton, 1st Baron Barham (1726–1813) who, as Comptroller of the Navy Board from August 1778 to March 1790, had overall command of the Navy's civil organisation.

William James
British (active 1754–71)
View of Charing Cross and Northumberland House
Oil on canvas
36 x 52in (91.5 x 132cm)
£4,000–5,000 *S*

Attributed to Edward Dayes
British (1763–1804)
Framlingham Castle
Inscribed, dated verso '1791', watercolour
8¾ x 10⅝in (22 x 27cm)
£650–750 *CAS*

English School (c1800)
Figures punting before a Country House
Oil on canvas
24¼ x 29½in (62 x 75cm)
£3,800–4,500 *P*

Hispanic Colonial School (late 18thC)
Views of a Country House with Figures crossing a Bridge in the foreground
A pair, oil on canvas
29½ x 20in (74.5 x 50.5cm)
£7,300–8,000 *Bon*

Giulio Parigi
Italian (active 1568–1635)
A Maid drawing water from a well
near a Farmhouse
Inscribed, pen and brown ink
over black chalk
9½ x 8in (24 x 20cm)
£450–550 *P*

Peter Tillemans
Flemish (c1684–1734)
A View of the Garden and main Parterre of
Winchendon House, Buckinghamshire, from
the East, with figures in the foreground
Oil on canvas
26¼ x 36in (67 x 99cm)
£30,000–35,000 *C*

*This picture can be dated to c1720.
Winchendon House was acquired in about
1642 by Philip, 4th Lord Wharton (1613–96),
a Parliamentarian and a noted art collector.
His son, Thomas, 5th Lord Wharton
(1648–1715), laid out the magnificent
gardens. Thomas was one of the great Whig
grandees at the courts of King William III
and Queen Anne, and famous for his love of
the ladies, as the following inscription
discovered on a beam in the servants' wing
suggests:*

> *May the Good Lord shorten
> the life of Lord Wharton
> And give us his son in his stead,
> For he drinks and he whores,
> and obeys no laws,
> And never goes sober to bed.*

*The servants experienced little joy when his
son Philip did indeed come into his
inheritance at the tender age of 17. Philip
gambled away the majority of his vast fortune
and in 1725, with debts amounting to some
£70,000, he sold Winchendon House and its
estates to Sarah, Duchess of Marlborough.*

George Stanley Repton (1786–1858) **in
the Office of John Nash** (1752–1835)
British
Perspective View of a Design for
Rockingham, Co. Roscommon
Watercolour over pen and black ink
18½ x 26in (47 x 66cm)
£4,000–5,000 *S*

Michael 'Angelo' Rooker, A.R.A.
British (1746–1801)
Usk Castle, Gwent
Signed, pencil and watercolour
10½ x 14⅛in (26.5 x 36cm)
£9,500–10,500 *C*

Francis Towne
British (1740–1816)
Windsor Castle from Clewer
Signed, inscribed, dated '1811', pencil,
pen and grey ink and watercolour
6¾ x 20¼in (17 x 51cm)
£3,800–5,000 *C*

Manner of Philips Wouwerman
Dutch (1619–68)
The Grounds of an Italiante Villa
with a Gentleman about to depart
Oil on panel
10½ x 12½in (26.5 x 31.5cm)
£2,000–2,500 *CSK*

19th Century

Cecil Charles Windsor Aldin
British (1870–1935)
The Post Office
An original etching, signed and
numbered '63/100'
10 x 8¼in (25 x 21.5cm)
£300–400 *CG*

American School (19thC)
An American Victorian House in
a Landscape with Flowers
A reverse oil painting on and under glass
28 x 36in (71 x 91.5cm)
£2,250–2,500 *S(NY)*

*What is unusual about this reverse painting
is that the paint is applied under as well as
on top of the glass. In its original carved
giltwood frame, probably executed in New
York State.*

Carlo Bossoli
Italian (1815–84)
Vorontsov Palace at Alupka, Yalta, Crimea
Signed and dated '1843', watercolour
and bodycolour
10 x 14¾in (25 x 37.5cm)
£5,000–6,000 *C*

*The palace of Alupka is one of the most
famous sites of the Crimea. It was first
occupied by Prince Potemkin (1739–91),
celebrated lover of Catherine the Great, who
built a residence there to receive the Empress
on her visit to the Crimea. Next inhabitant
was the Duc de Richelieu (1766–1822),
nephew of Cardinal Richelieu and the model
for Byron's Don Juan. The palace was built
(1828–48) by Mikhail Vorontsov, governor
general in the Crimea. Vorontsov was hugely
wealthy, his Russian estates totalled some
400,000 hectares and he was the proud owner
of 80,000 serfs. He spent an estimated nine
million rubles on the palace, which was
designed by Edward Blore, combining the
Gothic and Tudor styles, with a gateway
based on the Great Mosque at Delhi.
Vorontsov was famous for his opulence -
in one of his palaces every door handle was
made from polished amber, and when the
ceiling sprang a leak during a party guests
were convinced that it must be raining
eau-de-cologne. Visitors to Alupka had
divided opinions, either considering it 'the
finest building of its kind in Russia,' or 'very
peculiar' and extravagantly vulgar. Bossoli,
when in his 20s, was commissioned by the
Vorontsovs to paint a number of views of the
palace and its grounds, a selection of which
were exhibited in New York in 1988.*

Thomas Baker
British (1809–69)
Water Mill, Llandovery
Signed and dated '1862', oil on canvas
12 x 10in (30.5 x 25cm)
£2,800–3,100 *Dr*

John Buckler
British (1770–1851)
South West View of
Fountains Hall, Yorkshire
Signed, dated '1817' and inscribed, pen and
grey ink and watercolour over traces of pencil
12¼ x 16⅜in (31 x 43cm)
£1,000–1,500 *S*

William Callow, R.W.S.
Schloss Eltz on the Rhine
Signed and dated '1841', watercolour
over pencil
20½ x 14in (52 x 36cm)
£3,500–4,000 *S*

H. B. Carter
British (1803–67)
Scarborough Castle Arch
Signed, watercolour
14¼ x 10¼in (36.5 x 26cm)
£500–600 *IM*

Continental School (19thC)
A pair, architectural watercolours,
laid down on board
18 x 22½in (45.5 x 57cm)
£1,000–1,250 *S(NY)*

David Cox
British (1783–1859)
The Peacock Inn, Rowsley, Derbyshire
Signed and dated '1845', watercolour
over pencil
8 x 11in (20 x 28cm)
£2,000–2,500 *S*

George Samuel Elgood, R.I.
British (1851–1943)
Brympton d'Evercy House, Somerset
Signed, inscribed 'Brympton' on an
old label, watercolour
18½ x 14in (47 x 36cm)
£7,000–7,500 *CW*

George Samuel Elgood, R.I.
British (1851–1943)
Genoa
Signed, inscribed and dated '1891',
watercolour and bodycolour
12¼ x 10in (31 x 25cm)
£2,800–3,200 *CW*

English School (c1830)
A Coach and Four outside a Country House
Oil on canvas
13 x 17in (33 x 43cm)
£1,400–1,600 *CSK*

Robert Giles
British (19thC)
Prospect of Dilston Hall
Signed and dated '1825', pencil and
watercolour heightened with white
15¾ x 19in (40 x 48cm)
£275–350 *CSK*

*'Dilston Hall', reads the inscription, 'once
the seat of the unfortunate James, Earl of
Darwentwater, taken a short time after his
execution.' James, the 3rd Earl (1689–1716)
was beheaded for his part in the Jacobite
uprising of 1715, the death of this young,
handsome and popular man causing a huge
national outcry. Architectural drawings are
interesting not only for the buildings they
portray, but the stories of the people who
lived in them.*

Myles Birket Foster
British (1825–99)
Holyrood Palace
Monogrammed, watercolour
6 x 8in (15 x 20.5cm)
£4,500–5,000 *AG*

> **Miller's is a price GUIDE
> not a price LIST**

Albert Goodwin, R.W.S.
British (1845–1932)
Chichester
Signed and inscribed, watercolour
and bodycolour
7in x 10¼in (17.5 x 26cm)
£1,200–1,800 *P*

Paul Gauguin
French (1848–1903)
Chaumieres en Bretagne
Black crayon on paper
8 x 7in (20 x 17.5cm)
£3,000–4,000 *S(NY)*

Fred Hall
British (1860–1948)
Archer's Stores
Signed, oil on board
12½ x 15½in (32 x 39.5cm)
£3,500–4,500 *DN*

John Atkinson Grimshaw
British (1836–93)
Old English House, Moonlight after Rain
Signed and dated '1883+', oil on board
18 x 14in (45.5 x 35.5cm)
£40,000–50,000 *C*

Fanny Holden
British (1804–63)
An Hotel Particulier, Passy near Paris
Signed and dated 'Van Nye/1843', inscribed,
watercolour over pencil heightened with
touches of bodycolour
8½ x 11¼in (21.5 x 28.5cm)
£5,000–6,000 *S*

Richard Bankes Harraden
British (1778–1862)
West Front of the New Building,
St. John's College, Cambridge
Watercolour over pencil
5½ x 8¾in (14 x 22.5cm)
£700–800 *S*

Alexander Jamieson
British (1873–1937)
Le Petit Trianon
Signed and indistinctly inscribed,
oil on canvas
32 x 26in (81 x 66cm)
£1,800–2,400 *CSK*

Alfred William Parsons, R.A., P.R.W.S.
British (1847–1920)
The Boathouse
Signed and dated '1902', pencil and
watercolour with scratching out
14½ x 21in (36.5 x 53cm)
£3,500–4,500 *C*

William Joy
British (1803–67)
Lord Neville in conversation with Sir
Edmund Lacon and Captain Grenthorpe
outside Telegraph Cottage, Great Yarmouth
A pair, inscribed and dated '1853',
watercolours with touches of
white heightening
11½ x 17½in (29 x 44.5cm)
£4,500–6,000 *C*

J. Morat
German? (mid-19thC)
Maison de Conversation et Promenade à
Baden, Août 1842, and Baden et l'Allée de
Lichtenau, Août 1842
A pair, signed and inscribed, bodycolour
and watercolour on paper
10 x 12½in (25 x 32cm)
£10,000–12,000 *C*

James Rawlinson
British (1769–1848)
Lancaster Castle
Signed, watercolour
7½ x 10½in (18.5 x 26.5cm)
£450–550 *CSK*

Thomas Matthew Rooke
British (1842–1942)
Lincoln Cathedral
Signed, inscribed and dated '1921', pencil
and watercolour
17 x 11½in (43 x 29cm)
£600–700 *CSK*

*A designer for Morris and Co., Rooke worked
under Burne Jones and was employed by
Ruskin to make drawings of buildings.
He died in his 100th year and was still
producing watercolours at the age of 98.*

George Shepherd
British (1748–1862)
Beaufoy's Vinegar Yard, Cuper's
Gardens, Lambeth
Signed and dated '1823', pencil and
watercolour
8½ x 12¼in (21.5 x 31cm)
£2,000–2,500 *C*

Joseph Mallord William Turner, R.A.
British (1775–1851)
Smailholme Tower, Roxburghshire
Inscribed, watercolour, vignette in
a decorative cartouche
8¾ x 7½in (22 x 19cm)
£35,000–45,000 *C*

*This is one of the watercolours commissioned
from Turner in 1831 by Robert Cadell and
Sir Walter Scott as illustrations to Scott's
'Poetical Works', published in 1834. In
response to Cadell's first list of suggested
subjects, Scott wrote in a letter of 1 August
1831, 'You have omitted the eve of Saint John,
Smaylholm Tower, which is a striking subject
very appropriate...' Beyond the tower stands
Sandy-Knowe Farm, the property of Scott's
grandfather and the author's childhood home.*

*'Then rise those crags, that mountain tower.
Which charm'd my fancy's wakening hour.
It was a barren scene and wild
Where naked cliffs were rudely piled;
But ever and anon between
Lay velvet tufts of loveliest green...'
- Scott, Epistle to William Erskine
(Marmion, Canto III).*

Walter Henry Sweet
British (19th/20thC)
Old Quadrangle, in The Close, Exeter
Signed, watercolour
11 x 7in (28 x 17.5cm)
£250–300 *TAY*

John Varley, O.W.S.
British (1778–1842)
Old Houses, Clapham Common
Signed, watercolour
10¾ x 15in (27 x 38cm)
£7,500–8,500 *MCA*

John William Waterhouse, R.A.
British (1849–1917)
A Scottish Baronial House
Signed and dated '1907', oil on artist's board
13¾ x 15⅝in (35 x 40cm)
£2,250–2,750 *C*

John White, R.I.
British (1851–1933)
The Model, Beer, Devon
Signed, watercolour and bodycolour
14 x 9¾in (35.5 x 24.5cm)
£1,450–1,850 *P*

20th Century

Edward Bawden
British (1903–89)
Linsell Church
Signed, inscribed, 1960, numbered 30/50,
linocut, printed in colours on wove
26 x 62½in (66 x 157.5cm)
£300–400 *P*

Catherine Brennand
British (20thC)
Plane Tree, Cercle Fragonard, Grasse
Signed, watercolour
22 x 14½in (55.5 x 37cm)
£350–450 *TLB*

André Brasilier
French (20thC)
Chateau
Signed and inscribed, lithograph on wove
18 x 25in (46 x 64cm)
£550–650 *S*

Marc Chagall
French/Russian (1887–1985)
La Maison de mon Village
Lithograph, 1960
12⅛ x 9½in (31.5 x 24cm)
£300–365 *WO*

*Chagall often used imagery remembered from
his early life in Russia, as here - a self
portrait with his mother and father in their
village house.*

Jean Colyer
British (20thC)
Scotney Castle
Pastel, 1991
16 x 11in (41 x 28cm)
£280–310 *RGFA*

Graham Clarke
British (b1941)
Café Cochonique
No 1 of a set of 4, etching, hand coloured
10½ x 13½in (26.5 x 33.5cm)
£175–195 *GCP*

Peter Evans
British (b1943)
Shop at Catus
Acrylic
24in (61cm) square
£3,000–3,600 *CSG*

Sir William Russell Flint, R.A.
British (1880–1969)
Birdham Mill
Signed, tempera on paper
20 x 29in (51 x 74cm)
£7,000–8,000 *WH*

Maurits Cornelis Escher
Dutch (1898–1972)
Belvedere
Signed, numbered 'No. 33/107IV',
Lithograph, 1958
18 x 11½in (46 x 29cm)
£6,000–7,000 *S(NY)*

Kamesuke Hiraga
Japanese (1890–1971)
French Market
Signed, inscribed and dated '29', oil on board
24 x 18in (61 x 45.5cm)
£1,400–1,800   *SLN*

Michael Lyne
British (1912–89)
The late Duke of Beaufort talking to his
Huntsman outside Badminton House
Signed, watercolour over pencil heightened
with bodycolour
16¼ x 22¼in (41 x 56cm)
£1,600–2,000   *S(S)*

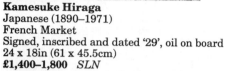

Brian Peacock
British (b1934)
Man with Newspaper, l'Aiguillon-sur-Mer
Oil on canvas
15in (38cm) square
£1,000–1,350   *CSG*

Paul Nagy
American? (b1959)
Abstract Schematic
Signed and dated '1989', acrylic on canvas
72¼in (183.5cm) square
£4,000–4,500   *C*

John Piper
British (1903–92)
Colby Lodge
Signed, pen, black ink, watercolour,
bodycolour heightened with white
16½ x 24½in (41.5 x 62cm)
£4,500–5,500   *C*

John Piper
British (1903–92)
Walsoken, Norfolk
Signed and numbered from the edition of 70,
1985, screenprint
20 x 26½in (50.5 x 67cm)
£890–940   *WO*

John Piper
British (1903–92)
A Palazzo in Vicenza, Italy
Signed, mixed media and collage
20½ x 27¼in (52 x 69cm)
£5,500–6,500 *P*

Anthony Proctor
British (1913–93)
Rooftop Geometry
Signed, oil on board, 1983
24 x 29in (61 x 73.5cm)
£800–1,000 *VCG*

Graham Sutherland
British (1903–80)
The Great Globe, Swanage, 1932
Signed, gouache
21¼ x 39½in (54 x 100cm)
£11,000–12,500 *P*

*This painting was Sutherland's first
commercial commission. It was used for the
highly successful series of Shell posters
'Everywhere you go - you can be sure of Shell'.*

Alex Williams
British (b1942)
Mary Evan's Shop, Talgarth
Oil on canvas
30 x 24in (76 x 61cm)
£1,550–1750 *JN*

Frank Taylor
British (20thC)
14 Kazantzakis Street
Signed, watercolour
19 x 25in (48 x 64cm)
£850–950 *PHG*

Interiors
17th–18th Century

Hendrik Cornelisz. van Vliet and Studio
Dutch (1611–75)
The Interior of Oude Kerk in Delft, from the
Choir to the north west, with a Grave Digger
and Gentleman
Oil with touches of gold leaf
41¼ x 35½in (105 x 90cm)
£6,500–8,000 *C*

19th Century

Attributed to Sir Thomas Armstrong
British (1835–1911)
Art School Interior
Oil on canvas
30 x 25in (76.5 x 63.5cm)
£1,000–1,200 *JDG*

Manner of Pieter Neeffs
Flemish (17thC)
A Gothic Church Interior
Oil on panel
8½ x 9½in (21 x 23.5cm)
£1,500–2,000 *CSK*

*Pictures of interiors are in demand in the
current market and frequently command
good prices. This picture more than
doubled its top estimate at Christie's
South Kensington.*

Attributed to Christian Stöcklin
Swiss (1741–95)
The Interior of a Baroque Cathedral,
with a Priest celebrating Mass
Oil on copper
7 x 9in (17.5 x 23cm)
£9,000–10,000 *S*

John Buckler
British (1770–1851)
The Staircase, Dodington House,
Gloucestershire
Signed and dated '1824', watercolour
over pencil
12¾ x 18in (32 x 45.5cm)
£3,000–3,500 *S*

*Dodington House was designed by James
Wyatt for Christopher Codrington, and built
between 1798 and 1813. The splendid central
staircase incorporates ironwork from the
Beckford mansion of Fonthill, Wiltshire,
demolished in 1808.*

English School (c1820)
Design for Staircase Hall
Pencil, pen and grey ink, and watercolour
12in (30.5cm) square
£600–800 *C*

H. B. Carter
British (1803–67)
Jarrow Church Interior Scene
with Bede Chair
Signed, watercolour
13½ x 9¾in (34 x 24.5cm)
£550–600 *IM*

English School c1840
The Interior of a Library
Pencil and watercolour
8¾ x 13in (22 x 33cm)
£2,600–3,000 *C*

English School c1800
The Staircase at the Villa Farnese, Caprarola
Pen and grey ink and watercolour, with a
black line border, indistinctly inscribed
'Payt.../16 April 1800'
13 x 10½in (33 x 26.5cm)
£1,200–1,600 *S*

*This is the circular open staircase designed by
Giacomo Barozzi da Vignola (1507–73) at the
Villa Farnese near Rome. The left half of the
drawing shows an elevation of the entire
staircase, and the right half shows a section
through it.*

Louis Haghe
Belgian (1806–85)
Figures before a Shrine in a Cathedral
Pencil and watercolour heightened
with white
11¾ x 8½in (30 x 21.5cm)
£450–550 *CSK*

Fanny Holden
British (1804–63)
Interior at Belmont, Bern
Signed, watercolour over pencil heightened
with gum arabic
7¾ x 10¾in (19.5 x 27.5cm)
£7,000–8,000 *S*

Fanny Holden (née Sterry) was the youngest
child of Benjamin Wasey Sterry and Mary
Davis. She also used the signature Van Nye,
which would seem to be a pseudonym based
on the phonetic sound of Fanny. In 1851 she
married Luther Holden, F.R.C.S., and they
spent part of their honeymoon at Passy where
they stayed in the Hôtel Particulier, and also
visited the Riviera and Switzerland where
they stayed at Belmont, Bern.

Fanny Holden
British (1804–63)
Fanny Holden's Room, Passy, near Paris
Signed 'Van Nye/1843', inscribed on mount,
watercolour over pencil heightened with
touches of bodycolour
8¼ x 11¼in (21 x 29cm)
£10,500–11,500 *S*

Bradford Rudge
British (1805–85)
The Great Hall of the Senate House,
Cambridge
Signed and inscribed, pencil and watercolour
heightened with white and gum arabic
12½ x 15in (31.5 x 38cm)
£650–750 *CSK*

Joseph Nash
British (1809–78)
Fireplace in the Gatehouse, Kenilworth
Signed and dated '1870' and inscribed
as title on the reverse, pencil, watercolour
and bodycolour
13 x 18½in (33 x 47cm)
£500–600 *CSK*

F. Schuster
Austrian? (active 1815)
Interior of a Classical Sculpture Gallery
Signed and dated '1815', pen and grey ink
and watercolour
19 x 25½in (48.5 x 65cm)
£1,500–2,000 *S*

Einar Wegener
Danish (1883–1931)
An Interior of a Boudoir
Signed and dated '1916', oil on canvas
32in (81.5cm) square
£2,500–3,500 *C*

Antonie Waldorp
Dutch (1803–66)
Figures in a Church Interior
Signed and dated 1839, oil on canvas
26 x 21¾in (66 x 55cm)
£2,500–3,500 *S(Am)*

R. H. Whitehead
British (1855–89)
Self Portrait in an Interior
Signed with initials and dated '1882',
oil on canvas
41 x 50in (104 x 127cm)
£10,000–11,000 *S(NY)*

*R.H. Whitehead studied for a short time
at Oldham School of Art and later at
Manchester. He died, aged 34, on Capri.*

20th Century

Carey Clarke, P.R.H.A.
Irish (20thC)
Evening Light, Notre Dame des Ardilliers, Saumur
Watercolour
28½ x 40in (72.5 x 101.5cm)
£5,000–5,500 *SOL*

Pamela Davis
British (20thC)
Morning Break
Acrylic
5 x 7in (12.5 x 17.5cm)
£200–225 *LA*

Roberto Ferruzzi
Italian (b1927)
Studio Interior, Venice
Signed, gouache
29½ x 39½in (75 x 100cm)
£4,500–5,500 *WFA*

Natalie Giltsoff
British (b1941)
The Top of My House
Watercolour
43 x 30in (109 x 76cm)
£600–675 *JN*

Geoffrey Scowcroft Fletcher
British (b1923)
Garrick Club Staircase with Irving's Chair
Signed, inscribed with title and dated '1962',
pen, ink and monochrome, watercolour
14½ x 11in (37 x 28cm)
£325–375 *CBL*

This was an illustration from The Sphere,
24th November 1962, page 312.

Martin Grover
British (b1962)
After Mrs Hope
Signed and dated '1993', acrylic on canvas
60 x 48in (152 x 122cm)
£1,600–1,800 *Mer*

Ludvig Karsten
Norwegian (1876–1926)
The Hall at Staur
Signed and dated '24', oil on canvas
48¾ x 39in (122 x 99cm)
£21,000–26,000 *S*

Kevin Hughes
British (20thC)
The Drawing Room
Watercolour
10 x 8in (25 x 20cm)
£300–350 *JN*

Stephen McCann
British (b1953)
Church Interior
Pencil on paper
26 x 30in (66 x 76cm)
£450–500 *FT*

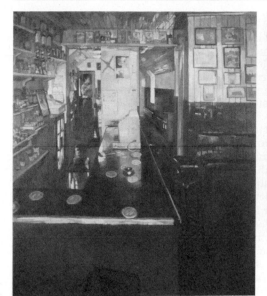

Richard Pikesley, N.E.A.C.
British (b1951)
Interior
Oil on canvas
25 x 30in (64 x 76cm)
£1,000–2,000 *AdG*

Hector McDonnell
Irish (b1947)
A Country Pub, Co. Kildare
Oil on canvas
36 x 30in (91.5 x 76cm)
£3,000–4,000 *SOL*

Rowland Suddaby
British (1912–72)
Elizabeth in Bedroom
Signed and dated '1943', watercolour
10 x 14in (25 x 35.5cm)
£1,000–1,500 *BRG*

Jacqueline Williams
British (b1963)
A Quiet Read
Oil on canvas
48 x 36in (122 x 91.5cm)
£2,500–3,500 *AdG*

David Tindle, R.A.
British (b1932)
Lightning
Signed with initials, also signed, dated '89'
and titled on reverse, egg tempera on panel
13 x 15¾in (33 x 40cm)
£2,200–2,500 *P*

Ian Weatherhead
British (b1932)
Folkingham from the Artist's Bedroom
Signed and inscribed, watercolour
15 x 19in (38 x 48cm)
£300–400 *MSW*

MARINE

The demand for marine pictures is strong, as long as the product is right. 'What is evident is that quality always achieves a high price and that quality is very rare,' explains Bernard Reed, who specialises in marine watercolours from 1750–1900. 'Fine works in good condition, by first class artists, are in short supply and make good results, but a substantial amount of minor pictures have been failing to sell at auction.'

'Really good, top of the range pictures have gone up in value quite dramatically,' agrees marine dealer John Morton Lee. 'Every lot I have bid for recently has gone over its top estimate.'

As in any other field, it is the big names that command the highest prices. 'A marine watercolour by Dixon fetches four or five times as much as a broadly similar work by Scarborough,' claims Reed. 'There is a big difference in price between first and second ranking artists.' Nevertheless, he adds, one of the great joys of collecting marine water-colours is their relative affordability. 'A good collection of marine watercolours would cost you about a fifth of its equivalent in oils. I think watercolours are very underpriced,

and you can have a lot of quality hanging on your walls for a lot less money.'

Certain areas of the marine market are currently undervalued. Academic pictures from the 18th and early 19th centuries – historically fascinating but more formal and less obviously decorative than Victorian pictures – are comparatively cheap in price. 'Early pictures in good condition are very rare,' says Morton Lee, 'and I think they are still selling well below their real worth.' Subject can also make a difference to value. 'Pictures of storms and wrecks generally fetch far less than pictures of calm seas,' notes Reed. 'Women in particular don't like the savagery of the sea. If you don't mind the rough weather you could assemble a fine collection at much lower prices than you would pay for more serene scenes.'

Whatever your tastes, always concentrate on good quality pictures and, above all, buy what you like personally. 'Now that we are better informed about how to look after watercolours, they are durable, and I do think that they are a safe way to invest,' concludes Reed, 'but the biggest dividend you get from a good watercolour is the pleasure of living with it.'

17th Century

Attributed to Jeronimus van Diest
Dutch (c1631–73)
Dutch Shipping in an Estuary with a Man-of-war Firing a Salute
Oil on canvas
39¼ x 54¼in (99.5 x 138cm)
£90,000–100,000 *S*

Cornelis Bouwmeester
Dutch (1670–1733)
The Battle of La Hogue, 1692
Signed, pen painting on panel
28¼ x 42¼in (71.5 x 107.5cm)
£25,500–30,000 *S*

Follower of Jan van Goyen
Dutch (1596–1665)
Dutch Coastal Vessels in an Estuary beside a Village
Indistinctly signed and dated
'1659', oil on panel
20½ x 31¾in (52 x 80.5cm)
£3,000–4,000 *S*

Attributed to Jan Claesz. Rietschoof
Dutch (1652–1719)
Shipping in an Estuary in a Calm
Bears initials on the jetty, oil on canvas
28 x 38in (71 x 96.5cm)
£27,000–30,000 *S*

Salomon van Ruysdael
Dutch (c1601–70)
An Estuary with Smalschips
and a Ferry by a Cottage
Signed with monogram and
dated '1666', oil on panel
11½ x 10½in (28 x 26.5cm)
£40,000–50,000 *C*

Abraham Storck
Dutch (c1635–1710)
The Departure of William of Orange
from Briel, 1688
Signed, oil on canvas
24 x 33¾in (61 x 85.5cm)
£70,000–80,000 *S*

After Willem van de Velde the Younger
Dutch (1633–1707)
Dutch Vessels mid-Channel, and Fisherfolk
on the Beach at Scheveningen
A pair, oil on canvas
18 x 27in (46 x 69cm)
£2,750–3,000 *CSK*

Follower of Willem van de Velde the Younger
Dutch (1633–1707)
A Dutch Flite, a Smalschip and other Shipping offshore in a Calm
Oil on canvas
26 x 31¼in (66.5 x 79.5cm)
£8,750–9,500 *S*

Herman Witmont
Dutch (1605–83)
Men-of-war at Anchor off a Fortified Rocky Coast
Signed, pen painting on panel
20¼ x 28¾in (51 x 73cm)
£16,500–18,000 *S*

18th Century

William Anderson
British (1757–1837)
British Frigate and other Shipping offshore
Signed and dated '1790', watercolour
8 x 13¼in (20 x 34cm)
£3,800–4,250 *JML*

William Anderson
British (1757–1837)
View of Greenwich and Deptford, showing Greenwich Hospital and the Royal Dockyard
Signed with initials and dated '1789', watercolour
15 x 20¼in (38 x 51cm)
£8,000–8,750 *JML*

William Anderson
British (1757–1837)
Dutch Vessel and British Man-o'-War
Watercolour
10½ x 16½in (27 x 43cm)
£3,800–4,300 *Mar*

Jean Henry d'Arles
French (1734–84)
Scenes of Imaginary Ports depicting Morning and Evening
A pair, signed and dated '1767' and '1768', oil on canvas
42½ x 62½in (108 x 159cm)
£130,000–140,000 *S(NY)*

Samuel Atkins
British (c1765–1810)
Frigates and a Cutter Offshore
Signed, watercolour
5½ x 7½in (14 x 19cm)
£1,800–2,100 *Mar*

Johann Wolfgang Baumgartner
Austrian (1712–61)
Sea Battle
Pen and grey ink with wash over black
chalk, heightened with white, 2 sheets joined
21½ x 26½in (54 x 67.5cm)
£20,000–30,000 *P*

*Born in the Tyrol, Baumgartner was initially
trained as a glass painter. By 1733 he had
established himself in Augsburg as one of
the leading artists of Augsburg 'rococo'.
He was much sought after, not only as a
decorative ceiling painter, but as a
draughtsman for engravings.*

Circle of Charles Brooking
British (1723–59)
An East Indiaman and Fishing
Craft off Sheerness
Oil on canvas
21½ x 29½in (55 x 75cm)
£9,500–10,500 *CSK*

John Cleveley, Snr.
British (c1712–77)
Frigate and other vessels off Flatholm,
Bristol Channel
Watercolour
5¾ x 7½in (15 x 20cm)
£3,000–3,500 *Mar*

John Cleveley
British (1747–86)
British Frigates in the West Indies,
and Azores
A pair, watercolours
5¼ x 7¾in (13 x 19cm)
£4,000–4,500 *JML*

John Cleveley
British (1747–86)
The British Fleet off Dover
Watercolour
15¾ x 22½in (40 x 57cm)
£1,500–2,000 *P*

Robert Cleveley
British (1747–1809)
A beached Hoy with Merchantmen beyond
Pen and black ink and watercolour
5¾ x 8¼in (15 x 21cm)
£1,700–2,200 *CSK*

Robert Dodd
British (1748–1815)
The Mutineers turning Lieutenant Bligh
and part of the Officers and Crew adrift
from H.M.S. 'The Bounty'
Oil on canvas
19 x 24in (49 x 61.5cm)
£35,000–45,000 *S*

*This painting depicts the dramatic moment on
April 28th 1789, when Bligh and eighteen of his
crew were cast adrift from the 'Bounty'. 'Just
before Sun Rise the People Mutinied, seized me
while asleep in my Cabbin tide my Hands
behind my back - carried me on Deck in my
Shirt - Put 18 of the Crew into the Launch and
me after them and set us adrift.' - Lieutenant
William Bligh, R.N., 28th April, 1789. With the
minimum of instruments and little food and
water Bligh skilfully navigated a 3,900 mile sea
journey to safety in the Dutch colony of Timor,
arriving on June 14th.*

English School (late 18thC)
Untitled
Oil on canvas
21 x 36in (53 x 91.5cm)
£1,000–1,400 *LT*

Thomas Luny
British (1759–1837)
The Battle of the Saints
Signed and dated '1782', oil on canvas
30½ x 48in (77.5 x 122cm)
£22,000–30,000 *Bon*

Thomas Luny
British (1759–1837)
Ships in Full Sail off Dungeness
Signed and dated '1827', oil on panel
8¼ x 11¾in (21 x 30cm)
£4,250–5,000 *Bon*

Peter Monamy
British (1689–1749)
Busy Coastal Scene
Oil on canvas
20 x 36in (51 x 92cm)
£6,500–7,500 *MEA*

Thomas Luny
British (1759–1837)
Unloading the Catch
Signed and dated '1826', oil on canvas
15 x 20in (38 x 50.5cm)
£8,000–8,500 *BuP*

After Lieutenant Philip Orsbridge
British (18thC)
Historical Views of the last glorious
Expedition of his Britannic Majesty's Ships
and Forces against the Havannah
A set of 12 engravings
18 x 25¾in (46 x 65.5cm)
£7,000–7,500 *CSK*

Nicholas Pocock
British (1740–1821)
Despatch Cutter Offshore
Signed on mount, grey wash
8½ x 12½in (22 x 32cm)
£500–700 *Mar*

Attributed to Charles Martin Powell
British (d1824)
Dutch Barges and other Sailing Vessels
at the Mouth of a Harbour
Oil on canvas
26¾ x 35in (68 x 89cm)
£12,500–14,000 *S(S)*

Nicholas Pocock
British (1740–1821)
English Frigates Offshore
Watercolour
8 x 11in (21 x 29cm)
£2,700–3,100 *Mar*

> **Miller's is a price GUIDE
> not a price LIST**

Dominic Serres, Snr., R.A.
French (1722–93)
English Invasion Squadron off
Belle Isle, 1761
Watercolour
8 x 13½in (20 x 35cm)
£4,500–5,000 *Mar*

Samuel Scott
British (1703–72)
The Capture of Porto Bello, 1739,
Commodore Charles Brown in the 'Hampton
Court 70', bombarding the 'Iron Fort'
Oil on canvas
40 x 54in (101.5 x 137cm)
£4,000–4,500 *CSK*

*This is one of several versions painted by
the artist.*

*The marine painters of the 18thC often served
on board ship or worked in some maritime
trade before becoming painters. William
Anderson was a shipwright and Nicholas
Pocock a naval commander, who began his
artistic career by illustrating the ship's log
that he wrote up every day. Born in France,
Dominic Serres ran away to sea to avoid
joining the priesthood. It was only after his
ship had been seized by the British in the
Seven Years War and he himself had been
imprisoned in London, that he turned to
marine painting. Serres was to enjoy great
commerical success and became one of the
founder members of the Royal Academy.*

Dominic Serres, Snr., R.A.
French (1722–93)
The Battle of the Saints, 12th April 1782
Oil on canvas
32½ x 49½in (82.5 x 126cm)
£17,500–19,000 *S*

Circle of Francis Swaine
British (c1715–82)
The Opening Shots of the Actions between
H.M.S. 'Quebec' and the French frigate
'Surveillante' and their accompanying cutters
on 6th October 1778.
Oil on canvas
20 x 24in (51 x 61cm)
£2,000–3,000 *S*

Lieutenant Thomas Yates
British (c1760–96)
Ships carrying a Vice-Admiral of the Blue
and a Rear-Admiral of the Red, possibly in
the Solent with Hurst Castle beyond
Oil on canvas
25¼ x 30½in (64 x 77.5cm)
£6,000–7,000 *C*

*Yates was an accomplished marine artist
whose oils are rare. This picture was painted
in 1788 - the first of six years in which he
exhibited at the Royal Academy.*

Francis Swaine
British (c1715–82)
The Surrender of the Spanish Fleet to
the British at Havana, 13 August 1762
Signed and dated '1768', oil on canvas
54 x 88in (137 x 224cm)
£52,000–60,000 *CSK*

*'Paintings of the Battle of Havana are
especially sought after because it was such
a major engagement in the Seven Years War
(1756–63), representing an important victory
for Britain,' explained the* Antiques Trade
Gazette, *reporting on the fact that Swaine's
painting had attracted enormous interest at
Christie's South Kensington.*

Joseph Mallord William Turner, R.A.
British (1775–1851)
Rochester
Signed, watercolour
8¼ x 10¾in (21 x 27.5cm)
£8,000–9,000 *P*

Thomas Whitcombe
British (1763–1824)
A 74-gun Man-of-war running
down the Channel
Signed and indistinctly dated
'1811', oil on canvas
20 x 27in (51 x 68.5cm)
£3,500–4,000 *CSK*

19th Century

Jackarias Maritini Aagard
Danish (b1863)
The Norwegian Coastal Defence
Vessel Tordenskjold
Signed and dated '1901', oil on canvas
29 x 41½in (74 x 105.5cm)
£3,000–5,000 *CSK*

*Although Norway was ruled by Sweden under
a joint monarchy until 1905, the Norwegian
mercantile marine, the fourth largest in the
world during the second half of the 19thC,
had its own separate naval force albeit of
a purely defensive nature.*

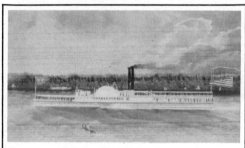

James and John Bard
American (twins 1815–97 and 1815–56)
The steam engine paddle wheeler Thomas
Powell, A Ship's Portrait
Signed and dated '1846', oil on canvas
31 x 55in (79 x 139.5cm)
£65,000–80,000 *S(NY)*

*The Bard twins were born in New York City
in 1815, of British parents. They painted their
first ship picture together at the age of 12 and
were to collaborate on marine watercolours
and oils until c1849 when their partnership
appears to have sundered. John Bard died in
an almshouse in 1856 recorded as a 'destitute
painter', and James went on to enjoy a
successful solo career painting ships for the
most important steamboat gentry of the day.*

Robert Weir Allan, R.W.S.
British (1851–1942)
Summer Morning
Signed and inscribed, pencil and watercolour
20¼ x 29½in (51.5 x 75cm)
£2,500–3,500 *C*

William Joseph Julius Caesar Bond
British (1833–1928)
Near Pwllheli
Signed, inscribed and dated '1878',
oil on panel
22¾ x 36½in (58 x 92.5cm)
£6,000–7,000 *C*

Eugène Boudin
French (1824–98)
Camaret, Le Port
Signed and dated '73', oil on canvas, 1873
19½ x 29in (49 x 74cm)
£185,000–200,000 *C*

*The philosopher-critic T.A. Castagnary so
admired Boudin's marine pictures that he
wrote, 'Monsieur Boudin is the only one who
treats the marine in this fashion', or rather,
to use the better expression of Courbet, 'the
landscape of the sea.' He has carved out a
charming little kingdom for himself in this
field, from which no one will dislodge him.'*

Thomas Shotter Boys
British (1803–74)
Fisherfolk on the French Coast
Signed and dated '1830', watercolour over
pencil with scratching out
9 x 12½in (23 x 31.5cm)
£6,500–7,500 *S*

Sir Oswald Walters Brierly, R.W.S.
British (1817–94)
La Reine Hortense, Yacht of His Imperial
Majesty Louis Napoleon arriving at Ledsund
Signed and inscribed, watercolour
9¾ x 16¾in (24.5 x 43cm)
£5,000–5,250 *JML*

British School (19thC)
Sailors of the Royal Navy
Part of a set of 8 lithographs, printed
in colour, published 1892
£350 the set of 8 *Lan*

John Callow
British (1822–78)
Hay Barges and Merchantmen entering the
mouth of the Thames
Remains of a signature, oil on canvas
36 x 56in (91.5 x 142cm)
£5,500–6,500 *CSK*

James Edward Buttersworth
British (1817–94)
Arriving in Port
Signed, oil on canvas
12 x 16in (30.5 x 40.5cm)
£10,000–11,000 *CSK*

John Callow
British (1822–78)
Merchantmen leaving The Downs Anchorage
Signed and dated '1861', watercolour
17¼ x 30in (44 x 76cm)
£5,500–6,250 *Mar*

R. Chappell-Goole
British (19thC)
Rosie of Bideford and Yacht in Full Sail
A pair, signed, watercolours
14½ x 22in (37 x 55.5cm)
£900–1,200 *AAV*

Chinese School (mid-19thC)
A View of Canton
Watercolour on ivory
4 x 5in (10 x 12.5cm)
£1,000–1,500 *Bon*

Miller's is a price GUIDE
not a price LIST

Paul-Jean Clays
Belgian (1819–1900)
A Naval Salute
Signed and dated '45', oil on panel
17¼ x 26½in (44 x 67.5cm)
£5,000–6,000 *S*

Continental School (19thC)
A portrait of the Greek Snowbrig,
'The Young Greek', off Piraeus
Gouache
20¼ x 28½in (51.5 x 72.5cm)
£5,500–6,500 *Bri*

Charles Edward Dixon, R.I.
British (1872–1934)
Merchantman in The Estuary
Signed and dated '98', watercolour
9 x 28in (23 x 71cm)
£6,500–7,200 *Mar*

Charles Edward Dixon, R.I.
British (1872–1934)
Above Greenwich
Signed and dated '1901', watercolour
11 x 30in (28 x 76cm)
£3,500–3,850 *WG*

Nora Davison
British (active 1881–1905)
Alongside the Quay
Signed, watercolour
13 x 8¼in (33 x 21cm)
£300–350 *JC*

Charles Edward Dixon, R.I.
British (1872–1934)
The Opening of Cowes Week, The Arrival
of the King and Queen, 1906
Signed, inscribed and dated '06'
17½ x 13½in (44.5 x 34.5cm)
£850–1,000 *CSK*

*Under the patronage of Edward VII both as
king, and earlier as Prince of Wales, Cowes
Week became one of the most glittering events
of the social calendar in the years preceding
WWI. Especially when Edward was also
Commodore of the Royal Yacht Squadron,
foreign monarchs were frequently invited to
join him for the week's festivities and, in
1906, it was the turn of King Alphonso XIII
of Spain. Assembled with their masters were
the British Royal yachts 'Victoria & Albert III'
and 'Osborne', chaperoned by the battleship
H.M.S. 'Renown', together with the Spanish
Royal yacht 'Giralda' accompanied by her
cruisers 'Princesa de Asturias', 6,888 tons,
and 'Estramadura', 2,030 tons, both
practically new vessels chosen with care to
impress the cosmopolitan crowds assembled
for the regatta.*

Edward Duncan
British (1803–82)
Hay Barge off the Dutch Coast
Signed, watercolour
8¼ x 12in (21 x 30.5cm)
£4,000–4,800 *Mar*

Edward Duncan
British (1803–82)
Swansea Bay
Signed and dated '1859', watercolour
15 x 21¾in (38 x 55cm)
£8,500–10,000 *Mar*

Jahn Ekenaes
Norwegian (1847–1920)
Fisherfolk on a Lake
Signed and dated '1909', oil on canvas
23¼ x 42in (59 x 106.5cm)
£6,500–7,500 *C*

After J. B. East
British (19thC)
Madras - Landing, and Madras -
The Embarkation, by C. Hunt
Coloured aquatints
14 x 19½in (36 x 49.5cm)
£1,300–1,500 *CSK*

William Evans
British (1798–1877)
Clovelly, Early Morning
Watercolour
16 x 22½in (41 x 57cm)
£1,275–1,475 *GG*

Themistocles von Eckenbrecher
German (1842–1921)
The 'Oihonna' in Ice, near Spitzbergen
Signed, inscribed, and dated '1905',
oil on canvas
14¾ x 21½in (38 x 54.5cm)
£3,000–4,000 *S*

J. Fannen
British (active 1893–1901)
The Trading Schooner 'Lilian'
Signed and dated '1889', oil on canvas
18¾ x 29½in (48 x 75cm)
£2,500–3,000 *CSK*

Anthony Vandyke Copley Fielding
British (1787–1855)
Beached Vessels
Signed and dated '1830', watercolour
8½ x 13in (21.5 x 33cm)
£2,000–2,400 *Mar*

Charles Gregory
British (19thC)
The 1851 schooner 'America', shown in
her trans-Atlantic ocean rig and flying the
ensign of the New York Yacht Club
Oil on canvas
16 x 24in (40.5 x 61cm)
£13,500–15,000 *CSK*

Thomas Greeenhalgh
British (19thC)
Battleships lying in the Pool of London
Signed and dated '1887', pencil and watercolour heightened with white
23½ x 35½in (60 x 90cm)
£1,000–1,200 *CSK*

*This scene almost certainly depicts ships of
the fleet visiting London during Queen
Victoria's Golden Jubilee celebration in the
summer of 1887.*

Haughton Forrest
British (1826–1925)
Duel in the Solent, a Racing Schooner,
thought to be British, neck and neck with
an American challenger from the Newark
(New Jersey) Yacht Club
Signed and indistinctly dated '188?', oil
on canvas
25 x 45in (64 x 114cm)
£42,000–50,000 *CSK*

*Forrest was born to a wealthy family whose
fortune came from slaves and extensive sugar
plantations in Jamaica. Several of his
forbears served in the Royal Navy, and
Forrest spent much of his childhood and early
youth travelling abroad. In 1848, he returned
to Britain, where he was to live for some
years, and which was to provide him with
artistic inspiration throughout his life. In
1876, Forrest emigrated to Australia, where
he became Tasmania's leading artist,
specialising in topographical scenes. Painted
in Tasmania, presumably using sketchbooks
from his years in England, 'Duel in the
Solent' achieved an auction record for the
artist at Christie's South Kensington,
quadrupling its lower estimate of £10,000 and
selling to an American gallery. This sale
reflects the current demand for racing yacht
scenes, the picture is particularly flamboyant
and the subject matter made it a perfect
purchase for the American market.*

Thomas Bush Hardy, R.B.A.
British (1842–97)
Tide going out, Katwijk-aan-Zee
Signed and dated '1883', watercolour
12½ x 19¼in (31.5 x 49cm)
£3,500–3,750 *JML*

Thomas Bush Hardy, R.B.A.
British (1842–97)
Squally Weather, Portsmouth
Signed and inscribed, watercolour
6 x 16in (15 x 40.5cm)
£2,000–2,200 *WG*

**Miller's is a price GUIDE
not a price LIST**

Thomas Bush Hardy, R.B.A.
British (1842–97)
Beached Fishing Boats at Equihen
Signed and dated '1872', watercolour
12 x 19in (30.5 x 49cm)
£1,800–2,400 *Mar*

Thomas Bush Hardy, R.B.A.
British (1842–97)
Hay Barges in the Medway
Signed and dated '1883' watercolour
5½ x 6¾in (14 x 17cm)
£2,000–2,250 *JML*

Thomas Bush Hardy, R.B.A.
British (1842–97)
Leigh-on-Sea, Essex
Signed and dated '1880', watercolour
4¾ x 6¾in (12 x 17cm)
£1,750–1,950 *JML*

Vassilios Hatzis
Greek (1870–1915)
A View near Piraeus and Xavierou
Beach, Greece
Signed, oil on canvas
20 x 34in (50.5 x 86cm)
£26,000–30,000 *S*

A marine and landscape painter, Hatzis studied at the School of Fine Arts in Athens with Nikiforos Lytras and Constantin Bolonakis as teachers. In naval themes, and especially naval battle scenes, Bolonakis was his primary influence. During the Balkan Wars, he painted themes about the action of the fleet, which are distinguished for their somewhat academic spirit.

T. Dyke Hart
British (active 1900–20)
The Harbour, Boscastle, Cornwall
Signed, watercolour
8 x 14¼in (20 x 36cm)
£250–350 *JC*

Joseph Heard
British (19thC)
The Barque 'Isis'
Oil on canvas
26 x 36in (66 x 91.5cm)
£12,000–13,000 *S*

Thomas Marie Madawaska Hemy
British (1852–1937)
Fishing Boats in Peel Harbour, Isle of Man
Signed and dated '1876', pencil and
watercolour heightened with bodycolour
20½ x 29½in (52 x 75cm)
£1,000–1,200 *CSK*

Frederick Haynes
British (active 1860–80)
St Michael's Mount
Signed, oil on canvas
30 x 50in (76 x 127cm)
£3,000–3,250 *FdeL*

William John Huggins
British (1781–1845)
Towing the Prize
Signed and dated '1831', oil on canvas
20 x 28½in (50.5 x 72.5cm)
£4,500–5,500 *Bon*

James Clarke Hook, R.A.
British (1819–1907)
Last Night's Disaster
Signed with monogram, oil on canvas
38 x 60½in (96.5 x 153cm)
£11,500–13,000 *S*

David James
British (active 1881–98)
Breaking Waves with Fishing Boats
in the Distance
Signed and dated '85', oil on canvas
25 x 50in (64 x 127cm)
£3,500–4,500 *CSK*

William and John Joy
British (1803–67 and 1806–66)
Sailing Craft in a Squall
Watercolour
8½ x 12in (21 x 30.5cm)
£3,200–3,500 *Mar*

William Joy
British (1803–67)
Frigate and other Vessels offshore with
Figures on the Beach
Watercolour, monochrome
7 x 10in (17.5 x 25cm)
£950–1,150 *JML*

William and John Joy
British (1803–67 and 1806–66)
Frigate and other Vessels off Gibralter
Signed and dated '1854', watercolour
14 x 20in (36 x 50.5cm)
£13,000–15,000 *Mar*

Frank Kelsey
British (19thC)
Square Rigged Clippers at Anchor
Signed, oil on canvas
19½ x 25½in (49 x 65cm)
£1,000–1,400 *LH*

William Joy
British (1803–67)
H.M.S. 'Serpent' dismasted off Spithead,
29 November 1836
Pencil and watercolour
14½ x 20½in (37 x 52cm)
£450–650 *CSK*

Charles Euphrasie Kuwasseg
French (1838–1904)
An Estuary with a Town beyond
Signed, oil on canvas
12¼ x 20in (31.5 x 50.5cm)
£1,700–2,000 *C*

*As has already been stated in the
introduction, shipwreck pictures often sell
for lower prices than portrayals of calm and
limpid seas. The Joy brothers demonstrate
this fact particularly well. Their patron,
Rear-Admiral Thomas Manby (1769–1834),
devised a number of life-saving maritime
devices and while working with him in
Great Yarmouth the Joys necessarily painted
storm-tossed views, including works that
illustrated Manby's inventions in action. 'You
can buy a really super wreck picture for far
less than you would pay for one of their more
serene subjects', notes Bernard Reed. 'From
an artistic and historical point of view, such
pictures can be fascinating, they are simply
not as commercial in today's market.'*

Richmond Markes
British (active 1860–80)
An Estuary at Low Tide
Signed with initials, watercolour
6¾ x 10½in (17 x 26cm)
£300–380 *JC*

Albert Markes
British (c1865–1901)
Fishing Boats Returning to Harbour
Signed, watercolour
16½ x 29½in (42 x 75cm)
£3,400–3,800 *Mar*

James Edwin Meadows
British (1828–88)
Shipping near the Promenade
Oil on canvas
20 x 30in (51 x 76cm)
£3,000–3,800 *HFA*

Captain Walter William May, R.I.
British (1831–96)
The Royal Yacht Squadron, Cowes
Signed, watercolour
8¼ x 12in (21 x 30.5cm)
£900–1,150 *JML*

> **Locate the Source**
> *The source of each
> illustration in Miller's
> can be found by checking
> the code letters below
> each caption with the list
> of contributors.*

Walter William May
British (1831–96)
Shipping off the Dutch Coast
Signed, watercolour
21 x 34in (53 x 86cm)
£2,250–2,500 *WrG*

Thomas Rose Miles
British (19thC)
After a Stormy Night
Signed, titled and inscribed 'Off the Buttery
Breakwater/Douglas, Isle of Man' on the
reverse, oil on canvas
51½ x 31¼in (131 x 79cm)
£6,000–7,000 *S*

Claude Monet
French (1840–1926)
Sainte-Adresse, Voilier Echoue
Pastel
8 x 11¼in (20 x 29cm)
£335,000–350,000 *C*

*Executed c1865 at Saint-Adresse, a small
fishing village on the Normandy coast, just
north of Le Havre, where Monet often spent
the summer months at the home of his aunt
Madame LeCadre. After his introduction to
'outdoor painting' by Boudin in 1856, Monet
made many studies of this shore which he
knew so intimately.*

Claude T. Stanfield Moore
British (1853–1901)
Her Majesty's Troopships receiving stores
in Portsmouth Harbour
Signed and dated '80', oil on canvas
20 x 30in (50.5 x 76cm)
£3,000–4,000 *S*

George F. Nicholls
British (active 1885–1939)
River Barge and Fisherman
Signed, watercolour, c1899
6½ x 9½in (16 x 24cm)
£400–500 *LH*

Charles-François Pécrus
French (1826–1907)
Boats in a Harbour
Signed, oil on canvas
15 x 21½in (38 x 54cm)
£3,750–4,500 *C*

Samuel Owen
British (c1768–1857)
Man-o'-War and other Craft offshore
Watercolour
6 x 8½in (15 x 21cm)
£2,000–2,300 *Mar*

T. G. Purvis
British (active late 19th/early 20thC)
Sail and Steam at Dawn
Signed and dated '1898', oil on canvas
20 x 30in (50.5 x 76cm)
£1,450–1,650 *HI*

Douglas Houzen Pinder
British (1886–1949)
The Harbour, Polperro, Cornwall
Signed and inscribed, watercolour
21¼ x 30¾in (54 x 78cm)
£1,400–1,600 *JC*

Thomas Miles Richardson, Snr.
British (1784-1848)
Low Light, North Shields about 1830
Signed with initials, oil on canvas
27¼ x 35in (69.5 x 89cm)
£10,500–12,000 *AG*

*This painting is interesting as one of the
earliest depictions of a steam paddle tug
(middle distance centre left) in operation on a
British river. Tugs revolutionised river traffic
and, on the Tyne, they were introduced from
about 1820, some years before their use on
the Thames.*

Thomas Sewell Robins
British (1814–80)
Shipping off the Dutch Coast
Signed and dated '1871', watercolour
12½ x 19½in (31.5 x 50cm)
£4,000–4,800 *Mar*

Thomas Sewell Robins
British (1814–80)
Fishing Boats in Swell
Signed and dated '1846', watercolour
14 x 22in (36 x 56cm)
£1,800–2,100 *LH*

William Stuart
British (19thC)
The Battle of Trafalgar
Oil on canvas
48 x 83¼in (122 x 211cm)
£30,000–35,000 *S(NY)*

*The battle of Trafalgar on October 21, 1805
marked the decisive end to Napoleon's long
campaign to secure the western approaches
to the English Channel and invade England.
The invasion was fought off Cape Trafalgar,
off the coast of Spain, and involved Lord
Nelson's fleet of 27 ships against the
combined French and Spanish contingent
of 33 ships under Comte de Villeneuve.*

John Francis Salmon
British (19thC)
Coastal Shipping Under Sail
Signed with initials, watercolour
9 x 16in (23 x 41cm)
£400–480 *LH*

Mark Thompson
British (1812–75)
A British Naval Squadron coming to Anchor
in Plymouth Sound, c1840
Signed, oil on canvas
24 x 36in (61 x 91.5cm)
£5,500–6,500 *Bon*

Charles Taylor, Jnr.
British (active 1841–83)
A Freshening Wind
Signed, watercolour
13¾ x 27in (35 x 68.5cm)
£1,000–1,200 *JC*

John Thirtle
British (1777–1839)
Fisherfolk by the Devil's Tower on
the River Yare
Signed and dated '1827', pencil and
watercolour with scratching out
9¼ x 13¼in (23.5 x 33.5cm)
£4,000–5,000 *C*

William Thornely, R.B.A.
British (active 1858–98)
Rye Harbour
Signed, oil on canvas
15½ x 23½in (39 x 60cm)
£3,000–4,000 *CGa*

William Turner of Oxford
British (1789–1862)
Boating on the Isis, a View of Oxford
from the South
Pencil and coloured washes
10½ x 15in (26 x 38cm)
£6,000–7,000 *P*

Louis Verboeckhoven
Belgian (1802–89)
Dutch Shipping in a Swell
Oil on canvas
7 x 19in (17.5 x 48.5cm)
£7,000–8,000 *WHP*

R. Weatherill
British (1810–90)
Harbour Scene Whitby, late 19th century
Signed, oil on board
10½ x 18½in (26 x 47cm)
£550–700 *PCh*

Archibald Webb
British (1866–93)
The Homecoming
Signed, watercolour
11½ x 15in (29 x 38cm)
£650–850 *TFA*

James Webb
British (1825–95)
The Beach at Scheveningen with
Fishing Craft
Signed and inscribed, watercolour
9¾ x 12¾in (24.5 x 32.5cm)
£2,000–2,250 *JML*

**Theodore Alexander
Weber**
French (1838–1907)
Fisherfolk unloading
their Catch, and
French Fishing Boats
returning Home
A pair, both signed,
oil on canvas
11¼ x 8in (29 x 20cm)
£5,000–6,000 *C*

William Edward Webb
British (1862–1903)
Beached Fishing Boats
Signed, oil on canvas
18 x 29in (46 x 74cm)
£2,000–3,000 *MSW*

John 'Jock' Wilson
British (1774–1855)
In the Firth of Forth
Oil on canvas
11 x 15in (28 x 38cm)
£2,400–2,800 *CGa*

Warren Williams
British (1863–1918)
Anglesey Harbour Scenes
A pair, signed, watercolours
11 x 15in (28 x 38cm)
£1,550–1,750 *WIL*

William Lionel Wyllie
British (1851–1931)
Coastal Scene, Thames Barges and
Fishing Smacks
Oil on canvas
10 x 18in (25 x 46cm)
£1,800–2,100 *F*

William Lionel Wyllie
British (1851–1931)
Thames Barges in the Estuary
Signed, watercolour
4½ x 11½in (11 x 29.5cm)
£2,000–2,500 *Mar*

William H. Yorke
British (late 19thC)
'Ladstock of Liverpool'
Signed, inscribed and dated '1893',
oil on canvas
20 x 30in (50.5 x 76cm)
£4,000–5,000 *Bon*

Alexander Young
British (active 1889–93)
On the Thames, near Windsor
Signed, inscribed and dated '88', oil on canvas
12 x 24in (30.5 x 61cm)
£1,000–1,500 *C(S)*

20th Century

Jennifer Bartlett
American (b1941)
At Sands Point No. 31
Oil on canvas, 1985
60 x 36in (152.5 x 91.5cm)
£35,000–40,000 *S(NY)*

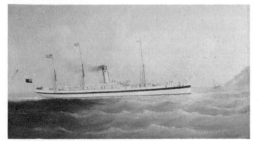

British Marine School (20thC)
The Hospital Ship 'Maine', c1914
Oil on canvas
17¾ x 23¾in (45 x 61cm)
£900–1,000 *S*

*The 1903 hospital ship 'Maine' was presented
by the USA at the time of the South African
War. She was wrecked in 1914.*

Owen Bowen
British (1873–1967)
Norfolk harbour scene
Signed, oil on canvas
13½ x 20½in (34 x 52cm)
£1,500–1,800 *AH*

David C. Bell
British (b1950)
'Ciceley' Racing of Cowes
Signed, pencil and watercolour
16½ x 25½in (41.5 x 54.5cm)
£1,500–1,800 *JS*

*Bell's maritime career began at the age of 14 when he
commenced a three year training course at Trinity House
Navigational School. He then served with the Merchant
Navy and it was not until his mid-twenties, after eight
years at sea, that he went to art school. Like the marine
painters of the 18thC, Bell's art has been formed by his
practical knowledge of the sea. Painter in both
watercolour and oils, his work can be found in collections
all over the world and patrons include the Queen and
Prince Charles.*

David Brackman
British (20thC)
'Westward' and 'Germania'
Signed and dated '86', gouache
16 x 26in (40.5 x 66cm)
£10,000–11,000 *S*

*'Westward' and 'Germania' are shown racing off
Cowes in 1910 and passing the Royal Yacht 'Albert'.*

Byron Browne
American (1907–61)
Docked Boats
Signed and dated '1953', ink wash,
watercolour and gouache on paper
18¾ x 25in (48 x 63.5cm)
£500–600 *SLN*

Charles Abel Corwin
American (1857–1938)
Inner Harbour, Gloucester
Signed, inscribed, oil on canvas
24 x 36in (61 x 91.5cm)
£5,000–5,500 *S(NY)*

John Gardiner Crawford
Scottish (b1941)
North Visitor
Signed, 1992, watercolour
14 x 21½in (35.5 x 54cm)
£2,000–2,500 *WH*

William Degouvre de Nuncques
Belgian (1867–1935)
Unloading Vessels on a Quay
Signed with initials, dated '17', black chalk
24½ x 29½in (62 x 74.5cm)
£1,600–2,000 *S(Am)*

Montague Dawson, R.S.M.A., F.R.S.A.
British (1859–1973)
Winging along the Solent
Signed, oil on canvas
24¼ x 36¼in (61.5 x 92cm)
£17,000–20,000 *S(NY)*

John Steven Dews
British (b1949)
Against the Tide, 'Big Class' working
up the North shore of the Solent against
a foul tide, 1934
Signed, oil on canvas
40 x 60in (102 x 153cm)
£25,000–35,000 *S*

*From left to right the yachts are 'Shamrock V',
'Westward', 'Britannia', 'Velsheda' and
'Astra'. The years immediately preceding
King George Vs death in 1936 are now seen
as a golden age in yachting history. Under
the enthusiastic patronage of the King
himself, Cowes Week became not only a
glittering social spectacle, but also the arena
for the countless exciting duels between the
great yachts of that day. Most famous of
them all was the King's boat 'Brittania',
built for his father when Prince of Wales in
1892 and refitted for big class racing in
1921. 'Shamrock V' was the last in a series of
legendary yachts built for the tea tycoon Sir
Thomas Lipton, and 'Velsheda' belonged to
the chairman of Woolworths.*

Louis Dodd
British (b1943)
The Sloop of War 'Queenborough'
Signed, oil on panel
15½ x 19½in (39.5 x 49.5cm)
£1,300–1,500 *CSK*

Marcel Dyf
French (1899–1985)
Port du Logeo, 1978
Signed, oil on canvas
18in (46cm) square
£6,500–7,500 *BuP*

John S. Goodall, R.I., R.B.A.
British (b1908)
Cowes
Signed, watercolour
7 x 9in (17.5 x 22.5cm)
£1,200–1,600 *JN*

Peter Graham
British (1959)
Yachts at Rhu
Signed, oil on canvas
30 x 24in (76 x 61cm)
£1,000–1,200 *Bne*

Karl Hagedorn, R.I., R.B.A., N.E.A.C.
British (b1889)
A Beach in Portugal
Signed, oil on canvas
20 x 24in (50.5 x 61cm)
£2,500–2,750 *JN*

Lawrence Irving
British (20thC)
Ketch Alongside, Flushing, Cornwall
Watercolour
9½ x 14in (23.5 x 35.5cm)
£300–400 *JN*

Brian Jones
British (20thC)
Clipper and Thames Barge
Oil on canvas
15½ x 19½in (39 x 49cm)
£300–400 *LH*

Jean Kévorkian
French (b1933)
Douarnenez
Signed, oil on canvas
23½ x 28½in (60 x 72cm)
£3,000–3,500 *Om*

Brian Knowler
British (b1937)
Low Tide
Signed, acrylics on board
12½ x 16½in (31.5 x 41.5cm)
£800–900 *JN*

Hayley Lever
American (1876–1958)
Fishing Town
Signed, oil on canvas
24 x 30in (61 x 72cm)
£5,500–6,500 *S(NY)*

Wilfred Knox
British (active 1920–50)
Into the Night
Signed, watercolour
9¾ x 14in (24 x 35.5cm)
£300–400 *JC*

Martyn R. Mackrill
British (b1962)
Shipping on the Thames
Signed, watercolour
9½ x 21½in (24 x 55cm)
£900–1,000 *CFA*

Donald McIntyre
British (b1923)
Mevagissey
Signed, oil on canvas
16 x 20in (40 x51cm)
£1,200–1,500 *A*

Frank Mason
British (1876–1965)
Shipping off the Coast
Signed, watercolour
7¾ x 12in (20 x 31cm)
£900–1,100 *Mar*

Paul Mathieu
Belgian (1872–1937)
Le Chenal, Zeebrugge
Signed, oil on canvas
39½ x 55½in (100.5 x 140.5cm)
£20,000–23,000 *HFFA*

Malcolm Morley
British (b1931)
Onsettant Moie
Signed, titled and dated'74', oil on canvas
20 x 27in (50.5 x 68.5cm)
£40,000–50,000 *S(NY)*

Ken Moroney
British (20thC)
On the Barge
Signed, oil on canvas
10 x 13½in (25 x 34cm)
£400–600 *GK*

Chrisopher Richard Wynne Nevinson A.R.A.
British (1889–1946)
The Thames at Limehouse
Signed, oil on panel
11¾ x 15¾in (30 x 40cm)
£4,500–6,000 *S*

Arthur Norris
British (20thC)
A Fair Breeze
Signed, watercolour
10½ x 14½in (26 x 37cm)
£300–380 *TFA*

Reginald E. Nickerson
American (b1915)
The American schooner 'May O'Neill'
Signed, oil on canvas
21 x 34in (53.5 x 86.5cm)
£2,000–2,500 *CSK*

*The American schooner 'May O'Neill' was
built in 1883 at Camden, Maine, for
J. P. Ellicott of Boston, Massachusetts.
Her Master was W. B. Crosby of Barnstable,
Mass., and her home port was Boston.*

Charles Oppenheimer, R.S.A., R.S.W.
British (1875–1961)
A Solway Port
Signed and inscribed, oil on canvasboard
16 x 20in (40.5 x 50.5cm)
£5,000–6,000 *C(S)*

Jack Pender
British (b1918)
Boat and the Single Figure
Signed, oil on board
4¼ x 27in (18 x 68.5cm)
£900–1,000 *C*

Stephen J. Renard
British (b1947)
'Westward' racing past Norris Castle, 1910
Signed, oil on canvas
40 x 50in (101.5 x 127cm)
£24,000–28,000 *JS*

*Pictures of yachting subjects are extremely
popular in the current market. Renard's
portrait of the 'Westward' tripled its £8,000
top estimate at Christie's South Kensington.
Renard, himself an enthusiastic and
knowledgable sailor, is one of the more
sought-after contemporary marine artists and
specialises in yachting pictures - seemingly a
lucrative choice. 'Westward' was designed and
built in Rhode Island in 1910.*

John Anthony Park
British (1880–1962)
Boats by the Tin Mines
Signed, oil on canvas
22½ x 28in (57 x 71cm)
£5,000–5,550 *Mon*

Lazlo Ritter
British/Hungarian (20thC)
Coastal Waters
Oil on board
27 x 19in (68.5 x 48cm)
£600–700 *SAV*

F. W. Scarborough
British (active 1893–1939)
The Pool of London
Signed, watercolour
13¾ x 17in (33.5 x 43cm)
£3,000–3,250 *AdG*

Frank W. Scarborough
British (active 1893–1939)
Fishing boats at Staithes
Signed, watercolour
7 x 9in (17.5 x 22.5cm)
£900–1,100 *LH*

Henry Scott
British (20thC)
The Night Watch
Signed and dated '66', oil on canvas
23 x 29½in (58.5 x 75cm)
£3,200–4,000 *WH*

Edward Seago
British (1910–74)
The Seine above Paris
Signed, oil on canvas
12 x 16in (30.5 x 40.5cm)
£7,500–8,500 *JN*

Frank Taylor
British (20thC)
Turkish Fishing Boat
Watercolour
17 x 23in (43 x 59cm)
£650–750 *PHG*

Anthony Thieme
American/Dutch (1888–1954)
Docked sailboards
Signed, oil on canvasboard
15¾ x 19½in (40 x 49.5cm)
£1,500–1,800 *CNY*

Epaminondas Thomopoulos
Greek (1878–1974)
From Poros, Fishing Boats in a Bay
Signed, oil on canvas
13¾ x 29½in (35 x 75cm)
£6,000–7,000 *C*

Richard Tuff
British (b1965)
Boats in the Harbour
Silkscreen, 28 colours
19¾ x 26¾in (50 x 60cm)
£150–190 *CCA*

Julian Trevelyan
British (1910–88)
The Thames at Chiswick
Signed and dated '59', oil on canvas
24 x 30in (61 x 76cm)
£1,100–1,500 *P*

Commander Eric Erskine Campbell Tufnell
British (b1888)
H.M.S. 'Devonshire'
Signed with monogram, watercolour
10 x 12in (25.5 x 30.5cm)
£300–350 *JC*

Carel Weight, R.A.
British (b1909)
The Shipwreck
Signed, 1951, oil on paper laid
down on canvas
20 x 60in (51 x 152cm)
£20,000–35,000 *BRG*

John Wheatley, A.R.A., R.W.S.
British (1892–1955)
A Corner Harbour
Oil on canvas
22 x 27in (55.5 x 68.5cm)
£1,200–1,500 *JN*

Neil Westwood
British (20thC)
Low Tide
Signed, watercolour
14 x 20in (35.5 x 51cm)
£800–900 *JN*

Edward Wadsworth
British (1889–1949)
Imaginary Harbour
Signed and dated '1934', tempera
16½ x 34¾in (42 x 87.5cm)
£42,000–50,000 *S*

*1933 marked Wadsworth's return to marine
subjects, from a biomorphic phase of the late
1920s and in the following years he produced
a short series of harbour subjects.*

Michael J. Whitehand
British (b1941)
'Velsheda' racing in the Solent around 1934
Signed, inscribed and dated '93', oil on canvas
24 x 42in (61 x 107cm)
£8,000–9,000 *Bon*

Fred Yates
English (b1922)
River Boats
Oil on board, 1993
40 x 30in (101.5 x 76cm)
£900–1,100 *Tho*

Bernd Zimmer
German (b1948)
Nächtlicher Fischzug
Signed, titled and dated '82', oil on linen
80 x 117¼in (203 x 297cm)
£4,000–5,000 *C*

Michael J. Whitehand
British (b1941)
'Shamrock I' and 'White Heather II' racing
with 'Britannia' off Cowes
Signed, inscribed and dated '93', oil on canvas
24 x 42in (61 x 107cm)
£4,000–4,500 *CSK*

Michael J. Whitehand
British (b1941)
'Britannia'
Signed and dated '93', oil on board
15½ x 11½in (39 x 29.5cm)
£900–1,000 *CSK*

Norman Wilkinson
British (1878–1971)
View of the S.S.'Invicta' sailing out
of Dover Harbour
Signed, oil on canvas
30 x 40in (76 x 101.5cm)
£2,000–2,500 *CAG*

Circle of Johann van der Hagen
Dutch (c1675–1745)
Rowing Vessels approaching a Ship Setting
Sail in Calm Waters
Oil on canvas
30 x 27½in (76 x 70cm)
£4,500–5,000 *P*

Jacob Adriaensz Bellevois
Dutch (1621–76)
A Dutch Merchantman with a Wijdschip and other
Shipping off Amsterdam
Oil on panel
35½ x 61½in (90 x 156cm)
£40,000–45,000 *S*

Adriaen van Diest
Dutch (1655–1704)
A Man of War firing a Salute with other Shipping,
Fishermen Hauling in their Nets on the Foreshore
Oil on canvas
19 x 24in (48 x 61.5cm)
£5,500–6,500 *CSK*

Francis Swaine
British (1720–83)
Men-of-War sailing through choppy Waters
Oil on canvas
26½ x 41¼in (67.5 x 104.5cm)
£5,000–6,000 *C*

William Anderson
British (1757–1837)
Frigate Preparing to Anchor
Signed and dated '1793', watercolour
12½ x 18in (32 x 46cm)
£5,000–5,500 *Mar*

Willem van de Velde the Younger
Dutch (1633–1707)
The Evening Gun - Shipping in a Flat Calm
with a Bezan Yacht Firing a Salute
Signed with initials 'WVV', oil on panel
14½ x 12½in (37 x 32cm)
£180,000–200,000 *S*

Pieter Christian Dommersen
Dutch (1834–1905)
Dutch Fishing Boats in a Calm
Signed, oil on panel
14 x 17in (35.5 x 43cm)
£3,500–4,000 *EG*

James Bard
American (1815–97)
The Steam Paddle Wheeler 'Mattano'
Inscribed and dated '1859', oil on canvas
29 x 48½in (73.4 x 123cm)
£100,000–120,000 *S(NY)*

Anglo-Chinese School (19thC)
The Clipper 'Blackadder'
Oil on canvas
15¼ x 23¼in (39 x 59.5cm)
£1,800–2,500 *Bon*

Frederick James Aldridge
British (1850–1933)
On the Lagoon, Venice
Signed, oil on canvas
14 x 12in (35.5 x 30.5cm)
£1,500–2,000 *JC*

John Wilson Carmichael
British (1800–68)
View of Hartlepool with Shipping and
Sailing Vessels
Signed and dated '1850', oil on canvas
20 x 29¼in (50.5 x 74cm)
£19,500–21,500 *BuP*

l. **George Gregory**
British (1849–1938)
Pilot Cutter and Merchantman
off Lundy
Signed and dated '1898', watercolour
12½ x 17¾in (32 x 45cm)
£1,800–2,200 *Mar*

l. **Thomas Bush Hardy**
British (1842–97)
Off Sandown
Signed, inscribed and dated '1896', watercolour
10 x 20in (25.5 x 50.5cm)
£1,800–2,000 *Dr*

r. **Edwin Hayes, R.A., R.H.A.**
British (1820–1904)
A Seascape - Genoa La Superba
Signed, oil on canvas
30¼ x 50¼in (77 x 128cm)
£8,000–9,000 *CCG*

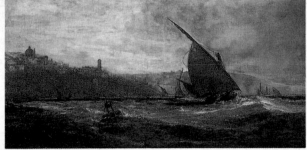

l. **Alfred Herbert**
British (c1820–61)
French Fishing Fleet
Watercolour
10½ x 21in (26 x 53cm)
£2,700–3,300 *Mar*

r. **Christian Cornelis Kannemans**
Dutch (1812–84)
Shipping off the Dutch Coast
Oil on canvas
22 x 30in (55.5 x 76cm)
£6,500–7,000 *WHP*

l. **William Adolphus Knell**
British (1805–75)
The Battle of Trafalgar
Signed and inscribed 'The Battle of
Trafalgar, October 21st 1805,/Vide,
James's Naval History,...Naval
Battles,..., W. A. Knell, Seur',
oil on canvas
34¼ x 51¼in (87 x 130cm)
£20,000–24,000 *C*

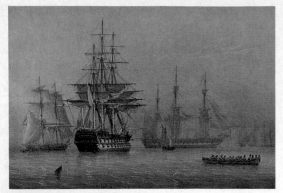

William Joy (1803–67) and
John Cantiloe Joy (1806–66)
British
HMS 'Melville', 74 guns, Preparing to Sail
Watercolour
10¾ x 15¾in (27 x 40cm)
£9,000–9,500 *JML*

Thomas Rose Miles
British (active 1869–88)
In a Breeze, off Killery Bay
Signed, oil on canvas
20 x 30in (50.5 x 76cm)
£5,000–5,750 *BuP*

Samuel Owen
British (c1768–1857)
Dutch Vessel and other Craft
Watercolour
9 x 7¼in (23 x 18cm)
£5,700–6,300 *Mar*

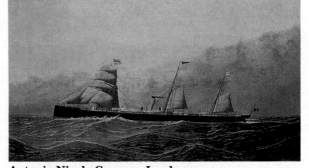

Antonio Nicolo Gasparo Jacobsen
American (1850–1921)
The Steamship 'Jan Breydel'
Signed, dated '1882' and inscribed, oil on canvas
29 x 49in (73.5 x 124.5cm)
£10,500–12,000 *S*

Carl Johan Neumann
Danish (1833–91)
Copenhagen Harbour
Signed and dated '1878', oil on canvas
16 x 23in (40.5 x 58.5cm)
£4,200–5,000 *S*

l. **Claude T. S. Moore**
British (1853–1901)
The Shore of England's Greatest Battlefield
Signed, oil on canvas
20 x 30in (50.5 x 76cm)
£7,000–7,500 *WG*

Robert Salmon
American (1775–1844)
Rough Seas
Signed and dated '1802', oil on canvas
18 x 24in (45.5 x 61.5cm)
£22,000–26,000 *S(NY)*

Thomas Sewell Robins
British (c1809–80)
Dutch Fishing Vessels and Merchantman off
The Needles
Signed and dated '1855', watercolour
12½ x 18¼in (32.5 x 46.5cm)
£2,800–3,500 *Mar*

Niels Simonsen
Danish (1807–85)
Arabs Storming a Boat
Signed and dated '1842', oil on canvas
27¾ x 37¼in (70.5 x 94.5cm)
£15,000–17,000 *C*

Henry Redmore
British (1820–1887)
Dutch Galjots - A Calm on the Humber Estuary
Signed and dated '1854', oil on canvas
12¼ x 18¼in (31.5 x 46cm)
£13,500–14,500 *BuP*

Francis A. Silva
American (1835–86)
Calm at Sunset
Signed, dated '1873', and inscribed, oil on canvas
29 x 50in (73.5 x 127cm)
£175,000–195,000 *S(NY)*

Charles Taylor, Snr.
British (c1880–75)
Aberdeen White Star Line Clipper
Watercolour
16 x 25in (40.5 x 63.5cm)
£4,100–4,500 *Mar*

r. **Frederick William Scarbrough**
British (1863–1945)
Wapping Reach, The Thames, London
A pair, signed and inscribed with title,
watercolour
8 x 15in (20 x 38cm)
£3,800–4,200 *WG*

Montague Dawson, F.R.S.A., R.S.M.A.
British (1895–1973)
Yachting off Cowes
Signed, oil on card
9 x 13⅛in (23 x 34cm)
£3,500–4,000 *JC*

James Brereton
British (b1954)
On the Crest of a Wave
Oil on canvas
40 x 50in (101.5 x 127cm)
£3,000–5,000 *JS*

Montague Dawson, F.R.S.A., R.S.M.A.
British (1895–1973)
High Seas
Signed, oil on canvas
40 x 50½in (101.5 x 128cm)
£50,000–60,000 *S(NY)*

David Brackman
Unknown (20thC)
'Westward' and 'Germania'
Signed and dated '86', gouache
16 x 26in (40.5 x 66cm)
£10,000–12,000 *S*

John Steven Dews
British (b1949)
'Ranger' and 'Endeavour II' Racing off Rhode Island
Signed, oil on canvas
20 x 30in (50.5 x 76cm)
£45,000–55,000 *S(NY)*

John Gardiner Crawford
Scottish (b1941)
The Nor' Reef
Signed, acrylic on masonite, 1990
48in (122cm) square
£18,000–20,000 *WH*

Norman Janes
British (20thC)
The Docks, c1935
Oil on canvas
16 x 20in (40.5 x 50.5cm)
£300–350 *JDG*

William Lee-Hankey
British (1869–1952)
St. Ives, Cornwall
Signed, oil on canvas
25 x 30in (63.5 x 76cm)
£20,000–22,000 *BuP*

John Duffin
British (20thC)
Seasearch
Signed, watercolour
16 x 11in (40.5 x 28cm)
£150–250 *GK*

Joe Hargan
Scottish (b1952)
Boats at Hania, Crete
Oil on canvas
20in (50.5cm) square
£1,600–1,800 *CON*

Axel Johansen
Danish (1872–1938)
The Race
Signed and dated '1921', oil on canvas
40½ x 64in (102 x 162.5cm)
£8,200–9,000 *C*

Martyn R. Mackrill
British (b1962)
'Columbia' leads 'Shamrock', Sandy Hook, 1899
Oil on canvas
24 x 35in (61.5 x 89cm)
£3,000–3,250 *CFA*

Paul Mathieu
Belgian (1872–1932)
Le Port d'Ostende
Signed, oil on board
15½ x 21½in (39 x 54cm)
£9,000–10,000 *HFFA*

Albert Marquet
French (1875–1947)
Le Port de la Ponche, Saint Tropez
Signed, oil on canvas, 1905
19¾ x 24in (50 x 60.5cm)
£120,000–130,000 *S(NY)*

John Anthony Park
British (1880–1962)
The Orange Sail
Signed, oil on canvas
19 x 23in (48 x 59cm)
£6,500–7,250 *Mon*

Robert Stirling Paterson
Scottish (active 1890–1940)
Inverness Fishing Boats
Signed, watercolour
20 x 30in (50.5 x 76cm)
£1,200–1,400 *EG*

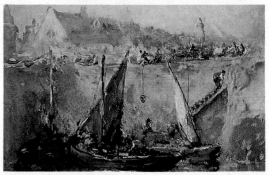

Lewis Charles Powles, R.B.A.
British (1860–1942)
Unloading the Fleet, Honfleur
Signed, watercolour
7 x 10in (17.5 x 25.5cm)
£1,500–2,000 *WG*

l. **Norman Smith**
British (20thC)
Douarnenez, Brittany
Oil on canvas
24 x 18in (61.5 x 46cm)
£700–800 *PHG*

After Pompeo Batoni
Italian (1708–87)
Portrait of The Hon. Humphrey Morice
Inscribed, oil on canvas, in a painted oval
29 x 24in (74 x 61.5cm)
£7,000–8,000 *S*

Workshop of Lucas Cranach the Elder
German (1472–1553)
A Portrait of the Elector Johann The Steadfast
of Saxony
Dated '1532', and the artist's device of a winged
serpent, inscribed, oil on panel
5½in (14cm) square
£25,000–35,000 *S*

John Kerseboom
British (active 1680–1708)
Portrait of a Gentleman
Oil on canvas
49 x 39in (124.5 x 99cm)
£8,000–9,000 *HFA*

Francis Hayman, R.A.
British (1708–76)
Portrait of David Garrick and William Windham
Oil on canvas
33¼ x 39½in (84.5 x 100cm)
£165,000–180,000 *S*

r. **Antonio David**
Italian (b1698)
Portrait of William Perry of Turville Park,
Buckinghamshire, aged 21
Inscribed, oil on canvas
87½ x 58¼in (222 x 148cm)
£11,000–12,000 *C*

Franz Xavier Wolfe
Austrian (1896–1989)
A Good Smoke, and
The Huntsman
A pair, both signed,
oil on panel
8⅞ x 7in (22 x 17.5cm)
£3,000–4,000 *C*

Richard Dadd
British (1817–86)
Portrait of Sir Thomas Phillips in Eastern
Costume, Reclining with a Hookhah
Inscribed, watercolour heightened with white
7 x 10¼in (17.5 x 25.5cm)
£38,000–45,000 *C*

r. **Artist unknown**
Irish (19thC)
Possibly members of
The Beamish Family
of Cork
Watercolour
13 x 16in (33 x 40.5cm)
£250–300 *STA*

German School (c1810)
Portrait of a Gentleman mounting
his horse with gundogs nearby
Oil on canvas
89½ x 59in (228 x 150cm)
£35,000–40,000 *C*

H. Melkus
Austrian (19thC)
Tavern Scenes
A pair, both signed and
inscribed 'München',
oil on panel
11¼ x 9in (28.5 x 22.5)
£4,000–5,000 *S*

l. **Isidor Kaufmann**
Austrian (1853–1921)
A pair of Shoes
Signed, oil on panel
15 x 12 (38 x 30.5cm)
£75,000–90,000 *S(NY)*

Giovanni Boldini
Italian (1845–1931)
Portrait of the Comte de Rasty
Signed, watercolour on paper,
laid down on board
28 x 15½in (71 x 39.5cm)
£60,000–70,000 *S(NY)*

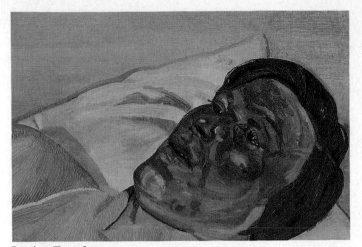

Lucian Freud
British (b1922)
Head and Shoulders of a Man
Oil on canvas
7½ x 10¾in (18.5 x 27cm)
£65,000–80,000 *S*

Harry Aaron Kernoff, R.H.A.
British (1900–74)
Portrait of James Joyce
Signed, pastel
14½ x 10¾in (37 x 27.5cm)
£800–1,000 *P*

John Duffin
British (20thC)
Shorebound
Signed, watercolour
16 x 11in (40.5 x 28cm)
£150–250 *GK*

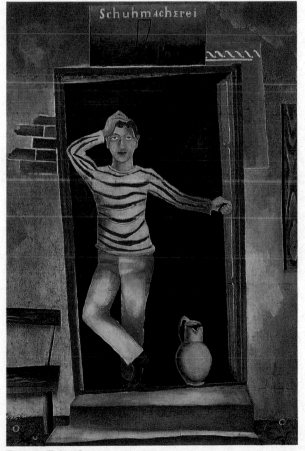

Ernest Fritsch
German (1892–1965)
Der Sohn des Schumachers
Signed and dated '22', oil on canvas
46 x 31in (116.5 x 79cm)
£25,000–30,000 *C*

l. **Christopher Reed**
British (b1962)
Day of the Gladioli
Signed, oil on canvas
30 x 36in (76 x 91.5cm)
£1,200–1,400 *FT*

Sir Peter Lely
British (1618–80)
Portrait of Jane, Countess of Northampton
Inscribed, oil on canvas
50 x 39½in (127 x 100cm)
£25,000–30,000 *S*

Bernardini de'Conti
Italian (1450-c1528)
Portrait of a Lady in profile
Oil on inset panel
30¾ x 23in (78 x 58.5cm)
£170,000–200,000 *C*

*Until 1892 this portrait was believed to have
been painted by Leonardo da Vinci, when an
Italian art historian reattributed it to
de'Conti. Bernardino de'Conti was a follower
of Leonardo and could possibly have been his
assistant. The Milanese artist painted several
profile portraits such as this one, and similar
examples can be seen in the Vatican, Rome,
and the Brooklyn Museum, U.S.A.*

Follower of Thomas Murray
British (1663–1735)
Portrait of a Lady before a Palladian House
Oil on canvas
48½ x 38in (123 x 96.5cm)
£5,000–6,000 *CSK*

Jacob van Loo
Dutch (c1614–70)
Portrait of a Lady
Oil on panel
28 x 23½in (71 x 60cm)
£16,500–20,000 *C*

Circle of Jean-Baptiste Morel
Flemish (1662–1732)
A Lady as Flora
Oil on canvas
31 x 34in (78.5 x 86cm)
£8,000–10,000 *C*

Maurice-Quentin de La Tour
French (1704–88)
Portrait of Marie Fel
Inscribed on the musical score 'Les yeux de
l'Amour/un cantatille', pastel with touches
of bodycolour on 5 sheets of paper
31¼ x 25in (79 x 63.5cm)
£160,000–180,000 *C*

Jean-Baptiste Pater
French (1695–1737)
Portrait of Mlle. Dangeville as Thalia
Oil on canvas
18½ x 22in (47 x 56cm)
£260,000–300,000 *S(NY)*

John Russell, R.A.
British (1745–1806)
Portrait of Mary Wood
Signed and dated '1784', pastel on paper laid
down on canvas
23½ x 17½ in (60 x 44.5cm)
£6,000–7,000 *C*

**Johann Friedrich August Tischbein
(the 'Leipziger')**
German (1750–1812)
A Portrait of Grand Duchess Catherine
Pavlovna of Russia
Oil on canvas
27½ x 22in (70 x 55.5cm)
£35,000–40,000 *S*

Vittorio Corcos
Italian (1859–1933)
Waiting by the Fountain
Signed and dated '96', oil on canvas
82 x 59in (208 x 149.5cm)
£90,000–100,000 *S*

Charles Baugniet
Belgian (1814–86)
La Lettre
Signed, oil on panel
25½ x 29½in (65 x 75cm)
£35,000–40,000 *S(NY)*

Henry Bacon
American (1839–1912)
A Scottish Lady on a Boat Arriving in New York
Signed, oil on canvas
19 x 27in (48 x 69cm)
£23,000–30,000 *S*

Mary Cassatt
American (1845–1926)
Woman Bathing
Drypoint and aquatint, 1890–1
14½ x 10½ in (37 x 27cm)
£200,000–225,000 *S(NY)*

Daniel Hernandez
Peruvian (1856–1932)
Portrait of a Lady
Oil on canvas
42 x 30in (106.5 x 76cm)
£30,000–40,000 *HFA*

William Lee-Hankey
British (1869–1952)
Reflections
Signed and dated '98',
watercolour
14¾ x 9½in (37.5 x 24cm)
£2,500–3,500 *AG*

Edward Hughes
British (1832–1908)
Portrait of a Lady
Signed and dated,
oil on canvas
49 x 41in (124.5 x 104cm)
£9,000–10,000 *RA*

Daniel Ridgway Knight
American (1839–1924)
A Pensive Moment
Signed and inscribed 'Paris', oil on canvas
23 x 30½in (59 x 77.5cm)
£18,000–22,000 *S(NY)*

George Dunlop Leslie, R.A.
British (1835–1921)
In the Park
Signed and dated '1866', oil on canvas
23½ x 17½in (60 x 44.5cm)
£17,000–18,000 *HFA*

John Melhuish Strudwick
British (1849–1937)
Song without Words
Signed with initials and dated '1875',
oil on canvas
29¼ x 39½in (74.5 x 99.5cm)
£70,000–90,000 *S*

Edward Naylor
British (1828–1922)
Contemplation
Signed and dated '1868', watercolour
16 x 12in (40.5 x 30.5cm)
£1,500–1,750 *EG*

Albert Ludovici, Snr.
British (1820–94)
Portrait of a Spanish Girl
Signed, oil on canvas
12 x 10in (30.5 x 25cm)
£2,500–3,000 *CGa*

Carlos Vazquez
Spanish (1869–1944)
Two Ladies
Signed, oil on canvas
41¾ x 53in (106 x 135cm)
£20,000–25,000 *S*

Alex Katz
American (b1927)
Salute No. 4
Signed, oil on canvas
43 x 46¾in (109 x 118.5cm)
£23,000–28,000 *S(NY)*

Olga Suvorova
Russian (b1966)
Tanya, 1991
Signed, oil on canvas
43 x 46in (113 x 116cm)
£2,000–2,500 *ALG*

Dorothy Lee Roberts
British (20thC)
Festive Occasion
Signed, mixed media
22 x 14½in (55.5 x 37cm)
£400–500 *LFA*

Raoul Dufy
French (1877–1953)
La Martiniquaise
Signed and dated '1931', oil on canvas
28½ x 23⅝in (72.5 x 60cm)
£130,000–150,000 *C*

Janet Owen
British (b1965)
You II, 1991
Signed and dated '1991', oil on panel
21 x 36in (53.5 x 91.5cm)
£900–1,000 *Mer*

MEN & WOMEN

Recent sales of British portraits have tended to show what the *Antiques Trade Gazette* described as 'keen bidding on the finest pictures contrasted with a very selective response to the more ordinary works.' 'Broadly speaking, if a portrait is of good quality, comes from a private source, is untouched and will clean well, a lot of people will be interested in it,' David Moore-Gwyn of Sotheby's British Pictures Department told Miller's. 'If it lacks these qualities, there aren't the buyers at the bottom of the market.'

What makes a desirable portrait, we asked John Stainton of Christie's British Pictures Department? 'Quality of work is vital, and condition is all important - both private buyers and dealers like their pictures to be, as far as possible, in original condition. Image is crucial and can be more significant than the identity of the artist. The sitter should be attractive or historically important and preferably both - and finally a good provenance can be a help.' Portraits that combine these myriad virtues have been

making strong prices but there are plenty of good works on offer in the middle and lower range of the market. 'In British art as a whole, portraiture is one of the few fields where we have excelled,' explains Stainton. 'Because of that there is a vast quantity of 18thC pictures about and prices can be very reasonable for quality works, representing tremendous value for money,' agrees Moore-Gwyn, 'especially when you think that many of them come in decorative hardwood frames that are valuable in their own right. Portraiture can be a very good area for the more modest collector, but it is important to buy known sitters - finding out about the subject raises the interest of work.'

A collection of British portraits represents not only a display of British art but a fascinating insight into British history. The more you research a sitter, the more interesting a picture becomes and amongst our home-grown art forms, portraiture cannot only be one of the more unappreciated areas of the market, but ultimately one of the most rewarding for the private collector.

MEN
16th Century

Attributed to Giulio Campi
Italian (c1502–72)
A Study of a Standing Figure
Inscribed '151', pen and brown ink over black chalk
6 x 3¾in (15 x 9.5cm)
£750–1,000 *P*

Follower of Pieter Breughel the Elder
Flemish (c1525–69)
A Head of a Peasant
Oil on panel
5½in (14cm) diam
£30,000–40,000 *S*

Circle of Barthel Bruyn the Elder
German (1493–1555)
Portrait of a Donor Cleric with Christ as the Man of Sorrows
Inscribed and dated '1545', oil on panel
18 x 13½in (45.5 x 34cm)
£10,500–12,000 *C*

English School (16thC)
Portrait of Cardinal Reginald Pole
Inscribed and dated '1557', oil on panel
15 x 11½in (38 x 29cm)
£4,500–5,500 *S*

*Reginald Pole, who was made both Cardinal
(1536) and Archbishop of Canterbury (1556),
enjoyed during his youth the friendship and
respect of Henry VIII. Their relationship,
however, was affected by Pole's tacit refusal to
campaign for acceptance of the Royal divorce.
After Henry's death in 1547, he tried in vain
to reconcile England with the Holy See. In
1556, he succeeded Cranmer as Archbishop
of Canterbury, and was also appointed
Chancellor of Cambridge University. He died
on 17th November 1558 at Lambeth Palace,
the same day as Queen Mary.*

Flemish School (c1529)
Portrait of Floris van Egmont,
Count of Bueren
Oil on panel
12¼ x 8½in (31 x 21.5cm)
£35,000–45,000 *S*

Florentine School (16thC)
Portrait of a Gentleman
Oil on panel
24 x 18¾in (61 x 47.5cm)
£1,300–1,500 *S(S)*

German School (16thC)
Portrait of a Gentleman standing in
an interior
Oil on panel
12½ x 8½in (31.5 x 21.5cm)
£5,600–6,600 *S*

Jacopo Palma, Il Giovane
Italian (1544–1628)
Portrait of a Pope, possibly Pius V Ghislieri
Oil on canvas
30 x 26in (76 x 66cm)
£8,000–9,000 *S*

Attributed to Robert Peake
British (c1551–1619)
Portrait of Robert Ker, 1st Earl of Somerset
Oil on panel
44½ x 34in (113 x 86cm)
£40,000–45,000 *S*

*It is not only royal mistresses who feature in
this year's Guide (see Lely), but also male
favourites. Robert Ker, or Carr, was a 'close
friend' of James I. In 1607, Ker broke his leg
at a royal tilting match, the King had him
nursed at the palace and, according to reports
at the time, fell in love with the patient.*

Francesco Maria Rondani
Italian (1490–1550)
Portrait of a bearded Gentleman
Signed and inscribed, oil on panel
23 x 18in (59 x 45.5cm)
£160,000–180,000 *C*

**Miller's is a price GUIDE
not a price LIST**

Circle of Frans Pourbus
Flemish (16th/17thC)
Portrait presumed to be Jean Le Veneur,
Comte de Tillières, Grand Panetier of Queen
Eleonore, second wife of François Premier
Oil on panel
17¾ x 14¼in (45.5 x 36cm)
£30,000–35,000 *S*

*The armorial baton bears the coat-of-arms
of the sitter.*

17th Century

Bolognese School (17thC)
A Study of a Young Man recto, and a
Sketch of a Youth's Head verso
Inscribed, black chalk heightened with white
14½ x 10½in (37.5 x 26cm)
£550–700 *P*

John Baptist Closterman
British (active c1690–1713)
Portrait of Thomas Eyre of
Hassop, Derbyshire
Inscribed with sitter's name, oil on canvas
50 x 40in (127 x 101.5cm)
£9,000–10,000 *HFA*

English School (17thC)
Portrait of a Clergyman
Oil on canvas
27 x 20in (69 x 51cm)
£200–300 *LF*

Follower of Domenico Feti
Italian (1589–1624)
Head of an Old Man
Oil on canvas
18¾ x 13¾in (47.5 x 35cm)
£1,000–1,200 *S(S)*

Cornelis Jonson
Dutch (1593–1661)
Portrait of a Gentleman
Oil on canvas
29¾ x 25in (76 x 63.5cm)
£2,600–3,500 *C*

Studio of Sir Godfrey Kneller
British (1646–1723)
Portrait of John Evelyn
Oil on canvas
33 x 27in (83.5 x 69cm)
£6,500–8,000 *S*

*John Evelyn (1620–1706) was 'a man of
means, of unblemished character, and
a dilettante, who helped to advance
civilisation,' (Oxford Companion to English
Literature, 4thEd.). Although he wrote
perceptively on many subjects from landscape
gardening to the perils of pollution in
London, it is for his diary that he is now
best remembered. The journal covered the
whole of his life containing brilliant portraits
of his contemporaries and current events.*

Follower of Jan Kupetski
German (1667–1740)
Portrait of a Warrior
Oil on canvas
28¾ x 23¼in (73 x 59cm)
£1,200–1,500 *CSK*

Manner of Judith Leyster
Dutch (1600–60)
A Portrait of a Jovial Man
Oil on canvas
22½ x 17¼in (57 x 44cm)
£4,500–6,000 *CSK*

Hendrick Heerschop
Flemish (c1620–after 1662)
A Cartographer in an Interior
Oil on panel
16½ x 14in (42 x 35.5cm)
£3,000–4,000 *S(Am)*

School of Lorraine (c1600)
Allegorical figure of a Soldier
crushing the Snake of Sedition
Red chalk
14 x 8½in (35.5 x 22cm)
£1,200–1,500 *P*

Willem van Mieris
Dutch (1662–1747)
A Bravo, holding a Clay Pipe
and a Roemer
Signed and dated '1699', oil on panel
7 x 5¾in (17.5 x 14.5cm)
£70,000–80,000 *S*

Pieter Jansz Quast
Dutch (1605–47)
A Standing Male Figure
Signed with initials in monogram,
red chalk
7¼ x 4¼in (18 x 10.5cm)
£950–1,100 *P*

**Follower of Rembrandt
Harmensz. van Rijn**
Dutch (1606–69)
Portrait of a Gentleman
Oil on panel
23¾ x 18½in (60 x 47cm)
£20,000–25,000 *C*

**Attributed to Jan Anthonisz.
van Ravesteyn**
Dutch (1570–1657)
Portrait of a Gentleman, probably
Sir Daniel de Ligne
Later inscribed, oil on canvas
89½ x 53½in (227 x 126cm)
£7,000–8,000 *S*

Rembrandt Harmensz. van Rijn
Dutch (1606–69)
Thomas Haaringh ('Old Haaringh')
Drypoint and burin on paper, c1655
7¾ x 6in (19.5 x 15cm)
£125,000–150,000 *S(NY)*

*'Old Haaringh' is executed entirely in burin
and drypoint, with no etching at all, though
here Rembrandt was working on an intimate
rather than a grand scale. The print is a study
in texture and drapery, and not least a telling
portrait of a man who was Bailiff to the Court
of Insolvents. By means of the most delicate
strokes of the needle and burin, Rembrandt
has created a picture of a man who had
witnessed scenes of great hardship, but who
had never lost sympathy with the sufferers.*

Jusepe de Ribera
Spanish (1588–1656)
Small Grotesque Head
Etching, dated '1622'
5¾ x 4½in (14.5 x 11.5cm)
£7,000–8,000 *S(NY)*

John Riley
British (1646–91)
Portrait of Dr. Peter Ball
Inscribed and dated '1671', oil on canvas in a
painted cartouche
29 x 24in (74 x 61cm)
£2,400–3,000 *S*

Salvator Rosa
Italian (1615–73)
A Bearded Man
Oil on canvas
26¾ x 21⅛in (68 x 53.5cm)
£10,500–12,000 *C*

Circle of William Segar
British (active 1585–1633)
Portrait of a Gentleman
Oil on panel
21¾ x 16½in (55 x 42cm)
£1,000–1,400 *P*

Robert White
British (1645–1703)
A group of 9 Portrait Studies, including
Dr. John Blow, Elias Keach, Thomas Manton
and William Salmon
The majority with inscriptions and date
'1503', pencil, a few with brown wash
4¾ x 4in (12.5 x 10cm)
£3,500–4,500 *C*

*Robert White, a pupil of David Loggan,
specialised in miniature portrait drawings,
over four hundred of which were engraved.
He drew most of the public and literary
characters of his day.*

18th Century

Lemuel Francis Abbott
British (c1760–1802)
Portrait of Warren Hastings
Oil on canvas
29¾ x 24¾in (73.5 x 63cm)
£8,000–25,000 *C*

Warren Hastings was one of the most important figures in Anglo-Indian history of the 18thC, and can largely be credited with laying the foundations of British supremacy in India. He joined the East India company in 1749 and rose to become the first Governor General of Bengal, the richest and most powerful state of India. Hugely successful, Hastings brought peace among the warring provinces. He introduced laws to protect Indian interests whilst at the same time improving the finances of the company and sought to stamp out corruption in every quarter. Hastings himself was ultimately to be impeached with fraud, embezzlement, and abuse of power. He was brought back to London in 1787 and put on trial before the House of Lords, with Edmund Burke, his arch enemy as Chief Prosecutor. 'I gave you all,' Hastings told the House 'and you have rewarded me with confiscation, disgrace and a life of impeachment.' The famous trial lasted for seven years and though Hastings was finally exonerated of all charges, he was never to return to India.

Thomas Beach, R.A.
British (1738–1806)
Portrait of John Edwin
Oil on canvas
49½ x 38½in (125 x 98cm)
£10,200–12,000 *S*

The sitter was a well known comedian and singer, according to essayist William Hazlitt. So great was Edwin's genius for comedy that 'he merely put his head out, the faces that he made threw the audience into a roar'.

Thomas Beach, R.A.
British (1738–1806)
Portrait of a Gentlemen, said to be Mr. P. Jones
Inscribed, oil on panel
30 x 25in (76 x 63.5cm)
£1,300–1,600 *C*

Louis-Léopold Boilly
French (1761–1845)
Portrait of André Augustin Delion
Inscribed, dated '1773', oil on canvas
8½ x 6½in (21 5 x 16.5cm)
£7,000–8,000 *Bon*

Francesco Saverio Candido
Italian (18thC)
Portrait of a Gentleman,
with a view of
Vesuvious beyond
Signed, oil on canvas
40¼ x 30⅛in (102 x 76.5cm)
£9,500–12,000 *C*

John Constable, R.A.
British (1776–1837)
Portrait of Henry Greswolde Lewis
Oil on canvas
30 x 25in (76 x 63.5cm)
£9,000–12,000 *S*

Henri-Pierre Danloux
French (1753–1809)
Portrait of a Gentleman
Oil on canvas
30½ x 25¾in (77.5 x 65cm)
£5,000–5,500 *C*

Gainsborough Dupont
British (1754–97)
Portrait of the Revd. Robert Heron
Oil on canvas
21 x 15in (53 x 38cm)
3,500–4,000 *S*

*Gainsborough Dupont was the nephew of
Thomas Gainsborough and his only studio
assistant. He imitated Gainsborough's artistic
style, and in the past his works have often
been attributed to the hand of his more
famous uncle.*

Arthur Devis
British (c1711–87)
Portrait of Frederick Montagu
Signed, inscribed and dated '1749', oil on canvas
23¾ x 16in (60 x 41cm)
£95,000–120,000 *S*

*This portrait fetched considerably more than its
estimate of £40,000–60,000 at Sotheby's.*

Thomas Gainsborough, R.A.
British (1727–88)
Portrait of Thomas Fane,
8th Earl of Westmorland
Oil on canvas
50 x 40in (127 x 101.5cm)
£23,000–30,000 *S*

English School (c1720)
Portrait of a Gentleman
Oil on canvas
40 x 50in (101.5 x 127cm)
£3,000–3,300 *SAV*

Ubaldo Gandolfi
Italian (1728–1871)
Study of a Man's Head
Black chalk heightened with white,
over traces of red chalk, laid down
6¾ x 5⅜in (17 x 14cm)
£1,000–1,200 *P*

Daniel Gardner
British (1750–1805)
Portrait of Sir John Taylor, Bt.
Pastel and bodycolour on laid paper
35½ x 23in (85 x 58cm)
£6,500–8,000 *S*

German School (18thC)
Portrait of an Officer
Oil on canvas
20 x 14½in (50.5 x 36.5cm)
£1,200–1,500 *CSK*

**Follower of Francisco José de
Goya y Lucientes**
Spanish (1746–1828)
Portrait of the Bullfighter Pedro
Joaquin Rodriguez Costillares
Oil on canvas
26 x 19⅝in (66 x 50cm)
£7,200–8,000 *C*

Thomas Hickey
British (1741–1824)
Portrait of Captain George Robertson
Oil on canvas
30 x 22in (76 x 56cm)
£1,500–2,000 *P*

Andrew Geddes, R.S.A.
British (1783–1844)
Portrait of Henry MacKenzie
Oil on panel
26 x 19⅝in (66 x 50.5cm)
£12,500–14,000 *C(S)*

*Scottish writer and literary
figure, Mackenzie was
certainly no oil painting in
the flesh. Contemporary
reports describe him as thin,
shrivelled and yellow, kiln
dried with smoking, and
when seen in profile, was said
to have the clever, wicked
look of Voltaire.*

Thomas Hudson
British (1701–79)
Portrait of Rear Admiral Richard Tyrrell
Oil on canvas
30 x 25in (76 x 64cm)
£3,000–4,000 *C*

*Hudson painted Tyrrell in 1759 after his
return from the West Indies, during which
commission the Admiral had lost three
fingers from his left hand in an engagement
between the French ship 'Florissant' and his
command, the 'Buckingham'. The hands are
concealed in this portrait.*

Charles Jervas
British (1675–1739)
Portrait of Colonel William Forward
Oil on canvas
49¾ x 40in (126.5 x 101.5cm)
£9,500–11,000 *C*

George Knapton
British (1698–1778)
Portrait of a Gentleman conducting
an Experiment
Inscribed, oil on canvas
49¾ x 39in (126 x 99cm)
£4,600–6,000 *S*

Angelica Kauffmann, R.A.
Swiss (1741–1807)
Portrait of William
Henry Lambton
Signed and dated '1797',
oil on canvas
86 x 55½in (218.5 x 140cm)
£100,000–120,000 *S*

*While minor portraits have
been suffering in the current
discriminating market, good
works by major artists have
fetched some strong prices.
Kauffmann's portrait had
been purchased for £130
in 1932.*

Manner of Nicolas de Largilliere
French (1656–1746)
Portrait of a Gentleman
Oil on canvas
40½ x 35¼in (103 x 89.5cm)
£2,000–2,500 *CSK*

Etienne Loys
French (1724–83)
Portrait of Guillaume Barcellon
Signed, inscribed and dated '1753',
oil on canvas
31 x 25in (79 x 63.5cm)
£79,000–100,000 *S*

*Guillaume Barcellon was a
distinguished French tennis
professional from Montpellier
who became paumier to King
Louis XV in 1753, the year of
this portrait. He also trained
his sons to become distinguished
players. His eldest son, Pierre
was the author of the* Regles et
Principes de Paume, 1800, *the
first published rules of tennis.*

Sir Thomas Lawrence, P.R.A.
British (1769–1830)
Portrait of Sir Samuel Shepherd
Oil on canvas
50 x 40in (127 x 101.5cm)
£100,000–120,000 *S*

Attributed to David Morier
Swiss (b1705)
Portrait of a Gentleman out riding
Oil on canvas
23½ x 19¾in (60 x 50.5cm)
£2,700–3,500 *L*

John Hamilton Mortimer, A.R.A.
British (1740–79)
Double Portrait of Thomas Somers Cocks and Richard Cocks
of Castleditch
Inscribed on the reverse, oil on canvas, 28¼ x 36in (71.4 x 91.5cm)
£100,000–120,000 *C*

*Christie's April 1994 sale of British pictures included two
portraits of the Cocks brothers from the collection of the late
Mary, Viscountess Rothermere. Though carrying the same
estimates, this example fetched a great deal more than its
companion piece, which showed its two sitters in an interior. The
attractive wooded landscape made this work far more popular,
resulting in the picture selling comfortably over the estimate.*

Follower of Antione Pesne
French (1683–1757)
Portrait of Frederick the Great
Oil on canvas
31½ x 25⅝in (80.5 x 65cm)
£3,000–3,800 *S*

**Attributed to the Revd. Matthew
William Peters, R.A.**
British (d1814)
Portrait of a Gentleman
Oil on canvas
29½ x 24½in (75 x 63cm)
£1,000–1,200 *S*

Attributed to Francesco Renaldi
British School (1755–98)
Portrait of Lieutenant Henry
Dove, R.N.
Oil on canvas, in a carved
wood frame
21¾ x 17¼in (55.5 x 44cm)
£6,000–7,000 *S*

Sir Henry Raeburn, R.A.
British (1756–1823)
Portrait of Archibald Constable
Oil on canvas
51 x 40in (129.5 x 101.5cm)
£4,000–5,000 *C*

*The sitter was the most important Scottish
publisher of his day and friend of Sir Walter
Scott. He set up his own printing shop in
Edinburgh at the age of 21. Within seven
years Constable had risen to prominence with
the publication of the* Edinburgh Review *and
achieved the envy of his rivals by paying the
highest prices for contributions and still being
the most profitable publication in Edinburgh.
In 1812 he purchased the copyright and stock
of the* Encyclopaedia Britannica *and in 1814
he started publishing Scott's* Waverley Novels.

George Romney
British (1734–1802)
Portrait of Frederick Montagu
of Papplewick
Oil on canvas
49 x 40in (125 x 102cm)
£35,000–45,000 *S*

*Romney painted this portrait
during the summer of 1780, and
was paid 36 guineas.*

Augustin de Saint-Aubin
French (1736–1807)
Portrait of a Gentleman
Pencil
4¾ x 3¾in (12 x 9cm)
£1,500–2,000 *P*

Follower of George Romney
British (1734–1802)
Portrait of Sir William Hope
Johnstone, K.C.B.
Inscribed, oil on canvas
29½ x 24½in (75 x 62cm)
£2,000–2,200 *S*

Attributed to Charles Smith
British (1749–1824)
Portrait of Asaf-ud-daula, Nawab of Oudh
Oil on canvas
16½ x 12¾in (42 x 32cm)
£13,000–15,000 *C*

*Asaf-ud-daula (d1797) succeeded his father
Shuja-ud-daula as Nawab Wazir of Oudh in
1775, and moved the capital back from
Faizabad to Lucknow which he developed
with great extravagance, attracting poets,
philosophers, calligraphers, artists, including
Europeans and adventurers. Lewis Ferdinand
Smith described him in a letter of 1 March
1795 to a friend, 'Asaf-ud-Dowlah is mild in
manner, generous to extravagance, and
engaging in his conduct, but he has not great
mental power. He is fond of lavishing his
treasures on gardens, palaces, horses,
elephants, and above all, on fine European
guns, lustres, mirrors, and all sorts of
European manufacturers, more especially ...
to the elegant paintings ...of a Lorraine and
a Zoffani ..Asaf-ud-Dowlah is absurdly
extravagant, he has no taste and less judgement.'*

Gilbert Stuart
British (1755–1828)
Portrait of Sir William
Barker, Bt.
Inscribed, oil on canvas
18 x 15¼in (46 x 39cm)
£3,000–4,000 *S*

Andrea Soldi
Italian (c1703–71)
Portrait of Richard Bendyshe
Signed and dated '1751', oil
on canvas
49 x 39½in (125 x 99cm)
£12,000–14,000 *S*

Henry Walton (c1746–1813) and
Sawrey Gilpin, R.A. (1733–1807)
British
Portrait of Richard Bendyshe
(1753–1824)
Inscribed, oil on canvas
29 x 24½in (74 x 62cm)
£99,000–120,000 *S*

Circle of Johann Georg Ziesenis
Danish (1716–76)
Portrait of a Nobleman
Oil on canvas
32½ x 25½in (82.5 x 64cm)
£2,500–3,500 *C*

Circle of Cornelius Troost
Dutch (1697–1750)
The Elegant Gentleman
Graphite on paper
11½ x 6½in (29.5 x 16cm)
£250–350 *S(NY)*

19th Century

Louis Anquetin
French (1861–1932)
Portrait d'Aristide Bruant
Signed, pastel on buff paper
18¾ x 12¾in (48 x 32cm)
£2,000–2,500 *S*

American School (19thC)
Portrait of a dark
haired Gentleman
Oil on canvas
28 x 21¾in (71 x 55cm)
£2,800–3,500 *S(NY)*

Sigismund von Ajdukiewicz
Austrian (b1861)
Portrait of a man, said to be Tolstoy
Signed, oil on canvas
32 x 25½in (81 x 65cm)
£1,000–1,200 *S(NY)*

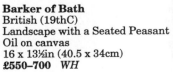

Barker of Bath
British (19thC)
Landscape with a Seated Peasant
Oil on canvas
16 x 13½in (40.5 x 34cm)
£550–700 *WH*

William Vierplanck Birney
American (1858–1909)
Lighting his Pipe
Signed, oil on canvas
8¼ x 10in (21 x 25.5cm)
£1,700–2,200 *CNY*

Gaetano Bellei
Italian (1857–1922)
A Good Smoke
Signed, oil on canvas
34 x 24in (87 x 61cm)
£11,000–13,000 *S*

F. Bühlmayer
German (19thC)
Portrait of a Gentleman
Signed and dated '1841',
oil on canvas
36 x 27¼in (91.5 x 69cm)
£2,000–2,300 *S(NY)*

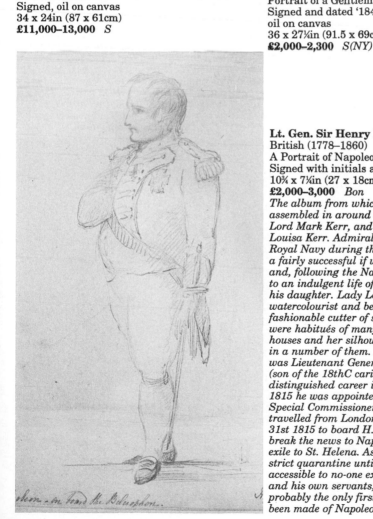

Lt. Gen. Sir Henry E. Bunbury
British (1778–1860)
A Portrait of Napoleon Bonaparte
Signed with initials and inscribed, pencil
10¾ x 7⅛in (27 x 18cm)
£2,000–3,000 *Bon*
*The album from which this work came was
assembled in around 1830 by Vice Admiral
Lord Mark Kerr, and his daughter, Lady
Louisa Kerr. Admiral Kerr had served in the
Royal Navy during the French wars, having
a fairly successful if undistinguished career
and, following the Napoleonic wars he retired
to an indulgent life of travel accompanied by
his daughter. Lady Louisa was an able
watercolourist and became a skilled and
fashionable cutter of silhouettes. The Kerrs
were habitués of many of Britain's grand
houses and her silhouettes are still be found
in a number of them. Among their friends
was Lieutenant General Sir Henry Bunbury
(son of the 18thC caricaturist), who had a
distinguished career in the British army. In
1815 he was appointed the War Department's
Special Commissioner to Napoleon and
travelled from London to Plymouth on July
31st 1815 to board H.M.S. 'Bellerophon' and
break the news to Napoleon of his impending
exile to St. Helena. As Napoleon was kept in
strict quarantine until his exile, and was
accessible to no-one except the ship's officers
and his own servants, Sir Henry's portrait is
probably the only first hand portrait to have
been made of Napoleon at this time.*

Franz von Defregger
German (1835–1921)
Bauernbursh mit Pfeife
Signed, oil on panel
16 x 12in (40.5 x 30.5cm)
£12,000–14,000 *C*

Richard Dadd
British (1817–86)
Portrait of Sir Thomas Phillips in Eastern costume
Watercolour with touches of white heightening
10¼ x 7in (26 x 17.5cm)
£25,500–35,500 *C*

*In July 1842, shortly before his 25th birthday, Dadd
set out on a tour of the Middle East, with his patron, the
Welsh lawyer Thomas Phillips. Dadd had been
recommended to Phillips both as gifted artist and a
charming companion, but the trip resulted in disaster.
Dadd returned to England in May 1843 insane, partly
as a result of the excitement of the journey and from
having suffered sunstroke in Egypt. That same year he
killed his father and was confined to Bedlam.*

English School (19thC)
Fisherman
Oil on canvas
16 x 20in (40.5 x 51cm)
£500–600 *LF*

Emil Fuchs
Austrian (b1866)
Portrait of a
Gentleman holding
a Cigar
Signed and dated
'1904', oil on canvas
36¼ x 32¼in
(92 x 81.5cm)
£500–700 *P*

English School (19thC)
Portrait of T. Cowburn, with a
model engine 'Perseverance'
Inscribed and dated '1839', oil on canvas
30 x 25in (76.3 x 63.5cm)
£4,000–5,000 *C*

James Green
British (1771–1834)
Portrait of an Officer
Signed and dated '1831',
oil on canvas
36 x 28in (91.5 x 71cm)
£5,500–6,500 *C*

Mrs Richard Hardey
American (19thC)
A Portrait of a
handsome Gentleman
Signed and dated '1855',
oil on canvas
36½ x 28in (93 x 71cm)
£1,800–2,200 *S(NY)*

George Peter Alexander Healy
British (1808–94)
Portrait of William Fleetwood
Signed and dated '1858', oil
on canvas
43½ x 32in (110.5 x 81.5cm)
£550–700 *CNY*

Johann Horrak
Austrian (1815–70)
A Group Portrait of the Brothers Klein
Signed and dated 'Nov.851', pencil and
watercolour heightened with white
18 x 22½in (46 x 57cm)
£1,600–2,000 *C*

*The Klein brothers were owners of the Zöptau
Ironworks from the 1840s, and played an
important role in the development of the
region, manufacturing the tracks for the
railway network.*

George Sherwood Hunter
British (active 1855–93)
'Porthaven' - a Study of an Old Man
Inscribed and dated '1873' on the reverse,
oil on board
12 x 6in (30.5 x 15cm)
£120–150 *AG*

Benjamin Hudson
British (active 1847–62)
Portrait of Bangso Gopal Nandi
Oil on canvas
30 x 24¾in (76 x 63cm)
£7,000–8,000 *C*

Jean Auguste Dominique Ingres
French (1780–1867)
Portrait of M. François Pouqueville
Signed, inscribed and dated '1834',
graphite on white wove paper
29¾ x 9½in (32 x 24cm)
£250,000–300,000 *S(NY)*

Ingres presented a very sympathetic portrait of this sitter, a gentleman who had managed to survive extraordinary misfortune. François-Charles-Hughues-Laurent Pouqueville (1770–1838) served with the Napoleonic forces in Egypt where he was taken prisoner by the Turks and the Barbary Pirates. He lived for years as a prisoner of war in Greece where he took advantage of his incarceration by studying both ancient and modern Greek art and literature, the geography of Greece, its customs and diseases. His resulting publications won him a Chevalier of the Legion of Honour and l'Ordre du Sauveur. He was given the responsibility of representing his country as the Consul General of France in Greece.

Henry Wright Kerr, R.S.W.
British 1857–1936
The Old Shepherd
Signed, watercolour
23 x 17in (59 x 43cm)
£1,300–1,500 *WH*

Sir William Orpen, R.A., R.H.A., R.W.S.
British (1878–1931)
The Valuers
Signed, oil on canvas
32¾ x 43in (83 x 109cm)
£46,000–55,000 *S*

Attributed to Stephen Pearce
British (1819–1904)
Portrait of an Officer
Oil on canvas
29 x 24½in (73.5 x 62cm)
£700–900 *S*

l. **Charles M. Padday**
British (active 1889–c1947)
An Old Salt
Signed and dated '89',
oil on canvas
40 x 30in (101.5 x 76cm)
£1,600–2,000 *CSK*

r. **John Pettie**
Scottish (active 1839–93)
Knight in a Suit of Armour
Signed, oil on canvas
14 x 9in (35.5 x 22.5cm)
£700–1,000 *GK*

Ammi Phillips
American (1788–1865)
Portrait of a Seated Gentleman
Oil on canvas
30¼ x 25¼in (76 x 64cm)
£1,400–1,800 *SK*

George Richmond
British (1809–96)
Portrait of the Reverend John Halford
Signed and dated '1850', pencil and
watercolour heightened with white
15½ x 12in (39 x 30.5cm)
£1,400–1,800 *CSK*

Anthony F. A. Sandys
British (1829–1904)
Portrait of Robert Browning
Signed, inscribed and dated '1881',
pencil and coloured chalks
27¼ x 20¼in (69 x 51.5cm)
£15,000–17,000 *C*

J. Walker West
British (19thC)
A Portrait of Alfred James Newton, who
served the last Shrievalty of London and
Middlesex (1888–89)
Oil on canvas
60 x 48in (152 x 122cm)
£500–700 *GH*

John Robert Wildman
British (active 1823–39)
Portrait of Arthur Wellesley,
1st Duke of Wellington
Oil on Canvas
30 x 25in (76 x 64cm)
£3,500–4,000 *C*

*'Wellington was 5ft 9in in height, spare and
muscular, with aquiline features and
penetrating grey eyes,' records the DNB. He
was described by one contemporary in 1814
as 'remarkably neat, and most particular in
his dress, considering his situation. He is well
made, knows it, and is willing to set off to the
best what nature has bestowed.' Among
nature's gifts was a very prominent nose.
As well as being nicknamed the 'Iron Duke',
Wellington was also called 'Old Nosey'.
'We would rather see his long nose in a fight
than a reinforcement of 10,000 men a day,'
claimed one of his captains.*

Henry Bryan Ziegler
British (1798–1874)
Portrait of the Marquis
of Westminster, and
another of The Lady
Elizabeth Lawley
Inscribed and
numbered '18',
watercolour over pencil
17 x 12⅜in (43 x 33cm)
£400–600 *P*

20th Century

Pietro Annigoni
Italian (1910–88)
Portrait of Mr. Austin Reidy
Signed, signed with monogram,
inscribed and dated '69',
oil on canvas
20 x 16in (51 x 40.5cm)
£7,000–8,000 *CSK*

Adam Birtwistle
British (20thC)
Münchausen by Proxy
Diptych, tempera and gouache
26 x 30in (66 x 76cm)
£2,000–2,250 each *PN*

William Conor, R.H.A.
Irish (1884–1968)
The Road Sweeper
Signed, coloured crayons
17 x 12½in (43 x 32cm)
£2,800–3,000 *S*

Francis Bacon
British (1909–92)
Study for a Portrait
Oil on canvas
20 x 16in (51 x 41cm)
£565,000–600,000 *S*

*Bacon tries to convey a presence
beyond likeness and which
transcends the mere depiction of
physical qualities. He once said to
David Sylvester, 'When I look at you
across the table I don't only see you
but I see a whole emanation which
has to do with personality and
everything else. And to put that over
in a painting, as I would like to be
able to do in a portrait, means that
it would appear violent in paint.' As
he explained to the Observer in
1985, 'I deform and dislocate people
into appearance, or hope to.'*

Edward Dawson, N.E.A.C.
British (b1941)
The Essay
Signed, oil on canvas
14 x 11in (35.5 x 28cm)
£600–700 *JN*

Margaret Dovaston
British (active 1908–1913)
Huntsman's Yarn
Signed, oil on canvas
18½ x 25in (46.5 x 63cm)
£9,000–10,000 *P*

William Gropper
American (1897–1977)
The Villagers
Signed, oil on canvas
26 x 30in (66 x 76cm)
£5,000–6,000   *S(NY)*

Dame Elisabeth Frink, C.H., R.A.
British (1930–93)
Green Man (blue)
Signed and numbered from the
edition of 70, original screenprint
in colours, 1992
22½ x 20½in (57 x 52cm)
£400–470   *WO*

Philip Harris
British (b1965)
Portrait of John Leather
Oil on canvas
20in (51cm) square
£6,000–6,500   *Mer*

Peter Howson
Scottish (b1958)
Studio
Etching, an edition of 50
10 x 13in (50 x 56cm)
£200–225   *GPS*

John Jensen
British (b1930)
Alfred Hitchcock
Signed, inscribed and punch below mount,
monochrome watercolour
4 x 4¾in (10 x 10.5cm)
£200–250   *CBL*

Augustus John
British (1878–1961)
William Butler Yeats
Signed, etching
7 x 5in (17.5 x 12.5cm)
£1,000–1,400   *Bon*

Henri Lebasque
French (1865–1937)
Le Jardinier
Signed, oil on paper laid
down on board
15¾ x 10¾in (39 x 27cm)
£3,000–3,500   *S*

Ken Moroney
British (20thC)
The Photographer
Signed, pencil
6½ x 4½in (16 x 11cm)
£100–200   *GK*

Pablo Picasso
Spanish (1881–1973)
L'Amateur ou Deux Personnages
Signed, 1901, conté crayon
8¾ x 6⅜in (22 x 17cm)
£130,000–140,000 *C*

Patrick Procktor
British (20thC)
Russians on Holiday
Signed and dated '67',
watercolour and wash
9 x 11in (22.5 x 28cm)
£500–700 *CSK*

Zsuzsi Roboz
Hungarian (20thC)
Sir George Solti
Signed, charcoal drawing
36 x 28½in (91.5 x 72cm)
£13,000–14,000 *RMG*

Ibrahim El Salahi
Sudanese (b1929)
Untitled
Signed and dated '1992', pen and
ink on paper
10 x 13¾in (25 x 35cm)
£1,800–2,000 *SG*

Julian Schnabel
American (b1951)
Portrait of Patrick, 1989
Oil, plates, bondo and epoxy
on wood
84 x 56in (213 x 142cm)
£35,000–45,000 *S(NY)*

Antoni Sulek
British/Polish (20thC)
Blue Figure
Oil on board
24 x 16in (61 x 40.5cm)
£250–350 *VCG*

Henry Scott Tuke, R.A.
British (1858–1929)
Chippy the Dog
Watercolour, c1924
10 x 7in (25.5 x 18cm)
£7,000–8,000 *C*

LAFITTE THE PIRATE

Jack Butler Yeats, R.H.A.
Irish (1871–1957)
Lafitte the Pirate
Signed and inscribed, pen black
ink and watercolour, 1905
14¾ x 10½in (37.5 x 26.5cm)
£22,000–25,000 *S*

*Yeats and his friend John
Masefield invented the character
of a foppish young pirate,
Théodore, and Jean Lafitte was
his captain. Although many
drawings exist of Théodore in
various escapades, this work is
the only known portrayal of
Lafitte, and unlike Théodore he
was based upon a real historical
figure whose story Masefield
researched. He was a French
smuggler and pirate of the late
18thC and early 19thC who,
despite a fearsome reputation,
was pardoned by the Americans
for his courage at the Battle of
New Orleans and eventually died
in penury in Honduras.*

WOMEN
16th–17th Century

Circle of Arnold Boonen
Dutch (1669–1729)
Portrait of a Lady, holding a Parrot
Oil on canvas
32 x 25in (81.5 x 63.5cm)
£1,800–2,200 *CSK*

After Hans van Aachen
German (1552–1616)
The Three Graces
Oil on panel
19¼ x 24¼in (49 x 62cm)
£1,400–1,600 *S(NY)*

Simon van der Does
Dutch (c1653–after 1718)
Portrait of a Lady
Signed, and date '1679' added later,
oil on canvas
27 x 21¾in (69 x 55cm)
£4,800–5,500 *S*

Carlo Cignani
Italian (1628–1719)
Study of a Head
Red chalk
7¾ x 5¾in (19 x 14cm)
£1,200–1,500 *P*

After Gerard Dou
Dutch (1616–75)
A Woman watering Flowers
at a Window Ledge
Oil on panel
14½ x 11in (37 x 28cm)
£2,700–3,500 *CSK*

Follower of Hans Eworth
British (active c1540–73)
Portrait of Elizabeth Bowes
Inscribed with sitter's
age '28', and dated '1562',
oil on panel
17¼ x 13¼in (44 x 34cm)
£9,000–10,000 *S*

*The sitter was the daughter
of Sir Martin Bowes, Lord
Mayor of London and
Jeweller to Elizabeth I. She
was born in 1534 and
married Sir George Hart
(1533–87) of Lullingstone
Castle, Kent.*

Domenikos Theotokopoulos, El Greco
Spanish (1541–1614)
Portrait of a Young Lady
Signed, oil on canvas
19¾ x 16½in (50.5 x 42cm)
£1,700,000–2,000,000 *C*

*Portraits by El Greco are extremely rare. This
work is one of only three women known to be
by the artist. A number of suggestions have been
made as to the sitter's identity, including the
possibility that she might be El Greco's
daughter-in-law. Although the condition of
the picture gave rise to some concern, the
portrait reached a record hammer price at
auction for El Greco of £1.5 million and
would, the auctioneers believe, have gone even
higher had the condition been better.*

Sir Peter Lely
British (1618–80)
Portrait of a Lady, called Nell Gwynne
Oil on canvas
48½ x 39½in (123.5 x 100.5cm)
£22,000–30,000 *S*

*If royal portraits can carry a premium, so can the
images of royal mistresses. This trio, portrayed
by Lely or his studio, were all the mistresses of
Charles II. 'Pretty, witty, Nell,' as Samuel Pepys
called her, was an actress and an orange seller at
the Theatre Royal, Drury Lane. Lively, funny and
down-to-earth she was extremely popular with
the British public who saw her as a home grown
rival to Charles's principal mistress, the French
Roman Catholic, Louise de Keroualle, Duchess of
Portsmouth.Once in Oxford, when an angry mob
surrounded Nell Gwynne's carriage, thinking it
to contain her rival, she thrust out her head and
told them: 'Pray good people be civil; I am the
Protestant whore.' 'She's now the darling
strumpet of the crowd,' noted the Earl of
Rochester, admiringly. Louise de Keroualle was
cordially hated for her race, her religion and the
influence she wielded over the king. 'This French
hag's poky bum / So powerful is of late / Although
it's both blind and dumb /
It rules both church and state,' jeered an
anonymous satire in 1680. Barbara Villiers was
another mistress famed for both her extravagance
(in one night alone she lost £20,000 at cards) and
her lust. In addition to the king, her list of
paramours ranged from dukes to rope dancers. It
was 'as if she sinned for exercise,' commented
Rochester cynically.*

Studio of Sir Peter Lely
British (1618–80)
Portrait of a Lady, probably Barbara Villiers,
Duchess of Cleveland
Oil on canvas
29½ x 24½in (75 x 62cm)
£1,800–2,200 *S*

Jacopo Ligozzi
Italian (1547–1626)
A Woman's Head in Profile
Pen and brown ink over black chalk,
laid down
11¾ x 8in (30.5 x 20cm)
£110,000–120,000 *P*

*Born in Verona in 1547, Jacopo Ligozzi was
called to the Medici Court in Florence in 1577
by Franceso I de' Medici, the beginning of a
long association with the Grand Dukes of
Tuscany. On Francesco's death in 1587,
Ligozzi continued to serve his successors,
Cosimo II and Ferdinando II.*

Thomas Murray
British (1663–1735)
Portrait of Henrietta Auverquerque,
Countess of Grantham
Oil on canvas
89 x 53in (226 x 134cm)
£6,500–8,000 *C*

Attributed to Frans van Mieris the Elder
Dutch (1635–1681)
Peasant Girl wearing a Head Shawl
Inscribed recto, black chalk
5¼ x 5in (13 x 12.5cm)
£2,000–2,500 *P*

Circle of Herman van de Mijn
Dutch or Flemish (1684–1741)
Portrait of Catherine Sedley,
Countess of Dorchester
Inscribed, oil on canvas
50 x 40¼in (127 x 102cm)
£3,500–4,500 *C*

John Michael Wright
British (1617–94)
Portrait of Lady Elizabeth Somerset,
Lady Powis
Oil on canvas
49 x 39in (124.5 x 99cm)
£22,000–25,000 *S*

Circle of Simon Verelst
Dutch (1644–1710)
Portrait of a Lady
Oil on canvas
30 x 25in (76.5 x 63.5cm)
£2,500–3,000 *WWG*

18th Century

Attributed to Thomas Bardwell
British (1704–67)
Portrait of Mary Jodrell
Dated '1755', oil on canvas
19 x 14½in (48 x 37cm)
£3,000–4,000 *S*

Thomas Beach, R.A.
British (1738–1806)
Portrait of Mrs Siddons in the
character of Melancholy, from
Milton's *'Il Penseroso'*.
Oil on canvas
48½ x 34¾in (123 x 88cm)
£19,000–22,000 *S*

William Redmore Bigg, R.A.
British (1755–1828)
Nutting
Signed, oil on canvas
29 x 24in (74 x 61cm)
£4,500–5,500 *S*

Giovanni Agostino Cassana
Italian (1658–1720)
A Peasant pouring Water into a Cauldron
Oil on canvas
53½ x 40in (136 x 101.5cm)
£26,000–30,000 *C*

Daniel Chodowiecki
German (1726–1801)
Portrait of a Young Woman
Inscribed verso, black and red chalk
14½ x 11¼in (37 x 28.5cm)
£4,000–6,000 *C*

George Dawe, R.A.
British (1781–1829)
Portrait of Mrs White (née Watford)
Signed and dated '1809', il on canvas
88½ x 54½in (223.5 x 138.5cm)
£180,000–200,000 *C*

*George Dawe is probably most celebrated
today as having been created 'First Portrait
Painter of the Imperial Court' by Tsar
Alexander I of Russia. The early part of his
career, however, was spent in London.
Estimated at only £20,000–30,000, this
beautiful portrait rocketed to fetch a final
hammer price of £160,000. 'It was highly
decorative, very unusual and a very rare
picture,' a delighted John Stainton told
Miller's. 'It really fetched an enormous
amount of money and I think we have set a
benchmark for prices of Dawe's work, which
will prove difficult to beat.'*

Balthasar Denner
German (1685–1749)
A Girl with Flowers in her Hair
Signed and inscribed recto, dated '1736',
oil on copper
15 x 12¼in (38 x 31cm)
£4,200–5,000 *C*

John Downman, A.R.A.
British (1750–1824)
Portrait of a Young Lady
Signed with initials, indistinctly dated,
watercolour and black chalk
5¾ x 4⅜in (14.5 x 12cm)
£520–700 *S(S)*

Manner of Jean-Baptiste Greuze
French (1725–1805)
A Milkmaid, and a Flower Girl
A Pair, oil on canvas
23½ x 19½in (60 x 50cm)
£4,000–4,500 *C*

Attributed to John Ellys
British (c1701–57)
Portrait of Lavinia Fenton, Duchess of Bolton
Oil on canvas
35½ x 27¼in (90 x 70cm)
£5,000–6,000 *S*

*The sitter was a successful actress and
mistress of the Duke of Bolton. He finally
married her in 1752, a few months after the
death of his first wife.*

John Hoppner, R.A.
British (1758–1810)
Portrait of Jane, Countess of
Westmoreland as Hebe
Oil on canvas
29½ x 24½ in (75 x 62cm)
£17,500–20,000 *S*

*The sitter was the second daughter of Richard
Huck Saunders. She married John, 10th Earl
of Westmoreland, in 1800.*

John Hoppner, R.A.
British (1758–1810)
Portrait of Miss Elizabeth Beresford
Oil on canvas
30 x 25in (76 x 63.5cm)
£45,000–50,000 *S*

Jens Juel
Danish (1745–1802)
Portrait of a Young Woman in
Circassian Costume
Oil on canvas
38½ x 29in (98 x 74cm)
£17,500–20,000 *C*

Follower of Angelica Kauffman
Swiss (1740–1807)
Portrait of Madame Andeval, née d'Aiguillon
Oil on canvas
25 x 20¾in (64 x 52.5cm)
£5,000–6,000 *S*

Circle of Louis-Jean-François Lagrenée
French (1725–1805)
Portrait of a Lady wearing a
blue lined Straw Hat
With signature and dated '1747'
39½ x 29½in (100.5 x 75cm)
£3,000–3,500 *C*

Follower of Antoine Pesne
French (1683–1757)
Portrait of a Lady
Oil on canvas, laid down on panel
17½ x 14in (45 x 35.5cm)
£850–1,000 *CSK*

After James Northcote, R.A.
British (1746–1831)
The Alpine Traveller, by J. Ward
Mezzotint, published by J. Jeffryes,
London, 1804
24 x 17¾in (61 x 45cm)
£400–500 *CSK*

Sir Joshua Reynolds, P.R.A.
British (1723–92)
Portrait of Annabella, Lady Blake,
as Juno Receiving the Cestus from Venus
Oil on canvas
93¼ x 57½in (237 x 146cm)
£48,000–55,000 *S*

George Romney and Studio
British (1734–1802)
Portrait of Mrs Jordan as Peggy in
The Country Girl
Oil on canvas
59½ x 47½in (150 x 120cm)
£13,000–15,000 *C*

George Romney
British (1734–1802)
Portrait of Emma Hamilton
Oil on canvas
17 x 13½in (43 x 34cm)
£22,000–25,000 *S*

*Emma Hamilton (1761–1815), wife
of Sir William Hamilton, mistress of
Admiral Horatio Nelson, and favourite
muse of George Romney, was regarded as
one of the most beautiful women of the
age. On first meeting her, Sir William
declared that she was lovelier 'than
anything found in nature; and finer
in her particular way than anything
that is to be found in antique art.'
Romney painted her ceaselessly, and
with his dying breath, Nelson begged
that the nation should look after her.
It did not, and Emma Hamilton died in
Calais, penniless and largely forgotten, in
1815. She is anything but forgotten today
and a statue was erected in Calais in 1994.*

**Miller's is a price GUIDE
not a price LIST**

Circle of George Romney
British (1734–1802)
Portrait of a Muse
Oil on canvas
30 x 25in (76 x 63.5cm)
£750–900 *CSK*

Pietro Antonio Rotari
Italian (1707–62)
A Young Woman
Oil on canvas
17¼ x 13½in (44 x 34.5cm)
£10,500–12,000 *S*

Circle of John Raphael Smith
British (1752–1812)
Portrait of a Lady, and a
Portrait of a Gentleman
A pair, oil on panel
9½ x 7½in (24 x 19cm)
£1,800–2,500 *CSK*

John Russell, R.A.
British (1745–1806)
Portrait of Mrs Carruthers
Pastel
24 x 19in (61 x 48cm)
£2,500–3,000 *S*

Jean-Joseph Taillasson
French (1745–1809)
A Study of a Young Woman
Signed and dated '1783',
oil on canvas
21¾ x 18in (55 x 46cm)
£3,000–3,500 *S*

Louis Vigée
French (1715–67)
Portrait of a Girl Holding a
Giamblette and her Dog
Signed, pastel on paper
mounted on canvas
22 x 18in (56 x 46cm)
£10,000–11,000 *S(NY)*

John Vanderbank
British (1694–1739)
Portrait of Elizabeth Innes
Signed and dated '1736', oil on canvas
49¼ x 39½in (125 x 100.5cm)
£7,000–7,500 *S*

John Zoffany, R.A.
British (1733–1810)
Portrait of Lady Elizabeth Noel
Inscribed, oil on canvas
30 x 25in (76 x 64cm)
£60,000–70,000
*The sitter was the daughter
of Baptist Noel, 4th Earl of
Gainsborough who married
in 1728, Elizabeth, daughter
of his gamekeeper, William
Chapman. This marriage
was not declared until 1736.
On Lord Gainsborough's
death in 1751, his widow
married Thomas Noel of
Walcot, Northamptonshire.*

Manner of Jean Antoine Watteau
French (18thC)
A Young Peasant Girl resting with
a dog at her side
Oil on panel
16 x 12in (40.5 x 30.5cm)
£850–1,000 *CSK*

Willem Verelst
British School (active 1734–56)
Portrait of Eleanor Mytton
Signed, inscribed and dated '1738',
oil on canvas
48¾ x 39½in (124 x 100cm)
£6,000–7,000 *S*

19th Century

The following section devoted to 19thC women shows the tireless demand for decorative pictures of attractive subjects. Many of the works illustrated are not portraits but genre pictures - pink cheeked peasant maids, young girls reading their first love letters, women contemplating in the garden or titivating in the dressing room. The women they represent are ideal rather than real, Victorian archetypes of female and feminine beauty.

American School (19thC)
Portrait of a Lady with a starched organdie collar
Oil on canvas
23 x 18in (59 x 45.5cm)
£1,000–1,500 *S(NY)*

Sophie Anderson
British (1823–1903)
The Love Letter
Signed, oil on canvas
53 x 38½in (134.5 x 97.5cm)
£32,000–40,000 *L*

Giuseppe Aureli
Italian (1858–1929)
Preparing for the Ball
Signed and inscribed, pencil and watercolour heightened with white
20¼ x 13¼in (51 x 34cm)
£800–1,000 *CSK*

Federico Andreotti
Italian (1847–1930)
The Love Letter
Signed, oil on canvas
31¾ x 27in (80.5 x 69cm)
£20,000–25,000 *S(NY)*

William F. Ashburner
British (19th/20thC)
The Squire's Daughter and
The Gardener's Daughter
A pair, both signed, watercolour
10¼ x 7in (26.5 x 17.5cm)
£1,000–1,200 *AH*

Jules Frederick Ballavoine
French (active 1880–1901)
Reminiscing
Signed, oil on canvas
18 x 12in (45.5 x 30.5cm)
£13,000–14,000 *HFA*

Charles Baugniet
Belgian (1814–86)
Expectation
Signed with initials, oil on canvas
23 x 17in (58.5 x 43cm)
£5,500–6,500 *EG*

Eugène de Blaas
Austrian (1843–1931)
A Rest from Washing
Signed and dated '1895', oil on panel
31½ x 15½in (80 x 39.5cm)
£30,000–35,000 *S(NY)*

Luigi Bechi
Italian (1830–1919)
Portrait of a Young Girl
Signed, oil on canvas
19½ x 15¾in (49.5 x 40cm)
£6,000–7,000 *P*

Mosè Bianchi
Italian (1840–1904)
A Fair Beauty
Signed, oil on board
27 x 19½in (68.5 x 49.5cm)
£11,500–12,500 *C*

Follower of Eugène de Blaas
Austrian (1843–1931)
The Love Token
With signature 'E. Ferroni',
oil on canvas
35 x 24½in (89 x 62cm)
£1,400–1,600 *CSK*

François Bonvin
French (1817–87)
La Lecture
Signed and dated '1853',
charcoal on paper
12½ x 9in (31.5 x 23cm)
£15,000–18,000 *S(NY)*

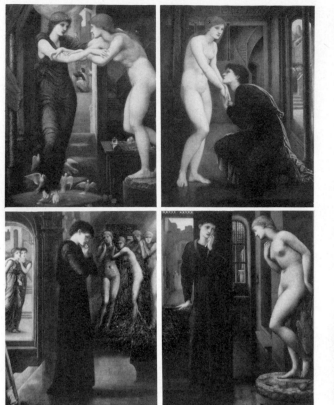

Sir Edward Coley Burne-Jones, A.R.A.
British (1833–98)
The Pygmalion Series
A series of 4, each signed and dated '1868'
or '1870', all oil on canvas
26 x 20in (66 x 50.5cm)
£675,000–700,000 *S*

*Burne-Jones's series of four pictures was
inspired by William Morris's poem*
Pygmalion and the Image, *but as Sotheby's
stressed in their catalogue entry, the works
also had a much more personal significance
for the artist.*

L. Borgognoni
Italian (19thC)
Secrets
Signed, oil on canvas
78¾ x 37¾in (200 x 96cm)
£5,200–6,000 *S*

> **Miller's is a price GUIDE
> not a price LIST**

Augustus Jules Bouvier
British (active 1866–94)
The Fruit Picker
Signed, pencil and watercolour
20 x 12in (50.5 x 30.5cm)
£950–1,200 *CSK*

Ulisse Caputo
Italian (1872–1948)
After the Ball
Signed and dated, oil on canvas
25¼ x 19¾in (65 x 50cm)
£5,000–6,000 *C*

William Adolphe Bouguereau
French (1825–1905)
La Faucheuse
Signed and dated '1872', oil on canvas
70½ x 45½in (179 x 116cm)
£130,000–150,000 *S(NY)*

What's in ANTIQUES BULLETIN?

☞ The most comprehensive Auction Calendar

☞ The only weekly Fairs Calendar

☞ More news and prices than any other antiques trade publication

Plus

Art Prices Index ◆ Saleroom Reports ◆ Fairs News
Exhibitions ◆ Talking the Trade ◆ Features

Subscribe NOW and receive a FREE subscription to the Antiques Fairs Guide – a publication that no serious fair goer can afford to miss.

1 years' subscription is £39.50 UK (46 issues), Europe £60.00, USA/Canada £80.00, Australia/New Zealand £120.00

Whether you are a dealer, a collector, or just furnishing your home, a subscription to Antiques Bulletin makes sense.

Subscribe to what interests you most

Each week on a four-weekly rotation, we focus on:

1. Furniture, clocks, bronzes and architectural items;
2. Silver, ceramics, glassware and jewellery;
3. Art and sculpture; and
4. Collectables.

Subscribe to all four if you wish, or choose one, two or three sectors from the four – please phone for details.

Mary Cassatt
American (1845–1926)
The Lamp or l'Abat-Jour
Drypoint, softground and
aquatint, 1890-91
12½ x 10in (32 x 25.5cm)
£60,000–65,000 *S(NY)*

Pierre J. Edmund Castan
French (b1817)
Reading the News
Oil on panel
13 x 10in (33 x 25.5cm)
£8,500–9,500 *HFA*

Edward Clifford
British (1844–1907)
Katrine, Countess Cowper
Signed, inscribed, and dated
'1875', watercolour heightened
with bodycolour, with
scratching out
25 x 19¾in (63.5 x 50cm)
£12,500–14,000 *C*

*Clifford was a follower of
Burne-Jones. He specialised in
portraits of the aristocracy,
generally painting life-sized
bust-length likenesses in
watercolour.*

John Watkins Chapman
British (active 1853–1903)
Waiting at the Gate
Signed, oil on panel
8¼ x 7in (21 x 18cm)
£500–600 *AG*

John da Costa
British (1867–1931)
The Glen Walker Sisters
Signed, oil on canvas
90 x 56in (228.5 x 142cm)
£45,000–55,000 *S(NY)*

*Commissioned in 1895 by his future father-in-
law, William Glen Walker, and exhibited at
the Royal Academy of 1904, this painting is
an entrancing and forceful symbol of
Edwardian opulence and aristocratic
confidence. Its grand size and bold brushwork
reinforce the Edwardian society portraitist's
idealised depiction of aristocracy and of
detached youthful beauty. Similar to the
work of his celebrated contemporary, John
Singer Sargent, da Costa mirrors the
Edwardian soul and its self-image with
calm brilliance.*

William Banks Fortescue
British (d1924)
Distant Thoughts
Signed, oil on canvas
16 x 12in (41 x 30.5cm)
£1,200–1,500 *CSK*

Fanny Fleury
French (19thC)
Young Parisian under a Tree
Signed and dated, oil on panel
8½ x 16in (21.5 x 41cm)
£3,200–4,000 S

Henri Fantin-Latour
French (1836–1904)
Tête de Femme
Stamped signature and dated '19 Oct 1865'
pen, brush, ink and charcoal on paper laid
down on card
7½ x 6¼in (19 x 16cm)
£5,200–5,500 S

Walter Gay
American (1856–1937)
Quiétude/An Interior Scene with
a Young Woman Reading
Signed and dated '1882',
watercolour on paper
15¼ x 21in (39 x 53cm)
£700–900 SK

Enrico Gobbi
Italian (19thC)
Lady Picking Roses
Signed, oil on canvas
28 x 39¼in (71 x 100cm)
£2,500–3,000 *S*

Louis Emile Pinel de Grandchamp
French (d1894)
Idle Moments
Signed, oil on canvas
31½ x 25½in (80 x 65cm)
£22,000–25,000 *C*

Kate Gray
British (19thC)
In Contemplation
Signed and dated '1887', oil on canvas
35 x 28in (89 x 71cm)
£4,000–4,500 *HLG*

Charles Edward Hallé
British (1846–1914)
Luna
Signed, oil on canvas
27 x 20in (69 x 51cm)
£30,000–35,000 *C*

Vincent van Gogh
Dutch (1853–90)
Tête de Paysanne
Oil on canvas, 1884
16 x 12in (40.5 x 30.5cm)
£180,000–220,000 *C*

Edwin Harris
British (1855–1906)
Arranging Irises
Signed and dated '1897', oil on canvas
24 x 30in (61 x 76cm)
£17,000–20,000 *S*

Sidney W. Hodges
British (19thC)
Portrait of a young Woman holding a Dog
Signed and dated '1867', oil on canvas
36 x 28in (91.5 x 71cm)
£250–350 *GH*

S. Hodgson
British (19thC)
Summer Contentment on the
River Thames at Pangbourne
Signed and dated '1870', oil on canvas
30 x 20in (76 x 51cm)
£1,600–1,900 *SAV*

Gustave de Jonghe
Belgian (1829–93)
The Confidante
Signed, oil on canvas
15 x 11½in (38 x 29cm)
£9,000–10,000 *C*

Paul-César Helleu
French (1859–1927)
Portrait of a Lady
Signed, pencil, charcoal and coloured
chalks heightened with white
28¾ x 14¾in (73 x 37.5cm)
£5,500–7,000 *P*

Elizabeth Alida Kiers Haanen
Dutch (1809–45)
The Fish Seller
Oil on panel
14 x 12in (35.5 x 30.5cm)
£11,000–12,000   HFA

George Goodwin Kilburne
British (1839–1924)
Miss Pinkerton's Academy
Signed, watercolour heightened
with bodycolour
27 x 38½in (69 x 98cm)
£18,500–20,000   S

H. J. Yeend King
British (1855–1924)
The Pretty Water Girl
Signed and dated '1854', oil on canvas
16 x 20in (40.5 x 50.5cm)
£8,500–9,500   C

Gustav Koller
German (b1870)
The Message
Signed, oil on panel
24 x 16in (61 x 41cm)
£18,000–20,000   HFA

Ivan Kramskoi
Russian (1837–87)
Lady in Black
Signed, oil on canvas
20 x 16in (51 x 41cm)
£4,000–5,000   EG

Henry le Jeune, A.R.A.
British (1819–1904)
The Love Letter
Monogrammed and dated '1871',
oil on panel
22 x 16in (56 x 41cm)
£14,000–15,000 HFA

Circle of Charles Robert Leslie
British (1794–1859)
A group portrait of the
Barclay Sisters
Oil on canvas
30 x 25in (76.5 x 64cm)
£1,750–2,000 CSK

John Linnell
British (1792–1882)
Portrait of Mrs Naysmith,
née Walker
Signed and dated '1836',
watercolour and coloured chalks
22 x 15¾in (56 x 40cm)
£600–800 P

Sir James Dromgole Linton, P.R.I.
British (1840–1916)
In the Library
Signed and dated '1897', oil on board
13 x 10¾in (33 x 27cm)
£1,300–1,800 C

François Martin-Kavel
French (1861–1931)
Jeune fille au Manchon et à la
Branche de Houx
Signed, oil on panel
32 x 25¼in (81 x 64cm)
£10,000–12,000 S(NY)

Edouard Menta
French (b1858)
Delivering the Wedding Dress
Signed, oil on canvas
32 x 24in (81 x 61cm)
£1,500–1,800 CSK

Jean-François Millet
French (1814–75)
Woman Sweeping her Home
Black chalk on paper laid down on board
12 x 9in (30.5 x 23cm)
£80,000–100,000 C

*Caught in the sunlight from her doorway, brushing dust and
scraps towards the threshold, the provincial housewife of 'Woman
Sweeping her Home' is one of a number of thoughtful depictions
of peasant women tending their hearths and their families that
appear throughout Millet's art. This drawing was probably
created about 1857–60, years when Millet devoted a large portion
of his time to making finished drawings for a small group of
devoted collectors, as well as a few supportive Paris dealers. It is
unusual to find so finished a Millet drawing that is unsigned.
Most carefully drawn scenes of peasant life were either
commissioned by private collectors or were created for sale in a
speculative art market where artists' signatures were an expected
feature of finished works. One can only guess that Millet may
have given 'Woman Sweeping' to a friend or artist colleague for
whom a signature might have seemed superfluous.*

Alphonse Mucha
Czechoslovakian (1892–1939)
The Ivy, final drawing for the
Paneau Decoratif
Signed, pencil and watercolour, Paris, 1901
12¾ x 12in (32 x 30.5cm)
£29,000–30,000 *GRO*

*Born in Moravia, Alphonse Mucha was one of
the leading exponents of Art Nouveau. He is
best known for his poster designs,
characterised by luxurious flowing lines and
light, clear colours. Many were made in Paris
in the 1890s for Sarah Bernhardt for whom
he also designed stage sets and costumes.*

Octavius Oakley, O.W.S.
British (1800–67)
The Midday Rest
Signed and dated '1860', pencil and
watercolour with scratching out
18¾ x 13½in (48 x 34cm)
£1,500–2,000 *C*

Antoine Emile Plassan
French (1817–1903)
Preparing for the Ball
Signed, oil on panel
16 x 12½in (40.5 x 31.5cm)
£3,500–4,500 *S*

Leo Putz
German (1869–1940)
Promenade
Signed, oil on canvas, c1903
39½ x 29½in (101 x 75cm)
£70,000–80,000 *C*

Edward H. Potthast
American (1857–1927)
The Washerwoman
Signed, oil on canvas
24 x 20in (61 x 50.5cm)
£4,000–5,000 *S(NY)*

Henrietta Rae
British (1859–1928)
Spring
Signed, oil on canvas
72½ x 37¾in (184 x 96cm)
£15,000–18,000 *S*

Pierre Auguste Renoir
French (1841–1919)
Jeune Fille portant une Corbeille de Fleurs, 1888
Signed, oil on canvas
32 x 26in (81 x 66cm)
£6,000,000–7,000,000 *C*

*'Jeune Fille portant une Corbeille de Fleurs' was one of the
major achievements of Renoir's oeuvre during 1888 and he
painted no less than three versions of it. It exemplifies
Octave Mirbeau's celebration of Renoir's qualities as a figure
painter. 'He is truly the painter of woman, in turn gracious
and moved, knowing and simple, always elegant with an
exquisite sensitiveness of eye, with caresses of the hand light
as kisses, with visions profound as those of Stendhal.'*

Sir William Blake Richmond, R.A.
British (1842–1921)
Study of a Woman's Head for
The Song of Miriam
Dated 'July 1880', black and white chalk
on blue grey paper
8¾ x 6in (22 x 15cm)
£1,000–1,400 *C*

Dante Gabriel Rossetti
British (1828–82)
Study for a Pall-bearer in *Dante's Dream*
Monogrammed and dated '1873', pencil with
red and brown chalk on grey-green paper, on
two joined sheets
33 x 22¼in (84 x 56.5cm)
£17,000–20,000 *C*

*This drawing is a study for the figure of the
pall-bearing attendant on the right in the
second version of* Dante's Dream at the Time
of the Death of Beatrice.

Félicien Joseph Victor Rops
Belgian (1833–98)
Modernité
Signed with initials, pencil, and
coloured chalk heightened
with white
8 x 6in (20 x 15cm)
£4,000–5,000 *C*

Harold Speed
British (1872–1957)
Portrait of the Artist's Wife
Signed and dated '1904', red chalk
13 x 9½in (33 x 24cm)
£1,500–2,000 *C*

Charles Spencelayh
British (1865–1958)
Ironing Day
Signed, oil on canvas
18 x 12in (46 x 30.5cm)
£4,000–5,000 *C*

Jules Emile Saintin
French (1829–94)
La Ménagère
Signed and dated '1886', oil on canvas
18 x 14in (46 x 36cm)
£20,000–25,000 *S(NY)*

Frederic Soulacroix
French (1825–79)
The Elegant Connoisseur
Signed, oil on canvas
29¾ x 18¼in (76 x 46.5cm)
£14,000–16,000 *P*

Henry Thomas Schafer
Franco/British (19thC)
On the Balcony
Signed, oil on canvas
28¾ x 17¾in (73 x 45cm)
£600–800 *P*

John Scott
British (1850–1918)
The Love Letter
Signed, watercolour
10½ x 14¾in (26 x 38cm)
£700–900 *AG*

Alfred Stevens
Belgian (1823–1906)
The Blue Bonnet
Signed, oil on canvas
19½ x 15¾in (49.5 x 40cm)
£20,000–25,000 *S(NY)*

Joaquín Sorolla y Bastida
Spanish (1863–1923)
Gitana
Signed and dated '1912', oil on canvas
43½ x 25in (110.5 x 64cm)
£220,000–250,000 *S(NY)*

This painting of a gypsy girl reflects the artist's lifelong interest in depicting aspects of Spanish life and culture.

Moritz Stifter
Austrian (1857–1905)
Portrait of a Woman in Elegant Dress
Signed, oil on panel
10 x 7¾in (25 x 19.5cm)
£2,000–2,500 *CNY*

Henri de Toulouse-Lautrec
French (1864–1901)
Divan Japonais
Lithograph printed in colours, 1893
31½ x 24¼in (80 x 61.5cm)
£11,500–13,000 *S(NY)*

James Jacques Joseph Tissot
French (1836–1902)
Octobre
Etching and drypoint, 1878
24½ x 15¾in (62 x 40cm)
£9,000–10,000 *S*

Ralph Todd
British (active 1880–93)
A Fishergirl
Signed, watercolour
17 x 13in (43 x 33cm)
£900–1,000 *BWe*

Thomas Uwins, R.A.
British (1782–1857)
Lacemakers
Signed, watercolour over pencil
9½ x 14½in (24 x 37cm)
£2,500–3,000 *S*

Arthur Langley Vernon
British (active 1871–c1922)
The Fortune Teller
Signed and dated '80',
oil on canvas
21 x 14in (53 x 36cm)
£2,000–2,500 *CSK*

Locate the Source

*The source of each
illustration in Miller's
can be found by checking
the code letters below
each caption with the list
of contributors.*

Eugène Verdyen
Belgian (1836–1903)
Portrait of a Lady with a Fan
Signed, oil on canvas
21¼ x 15¾in (54 x 40cm)
£3,500–4,500 *S*

Charles Louis Verwée
Belgian (19thC)
La Lecture
Signed, oil on panel
30¾ x 23½in (78 x 60cm)
£10,000–12,000 *S(NY)*

Arthur Wardle
British (1864–1949)
Fanny
Signed and dated '93', watercolour
7 x 5¼in (17.5 x 13cm)
£875–975 *WrG*

A. C. Weatherstone
British (active 1888–1929)
Summer
Signed, watercolour
14 x 10in (36 x 25cm)
£1,650–1,850 *HLG*

John William Waterhouse, R.A.
British (1849–1917)
Ophelia
Signed, oil on canvas
49 x 29in (124.5 x 74cm)
£450,000–500,000 *S*

The subject of Ophelia was treated by many of the Pre-Raphaelite painters and Waterhouse returned to it three times. Though when the present work was first exhibited in 1894, critic F.G. Stephens complained caustically that it showed 'little of Ophelia's madness and distress, and not much of her pain or sorrow,' no one could argue with the work's seductive and decorative beauty. Auctioned by Sotheby's in 1993, it shot way over its £180,000–220,000 estimate.

Driven mad by Hamlet's neglect and the murder of her father, Polonius, Ophelia decks herself with garlands of flowers prior to her death by drowning. The scene is graphically described by Queen Gertrude in Hamlet, *Act IV, scene 7:*

There is a willow grows aslant a brook,
That shows his hoar leaves in the glassy stream;
There with fantastic garlands did she come,
Of crow-flowers, nettles, daisies, and long purples,
That liberal shepherds give a grosser name,
But our cold maids do dead man's fingers call them:
There, on the pendant boughs her coronet weeds
Clambering to hang, an envious sliver broke,
When down her weedy trophies and herself
Fell in the weeping brook.

Micah Williams
American (1782–1837)
Portrait of a Young Woman
Oil on canvas, c1830
29¾ x 24in (76 x 61cm)
£3,500–4,500 *S(NY)*

John Riley Wilmer
British (active 1905–26)
Constance in Captivity
Signed and dated '1929',
watercolour
11 x 9in (28 x 22.5cm)
£2,500–3,000 *S*

H. Wyatt
British (1794–1840)
Portrait of a Lady with a
King Charles Spaniel
Oil on canvas
50 x 40in (127 x 101.5cm)
£12,000–12,500 *SAV*

David Woodlock
British (1842–1929)
Lady on the Rose Terrace
Signed, watercolours heightened
with white
12 x 6¾in (30.5 x 17cm)
£2,000–2,250 *FL*

Franz Xavier Winterhalter
German (1806–73)
Portrait of a Lady
Signed, oil on canvas
39½ x 32in (101 x 81cm)
£21,000–25,000 *C*

*Winterhalter was the most
successful court painter of his
day, portraying Europe's royalty
and leading aristocracy, with a
lavish, glossy and romantic charm.
At the same period, Worth was
the most fashionable couturier in
Europe and many of Winterhalter's
women are portrayed in the
spectacular white silk and tulle
confections of the great Parisian
designer. At times it seemed almost
as though artist and couturier
were working as a team, combining
their decorative talents to idealize
their sitters and creating a shared
vision of opulent, courtly beauty.*

Karl Zewy
Austrian (1855–1929)
Die Weissen Lilien
Signed, oil on canvas
41½ x 27¼in (105 x 69cm)
£4,500–5,500 *S(NY)*

20th Century

Giuseppe Amisani
Italian (1881–1941)
Princess Ostheim
Signed, oil on canvas
29½ x 36in (75 x 91.5cm)
£3,500–4,500 *S(NY)*

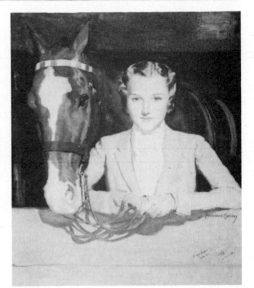

McClelland Barclay
American (1891–1943)
A Horse and Rider
Signed, inscribed and dated
'July 2 1933', oil on canvas
35 x 30in (89 x 76cm)
£800–1,000 *CNY*

Edward Burra
British (1905–76)
Kiss Me Again, I'm Still Conscious
Signed and dated '1929', pen, brush,
black ink and collage
20 x 15in (50.5 x 38cm)
£7,500–8,500 *C*

Sir Max Beerbohm
British (1872–1956)
Portrait of Rebecca West
Signed and dated '1918', watercolour and ink
9½ x 7⅞in (24 x 19.5cm)
£2,000–2,500 *P*

*This picture is in the form of a letter from
the artist to George Bernard Shaw, dated
June 28, 1918.*

*Rebecca West has become almost as celebrated
for her personal life as for her writings.
In 1913 she met H.G. Wells who was married
and at the height of his fame. They became
lovers and she bore him a son, Anthony West.
Although the stormy relationship came to an
end, her passionate love for Wells did not, and
it blighted her life. She had an equally
unhappy relationship with her son, who never
forgave her for neglecting him as a child.
As Bernard Levin notes severely, 'Until her
death, they were constantly at loggerheads,
sometimes legal ones, and after her death, he
took his revenge by publishing accounts of
her, Wells, and himself which make wretched
reading, whatever view is taken of the rights
and wrongs of the matter.' Paradoxically,
these bitter accounts also ensured his mother's
enduring celebrity.*

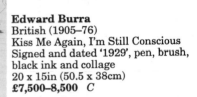

Francis Campbell Boileau Cadell, R.S.A., R.S.W.
British (1883–1937)
Crème de Menthe
Signed and inscribed, oil on canvas
25in (63.5cm) square
£45,000–55,000 *C(S)*

*From around 1910 Francis Cadell became particularly
fond of painting interiors often incorporating elegantly
dressed women either seated or standing by a table
within an Edwardian interior. As the* Antiques Trade
Gazette *noted, these works are one of the high points of
Scottish Colourism.*

Joyce Cairns
British (20thC)
A Reasonable Offer, 1992
Watercolour on paper
19¼ x 15in (49 x 38cm)
£400–500 *LG*

Charles Camoin
French (1879–1965)
Madame Camoin sur la Terrasse
de la Ville à St. Tropez
Signed, oil on canvas, c1921
18¼ x 21¾in (46 x 55.5cm)
£7,000–9,000 *CSK*

Albert Henry Collings
British (19th/20thC)
A Portrait of a seated Lady
Signed, watercolour
14½ x 10½in (37 x 26.5cm)
£350–450 *Bon*

William Conor, R.H.A.
Irish (1884–1968)
Washing Day
Signed, oil on canvas
20 x 24in (50.5 x 61cm)
£10,000–11,000 *S*

Ernest Copestick
British (active 1927)
An Elegant young Lady
Signed, oil on canvas
19 x 16in (48 x 41cm)
£1,300–1,500 *HLG*

Jane Corsellis, N.E.A.C.
British (20thC)
The Corner Table
Oil on canvas
32 x 36in (81 x 91.5cm)
£5,000–5,500 *WHP*

Emile Deckers
Belgian (20thC)
Femme allongée
Signed, inscribed 'Alger' and dated '1927',
oil on canvas
24 x 33½in (61 x 85cm)
£1,500–2,500 *Bon*

Ivan Dmitriev
Russian (b1958)
Two Women
Signed, oil on canvas
31½ x 36½in (80 x 93cm)
£1,300–1,500 *Ch*

Otto Dix
German (1891–1969)
Schwangerschaft (Karsch 46/2)
Signed and dated '1922', drypoint
printed with tone
19¼ x 17in (49 x 43cm)
£4,500–5,500 *S*

Pedro Creixams
Spanish (1893–1965)
Portrait de Femme à la Chemise rose
Signed, oil on canvas, 1918
36 x 28¾in (91.5 x 73.5cm)
£10,500–12,500 *C*

Ronald Ossory Dunlop, R.A.
British (1894–1973)
Portrait of a young Woman wearing
a white Blouse
Signed, oil on canvas
27 x 22in (69 x 56cm)
£750–900 *CSK*

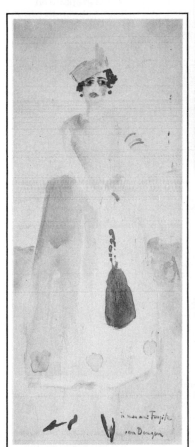

Kees van Dongen
French (1877–1968)
Femme du Grande Monde
Signed and inscribed, watercolour
on paper, c1925
15 x 6¼in (38 x 16cm)
£7,000–8,000 *CSK*

James Durden
British (1878–1964)
The Orange Frock
Signed and inscribed with title on
artist's label on stretcher, oil on canvas
20 x 16in (51 x 40.5cm)
£1,500–1,800 *P*

*James Durden was born in
Manchester and studied at the
Manchester College of Art and at the
R.C.A.. A painter in oil and
watercolour, mainly of landscapes
and portraits, he exhibited at the
Royal Academy from 1909
to 1937 and at the Royal Society of
Portrait Painters, and abroad, where
he won a silver medal at the Paris
Salon in 1927.*

Sir William Russell Flint, R.A.
British (1880–1969)
Madeleine in her Finery
Signed, watercolour
20 x 27in (50.5 x 69cm)
£28,000–30,000 *WH*

Sir William Russell Flint, R.A.
British (1880–1969)
Girl from Orio
Reproduction, in colours
15 x 22½in (38 x 57cm)
£700–900 *Bon*

Edwin A. Georgi
American (1896–1964)
The Golden Flower
Watercolour, gouache and graphite on
paperboard, artist's estate stamp on reverse
30 x 22in (76 x 56cm)
£150–250 *SK*

Eric Gill
Rachel Rothenstein
British (1882–1940)
Signed engraving, inscribed 'Portrait',
on thick wove
10 x 7in (25 x 17.5cm)
£300–400 *P*

Harold Gilman
British (1876–1919)
Interior (Mrs Mounter)
Signed, oil on canvas, 1917
15 x 13in (38 x 33cm)
£115,000–140,000 *C*

*Gilman's portrayal of Mrs Mounter, his
landlady at 47 Maple Street, during 1916–17,
provided a pleasurable surprise for Christie's.
The painting was estimated at £20,000–30,000
and after much serious bidding sold for an
auction record for the artist.*

Harold Gilman
British (1876–1919)
Miss Ruth Doggett
Oil on canvas, with stamped signature, c1915
23½ x 17½in (60 x 44.5cm)
£18,500–22,000 *C*

Imre Goth
Hungarian (1893–1982)
Berlin Portrait, 1928
Signed, oil on canvas
35¼ x 29½in (90 x 75cm)
£2,200–2,500 *JDG*

Emile Grau-Sala
Spanish (1911–75)
Femme Allongée sur un Lit
Signed and dated '40', oil on canvas
15 x 18in (38 x 46cm)
£5,750–7,000 *S*

Peter Graham
British (b1959)
Tropical Discussion
Oil on canvas
47 x 59in (119 x 149.5cm)
£4,500–4,800 *Bne*

Louis Icart
French (1888–1950)
Lady with Cat
Signed in pencil,
drypoint engraving
14 x 12in (36 x 30.5cm)
£800–1,200 *GK*

Cheryl Howeld
English (b1944)
Letting Down Her Hair
Signed, oil on canvas
25 x 20in (64 x 50.5cm)
£700–800 *Ch*

Augustus John, R.A.
British (1878–1961)
Portrait of Mrs Cheever Cowdin
Signed, oil on canvas
26 x 22in (66 x 56cm)
£4,500–5,000 *P*

Fraser King
British (20thC)
Shoppers' Break
Signed, acrylic
15¾ x 23½in (40 x 60cm)
£450–550 *LA*

Dame Laura Knight
British (1877–1970)
Signed, inscribed 'Romeo & Juliet,
Regent Theatre, 1922', charcoal
13¼ x 9⅜in (34 x 24.5cm)
£900–1,000 *P*

Jacob Kramer
British (1892–1962)
Portrait of his sister Sarah, 1916
Signed and dated, charcoal
22½ x 18in (57 x 46cm)
£750–850 *JDG*

Marie Laurencin
French (1883–1956)
Columbine
Signed, oil on canvas
21½ x 18in (55 x 46cm)
£85,000–95,000 *C*

Fernand Léger
French (1881–1955)
Deux Femmes
Signed with initials and dated '48',
gouache on paper
11 x 7¼in (28 x 18cm)
£19,000–22,000 *C*

Henri Matisse
French (1869–1954)
Femmes dans un Intérieur, Hotel
Regina, Cimiez, Nice
Signed and dated 'février 40',
pencil on paper
21 x 16in (53 x 41cm)
£40,000–50,000 *C*

Jean Metzinger
French (1883–1956)
Tête de Femme
Signed, oil on canvas, 1916
29 x 21in (74 x 53cm)
£138,000–150,000 *C*

*'Tête de Femme' was probably
painted just after Metzinger
completed his military service.
It belongs to a whole series of
fine cubist representations of
fashionable women begun in 1912.*

Locate the Source

*The source of each
illustration in Miller's
can be found by checking
the code letters below
each caption with the list
of contributors.*

Richard Edward Miller
American (1875–1943)
Portrait of Eva and Self Portrait
of the Artist, a double sided painting
Signed, oil on board
34 x 36in (86 x 91.5cm)
£23,000–26,000 *S(NY)*

Amedeo Modigliani
Italian (1884–1920)
Tête de Jeune Fille
Signed, oil on canvas, 1916
26 x 20in (66 x 51cm)
£3,000,000–3,500,000 *C*

Although Moigliani's pictures now fetch millions, during his lifetime the artist traded his canvases and drawings for food and drink. The Parisian shopkeepers who took the pictures often regarded them as worthless. One local potato seller with whom Modigliani used to barter regularly, is said to have used his drawings to wrap up her chips.

When selecting this picture for the Tate Gallery Modigliani exhibition of 1963, John Russell considered it one of the first truly successful portraits of a female sitter that Modigliani had painted. Russell wrote that it is a picture which, 'demonstrated the monumentality which Modigliani could achieve when he combined the flawless ovals of sculpture with eyes no longer sightless ... This painting keeps an exemplary balance between the stylisation of the head and neck and the individual living presence of the sitter; and the rectilinear background which looks so casual, has a formal function as precisely calculated as that of the picture frames in Poussin's self-portrait in the Louvre.'

Gani Odutokun
Ghanaian (b1946)
African Womanhood IV:
At the Dressmaker
Signed, gouache on paper, 1990
14¾ x 19¼in (38 x 49cm)
£400–500 *SG*

Pablo Picasso
Spanish (1881–1973)
Femme dans un Fauteuil
Dated on both sides '12.4.45',
oil on canvas
36¼ x 25½in (93 x 67cm)
£350,000–450,000 *C*

Amanda Rabey
British (20thC)
The Story Spinner
Signed, oil on canvas
60 x 48in (152 x 122cm)
£800–900 *VCG*

Locate the Source
The source of each illustration in Miller's can be found by checking the code letters below each caption with the list of contributors.

Walter Nessler
German (20thC)
Veronique, 1952
Gouache
44 x 38in (111.5 x 96.5cm)
£1,400–1,600 *JDG*

Sir Alfred Munnings, P.R.A.
British (1878–1959)
Poster design for Caley's
Chocolates
Signed, gouache
18 x 10½in (46 x 26cm)
£3,000–3,500 *C*

F. A. Sotomayor y Zaragoza
Spanish (1875–1960)
Portrait of Mrs Joos E. Wolf
Signed, oil on canvas
51¼ x 43¼in (130 x 110cm)
£5,000–6,000 *S*

Lorna Smith
British (20thC)
Lady in Grey
Gouache
8 x 7½in (20 x 19cm)
£250–300 *JN*

Olga Suvorova
Russian (b1966)
La Chansonette, 1991
Signed, oil on canvas
50½ x 41in (128 x 104cm)
£1,600–1,800 *ALG*

Leon Underwood
British (b1890)
Seated Woman
Signed, wood engraving
6 x 5in (15 x 12.5cm)
£150–200 *BLD*

> **Miller's is a price GUIDE
> not a price LIST**

Colin Vincent
British (b1965)
Kate in the Window, c1992
Oil on board
24½ x 20½in (62 x 52cm)
£400–450 *A*

Jack Vettriano
Scottish (20thC)
The Model and The City Boys, 1951
Oil on canvas
20 x 16in (51 x 40.5cm)
£2,750–2,950 *VCG*

Walter Ernest Webster
British (1878–1959)
Girl in a Blue Dress
Signed, watercolour
22¾ x 17in (58 x 43cm)
£2,800–3,250 *FL*

Anna Zinkeisen
British (1901–72)
The Spinning Lady
Signed, oil on canvas
24 x 30in (61.5 x 76cm)
£4,000–4,500 *HLG*

COUPLES

Durer's 'Adam and Eve', van Eyck's 'Arnolfini Marriage', Gainsborough's 'Mr and Mrs Andrews', Rodin's 'The Kiss' - the couple has been one of the most celebrated themes throughout the history of Western art. The following section includes both double-portraits and imaginary portrayals of couples, ranging from anonymous, if decorative, courting peasants to Anthony and Cleopatra, Petrarch and Laura, Napoleon and Josephine, and the most famous lovers in history and in literature.

17th–18th Century

John Eycke
British School (active 1618–after 1640)
Portrait of Sir Francis Vincent, and
another of Lady Vincent
The former signed and inscribed, the latter
inscribed, both dated '1627', oil on canvas
80 x 50in (203 x 127cm)
£23,000–30,000 *C*

Circle of Louis Léopold Boilly
French (1761–1845)
A young Couple plighting their Troth
Signed with monogram, oil on canvas
21 x 17¼in (53 x 44cm)
£8,500–9,500 *C*

Mathaus Terwesten, called Arents
Dutch (1670–1757)
Anthony and Cleopatra
Signed and dated '1701', oil on canvas
47 x 30in (119 x 76cm)
£5,500–6,500 *C*

Jean-Baptiste Hüet
French (1745–1811)
The Dove's Nest, and The Basket of Roses
A pair, signed, oils on canvas
27½ x 33½in (70 x 85cm)
£130,000–160,000 *S*

With their courting couples in idealised pastoral surroundings, these two pictures epitomise the romantic frivolity of the rococo style. This attractive pair of paintings sold for more than double their top estimate.

George Knapton
British (1698–1778)
Portrait of John, 1st Earl of Moira
and his wife Elizabeth
Oil on canvas
87¼ x 59½in (222 x 151cm)
£16,500–18,000 *S*

After Pierre Etienne Moitte
French (1746–1810)
Le Jaloux Endormi, and l'Infidelité
Reconnue, by Vidal and
Dambrun respectively
A pair, mixed method engraving,
laid paper
14¾ x 10½in (38 x 26.5cm)
£600–700 *C*

Angelica Kauffmann
Swiss (1741–1807)
La Bergère des Alpes
Oil on canvas
50 x 39¾in (127 x 101cm)
£82,000–90,000 *P*

Locate the Source
*The source of each
illustration in Miller's
can be found by checking
the code letters below
each caption with the list
of contributors.*

Circle of Anton Raphael Mengs
German (1728–79)
Angelica and Medoro
Oil on canvas
29 x 23½in (74 x 60cm)
£3,500–4,500 *CSK*

*A favourite artistic subject, the couple are
taken from the romantic epic poem 'Orlando
Furioso', by the Italian poet Aristo
(1474–1533). Angelica was a Princess of
Cathay, loved by several knights, both
Christian and Pagan. Amongst the former
was Orlando who was maddened (furioso)
with grief and jealousy, because she fell in
love with and married Medoro. Angelica
found Medoro terribly wounded after a battle,
she cured him, and the painting shows the
couple together under a tree, carving their
names into the bark. it was the discovery of
this 'ocular proof' that caused Orlando's
jealous madness.*

Thomas Rowlandson
British (1756–1827)
Infidelity Discovered
Pen and grey ink and watercolour over
traces of pencil
5¼ x 3¼in (13 x 8cm)
£1,000–1,200 *S*

19th Century

Jacques-Laurent Agasse
Swiss (1767–1849)
A Portrait of Edward Cross, and another of Mrs Edward Cross
A pair, oil on canvas
36 x 28in (92 x 71cm) and 35¼ x 28in (90 x 70.5cm)
£200,000–220,000 *C*

This pair of pictures was sold by the Zoological Society of London, as part of their much advertised and much needed campaign to raise funds for the Society and London Zoo. Animal painter par excellence, Agasse was a regular visitor to the popular Exeter menagerie owned by Edward Cross, who was also supplier of exotic animals to the extravagant and genuinely curious Prince Regent (later George IV). In 1829, the Cross Zoo moved to London, first to the site now occupied by the National Gallery, and then to Kennington. The centrepiece of his zoological gardens was a remarkable circular glass building, 300 feet in diameter, which housed the wild cats and large mammals in the centre, with tropical birds in cages on the outside edge of the building. It is in this structure, lion cub in hand, that Edward Cross is portrayed.

Albert Emile Artigue
French (19thC)
The Flirt
Signed, oil on canvas
78¾ x 59in (200 x 149.5cm)
£3,000–3,500 *S(NY)*

William A. Breakspeare
British (1855–1914)
A Small Dispute
Signed, oil on canvas
13½ x 10in (34 x 25cm)
£1,500–2,000 *S(S)*

Giuseppe Aureli
Italian (1858–1929)
The Toilet
Signed and inscribed 'Roma',
oil on canvas
21½ x 14½in (54.5 x 37cm)
£950–1,200 *AG*

Luigi Bechi
Italian (1830–1919)
Flirtation
Signed, oil on canvas
39½ x 29in (100 x 73.5cm)
£18,500–20,000 *C*

r. **Francesco Coleman**
Italian (b1851)
The Musician's Distraction
Signed and inscribed, pencil and
watercolour heightened with white
21¼ x 14¼in (54 x 36.5cm)
£800–1,000 *CSK*

l. **Jean Henri de Coene**
Flemish (1798–1866)
The Amorous Author
Signed and inscribed, oil on panel
26¾ x 20½in (68 x 52cm)
£4,000–5,000 *P*

Cesare Augusto Detti
Italian (1847–1914)
Caught!
Signed, oil on panel
14 x 10¼in (35.5 x 26cm)
£8,500–10,000 *C*

Alfred W. Elmore, R.A.
British (1815–81)
The Proposal
Signed and dated '1860',
oil on canvas
36 x 30in (91.5 x 76cm)
£15,000–18,000 *C*

Albert Guillaume
French (1873–1942)
The Wedding
Signed, oil on panel
15¾ x 12½in (40 x 31.5cm)
£1,500–1,800 *S*

George Goodwin Kilburne
British (1839–1924)
The Wounded Duellist
Signed, watercolour and bodycolour
on buff paper
5½ x 7½in (14 x 19cm)
£400–500 *MSW*

Nicaise de Keyser
Flemish (1813–87)
Petrarch and Laura
Signed and dated '1842', oil on panel
41½ x 32in (105 x 81cm)
£11,000–13,000 *C*

*Petrarch (1304–74), Italian poet and
humanist, is today most famous for his series
of love sonnets to Laura, a woman he met in
1327, but whose true identity is unknown. If
she was a real person she was probably Laura
de Noves, who married Hugues de Sade and
had 11 children by him before dying of the
plague. Petrarch's relationship with her was
almost certainly purely poetical, as Byron
cynically remarked:
'Think you, if Laura had been Petrarch's wife,
He would have written sonnets all his life?'
Petrarch's poetry did much to popularise the
Christian name Laura.*

Arthur Hughes
British (1832–1915)
Enid and Geraint
Signed, oil on canvas
10¼ x 14¾in (26 x 38cm)
£65,000–100,000 *C*

The subject is taken from The Marriage of
Geraint *in Tennyson's Idylls of the King.*

*The theme of love was one of Hughes'
favourite pictorial subjects and, like many of
the Pre-Raphaelites, he was strongly attracted
to Arthurian subject matter.*

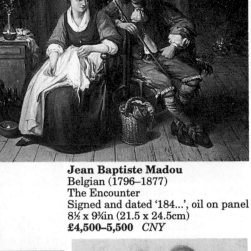

Jean Baptiste Madou
Belgian (1796–1877)
The Encounter
Signed and dated '184...', oil on panel
8½ x 9¾in (21.5 x 24.5cm)
£4,500–5,500 *CNY*

Edmund Blair Leighton
British (1853–1922)
Forget-me-nots
Initialled and dated '95' and inscribed,
oil on panel
13 x 10½in (33 x 26cm)
£9,500–11,000 *C*

Ferdinand Marohn
French (19thC)
Young Lovers at a Spinning Wheel
Signed and dated '1847', pencil
and watercolour
10½ x 12in (26.5 x 31.5cm)
£850–1,000 *CSK*

Pompeo Massani
Italian (1850–1920)
The Courtship
Signed, oil on canvas
12 x 10in (30.5 x 25cm)
£2,000–2,500 *C*

Sir John Everett Millais, P.R.A.
British (1829–96)
The Proposal
Black chalk with pen and black
and grey ink
8½ x 6¾in (21.5 x 17cm)
£1,400–1,600 *C*

19th Century School
A Samoan Chief, and Wife
A pair, inscribed in pencil on reverse, watercolours
11½ x 9½in (29 x 24cm)
£700–800 *TER*

*This Chief went to Washington DC in 1877 for support
in order to persuade America to annexe Samoa.*

Alonzo Perez
Spanish (active 1893–1914)
A Walk in the Garden
Signed, oil on panel
25½ x 14½in (65 x 37cm)
£1,700–2,000 *CNY*

Vilhelm Rosenstrand
Danish (1838–1915)
The Proposal
Signed and dated '1880',
oil on canvas
32½ x 22½in (82.5 x 57cm)
£6,000–8,000 *CSK*

James Jacques Joseph Tissot
French (1836–1902)
The Ferry
Signed, oil on panel
12 x 7¾in (30.5 x 19.5cm)
£190,000–210,000 *C*

**Phoebe Anna Traquair,
H.R.S.A.**
British (1852–1936)
Love's Testament
Signed with monogram and
dated '1898', oil on canvas
21 x 14in (53.5 35.5cm)
£35,000–40,000 *C(S)*

*Phoebe Traquair was one of the
leading artists of the Celtic
Revival and the Arts and Crafts
movement in Edinburgh. The
many admirers of her work
included Ruskin, Walter Crane
and W. B. Yeats: 'I find her work
far more beautiful than I had
foreseen,' wrote Yeats in 1906.
'...She has but one story, the
drama of the soul ... She herself
is delightful, a saint and a little
singing bird.'
A recent exhibition of Traquair's
 work at the Scottish National
Portrait Gallery led to this picture
 being rediscovered. It had been
purchased by its owner some 20
years ago for only £3 in an
Edinburgh antique shop.*

William Aiken Walker
American (1839–1921)
The Cotton Field
Signed with monogram, oil on board
9¼ x 12¼in (23.5 x 31.5cm)
£4,000–5,000 *S(NY)*

Alexander Friedrich Werner
German (1827–1908)
The After Dinner Pipe
Signed, oil on panel
13¾ x 10½in (35 x 26.5cm)
£5,000–6,000 *S*

Berthold Woltze
German (1829–96)
Off to America
Signed, oil on canvas
29 x 23in (74 x 59cm)
£7,000–8,000 *S*

John William Waterhouse, R.A.
British (1849–1917)
A Study for 'La Belle Dame sans Merci'
Oil on board, laid down on panel
14½ x 11½in (37 x 29cm)
£50,000–60,000 *C*

20th Century

Marc Chagall
French/Russian (1887–1985)
Mein Leben: Der Spaziergang I
Etching and drypoint, 1922,
signed in pencil
12¾ x 9in (33 x 23cm)
£4,500–5,500 *S(NY)*

Howard Chandler Christy
American (1873–1952)
After the Match
Signed and dated '1929',
wash on board
38¼ x 28¾in (98 x 73cm)
£1,000–1,500 *CNY*

Jean Cocteau
French (1889–1963)
N'était-il pas de son devoir conjugal
de partager les preferences de
son epoux
Original etching 1953, No. 108
from an edition of 250 from the
series of etchings 'Le Bal'
12¾ x 10in (32 x 25cm)
£145–185 *WO*

Alex Katz
American (b1927)
Study for Peter and Lauren
Signed and dated '88',
oil on masonite
13 x 12in (33 x 30.5cm)
£6,500–7,500 *S(NY)*

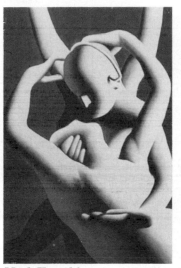

Mark Kostabi
American (b1960)
Beauty, Wit, Sensuality, Intensity
and Style
Signed and dated '1984', oil on canvas
72 x 48in (182.5 x 122cm)
£2,000–2,500 *CNY*

David Kirk
British (20thC)
Love by the Greenhouse
Signed, acrylic
23 x 20in (59 x 51cm)
£750–850 *SJG*

Michael Heath
British (b1935)
But I can't live without you!
Signed, pen and ink
5½ x 11½in (14 x 29.5cm)
£175–200 *CBL*

Per Krohg
Norwegian (1889–1965)
Conversation
Signed, oil on canvas, c1930
39½ x 32in (100 x 81cm)
£16,000–20,000 *C*

Osbert Lancaster
British (1908–86)
Colonel and Lady
Inscribed with title, watercolour
with pencil
11¾ x 8in (30 x 20cm)
£750–850 *CBL*

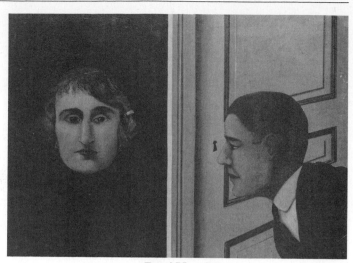

René Magritte
Belgian (1898–1967)
L'Espion
Signed and inscribed, oil on canvas, 1928
21¼ x 28½in (51.5 x 72cm)
£135,000–150,000 *C*

Bronwen Malcolm
British (b1963)
Healing Hands
Oil on canvas
30 x 40in (76 x 101.5cm)
£1,600–1,800 *TRG*

Tony Peart
British (20thC)
November the Fifth
Signed and dated 1990, oil on canvas
32 x 22in (81 x 56cm)
£1,800–2,000 *VCG*

Peter Peri
British (1899–1967)
Yet to be Convinced, 1946
Etching
7 x 6¼in (17.5 x 16cm)
£150–175 *BLD*

Glyn Philpot, R.A.
British (1884–1937)
The Juggler of
Notre Dame
Signed and dated '1928',
oil on canvas
20 x 16in (51 x 40.5cm)
£5,500–6,500 *S*

*This work is based upon
Massenet's opera The
Juggler of Notre Dame.
The hero of the story, a
destitute and dying street
artist, has blasphemously
performed his act in front
of a statue of the Virgin,
to the pious horror of the
priest and congregation.
As he dies, the statue
miraculously leans
forward to bless him.*

Ben Sunlight
British (20thC)
Variation on a theme of Tintoretto
Signed and dated, oil on canvas
19 x 11¾in (48 x 30cm)
£1,000–2,000 *GK*

Haywood Hardy, A.R.W.S., R.P.E.
British (1843–1933)
The Morning Ride
Oil on canvas
30 x 21in (76 x 53.5cm)
£25,000–30,000   *JN*

Ford Madox Brown
British (1821–93)
Romeo and Juliet
Signed with monogram and dated '68–71',
watercolour and bodycolour with gum arabic
12½ x 9¾in (32 x 24cm)
£45,000–55,000   *C*

Sir John Everett Millais, Bt., P.R.A.
British (1829–96)
The Crown of Love
Signed with monogram and dated '1875',
oil on canvas
51 x 34½in (130 x 88cm)
£65,000–85,000   *S*

James Jacques Joseph Tissot
French (1836–1902)
L'Esthetique (au louvre)
Signed, oil on canvas
25½ x 17½in (65 x 44.5cm)
£150,000–170,000   *S(NY)*

Graham Knuttel
Irish (20thC)
Life on the Ocean Wave
Oil on canvas
72 x 60in (182.5 x 152cm)
£7,000–7,500 *NAG*

Michael Scott
Scottish (b1946)
The Meeting
Oil on canvas
40 x 32in (101.5 x 81cm)
£3,500–4,000 *RB*

Edmund Blair Leighton
British (1853–1922)
The Lord of Burleigh, Tennyson
Signed with initials and dated '1919',
oil on canvas
13¾ x 9½in (35 x 24cm)
£6,000–7,000 *AG*

Archie Forrest
Scottish (b1950)
Love, Here is my Hat
Oil on canvas
40 x 36in (101.5 x 91.5cm)
£10,000–12,000 *PG*

French School (c1700)
Portrait of a Young Girl
Oil on canvas, in a
painted oval
26¾ x 22¼in (67.5 x 57cm)
£3,700–4,200 *S*

Nicolas de Largillière
French (1656–1746)
Portrait of François Pommyer and
Yves-Joseph-Charles Pommyer
Oil on canvas
29½ x 36¼in (75 x 92cm)
£530,000–550,000 *C*

Maria Cosway
British (1759–1838)
Portrait of the Hon. George Lamb
as the Infant Bacchus
Oil on canvas
27¾ x 35¾in (70 x 91cm)
£5,000–6,000 *C*

Alonso Sanchez Coello and Studio
Spanish (1515–90)
Portrait of a Child, Caterina, Aged One, Seated
in her Andador
Inscribed, oil on canvas
40 x 30½in (101.5 x 77.5cm)
£25,000–35,000 *S(NY)*

l. **Francis Alleyne**
British (active 1774–90)
Portrait of two Eton
Schoolboys
Oil on panel
23 x 17¾in (58.4 x 45cm)
£9,500–10,500 *C*

r. **George Geldorp**
British (c1595–1665)
Portrait of a Boy with a Dog
Inscribed and dated '1617',
oil on canvas
47 x 35in (119 x 89cm)
£20,000–25,000 *S(NY)*

Edmund Adler
Austrian (1871–1957)
The New Puppies
Signed, oil on canvas
18 x 24in (45.5 x 61.5cm)
£15,500–16,500 *HFA*

Mark W. Langlois
British (active 1862–73)
The Naughty Schoolboy
Signed, oil on canvas
21 x 17in (53 x 43cm)
£1,700–2,200 *CAG*

William Marshall Brown
British (1863–1936)
A Motor Boat
Signed and inscribed on label, oil on canvas
10 x 14in (25.5 x 36cm)
£9,500–10,500 *BuP*

r. **P. Harland Fisher**
British (1865–1944)
The Green Ball
Signed, oil on canvas
27 x 25in (69 x 64cm)
£7,000–8,000 *JN*

James Drummond
British (1816–77)
A Young Cockle-Gatherer
Signed and dated, watercolour
20 x 14in (50.5 x 36cm)
£2,000–2,200 *WrG*

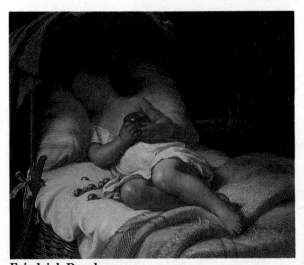

Friedrich Durck
German (1809–44)
Sweet Dreams of Christmas
Signed and dated '1852', also inscribed on old label
on reverse, oil on canvas
35 x 39½in (89 x 100cm)
£6,000–7,000 *P*

Matthias Robinson
British (active late 19thC)
Playing Trains
Signed with monogram and dated '90', oil on canvas
28 x 36in (71 x 91.5cm)
£6,500–7,500 *CGa*

Fredrico Mazzotta
Italian (19thC)
The Favourite Calf
Signed, oil on canvas
23¼ x 17¾in (59 x 45cm)
£17,500–18,500 *BuP*

l. **Octavius Oakley**
British (1800–67)
Out of School
Signed verso,
watercolour
25 x 19in
(63.5 x 48.5cm)
£2,500–2,750 *WrG*

Sir William Blake Richmond
British (1842–1921)
Portrait of Henrietta Green
Oil on canvas
30 x 48in (76 x 122cm)
£34,000–38,000 *HFA*

Jacob Thompson
British (1806–79)
Portrait of George and Ann Harvey
Signed and dated '1846', oil on canvas
41 x 32in (104 x 81.5cm)
£17,000–20,000 *S*

Emile Vernon
French (19th/20thC)
Little Kittens
Signed and dated '1917',
oil on canvas
25½ x 21¼in (65 x 54cm)
£35,000–40,000 *C*

Muriel Owen
British (20thC)
Fish for Supper
Signed, watercolour
7¾ x 9½in (19 x 24.5cm)
£300–350 *LA*

Frederick C. Frieseke
American (1874–1939)
The Pet Rabbit
Signed and dated '21', oil on canvas
31¼ x 25¼in (79.5 x 64cm)
£75,000–90,000 *S(NY)*

Zhung Chang
Chinese (20thC)
Christmas Morning, 1992
Mixed media under glass
21 x 31in (53 x 79cm)
£200–300 *RMG*

r. **Cheryl Howeld**
British (b1944)
Lion Child
Oil on canvas
32 x 24in (81 x 61.5cm)
£1,000–1,300 *Ch*

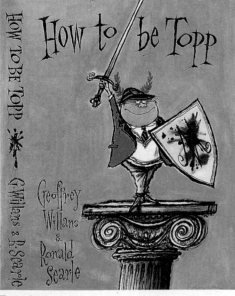

Ronald Searle
British (b1920)
How to be Topp
Watercolour and pen
13½ x 9in (34.5 x 23cm)
£2,000–2,250 *CBL*

Jean Young, R.B.A., N.E.A.C.
British (1914)
Children at a Table
Oil on canvas
25 x 30in (64 x 76cm)
£1,000–1,350 *JN*

Angelo Martinetti
Italian (19thC)
Happy Birthday
Signed and inscribed 'Roma', oil on canvas
20¼ x 29¼in (51.5 x 74.5cm)
£5,500–7,000 *P*

Herbert Blande Sparks
British (active 1892-3)
In the Garden
Signed, oil on canvas
30¼ x 24in (77 x 61cm)
£1,800–2,300 *S*

Mané-Katz
French (1894–1962)
Maternité
Signed, oil on canvas
28¾ x 24in (73 x 61cm)
£12,000–14,000 *S*

Carlton Alfred Smith
British (1853–1946)
The New Friend
Signed and dated '1900', watercolour
18 x 26in (46 x 66cm)
£14,000–16,000 *HFA*

Eugenio Zampighi
Italian (1859–1944)
Amusing Baby
Signed, oil on canvas
20 x 30in (51 x 76cm)
£17,500–20,000 *C*

Colin Middleton, R.H.A.
British (1910–83)
Nomads
Signed, inscribed, and dated
'1951' verso, oil on canvas
30 x 24in (76 x 61cm)
£6,000–7,000 *CCG*

François Boucher
French (1703–70)
L'Heureuse Fécondité
Signed and dated '1764', oil on canvas
25½ x 21¼in (65 x 54cm)
£540,000–600,000 *S(NY)*

Amédée Guérard
French (1824–1908)
A Young Mother Playing with Her Child
Signed and dated '1868', oil on canvas
33½ x 48in (85 x 122cm)
£10,000–11,000 *S*

Edward Killingworth Johnson, R.W.S.
British (1825–1923)
Happy as the Day is Long
Signed and dated '1881', watercolour
heightened with bodycolour
16¾ x 21¼in (42.5 x 54cm)
£8,000–9,000 *S*

George Chinnery
British (1774–1852)
A Tanka Woman with her Child on a Boat
Pen and brown ink and watercolour
4¾ x 6½in (12 x 16.5cm)
£5,600–6,500 *C*

William Lee-Hankey
British (1869–1952)
Mother and Child
Signed, oil on canvas
11½ x 17½in (29 x 44.5cm)
£7,500–8,500 *MI*

Artistide Maillol
French (1861–1944)
Mère et Enfant
Signed with initial 'M', oil on board
17 x 14in (43 x 36cm)
£85,000–100,000 *C*

r. **Jean Béraud**
French (1849–1936)
Le Chalet du Cycle
Signed and copyrighted,
oil on canvas
28 x 35in (71 x 88.5cm)
£260,000–280,000 *S(NY)*

John Evan Hodgson, R.A., H.F.R.P.E.
British (1831–95)
The Arrest
Signed with monogram and dated '1857', oil on canvas
21½ x 28¾in (54.5 x 73cm)
£3,500–4,500 *C(S)*

Julius Frank
German (b1826)
The Meeting of the Two Queens
Signed, oil on canvas
20½ x 17in (52 x 43cm)
£1,200–1,500 *AH*

Ludovico Marchetti
Italian (1853–1909)
Courtly Entertainment
Signed and dated '1884', oil on panel
11¾ x 16in (30 x 40.5cm)
£6,500–7,500 *P*

Gugwelmo Innocenti
Italian (late 19thC)
The Marriage Festival
Oil on canvas
16 x 23in (40.5 x 58.5cm)
£34,000–38,000 *HFA*

Margaret Dovaston
British (active 1908–50)
Back From the South Seas
Signed, oil on canvas
20 x 27in (50.5 x 68.5cm)
£8,200–9,000 *C*

Helen Bradley
British (1900–79)
Flood in Lees
Signed and signed with fly device, inscribed on label
on reverse, oil on board
18 x 24in (45.5 x 61.5cm)
£12,000–15,000 *S*

Dean Cornwell
American (1892–1960)
Bar Room Scene
Signed and dated '22', oil on canvas
28 x 46¼in (71 x 117.5cm)
£12,000–14,000 *S(NY)*

Joe Hargan
Scottish (b1952)
Two Plus One
Oil on canvas
41 x 37in (104 x 94cm)
£4,500–5,000 *CON*

Kyra Markham
American (1891–1967)
New Year's Eve in Greenwich Village
Signed and dated '37', oil on canvas
32 x 40in (81 x 101.5cm)
£18,000–22,000 *S(NY)*

Carel Weight
British (b1908)
Trying on Masks
Signed on reverse, oil on board, 1972
30 x 24in (77.5 x 61cm)
£14,000–19,000 *BRG*

Abraham Willemsens
Flemish (active 1627–72)
The Interior of a Barn with a Woman Spinning
Oil on panel
21 x 29½in (53 x 75cm)
£16,500–18,000 *C*

Maerten van Cleve
Flemish (1527–81)
The Procession of the Fiancé Led by a Piper
Oil on panel
10½ x 15in (26.5 x 38cm)
£10,000–15,000 *P*

Follower of Gillis van Tilborch
Flemish (c1625–78)
A Tavern Interior
Oil on panel
27½ x 23½in (70 x 60cm)
£2,800–3,500 *C*

William Williams of Norwich
British (active 1758–97)
The Cottager's Return
Signed and dated '1786', oil on canvas
29½ x 36¼in (75 x 92cm)
£5,000–6,000 *C*

r. **Charles Beschey**
Flemish (1706–76)
A Hamlet in a Wood with
Peasants going to Market
Oil on panel
10½ x 14½in (27 x 37cm)
£28,000–30,000 *C*

Myles Birket Foster, R.W.S.
British (1825–99)
The Donkey Ride
Signed with monogram, watercolour
8 x 11in (20 x 28cm)
£7,000–8,000 *WG*

Sir George Clausen, R.A.
British (1852–1944)
Springtime
Signed and dated '1882', signed again and
inscribed on reverse, oil on canvas
20¾ x 16in (53 x 40.5cm)
£100,000–120,000 *C*

David Fulton, R.S.W.
British (1848–1930)
Daydreams
Signed and dated '1889', oil on canvas
24 x 36in (61 x 91.5cm)
£5,500–6,000 *S*

l. **Frederick George Harris**
British (active 1858–81)
Idle Moments
Watercolour
6¾ x 9¾in (17 x 24cm)
£1,200–1,500 *JC*

Jacob Meyer de Haan
Dutch (1852–95)
Labor, Paysannes Broyant du Lin
Inscribed and dated '1889', fresco, mounted on canvas
52½ x 79¼in (133.5 x 201cm)
£660,000–700,000 *S(NY)*

Hector Caffieri, R.I., R.B.A.
British (1847–1932)
Mussel Gathering at Boulogne
Signed, watercolour
19½ x 13½in (49.5 x 34.5cm)
£4,250–4,750 *WrG*

Edward Masters
British (late 19thC)
A Rural Village
Oil on canvas
20 x 30in (50.5 x 76cm)
£8,250–9,250 *HFA*

Henry H. Parker
British (1858–1930)
The Harvest Field
Signed, oil on canvas
28 x 18in (71 x 46cm)
£13,000–14,000 *BuP*

James Clarke Waite, R.B.A.
British (late 19thC)
A Penny for Yourself
Watercolour
11 x 14in (28 x 35.5cm)
£2,500–3,500 *JN*

John Linnell
British (1792–1882)
Carrying Wheat
Signed and dated '1862', oil on board
19½ x 24½in (49 x 63cm)
£10,500–12,000 *S*

Jules Jacques Veyrassat
French (1828–93)
Harvesting
Signed, oil on canvas
15 x 23in (38 x 59cm)
£5,500–6,500 *HLG*

r. **Walter Henry Sweet**
British (1890–1943)
Fisherfolk, Polperro
Signed, watercolour
24¼ x 18½in (62 x 47cm)
£1,500–2,000 *JC*

Jean Frelaut
French (20thC)
La Ferme
Oil on canvas, 1921
32 x 24in (81 x 61cm)
£1,300–1,500 *JDG*

Klim Forster
British (20thC)
Haymaking
Watercolour
15 x 12in (38 x 30.5cm)
£175–200 *RGFA*

D. Drey
British (b1962)
Cutback
Oil on hardboard
49 x 24½in (124.5 x 62.5cm)
£700–800 *FT*

Mick Rooney
British (b1944)
Greek Life
Signed and dated '1993', mixed media
9 x 7in (23 x 17.5cm)
£6,000–8,000 *BRG*

Judy Talacko
Australian (b1941)
The Road to Oz
Oil on canvas
16 x 22in (41 x 55.5cm)
£1,500–1,750 *Om*

l. **Frank Taylor**
British (20thC)
Baking Bread, Soganli, Cappadocia
Watercolour
16 x 24in (41 x 61.5cm)
£850–950 *PHG*

John de Critz the Elder
British (c1522–1642)
Portrait of King James VI of Scotland,
James I of England
Oil on panel
44¾ x 32⅛in (113.5 x 83cm)
£35,000–45,000 *C*

After Daniel Mytens
Dutch (1590–1648)
King Charles I and Queen Henrietta Maria
Oil on canvas
35½ x 53½in (90.5 x 135cm)
£15,000–17,000 *C*

After Sir Anthony van Dyck
Flemish (1599–1641)
The Three Children of Charles I
Oil on canvas
23½ x 28in (60 x 71cm)
£10,500–12,000 *S*

l. **Follower of Franz Xavier Winterhalter**
German (19thC)
Portraits of Emperor Napoléon III and Princess Eugénie
A pair, oil on canvas
35 x 23½in (89 x 60cm)
£12,000–15,000 *S*

Sir Peter Lely
British (1618–80)
Portrait of Mary II
Oil on canvas
49 x 39in (124 x 99cm)
£55,000–70,000 *S*

Charles Lucy
British (1814–73)
The Forced Abdication of Mary Queen of Scotland at Lochleven
Castle, July 25, 1567
Signed and dated '1868', oil on canvas
83½ x 62¾in (213 x 159cm)
£30,000–40,000 *C*

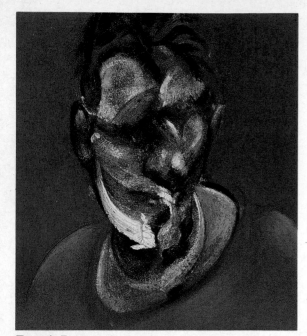

Francis Bacon
British (1909–92)
Portrait of Lucian Freud
Signed, titled, dedicated and dated
'1965' on reverse, oil on canvas
14 x 12in (35.5 x 30.5cm)
£220,000–250,000 *S*

A. Orselli
Italian (19thC)
The Rejected Artist
Signed, oil on canvas
24¼ x 20in (62 x 51cm)
£8,500–10,000 *P*

l. **Russell Sydney Reeve**
British (1895–1970)
Self-portrait with Merry
and Polly
Signed, oil on canvas
39½ x 30in (100 x 76cm)
£9,000–10,000 *PN*

Douglas Percy Bliss, R.B.A.
British (1900–84)
Renoir Old
Signed and inscribed with title, watercolour
9½ x 11in (24 x 28cm)
£750–850 *CBL*

Jean-Baptiste Marie Pierre
French (1713–89)
The Sculptor's Studio
Signed and dated '1756', oil on canvas
12½ x 16in (32 x 40.5cm)
£130,000–150,000 *S(NY)*

r. **Bob Robinson**
Irish (b1951)
Beast of Burden
Oil on canvas, 1993
27½in (70cm) square
£4,000–4,500 *Tr*

Henry Mayo Bateman
British (1887–1970)
Double Seven, No Trumps – What!
Signed with initials, inscribed
with title on reverse, pen, ink
and watercolour
4in (10cm) square
£850–950 *CBL*

Johann Hamza
Austrian (1850–1927)
The Chess Players
Signed, oil on panel
22 x 27⅛in (56 x 69cm)
£40,000–50,000 *S*

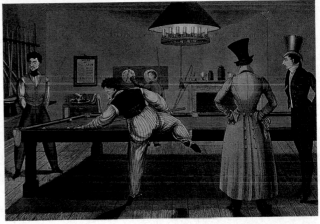

W. H. Pyne
British (19thC)
Billiards
Original hand coloured aquatint,
by Williams & Hunt, c1824
8¾ x 11¾in (22 x 30cm)
£850–950 *Bur*

Alexander Christie, Jnr.
British (b1901)
The Chess Problem (Candlelight)
Signed and dated '1923', oil on canvas
28 x 32¼in (71 x 82cm)
£2,000–3,000 *Bon*

r. **Kees van Dongen**
French (1877–1968)
Les Salons du Casino de
Deauville, Le Privé
Signed, titled on the reverse,
oil on canvas
21¼ x 25¾in (54 x 65cm)
£280,000–320,000 *C*

John Angus
Belgian (b1823)
A Flemish Scene of a Serving Wench Pouring
Wine on the Terrace
Oil on canvas
19¾ x 17¼in (50 x 44cm)
£550–750 *Bri*

John Mallard Bromley, R.B.A.
British (active 1876–1904)
Don't Touch
Signed, indistinctly inscribed on reverse
14 x 18in (35.5 x 45.5cm)
£11,500–12,500 *BuP*

Herbert Johnson Harvey
British (1884–1928)
Preparing Fruit
Signed and dated '1910', oil on canvas
24 x 30in (61 x 76cm)
£5,500–6,000 *NZ*

Graham Knuttel
Irish (20thC)
Taut Cuisine
Oil on canvas
48 x 36in (122 x 91.5cm)
£4,500–5,000 *NAG*

Alexander Sonnis
Czech/British (20thC)
In the Kitchen
Oil on canvas
20 x 16in (51 x 41cm)
£350–450 *JDG*

Guillaume Koller (1829–84) and
David Emil Josef de Noter (1825–75) Belgian
In the Pantry
Signed and inscribed, oil on panel
25¼ x 32½in (64 x 82.5cm)
£12,000–15,000 *C*

Cesare Tiratelli
Italian (b1864)
Market Day, near Rome
Signed and inscribed, oil on canvas
24½ x 53in (62 x 134.5cm)
£125,000–150,000 *C*

Petrus van Schendel
Belgian (1806–70)
Avondmarkt
Signed, oil on panel
25 x 20in (64 x 51cm)
£60,000–80,000 *S*

Mary S. Hagarty
British (active 1882–1938)
Market Day, Caudebec
Watercolour
15¼ x 11¼in (39 x 29cm)
£600–900 *GG*

Walter Frederick Roofe Tyndale, R.I.
British (1855–1943)
Fish Market at Bruges
Signed, watercolour
9 x 11in (22.5 x 28cm)
£1,650–1,850 *HO*

Moya Cozens
British (1920–90)
The Fruit Market
Signed, oil on board
13 x 19in (33 x 48cm)
£300–385 *TFA*

Edward H. Potthast
American (1857–1927)
At The Beach
Signed, oil on canvas
16¼ x 20in (41.5 x 50.5cm)
£120,000–140,000 *S(NY)*

William Marsh Brown, R.S.A., R.S.W.
British (1863–1936)
Wading
Oil on canvas
10 x 8in (25 x 20cm)
£7,000–7,750 *BuP*

John Reay
British (b1932)
The Bathers
Oil on board
11½ x 15in (29 x 38cm)
£550–625 *ULG*

Lionel Aggett
British (20thC)
Sennen, Cornwall
Pastel
16 x 20in (40.5 x 50.5cm)
£700–800 *LA*

George Charlton
British (b1899)
Bathers on the Beach
Oil on board
20 x 29in (51 x 74cm)
£2,500–2,750 *GG*

Ken Howard, R.A.
British (b1932)
Sennen, August '92
Oil on canvas
20 x 24in (51 x 61cm)
£2,500–3,000 *WHP*

Marcel Cosson
French (1878–1956)
Danseuse au Miroir
Signed, oil on board
18 x 15in (45.5 x 38cm)
£3,500–4,500 *C*

Jan Tilius
Italian (1660–1719)
A Hurdy-Gurdy Player and an Old Woman Singing
Signed and dated '1681', oil on panel
13¾ x 11½in (34.5 x 29.5cm)
£30,000–40,000 *C*

Andrew Curtis
British (20thC)
Blowing up a Storm
Signed, watercolour and charcoal
15 x 12in (38 x 30.5cm)
£225–275 *TFA*

James McBey
British (1884–1959)
A Spanish Guitarist –
Portrait of Consuela Carmona
Signed and dated '1929',
oil on canvas
46½ x 38in (118 x 96.5cm)
£5,500–7,000 *C(S)*

r. **Christian Holm**
Danish (1815–1907)
The Music Lesson
Oil on canvas
22 x 18in (56 x 46cm)
£13,000–14,000 *HFA*

Herman W. Hansen
American (1854–1924)
Shooting a Rattlesnake
Signed, watercolour on paper
21½ x 14½in (54.5 x 37cm)
£14,000–16,000 *S(NY)*

Charles Schreyvogel
American (1861–1912)
The Messenger
Signed and dated '1912', oil on canvas
34 x 24in (86 x 61cm)
£175,000–200,000 *S(NY)*

*Charles Schreyvogel became one of the most
popular artists to paint the American West,
despite an early life of poverty and struggle.
He had a particular interest in depicting
American cavalry officers.*

John Berry
British (b1920)
The Scouts
Signed, oil on canvas
30 x 24in (76 x 61cm)
£3,000–3,600 *Dr*

Gordon Phillips
American (b1927)
Rise and Shine
Signed, oil on canvas
24 x 20in (61 x 51cm)
£5,500–7,000 *S(NY)*

Giuseppe Guidi
Italian (19th/20thC)
Baby's Birthday
Signed and dated '1918', oil on canvas
15¾ x 22in (40 x 55.5cm)
£10,000–12,000 *S*

François Brunery
Italian (late 19thC)
Le Vendredi on fait Pénitence
Signed, oil on canvas
18¼ x 15¼in (46.5 x 39cm)
£22,000–25,000 *C*

Georges Croegaert
French (1848–1923)
The Connoisseur
Signed, oil on panel
13¾ x 10½in (35 x 26.5cm)
£6,500–7,500 *BuP*

Andrea Landini
Italian (b1847)
Un Passage de Rabelais – Salon du Conseil du Roi
Louis XIV à Versailles
Signed, titled on a label on reverse, oil on canvas
37 x 29½in (94 x 75cm)
£35,000–45,000 *S(NY)*

r. **Frank Moss Bennett**
British (1874–1953)
D'Artagnan and Richelieu
Signed and dated '1947',
oil on canvas
19½ x 23½in (49.5 x 60cm)
£4,200–5,000 *S(S)*

Sir Laurence Alma-Tadema, R.A.
British (1836–1912)
Egyptian Players
Signed and inscribed, oil on panel
16 x 21¾in (40.5 x 55cm)
£75,000–90,000 *S*

John William Godward
British (1861–1922)
Cestilia
Signed and dated '19', oil on canvas
31½ x 16in (80 x 40.5cm)
£38,000–45,000 *C*

Henry Ryland
British (1856–1924)
Melody
Signed, pencil and watercolour
15 x 21¾in (38 x 55cm)
£4,200–5,000 *C*

Gustave Clarence Rodolphe Boulanger
French (1824–88)
The Slave Market
Signed and dated 'MDIIILXXXVI', oil on canvas
30½ x 39in (77.5 x 99cm)
£62,000–70,000 *S*

Adolphe Alexandre Lesrel
French (1839–1929)
Le Lis est Mort
Signed and dated '1873', oil on canvas
62¾ x 47in (159 x 119.5cm)
£46,000–50,000 *C*

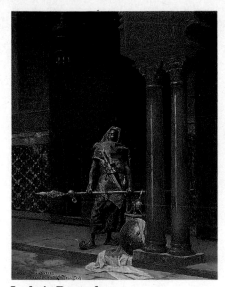

Ludwig Deutsch
Austrian (1855–1935)
The Nubian Guard
Signed and dedicated, oil on panel
12¼ x 9½in (31 x 24cm)
£24,000–30,000 *S*

Theodor van der Beek
German (b1838)
Arabischer Tanz
Signed, oil on canvas
43¾ x 53½in (111 x 136cm)
£10,000–12,000 *C*

Sir Frank Dicksee, P.R.A.
British (1853–1928)
Leila
Signed with initials, signed and inscribed with
title on the reverse, watercolour and bodycolour
5½ x 6¾in (14 x 17cm)
£40,000–50,000 *S*

Rudolf Ernst
Austrian (1854–1920)
An Arab in a Palace Interior
Signed, oil on panel
25½ x 21in (65 x 53.5cm)
£80,000–95,000 *C*

Jean-Léon Gérôme
French (1824–1904)
Femme de Constantinople, Debout
Signed, oil on canvas, 1876
16¼ x 12¾in (41 x 32cm)
£110,000–130,000 *S(NY)*

Adrien-Henri Tanoux
French (1865–1923)
The Odalisque
Signed and dated '1913', oil on canvas
23¼ x 30½in (59.5 x 77.5cm)
£13,500–15,000 *C*

Guillaume François Gabriel Lépaulle
French (1804–86)
A Turkish Lady
Signed and dated '1843',
oil on canvas
39¾ x 32in (101 x 81cm)
£35,000–40,000 *S*

George Antoine Rochegrosse
French (1859–1938)
Dans les Jardins de
Djenan Meriem
Signed and dated '1908',
oil on canvas
40½ x 60¾in (103 x 154cm)
£25,000–35,000 *S(NY)*

Maurice Brianchon
French (1899–1979)
Le Page
Signed, oil on canvas
21¼ x 25¾in (54 x 65cm)
£20,000–25,000 *S(NY)*

l. **José Villegas y Cordero**
Spanish (1848–1922)
Le Fumeur Oriental
Signed and dated '1875', oil on canvas
62½ x 33½in (158.5 x 85cm)
£200,000–225,000 *S(NY)*

Rosalba Carriera
Italian (1675–1757)
Flora, Holding a Basket of Flowers
Pastel
24¾ x 19½in (63 x 49cm)
£26,000–30,000 *C*

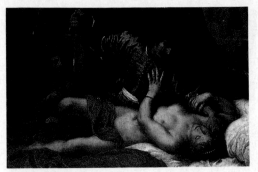

Felice Ficherelli, called Felice Riposo
Italian (1605–69)
Tarquin and Lucretia
Oil on canvas
39¼ x 58¼in (99 x 148cm)
£85,000–100,000 *S*

Anton Raphael Mengs
German (1728–79)
Truth
Pastel
24 x 19½in (61 x 49.5cm)
£110,000–120,000 *C*

Lucas Cranach I
German (1472–1553)
Lucretia
Signed with a serpent device and dated,
oil on panel
22¼ x 15½in (56.5 x 39.5cm)
£310,000–340,000 *C*

r. **Pietro Liberi**
Italian (1614–87)
Venus with Putti
Bears inventory number
on reverse, oil on canvas
54¾ x 69¾in (139 x 177cm)
£38,000–45,000 *S*

Hans von Staschiripka Canon
Austrian (1829–85)
A Male Nude
Oil on canvas
20¾ x 16⅜in (53 x 43cm)
£4,200–5,000 *C*

Franz von Stuck
German (1863–1928)
Amor auf dem Maskenball
Signed, mixed media on board
21½ x 17¾in (55 x 45cm)
£26,000–30,000 *C*

Auguste Raynaud
French (late 19thC)
Tending the Garden
Signed, oil on canvas
31 x 21½in (78.5 x 54.5cm)
£10,500–12,000 *C*

Delphin Enjolras
French (1857–1945)
The Boudoir
Signed, pastel on paper
24½ x 35½in (62.5 x 90.5cm)
£15,000–18,000 *S(NY)*

r. **Paul Merwart**
Polish (1855–1902)
Bacchante aux Raisins
Signed and dated '1887',
oil on canvas
62¼ x 79in (158 x 201cm)
£11,000–13,000 *S(NY)*

John Armstrong, A.R.A.
British (1893–1973)
Nude Reading
Oil on canvas
18½ x 21½in (47 x 54.5cm)
£3,500–4,000 *AdG*

Kitty Blandy
British (b1966)
Exuberance
Oil on canvas
36in (91.5cm) square
£800–1,200 *AMC*

Laureano Barrau
Spanish (1864–1957)
After the Swim
Signed, oil on canvas
74 x 54in (188 x 137cm)
£40,000–50,000 *S*

Elizabeth Cope
Irish (b1952)
Kristine
Oil on canvas
32 x 26in (81.5 x 66cm)
£1,000–1,100 *SOL*

Jane Corsellis
British (20thC)
The Regency Chaise Longue
Oil on canvas
20 x 24in (50.5 x 61cm)
£2,500–3,000 *WHP*

Clifford Cundy
British (1925–92)
Three Graces
Signed, oil on canvas, c1960s
36 x 48in (91.5 x 122cm)
£11,000–12,000 *PN*

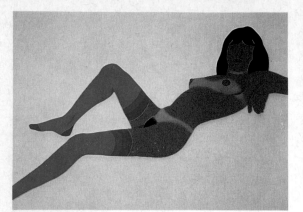

Tom Wesselmann
American (b1931)
Reclining Stockinged Nude No. 2
Oil on canvas on board, 1982
29½ x 51¼in (75 x 130cm)
£38,000–45,000 *S(NY)*

Dennis Gilbert, N.E.A.C., N.S.
British (b1922)
What to Wear?
Oil on canvas
14 x 18in (35.5 x 46cm)
£550–650 *JN*

Mary Gamlin
British (20thC)
Nude
Oil on canvas, 1936
30 x 20in (76 x 50.5cm)
£400–450 *JDG*

Lin Jammet
British (b1958)
Earth Rests
Gouache
48 x 30in (122 x 76cm)
£1,000–1,200 *CON*

l. **Milan Kunc**
Czechoslovakian (b1944)
Yellow Venus
Signed and dated '82', inscribed on
stretcher 'Gelbe Venus', oil on canvas
63 x 94½in (160 x 240cm)
£6,500–7,500 *C*

CHILDREN

'Men are generally more careful of the breed of their horses and dogs than of their children,' fulminated Quaker and founder of Pennsylvania, William Penn, in 1695. Looking through portraits of children from the 17thC and 18thC, it is notable how many of them are portrayed alongside the family dogs or with other domestic pets. These animals served a variety of functions. In Maria Cosway's picture of William Lamb, the dog underlines the gentle playfulness of childhood. In Robert Byng's portrait of a young aristocrat, the obedient hound serves to emphasise the child's authority and his presentation as a miniature adult rather than a small boy. Animals mirror the natural innocence of childhood and frequently carry an allegorical significance – the lamb that appears in so many pictures of children was not only a familiar farmyard beast but an emblem of the infant Christ – a bird's nest with eggs or fledglings stood for spring and the creation.

Pictures of children are often full of images that are both decorative and symbolic – cherries not only reflected rosy cheeks and rosebud lips but were the fruit of paradise and an emblem of heaven, again associated with the infant Christ; blowing bubbles signified the transience of youth. Much of the sentiment in Victorian portrayals of childhood lies in the implication that it will soon be lost; girls are portrayed as embryonic mothers cradling dolls, little boys bring them gifts of fruit and flowers in an innocent parody of future courtship. Such pictures were much loved by the 19thC public and are equally in demand today. 'Children are always extremely popular and certainly attract a premium,' agrees James Lloyd of Burlington Paintings. 'Children and animals are a perfect combination,' another dealer told Miller's. 'It's that 'aaah' factor that sells a picture.'

17th–18th Century

Attributed to Jacopo Chimenti, called Jacopo da Empoli
Italian (1554–1640)
Portrait of a Boy holding a staff and two flowers
Oil on canvas
40¼ x 28½in (102 x 72.5cm)
£15,000–18,000 *S(NY)*

Robert Byng
British (1666–1720)
Portrait of a Young Boy
Oil on canvas
49 x 38¾in (124.5 x 100cm)
£10,500–12,500 *C*

This picture bears similarities to the portrait of General Charles Montagu (Buccleuch Collection, Boughton House).

Attributed to Robert Byng
British (1666–1720)
Portrait of a Boy
Oil on canvas
30 x 25in (76 x 63.5cm)
£7,000–7,800 *HFA*

Attributed to John Closterman
German (1660–1713)
Portrait of a boy, holding a rabbit
Oil on canvas
44 x 34in (111.5 x 86cm)
£3,500–4,000 *WWG*

Dutch School (17thC)
Portraits of a Boy holding a Rabbit, and a Girl feeding a Sheep
A pair, one bears signature, oil on panel
21 x 16¼in (53 x 41cm)
£22,000–27,000 *S(NY)*

English School (c1685)
Portrait of a Young Girl
Indistinctly signed and dated '1685(?)',
oil on canvas
30 x 24in (76 x 61cm)
£2,800–3,500 C

School of Friesland (c1610)
Portrait of a Girl
Oil on panel
33¼ x 25⅜in (84 x 65.5cm)
£5,600–6,000 C

Circle of George Geldorp
British (c1595–1665)
Portrait of a young boy
Oil on canvas
49 x 34½in (124.5 x 88cm)
£10,500–12,500 S

Jan van Noort
Dutch (active 1644–76)
A Young Boy holding a Nest
Bears signature 'Flink', oil on panel
28¾ x 22⅛in (73 x 56cm)
£6,000–7,000 S(Am)

Johannes Vollevens II
Dutch (1685–1758)
Portrait of a Boy, aged 1 year 3 months,
with a spaniel in an ornamental garden
Signed, inscribed and dated '1729',
oil on canvas
33½ x 26¼in (85.5 x 66.5cm)
£8,200–10,000 C

Thomas Bardwell
British (1704–67)
Portrait of Lady Jane Elizabeth Leslie, later
Countess of Rothes, and her brother John,
later 11th Earl of Rothes
Oil on canvas
72 x 48in (182.5 x 122cm)
£12,000–15,000 C

Thomas Barber
British (c1768–1843)
Portrait of two boys
Oil on canvas
65 x 54in (165 x 137cm)
£14,000–16,000 *S(NY)*

After Giovanni Battista Cipriani
Italian (1727–85)
Le Bain, by J. B. Lucien
Soft ground etching in sepia on laid paper
11½ x 15in (29 x 38cm)
and a quantity of engravings, stipple
engravings by N. De Launay, W. Walker,
C. Galle and others
£350–400 *CSK*

*William Lamb, later Viscount Melbourne,
married Lady Caroline Ponsonby in 1805,
who was to become celebrated for her love
affair with Lord Byron. She famously
described Byron as 'mad, bad and dangerous
to know'. Their affair ended publicly and
badly, and in 1825 Melbourne separated from
his wife. He became Prime Minister in 1834,
and worked closely with the young Queen
Victoria who held him in great favour. The
statesman Charles Greville noted Melbourne's
great fatherly affection for the new Queen,
'and the more because he is a man with a
capacity for loving without anything to love,'
be concluded, providing a sad epitaph for the
affectionate child in this picture.*

Maria Cosway
British (1759–1838)
Portrait of the Hon. William Lamb, later
2nd Viscount Melbourne, playing with a dog
Oil on canvas
29¾ x 33⅝in (75.5 x 85.5cm)
£6,500–8,000 *C*

Manner of Joshua Cistall
British (1767–1849)
Portrait of a young girl
carrying a dish of water
Indistinctly signed,
oil on canvas
21 x 15in (53 x 38cm)
£850–1,000 *L*

Bartholomew Dandridge
British (1691–1755)
Portrait of a Girl
Oil on canvas
62½ x 41¾in (158.5 x 106cm)
£17,500–20,000 *C*

Studio of Georgio Domenico Dupra
Italian (1689–1770)
Portrait of Victor Amadeus III of Savoy
Oil on canvas
32 x 25½in (81 x 64.5cm)
£7,500–8,500 *S*

Jean-Honoré Fragonard
French (1732–1806)
Portrait of a young Boy
Oil on canvas
15¾ x 12½in (40 x 31.5cm)
£60,000–70,000 *S*

French School (c1700)
Portrait of a young Boy, his hat
under his arms
Oil on canvas
29 x 23½in (73.5 x 60cm)
£3,300–4,000 *S*

German School (c1790)
A Young Child seated on a red
velvet chair holding a biscuit
for her Dog
Oil on canvas
30¼ x 25½in (76.5 x 64.5cm)
£1,400–1,800 *P*

John Theodore Heins, Snr.
British (1697–1756)
Portrait of a Boy, holding a cherry
to a parrot, a spaniel at his side
Signed and dated '1741',
oil on canvas
50 x 40in (127 x 101.5cm)
£12,000–14,000 *C*

George Henry Harlow
British (1787–1819)
Portrait of a Child
Pencil, red and black chalk
13¼ x 10¼in (33.5 x 26.5cm)
£1,200–1,500 *C*

Nicolas de Largillière
French (1656–1746)
Portrait of François-Emmanuel
Pommyer wearing a grey jacket
Inscribed and dated '1722',
oil on canvas
21¾ x 17¾in (55 x 45cm)
£28,000–33,000 *C*

Sir Thomas Lawrence, P.R.A
British (1796–1830)
Portrait of Fanny Hamond and Jane
Hamond, later Marchesa Bocella
Oil on canvas
36 x 32½in (91.5 x 82.5cm)
£190,000–220,000 *S(NY)*

*Born in Bristol in 1869, Lawrence was an
infant prodigy and by the age of five could
already draw remarkable likenesses, further
stunning his sitters by reciting vast chunks
of Milton. Barely into his teens, he had a
flourishing portrait business completing
three to four portraits a week at two or
three guineas each.*

Circle of John Opie
British (1761–1807)
Portrait of a young Boy
carrying a basket
Oil on canvas
26½ x 22½in (67 x 57cm)
£1,000–1,400 *P*

**Attributed to Charles
Willson Peale**
American (1741–1827)
Portrait of Sarah Latimer
Oil on canvas
23 x 18¾in (58.5 x 47.5cm)
£7,500–9,000 *S(NY)*

Attributed to Jan Maurits Quinkhard
Dutch (1688–1772)
Portrait of a young Girl in a garden
Signed and dated '1741', oil on canvas
19¼ x 16¾in (48.5 x 41.5cm)
£2,700–3,500 *CSK*

Sir Henry Raeburn, R.A., P.R.S.A.
British (1756–1823)
Portrait of Miss Maitland
Oil on canvas
29½ x 25in (75 x 64cm)
£5,200–6,000 *S*

*The sitter was possibly a relative of Admiral
Sir F. L. Maitland who, as Commander of
H.M.S. 'Bellerophon', took Napoleon to St.
Helena, Raeburn painted both his portrait
and that of his wife.*

**Follower of Joseph Wright
of Derby**
British (1734–97)
Portrait of a young member
of the Powell Family with
his pet dog
28½ x 23¾in (72.5 x 60.5cm)
£950–1,250 *S(S)*

Jakob Mathias Schmutzer
Austrian (1733–1811)
Head of a Girl, recto, a Sketch
of a Girl's Head detailing the
eyes, verso
Red chalk, watermark
22½ x 17½in (57 x 44.5cm)
£550–700 *P*

19th Century

Louise Emile Adan
French (1839–1937)
The Bird's Nest
Signed, oil on canvas
21½ x 29in (54.5 x 73.5cm)
£25,000–30,000 *C*

Helen Allingham, R.W.S.
British (1848–1926)
Edith
Signed, inscribed and extensively
annotated verso, watercolour
4⅓in (11cm) diam
£6,000–7,000 *WrG*

American School (19thC)
Two Sisters in white dresses and red slippers
holding a delicate floral vine
Oil on panel
34¼ x 48½in (87 x 123cm)
£30,000–35,000 *S(NY)*

*Painted c1815, the sisters are posed in a
fashionable interior of the early 19thC with
wide painted floorboards, flower decorated
wainscoting and period wallpaper.*

Edmund Adler
Austrian (1871–1957)
The Daisy Chain
Signed, oil on canvas
22 x 27in (55.5 x 68.5cm)
£20,000–21,800 *HFA*

Helen Allingham, R.W.S.
British (1848–1926)
On the Sands
Watercolour
6 x 7in (15 x 17.5cm)
£14,000–15,000 *JN*

Attributed to Edward Charles Barnes
British (19thC)
A Country Girl
Oil on canvas
30 x 20in (76 x 51cm)
£1,900–2,500 *CSK*

Montagu Barstow
British (19th/20thC)
The Morning News
Signed, monochrome watercolour
11 x 8½in (28 x 21cm)
£300–400 *Bon*

Francesco Bergamini
Italian (1815–83)
Sunday School
Signed and inscribed, oil on canvas
17½ x 26½in (44.5 x 67cm)
£7,500–8,500 *C*

 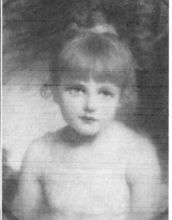

A. Bonifazi
Italian (19thC)
A Peasant Girl, and a Peasant Boy
A pair, signed, inscribed, dated '75',
oil on board
8¾ x 7⅜in (22 x 19.5cm)
£3,000–3,800 *CSK*

John Ernest Breun, R.B.A.
British (1862–1921)
Simplicity and Innocence
A pair, both signed and dated
'1900', pastel
15 x 12in (38 x 30.5cm)
£8,000–9,000 *HFA*

Camille Léopold Cabaillot
French (b1839)
The Pet Lamb
Signed and dated '1877', oil on panel
12½ x 9½in (32 x 23.5cm)
£3,300–4,300 *Bon*

Robert Carrick
British (1829–1905)
The Red Squirrel
Signed and dated '1889',
watercolour heightened with white
17¾ x 11½in (45 x 29cm)
£1,500–1,800 *C*

Niccolò Cannicci
Italian (1846–1906)
Una Conchiglia
Signed, inscribed and dated '1895',
oil on canvas
21¾ x 11¾in (55 x 30cm)
£18,000–20,000 *Bon*

Circle of Margaret Carpenter
British (1793–1872)
Two Children with a pet finch in a Cage
Oil on board
18½ x 24½in (47 x 62cm)
£6,000–7,000 *S(S)*

The goldfinch, a favourite children's pet, was
another symbol associated with Christ, often
appearing in religious pictures and paintings
of the Christ child. Legend has it that the bird
acquired its red spot from being splashed
with the Saviour's blood as it pulled a thorn
out of Christ's head on the road to Calvary.

Louis-Robert Carrier-Belleuse
French (1848–1913)
The Doll
Signed, oil on canvas
26 x 18½in (66 x 46.5cm)
£25,000–30,000 *C*

Milly Childers
British (19th/20thC)
Aromanches
Signed, inscribed with title and dated '1903'
23¼ x 19¼in (59 x 49cm)
£350–450 *S(S)*

Gaetano Chierici
Italian (1838–1920)
Gioia and Dolore
A pair, each signed and dated '1871',
oil on canvas
22¾ x 18½in (58 x 47cm)
£100,000–120,000 *S(NY)*

Thomas Cooper Gotch
British (1854–1931)
Golden Youth
Signed and inscribed, oil on canvas
48 x 84½in (122 x 214cm)
£50,000–60,000 *C*

Joseph Clarke, R.A.
British (1835–1926)
With Smiles of Peace and Looks of Love
Signed and dated '1886', oil on canvas
25 x 30in (64 x 76cm)
£13,000–14,000 *TOT*

William Charles Thomas Dobson R.A.
British (1817–1998)
Christmas Roses
Signed with monogram and dated '1881',
pencil and watercolour with scratching out
18 x 14in (45.5 x 35.5cm)
£8,800–10,000 *C*

Ebenezer Newman Downard
British (active 1849–89)
The Loiterers
Signed and inscribed, oil on panel
17 x 13¾in (43 x 32.5cm)
£1,500–1,800 *Bea*

English School (c1850)
Boy with a Drum
Oil on canvas
8 x 11½in (20 x 29cm)
£1,600–1,800 *CGa*

Arthur John Elsley
British (b1861)
Playtime
Signed, oil on canvas
38¼ x 29in (97 x 74cm)
£19,000–24,000 *C*

Angele Dubos
French (b1844)
Sisters
Signed, oil on canvas
30 x 24in (76 x 61cm)
£50,000–55,000 *HFA*

English School (late 19thC)
Three children in a rustic interior
Signed indistinctly, watercolour and pencil
13½ x 15½in (34 x 39.5cm)
£800–1,000 *DN*

English School (19thC)
The Twins, purported to be
of the Howard family
Oil on canvas
34¾ x 28¼in (87 x 71.5cm)
£6,000–7,000 *DA*

English School (c1860)
Portrait of a Boy, walking
on a path with two Dogs
Oil on canvas
54 x 41½in (137 x 105cm)
£1,900–2,400 *CSK*

Elizabeth Adela Forbes
British (1859–1912)
Young Girl with her Puppy
Signed, black crayon,
watercolour and bodycolour
heightened with white
16¾ x 11¾in (43 x 30cm)
£1,700–2,300 *CSK*

E. Frère
French (1819–86)
Bird Catchers
Signed and dated '1859', oil on paper
13 x 17in (33 x 43cm)
£12,000–12,800 *HFA*

> **Miller's is a price GUIDE
> not a price LIST**

Manuel Mendez Gonzalez
Spanish (19thC)
Portrait of a Boy wearing
a Sailor Suit, on a beach
Signed and dated '1889',
oil on canvas
58 x 36¾in (147.5 x 93.5cm)
£2,000–2,500 *C*

Kate Greenaway
British (1846–1901)
A Fern Gatherer
Signed, pencil and watercolour
heightened with touches of
bodycolour and scratching out
23¾ x 15½in (60 x 39.5cm)
£4,000–5,000 *C*

*This is a typical drawing of
c1872 when Greenaway was
in the habit of using models
she found on the street.*

Guerrino Guardebassi
Italian (b1841)
A Pageboy standing by a Column
Signed, pencil and watercolour
heightened with white
13¼ x 9in (34 x 22.5cm)
£160–250 *CSK*

Alexei Alexeiwicz Harlamoff
Russian (1842–1915)
The Arrangement
Signed, oil on canvas
29 x 40⅝in (73.5 x 103cm)
£100,000–125,000 *C*

Alexei Alexeiwicz Harlamoff
Russian (1842–1915)
The Two Sisters
Signed, oil on canvas
42 x 33in (106.5 x 83.5cm)
£160,000–200,000 *WH*

Harlamoff's recognisable and attractive pictures of young girls are becoming increasingly sought after. His picture 'The Two Sisters' offered by William Hardie, shot way over its £20,000–£25,000 estimate to create an auction record for the artist. Two months later at Sotheby's, 'The Arrangement' quadrupled its lower £25,000 estimate. Pretty and finely painted, if somewhat sentimental and predictable, Harlamoff's pictures continue to weave their magic in the current market, proving that if the product is right, both the demand and the money are certainly there to meet it.

Alexei Alexeiwicz Harlamoff
Russian (1848–1915)
A Peasant Girl on a Footbridge
Signed, oil on canvas
33 x 19¼in (83.5 x 49cm)
£17,500–20,000 *S*

Alexei Alexeiwicz Harlamoff
Russian (1848–1915)
Portrait of a Girl
Signed, charcoal and pastel on paper
22 x 18¼in (55.5 x 46cm)
£4,500–6,000 *C*

William Hemsley, R.B.A.
British (active 1848–93)
Puzzled
Signed, oil on canvas
10 x 8in (25 x 20cm)
£6,000–7,000 *HFA*

Léon Herbo
Belgian (1850–1907)
The Red Dress
Signed and dated '1881', oil on panel
26½ x 21in (67 x 53.5cm)
£2,400–3,000 *C*

Attributed to Robert Hills, O.W.S.
British (1797–1844)
A Thatcher's Apprentice
Watercolour
7¾ x 3¼in (19.5 x 8.5cm)
£350–450 *P*

Arthur Hopkins
British (1848–1930)
Courting Danger, and A Garden in
the Cotswolds
A pair, both signed, inscribed and dated
'29 Oct' and '9 Sept' respectively, watercolour
and bodycolour
10½ x 15in (26.5 x 38cm)
£900–1,200 *CSK*

Edward Atkinson Hornel
British (1864–1933)
Gathering Mushrooms
Signed and dated '1901'
30 x 24in (76 x 61cm)
£18,500–22,000 *WH*

Charles Hunt
British (1803–77)
The Tribunal
Signed and dated '1870', oil on canvas
29¼ x 44½in (75 x 113cm)
£9,000–11,000 *S(NY)*

Charles Hunt specialised in scenes of
children at play, dressing up and acting
out adult scenes.

Gustav Igler
Hungarian (b1842)
Left to their own Devices
Signed and dated '1881', oil on canvas
27¼ x 75in (69 x 190.5cm)
£35,000–45,000 *C*

Gottlieb Theodor Kempf von Hartenkampf
Austrian (1871–1964)
Little Red Riding Hood
Signed and inscribed, oil on panel
25¾ x 31½in (65.5 x 80cm)
£12,000–14,000 *C*

An attractive juvenile subject, a bright and sunny picture, a clear and crisp style, all these qualities gave Gottlieb von Hartenkampf's painting instant commercial appeal and it shot several times over its £2,000–3,000 estimate at Christie's.

Johan Mari Henri Ten Kate
Dutch (1831–1910)
Native School at Sinagar
Signed and inscribed 'Java', oil on canvas
19 x 23½in (48 x 60cm)
£12,000–14,000 *P*

This painting was given to Thomas Pryce by the artist as a souvenir of the journey they made together to Java in 1883, the same year as the eruption of Krakatoa. This School was established and maintained by Mr. E. J. Kerkhoven, the owner of Sinagar Estate, for the education of native children on the tea estate.

Joseph Kirkpatrick
British (1872–c1930)
Lost in the Woods
Signed, pencil and watercolour
9¾ x 6¾in (24.5 x 17cm)
£500–600 *CSK*

Frederik Lintz
Belgian (1824–1909)
The Playful Pet
Signed, oil on canvas
35¾ x 23¾in (91 x 65.5cm)
£9,500–10,500 *S(NY)*

Agnes Gardner King, A.S.W.A.
British (active 1880–1902)
The Page Boy
Signed, watercolour
21 x 13in (53 x 33cm)
£1,400–1,600 *HO*

Basile de Loose
Dutch (1809–85)
The School Room
Signed and dated '1847', oil on panel
27½ x 33½in (70 x 85cm)
£55,000–65,000 *C*

Aristide Maillol
French (1861–1944)
Profil de Jeune Fille
Signed with monogram, dated '1843', oil
on canvas
13 x 16in (33 x 40.5cm)
£80,000–90,000 *C*

*'Profil de Jeune Fille' illustrates the influence
of three different forces on Maillol's work in
the 1890s, the flatness of the picture plane
owes much to Gaugin, whom Maillol had met
in 1892, the range of Maillol's colours and
'classical order' of the composition owes much
to the Nabis, whom he joined in the mid-
1890s, and the choice of subject reflects the
Symbolists' infatuation with the spirituality
of young women, 'innocent and virginal,
sinless Eve's before the fall'.*

Ferdinand Marohn
French (19thC)
The young Look-Out
Signed, inscribed and dated
'1847', pencil and watercolour
10½ x 8½in (26.5 x 21cm)
£350–450 *CSK*

Harry Humphrey Moore
American (1844–1926)
Best of Friends
Signed and inscribed, oil on canvas
32½ x 25¼in (81.5 x 64cm)
£18,000–20,000 *C*

Alfred Morgan
British (active 1862–1904)
Grandmother's Visit
Signed, inscribed and dated '1871',
oil on canvas
28 x 36in (71 x 92cm)
£9,500–12,000 *P*

*The eggtimer in the child's hand is a
standard symbol of the passing of time
and the transience of youth.*

Follower of Fred Morgan
British (1856–1927)
Teatime, The First Introduction
A pair, oil on canvas
17½ x 23½in (44.5 x 60cm)
£950–1,200 *S(S)*

Emily Mary Osborn
British (active 1851–1908)
The Oyster Girl
Oil on canvas
24 x 20in (61 x 50.5cm)
£1,000–1,250 *CAG*

William McWhannel Petrie
British (1870–1937)
Eva
Signed and inscribed, pastel on canvas
54 x 28in (137 x 71cm)
£4,700–6,000 *C(S)*

Ludwig Passini
Australian (1832–1903)
Il Pastorello, and La Piccola Fioraia
One signed and dated '1865', the other
signed '1863', watercolour on paper laid
down on board
16¾ x 12¼in (42.5 x 31cm)
£5,000–6,000 *C*

**Miller's is a price GUIDE
not a price LIST**

Camille Pissarro
French (1830–1903)
Portrait de Ludovic-Rodo-Pissarro
Signed with initials, pastel on paper, 1880
9½ x 8¾in (24 x 22cm)
£15,000–17,000 *C*

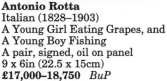

William Matthew Prior
American (1806–73)
Portrait of a Child in green holding a Whip
Oil on paperboard
14¾ x 10¼in (37.5 x 25.5cm)
£3,000–4,000 *SK*

Antonio Rotta
Italian (1828–1903)
A Young Girl Eating Grapes, and
A Young Boy Fishing
A pair, signed, oil on panel
9 x 6in (22.5 x 15cm)
£17,000–18,750 *BuP*

Ernest Howard Shepard
British (1879–1976)
The Only Child
Oil on canvas
27¾ x 37¼in (71 x 95cm)
£16,500–17,500 *CBL*

*This powerful image of childhood
was created by the artist who
provided the immortal illustrations
to A. A. Milne's Winnie the Pooh,
and whose work is now familiar to
generations of children.*

Henry Terry
British (1879–1920)
Knitting for Grandma
Signed, watercolour
17¾ x 12¾in (45 x 32cm)
£1,600–2,200 *Bon*

Frederick Smallfield, A.W.R.S.
British (1829–1915)
Summer's Harvest
Signed and dated '1868', watercolour
26 x 18in (66 x 45.5cm)
£15,500–16,500 *HFA*

Fred Stratton
British (19th/20thC)
Threading the Needle
Watercolour
20½ x 14½in (51 x 36.5cm)
£2,250–2,450 *AdG*

Franz Schams
Austrian (1823–83)
The Thief
Signed, and dated '882', oil on panel
15¾ x 12in (40 x 30.5cm)
£4,000–5,000 *S*

Virgilio Tojetti
Italian (1851–1901)
Children with a Lute
Signed and dated '99', oil on board
9½ x 20¼in (23.5 x 51cm)
£1,500–2,000 *P*

Harold Waite
British (active 1880–1920)
Collecting Eggs
Signed, watercolour
11 x 8in (28 x 20cm)
£600–700 *HI*

Joseph Watter
German (1838–1913)
A Moment's Thought
Signed, oil on canvas
17 x 13in (43 x33cm)
£9,500–10,500 *HFA*

Charles Edward Wilson
British (active 1891–c1936)
A Special Treat
Signed, watercolour
14 x 10in (35.5 x 25cm)
£12,750–13,750 *HFA*

David Woodlock
British (1842–1929)
Young Boy playing a tin whistle
in the Garden
Signed and inscribed, watercolour
11½ x 4in (29 x 10cm)
£1,000–1,200 *LH*

Aurelio Zingoni
Italian (1853–1922)
Una Cruna Difficile
Signed and dated '1875', oil on canvas
41¼ x 34in (104.5 x 86.5cm)
£6,000–7,000 *C*

20th Century

Mabel Lucie Attwell, S.W.A.
British (1879–1964)
Lucie Attwell's Annual front cover and spine
Watercolour and bodycolour
13½ x 12½in (34 x 32cm)
£4,000–4,500 *CBL*

Mabel Lucie Attwell was a remarkable woman. Born in Mile End, London, the daughter of a butcher, she attended art classes at Regent Street and Heatherley's Art Schools. Unimpressed by the rigorous routine of still life drawing and copying classical casts, she preferred to create her own imaginary sketches and was soon selling drawings to magazines. Attwell illustrated a whole range of celebrated children's books and soon the artist became a marketing phenomenon. Lucie Attwell's grinning and bun-faced infants appeared on everything from nursery equipment to biscuit tins. Chad Valley produced Lucie Attwell dolls, and the Lucie Attwell Annual ran from 1922–74. The artist designed postcards, calendars, crockery, wall plaques ... and by the 1920s, she was a household name. In 1908, Attwell married painter and illustrator Charles Earnshaw and the couple had three children. During WWI, Earnshaw was gravely wounded and lost his right arm - much of the responsibility for supporting the family fell on Attwell's shoulders, a task she seems to have relished.

Alexander Averianov
Russian (b1948)
The White Dress
Signed and dated '1987', oil on canvas
47in (119cm) square
£2,750–3,000 *EG*

Cicely Mary Barker
British (1895–1973)
Holiday Pictures, London, Blackie's 'It Won't Tear' Series front cover
Signed with initials, 1928, watercolour with bodycolour,
13¾ x 10¼in (35 x 26cm)
£1,550–1,750 *CBL*

Mary Beresford-Williams
British (b1931)
Ennui
Signed with initials, oil on canvas
10 x 8in (25 x 20cm)
£400–490 *JN*

Peter Blake, R.A.
British (b1932)
Girl in a Poppy Field
Signed and dated '1974', original
screenprint in colours
16 x 10¾in (41 x 27cm)
£700–750 *WO*

Sue Broadley
British (b1943)
Rosie in a Hat
Signed and dated '1992',
watercolour
14 x 18in (35.5 x 45.5cm)
£500–600 *HI*

Robert Cree Crawford
British (1842–1924)
My Best Friend
Oil on canvas
60 x 40¼in (152 x 102cm)
£14,500–16,500 *C*

*The sitter is the artist's
granddaughter, Sarita, aged 5.*

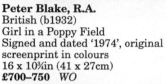

Beryl Cook
British (b1926)
Children in a Playground
Signed, inscribed and dated '1991',
oil on panel
15½ x 11½in (39.5 x 29.5cm)
£2,400–3,400 *Bea*

Phillippa Clayden
British (b1955)
Hopscotch
Pastel
22 x 30in (56 x 76cm)
£1,300–1,500 *BOU*

Harold Harvey
British (1874–1941)
The Village Shop
Signed, inscribed and dated '13',
oil on canvas
18 x 16in (46 x 41cm)
£13,000–14,000 *C*

Grace Henry, H.R.H.A.
British (1868–1953)
Feeding the Ducks
Signed, oil on board
14 x 11in (35.5 x 28cm)
£2,000–2,500 *CCG*

Normal Hepple, R.A., R.P.
British (1909–94)
The Woolly Hat
Signed, oil on panel
16 x 12in (40.5 x 30.5cm)
£2,000–3,000 *BRG*

*Norman Hepple died in January 1994 at the
age of 85. He 'was the epitome of an almost
extinct breed, the Royal Academy painter,'
noted his obituary in* The Daily Telegraph.
*'His traditional portraits of the Royal family,
belted earls, boardroom worthies, well
groomed debutantes and well brushed
children, were once a regular feature of the
R.A.'s Summer Exhibition.' When people
criticised the traditionalist elegance of his
work, Hepple's response was robust. 'They're
not paying you to make them look as if
they've just been pulled out of the river,'
he would declare. 'It isn't really flattery, it's
a question of selection.' Hepple painted many
pictures of children throughout his career.*

Sir Gerald Festus Kelly, P.R.A., R.H.A.
British (1879–1972)
Ma Aung Saw Myaing
Inscribed, oil on canvas
41 x 32in (104.81cm)
£5,500–6,500 *C*

John Heseltine
British (20thC)
Children with a Kitten
Signed, watercolour
16½ x 13in (41.5 x 33cm)
£400–500 *LH*

Moïse Kisling
French (1891–1953)
La Fillette
Signed, 1918, oil on canvas
21¾ x 15in (55 x 38cm)
£42,000–50,000 *S(NY)*

Madeleine Luka
French (20thC)
Le Champagne
Signed, oil on canvas
28¾ x 23½in (73 x 59.5cm)
£900–1,100 *CSK*

Constant Montald
Belgian (1863–1944)
Jeune Fille et sa Dame de Compagnie
Signed and dated '15', gouache on board
28 x 35in (71 x 89cm)
£11,500–13,000 *C*

Orovida Pissarro
Anglo-French (1893–1968)
Winter (The Skaters)
Signed and dated '1936–38'
Tempera on linen
36 x 45in (91.5 x 114cm)
£4,500–5,000 *STD*

Dorothea Sharp
British (1874–1955)
Girl on a grassy cliff top
Signed, oil on board
15 x 18in (38 x 45.5cm)
£1,600–3,500 *AH*

Lev Soloviev
Russian (1907–86)
Lionka
Signed and dated '1939', oil on canvas
20 x 16in (50.5 x 40.5cm)
£700–800 *EG*

MOTHERS & CHILDREN

'Here all mankind is equal:
Rich and poor alike, they love their children.'
Euripides, c422 B.C.

In the following section, the formal family
portraits of the 18thC gradually give way to
the sentimental, non-specific, depictions of
motherhood ever-popular with a Victorian
audience. Aristocratic mamas are replaced by
middle and working class mothers. Settings
are often rural and humble, reflecting the
influence of Dutch genre paintings with their
dim cottage interiors and crib scenes. The
function of such pictures is moral as much
as representational. Mothers are not shown
posing for their portraits, but busily involved
in domestic pursuits, caring for the physical
and spiritual well-being of their offspring
(supervising prayers was a particularly
popular subject).

After Henri Gascars
French (1635–1701)
A portrait of an Elegant Lady, believed
to be Barbara, Duchess of Cleveland,
with her daughter, Lady Barbara Fitzroy,
Countess of Lichfield
Oil on canvas
39¾ x 47¾in (100 x 121cm)
£5,000–6,000 *P*

*Inscribed on the reverse with the identities of
the sitters. The original composition by Henri
Gascars is in Lord Dillon's Collection, Ditchley.*

Attributed to Richard van Bleeck
Dutch (c1670–c1733)
Portrait of Selina, Countess of Huntingdon
and her daughter, Elizabeth
Oil on canvas
73¾ x 52in (187 x 132cm)
£4,500–5,500 *C*

Henry Edridge, A.R.A.
British (1769–1821)
Portrait of Mrs Whalley and her Daughter
Signed, inscribed and dated '1809',
pencil and watercolour with touches
of white heightening
13½ x 10in (34 x 25cm)
£2,200–2,800 *C*

After James Ward
British (1769–1859)
Compassionate Children
Coloured mezzotint, wove paper
19 x 25in (48 x 63.5cm)
£700–900 *CSK*

George Washington Brownlow
British (1835–76)
The Joys of Home
Signed and dated '1857', oil on canvas
31 x 27½in (79 x 70cm)
£14,000–16,000   P

Pierre Jean Edmond Castan
French (b1817)
The Toy Sailboat
Signed and dated '1862', oil on panel
10 x 7in (25 x 17.5cm)
£9,000–9,800   HFA

George Chinnery
British (1774–1852)
A Tanka Woman with her Child
Inscribed and dated in the artist's shorthand
'July 6, 1846', pencil and pen and brown ink
3½ x 4in (9 x 10cm)
£800–1,000   C

*Although in the 1840s the Tanka boatwomen
of Macau made up an estimated quarter of
the local population, they were discouraged
from mixing with the mainland Chinese, who
forced them to remain at night on the Praya
Pequera, the beach opposite the official
'Hoppo-house'. They were a distinct ethnic
class, their feet left unbound and their long
hair parted at the front. To the largely male
expatriate community they were a female
symbol of the China coast. In 1848 Chinnery
sent a picture of a demure and smiling
Tanka woman to a client as a souvenir.
In Chinnery's words 'They were good-natured,
pretty-looking young women, and smiled
frequently, exhibiting beautiful teeth.'*

William Merritt Chase (1849–1916) **and
Irving R. Wiles** (1861–1948)
American
Mrs William Merrit Chase and her Son,
Roland Dana
Signed, oil on canvas
62 x 50¼in (157 x 128cm)
£20,000–25,000   S(NY)

*Irving R. Wiles was one of Chase's earliest
pupils at the Art Student's League and later
taught at the Chase School of Art. The
unfinished portrait of Mrs Chase was
completed by Wiles at the request of the Chase
family. On his deathbed, Chase had requested
that Wiles complete any unfinished portrait
commissions that remained in his studio.*

English School (19thC)
The Bible Lesson
Oil on panel
14 x 11in (35.5 x 30cm)
£300–400 *C*

Adolphe Eberle
German (1843–1914)
The New Puppies
Signed and inscribed, oil on panel
16¾ x 20½in (43 x 52cm)
£28,000–35,000 *S(NY)*

William Powell Frith, R.A.
British (1819–1909)
'When we Devote our Youth to God,
'Tis pleasing in his eyes,
A Flower when offered in the bud, is no vain sacrifice'
Signed and dated '1852', oil on canvas
36½ x 28¾in (93 x 73cm)
£25,000–30,000 *S*

Frith spent much of the summer of 1851 at Ramsgate and, as he reported in his autobiography, 'weary of costume painting', he decided to turn his hand to 'modern life, with all its drawbacks of unpicturesque dress.' In September, Frith began the oil sketch for this composition and the next April began the large oil of Ramsgate Sands. Laboured over for two years, the picture was exhibited at the Academy in 1854. It was bought by Queen Victoria for 1,000 guineas, and immediately established Frith as the chronicler in paint of the age. 'When we devote our youth to God...' was the first painting of contemporary life which Frith sent to the Royal Academy, and as such marks that turning point in his career.

Circle of Sir Francis Grant
British (1803–78)
A Mother and Daughter, in widow's weeds
Oil on canvas
20 x 16in (50.5 x 40.5cm)
£500–700 *CSK*

Carl Hirschberg
American (1854–1923)
Good Morning
Signed and dated '10', oil on canvas
28¾ x 21¼in (73 x 54cm)
£6,000–6,500 *P*

Edwin Harris
British (1855–1906)
Faraway Thoughts
Signed, oil on canvas laid down on panel
20 x 16¼in (50.5 x 41.3cm)
£4,000–5,000 *C*

James John Hill
British (1811–82)
'She looks and looks, and still with new delight'
Signed, oil on canvas
23¼ x 19½in (59 x 49cm)
£3,000–4,000 *Bon*

Gustave Leonhard de Johnghe
Belgian (1829–93)
Family Prayers
Signed and dated '1894', oil on panel
22 x 17¾in (55.5 x 45cm)
£15,000–18,000 *S(NY)*

George Goodwin Kilburne
British (active 1880–1920)
A Mother's Love
Signed, watercolour
10 x 14in (25 x 35.5cm)
£2,500–3,000 *WG*

Angelo Martinetti
British (active 1880)
Mamma's Birthday
Signed, oil on canvas
20 x 30in (50.5 x 76cm)
£20,000–25,000 *HFA*

**William McTaggard,
R.S.A., V.P.R.S.W.**
British (1835–1910)
The Mother's Song
Signed and dated '1868', oil on panel
22 x 16½in (55.5 x 41.5cm)
£5,000–6,000 *C(S)*

Albert Neuhuys
Dutch (1844–1914)
Mother and Child at a Spinning Wheel
Signed, watercolour
25 x 18¼in (63.5 x 46.5cm)
£1,800–2,400 *P*

Federico Mazzotta
Italian (late 19thC)
L'Ora de Bagno
Signed, oil on canvas
28½ x 45in (72.5 x 114cm)
£20,000–30,000 *C*

Sir William Orpen, R.A., H.R.A.
British (1878–1931)
Lottie Feeding a Baby
Signed, oil on canvas
30 x 25in (76.5 x 63.5cm)
£57,000–70,000 *S*

Evert Pieters
Dutch (1856–1932)
Maternité
Signed, oil on canvas
42¾ x 35in (108.5 x 89cm)
£7,000–9,000 *S(NY)*

Bernard Pothast
British (1882–1966)
Blowing Bubbles
Signed, oil on canvas
29¾ x 25¾in (76 x 66cm)
£25,000–30,000 *BuP*

l. **Sir James Jebusa Shannon**
British (1892–1923)
Lady Dickson-Poynder and
her daughter Joan
Signed, oil on canvas
72¼ x 43¾in (183.5 x 111cm)
£55,000–65,000 *C*

Alfred Provis
British (active 1843–86)
Family Feeding the Kitten
Signed with initials, oil on canvas
8 x 10½in (20 x 26cm)
£3,000–3,300 *LH*

Jules Trayer
French (1824–1908)
Morning Prayer
Signed, oil on panel
14 x 11in (35.5 x 28cm)
£9,000–9,500 *S*

Christian Mary Wilbee
British (active 1903–12)
A Waif from the Sea
Signed, indistinctly inscribed and
dated '1912', oil on canvas
30¼ x 20¾in (77 x 52.5cm)
£5,000–6,000 *C*

Eugenio Zampighi
Italian (1859–1944)
Feeding the Baby
Signed, watercolour
20¾ x 13¾in (52.5 x 35cm)
£2,500–3,500 *P*

William Kay Blacklock
British (b1872)
A Mother and Child paddling
in the Sea
Signed and dated '15',
pencil and watercolour
13¾ x 10in (35 x 25cm)
£3,800–4,800 *CSK*

**Le Corbusier (Charles
Edouard Jeanneret)**
French (1887–1967)
L'Africaine portant son Enfant
au Dos
Signed with initials, red crayon
and pencil on paper
12¾ x 8½in (32.5 x 22cm)
£900–1,200 *CSK*

William Lee-Hankey, R.A.
British (1869–1952)
Maternity
Signed, watercolour
39¾ x 24¾in (101 x 63cm)
£4,200–6,000 *P*

Fernand Léger
French (1881–1955)
Plaque: Mère et Enfant
Signed and numbered, glazed ceramic
11 x 7¼in (28 x 18.5cm)
£4,000–5,000 *CNY*

Bernard Heninsky
Ukrainian (1891–1950)
Mother and Child
Gesso
13¾ x 8¾in (35 x 22cm)
£2,000–2,200 *GG*

Peter Peri
British (1899–1946)
Up in the Air, 1946
Etching
12¾ x 7in (32.5 x 17.5cm)
£175–200 *BLD*

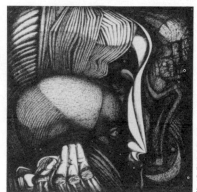

Peter Augustave Rasmussen
British (b1927)
Near Cagnes sur Loup
Signed, pastel
19 x 24in (48 x 61cm)
£1,200–1,600 *RBB*

Ibrahim El Salahi
Sudanese (b1929)
Mother and Child
Signed and dated '1990'
9½in (24cm) square
£800–1,000 *SG*

FAMILY GROUPS

Michiel van Musscher
Dutch (1645–1705)
A Family in an Interior
Traces of signature, oil on canvas
28½ x 24½in (72.5 x 62cm)
£30,000–35,000 *S*

Circle of Francis Wheatley, R.A.
British (1747–1801)
Portrait of the Bankes Family in a Garden
Oil on canvas
29¾ x 24¾in (75.5 x 63cm)
£33,000–45,000 *C*

Circle of Richard Buckner
British (active 1830–97)
The Fremlin Family, Brewers of Kent
Oil on canvas
52¼ x 68in (133 x 173cm)
£2,500–3,500 *P*

Circle of Alfred-Edward Chalon
British (1780–1860)
Mrs. Robert Ibbetson and Family
Oil on panel, c1825
14 x 17in (35.5 x 43cm)
£900–1,200 *S(NY)*

English School (mid-19thC)
A Family Group in a Drawing Room
Watercolour over pencil
21¼ x 28½in (54 x 72.5cm)
£4,000–5,000 *S*

English School (early 19thC)
A Gentleman with his family and
others assembled on a lawn
Oil on canvas
37 x 49¼in (94 x 125.5cm)
£9,000–11,000 *S*

George Goodwin Kilburn, R.I., R.B.A.
British (1839–1924)
Sunday Morning
Watercolour
19 x 27in (48 x 68.5cm)
£12,000–13,000 *HFA*

George Sheridan Knowles, R.I., R.B.A.,
British (1863–1931)
The Money Box, and The Painting Lesson
A pair, each signed and dated '1909', oil
on canvas
31½ x 22½in (80 x 57cm)
£6,000–7,000 *S(NY)*

Alexander Ivanov
Russian (b1950)
Weekend
Signed and dated '1989–1990', etching,
watercolour and inks on paper
18in (46cm) square
£400–500 *Mer*

Il'ia Efimovich Repin
Russian (1844–1930)
The Artist's Daughter, Tat'iana
and her family
Signed in Cyrillic, oil on canvas
34½ x 70¾in (87.5 x 179.5cm)
£115,000–140,000 *C*

Alessandro Milesi
Italian (1856–1945)
The Fisherman's Return
Signed and inscribed, oil on canvas
37¾ x 51¼in (96 x 130cm)
£50,000–60,000 *C*

Laurence Stephen Lowry, R.A.
British (1887–1976)
Family Group
Signed and dated '1951', oil on panel
12 x 8½in (30.5 x 21.5cm)
£10,000–11,000 *S*

*Lowry claimed to have few fond memories
of his childhood. 'I never had a family - all
I had round me was a garden and a fence'
he declared grimly. Perhaps significantly,
the artist painted pictures of family groups
throughout his career – stiff and cool images,
in which figures often appear isolated from
one another.*

FIGURES & GROUPS

The following section includes a number of
Victorian 18thC genre pieces. Costume
pictures, whether portraying Greeks and
Romans, cavaliers or 18thC nobility at play,
appealed greatly to a 19thC audience. These
were not grand and portentous history
paintings in the tradition of the past, but
decorative and domestic dressing-up pictures:
'the public are attracted to costume subjects
in the same way that they fall in love with
the fancy-dress of a masked ball,' explained
the Victorian sculptor, Alfred Stevens.
The 18thC, as a pre-revolutionary age of
elegance, aristocratic supremacy and
decorative luxury, was a particularly favourite
subject. The French artist, Meisonnier,
achieved international popularity with his
painstakingly detailed historical genre
pictures, and his portrayals of the everyday
life of titled 18thC folk spawned a host of
imitators across Europe. What such pictures
lacked in intellectual content, they made up
for in slick technique and superb decorative
detail. Often masterpieces of craftsmanship,
they continue to find a ready audience in the
current market.

After J. Verkolje
Dutch (1650–93)
A Lady, Gentleman and
Attendants in an Interior
Oil on board
16½ x 13in (42 x 33cm)
£700–1,000 *MSW*

17th–18th Century

Dirk Maas
Dutch (1659–1717)
A Boy begging from elegant
Horsemen halted on a Track
Signed, oil on canvas
19½ x 24½in (49.5 x 62cm)
£12,000–13,500 *C*

After George Morland
British (1763–1804)
The Story of Laetitia
A set of six stipple engravings, by John
Raphael Smith, 1789, printed in colours
with touches of hand colouring
13¾ x 11in (35 x 28cm)
£600–800 *P*

François de Troy
French (1645–1730)
Fête aux Porcherons
Oil on canvas
35½ x 46in (90 x 116.5cm)
£245,000–270,000 *S(NY)*

*Les Porcherons was a famous amusement
park in the open country outside Paris. In the
18thC it became fashionable to visit this area
particularly on Sundays, and to frequent the
equally famous Tambour-Royale owned by
Ramponneau. Today this section of Paris is
occupied by the Church of La Trinité, near
the intersection of the rue Saint-Lazare and
the rue Clichy. In 1850, a comic opera was
written by Thomas Sauvage and Albert
Grisar which commemorated the gaiety of
Sunday afternoons there.*

19th Century

Sir Edward Coley Burne-Jones, A.R.A., R.W.S.
British (1833–98)
Study for *The Garden Court*
Pencil and watercolour heightened with white
12¾ x 23¾in (32.5 x 60.5cm)
£55,000–70,000 *C*

This drawing corresponds to the third painting in the Briar Rose series which occupied Burne-Jones for so much of his career. The story of Sleeping Beauty first attracted Burne-Jones' attention in the early 1860s, when it was one of several fairy stories to inspire the sets of tiles which he designed for Birket Foster's house, The Hill, at Witley. By 1869 he had conceived the idea of treating the story in terms of a series of paintings, and in 1871 he began the so-called 'small' set of three canvases for his patron, William Graham, completing them in 1873. By the following year he had started a much larger set, adding a fourth subject of girls asleep at a loom which he placed third in the series and called The Garden Court. *The paintings were finally completed in 1890.*

Frederico Bartolini
Italian (late 19thC)
A Daring Challenge
Signed, oil on panel
8 x 6in (20 x 15cm)
£6,000–6,500 *HFA*

Samuel S. Carr
British (1837–1908)
Westward Ho for New York
Signed and inscribed, oil on canvas
10¼ x 14¼in (26 x 36cm)
£14,000–16,000 *S(NY)*

George Cattermole
British (1800–68)
Preparing for the Feast
Signed with monogram, watercolour
8¼ x 11½in (21 x 29cm)
£350–450 *JC*

Emma Ciardi
Italian (1879–1933)
Primavera
Signed and dated '1923', oil on canvas
29 x 26½in (74 x 67cm)
£10,000–12,000 *S*

Hendrick-Joseph Dillens
Belgian (1812–72)
The Centre of Attraction
Signed, indistinctly inscribed and
dated '1850', oil on panel
28½ x 41⅛in (72.5 x 105cm)
£15,000–17,000 *C*

South Italian School (19thC)
Naïve Scene
Signed with monogram, inscribed 'Emilio
Generoso', watercolour
9½ x 13in (24 x 33cm)
£250–275 *MBA*

After Théodore Gericault
French (1791–1824)
The Raft of Medusa
Oil on canvas
27½ x 39¾in (70 x 101cm)
£1,200–1,800 *CSK*

Wenceslao de la Guardia
American (b1861)
Embarquement de Lafayette a
Passages pour son premier voyage
en Amérique
Signed and dated '83', oil on canvas
45 x 64in (114.5 x 162.5cm)
£14,000–16,000 *S(NY)*

Joseph John Jenkins
British (1811–85)
A Charitable Act
Signed and dated '1868', pencil and
watercolour heightened with white
19 x 13½in (48 x 34.5cm)
£450–650 *CSK*

Robert Scott Lauder, R.S.A.
British (1803–69)
Claverhouse ordering Morton to be carried
out and shot for having given refuge to
Balfour of Burley
Oil on canvas
65 x 96in (165 x 244cm)
£14,000–16,000 *S*

The scene is taken from Old Mortality, *by
Sir Walter Scott, a dramatic romance set in
the time of Charles II.*

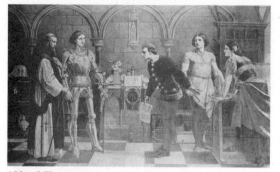

Alfred Keeson
British (19thC)
The Homecoming
Signed on the stretcher, oil on canvas
31 x 50¼in (78.5 x 127.5cm)
£1,000–1,500 *S(S)*

Julien Le Blant
French (b1851)
Les Sans Culottes - Highway Robbery
Signed, oil on canvas
58 x 87in (147 x 221cm)
£12,000–15,000 *S(NY)*

Maurice Leloir
French (1853–1940)
Rousseau reading the Manuscript of Julie to
the Marquis Bonnaval
Watercolour
10 x 7in (25 x 17.5cm)
£1,500–2,000 *L&E*

Maurice Leloir
French (1853–1940)
Scenes from *La Rampe*
A set of twelve, signed, watercolours
14 x 10in (35.5 x 25cm)
£7,000–8,000 *C*

La Rampe *by Henri Rothschild was published in Paris in 1913 with engravings by Charles Wittman and Léon Boisson.*

Max Klinger
German (1857–1920)
Ein Handschuh, Opus VI
A set of ten etchings, 1880
13¾ x 6¼in (34 x 15.5cm)
£22,000–28,000 *S*

Henry Stacy Marks, R.A., R.W.S.
The Author and the Critics
Signed and dated '1881', oil on canvas
laid on board
34 x 46in (86 x 116.5cm)
£15,000–20,000 *S*

Marks' gently humorous historical picture is characteristic of the group of artists who became known as the St. John's Wood Clique, the name taken from the prosperous area of London where Marks himself lived. The group, which included artists such as J. E. Hodgson, W. F. Yeames and G. D. Leslie, painted scenes from British history, concentrating on domestic genre pieces showing 'the home life of past times', rather than the great historical events. Their pictures were well crafted and often colourful. The club met regularly on Sunday mornings for tea and sketching, and organised outings and theatrical events, preferably in historical costume.

Charles Robert Leslie, R.A.
British (1794–1859)
Jeanie Deans and Queen Caroline
Oil on canvas
39 x 33in (99 x 83.5cm)
£6,000–8,000 *S*

Mariano Alonso Pérez y Villagrosa
Spanish (active 1893–1914)
The Farewell
Signed, oil on panel
28¼ x 36in (71.5 x 91.5cm)
£12,000–14,000 *C*

Francesco Peluso
Italian (b1836)
The Surprise Visit
Signed, oil on canvas
27¼ x 19½in (69.5 x 49.5cm)
£6,500–8,000 *C*

Arturo Ricci
Italian (b1854)
Presenting the Heir
Signed, oil on canvas
27 x 37in (68.5 x 94cm)
£25,000–35,000 *S(NY)*

John Ritchie
British (19thC)
The Challenge
Signed and dated '75', oil on canvas
28 x 36in (71 x 91.5cm)
£450–650 *CNY*

Vittorio Reggianini
Italian (b1858)
The Love Poem
Signed, oil on canvas
22 x 27¾in (55.5 x 70.5cm)
£38,000–45,000 *C*

Henrich Engelbert Reyntjens
Dutch (1817–1900)
Figures in an Interior
Signed, oil on board
7¼ x 9½in (18 x 24cm)
£1,400–1,800 *Bon*

James Jacques Joseph Tissot
French (1836–1902)
Goodbye, on the Mersey
Signed and dated '1880', watercolour and
gouache over traces of pencil laid down
on board
16¾ x 12in (43 x 30.5cm)
£70,000–90,000 *S(NY)*

20th Century

Max Beckmann
German (1884–1950)
Der Zeichner in Gesellschaft
Signed, 1922, drypoint on pale pink
Japan paper
12¾ x 9¼in (32.5 x 23.5cm)
£3,500–4,500 *S(NY)*

According to Hofmaier, the 'draftsman' in this print is Rudolf Grossmann, painter and print maker, who was known for 'his compulsive drawing, whether alone or in public'.

Helen Bradley
British (1900–79)
Uncle John's Wedding was in a
Strange Church
Signed with fly, canvas on board
15½ x 19½in (39 x 49cm)
£6,000–8,000 *JNic*

On a postcard on the reverse is the following: 'Uncle John's Wedding was in a strange church on a cold January day. Mother looked lovely in blue and father had to carry George because he wasn't big enough to walk. Aunt Frances and Aunt Mary were the bridesmaids in claret red velvet trimmed with white fur. The Best Man was James Alfred who had a secret passion for Aunt Frances and as soon as he got the chance he slipped out round the back and Aunt Frances out of the front where they met by the gravestones. "Oh Frances," he said, taking her hand, "Will you become..." but his mother had seen him and before he could finish the sentence she called "James Alfred, come here," so they waited and waited, until Aunt Frances was 52 and James Alfred was 60 until they would marry, and the year was 1904.' Signed Helen Mayfield Bradley, 1969.

Paul Emile Boutigny
French (1854–1929)
Arrival for the Wedding
Oil on canvas
28 x 36in (71 x 91.5cm)
£6,000–7,000 *JN*

Frank Moss Bennett
British (1874–1953)
Dr. Johnson at the Cheshire Cheese
Signed and dated '1948', oil on canvas
15½ x 19½in (39.5 x 49.5cm)
£6,000–7,000 *S(S)*

Marcel Cosson
French (1878–1956)
Le Bar à l'Entracte
Signed, oil on board
24 x 19¾in (61 x 50cm)
£4,000–5,000 *C*

Margaret Dovaston, R.B.A.
British (active 1908–13)
Forgotten Treasure
Signed, oil on canvas
20 x 27in (50.5 x 68.5cm)
£14,000–15,000 *HFA*

Boris Deutsch
American (1892–1978)
One World or None
Signed and dated '1947', oil on canvas
60 x 45in (152.5 x 114cm)
£4,000–5,000 *S(NY)*

*Deutsch was considered an important
figurative painter in southern California
during the 1930s and 1940s. The present
work exhibits his interest in the emotional
power of form and colour combined with his
concern of the effects of war.*

Sir William Russell Flint
British (1880–1969)
Chattels
Signed, colour print
16 x 20in (40.5 x 50.5cm)
£200–300 *TAY*

Giuseppe Guidi
Italian (20thC)
Figures in a Drawing Room
Signed and dated '1818', oil on canvas
17 x 22in (43 x 56cm)
£3,400–4,000 *GH*

Martin Grover
British (b1962)
And they just don't last as long
Signed and dated '1993', acrylic on canvas
18in (46cm) square
£380–420 *Mer*

Edward Irvine Halliday
British (20thC)
A.D. 353 Hilary, a Philosopher of Poictiers,
was invited by the Priests and People of that
City to become their Bishop
Signed and dated '1931', oil on canvas
39½ x 61in (100.5 x 155cm)
£1,000–1,500 *CSK*

Graham Knuttel
Irish (20thC)
Off the Coast at Calabar
Signed, oil on canvas
60 x 72in (152 x 182.5cm)
£2,000–2,500 *NAG*

Laurence Stephen Lowry, R.A.
British (1887–1976)
People Walking
Signed and dated '1961', oil on canvas
30 x 20in (76 x 50.5cm)
£45,000–60,000 *S*

Fikret Moualla
Turkish (1905–68)
Le Marchand de Ballons
Signed and dated '61', gouache on board
21¾ x 25⅜in (55 x 65cm)
£8,500–10,000 *CSK*

Miller's is a price GUIDE not a price LIST

Jack Butler Yeats, R.H.A.
Irish (1871–1957)
The Great Tent has Collapsed
Signed, oil on canvas
24 x 36in (61 x 91.5cm)
£110,000–140,000 *S*

The present work more than doubled its estimate of £30,000–40,000 when sold at Sotheby's, making the highest auction price for a Yeats since the 1989–90 season. Painted in 1947, and the first picture produced by the artist after the death of his wife, critics have interpreted this expressionistic scene as reflecting both the artist's grief at his loss and his determination to carry on regardless, the Ringmaster steps from the collapsed tent, head held high, to brave the storm and the public outside.

Margaret Pullee
British (b1910)
Street in Antalya
Signed and inscribed, oil on board
24in (61cm) square
£900–1,200 *C*

PEASANTS & COUNTRY LIFE

The following pictures range from the rumbustious tavern scenes of the 17thC, through to a genteel village fête in the 20thC countryside. Agricultural life and labour has been a continuous theme throughout the history of art. As Western society became more urbanised and more industrialised in the 19thC, the middle-class hunger for pictures of rural life and peasant subject only increased, and the theme remains one of the great providers of the current market.

16th–17th Century

Pieter Brueghel the Younger
Flemish (1564–1637)
The Birdnester
Oil on panel
16¾ x 22⅜in (42.5 x 58cm)
£175,000–210,000 *S*

Various interpretations have been advanced for the possible meaning of the subject of this composition, which derives from the famous painting by Pieter Brueghel the Elder of 1568, now in the Kunsthistorisches Museum in Vienna. The most widely accepted view was that suggested by Hulin de Loo in 1907, who believed that this work illustrated the Flemish proverb, 'He who knows where the nest is, knows that and nothing else; he who steals the nest, has it.'

Follower of Jacopo da Ponte, called Jacopo Bassano
Italian (1515–92)
Peasants tending Farm Animals in a Landscape
Oil on canvas, laid down on panel
37 x 44¾in (94 x 113.5cm)
£9,500–11,500 *CSK*

Joost Cornelisz. Droochsloot
Dutch (1586–1666)
A Village Street with a Brawl outside an Inn
Bears Teniers monogram and dated '1647',
oil on canvas
40¾ x 61in (103 x 155cm)
£44,000–55,000 *S*

Cornelis Dusart
Dutch (1660–1704)
A Village with a Peasant Couple on a Vegetable Cart outside an Inn
Signed and dated '168(0?)'
Oil on panel
11 x 13¾in (28 x 34.5cm)
£35,000–45,000 *C*

Dutch School (17thC)
A Seated Male Traveller Drinking
Inscribed in pen and brown ink,
black chalk, laid down
9 x 6¾in (22 x 17cm)
£200–300 *P*

Attributed to Matheus van Helmont
Flemish (1623–79)
Peasants making Merry in a Tavern Interior
Bears signature, oil on canvas
19½ x 26½in (49.5 x 67cm)
£4,000–5,000 *CSK*

Manner of Mattheus Helmont
Flemish (1623–79)
An Old Man Teaching a Dog Tricks,
a Pedlar with a Hurdy-Gurdy
A pair, oil on panel
6¼ x 4¾in (16 x 12cm)
£1,500–2,000 *S(Am)*

Manner of David Teniers
Flemish (17thC)
A Toper Lighting a Pipe in a Tavern Interior
With signature, oil on copper
7½ x 9¾in (19 x 24.5cm)
£850–1,000 *CSK*

*Smoking features in many Dutch and
Flemish tavern interiors of the 17thC.
Whilst the Catholic countries tended to take
their tobacco in the form of snuff, Protestant
nations preferred the pipe, and smoking was
extremely popular in the Netherlands.
Contemporary pictures often give a very
precise account of the smoker's accoutrements
which included clay pipes of varying lengths,
a hand-held clay brazier and a selection of
spills to light the pipe, a paper twist
containing tobacco and almost invariably
a jug or tankard of ale to wash it down. In
genre painting depicting the 'Five Senses',
a particularly popular theme in 17thC Dutch
painting, smoking represented the sense of
smell, and beer that of taste.*

Klaes Molenaer
Dutch (1630–76)
Skaters on a Froken Lake outside a House
Signed, oil on panel
10 x 12½in (25 x 31.5cm)
£2,200–3,000 *S(Am)*

David Teniers the Younger
Flemish (1610–90)
Peasants in a Tavern
Signed, oil on panel
13½ x 20in (34.5 x 50.5cm)
£25,000–35,000 *S(Am)*

David Teniers the Younger
Flemish (1610–90)
Peasants playing Skittles by Cottages
Signed with monogram 'DT.F', oil on panel
8 x 11in (20 x 28cm)
£16,500–20,000 *C*

18th Century

Franz de Paula Ferg
Austrian (1689–1740)
Peasants merrymaking amongst
Ruins in an Italianate Landscape
Oil on copper
13 x 16½in (33 x 42cm)
£14,000–16,000 *C*

Circle of Jan Anton Garemyn
Flemish (1712–99)
Peasants Merrymaking Outside a Farm
Oil on canvas, laid down on panel
25½ x 34in (65 x 86cm)
£5,000–6,000 *C*

Peter La Cave
British (active 1769–1810)
A Landscape with Figures and Donkeys,
with Candle Snuffers
Signed and inscribed, pencil, pen and
brown ink and watercolour
7½ x 9½in (19 x 24.5cm)
£750–1,000 *C*

Peter La Cave
British (active 1769–1810)
Peasant Couple with Donkey
Watercolour
8 x 12in (20.5 x 30.5cm)
£580–630 *LH*

After George Morland
British (1763–1804)
Cottage Family, and Shepherd's Meal
A pair, mezzotints
22 x 16in (56 x 40.5cm)
£350–550 *CSK*

George Morland
British (1763–1804)
Figures gathering Wood in a
Winter Landscape
Bears signature, oil on canvas
11½ x 9½in (29 x 24cm)
£1,800–2,500 *S*

19th Century

John White Abbott
British (1763–1851)
Returning from Market
Dated '1815', ink and wash
6in (15cm) square
£380–450 *TAY*

Jules Bouvier
French/British (1800–67)
The Shepherdess
Signed and dated '1854', pencil and
watercolour heightened with white
26½ x 19½in (68 x 49.5cm)
£550–800 *CSK*

Rudolf Epp
German (1834–1910)
Die Hopfenernte
Signed and dated '1870', oil on canvas
laid down on board
36 x 48in (91.5 x 122cm)
£45,000–55,000 *S(NY)*

John Califano
Italian/American (1862–1946)
Bringing in the Catch
Signed, oil on canvas laid down on masonite
33½ x 24in (85 x 61cm)
£950–1,200 *CNY*

Kathleen Davis
British (active 1892–93)
Peasant Girls
Oil on canvas
30 x 25in (76 x 63.5cm)
£3,250–3,500 *FdeL*

Thomas Faed, R.A., H.R.S.A.
British (1826–1900)
Highland Tramp crossing a Headland
Signed and dated '1890', oil on canvas
48 x 38in (122 x 96.5cm)
£9,000–12,000 *C(S)*

Miller's is a price GUIDE
not a price LIST

Myles Birket Foster, R.W.S.
British (1825–99)
The Fisherman's Children
Signed with monogram, pencil and
watercolour heightened with white
10½ x 15½in (26.5 x 39cm)
£25,000–35,000 *C*

*Myles Birket Foster specialised in pretty,
rustic scenes peopled with pretty, rustic
characters. 'We may deplore the sentiment,
but we shall be narrow minded if we fail to
respect the artistry,' commented the great
historian of the English watercolour, Martin
Hardie. Today, considerable respect is given
to Foster's extremely attractive works,
expressing itself in hard cash terms. Sold at
Christie's, this work went well over its
£12,000–18,000 estimate.*

Horace Hammond
British (active 1920s–50s)
The Donkey Ride
Signed, watercolour
6¾ x 9¾in (16.5 x 25cm)
£450–550 *JC*

David Hardy
British (19thC)
The Fortune Teller
Signed and dated '1865',
watercolour
19½ x 13½in (50 x 34cm)
£1,200–1,500 *LH*

G. Hardy
British (1822–1909)
Figures at a Cottage Door
Oil on panel
13½ x 11½in (34.5 x 29.5cm)
£1,500–2,000 *AH*

Adelaide L. Haselgrave
British (active 1901–16)
Early Morning, Going to Work
Signed and inscribed verso, watercolour
15 x 22in (38 x 56cm)
£900–975 *WrG*

Ralph Hedley
British (1851–1913)
Washing Day, Runswick Bay
Signed and dated '96', oil on canvas
29½ x 19½in (75 x 50cm)
£7,000–8,000 *AG*

*Hedley's original title for this work is
unknown, but it is clear that the painting is
intended to convey the common predicament
of fisherwives who lost their husbands at sea -
the young widow, wearing a black bonnet, is
forced to take in washing, whilst her mother
looks after her child. This became a recurrent
theme by later artists of the Staithes School.*

John Frederick Herring, Snr.
British (1795–1865)
The Hop Pickers
Signed, dated '1854 to 69', oil on canvas
24¾ x 42½in (63 x 108cm)
£65,000–85,000 *S*

José Jara
French (active in Mexico) (1867–1939)
Indigena con Niño, Muchacho con Itacate
A pair, one signed, watercolour, c1900
13½ x 9½in (34.5 x 24cm)
£12,500–14,500 *S(NY)*

Henry John Yeend King
British (1855–1924)
The Duck Pond
Signed and inscribed on an old label
on reverse, oil on canvas
41 x 59¼in (104 x 150cm)
£18,000–20,000 *C*

John Linnell
British (1792–1882)
Reaping
Signed and dated '1855', oil on canvas
26 x 38½in (66 x 98cm)
£30,000–40,000 *S*

Léon Augustin l'Hermitte
French (1844–1925)
En Moisson
Signed, oil on canvas, 1913
37 x 50in (94 x 127cm)
£90,000–110,000 *C(S)*

*Pictures of rural life by the French painter
l'Hermitte have certainly increased in price
since the recession. 'En Moisson' more than
doubled its top auction estimate of £35,000 at
Christie's recently.*

Eugène Remy Maes (1849–1931) and
Jan David Col (1822–1900)
Belgian
Feeding the Chickens
Signed, oil on canvas
26 x 19in (66 x 48cm)
£12,500–14,000 *C*

Robert Walker Macbeth, R.A.
British (1848–1910)
Potato Harvest in the Fens
Signed with initials and dated '1877',
oil on canvas
70 x 53¾in (177.5 x 136cm)
£9,500–12,000 *C*

*The son of the Scottish portrait painter,
Norman Macbeth, Robert Walker Macbeth
trained in London and worked, like so many
up-and-coming young artists in the 1870s,
on The Graphic. He evolved an heroic-pastoral
style owing much to George Heming Mason
and Fred Walker, which led James Caw, the
historian of Scottish painting, to compare his
work to the novels of Thomas Hardy.*

Attributed to W. Norris
British (19thC)
Harvesting Scene
Indistinctly signed, oil on panel
7 x 9½in (17.5 x 24cm)
£450–550 *LH*

Phiz, (Hablot Knight Browne)
British (1815–82)
Fisherman Mending his Nets on the Beach
Signed, watercolour with bodycolour
and pencil
4¾ x 10½in (12 x 27cm)
£850–950 *CBL*

Alfred Provis
British (active 1843–86)
Cottage Interior
Oil on canvas
7¾ x 12in (19 x 30.5cm)
£2,750–2,950 *AdG*

Jean François Portaels
Belgian (1818–95)
The Shepherdess
Signed and dated '1870', oil of canvas
34½ x 59¼in (87.5 x 150.5cm)
£6,000–6,500 *C*

*Portaels' shepherdess is distinctly more erotic
than pastoral in her pose and presentation.*

William Shayer
British (1787–1879)
A Passing Word
Oil on canvas
18 x 24in (46 x 61cm)
£8,000–8,500 *HFA*

Snaffles (Charles Johnson Payne)
British (1884–1967)
The Wheat is My Care – The Rest is the
Will of God (Rudyard Kipling)
Signed, inscribed on the mount, gouache
14½ x 22in (37 x 56cm)
£9,000–11,000 *AG*

Ralph Todd
British (active 1880–93)
The Cornish Fishergirl
Signed, inscribed as title on reverse, pencil
and watercolour
15½ x 11½in (39.5 x 29.5cm)
£1,000–1,500 *CSK*

William Aiken Walker
American (19thC)
A Southern Farmstead, and Cotton Pickers
A pair, both signed, oil on board
6 x 12in (15 x 31.5cm)
£6,000–8,000 *Bon*

Jean Georges Vibert
French (1840–1902)
At the Well
Signed and dated '1867', oil on canvas
39 x 29in (99 x 73.5cm)
£2,000–2,600 *TAY*

Sir Ernest Albert Waterlow, R.A., P.R.W.S.
British (1850–1919)
The Two Paths
Signed and dated '1878', watercolour
18 x 31in (45 x 78.5cm)
£3,000–4,000 *WG*

Robert W. Wright
British (active 1871–89)
Playing Fives, and The Fruit Seller
A pair, both signed and dated '1895',
oil on panel
7 x 9in (18 x 22.5cm)
£8,000–9,000 *WG*

Annie Mary Youngman
British (1860–1919)
After Supper
Signed, oil on canvas
25 x 30in (64 x 76cm)
£3,000–4,000 *S*

20th Century

Michael Ayrton
British (1921–75)
Fishermen at Midday, Ischia
Signed and dated 'June 48',
oil on aluminium sheet
9¾ x 13¾in (24.5 x 35cm)
£4,200–5,000 *S*

Adrian Paul Allinson
British (1890–1959)
Marble Transport, Carrara, Tuscany
Signed, oil on canvas
25½ x 49½in (65 x 125cm)
£6,000–6,800 *JG*

Marc Chagall
French (1887–1985)
La Basse-Cour
Signed, gouache and pencil on paper, c1925
24½ x 18½in (62.5 x 47cm)
£85,000–100,000 *C*

William Conor, P.R.U.A., R.H.A.
Irish (1881–1968)
Pedlars
Signed, inscribed with title on original
label verso, oil on canvas
24 x 20in (61 x 50.5cm)
£14,000–15,000 *CCG*

Mary Fedden, R.A.
British (b1915)
Gathering Storm
Signed, watercolour
10 x 12in (25.5 x 31.5cm)
£450–550 *OLG*

Fred Cuming, R.A.
British (b1930)
Iden Fête
Signed, oil on canvas
24 x 28in (61 x 71cm)
£4,200–4,500 *WHP*

Jac Martin-Ferrieres
French (1893–1972)
Collioure - Fishermen Drying Nets
on the Beach
Signed, oil on canvas
23¼ x 31½in (59 x 80cm)
£6,000–8,000 *L*

W. Harrison
British (active 1900–40)
The Day's Catch
Signed and dated '21', watercolour
5 x 7½in (12.5 x 19cm)
£200–250 *JC*

> **Miller's is a price GUIDE
> not a price LIST**

Sir Alfred Munnings, P.R.A.
British (1878–1959)
Field of Poppies
Signed and dated '1911', oil on canvas
20 x 24in (61 x 61cm)
£130,000–150,000 *C*

*Munnings' impressionistic 'Field of Poppies'
inspired fierce competition when it was
offered by Christie's recently. For once in the
artist's work, horses were relegated to the
back of the picture, and pride of place was
given to the brilliantly coloured and boldly
painted sway of scarlet flowers. The low
estimate of £15,000–20,000 was soon doubled,
then tripled and finally more than quadrupled.
Given its auction result, it is perhaps ironic
that the picture was given by the artist to its
original owner, Norfolk businessman James
Hardy, in return for food and whisky in the
days before he became well-known.*

Ken Moroney
British (20thC)
Fence Making
Signed, oil on canvas
15¾ x 10in (40 x 25cm)
£400–600 *GK*

Anna Mary Robertson (Grandma) Moses
American (1860–1961)
In Maple Sugar Time
Signed and titled, oil on board
18 x 20in (46 x 51cm)
£24,000–30,000 *S(NY)*

Diego Rivera
Mexican (1886–1957)
Campesino Sembrando
Signed and dated '41', watercolour
on rice paper
15½ x 10½in (39.5 x 27cm)
£30,000–35,000 *S(NY)*

Mick Rooney, R.A.
British (b1944)
Greek Life
Signed and dated '1993', mixed media
9 x 7in (22.5 x 17.5cm)
£600–800 *BRG*

*'Mick Rooney is a major artist who captures
the spirit of all the countries in which he
worked, whether Mexico, Greece or England.
He manages to convey the life blood of all
these cultures,' comments J. Brandler of the
Brandler Galleries.*

William Strang, R.A.
British (1859–1921)
The Swineherd
Signed in pencil, original etching
8 x 6¾in (20 x 17cm)
£125–160 *CG*

Judy Talacko
Australian (b1941)
Early Morning Heaven
Signed, oil on canvas
16 x 20in (41 x 51cm)
£1,450–1,650 *Om*

Ethelbert White
British (1891–1972)
Hay Wagons
Signed, watercolour over
traces of pencil
15 x 21¾in (38 x 55cm)
£600–700 *JG*

ROYALTY

The following section is devoted to royal portraits, and historical and imaginary pictures of royalty.

John Stainton of Christie's British Picture Department told us, 'there are always pictures of royals, particularly from the 17thC and 18thC, in any major portrait sale. Prices can vary enormously from millions of pounds for a van Dyck royal portrait, to a "tenth-down-the-road" copy of the same work which will go for perhaps £1,000.' Royal portraits have always been copied extensively, hence their proliferation in the salerooms. 'Patrons commissioned copies of famous royal portraits for their own collections, for diplomatic gifts, and many other purposes,' explains Stainton. 'They were also used as art school exercises, which is why they turn up so frequently and range so much in quality.' Though there is often a premium for a kingly or queenly face, as in every field it is the best pictures that command the best prices. 'There is an enormous demand for good quality royal pictures,' concludes David Moore-Gwynne of Sotheby's, 'and fine examples can make spectacular prices.'

16th–17th Century

Circle of Charles Beaubrun
French (1604–92)
Portrait of Princess Henrietta of England, as Cleopatra
Oil on canvas
69 x 42¼in (175 x 107.5cm)
£11,000–15,000 *S*

The sitter was the youngest daughter of Charles I by his consort Henrietta Maria of France.

Follower of John de Critz
British (16th/17C)
Portrait of King James I, and another of Queen Anne of Denmark
A pair, oils on panel
10½ x 8½in (26 x 21cm)
£3,750–4,750 *C*

English School (c1677)
The Presentation of a Pineapple to Charles II
Oil on canvas
40½ x 46½in (103 x 118cm)
£470,000–600,000 *S*

By tradition, this celebrated image shows John Rose, the Royal Gardener, presenting the first pineapple raised in England to Charles II. The fine house in the background has also been identified as Dorney Court, near Windsor, seat of Roger Palmer, Earl of Castlemaine, whose wife Barbara Villiers became Charles II's mistress.
By an unknown hand, this is one of two versions, and there are also two copies of the same subject. Like many of the most fascinating pictures, the work owes some of its interest to myth. Pineapples were not in fact grown in Britain until later in the century and doubts have been raised as to the identification of the house. Nevertheless, the work is undoubtedly a rare portrait of Charles II in ordinary day dress. 'It is by far the best likeness of the King I ever saw,' enthused Horace Walpole in 1780, 'the countenance cheerful, good-humoured and very sensible.' The man holding the pineapple is almost certainly John Rose, 'Gardener to His Majesty at his Privy Garden in St. James's,' and the work is one of the earliest conversation pieces in British art. A remarkable picture, it inspired considerable interest from both British and American bidders at Sotheby's recently, and sold for well over its £200,000–300,000 estimate.

Studio of Sir Godfrey Kneller, Bt.
British (1646–1723)
Portraits of William III, and Queen Mary II,
wearing Coronation robes
A pair, oils on canvas
52¼ x 41¾in (133 x 106cm)
£6,000–7,000 *S*

Studio of Godfrey Kneller
British (1646–1723)
William III, in Robes of State
Oil on canvas
33½ x 26in (85 x 66cm)
£1,500–2,000 *SLN*

*The prototype for this painting is a full length
work by Kneller depicting 'William III in
Robes of State with his Crown' in the Queen's
collection at Windsor Castle. This image was
the approved official likeness of the Sovereign,
and Kneller and his studio painted versions
of it for the King's ministers, friends and
ambassadors, as well as foreign sovereigns
and governments.*

Circle of Sir Peter Lely
British (1618–80)
Portrait of Catherine of Braganza
Oil on canvas
50 x 40¼in (127 x 102cm)
£4,000–5,000 *C*

Follower of Marten Mytens
Swedish (1695–1770)
Portrait of the Empress Maria Theresa
Oil on canvas
32½ x 25¾in (83 x 66cm)
£1,000–2,000 *Bon*

Circle of François de Troy
French (1645–1730)
Portrait of a Nobleman, probably
the young Philippe V of Spain
Oil on canvas
15 x 11¼in (38 x 29cm)
£600–800 *S*

*Philippe V of Spain, a grandson of Louis XIV,
was born at Versailles in 1683. He was King
of Spain from 1700–46.*

Willem Wissing
Dutch (1656–87)
Portrait of Queen Anne when Princess
of Denmark
Signed and dated '1687', oil on canvas
49 x 39¾in (124.5 x 101cm)
£55,000–70,000 *S*

Willem Wissing
Dutch (1656–87)
Early portrait of Charles II,
seated, wearing Ceremonial
Robes and Order of the Garter
Oil on canvas
49 x 40in (124.5 x 101.5cm)
£2,000–3,000 *MEA*

Circle of Charles Boit
Swedish (1663–1727)
Portrait of King William and
Queen Mary
Oil on canvas
21½ x 16in (54.5 x 41cm)
£3,800–4,800 *CSK*

18th Century

French School (18thC)
Portrait of Anne Charlotte of Lorraine
Inscribed, oil on copper
7¼ x 9¼in (18.5 x 23.5cm)
£650–850 *S(S)*

William Hamilton, R.A.
British (1750–1801)
Marie Antoinette being led to her Execution
Signed and dated '1794', oil on canvas
59¾ x 77½in (151.5 x 197cm)
£30,000–40,000 *S*

*This is perhaps the most impressive British
painting depicting a French Revolutionary
subject to survive from the period. Marie
Antoinette is portrayed here as a Christian
martyr, leaving the conciergerie accompanied
by a priest on the way to her execution on 16th
October 1793. She looks particularly tragic,
wearing a bright white dress, and surrounded
by soldiers of the Parisian guard. The picture
reflects English sympathies towards the
French royal family and aristocracy. Louis
XVI had been executed on 21st January 1793,
and Marie Antoinette had been imprisoned
alone, separated from her ten year old son,
the Dauphin since July of that year. The
image of the French Queen as martyr differs
dramatically from contemporary French
pictures, which tend to show her as an
immoral woman, who influenced her
weaker husband.*

David Morier
Swiss (c1705–70)
Equestrian Portrait of George II
Oil on canvas
49 x 39¼in (124.5 x 100cm)
£35,000–45,000 *S*

Martin Maingaud
French (active early 18thC)
The Princesses Anne, Amelia and Caroline,
the daughters of George II
Oil on canvas
38 x 48in (96.5 x 122cm)
£25,000–35,000 *S*

James Northcote, R.A.
British (1746–1831)
Dr Feckenham, Dean of St. Paul's, trying by
argument to convert Lady Jane Grey to the
Romish faith, three days before her execution
Signed, pencil and watercolour
11½ x 12½in (29 x 31.5cm)
£450–650 *C*

James Northcote, R.A.
British (1746–1831)
The Princes in the Tower
Oil on canvas
71 x 54in (180 x 137cm)
£9,500–10,500 *C*

*This picture is a second version of a work
illustrating Act IV, Scene iii from
Shakespeare's* Richard III: *the murder of the
two young Princes, King Edward V and his
brother Richard, Duke of York, on the orders
of their uncle Richard, Duke of Gloucester.*

19th Century

Sir Lawrence Alma-Tadema, R.A.
British (1836–1912)
The Education of the Children of Clovis
(School of Vengeance; Training of
Clotilde's Sons)
Signed and dated '1861', oil on canvas
51 x 70½in (129.5 x 179cm)
£140,000–160,000 *S*

Thomas Barker of Bath
British (1769–1847)
Portrait of Princess Caraboo of Javasu
Oil on canvas
23¾ x 19½in (60.5 x 49.5cm)
£6,500–7,500 *S*

*Not a real royal, but a remarkable pretender,
born Mary Willcocks, a cobbler's daughter
from Devon. She managed to convince
Regency England that she was an exotic Far
Eastern Princess who had been kidnapped by
pirates but had managed to escape to
England. Regency society at that time was
consumed by an interest in all things Oriental
and readily took the 'Princess' to their heart.*

H.R.H. Queen Victoria
British (1819–1901)
Annie McDonald's Mother
Signed and dated '1888', 'Victoria',
oil on panel
12 x 8¾in (30.5 x 22cm)
£40,000–75,000 *BRG*

Not a portrait of a queen, but a portrait by one!

John McKirdy Duncan, R.S.A.
British (1866–1945)
Mary Queen of Scots
Signed, inscribed and dated '1587', egg
tempera, 1912
36 x 30in (91.5 x 76cm)
£15,000–18,000 *C*

20th Century

After Susan L. Crawford
British (b1941)
Her Majesty Queen Elizabeth, The Queen
Mother, with Desert Orchid at Cheltenham
Limited edition colour reproduction, signed
and numbered 5/250 in the margin
17½ x 19in (44.5 x 48cm)
£850–1,000 *C(S)*

John Leigh-Pemberton
British (20thC)
King George IV, at the Royal Pavilion,
Brighton, c1820
Oil on canvas
22½ x 25½in (57 x 65cm)
£1,400–1,600 *P*

Andy Warhol
American (1930–86)
Queen Elizabeth II of the United Kingdom
Silkscreen printed in colours, 1985,
signed in pencil
39 x 31½in (99 x 80cm)
£2,500–3,000 *S*

Barnet Freedman
British (1901–58)
God Save Our Queen
Signed and dated '1953' and inscribed
'Design for Shell-Mex and BP Ltd', gouache
19 x 39½in (48 x 100cm)
£600–800 *P*

**Published by the Society of
Antiquaries, London**
British (20thC)
Two original engravings from a new limited
edition, by James Basire in 1774 and 1781
The Field of the Cloth of Gold, and The
Embarkation of Henry VIII at Dover 1520
27 x 49in (69 x 124.5cm)
£1,000–1,100 each *RGFA*

*The copperplates engraved for the Society in
1774 and 1781 have survived in near perfect
condition. The impressions taken for this
20thC edition are, claim the Society, as vivid
today as when the subjects were first
published. The reprint has been limited to 400
copies of each, and no further printing will be
permitted for 50 years.*

John Leigh-Pemberton
British (20thC)
Queen Victoria travels by Train, 1855
Signed and dated '52', oil on canvas
23 x 25½in (59 x 65cm)
£800–1,000 *P*

ARTISTS' PORTRAITS & PICTURES
17th–18th Century

Rembrandt Harmensz. van Rijn
Dutch (1606–69)
Self Portrait with Saskia
Etching, 1636
4 x 3¾in (10 x 9cm)
£4,500–5,500 *S*

Pieter Snyers
Flemish (1682–1752)
Portrait of a Collector, said to
be a self portrait
Signed and dated '1747',
oil on panel
11¾ x 10¾in (30 x 27.5cm)
£12,000–14,000 *S*

Studio of Sir Anthony van Dyck
Flemish (1599–1641)
A Self Portrait
Oil on canvas
18 x 15in (46 x 38cm)
£1,500–2,000 *P*

Thomas Gainsborough, R.A.
British (1727–88)
Portrait of the Artist
Oil on canvas
25 x 18¾in (66 x 48cm)
£300,000–350,000 *C*

In the market place there is often a premium
attached to self portraits and Gainsborough's
elegant head and shoulders view, more than
doubled its top auction estimate.

John Opie, R.A.
British (1761–1807)
Portrait of the Artist
13½ x 11in (34 x 28cm)
£3,300–4,300 *C*

The son of a Cornish carpenter, Opie came to
London at the age of 19 in 1780:

'There is a wondrous Cornishman
who is carrying all before him...
(he is) like Caravaggio and
Velasquez in one,'
Sir Joshua Reynolds excitedly told painter
James Northcote. Not all Opie's fellow artists
were quite so welcoming or as enthusiastic.
'I have been introduced to Mr Opie', wrote
Martin Archer Shee in 1789, 'who is in
manners and appearance as great a clown
and as stupid a looking fellow as ever I set my
eyes on. Nothing but incontravertible proof of
the fact would force me to think him capable
of anything above the sphere of a journeyman
carpenter, so little, in this instance, has
nature proportioned exterior grace to inward
worth. I intend calling upon him occasionally;
for I know him to be a good painter, and
though appearances are so much against
him, he is, I am told, a most sensible and
learned man.'

Thomas Rowlandson
British (1756–1827)
Genius Crumpled, the Artist painting
his Gaoler
Pen and red ink and watercolour over pencil
6 x 8¼in (15 x 21cm)
£2,400–3,400 *S*

19th Century

John Absolon
British (1815–95)
An Artist Sketching
Signed and dated '1874', watercolour over
pencil heightened with touches of bodycolour
9½ x 14in (24 x 36cm)
£900–1,200 *S*

John Constable, R.A.
British (1776–1837)
Portrait of Ramsay Richard Reinagle, R.A.
Signed, inscribed and dated '1835',
oil on canvas
30 x 24¾in (76 x 63cm)
£3,500–4,500 *S*

Richard Dadd
British (1817–86)
Portrait of the Artist
Oil on panel
22 x 18in (56 x 46cm)
£6,500–7,500 *S*

*This portrait of the artist shows him in his
early twenties and was painted in c1841
before his travels to Europe and the Middle
East with Sir Thomas Phillips between 1842
and 1843. It was shortly after his return from
this trip that he murdered his father and was
confined to an asylum.*

Théodore Gérard
Belgian (1829–95)
Rustic Connoisseurship
Signed and dated 'Bruxelles 74', oil on panel
23¼ x 35¼in (59 x 90cm)
£20,000–25,000 *S(NY)*

English School (19thC)
Portrait of a girl painting by a window
Watercolour
12 x 9½in (30.5 x 24cm)
£2,000–2,500 *Bea*

Léon Herbo
Belgian (1850–1907)
A Portrait of a Paintress
Signed and dated '1891', oil on panel
26½ x 21½in (67 x 54.5cm)
£750–1,000   *S(Am)*

Charles Green
British (1840–98)
The Artist, Seymour Lucas
Signed and inscribed, pencil and watercolour
10¾ x 8½in (27 x 21cm)
£450–650   *CSK*

Edward Lear
British (1812–88)
The Artist playing the Piano,
a self caricature
Pen and ink on blue paper
3½ x 5in (9 x 12.5cm)
£5,000–6,000   *S*

Francesco Paolo Michetti
Italian (1851–1929)
Self Portrait (Scherzo)
Signed, dated '1877' and inscribed 'Napoli',
pastel on coloured paper
18 x 11¼in (46 x 29cm)
£25,000–30,000   *S(NY)*

*This self-portrait depicts the artist at the age
of 26, the same year in which he received
great acclaim from his fellow Neapolitans for
the exhibition of his first major canvas, 'The
Procession of the Corpus Domini at Chieti.'*

Maximilien Luce
French (1858–1941)
Peintre a Son Chevalet
Signed, pastel
9 x 12¼in (23 x 31cm)
£5,000–6,000   *S*

Gabriele Rottini
Italian (1797–1858)
A Portrait of the Artist
Oil on canvas
28½ x 22¾in (72 x 58cm)
£3,750–5,000 *C*

Edouard Vuillard
French (1868–1940)
Autoportrait
Stamped with initials, pencil on
buff paper, c1888
9¼ x 7in (23.5 x 17.5cm)
£9,000–11,000 *C*

20th Century

Vanessa Bell
British (1879–1961)
Self Portrait
Initialled, dated '50', and inscribed
on reverse, oil on canvas
16½ x 12in (42 x 30.5cm)
£6,000–7,000 *C*

*Painted in the attic studio at Charleston, the
artist is seated on an armchair covered in a
textile she designed in the early 1930s for
Allan Walton Ltd., and an early painting of
Italy from 1912 is placed upside down by her
chair. According to Bell's contemporaries,
though the artist's portraits rarely contained
defined facial features, the people she painted
were always instantly recognisable and
infallible likenesses.*

John Bellany
British (b1942)
Self Portrait with Lobster
Signed and titled on reverse,
oil on canvas
36 x 24in (92 x 61cm)
£4,000–4,500 *P*

John Byrne
Scottish (b1940)
Self Portrait with Dowt
Drypoint, 1992
21 x 13½in (53.5 x 34cm)
£145–165 *GPS*

Ffolkes (Brian Davis)
British (20thC)
Same Time Tomorrow Miss Barstow?
Pen, ink and monochrome, watercolour
9½ x 11¼in (24 x 29cm)
£850–950 *CBL*

Cyril Mann
British (1911–80)
Self Portrait
Signed and dated '1972', oil on panel
16in (41cm) square
£7,000–7,500 *PN*

Henry Lamb, R.A.
British (1883–1960)
Roger Fry
Signed and dated '1911', pencil
11½ x 9in (29 x 23cm)
£6,500–7,500 *C*

Ken Howard
British (b1932)
Self Portrait in Studio
Oil on canvas
72 x 36in (182.5 x 91.5cm)
£5,000–7,000 *BRG*

Richard Pikesley, N.E.A.C.
British (20thC)
Landscape Painters,
the Loire Valley
Oil on canvas
36 x 40in (91.5 x 101.5cm)
£3,000–3,500 *WHP*

Nicholas Remisoff
Russian (1887–1979)
A Quartet of Merry Artists
Signed, gouache
9½ x 15in (24 x 38cm)
£650–750 *MTG*

Walter Richard Sickert
British (1860–1942)
Portrait of a Lady
Oil on canvas
16 x 13in (41 x 33cm)
£5,000–7,000 *BRG*

Andy Warhol
American (1930–86)
Self Portrait 1978
Signed, silkscreen
48 x 40in (122 x 101.5cm)
£4,500–5,000 *BRG*

Mick Rooney
British (20thC)
Artist's Studio
Oil on panel
10 x 7½in (25 x 19cm)
£1,750–2,000 *BRG*

Carol Weight
British (b1908)
Royal Academy Banquet
Painted print
7½ x 9in (19 x 23cm)
£550–650 *BRG*

Adrian Wiszniewski
Scottish (b1958)
Alter Ego/Self Portrait
Screenprint, 1992
27¼ x 42in (69.5 x 106cm)
£250–300 *GPS*

CARDS & INDOOR GAMES

French School (18thC)
The Gambling Salon
Oil on canvas
11 x 14½in (28 x 37cm)
£1,200–1,500 *CSK*

Thomas Rowlandson
British (1756–1827)
The Gaming Table at Devonshire House
Signed, and dated '1787', pen and black and
grey ink and watercolour over traces of pencil
11½ x 16¼in (29 x 41.5cm)
£35,000–45,000 *S*

*This watercolour appears to be the earliest
version of one of Rowlandson's best known
subjects. It depicts a game of faro at
Devonshire House, Piccadilly, the home of
the 5th Duke of Devonshire and his wife
Georgiana Cavendish (1757–1806), who was
well known for her love of gambling.*

Francesco Beda
Italian (b1879)
The Billiard Game
Signed, oil on canvas
24 x 40½in (61 x 103cm)
£6,500–7,500 *CSK*

John Arthur Lomax
British (1857–1923)
The Victim
Signed and inscribed, oil on panel
11¾ x 18in (30 x 46cm)
£4,000–5,000 *C*

Girolamo Induno
Italian (1815–78)
Una Partita a Scacchi
Signed and inscribed, oil on canvas
33 x 47½in (84 x 120.5cm)
£30,000–40,000 *S*

George Ogilvy Reid, R.S.A.
British (1851–1928)
The Winning Hand
Signed and dated '1884', oil on canvas
32 x 22in (81 x 55.5cm)
£4,500–5,250 *HFA*

L. Thackeray
British (20thC)
A set of four Billiard prints
11 x 14in (28 x 36cm)
£200–400 *MSh*

Frank Gascoigne Heath
British (1873–1936)
Cut Throat Euchre
Signed and dated '1909', oil on canvas
50½ x 60in (128 x 152cm)
£4,000–5,000 *P*

Henry Mayo Bateman
British (1887–1970)
A set of four pen ink and watercolour
designs for a bridge scoring card
4in (10cm) square
£850–950 *CBL*

Edouard Vuillard
French (1868–1940)
Le Bridge
Signed, peinture à la colle on paper laid
down on canvas
39¼ x 29⅜in (100 x 76cm)
£410,000–450,000 *C*

*'Le Bridge' was painted in 1923 at the home
of the Hessels. Lucie Hessel, the wife of the
successful art dealer Jos Hessel, was first
introduced to Vuillard by the painter Felix
Vallotton, at Omanel, near Lausanne, in
1900. The two became great friends and
Vuillard was a regular visitor at her salon,
where he frequently painted Madame Hessel
and her guests. In this work, the figures
shown are Alfred Natanson, Jos Hessel,
Madame Aron and Tristan Bernard.*

Sano di Pietro
Italian (1405–81)
The Madonna and Child with Saint John the Baptist
and Saint Leonard and two adoring Angels
Tempera on gold ground panel
18¾ x 15in (47.5 x 38cm)
£90,000–120,000 *C*

German School (c1520)
The Crucifixion with the Virgin and Saint
John the Evangelist
Black chalk, bodycolour heightened with
gold, the borders with bodycolour and gold,
on vellum
15 x 9½in (38.5 x 24cm)
£110,000–120,000 *C*

Studio of Sandro Botticelli
Italian (1444–1510)
Madonna and Child Seated in a Marble Niche
Oil on panel
25 x 17¼in (63.5 x 44cm)
£115,000–130,000 *S(NY)*

Giorgio Giulio Clovio
Italian (1498–1578)
The Lamentation
Watercolour and bodycolour heightened with
gold, on vellum
8½ x 5¾in (22 x 15cm)
£35,000–45,000 *C*

r. **Pieter Brueghel the Younger**
Flemish (c1564–1637)
The Adoration of the Magi
Signed and dated '1617',
oil on panel
15¼ x 22⅜in (39 x 58cm)
£225,000–250,000 *S(NY)*

l. **Jan Brueghel I** (1568–1625)
and **Hendrick van Balen I**
(1575–1632) Flemish
The Four Elements
Oil on panel
24¾ x 43in (63 x 109cm)
£150,000–200,000 *C*

Flemish School (17thC)
Nimrod Supervising the Construction of the
Tower of Babel
Oil on copper
8¾ x 11in (22.5 x 28cm)
£18,000–22,000 *S*

Jan van Neck
Dutch (1635–1714)
The Bath of Diana
Signed, oil on copper
12¾ x 16½in (32 x 42cm)
£8,200–9,000 *C*

l. **French School** (17thC)
The Garden of Venus
Oil on panel
16⅛ x 28¼in (42 x 72cm)
£4,000–5,000 *S*

Edward Reginald Frampton
British (1872–1923)
St. Cecily
Signed and dated '1905', oil on canvas
45¼ x 49½in (115 x 125.5cm)
£75,000–90,000 S

William Adolphe Bouguereau
French (1825–1905)
La Vierge, l'Enfant Jésus et Jean-Baptiste
Signed and dated '1875'
Oil on canvas
79 x 48in (200.5 x 122cm)
£470,000–520,000 S(NY)

Walter Crane, R.W.S.
British (1845–1915)
Pandora
Signed with pictogram and dated, watercolour
21 x 29in (53 x 73.5cm)
£28,000–35,000 S

Sir Edward Coley Burne-Jones, A.R.A.
British (1833–98)
Caritas
Signed, inscribed and dated 'MDCCCLXVII',
watercolour heightened with gold
60 x 27in (152 x 68.5cm)
£100,000–120,000 S

r. **Xavier Mellery**
Belgian (1845–1921)
L'Eternité et la Mort
Signed, watercolour over pencil
and gold paint
25½ x 38½in (65 x 98cm)
£14,000–16,000 S

Sidney Harold Meteyard
British (1868–1947)
St. George and the Dragon
Oil on canvas
43½ x 44¼in (110.5 x 112cm)
£105,000–120,000 *C*

Charles Napier Kennedy
British (1852–98)
Perseus and Andromeda
Signed and dated '1890', oil on canvas
101¾ x 68¼in (258 x 173cm)
£25,000–35,000 *S(NY)*

Joseph Schönmann
Austrian (1799–1879)
David and Abigail
Oil on canvas
52¼ x 67in (133 x 170cm)
£16,000–20,000 *S*

Sir Edward John Poynter, P.R.A.
British (1836–1919)
The Siren
Signed with monogram and dated '1864',
oil on canvas
36 x 30in (91.5 x 76cm)
£25,000–35,000 *C*

John William Waterhouse, R.A.
British (1849–1917)
A Song of Springtime
Signed and dated '1913', oil on canvas
28¼ x 36¼in (72 x 92cm)
£120,000–150,000 *S*

Tom Wood
British (b1955)
Redemption 1993
Oil on paper and board
43⅜ x 47⅛in (110 x 120cm)
£4,000–4,500 *HaG*

Helen F. Wilson
Scottish (b1954)
Medusa
Mixed media
7 x 6in (17.5 x 15cm)
£400–450 *RB*

Victor Brauner
French (1903–66)
Frica la Peur
Signed and dated '1950', oil on board
25½ x 32in (65 x 81cm)
£55,000–65,000 *C*

William Arthur Chase
British (1878–1944)
The Annunciation
Pastel
13 x 8in (33 x 20cm)
£450–550 *HI*

l. **Georges Rouault**
French (1871–1958)
Christ en Croix
Aquatint printed in colours, 1936
26 x 19½in (66 x 49.5cm)
£19,000–24,000 *S(NY)*

r. **Else Meidner**
German (1901–87)
Angel
Watercolour, c1950
27½ x 22¼in (70 x 56cm)
£750–850 *JDG*

Jan van den Hoecke
Flemish (1611–51)
A Still Life of a Basket of Fruit
Oil on canvas
46¾ x 38in (118.5 x 96.5cm)
£60,000–80,000 *S(NY)*

Pieter Adriaensz. van de Venne
Dutch (c1600–57)
A Still Life of a Vase of Flowers
Oil on canvas
29 x 22¼in (73.5 x 56.5cm)
£50,000–70,000 *S(Am)*

Jan Davidsz. de Heem
Dutch (1606–84)
Oysters, Cobnuts, a Peeled Lemon and an Orange
Signed, oil on panel
9½ x 13⅜in (24 x 34cm)
£245,000–260,000 *C*

Attributed to John Crome
British (1768–1821)
Still Life of Flowers
Oil on panel
16½ x 13in (42 x 33cm)
£3,000–4,000 *S*

l. **Justus van Huysum**
Dutch (1659–1716)
Still Life of Flowers
Signed, oil on canvas
37½ x 33¼in (95 x 84cm)
£20,000–25,000 *S(NY)*

Attributed to Peter Willebeeck
Flemish (1620–after 1652)
Still Life of Fruit in a Basket
Oil on canvas
21 x 26½in (53.5 x 67cm)
£10,000–12,000 *S*

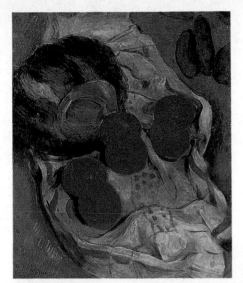

Emile Bernard
French (1868–1941)
Nature Morte a l'Eventail de Plumes
Signed and dated '1895', oil on canvas
23½ x 19⅝in (60 x 50cm)
£9,500–10,500 *S*

Henri Fantin-Latour
French (1836–1904)
Roses
Signed and dated '84', oil on canvas
20¾ x 17½in (52.5 x 44.5cm)
£340,000–380,000 *S(NY)*

Oliver Clare
British (c1853–1927)
Still Life of Flowers, and a Bird's Nest
A pair, signed and dated '1920', oil on board
9 x 12in (22.5 x 3.5cm)
£5,000–6,000 *HFA*

Charles Thomas Bale
British (19thC)
Still Life
A pair, signed with monogram
and dated '1875'
14 x 18in (35.5 x 46cm)
£7,500–8,250 *BuP*

l. **Mary Elizabeth Duffield**
British (1819–1914)
Still Life with Orchid
Signed, watercolour
8½ x 11½in (21.5 x 29.5cm)
£750–850 *WrG*

Roger Godchaux
French (b1878)
Vase de Fleurs
Signed, oil on canvas
32 x 45½in (81 x 115.5cm)
£7,500–8,500 *S(NY)*

Maria Harrison, A.R.W.S.
British (active 1845–1904)
Grapes and Chrysanthemums
Signed and dated '1869', watercolour
14¾ x 18¾in (37.5 x 47.5cm)
£1,500–1,700 *WrG*

William Hough
British (active 1857–94)
Still Life with a Bird's Nest,
Primroses and Violets
Signed, pencil, watercolour and bodycolour
11 x 14½in (28 x 37cm)
£3,500–4,000 *C*

George Lance
British (1802–64)
Grapes, Peaches, Plums and Cornucopia and a
Tazza on a Draped Table
Signed and dated '1832', oil on panel
23¾ x 20in (60.5 x 50.5cm)
£13,000–14,000 *C*

Odilon Redon
French (1840–1916)
Nature Morte au Coquelicot
Signed, oil on canvas
9½ x 7in (24 x 17.5cm)
£55,000–65,000 *C*

Pericles Pantazis
Greek (1849–84)
Le Fromage de Brie
Signed, oil on canvas
13½ x 18½in (34.5 x 47cm)
£7,500–8,500 *S*

Georg Seitz
German (1810–70)
Still Life with Fruit and Flowers on a Stone Ledge
Signed, oil on canvas
31¼ x 39¾in (79.5 x 101cm)
£5,000–6,000 *P*

William E. D. Stuart
British (active 1846–58)
Still Life of Fruit
Oil on canvas
35 x 48in (89 x 122cm)
£15,000–17,000 *HFA*

John Sherrin
British (1819–96)
Apples and Plums on a
Mossy Bank
Signed, bodycolour
10 x 13½in (25.5 x 34.5cm)
£3,000–4,000 *Bon*

Henry George Todd
British (1847–98)
Still Life
Signed and dated '1892', oil on canvas
17½ x 14in (44.5 x 35.5cm)
£10,500–11,500 *BuP*

Leopold Zinnögger
Austrian (1881–72)
An elborate Still Life with Animals
Signed and dated '1851', oil on canvas
57 x 40½in (144.5 x 103cm)
£50,000–60,000 *S(NY)*

Leopold von Stoll
German (active 1828–69)
Still Life of Hyacinth, Primula and Apples
Signed and dated '1838', oil on canvas
29in (73.5cm) square
£7,500–9,000 *S(NY)*

Vanessa Bell
British (1879–1961)
Still Life with Kitchen Table
Signed, oil on canvas
30 x 25in (76 x 63.5cm)
£9,000–10,000 *EG*

Olga Costa
German (b1913)
Naturaleza Muerta
Signed and dated '52', oil on canvas
16 x 21¾in (40.5 x 55cm)
£20,000–30,000 *S(NY)*

Jenny Devereux
British (20thC)
Tulips and Daffodils
Etching
17½ x 18½in (44.5 x 47.5cm)
£100–125 *CCA*

Robert Chandler
British (b1952)
Still Life with Orange and Apple
Oil on canvas
22 x 19in (56 x 48cm)
£700–800 *AMC*

Ronald Bone
British (b1950)
The Chinese Chair
Acrylic
7 x 5½in (17.5 x 14cm)
£450–550 *JN*

Willem Dolphyn
Belgian (b1932)
Study in Blue
Oil on canvas
17 x 19in (43 x 48.5cm)
£5,700–6,000 *WHP*

Edna Bizon
British (20thC)
Strawberries and Blue and White China
Oil on canvas
12 x 16in (30.5 x 41cm)
£2,500–2,800 *LA*

Florence Engelbach
British (1872–1951)
Still Life with Fruit on a Table
Signed, oil on canvas
30 x 25in (76 x 64cm)
£3,500–4,000 *EG*

Archie Forrest
Scottish (b1950)
Midnight Omelette
Oil on canvas
28 x 30in (71 x 76cm)
£7,000–7,500 *PG*

r. **Roy Freer**
British (b1938)
Red Chair
Oil on canvas
24 x 20in (61 x 51cm)
£1,000–1,200 *AdG*

Darrell Gardner
British (20thC)
Quinces
Oil on canvas
26 x 20in (66 x 51cm)
£800–900 *RGFA*

Elaine Fine
British (20thC)
Still Life with Lace Cloth
Oil on canvas
29¾ x 24in (76 x 61cm)
£800–875 *AMC*

Mark Gertler
British (1891–1939)
Still Life with Red Tulips
Signed and dated '1931', oil on canvas
17½ x 21½in (44.5 x 54.5cm)
£9,000–10,000 *S*

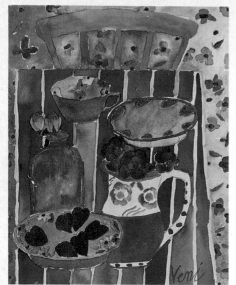

Veni Gligorova-Smith
Macedonian (20thC)
Kitchen Table
Signed, watercolour
17¾ x 13½in (45 x 34.5cm)
£450–500 *AMC*

Genrich Khozatsky
Russian (b1931)
Florence Duomo and Still Life
Oil on wood, 1991
32½ x 45in (82 x 114cm)
£6,000–6,500 *ALG*

Childe Hassam
American (1859–1935)
Tulip Tree in Blossom
Signed, dated 'June 19, 1932', and inscribed 'Easthampton',
oil on canvas
24½ x 36⅓in (62 x 92.5cm)
£140,000–160,000 *S(NY)*

Michael John Hunt
British (b1941)
Still Life with Chair
Signed, oil on canvas
26 x 24in (66 x 61cm)
£2,000–2,500 *THG*

Khrustalyova
Russian (20thC)
Sunflowers
Oil on canvas
32 x 40in (81 x 101.5cm)
£1,000–1,200 *SAV*

Joe Hargan
Scottish (b1952)
Fish Platter
Oil on canvas
28in (71cm) square
£1,800–2,200 *CON*

Sonia Lawson, R.A.
British (b1934)
Irises
Initialled and dated '1992'
Oil and filler on canvas
40 x 30in (101.5 x 76cm)
£6,000–10,000 *BRG*

Elizabeth Jane Lloyd
British (20thC)
Terrine of Polyanthus
Oil on canvas
20 x 24in (51 x 61cm)
£500–600 *AMC*

James McDonald
Scottish (20thC)
Two Weeks Last Summer
Oil on canvas
84 x 60in (213 x 152cm)
£4,500–5,000 *RB*

John E. Nicholls
British (20thC)
Magnolia and Spring Blossom
Signed, oil on board, c1960
20 x 24in (51 x 61cm)
£6,500–7,250 *BuP*

Bernard Lorjou
French (1908–93)
Vase de Chrysanthèmes
Signed, oil on canvas
32 x 25½in (81 x 65cm)
£12,500–14,000 *CSK*

Leon Morrocco
British (b1942)
Vegetables on a Kitchen Table
Gouache and pastel
30 x 32in (76 x 81cm)
2,500–2,750 *RB*

Pat Moran
Australian (20thC)
Summer Hues
Oil on canvas
36 x 30in (91.5 x 76cm)
£5,000–6,000 *Om*

Noelle O'Keeffe
Irish (20thC)
Wedgwood
Oil on paper
20½ x 28in (52 x 71cm)
£500–600 *SOL*

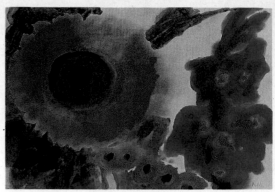

Emil Nolde
German (1867–1956)
Sonnenblumen
Signed, watercolour on paper
12¾ x 18½in (32 x 47cm)
£50,000–60,000 *S(NY)*

Georgia O'Keeffe
American (1887–1986)
Pink Roses and Larkspur
Signed with initials and with star on reverse,
pastel on paper
16 x 12in (41 x 30.5cm)
£90,000–110,000 *S(NY)*

Edward Noott
British (b1965)
Lobster Lunch
Oil on canvas
25 x 30in (64 x 76cm)
£1,200–1,400 *JN*

John Pawle
British (b1915)
Mirror
Oil on canvas
20 x 16in (51 x 41cm)
£600–700 *A*

Adrian Ryan
British (b1920)
Pears and Lemons on a Blue Plate
Signed, oil on canvas board
10 x 14in (25 x 35.5cm)
£1,200–1,500 *NZ*

Edgars Vinters
Latvian (b1919)
Tulips
Oil on canvas, 1989
28 x 37in (71 x 94cm)
£3,500–4,500 *RMG*

Derrick Sayer
British (1917–92)
Still Life
Gouache on paper
24 x 32in (61 x 81cm)
£500–600 *HI*

Jenny Webb
British (20thC)
Japanese Anemones
Watercolour
24 x 30in (61 x 76cm)
£180–220 *LS*

Tanya Short
British (b1955)
Etruscan Vase
Watercolour
22 x 29in (56 x 73.5cm)
£900–1,000 *AMC*

Susan Ryder, N.E.A.C.
British (20thC)
The Prince Albert Jacket
Oil on canvas
42 x 28in (106.5 x 71cm)
£4,000–4,500 *WHP*

Lev Soloviev
Russian (1907–86)
Camomile and Cornflowers
Oil on canvas
19 x 25in (48 x 64cm)
£700–800 *EG*

Jackie Simmonds
British (20thC)
Apples and Roses
Pastel
20 x 25in (51 x 64cm)
£750–850 *TLB*

l. **Shirley Trevena**
British (20thC)
Large Plate of Fruit
Watercolour
14 x 19in (36 x 48cm)
£750–850 *NBO*

Jan van Kessel the Younger
Flemish (1627–79)
A Still Life of Gooseberries,
and a Still Life with Bluebells, with Butterflies
A pair, oil on copper
4¼ x 7½in (11 x 19cm)
£80,000–100,000 *S*

Franz Horny
German (1798–1824)
Asters, a Bunch of Grapes, Two
Mespilus Fruits and Part of a Walnut
Watercolour, bodycolour and graphite
on paper
13¼ x 9in (34 x 23cm)
£18,000–20,000 *S(NY)*

Patricia Jorgenson
Irish (20thC)
In Full Bloom
Watercolour
28 x 20in (71 x 50.5cm)
£600–700 *SOL*

Lynne Broberg
British (20thC)
Tulips
Signed, ink print reproduced
on handmade paper
11 x 15in (28 x 38cm)
£2,250–2,500 *LyB*

Albert Durer Lucas
British (1828–1918)
Harebells and a Red Admiral
Butterfly and Blackberries
A pair, signed and dated '1877',
oil on ivory
5½ x 4½in (14 x 11.5cm)
£6,000–7,000 *S*

r. **Frieda Hughes**
British (b1960)
Golden Hibiscus
Oil on canvas
32¾ x 40½in (83 x 103cm)
£3,000–3,500 *AMC*

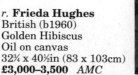

DOCTORS

'Doctors cut, burn, and torture the sick, and then demand of them an undeserved fee,' claimed Heraclitus, circa 500 B.C. 'Men who are occupied in the restoration of health to other men, by the joint exertion of skill and humanity, are above all the great of the earth, they even partake of divinity...' wrote Voltaire in 1764.

Separated by over 2,000 years, these two comments sum up how the medical profession has been viewed in art and literature down the centuries. Throughout the history of painting, doctors have been either vilified as money-grabbing charlatans or venerated as human saviours. In the 19thC, for example, Honoré Daumier satirised the medical profession in his drawings with the same vicious wit that he reserved for lawyers and politicians. Conversely, Sir Luke Fildes' sentimental painting 'The Doctor' in the Tate Gallery, showing the doctor as a compassionate, tragic hero, was one of the most popular paintings of the late Victorian period. Agnew's photogravure of the work was the most successful print that the firm ever produced, and the picture was subsequently reproduced on two postage stamps.

Albrecht Dürer
German (1471–1528)
The Dream of the Doctor
Engraving, after 1497
7½ x 4¾in (18.5 x 12cm)
£20,000–25,000   *S(NY)*

Follower of Adriaen van Ostade
Dutch (1610–84)
A Doctor's Surgery
Oil on panel
9½ x 13½in (23.5 x 33.5cm)
£2,800–3,500 *S*

Probably based on one of a series of paintings (now lost) by Adriaen van Ostade which must have been in Antwerp in the 17thC, judging from the existence of a number of copies by contemporary Flemish artists.

Circle of Adriaen van Ostade
Dutch (1610–84)
A Doctor casting the Water in an Interior
Bears indistinct signature and dated '16',
oil on panel
13½ x 12in (34.5 x 30.5cm)
£1,200–1,800 *CSK*

Rembrandt Harmensz. van Rijn
Dutch (1606–69)
Abraham Francen, Apothecary
Etching, drypoint and burin, c1657
6¼ x 8¼in (15.5 x 20.5cm)
£4,800–5,800 *S(NY)*

Rembrandt Harmensz. van Rijn
Dutch (1601–69)
Ephraim Bonus, Jewish Physician
Etching, drypoint and burin, c1657
9½ x 7in (23.5 x 17.5cm)
£45,000–55,000 *S(NY)*

Follower of David Teniers the Younger
Flemish (1610–90)
A Quack Doctor
Bears signature, oil on canvas
9¾ x 8in (24.5 x 20.5cm)
£3,300–4,000 *S*

After James Northcote, R.A.
British (1746–1831)
The Village Doctoress, by J. Walker
Mezzotint printed in colours
26 x 18½in (66 x 47cm)
£450–650 *CSK*

Honoré Daumier
French (1808–79)
Les deux Médecins et la Mort
Crayon and wash on paper
15 x 9½in (38 x 24cm)
£16,500–18,000 *C*

Jean-Louis Forain
L'Accouchement
Signed, Indian ink and black crayon
on paper, c1910
14½ x 20¼in (36.5 x 51cm)
£700–900 *S(NY)*

EATING & DRINKING

The following section is devoted to pictures of eating, drinking and preparing food. Food also appears in many other parts of the book - in landscape and peasant pictures, as labourers harvest the crops, in portraits and pictures of people, where items such as an apple or a bunch of cherries often carry symbolic as much as a decorative significance and, above all, in the still life section, where from the 17thC onwards, artists celebrate the glory of food in all its infinite, colourful variety.

17th–18th Century

Circle of Richard Brakenburgh
Dutch (1650–1702)
Peasants eating in a Cottage
Oil on panel
9 x 13½in (22.5 x 34cm)
£1,000–1,500   *C*

After Annibale Carracci
Italian (1560–1609)
The Bean Eater
Oil on canvas
30½ x 39⅛in (77.5 x 100cm)
£1,000–1,500   *S(S)*

This painting is after the original in the Colonna Gallery, Rome. Annibale Carracci's 'Bean Eater' is one of the earliest known portrayals of a man eating what seems to be a typical peasant meal. This includes black-eyed beans which originally came to Europe from North Africa, bread, wine, and onions - a staple element of the 16thC meal and often served as a substitute for meat.

Quiringh Gerritsz. Van Brekelenkam
Dutch (c1620–68)
A Woman gutting Fish, and
An Old Man with a Beer Jug and a Pipe
A pair, both signed and dated
'1664', oil on panel
12 x 11in (30.5 x 28cm)
£20,000–25,000   *C*

Follower of Matheus Helmont
Flemish (1623–79)
The Interior of an Inn with a Toper
Signed with monogram, oil on canvas
12¼ x 10in (31 x 25cm)
£2,200–3,000   *C*

North Italian School (17thC)
A Boy Pouring Wine
Oil on canvas
29¼ x 24½in (74 x 62cm)
£15,000–20,000   *S*

Jusepe de Ribera
Spanish (1588–1656)
Drunken Silenus
Etching, 1628
10¾ x 13¾in (27 x 35cm)
£11,000–15,000 *S(NY)*

Studio of Frans Snyders
Dutch (1579–1657)
A Still Life of Fruits in Baskets and Plates,
with a Monkey, a Parrot and a Maidservant
Oil on canvas
56½ x 84½in (143.5 x 214.5cm)
£40,000–60,000 *S*

*The Dutch could indulge their passion for exotic
fruit as a consequence of the prosperity brought by
the Dutch East India Company, founded in 1602.
Merchants brought back new fruits along with new
flower bulbs and they were greatly prized. Unlike
vegetables, fruit was often considered upper class
food. The prices it commanded, particularly when
it was somewhat out of season, were extremely high
and a variety of rarified techniques were devised to
preserve it for as long as possible.*

After Jan Verbeeck
Dutch (died after 1619)
Dirty Sauce
Etching and engraving
7¾ x 11⅛in (19.5 x 28.5cm)
£3,500–4,500 *S*

A. M. Broadley (Compiler)
British (18th/19thC)
Tea in Three Centuries
A collection of over 200 prints on 198 leaves
including mezzotints, aquatints and
lithographs, many hand coloured, 1910
£5,000–6,000 *Bon*

French School (18thC)
The Chocolate Seller
Pastel
33 x 20½in (84 x 52cm)
£1,600–2,000 *P*

*Chocolate was discovered in the 16thC
in Mexico by the Spanish conquistadors.
According to Bernard Diaz, who
visited Mexico with Cortez. The Aztec
chiefs drank chocolate from solid
gold cups, mixing the drink with
honey, vanilla and even chilli powder.
Brought back from the New World,
chocolate first became popular in
Spain, where it was drunk flavoured
with cinnamon, nutmeg, pepper
and ginger.*

19th Century

Gaetano Bellei
Italian (1857–1922)
A Good Brew
Signed, oil on canvas
34 x 24in (86.5 x 61.5cm)
£7,000–8,000 *S*

V. Chavigny
French? (19thC?)
A Picnic
Signed, oil on canvas
24 x 36in (61 x 91.5cm)
£3,000–3,500 *Bon*

*This picture, by a little known artist, was
sold purely on its decorative merit.*

Chinese School (early 19thC)
The Production of Tea, The Production of
Porcelain, The Production of Silk, and The
Cultivation of Rice and Corn
A collection of four sets of 12 gouaches
recording the four great areas of production
in China, all inscribed and numbered, the
album bound in embroidered boards, a paper
crest attached to the cover
15¼ x 20½in (39 x 52cm)
£46,000–60,000 *S*

James Ensor
Belgian (1860–1940)
La Mangeuse d'Huîtres
Signed and dated '1882', oil on canvas
55¾ x 42½in (142 x 108cm)
£280,000–330,000 *C*

*Oysters were long considered a lowly food
and it was only gradually that they began
to be accepted on the rich man's table. As
early as 1600, William Vaughan in
Directions for Health was warning his
readers that 'Oysters must not be eaten in
those months which, in pronouncing, want
the letter R.' Subsequent writers reiterated
the safest times to enjoy this delicacy and
also stressed its medicinal virtues.*

European School (19thC)
Interior scene with Dead Game
being blessed by an Abbot
Oil on canvas
24 x 30in (61.5 x 76cm)
£200–400 *GH*

Jan Hendrich Van Grootvelt
Dutch (1808–65)
Preparing the Meal
Signed and dated '1844', oil on canvas
15 x 9in (38 x 22.5cm)
£18,000–19,000 *HFA*

George Elgar Hicks, R.B.A.
British (1824–1914)
The Soup Kitchen
Signed and dated '1851', oil on canvas
26 x 35in (66 x 89cm)
£7,500–8,500 *GAK*

Harold Gilman
British (1876–1919)
The Cook
Signed, oil on canvas, c1908
16¼ x 10¼in (41.5 x 26cm)
£20,000–30,000 *C*

Hermann Kern
Hungarian (1839–1912)
Preparing Vegetables
Signed, artist's seal on reverse,
oil on panel
18¾ x 12¼in (47.5 x 31.5cm)
£3,500–4,500 *P*

Circle of John Arthur Lomax
British (1857–1923)
A Celebratory Drink
Oil on canvas
21 x 15½in (53 x 39.5cm)
£1,500–2,000 *S(S)*

Adrien-Emmanuel Marie
French (1848–91)
Feeding the Hungry after the Lord Mayor's
Banquet, interior of the Guildhall
Signed and dated '1882', oil on vcanvas
36 x 52½in (92 x 132cm)
£56,000–75,000 *P*

Erskine Nicol, A.R.A.
British (1825–1904)
Her Ain Auld Man
Signed, inscribed and dated '1886', pencil
and watercolour heightened with bodycolour
10 x 14¾in (25.5 x 37.5cm)
£1,500–2,000 *C*

Alfred Provis
British (active 1843–86)
Helping Mother
Oil on canvas
9 x 13in (22.5 x 33cm)
£2,700–3,200 *HFA*

Ferdinand Wagner, Snr.
German (1819–81)
The Banquet
Signed, oil on canvas
36 x 65¾in (91.5 x 167cm)
£25,000–35,000 *S(NY)*

20th Century

Frank Moss Bennett
British (1874–1953)
A Good Vintage
Signed and dated '1930'
19¾ x 14½in (50 x 37cm)
£11,000–15,000 *S(S)*

*An oenophilist is a lover of wine, and
oenological elements in a picture can often
serve to increase its value. Frank Moss
Bennett's decorative historical oils are always
popular in the saleroom. The picture went
comfortably over top estimate thanks to the
desirable wine-orientated subject matter.*

Lawson Wood
British (1878–1957)
Old English Interior
Signed and dated '09, watercolour
with bodycolour
10 x 13¼in (25 x 33.5cm)
£350–400 *CBL*

Nicholas Africano
American (b1948)
Oysters in Vinegar again!
Signed and dated '1981' on the reverse,
oil on masonite
12 x 23¼in (30.5 x 59.5cm)
£3,000–4,000 *S(NY)*

Locate the Source
*The source of each
illustration in Miller's
can be found by checking
the code letters below
each caption with the list
of contributors.*

Gerard Dillon, R.H.A.
Irish (1916–71)
The Fish Eaters
Signed, oil on board
17 x 20¾in (43 x 53cm)
£12,000–15,000 *S*

Graham Knuttel
Irish (20thC)
Fish Soup
Oil on canvas
36 x 48in (91.5 x 122cm)
£4,500–5,000 *NAG*

Karolina Larusdottir, R.W.S., N.E.A.C.
British (b1944)
Tea with a little Woman
Signed and dated '1993', oil on canvas
10 x 14in (25 x 35.5cm)
£1,000–1,250 *BRG*

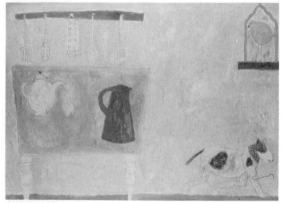

Annora Spence
British (b1963)
In the Kitchen
Mixed media
19 x 23in (48 x 58.5cm)
£350–400 *TRG*

Nikolai Obriynba
Russian (b1913)
The Picnic
Signed and dated '1958', oil on board
6½ x 8in (16.5 x 20cm)
£900–1,000 *CE*

Ruskin Spear
British (1911–90)
The Enthusiast
Oil on panel
20 x 30in (50.5 x 76cm)
£13,500–14,250 *BRG*

Andy Warhol
American (1930–86)
Tom 'n' Jerry Recipe
Hand coloured blotted ink line
drawing, pen and ink on paper
24 x 18in (61 x 45.5cm)
£2,000–2,500 *S(NY)*

Charles Walter Simpson
British (1885–1971)
Skinning Fish, St. Ives
Indistinctly signed, oil on canvas
24 x 30in (61 x 76cm)
£2,600–3,400 *C*

SHOPS & MARKETS

Peeter van Bredael
Dutch (1629–1719)
Village Market Scenes
A pair, oil on panel
10½ x 15½in (25.5 x 39cm)
£10,500–15,000 *S*

Attributed to Justus Junker
German (1703–67)
A Cobblers Shop, and An Apothecary
A pair, oil on panel
16 x 19in (40.5 x 48.5cm)
£13,000–16,000 *S(Am)*

North German School (17thC)
A Fish Market in a Baltic Coastal Town
Oil on canvas
16 x 29in (40.5 x 74cm)
£3,500–4,500 *S*

Abraham van Stry
Dutch (1753–1826)
Figures in a Cloth Shop
Signed, oil on panel
24½ x 22½in (62 x 57cm)
£13,000–15,000 *S(Am)*

Follower of Casper Netscher
Dutch (1639–84)
The Game Seller
Oil on panel
16¾ x 13in (42.5 x 33cm)
£3,500–4,500 *CSK*

William Raymond Dommersen
Dutch (d1927)
The Place des Halles, Paris
Signed, oil on canvas
24 x 20in (61 x 50.5cm)
£1,600–2,200 *CSK*

Charles-Edouard Delort
French (1841–95)
The Bargain
Signed and dated '1894', oil on canvas
14 x 11in (36 x 28cm)
£2,500–3,500 *C*

William Mark Fisher, R.A.
British (1841–1923)
Outside the Blacksmith's Shop
Watercolour
28 x 42in (71 x 106.5cm)
£7,000–8,000 *WG*

Xavier Della Gatta
Italian (active 1777–1817)
A collection of 25 watercolours on paper laid
down on paper, 4 signed and dated '1818',
13 signed, bound in an album
£25,000–35,000 *C*

Alexander Fraser, Snr., A.R.S.A.
British (1786–1865)
The Cobbler
Signed and dated '1839', oil on panel
18 x 14½in (45.5 x 37cm)
£1,900–2,400 *S*

H. Gillard Glindoni
British (1852–1913)
A Fishy Tale
Signed and dated '1897', watercolour
21 x 29in (53 x 73.5cm)
£3,000–4,000 *GH*

Ralph Hedley
British (1851–1913)
Christmas Market
Signed and dated '1909', oil on canvas
50 x 40in (127 x 101.5cm)
£14,500–15,500 *HFA*

*Ralph Hedley was a Newcastle genre painter
who worked in both oil and watercolour.
He was born in Richmond, Yorkshire and
studied at the Newcastle School of Art. Later
he became President of the Berwick Clun
and Northumbrian Art Institute, as well
as a Member of the Society of British Artists.
The subjects of his paintings are usually
scenes of the working lives of ordinary
people, beautifully observed and well
executed. Hedley exhibited at the Society of
British Artists as well as the Royal Academy
from 1879.*

Edith Mary Lee-Hankey (née Garner)
British (b1881)
Market Day
Signed, oil on canvas
24 x 25¼in (61 x 64cm)
£1,400–1,800 *P*

Petrus van Schendel
Belgian (1806–70)
Avondmarkt
Signed and dated '1867', oil on panel
27½ x 21in (70 x 53.5cm)
£75,000–90,000 *S(NY)*

F. H. Moller
Continental (19thC)
At the Cobbler's Door, and A Visit to
the Forge
A pair, one signed and dated '1853',
oil on canvas
35 x 28in (89 x 71cm)
£2,000–2,500 *CSK*

Benjamin Walter Spiers
British (c1860–c1910)
A Bit of London Town
Signed with initials, inscribed and
dated '81', pencil and watercolour
heightened with bodycolour
7 x 19½in (17.5 x 49.5cm)
£7,500–9,500   *C*

Percy Lancaster
British (1878–1951)
A Flower Girl
Watercolour
27¼ x 16½in (69 x 42cm)
£4,500–4,750   *GG*

Karolina Larusdottir, R.W.S., N.E.A.C.
British (b1944)
Trying on Hats
Signed amd dated '1993', oil on canvas
10 x 14in (25 x 35.5cm)
£1,000–1,250   *BRG*

Takanari Oguiss
Japanese (1901–86)
Signed and dated '33', oil on panel
10¼ x 13¾in (25.5 x 35cm)
£14,000–16,000   *S*

Janet Ledger
British (20thC)
Sunday Morning - Columbia Road
Signed, oil on canvas
12 x 10in (30.5 x 25cm)
£550–650   *TLB*

Edwin Morrow
British (active 1903–36)
Could I have a pound of tomatoes,
top ones please?
Pen and ink, 1935
14 x 10in (35.5 x 25cm)
£300–350   *CBL*

ON THE BEACH

As the following pictures suggest, seaside holidays took off in the 19thC, when coastal resorts began to replace inland spa towns as popular retreats. As Christopher Hibbert has noted, (see bibliography), it was the development of the railways that enabled the general public to see the sea. In the days of the stage coach, it cost a prohibitive 21 shillings to travel inside from London to Brighton - by 1844 the 3rd Class rail fare was only 4s 2d, and tourists came in droves. Subtle social divisions separated the seaside resorts. Those locations furthest away from London and the large towns and, as such, most difficult to reach, were the more fashionable and most upper-class - Scarborough and Blackpool were both favoured by the well-off Victorian gentry. Margate, notes Harold Perkin in *The Age of the Railway* (1970) was 'merely for tradespeople, Ramsgate for the somewhat higher class depicted in broad cloth and silk in W. P. Frith's painting of Ramsgate Sands... Gravesend and Southend were "low", a target for day tripping clerks, shop assistants and artisans.'

19th Century

Bernardus Johannes Blommers
Dutch (1845–1914)
Children on the Beach
Signed, oil on canvas
13½ x 19½in (34 x 49.5cm)
£15,000–18,000   *S(Am)*

Wenceslas de Brozik
Bohemian (1851–1901)
The Croquet Game
Oil on canvas
22 x 32in (55.5 x 81cm)
£18,000–19,500   *HFA*

Johannes Evert Akkeringa
Dutch (1861–1942)
Children on the Beach
Signed, oil on canvas
14½ x 18¼in (37 x 46.5cm)
£10,500–13,500   *S(Am)*

Albert Aublet
French (1851–1938)
Sur les Galets, le Tréport
Signed and dated '1883', oil on canvas
33¾ x 54½in (86 x 138.5cm)
£270,000–300,000   *S(NY)*

Eugène Boudin
French (1824–98)
Trouville, l'Heure du Bain
Signed and dated '1863', oil on panel
10¼ x 19in (26 x 48.5cm)
£100,000–120,000   *C*

Trouville is located at the mouth of the river La Touques in Normandy. It was a small, quiet village without the distinguished maritime importance of neighbouring Honfleur or Le Havre. From the 1820s, however, Trouville became a fashionable and elegant summer retreat of the Parisians as well as English visitors. Boudin began painting his first beach scenes in oil in 1862. 'People really like my ladies on beaches, some claim that there is a gold mine there to be exploited,' the artist wrote excitedly to his friend, Ferdinand Martin. A gold mine these paintings certainly proved. In between 1862–95, Boudin was to execute over 300 pictures showing fashionable holiday makers on the beach at Trouville and Deauville.

Virginie Demont-Breton
French (1859–1935)
Playing in the Surf
Signed, oil on canvas
30½ x 41½in (77.5 x 105.4cm)
£7,000–8,000 S(NY)

*Demont-Breton was the daughter and student
of Jules Breton, the realist painter.*

Paul Michel Dupuy
French (b1869)
A Beach Scene
Signed, oil on canvas
14½ x 21in (36.5 x 53cm)
£11,000–13,000 S

Julian Drummond
British (late 19thC)
The Toy Yachts
Signed and dated '76', pencil and
watercolour heightened with white
17½ x 28½in (44 x 72cm)
£750–1,000 CSK

Winslow Homer
American (1836–1910)
Children on the Beach
Signed and dated '1881', watercolour
and pencil on paper
13¼ x 19in (33.5 x 48.5cm)
£190,000–220,000 S(NY)

Robert Gemmell Hutchison
British (1855–1936)
Sings ring in the Sea
Signed and inscribed, watercolour
heightened with white
14 x 20½in (35.5 x 52cm)
£3,500–4,500 CSK

John William Buxton Knight
British (1843–1908)
On the Beach at Ramsgate
Signed, watercolour
12¾ x 19½in (32.5 x 49.5cm)
£4,200–4,500 GG

Alfred Glendening Junior, R.B.A.
British (active 1861–1907)
On the Sands
Signed with monogram and
dated '1895', watercolour
13 x 19in (33 x 48cm)
£7,000–7,850 WG

Charles-François Pécrus
French (1826–1907)
Elegant Figures on a Beach
Signed and dated '91', oil on canvas
15 x 25in (38 x 61cm)
£12,000–14,000 *C*

Edward H. Potthast
American (1857–1927)
In the Summertime
Signed, oil on board
12 x 16in (30.5 x 40.6cm)
£20,000–25,000 *S(NY)*

Joaquín Sorolla y Bastida
Spanish (1863–1923)
Niños en el Mar: Study for Triste Herencia
(Sad Inheritance)
Signed, oil on canvas
16 x 21¾in (40.5 x 55cm)
£125,000–150,000 *S(NY)*

*This study is one of several images painted
in 1899 which lead up to the pivotal Triste
Herencia, Sorolla's last great masterpiece,
painted to provoke social consciousness. Triste
Herencia won Sorolla the Grand Prix and a
medal of honour in the Paris Exposition
Universelle of 1900. Sorolla poignantly
depicted crippled children bathing in the sea
at the Cabíral beach, Valencia, under the
protective guidance of a monk from the Order
of San Juan de Dios.*

Hermann Seeger
German (b1857)
On the Beach
Signed, oil on canvas
33½ x 42½in (85 x 108cm)
£5,250–7,000 *C*

20th Century

Jan Zoetelief Tromp
Dutch (1872–1947)
At the Seaside
Signed, oil on canvas
14 x 20in (35.5 x 50.5cm)
£19,000–22,000 *C*

Charles-Garabed Atamian
Turkish (20thC)
Children of the Sea
Indistinctly signed, oil on canvas
21 x 25in (54 x 63cm)
£10,000–12,000 *HSS*

Mary Beresford-Williams
British (20thC)
Sea Defences
Signed, oil on canvas
10 x 14in (25 x 35.5cm)
£450–500 *JN*

David Burliuk
Russian/American (1882–1967)
Bradenton Beach, Florida
Signed, numbered and dated 1946',
oil on canvas board
11½ x 15½in (29 x 39cm)
£1,400–1,800 *CNY*

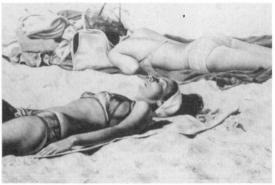

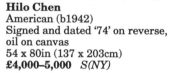

William Burns
British (b1923)
The Yellow Umbrella
Signed, oil on canvas
7 x 9in (17.5 x 22.5cm)
£400–450 *JN*

Hilo Chen
American (b1942)
Signed and dated '74' on reverse,
oil on canvas
54 x 80in (137 x 203cm)
£4,000–5,000 *S(NY)*

Carlos Alberto Castellanos
South American (20thC)
Personajes en la Playa
Signed, oil on canvas, 1930
32 x 39½in (81 x 100cm)
£8,000–10,000 *S(NY)*

Henry Davenport
American (b1882)
Late Afternoon, Old Garden Beach,
Rockport, MA
Signed, oil on canvas
24 x 30¼in (61 x 76.5cm)
£1,000–1,500 *SK*

Emily Court
British (d1957)
Beach Scene
Signed, oil on canvas
24 x 32in (61 x 81cm)
£1,450–1,650 *TFA*

Sir William Russell Flint, R.A.
British (1880–1969)
Phyllis Alone
Signed, watercolour
13 x 20in (33 x 50.5cm)
£12,000–13,000 *JN*

Ken Howard, R.A.
British (b1932)
Sennen Sparkle
Watercolour
7 x 9in (17.5 x 22.5cm)
£550–650 *WHP*

Robert Greenham
British (1906–75)
Beach Paraphanalia
Signed, inscribed and dated '68',
oil on canvas
30½ x 20in (76.5 x 50.5cm)
£2,750–3,500 *C*

George Large, R.I.
British (20thC)
Beachboys
Watercolour
22 x 19in (55.5 x 48cm)
£850–950 *GL*

Isaac Israëls
Dutch (1865–1934)
Figures on Viareggio Beach
Signed, oil on canvas
15½ x 19½in (39 x 49.5cm)
£20,000–25,000 *S(Am)*

Janet Ledger
British (20thC)
Childhood Walks, Stormy Days
Signed, oil on canvas
6in (15cm) square
£300–400 *TLB*

Campbell Mellon
British (1876–1955)
Children playing on the Beach
Signed, oil on panel
12 x 16in (30.5 x 40.5cm)
£2,750–3,750 *C*

Adrianus Cornelis van Noort
Dutch (b1914)
At Zandvoort
Signed, oil on canvas
12 x 16in (30.5 x 40.5cm)
£1,000–1,250 *JN*

Judy Talacko
Australian (b1941)
The Kit Launch
Signed and dated '93', oil on canvas
24 x 30in (61 x 76cm)
£2,750–3,250 *Om*

Dorothea Sharp, R.B.A.
British (1874–1955)
Paddling in the Shallows
Signed, oil on canvas
22in (55.5cm) square
£14,000–15,000 *JN*

Frederick John Widgery
British (1861–1942)
The Cockle Rakers, Dawlish Warren
Signed and inscribed, watercolour
7½ x 19in (18.5 x 48cm)
£950–1,200 *WrG*

Jonathan Trowell, N.E.A.C.
British (b1938)
Summer Outing
Oil on canvas
7 x 9in (17.5 x 22.5cm)
£500–600 *JN*

George Russel Woolway
British (1879–1961)
French Beach
Signed, watercolour, c1930
11 x 15in (28 x 38cm)
£300–350 *JDG*

MUSIC & DANCE
17th–18th Century

Maerten van Cleve
Flemish (1527–81)
A Wedding Dance
Oil on panel
9½ x 13½in (24 x 34.5cm)
£18,500–22,000 *S*

Studio of Bartolomeo Veneto
Italian (active 1502–46)
A Lady playing the Lute
Oil on panel, in a period painted wood frame
23½ x 17¼in (60 x 44cm)
£25,000–30,000 *S*

This painting is a version of Bartolomeo Veneto's celebrated painting in the Pinacoteca di Brera, Milan.

Egbert van Heemskerck
Dutch (c1634–1704)
Boers Singing in a Tavern Interior
Signed and dated '1686', oil on canvas
14 x 11¾in (35.5 x 30cm)
£4,500–5,000 *S*

Renier de la Haye
Dutch (1640–95)
A young Lady playing a Violoncello
Signed, oil on panel
12¼ x 9½in (31 x 24cm)
£8,500–10,000 *S*

Follower of Hendrik Martensz. Sorgh
Dutch (1611–70)
Boers making Music in a Tavern
Oil on panel
16 x 13in (40.5 x 33cm)
£2,200–2,500 *CSK*

Franz Christoph Janneck
Austrian (1703–61)
An Elegant Trio playing in
an Elaborate Baroque Interior
Oil on copper
10¾ x 8½in (27.5 x 21.5cm)
£15,000–17,000 *S*

Leonardo Marini
Italian (1730–97)
Bacco, Satiri al Seguito di Bacco,
Seguaci di Bacco, Baccante,
and Figuranti
A set of 5, black chalk, pen and
black ink, watercolour, inscribed
as titles and numbered '17'
13 x 9in (33 x 23cm)
£1,200–1,500 *C*

Joseph Grassi
Austrian (1758–1838)
Portrait of Countess
Augusta Nimptsch
Signed and dated '1800',
oil on canvas
52¾ x 41⅛in (134 x 105cm)
£7,000–8,000 *S*

19th Century

Micheline Blenarska
Russian (early 19thC)
A Russian Interior
Signed, watercolour over pencil
4¼ x 7½in (11 x 19cm)
£2,750–3,000 *CW*

John G. Brown
American (1831–1913)
The Two Musicians
Signed and dated '1874', oil on canvas
18 x 14in (46 x 35.5cm)
£12,500–14,500 *S(NY)*

John Bagnold Burgess, R.A.
British (1830–97)
A Neapolitan Dancer
Signed, oil on canvas
26 x 19in (66 x 48cm)
£8,000–9,000 *C*

George-Jules-Victor Clarin
French (1843–1919)
The Spanish Dancers
Signed and dated '1875',
oil on canvas
39¼ x 32¼in (100 x 82cm)
£8,200–10,000 *C*

Christian Frederick Carl Halm
Danish (1804–46)
The Music Lesson
Signed, oil on canvas
21 x 17in (53 x 43cm)
£13,000–14,000 *HFA*

Paul Heyman
German (19th/20thC)
Evening Relaxation
Signed, oil on canvas
43 x 60in (109 x 152cm)
£35,000–38,000 *HFA*

Albert Ludovici, Jnr.
British (1852–1932)
A Grand Ball
Signed, watercolour
14¼ x 21¾in (36 x 55cm)
£900–1,000 *JML*

Hermann Kern
Hungarian (1839–1912)
The Maestro
Signed, oil on panel
27 x 18¾in (68.5 x 47.5cm)
£5,000–6,000 *P*

Raphael de Ochoa y Madrazo
Spanish (b1858)
The Ballerinas
Signed, oil on panel
18½ x 15in (47 x 38cm)
£700–900 *CSK*

Jean P. Platteel
Belgian (active 1839–67)
The Organ Grinder
Signed and dated '45',
watercolour heightened
with silver
6 x 4¾in (15 x 13cm)
£200–300 *P*

Franciso Rodriguez San Clement
Spanish (1861–1956)
The Flamenco Dancer
Signed, oil on canvas
31½ x 25in (80 x 63.5cm)
£800–1,000 *CSK*

Otto Ludwig Sinding
Norwegian (1842–1909)
La Tarantella
Signed and dated '1905',
oil on canvas
41½ x 80¾in
(105.5 x 205cm)
£7,250–8,000 *C*

L. Willems
Dutch (19thC)
The Music Lesson
Signed, faintly inscribed
on label on reverse,
oil on panel
9½ x 11in (24 x 28cm)
£350–450 *SLN*

Charles Spencelayh
British (1865–1958)
Failing Memories
Signed and inscribed,
dated 'August 4th 1926',
oil on canvas
20 x 15¼in (50.5 x 38.5cm)
£27,000–30,000 *C*

20th Century

British School (c1900)
The Revellers
Gouache
3½ x 7¼in (9 x 18.5cm)
£300–350 *JDG*

Milton Avery
American (1885–1965)
Girl with Mandolin
Signed, inscribed and titled on the reverse,
gouache on paper
12 x 18in (30.5 x 45.5cm)
£11,000–12,000 *S(NY)*

> **Miller's is a price GUIDE
> not a price LIST**

Corneli
Italian (c1920)
The Band
Signed, ink and wash
9½ x 8½in (24 x 21.5cm)
£300–350 *JDG*

André Dignimont
French (1891–1965)
Danseurs dans la Rue
Stamped signature, watercolour on card
21¼ x 18½ in (54 x 47cm)
£1,800–2,500 *CSK*

John Duffin
British (20thC)
Three Musicians
Signed, watercolour
16 x 11in (40.5 x 28cm)
£150–250 *GK*

Klim Forster
British (20thC)
Rosie
Watercolour
16 x 12in (41 x 30.5cm)
£200–240 *RGFA*

Anthony Gross
British (b1905)
Charivari Series, Tuba Player, 1960
Etching, signed, inscribed and
numbered '49/50'
14¾ x 18in (37.5 x 45.5cm)
£400–450 *BLD*

Louis Icart
French (1888–1950)
Fairy Dancer
Drypoint with aquatint, 1939
19½ x 23in (49.5 x 58cm)
£750–1,000 *P*

Percy Wyndham Lewis
British (1882–1957)
Three Figures, 1919–20
Signed, black chalk and coloured washes
14¾ x 19½in (37.5 x 49.5cm)
£3,800–4,200 *S*

André Lhote
French (1885–1962)
Gypsies Dancing
Signed, watercolour and gouache on paper
8½ x 6¾in (21 x 17cm)
£12,000–14,000 *CSK*

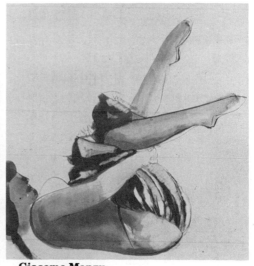

Giacomo Manzu
Italian (1908–91)
Ballerina
Signed, brush, pen, blue ink and blue ink wash
heightened with white gouache on paper
21½ x 17½in (55 x 44.5cm)
£3,300–4,300 *CNY*

Larry Otoo
Ghanaian (b1956)
Perception for Percussion
Oil on canvas, 1990
28½ x 47½in (72 x 120cm)
£700–800 *SG*

Ken Paine
British (20thC)
The Saxophone Player
Pastels
27 x 21in (68.5 x 53cm)
£2,000–2,500 *TLB*

Steven Spurrier, R.A.
British (1878–1961)
The Recital
Signed, oil on canvas
40½ x 50in (103 x 127cm)
£1,500–2,000 *C*

Russell Sydney Reeve, R.E., R.B.A.
British (1895–1970)
Drums and Brass
Signed, copperplate etching
7½ x 10in (19 x 25cm)
£600–650 *PN*

Locate the Source
*The source of each
illustration in Miller's
can be found by checking
the code letters below
each caption with the list
of contributors.*

Moses Rynecki
Polish (1885–1943)
Café Scene, and The Accordianist
A pair, signed and dated '1934', watercolour
14 x 20in (35.5 x 50.5cm)
£1,400–1,800 *S(NY)*

CIRCUS & FAIRGROUND

Like the fool in literature, the clown is one of the great archetypes of Western art, celebrated in the work of artists from Watteau to Rouault. In the 18thC, the Italian Commedia dell'Arte had a huge effect on the fine and decorative arts, with stock characters such as Pierrot and Columbine appearing in every medium from rococo paintings to the porcelain figurines produced by the great ceramics factories of the period. As Claude Harrison's work shows, these figures continue to inspire the artists of the 20thC. Principal Commedia dell'Arte characters include: Pierrot - the white-faced clown, Scaramouch - a braggart dressed in black, Harlequin - a mischievous fellow in a tight fitting spangled dress. He was beloved by the beautiful Columbine, daughter of Pantaloon, the foolish old Venetian, who dressed in loose trousers and from whom pantaloons or pants derive their name.

Philippe Mercier
French (1689–1760)
Comédie Italienne
Oil on canvas
41 x 46½in (104 x 118cm)
£20,000–25,000 *S*

Honoré Daumier
French (1808–79)
Deux Saltimbanques
Pen and ink and grey wash on paper
9½ x 6in (24 x 15cm)
£58,000–65,000 *S(NY)*

Ridolfo Bernard
Italian (20thC)
Il Circo
Oil on board, c1930
11 x 14in (28 x 36cm)
£400–485 *JDG*

Byron Browne
American (1907–61)
Head of a Clown
Signed, inscribed and dated '1947',
oil on canvas
14 x 12in (36 x 30.5cm)
£2,000–2,500 *CNY*

Dame Laura Knight
British (1877–1970)
The Merry-Go-Round
Etching, signed in pencil,
inscribed 'state trial proof'
11 x 8in (28 x 20cm)
£200–300 *CSK*

Margaret Mitchell
British (20thC)
Balloon Clown
Signed, oil on board
16 x 12in (41 x 30.5cm)
£200–300 *GK*

Ken Moroney
British (20thC)
The Suitor
Signed, oil on canvas
14 x 12in (36 x 30.5cm)
£800–1,000 *GK*

Jules Pascin
American (1885–1930)
Le Cirque
Oil on canvas
29 x 32in (74 x 81cm)
£60,000–75,000 *S(NY)*

Patricia Terrell
British (20thC)
Mask
Signed, oil on board
18 x 12in (46 x 31cm)
£200–400 *GK*

Helen Peters
British (b1912)
On Stage
Engraving, signed in pencil, c1910
9 x 7in (23 x 17.5cm)
£250–300 *GK*

George Weissbort
British (20thC)
Waiting to Go On
Signed, oil on board
12 x 10in (31 x 25cm)
£400–800 *GK*

MILITARY

The following collection of pictures runs
from the cavalry engagements of the 17thC
to the tank warfare of the 20thC, and
includes both genre paintings and historical
military pictures. The latter can often yield
a fascinating amount of information,
permitting the collector to identify specific
battles, uniforms and individuals, thus
providing a decorative introduction to the
history of warfare. Such pictures are often
well worth researching and the following
specialist museums can offer invaluable
assistance. The National Army Museum,
Chelsea, London, covers the history of the
armies of Britain and is home to one of the
largest collections of military costume in the
world. Its library is open to the public (apply
for a reader's ticket from the Director) and
the museum will help identify objects by
appointment. The Imperial War Museum,
Lambeth, London, is the place to visit with
enquiries about 20thC material, particularly
pertaining to the two World Wars, and many
individual regiments have their own small
museums or art and object collections.

17th–18th Century

Francesco Simonini
Italian (1686–1753)
A Battle with Horses and Infantrymen
Inscribed on verso in black chalk, pen and
brown ink with wash over black chalk
11 x 15in (28 x 38cm)
£450–600 *P*

Follower of Adam Frans van der Meulen
Flemish (1632–90)
A Cavalry Engagement
Monogram 'GPR', and signature
'J.V. Huchtenburg'
43½ x 63¼in (110 x 160.5cm)
£7,000–8,000 *C*

Follower of Christian Reder
German (1656–1729)
A Cavalry Battle between Turks
and Christians
Oil on canvas
23 x 35in (59 x 89cm)
£5,500–6,500 *S*

Jean Tassel
French (1608–67)
Soldiers arguing over a Game of Cards,
and Musicians entertaining Soldiers
at a Table
A pair, oil on copper
10 x 12¼in (25.5 x 31cm)
£14,000–16,000 *C*

Circle of Thomas Beach
British (1738–1806)
A Portrait of an Officer of a
Volunteer Regiment
Oil on canvas
28½ x 22in (72.5 x 56cm)
£750–900 *CSK*

French School (early 18thC)
A Moroccan Military Encampment,
probably in the Atlas Mountains
Oil on canvas
61¼ x 108 (155.5 x 274cm)
£44,000–60,000 *C*

John Thomas Seton
British (c1735–c1806)
Portrait of a Gentleman with his Clerk,
probably Giles Stibbert and William Hickey
Oil on canvas
35¾ x 32¼in (91 x 82cm)
£5,000–6,000 *S*

Thomas Rowlandson
British (1756–1827)
Soldiers on the March
Inscribed on reverse, pencil, pen,
ink and watercolour
9¼ x 11½in (23 x 29cm)
£3,750–4,750 *C*

*The soldiers are the 'Old Buffs', members of
the 3rd Regiment of the Line, now the East
Kent Regiment.*

Scottish Provincial School (late 18thC)
Sir Neil Menzies at the Head of his Clan
Oil on canvas, unlined
29 x 48in (73.5 x 122cm)
£5,000–6,000 *S*

19th Century

'It is not surprising that military painters
should abound in a century which was
devoted to imperialism, colonial
expansionism, and a good deal of sabre
rattling,' note the writers of *Popular 19th
Century Painting,* Antique Collectors' Club,
1986. The Napoleonic wars, the Crimea and
the Franco-Prussian conflict provided
endless heroic subject matter for Victorian
military artists. Battle scenes offered drama,
pathos and patriotism, and in a pre-khaki,
pre-technological age, and had the added
decorative attractions of cavalry horses,
flashing steel and glamorous uniforms.

Louis Marie Baader
French (1828–1919)
Les Conseils de l'Ancien
Oil on canvas
32 x 39¾in (80 x 101cm)
£17,000–20,000 *S(NY)*

François Auguste Biard
French (1798–1882)
The Inspection
Signed, oil on canvas
25 x 41½in (63.5 x 105.5cm)
£14,000–16,000 *S(NY)*

Caran d'Ache
French (1858–1909)
Soldiers by a Fire
Signed, monochrome watercolour
7¾ x 10in (19.5 x 25.5cm)
£400–450 *CBL*

Jules-Resnard Draner
French (b1853)
Etats-Unis, 1862, Missouri Emmet Guard
Signed, inscribed with title, watercolour
with pencil
11¼ x 7½in (29 x 19cm)
£750–850 *CBL*

Joshua Dalby of York
British (1794–1836)
A Troop Sergeant Major of the 7th Dragoon
Guards mounted on his Charger
Signed, dated '1838', oil on canvas
14 x 18in (35.5 x 46cm)
£3,500–4,500 *S*

Sir Francis Grant, P.R.A.
British (1803–78)
Portrait of General Sir Josiah Champagne
Oil on canvas
54 x 46in (137 x 116.5cm)
£8,500–10,000 *S(NY)*

Attributed to Sir Charles Lock Eastlake
British (1793–1865)
The Death of Lord Nelson
Oil on canvas
94½ x 67in (240 x 170cm)
£14,000–16,000 *S(NY)*

Paul Louis Narcisse Grolleron
French (1848–1901)
Storming the Gate
Signed, oil on canvas
25½ x 21½in (65 x 54.5cm)
£2,000–2,500 *S(NY)*

Winslow Homer
American (1836–1910)
The Union Cavalry and Artillery
Starting in Pursuit of the Rebels up the
Yorktown Turnpike
Signed and dated 'May 5th 1862',
pencil on paper
8¾ x 14in (22 x 40cm)
£12,000–14,000 *S(NY)*

Emil Johann Hunten
German (19thC)
An Incident on the Field - German Artillery
Signed and dated '73', oil on canvas
28½ x 38¼in (72.5 x 97cm)
£3,500–4,500 *CSK*

Paul Léon Jazet
French (b1848)
The Death of Lord Nelson
Signed and inscribed 'Nelson 1882',
oil on canvas
42 x 61½in (106.5 x 156cm)
£33,000–40,000 *S(NY)*

Hermanus Willem Koekkoek
Dutch (1867–1929)
Defendants of the Empire Keeping
the Boers at Bay at Mafeking
Signed and inscribed on old label on
stretcher, oil on canvas
39½ x 59½in (100 x 151cm)
£3,500–4,500 *P*

*Hermanus Willem Koekkoek was the son of
Willem, and a member of the extensive
Koekkoek family of artists. He specialised in
military paintings, working in both London
and Holland and as an illustrator for* The
Sketch *and* The Illustrated London News.

Sir James Dromgole Linton
British (1840–1916)
A Man at Arms
Signed with initials, watercolour
15 x 10in (38 x 25cm)
£500–600 *CSK*

Orlando Norie
British (1832–1901)
Cavalry Officers in an Encampment
Signed, watercolour over traces of pencil
heightened with touches of bodycolour
12½ x 18¾in (32 x 48cm)
£1,000–1,400 *S*

Richard Thomas Moynan
British (1856–1906)
The Last of the 24th,
Isandula, 1879
Signed and dated '1883',
oil on canvas
50 x 40in (127 x 101.5cm)
£25,000–35,000 *S*

*Moynan's picture is one of the few
paintings inspired by the Zulu wars
of 1878–9. It depicts the last moment
of the Battle of Isandlwana, the worst
defeat ever suffered by the British at
the hands of native armies. Nine
hundred and fifty European troops
and eight hundred and fifty Natal
levies were massacred by the Zulu
regiments, partly because the British
force was poorly commanded and,
also, owing to the horrifying fact that
soldiers experienced great difficulty
in opening faulty ammunition boxes.
The 24th Regiment was entirely
decimated and Moynan shows the
last dying soldier in a Christ-like
pose, as a martyr of the Empire, with
one hand outstretched as though
in foregiveness.*

Amadeo, Count Preziosi
Italian (1816–82)
The Albanian Guard
Signed and dated '1863',
pencil and watercolour on paper
16½ x 11¼in (42 x 28.5cm)
£1,400–2,000 *C*

Philip Meadows Taylor
British (1808–76)
Portrait of General Henry
Darby Griffith
Signed and dated '1871',
oil on canvas
45¾ x 55in
(116 x 139.5cm)
£2,000–2,500 *S(NY)*

Sir David Wilkie, R.A.
British (1785–1841)
A Study for 'Sir David Baird discovering the Body
of Tipu Sahib'
With inscription on the reverse of the mount, pencil,
black chalk and watercolour
16 x 10¾in (40.5 x 27cm)
£35,000–45,000 *C*

*Tipu Sahib, son and successor to Haidar Ali, ryler of
Mysore, had resisted the British in the second, third and
fourth and final Mysore Wars. The last ended on 4 May
1799, when the British stormed Tipu's capital city
Seringapatan, sending in a flag of truce and promising
to protect Tipu should he surrender. He was, however,
dead already, and his body was discovered under a heap
of corpses.
This drawing, relating to Wilkie's famous painting of
1838 (National Gallery of Scotland) went to two and a
half times its top estimate of £12,000 at Christie's in April
1994, with Tipu Sahib's own descendants participating
in the bidding.*

20th Century

Sir David Low
British (1891–1963)
Lesser Breeds (Hitler and Mussolini)
Monochrome watercolour
7in (17.5cm) square.
£550–650 *CBL*

Snaffles (Charles Johnson Payne)
British (1884–1967)
Ubique Means – Here we're suffering grief
and pain, over the road they're just the same'
Signed and inscribed, watercolour
14 x 13½in (35.5 x 34.5cm)
£1,500–2,000 *AG*

Peter Peri
British (1899–1967)
Get Out or Perish c1943
Etching
5½ x 7½in (13.7 x 19cm)
£150–175 *BLD*

Snaffles (Charles Johnson Payne)
British (1884–1967)
Cavalree, an Indian Officer of the 9th Horse
Signed and inscribed, watercolour heightened
with bodycolour
13½ x 10in (34 x 25.5cm)
£750–950 *Bon*

Kenneth Riley
American (b1919)
Soldiers
Signed, oil on board
13 x 15in (33 x 38cm)
£2,000–2,500 *CNY*

Ken Riley's work has appeared in Reader's
Digest, The Saturday Evening Post *and* Life.
*Along with being a well-known illustrator, he
is considered to be one of the best painters of
the American West. Riley is a charter member
of the National Academy of Western Art and
is a member of the Cowboy Artists of America.
Born in Missouri, Riley studied under
Thomas Hart Benton and at the Kansas City
Art Institute. He later came to New York
where he studied with Dunn at the Grand
Central School. Riley's most famous
illustrations are those he did for C.S.
Forester's* Captain Hornblower, *stories in the*
Saturday Evening Post.

COWBOYS & INDIANS

At first glance it might seem strange to include Wild West heroes alongside the cavaliers, cardinals and classical beauties, so sought after by Victorian collectors. In reality these popular, and often extremely expensive, American pictures have much in common with European genre painting. Cowboy and Indian pictures could be as imaginary as any 19thC portrayal of Ancient Rome - romantic visions of the Wild West concocted in New York studios for a nostalgic bourgeois clientele. Like the Victorian Orientalists, some artists travelled to the regions they were painting, making faithful records of native life, whilst others were happy to work predominantly from imagination and secondary sources.

M. Guzmán
South American (19thC)
Alegoría de America
Signed, inscribed and dated '1836', oil and feather collage on sheet metal
14 x 20in (35.5 x 51cm)
£40,000–45,000 *S(NY)*

This exotic medium uses the iridescent feathers of quetzals, hummingbirds, and other tropical species, set into mosaics on panels or woven into garments, headdresses, liturgical vestments etc. The final effect was created by overlapping fine layers of the most precious feathers, with matte and iridescent types alternating for effect.

Alfred Jacob Miller
American (1810–74)
Profile of a Sioux Indian
Watercolour on paper, c1833
4½ x 3¾in (11.5 x 90.5cm)
£14,000–15,000 *S(NY)*

Alfred Miller recorded in a letter that the tuft on the Sioux's head was left both for ornament, and so that the enemy should be able to secure their scalp as easily as possible in case of defeat.

E. Irving Couse
American (1866–1936)
Taos Turkey Shooters
Signed, oil on board
8½ x 10in (21 x 25cm)
£11,000–12,000 *S(NY)*

Edward Borein
American (1872–1945)
The Long Drive
Signed, watercolour on paper
12 x 20in (30.5 x 50.5cm)
£30,000–35,000 *S(NY)*

Frank Tenney Johnson
American (1874–1939)
Return from the Hunt
Signed, titled on the stretcher, dated '1934', oil on canvas
25 x 30in (63.5 x 76cm)
£40,000–45,000 *S(NY)*

William R. Leigh
American (1866–1955)
The Hopi Indian Runners
Signed and dated '1913', oil on canvas
40 x 60in (101.5 x 152.5cm)
£90,000–110,000 *S(NY)*

Charles Marion Russell
American (1864–1926)
Bucking Bronco
Signed with skull and dated '1899',
watercolour on paper
14 x 22in (35.5 x 56cm)
£110,000–130,000 *S(NY)*

Joseph Henry Sharp
American (1859–1953)
Taos Drummers
Signed, inscribed on the stretcher,
oil on canvas
20 x 16in (50.5 x 40.5cm)
£34,000–40,000 *S(NY)*

Worthington Whittredge
American (1820–1910)
Indian Encampment on the
Platte River, Colorado
Signed, oil on canvas, c1875
14½ x 22in (36.5 x 56cm)
£95,000–120,000 *S(NY)*

*In his efforts to develop a native landscape
style and become one of America's premier
landscape painters, Whittredge made
three separate excursions West, beginning
in the 1860s.*

Spencer Roberts
British (20thC)
Grey Owl in his Beaver Area
Oil on canvas
48 x 60in (122 x 152cm)
£3,500–4,000 *RGFA*

Saul Steinberg
American (b1914)
The Sheriff
Signed and dated '1951', black ink,
coloured crayons and foil collage on paper
14¾ x 11½in (37 x 29cm)
£5,500–6,500 *CNY*

CAVALIERS

Like the Regency buck, and the scarlet
gowned cardinal (see following section), the
cavalier was one of the favourite subjects of
19thC genre painters. Cavalier pictures
typify the Victorian love of romanticising
and popularising the past, history seen as a
costume drama and told as an anecdote.
The success of such painters can be related
to the literary vogue for the historical
romance. Walter Scott was undoubtedly the
greatest exponent of this genre. 'He was,'
notes one commentator 'the favourite of his
age, read over the whole of Europe, was
compared and almost equalled to Shakespeare,
had more popularity than Voltaire, made
dressmakers and duchesses weep and earned
about £200,000.' (For further information,
see P. Hook and M. Poltimore, bibliography).

Attributed to Willem Pietersz. Buytewech
Dutch (1591–1624)
A Merry Company Smoking and Drinking
in an Interior
Oil on panel
10½ x 14½in (26.5 x 36.5cm)
£9,500–12,000 *S*

*Buytewech is justly celebrated as a great
draughtsman and print maker, but he is less
well known as a painter since few of his pictures
survive. Buytewech's distinctive caricatural faces
which characterise his drawings and prints, are
also found in his paintings, and allow them
easily to be distinguished from similar works
by contemporary exponents of the merry company
genre such as Dirk Hals and Esaias van de Velde.
His colour scheme with strongly predominant
deep reds, is also distinctive.*

Francesco Bergamini
Italian (1815–83)
A Tavern Scene
Signed, oil on canvas
14 x 20in (35.5 x 51cm)
£3,300–4,300 *S*

J. E. Buckley
British (19thC)
Warwick Castle and Haddon Hall
A pair, watercolours
15 x 11in (38 x 28cm)
£5,500–5,900 *HFA*

Alfred François Gues
French (b1837)
A Game of Dice
Signed, oil on panel
18½ x 11in (47 x 28cm)
£1,700–2,200 *CSK*

**Herman Frederik
Carel Ten Kate**
Dutch (1822–91)
The Game of Cards
Signed, oil on panel
25½ x 37in (64.5 x 94cm)
£18,000–20,000 *C*

Adolphe Alexandre Lesrel
French (b1839)
The Latest Model
Signed and dated '1912', oil on cradled panel
23½ x 29in (59.5 x 73.5cm)
£18,000–20,000 *S(NY)*

After Franz Mieris
Dutch (17th/18thC)
Sleeping Cavalier with Companion and
Servant in an Interior
Oil on board
16 x 12in (40.5 x 30.5cm)
£800–1,000 *MSW*

J. Della Rocca
Italian (19thC)
The Cavaliers' Fancy
Signed, oil on canvas
19½ x 25in (49.5 x 64cm)
£2,000–2,500 *S(S)*

Francesco Vinea
Italian (1845–1902)
Good Health and Good Fortune
Signed and dated '1890', oil on canvas
22½ x 27½in (57.5 x 69.5cm)
£17,000–20,000 *CSK*

Ferdinand Roybet
French (1840–1920)
A Musketeer standing with his Dog
Signed, oil on canvas
59 x 33½in (149.5 x 85cm)
£9,000–11,000 *S(NY)*

MONKS & CARDINALS

Salvador Sanchez Barbudo
Spanish (1858–1917)
The First Steps
Signed and dated '1907', oil on canvas
21½ x 33in (54 x 84cm)
£24,000–30,000 *S*

Francesco Bergamini
Italian (1815–83)
A Lesson in Scripture
Signed, oil on canvas
20¼ x 32¼in (51.5 x 82cm)
£7,000–8,000 *C*

François Brunery
Italian (late 19thC)
Un Passage Difficile
Signed, oil on panel
18¼ x 14⅜in (46 x 37cm)
£11,000–13,000 *C*

Giuseppe Bortignoni
Italian (1778–1860)
Just a Tipple
Signed, oil on canvas
16 x 12in (41 x 30.5cm)
£7,200–8,000 *S*

Marcel Brunery
French (19th/20thC)
La Sonate
Signed, oil on canvas
22¾ x 28¼in (58 x 72cm)
£15,000–17,000 *S*

Adolf Humborg
Austrian (1847–1913)
Cleaning out the Wine Cellar
Signed and inscribed, oil on panel
17 x 23⅜in (43 x 60.5cm)
£6,000–7,000 *S(NY)*

Andrea Landini
Italian (b1847)
Impatience
Signed, oil on canvas
18½ x 15in (47 x 38cm)
£10,000–12,000 *C*

Horace Mummery
British (active late 19thC)
A Dominican Friar
Signed and dated '92', watercolour
11 x 9in (28 x 22.5cm)
£250–350 *TAY*

Stefano Novo
Italian (b1862)
The Cardinal's Toast
Signed, oil on canvas
19½ x 29¾in (49.5 x 75.5cm)
£3,500–4,500 *S(S)*

Fritz Steinmetz-Noris
German (b1860)
The Last Drop
Signed, oil on panel
4¼ x 4½in (10.5 x 11.5cm)
£1,000–1,500 *Bon*

Jean-Georges Vibert
French (1840–1902)
A Tasty Treat
Signed, oil on cradled panel
15 x 18¼in (38 x 46.5cm)
£13,000–15,000 *S(NY)*

Max Scholz
German (b1855)
A Cardinal reading in his Study
Signed and inscribed, oil on panel
12½ x 16¼in (32 x 41cm)
£3,500–4,500 *CNY*

VICTORIAN ROMANS: CLASSICAL GENRE

Hugely popular and often highly expensive in the late Victorian period, classical genre pictures spent much of the 20thC being sneered at by critics and ignored by collectors. It is only within the last 30 years that they have returned to favour. Perhaps no single picture could provide a better illustration of the ups-and-downs of artistic fashion than 'The Roses of Heliogabalus', by Sir Lawrence Alma-Tadema, one of the most popular painters of his day, one of the most derided after his death and the current darling of the salerooms. The picture was commissioned by Sir John Aird, M.P. in 1888, for the then enormous sum of £4,000. It was exhibited at the Royal Academy that same year to rapturous applause, *The Art Journal* describing it as 'the painter's chef d'oeuvre'. Sold at Christie's in 1935, the picture fetched only 483 guineas, and when it was offered by the same auction house in 1960, it failed to find a buyer. The next decade saw Victorian pictures coming back into vogue and at Sotheby's in 1973 the picture made £28,000. Twenty years on, and back at Christie's, the picture sold for £1.5 million, a sterling record for the artist at auction.

Sir Lawrence Alma-Tadema, R.A.
British (1836–1912)
A Question
Signed, inscribed and dated 'CLXXXV',
oil on board
6¾ x 15in (17 x 38cm)
£100,000–120,000 *S(NY)*

Abbey Alston
British (1864–1937)
The Fruit Seller
Signed, oil on canvas
36¼ x 28in (92 x 71cm)
£3,500–4,500 *C*

George Lawrence Bulleid, A.R.W.S.
British (1858–1933)
Feeding the Doves
Signed, pencil and watercolour
20½ x 11¼in (52 x 28.5cm)
£4,500–5,500 *C*

The Hon. John Collier
British (1850–90)
Study for Horace and Lydia
Signed, inscribed, oil on canvas
24 x 30in (61 x 76cm)
£2,000–2,500 *C*

Francis Criss
American (1901–73)
Romans
Signed, oil on masonite
24 x 36in (61 x 91.5cm)
£2,500–3,000 *CNY*

Ettore Forti
Italian (19thC)
Conflitto de Interessi
Signed and inscribed, oil on canvas
24 x 39½in (61 x 100.5cm)
£16,000–20,000 *C*

Pietro Gabrini
Italian (1856–1926)
The Forum
Signed and inscribed, oil on canvas
41 x 55½in (104 x 141cm)
£2,000–3,000 *S(NY)*

W. Anstey Dollond
British (active 1880–1911)
Fresh from the Vineyard
Signed and inscribed on
the reverse, watercolour
17½ x 7¾in (44.5 x 19.4cm)
£1,500–2,500 *AG*

John William Godward
British (1861–1922)
A Greek Beauty
Signed and dated '1905', oil on canvas
30 x 15in (76 x 38cm)
£50,000–60,000 *S*

*A Godward classical maiden also
decorates the front cover of* Miller's
Picture Price Guide. *Godward's
highly polished and precisely painted
classical scenes have been fetching
strong prices in the current market.*

Edwin Long, R.A.
British (1829–91)
The Artist's Model
Signed with monogram and dated '1890',
oil on panel
5¾ x 9⅜in (15 x 24.5cm)
£2,000–3,000 *P*

Richard Linderum
German (b1851)
The Soothsayer
Signed and dated '82', oil on panel
24½ x 17in (62 x 43cm)
£2,500–3,500 *C*

Percy Thomas MacQuoid
British (1852–1925)
Penelope
Signed, inscribed and dated '1883',
oil on canvas
36 x 47in (91.5 x 119cm)
£20,000–25,000 *P*

Sidney Harold Meteyard
British (1868–1947)
Love in Idleness
Oil on canvas
34½ x 41⅜in (87.5 x 106cm)
£60,000–70,000 *C*

*Meteyard was a leading member of the
Birmingham Group, the circle of young artists
who emerged in the 1880s as a distinct local
offshoot of the Pre-Raphaelite movement.
In addition to painting pictures he was a
prolific designer of stained glass, carried out
altarpieces at Bordesley (1916) and Southport
(1921), illuminated rolls of honour, made
enamel plaques (often in collaboration with
his wife and former pupil, Kate Eadie), and
illustrated books.*

Guillaume Seignac
French (1870–1924)
The Muse
Signed, oil on canvas
61 x 35in (155 x 89cm)
£11,000–14,000 *S(NY)*

Harold Piffard
British (active 1895–99)
At the Colosseum
Signed, oil on canvas
25¼ x 30in (64 x 76cm)
£7,000–8,000 *S*

Norman Prescott-Davies
British (1862–1915)
A Lullaby
Signed, inscribed and dated '1894',
pencil and watercolour
17¼ x 26¼in (44 x 67cm)
£3,750–4,750 *C*

Henry Ryland
British (1856–1924)
Greeting
Signed and inscribed, watercolour
14½ x 21in (37 x 53cm)
£5,500–6,500 *S*

Sir Edward John Poynter, P.R.A., R.W.S.
British (1836–1919)
The Sandal
Signed with monogram, dated '18EJP71',
oil on panel
8in (20cm) square
£22,000–30,000 *S*

Hendrik Siemiradzki
Russian (1843–1902)
Fête à Capri
Signed, inscribed and indistinctly
dated, oil on canvas
21 x 40in (53.5 x 101.5cm)
£13,000–16,000 *S(NY)*

Eugene Steinsberg
Continental (19thC)
Cupid asleep beneath the Sphinx
Signed and dated '1889', oil on canvas
71¾ x 51¼in (182 x 130cm)
£30,000–35,000 *S(NY)*

ORIENTALIST

From the 1970s until the mid-1980s, demand for Orientalist pictures enjoyed a tremendous boom, with even inferior works fetching record sums. The fall of the Shah of Iran, the collapse of oil prices, the Gulf War and the effect of international recession severely affected the largely Arab based market and prices tumbled. Currently, the market seems to be flourishing again. Many works have achieved very strong prices at auction, although buyers are tending to be more discriminating than they were in the 1970s and 1980s, concentrating on quality and not just decoration. With certain exceptions, figure subjects tend to fetch higher prices than landscapes, and the more attractive the subject matter, usually female, the more desirable the picture.

17th–18th Century

Georges Antoine Keman
French (1765–1830)
The Arrival by Camel, and A Woman
Pleading with the Centurion
A pair, both signed, pencil and watercolour
16 x 22½in (40.5 x 57cm)
£500–700 *CSK*

Albrecht Dürer
German (1471–1528)
The Turkish family
Engraving
4½ x 3¼in (11 x 7.5cm)
£1,200–1,600 *S*

Circle of Jacques Callot
French (1592–1635)
A Figure à la Turque
A set of 7 drawings of a single figure in movement on one sheet, pen and black ink
Each drawing 2¼ x 3in (5.8 x 7.5cm)
£1,600–2,000 *P*

Francesco Santini
Italian (1763–1840)
A Standing Moor
Signed with monogram, pen and brown ink over traces of black chalk
8¼ x 6¼in (20.5 x 15cm)
£350–450 *P*

19th Century

I. Clark, after Henry Alken Snr.
British (1785–51)
The Arabian
Aquatint with hand colouring, 1820
6 x 8½in (15 x 21.5cm)
£300–400 *CG*

J. Alsina
French (19th/20thC)
Oriental Weavers
Signed, oil on canvas
17¾ x 23½in (45 x 60cm)
£6,500–8,000 *S*

Filippo Baratti
Italian (late 19thC)
The Game of Chess
Signed and dated '1880', oil on panel
14 x 9¾in (35.5 x 25cm)
£15,000–17,000 *C*

Joseph Austin Benwell
British (c1830–90)
The Head of the Caravan passing
Mount Sinai
Signed, inscribed and dated '1877', pencil
and watercolour heightened with bodycolour
10¾ x 18¾in (27.5 x 48cm)
£3,300–4,000 *C*

Edmund Berninger
German (b1843)
At the Oasis, and On the Nile
A pair, both signed and inscribed,
oil on canvas
17¾ x 33½in (45 x 85cm)
£6,500–7,500 *C*

John Bagnold Burgess
British (1830–97)
East meets West
Signed and dated '1874', oil on canvas
21¼ x 28½in (54 x 71.5cm)
£11,000–13,000 *S(NY)*

A. Buzzi
Italian (late 19thC)
Arab Carpenters
Signed, pencil and watercolour on
paper laid down on board
20 x 14in (50.5 x 35.5cm)
£3,300–4,000 *C*

Alfred de Dreux
French (1810–60)
The Mounts of Abd El Kader
Signed and dated '58', oil on canvas
34 x 44¼in (86.5 x 112.5cm)
£465,000–500,000 *S*

*Alfred de Dreux is regarded as the leading
19thC equestrian artist. From an early age
he specialised in horse portraits and riding
subjects almost to the exclusion of anything
else, and the many prizes that he won in his
illustrious career indicate his enormous
popularity. Amongst his many patrons were
the Duc de Chartres, the Duc d'Orléans and
Napoleon III. He also worked often in England.
Through his work for the Duc d'Orléans he
came to paint this work depicting the mounts
of the exiled Abd El Kader, the former leader
of the Algerian forces in the war with the
French. De Dreux was at the height of his
career in the 1850s, having completed in
1853 an equestrian portrait of the Emperor
and been made a Chevalier of the Légion
d'Honneur in 1857.
De Dreux's work comes up for auction quite
regularly, but this picture, sold by Sotheby's,
was a particularly fine example, probably
better than anything else seen on the market
in recent years.*

Rudolf Ernset
Austrian (1854–1932)
Lighting the Mosque
Signed and dated '1885', oil on cradled panel
24 x 19¼in (61 x 49cm)
£24,000–30,000 *S(NY)*

***Donze
Swiss (19thC)
A Dancing Beauty
Signed, oil on canvas
23½ x 19¼in (60 x 49cm)
£1,200–1,500 *S*

Joseph Farquharson, R.A.
British (1846–1935)
In Cairo, the Ferry from the Island of
Gazirie on the Nile to Boulach, the
Port of Cairo
Signed, oil on canvas
44 x 78in (112 x 198cm)
£28,000–35,000 *S*

Kitty Fornier
French (d1908)
A Slave Girl
Signed and dated '01'(?), oil on canvas
40½ x 25¾in (102.5 x 65.5cm)
£5,400–6,400 *C*

Frederick Goodall, R.A.
British (1822–1904)
The Sugar Cane Harvest
Signed with monogram and dated
'1869', oil on canvas
7¾ x 21¼in (19.5 x 54cm)
£5,800–6,500 *C*

Laurent-Lucien Gsell
French (1860–1944)
An Odalisque
Signed, oil on canvas
36½ x 29in (92.5 x 73.5cm)
£17,500–19,500 *C*

Louis Eugène Ginain
French (1818–86)
The Falcon Hunt
Signed and dated '1855', oil on canvas
81 x 51½in (204 x 130cm)
£25,000–30,000 *S*

Ginain studied at the Ecole des Beaux-Arts
under Charlet and Abel de Pujol. He
exhibited regularly at the Paris Salons from
1840 to 1879. He painted mainly military
and Oriental subjects, and was awarded the
Légion d'Honneur in 1878.

E. Ansen Hofmann
German (late 19thC)
The Slave Market
Signed, oil on canvas
35¼ x 49in (89.5 x 124.5cm)
£18,000–20,000 *C*

Victor Pierre Huguet
French (1835–1902)
Desert Caravan
Signed, oil on canvas
26 x 34in (66 x 86cm)
£18,000–20,000 *S(NY)*

*Slave markets and hareems were a
particularly popular subject with Western
artists and their audiences, since the theme
allowed for a liberal display of female flesh.
The Arabian beauty, preferably at least
partially unclothed, was one of the archetypes
of Oriental genre painting, although ironically,
since Muslim women were forbidden to sit for
artists, most of these exotic ladies were based
on European models.*

José Laguna y Pérez
Spanish (late 19thC)
The Palace Courtyard
Signed and dated '1871',
oil on canvas
10¾ x 8¾in (27 x 22cm)
£5,800–6,800 *C*

Charles-Edouard Lemaitre
French (late 19thC)
Arab Watercarriers at Rest
Signed, oil on canvas
10¾ x 8½in (27.5 x 21.5cm)
£6,000–7,000 *C*

Paul Joanovitch
Austrian (b1859)
An Arnaut Warrior
Oil on panel
16 x 12⅜in (40.5 x 32cm)
£23,000–30,000 *C*

Paul Dominique Philippoteaux
American (b1846)
The Odalisque
Signed, oil on panel
10½ x 8in (27.5 x 20.5cm)
£7,500–9,000 *C*

Leopold Carl Müller
German (1834–92)
An Arab Encampment
Signed and dated '1880', oil on canvas
29¼ x 48in (74.5 x 122cm)
£52,000–60,000 *C*

Sir Edward John Poynter, P.R.A., R.W.S.
British (1836–1919)
Zenobia Captive
Signed with monogram and dated '1878',
oil on canvas
28½ x 21½in (72 x 54.5cm)
£26,000–35,000 *S*

Georges Antoine Rochegrosse
French (1859–1938)
Salome's Dance
Signed, oil on canvas
22 x 35¾in (56 x 91cm)
£14,000–16,000 *S*

Ellis Silas
British (b1883)
Bondage
Signed, watercolour
13 x 12in (33 x 30.5cm)
£350–400 *G*

Adolf Schreyer
German (1828–99)
Lone Arab on Horseback
Signed, oil on canvas
45 x 67½in (114.5 x 171.5cm)
£22,000–28,000 *S(NY)*

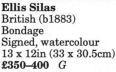

Gustavo Simoni
Italian (b1846)
At the Arms Dealer's Shop
Signed and dated 'Roma 1902',
watercolour on paper
20¾ x 29in (53 x 74cm)
£18,000–20,000 *S(NY)*

Enrico Tarenghi
Italian (b1848)
Prière à la Mosquée
Signed, watercolour on board
29½ x 21½in (80 x 54.5cm)
£8,000–10,000 *C*

Georges Washington
French (1827–1910)
Arab Horsemen Crossing a Ford
Signed, oil on canvas
19½ x 24in (50 x 61cm)
£10,000–12,000 *S*

Casimiro Aldini Tomba
Italian (1857–1929)
Odalisques
A pair, both signed, and one inscribed 'Roma',
oil on canvas
20 x 27½in (51 x 70cm)
£55,000–75,000 *C*

Edwin Lord Weeks
American (1849–1903)
Ispahan
Signed and inscribed, oil on canvas
56 x 74½in (142 x 188cm)
£90,000–120,000 *S(NY)*

*'Ispahan', one of Edwin Lord Weeks' most
important monumental compositions, and the
most significant of his Persian paintings, was
executed c1900–01 in the artist's Paris studio.
Weeks travelled through Persia in 1892–93,
and considered his visit to the city of Ispahan
as the highlight of his entire expedition.
'Ispahan,' he wrote, 'the most sumptuous
court in the world...no spot in the world could
appeal more touchingly to the imagination...
it was once the perfect flower of Persian art...'*

Attributed to Alfred Joseph Woolmer
British (1805–92)
A Moor standing beside a Salver of Fruit
Oil on canvas
14 x 10in (35.5 x 25.5cm)
£900–1,200 *CSK*

Achille Zo
French (1826–1901)
An Arab Smoking a Pipe
Signed, watercolour
11¾ x 10in (30 x 25cm)
£1,000–1,500 *S*

20th Century

Sir Frank Brangwyn, R.A., R.W.S.
British (1867–1956)
An Eastern Market
Signed with initials and indistinctly
dated '55', oil on board
20 x 16in (51 x 40.5cm)
£4,200–5,000 *S*

Henri Matisse
French (1869–1954)
Odalisque à la Coulotte de Satin Rouge
Lithograph, 1925
7¾ x 10½in (19 x 26.5cm)
£26,000–35,000 *C*

Frank Taylor
British (20thC)
Turkish Family at Pamukkale
Watercolour
20 x 26in (50.5 x 66cm)
£900–1,000 *PHG*

Dudley Hardy
British (1865–1922)
Arab Traders
Signed, gouache
13 x 19in (34 x 48cm)
£450–600 *WIL*

Constantin Georges Macris
French (1917–84)
Egyptian Girls
Signed and dated '38', oil on canvas
24¾ x 30in (63 x 76cm)
£5,000–6,000 *C*

Georges Manzana Pissarro
French (b1871)
Two Oriental Girls
Stamped signature, charcoal with gold
38 x 25in (96.5 x 64cm)
£3,000–3,500 *STD*

NUDES

Generally speaking, it was only from the late 19thC that artists began to paint nudes without dressing them up in some story that provided a cover for their nakedness. Religious and classical myths offered endless opportunities for the display of rolling flesh. Orientalist and classical genre subjects allowed Victorian artists to portray naked European models in settings that concealed their origins. Nudity was acceptable as long as the subjects were distanced either historically, geographically or allegorically from real life and contemporary womanhood. Manet's 'Olympia' inspired almost universal hostility when exhibited at the Paris Salon in 1865, because the artist portrayed a contemporary woman in the nude, gazing out of the canvas, unashamed, at her then largely scandalised spectators.

For the collector in this field, quality of painting is all important. Pass over the more titillating areas and check the hands and feet of a figure. Since these are perhaps the hardest part of the body to portray, they can provide a reliable indicator of an artist's skill. Attractive nudes are likely to fetch better prices than more unattractive bodies but, as Baudelaire noted in a Salon review of 1846, 'there are as many kinds of beauty as there are habitual ways of seeking happiness.'

16th–18th Century

Italian School (c1580)
Venus and Cupid
Oil on panel
40½ x 67¾in (103 x 172cm)
£35,000–45,000 *S*

Attributed to Jan van Haensbergen
Dutch (1642–1705)
Nymphs in an Italianate Landscape by Ruins
Oil on panel
9¾ x 11½in (23.5 x 29.5cm)
£4,500–5,500 *C*

Manner of Correggio
Italian (16thC)
Venus and Cupid
Oil on panel
20 x 11¾in (51 x 30cm)
£2,500–3,500 *C*

Bartolomeo Passarotti
Italian (1529–92)
A Study of a Standing Male Nude
Pen and brown ink over traces of black chalk
16½ x 7½in (42 x 19cm)
£1,000–1,400 *P*

Follower of Gerard de Lairesse
Flemish (1641–1711)
The Death of Cleopatra
Oil on canvas
35 x 26½in (89.5 x 67cm)
£3,500–4,500 *CSK*

Pietro Liberi
Italian (1614–87)
Venus
Oil on canvas
44½ x 59in (113 x 149.5cm)
£14,000–16,000 *S*

Rembrandt Harmensz. van Rijn
Dutch (1606–69)
Nude Man Seated Before a Curtain
Etching, 1646
6½ x 3¾in (16 x 9cm)
£32,000–40,000 *S(NY)*

Sebastiano Conca
Italian (c1680–1764)
A Draped Male Youth lying on a Bed
Red chalk, some stamping, laid down,
inscribed on mount
15¾ x 10in (40 x 25cm)
£1,600–2,000 *P*

Rosalba Carriera
Italian (1675–1757)
Flora, holding Plums
Pastel
24 x 19in (61 x 49cm)
£38,000–45,000 *C*

Follower of Bartholomeus Spranger
Flemish (1546–1611)
Venus and Mars
Oil on panel
13¼ x 10in (34 x 25cm)
£3,300–4,300 *C*

Johann Heinrich Fuseli, R.A.
British (1741–1825)
A Male Nude seated against a Wall
Pen and grey ink over traces of pencil
4¼ x 7in (11 x 17.5cm)
£1,200–1,600 *S*

19th Century

Jean Beauduin
Belgian (1851–1916)
Jeune Fille a L'Eventail
Signed, oil on canvas
21 x 28¾in (53 x 73cm)
£3,000–4,000 *S(NY)*

Johannes Arnoldus Boland
Dutch (1838–1922)
Nude in a Forest Clearing
Signed, inscribed and dated 'Juin 1881',
oil on canvas
92 x 51in (233.5 x 129.5cm)
£5,500–7,000 *S*

Hans von Staschiripka Canon
Austrian (1829–85)
A Seated Male Nude
Signed, oil on board
17½ x 14in (44.5 x 36cm)
£4,500–6,000 *C*

Paul Cézanne
French (1839–1906)
Esquisse de Baigneurs
Oil on canvas, c1900
8 x 13in (20 x 33cm)
£750,000–950,000 *S(NY)*

*Cézanne's bathers have proved to be a rich mine for generations
of art historians, each initiating explorations into the sources,
formal inventions and meanings of these benchmarks of
modern art. He explored the theme of the Bathers from 1870
until his death in 1906. As Cézanne was never able to realise
his dream of posing nude figures out of doors, he had to
rely on the few sketches of nude models which he had made
in his Paris studio and, more importantly, his study and copy
of figurative elements from past masters' works, such as
those of Michaelangelo, Veronese, Signorelli and Delacroix.*

John Constable, R.A.
British (1776–1837)
Male Nude
Oil on canvas
24 x 19¾in (61 x 50cm)
£5,000–6,000 *S*

Georges de Dramard
French (1839–1900)
The Dancer
Signed and dated '1873', oil on canvas
41 x 29in (104 x 74cm)
£15,000–17,000 *C*

Ebenezer Wake Cook
British (1843–1926)
An Eastern Princess
Signed and dated '96',
pencil and watercolour
20 x 9½in (51 x 24cm)
£1,200–1,600 *CSK*

Thomas Cooper Gotch
British (1854–1931)
Standing Male Nude
Initialled, charcoal
23 x 14in (59 x 36cm)
£400–450 *EG*

French School (19thC)
Leda and the Swan
Oil on canvas
23 x 41in (59 x 104cm)
£2,750–3,750 *S(NY)*

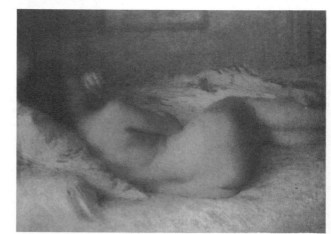

Arthur Hill
British (active 1858–93)
The Naked Piper
Signed, oil on canvas
62 x 24⅜in (157 x 63cm)
£14,000–16,000 *C*

Ernest Joseph Laurent
French (1859–1929)
Nu Etendu sur un Lit
Oil on canvas
19 x 25½in (48 x 65cm)
£24,000–30,000 *S(NY)*

Hans Lietzmann
German (b1872)
Boys Picking Grapes
Signed and dated '1920',
oil on canvas
50½ x 39½in (128 x 100cm)
£6,500–8,000 *C*

Edvard Munch
Norwegian (1863–1944)
Der Kuss
Etching with drypoint and
aquatint, 1895, on wove paper,
with Felsing's pencil signature
13¼ x 10¾in (34 x 27.5cm)
£30,000–35,000 *C*

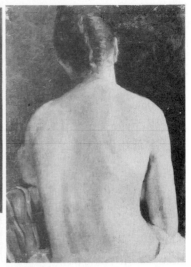

Circle of Ilia Efimovich Repin
Russian (1844–1930)
Study of a Female Nude
Oil on canvas
27½ x 19¼in (70 x 49cm)
£1,500–2,000 *P*

Julius Schnorr von Carolsfeld
German (1794–1872)
Double Academy with Two Male Models
Signed with monogram and dated 'August
1815', brown ink and graphite on paper
heightened with white
24 x 16½in (61 x 42cm)
£2,750–3,500 *S(NY)*

Sascha Schneider
Russian (1870–1927)
Gefühl der Abhängigkeit
Initialled, oil on canvas
98¾ x 65¼in (251 x 166cm)
£17,500–20,000 *C*

Charles Robinson
British (1870–1937)
Nymphs in the Park
Signed, pen and ink and watercolour
17¾ x 13¾in (45 x 35cm)
£800–1,000 *P*

Félicien Joseph Victor Rops
Belgian (1833–98)
Masques Parisiens
Signed, black crayon on paper
14¼ x 9¼in (36 x 23cm)
£10,000–12,000 *C*

Henry Scott Tuke, R.A.
British (1858–1929)
The Three Companions
Signed and dated '1905', oil on canvas
24¾ x 36½in (63 x 93cm)
£15,000–18,000 *C*

Henry Scott Tuke, R.A.
British (1858–1929)
Male Nude
Signed with initials, oil on canvas
20 x 16in (51 x 41cm)
£2,750–3,000 *EG*

Lorenzo Valles
Italian (1830–1910)
Paulina Borghese in the Sculptor's Studio
Signed, oil on canvas
22 x 29in (56 x 74cm)
£12,500–14,000 *S*
*According to William Hazlitt, writing in
1830, 'The Princess Borghese, Bonaparte's
sister, who was no saint, sat to Canova as a
reclining Venus and, being asked if she did
not feel a little uncomfortable, replied, "No.
There was a fire in the room".'*
*This picture records Canova's celebrated
sculpture (1805–7) of Paulina Borghese,
Napoleon's sister, as the reclining Venus
Victrix. Set in the sculptor's studio, the
painting entirely lacks the cool eroticism
that so distinguishes Canova's masterpiece.*

Eduard Veith
Austrian (1856–1925)
The Sirens
Signed and dated '1889', oil on canvas
29½ x 59¼in (75 x 150.5cm)
£12,750–14,000 *C*

François Edouard Zier
French (1856–1924)
Acis and Galatea Hiding from Polyphemus
Signed, oil on canvas
39½ x 58¼in (100 x 148cm)
£16,000–18,000 *S(NY)*

Anders Zorn
Swedish (1860–1920)
Solnedgöng
Signed and dated '1910', oil on canvas
25½ x 17in (65 x 43cm)
£47,000–57,000 *S(NY)*

20th Century

Karl Barrie
British (20thC)
Vanity
Signed and dated '66', oil on board
20 x 15in (51 x 38cm)
£500–600 *GK*

Fernando Botero
Columbian (b1932)
Mujer Fumando, and Mujer ante el Espejo
Two lithographs, 1985, signed in pencil and
numbered IX/L, on wove paper
16 x 13in (41 x 33cm)
£9,500–11,000 *S(NY)*

Robert Brackman
American (1898–1980)
Two Women
Signed, pastel and charcoal
on green paper
28¼ x 16¾in (72 x 43cm)
£600–800 *CNY*

Chester Browton
British (20thC)
Oh Gabrielle
Signed and inscribed, oil on canvas
36½ x 54in (93 x 137cm)
£450–550 *CSK*

P. J. Crook
British (20thC)
Jathan Namesc Rock
Signed, oil on board
24 x 14in (61 x 36cm)
£600–800 *GK*

Hilo Chen
American (b1942)
Beach
Signed, titled, numbered and dated '84'
on reverse, acrylic on canvas
12 x 16in (30.5 x 41cm)
£1,400–1,800 *CNY*

André Derain
French (1880–1954)
Nu
Signed, red chalk
17¾ x 23½in (45 x 60cm)
£2,500–3,000 *S*

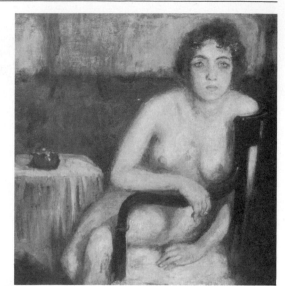

Kees van Dongen
French (1877–1968)
Nu au Fauteuil
Signed and dated '1896', oil on canvas
13¾in (35cm) square
£45,000–55,000 *S*

Raoul Dufy
French (1877–1953)
Nu Couché
Signed, oil on board, 1939
10 x 15in (25 x 38cm)
£17,000–20,000 *C*

Bernard Dunstan, R.A.
British (b1920)
Sitting Pretty
Signed with initials, oil on panel
18 x 14in (46 x 36cm)
£8,000–15,000 *BRG*

Nigel Ellis
British (b1960)
Drawing
Acrylic on paper
16 x 36in (41 x 92cm)
£250–300 *FT*

Sir Jacob Epstein
British (1880–1959)
Juanita
Signed, pencil drawing
17¼ x 22in (44 x 56cm)
£1,800–2,500 *C*

*When Epstein's first major public sculpture of
nude figures was unveiled in 1908 on the new
building of the British Medical Association,
the* Evening Standard *described the work as
'a form of statuary which no careful father
would wish his daughter to see, or no
discriminating young man his fiancée to see.'*

Sir William Russell Flint, R.A., P.R.W.S.
British (1880–1969)
Gisele
Signed and inscribed 'For Helen with loving
gratitude for all her dear care of me' and
dated 'June 29–30, 1961', watercolour
10 x 15½in (25 x 39.5cm)
£18,000–22,000 *Bon*

*The demand for Russell Flint's scantily
clad females shows no signs of flagging, and
prices are even beginning to climb back to
their pre-recessionary heights. For obvious
reasons, nudes tend not to be featured on
chocolate boxes, but if they were, Russell
Flint's decorative pictures would surely be
a prime contender.*

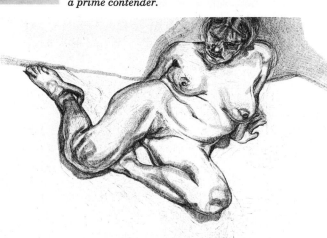

Tsuguharu Foujita
French/Japanese (1886–1968)
Femmes (Two Nudes Seated on a Bed)
Etching and aquatint printed in colours,
signed in pencil and inscribed 'EA -D/J',
an artist's proof, 1930
23 x 15½in (60 x 39.5cm)
£6,500–8,000 *S*

Lucian Freud
British (b1922)
Girl Sitting
Etching printed with tone,
1987, initialled in pencil
20½ x 27¼in (52 x 69.5cm)
£3,750–4,500 *S*

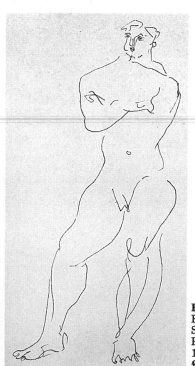

Jürgen Görg
German (b1951)
Rückenakt
Lithograph, in six colours
18¾ x 14in (48 x 36cm)
£200–225 *CCA*

Henri Gaudier-Brzeska
French (1891–1915)
Standing Male Nude
Pen and brown ink
12 x 8in (30.5 x 20cm)
£1,300–1,600 *C*

Eric Gill
British (1882–1940)
Eve
Wood engraving, signed and
numbered 22/50 in pencil,
and 4 others
14 x 7½in (36 x 19cm)
£2,000–2,500 *CSK*

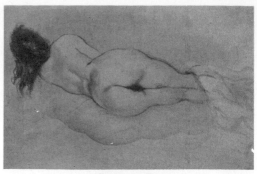

James Gorman
British (20thC)
Dreamshore
Signed, watercolour
16 x 21in (41 x 53cm)
£500–600 *GK*

Georges Grosz
German (1893–1959)
Liegende Akt
Stamped signature, watercolour
11½ x 17¼in (29.5 x 44cm)
£4,500–6,000 *C*

Ken Howard
British (b1932)
Debora and Daffodils, Morning Light
Signed, oil on canvas
36 x 30in (91.5 x 76cm)
£4,500–4,750 *MI*

Lin Jammet
British (b1958)
Two Men and a Horse
Gouache
48 x 60in (122 x 152cm)
£1,400–1,600 *CON*

The inspiration for Jammet's bold romantic gouaches come from a period in his life that he spent in the Cevennes in the South of France with his mother and step-father. Here on the edge of the Camargue, that strange pastoral region of horses and bulls, Jammet grew out of boyhood and spent his formative years. These paintings grew from the memories of early adolescence; of breaking from the local legends told to children of ogres and giants; memories of his father as a strong guiding figure; memories of learning to ride; memories of approaching manhood and its accompanying strivings for machismo.

Sir Gerald Kelly, P.R.A.
British (1879–1972)
Negress Kneeling
Oil on canvas
20 x 16in (51 x 41cm)
£1,800–2,800 *CSK*

Tom Keating
British (1917–84)
Renoir Nude
Signed, oil on canvas
30 x 24in (76.5 x 61cm)
£2,000–4,000 *BRG*

*Born in London, Keating was the son of a
house painter and a charlady. As a child, he
won a box of paints for swimming a length
of the local swimming baths underwater,
and painting became his obsession. It was
only during the war, invalided out of the
navy with an ex-serviceman's grant, that he
was able to become a full-time student at
Goldsmith's Art School. Keating twice failed
his exams, which meant that he was not able
to become an art teacher, and this marked
the beginning of his antagonism towards the
art establishment.*
*Keating joined a restoration studio and while
there was asked to make a number of copies
of famous paintings. He was later horrified to
discover them being sold as genuine. It was
then that he decided to flood the market with
fakes ('Sexton Blakes' as the artist called
them, in his own personal rhyming slang), to
confound the rich collectors and dealers and
get back at the art world. Fooling the experts
he claimed was the greatest joy in his life and
made him literally helpless with laughter.
Keating later admitted to putting some 2,000
fakes on the market in the style of 130 artists.
His counterfeiting only came to light in 1976
when he wrote to* The Times *admitting that
a major collection of 13 Samuel Palmer
watercolours was by his hand. Keating
became a popular anti-hero, with his own
successful television series and lived to see his
fakes become collectable Keating originals.*

Janka Malkowska
Polish (b1912)
The Source
Silkscreen, on Somerset satin paper
24½ x 36½in (75 x 105cm)
£125–150 *GPS*

Henri Matisse
French (1869–1954)
Nu au Turban (Henriette)
Signed, oil on canvas, 1921
36¼ x 29in (92 x 73.5cm)
£2,450,000–2,650,000 *C*

Paul R. Meltsner
American (b1905)
A Reclining Nude
Signed and inscribed on the reverse,
oil on canvasboard
18 x 24in (46 x 61.5cm)
£400–500 *CNY*

John Minton
British (1917–57)
The Life Model
Signed and dated '1948', oil on canvas
25 x 30in (66 x 76cm)
£16,000–18,000 *S*

Dhruva Mistry
Indian (b1957)
Untitled (Reclining nude)
Drypoint, on Somerset Satin Waterleaf, 1989
12¾ x 15in (32 x 38cm)
£200–250 *GPS*

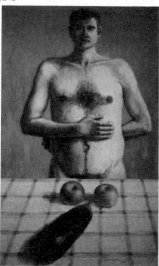

Henry Moore
British (1898–1986)
Seated Figure
Etching with drypoint,
signed in pencil, 1979
8½ x 6½in (21 x 16.5cm)
£450–550 *S*

Fried Pal
Hungarian (b1914)
Female Nude
Signed, oil on canvas
30 x 24in (76 x 61cm)
£475–600 *S(NY)*

Christopher Reed
British (b1962)
A Meeting with My Tailor
Oil on board
24 x 15in (61 x 38cm)
£900–1,000 *FT*

*One of the more unusual nudes
that we have received for this year's
guide, if not one of the most modest.*

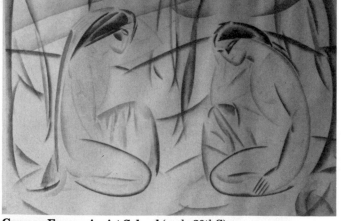

German Expressionist School (early 20thC)
Two Women Kneeling
Watercolour
18½ x 25in (47 x 64cm)
£1,000–1,200 *JDG*

Diego Rivera
Mexican (1886–1957)
Desnudo Sentado con Brazos
Levantados (Frida Kahlo)
Lithograph, signed in crayon,
dated '1930'
16½ x 11in (42 x 28cm)
£11,000–13,000 *S(NY)*

Leonard Sarluis
French (1874–1949)
Portrait of a Nude Woman
Signed and dated '1931',
oil on canvas
40 x 29¾in (101.5 x 76cm)
£1,600–2,000 *S(NY)*

Derrick Sayer
British (1917–92)
Life Studies
Pastel
24 x 32in (61 x 81cm)
£500–550 *HI*

Ellis Silas
British (b1883)
Nude Study
Signed, watercolour
14 x 9½in (36 x 24cm)
£220–250 *Gan*

Leon de Smet
Belgian (1881–1966)
Nu debout–staand naakt
Signed, oil on canvas, c1928
52½ x 26in (133 x 66cm)
£14,000–18,000 *C*

Frank Taylor
British (20thC)
Jenny
Pencil drawing
18 x 13in (46 x 33cm)
£200–250 *PHG*

Locate the Source
*The source of each
illustration in Miller's
can be found by checking
the code letters below
each caption with the list
of contributors.*

William E. Gladstone Solomon
British (active 1903–40)
Signed, watercolour
17½ x 23in (44 x 59cm)
£1,200–1,400 *GG*

Patricia Terrell
British (20thC)
Study
Signed, oil on canvas
12 x 18in (30.5 x 46cm)
£200–400 *GK*

Philip Tyler
British (b1964)
The Seed Carrier (Study for Leda)
Acrylic on paper
47½in (120cm) square
£180–200 *Mer*

*'The male nude is much more than genitalia,'
writes Philip Tyler, about his series of
paintings 'The Seed Carriers'. 'These figures
perform an unscripted drama. In this play sex
is the point of contact where we meet in our
desire to become whole; but the seed of this
union has taken on a new meaning. Conscious
of their potential for life and death these
figures search for their identity. Sometimes on
their own, or in groups, they speak of human
presence stripped bare and the basic need
to communicate.'*

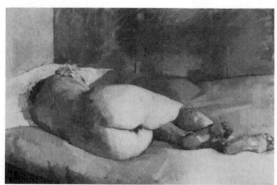

Euan Uglow
British (20thC)
Beautiful Girl Lying Down
Oil on canvas
24 x 37in (61 x 94cm)
£23,000–27,000 *CSK*

Leon Underwood
British (b1890)
Music From Behind the Moon 1926
Signed and dated, wood engraving,
1st state trial proof with alterations
in white gouache
6¼ x 4in (16 x 10cm)
£175–200 *BLD*

Tom Wesselmann
American (b1931)
Study for Great American Nude #6 Plus 23
Titled and dated '84', oil on canvas
24in (61cm) diam
£28,000–35,000 *S(NY)*

Stephen Elmer, A.R.A.
British (1717–96)
Ptarmigan in a Landscape
Oil on canvas
28¼ x 35½in ((72 x 90cm)
£4,200–5,000 *S*

Harry Bright
British (active 1867–92)
The Lark
Signed, watercolour
16 x 12in (40.5 x 30.5cm)
£2,000–2,500 *HLG*

S. Dixon
British (active from 1755)
The Traco, and The Red Barbary Partridge
A pair, watercolour
10 x 8in (25 x 20cm)
£2,000–2,500 *MEA*

Robert Morley
British (1857–1941)
Union is Strength
Signed, oil on panel
10½ x 15in (26.5 x 38cm)
£4,500–5,000 *C*

Archibald Thorburn
British (1860–1935)
Black Game
Signed and dated '1928', watercolour and bodycolour
14¼ x 21½in (36.5 x 54.5cm)
£30,000–35,000 *S*

John Gould
British (1804–81)
Pitta Nipalensis
Lithograph and
original hand colour
20½ x 13in (52 x 33cm)
£125–150 *SRAB*

Emma Faull
British (b1956)
Green Peacocks
Signed and dated '89', pencil, pen and black
ink and watercolour
31 x 43in (78.5 x 109cm)
£1,600–2,000 C

Mary Fedden
British (1915)
The Oyster Catcher
Signed and dated '1992', oil on canvas
20 x 24in (50.5 x 61cm)
£2,500–3,000 BRG

Alison Guest
British (20thC)
Grouse
Oil on canvas
10 x 8in (25 x 20cm)
£350–400 RGFA

Veni Gligorova-Smith
Macedonian (20thC)
Cockerel's Celebration
Signed and dated '89', watercolour
11¾ x 15¼in (30 x 39cm)
£450–550 AMC

Edgar Hunt
British (1876–1953)
The Upturned Basket
Signed and dated '1930', oil on canvas
11 x 16in (28 x 41cm)
£14,000–16,000 C

George Morrison Reid Henry
British (1891–1983)
A sketchbook of Bird and Plant Studies
63 drawings, signed, inscribed and
dated, pencil and watercolour
9¾in (24.5cm) square
£10,500–12,000 C

Sir Peter Scott, C.H.
British (1909–89)
Red-breasted Geese, at Tulcea, Romania
Signed and dated '1972', oil on canvas
19¾ x 23¾in (50 x 60cm)
£7,500–9,000 *C*

Mariano Rodriguez
Cuban (1912–90)
El Gallo Pintado
Signed and dated '41', oil on canvas
25¾ x 21in (65.5 x 53cm)
£200,000–225,000 *S(NY)*

Clifford Cyril Webb
British (1895–1972)
Flamingoes
Pen and ink with scratching out
10½ x 8½in (26.5 x 21.5cm)
£550–650 *CBL*

r. **Owen Williams**
Welsh (b1956)
Shoveler Drake
Signed, watercolour
10½ x 14½in
(26.5 x 37cm)
£375–425 *MWe*

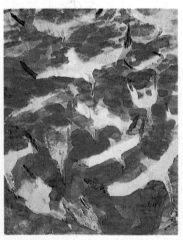

Jim Manley
British (b1934)
Gannets Fishing I
Signed, watercolour
32 x 27in (81 x 69cm)
£700–800 *SOL*

Charles Frederick Tunnicliffe
British (1901–79)
Rock Pool - Eight Widgeon Drinking and Bathing
Signed, watercolour
14 x 20in (36 x 50.5cm)
£5,500–7,000 *CAG*

George Armfield
British (1840–75)
Spaniels with a Covey of Partridge
Oil on canvas
10 x 12in (25 x 30.5cm)
£4,200–4,800 *BuP*

Maud Earl
British (d1943)
A Red and a Tri-colour Pekinese in a
River Landscape
Signed and dated '1916', oil on gold
ground silk laid down on board
25¾ x 23⅜in (65.5 x 60.5cm)
£9,000–10,000 *C(S)*

Charles Henry Blair
British (19thC)
Pride of Place
Signed, oil on canvas
14¾ x 18⅜in (37.5 x 47.5cm)
£6,500–7,000 *Bon*

Samuel Fulton
British (1855–1941)
Two Golden Retrievers and a Boxer
Signed, oil on canvas
27 x 35in (68.5 x 89cm)
£8,500–10,000 *C*

Walter Harrowing
British (late 19thC)
Tottie II, a Skye Terrier
Signed, oil on canvas
23 x 28in (58 x 71cm)
£6,500–8,000 *C*

Léon Charles Huber
French (1858–1928)
Up to No Good!
Oil on canvas
18¼ x 21⅜in (46.5 x 55cm)
£20,000–22,000 *BuP*

John Sargeant Noble
British (1848–96)
In the Lap of Luxury
Signed and dated '1881', oil on canvas
40 x 60½in (101.5 x 153.5cm)
£30,000–40,000 *S(NY)*

Adrienne Lester
British (active from 1885)
A Bowlful of Mischief
Signed, oil on canvas
19½ x 23½in (49 x 60cm)
£5,000–5,500 *FL*

William Henry Trood
British (1860–99)
Wait 'till the Clouds Roll By
Oil on canvas
7½ x 10½in (19 x 26.5cm)
£3,500–4,500 *L*

Frank Paton
British (1856–1909)
The Folly of Innocence
Signed and dated '1881', oil on canvas
18 x 15in (45.5 x 37.5cm)
£17,000–19,000 *HFA*

Arthur Wardle
British (1864–1949)
Two Setters
Signed, pastel
22 x 17in (56 x 43cm)
£12,000–13,000 *HFA*

Henriette Ronner-Knip
Dutch (1821–1909)
Making Mischief
Signed, inscribed on reverse, oil on panel
18 x 25¼in (46 x 64cm)
£65,000–80,000 *P*

Anne Hewson
British (20thC)
Cat on a Chest of Drawers
Oil on board, 1986
10 x 12in (25.5 x 30.5cm)
£250–300 *JDG*

Lesley Anne Ivory
British (20thC)
The China Doll, Dorothy… Sits on the
Window Seat Nowadays
Signed, watercolour with bodycolour
8½ x 10½in (21.5 x 27cm)
£2,000–2,500 *CBL*

John Arnold Wheeler
British (19th/20thC)
Heads of Hounds
Signed and dated '1914', oil on board
11¾ x 17½in (30 x 44.5cm)
£2,500–3,500 *Bon*

After Louis Wain
British (1860–1939)
A set of 6 postcards depicting Cats
playing with a Diabolo
5½ x 3¼in (14 x 8cm)
£200–300 *Bon*

Ronald Searle
British (b1920)
Kool Cat
Signed and dated '1987',
watercolour pen, ink and pencil
11½ x 8⅜in (29.5 x 21.5cm)
£2,500–2,750 *CBL*

Louis Wain
British (1860–1939)
A Class Outing
Signed, gouache
5¼ x 16¾in (13.5 x 42.5cm)
£3,800–4,200 *Bon*

Claude Cardon
British (active 1892–1915)
Farmyard Friends
Signed, oil on canvas
14 x 18in (35.5 x 46cm)
£5,000–6,000 *WG*

George W. Horlor
British (active 1849–51)
Guardians of the Flock
Oil on canvas
24 x 36in (61 x 91.5cm)
£8,000–8,500 *WHP*

Johann Wenzel Peter
German (1745–1829)
A Ram and a Sheep
Oil on canvas
38½ x 53in (97.5 x 134.5cm)
£11,000–12,000 *C*

English Provincial School (early 19thC)
A Prize Hog in a Landscape
Oil on canvas
24⅛ x 29½in (62 x 75cm)
£3,800–4,500 *S*

Henry Charles Fox
British (1860–1929)
A Shepherd with his Flock
Signed and dated, watercolour
20 x 13in (50.5 x 33cm)
£1,900–2,100 *ChG*

Thomas Sidney Cooper, R.A.
British (1803–1902)
Canterbury Meadows
Signed and dated '1848', oil on canvas
47 x 77in (119 x 195.5cm)
£55,000–65,000 *HFA*

Louis B. Hurt
British (1856–1929)
Highland Beside a Loch
Signed and dated '93', oil on canvas
24 x 36in (61 x 92cm)
£24,000–26,000 *BuP*

Elmer Keene
British (active from 1895)
Homeward Bound
Signed, oil on canvas
25 x 16in (63.5 x 40.5cm)
£1,250–1,450 *HLG*

Arthur W. Redgate
British (19th/20thC)
Milking Time, near Kegworth, Leicestershire
Signed, inscribed and dated '1906', oil on canvas
28 x 36in (71 x 91.5cm)
£280–320 *TAY*

Vernon Ward
British (1905–88)
Sheep on the Hill
Signed, oil on canvas
15 x 22in (38 x 55.5cm)
£3,500–4,000 *HLG*

John Gardiner Crawford
Scottish (b1941)
Painted Clown
Signed, acrylic on masonite, 1991
27¼ x 18in (69.5 x 45.5cm)
£8,000–8,500 *WH*

William Weekes
British (1864–1904)
Our Member of the Commons
Signed, oil on canvas
10¾ x 14¾in (27.5 x 37.5cm)
£5,250–5,750 *BuP*

Thomas Spencer
British (active 1730–63)
Charles Montagu with his Racehorse
Oil on canvas
35½ x 41½in (90.5 x 105cm)
£35,000–40,000 *S*

Circle of Henry Alken
British (1785–1851)
A Race Meet
Oil on canvas
21¼ x 26½in (54 x 67.5cm)
£1,450–1,650 *CGa*

René Choquet
French (19thC)
Horse and Dogs
Signed, oil on canvas
17 x 21in (43 x 53cm)
£5,000–5,500 *HLG*

James Seymour
British (c1702–52)
Sedbury with Two Grooms
Signed and dated '1740', inscribed on the reverse with
details of his races, oil on canvas
28 x 35in (71 x 89cm)
£55,000–60,000 *S*

William Shayer, Snr.
British (1787–1879)
Noontime in the New Forest
Oil on canvas
30 x 40in (76 x 101.5cm)
£18,000–20,000 *WHP*

John Alfred Wheeler
British (1821–77)
Three Horses at a Trough
Signed and inscribed 'Bath 1863'
27½ x 35in (70 x 89cm)
£5,500–6,000 *S(S)*

Charles Church
British (20thC)
Jockey Study 2, Florence
Signed, oil on canvas
29 x 25½in (74 x 65cm)
£500–600 *EAG*

Norman Hoad
British (20thC)
A Flying Start
Oil on canvas
20 x 25in (51 x 64cm)
£575–675 *EAG*

Stephen Park
British (20thC)
Desert Orchid at Cheltenham
Oil on canvas
24 x 16in (61 x 40.5cm)
£650–750 *LIO*

Henry Koehler
American (b1927)
Groom with Yellow Cooler
Signed, inscribed and dated '1961' verso,
oil on canvas
20 x 24in (51 x 61cm)
£3,000–3,500 *TOT*

Rosemary Sarah Welch
British (b1943)
Saturday's Child
Oil on canvas
30 x 24in (76 x 61cm)
£4,000–4,500 *CSG*

Russell Sydney Reeve, R.E., R.B.A.
British (1895–1970)
Shires at Islington
Signed and dated '32', watercolour and conté crayon on paper
12½ x 20in (32 x 51cm)
£1,500–1,800 *PN*

I. Clark, after Henry Alken, Snr.
British (1785–1851)
Pheasant Shooting
A set of 4 aquatints, original hand
colouring, published by T. McLean,
Jan 1, 1820
7¾ x 11½in (19.7 x 29.5cm)
£1,650–1750 *CG*

John Nost Sartorius
British (1759–1828)
Well Over
Signed, oil on canvas
24½ x 29½in (62 x 75cm)
£9,000–10,500 *S*

After E. A. S. Douglas
British (19thC)
Off to the Meet
A set of 4 aquatints, original hand colouring, 1889
18¾ x 25½in (47.5 x 65.5cm)
£1,600–1,800 *Bur*

Henry Jutsum
British (1816–69)
The Hunting Party
Oil on panel
19 x 13in (48 x 33cm)
£6,000–6,500 *HFA*

Harris, after John Frederick Herring, Snr.
British (1795–1865)
Full Cry
A set of 4 aquatints, original hand colouring
17¼ x 30½in (44 x 77.5cm)
£4,250–4,750 *Bur*

Klavdi Vasilievich Lebedev
Russian (1852–1916)
A Falcon Hunt
Signed, oil on canvas
23½ x 35½in (60 x 90cm)
£11,000–12,000 *S(NY)*

Bentley, after Henry Alken, Snr.
British (1785–1851)
The Leap
A set of 4 aquatints, original hand colouring
12 x 16½in (30.5 x 42cm)
£3,000–3,500 *Bur*

**Gilbert Keith
Chesterton**
British (1874–1936)
Nocturnal Huntsman
Signed, pastel on paper
13 x 9¾in (33 x 24.5cm)
£550–650 *CBL*

Sir Alfred Munnings, P.R.A.
British (1878–1959)
Huntsman with Hounds, Zennor Hill, Cornwall
Signed, oil on canvas, c1913
31 x 36in (78.5 x 91.5cm)
£110,000–125,000 *C*

Gilbert Scott Wright
British (1880–1958)
On the Scent
Oil on canvas
8 x 12in (20 x 30.5cm)
£4,000–4,500 *JN*

In the manner of Cecil Aldin
British (1870–1935)
Hunting Scenes
A set of 4 prints, c1900
33 x 72in (83.5 x 182.5cm)
£2,000–3,000 *MSh*

Murray Robertson
British (b1961)
Calydonian Boar Hunt
Silkscreen, 1989
23½ x 31½in (60 x 80cm)
£175–200 *GPS*

Orivida Pissarro
British (1893–1968)
The Hunt
Signed and dated '1952', oil on board
35¾ x 48in (90.5 x 122cm)
£4,500–5,000 *STD*

Claude Charles Bourgonnier
French (d1921)
The Knock Out
Signed, oil on canvas
23 x 32in (59 x 81cm)
£3,500–4,500 *C*

l. **John C. Anderson**
British (mid-19thC)
Caffyn
Lithograph, original
hand colouring, c1854
12¾ x 8in (32 x 20cm)
£650–750 *Bur*

James Cole
British (active 1856–85)
The Young Chickens
Oil on canvas
8 x 6in (20 x 15cm)
£7,000–7,500 *BuP*

Henry Sandham
Canadian (1842–1912)
The Club's the Thing
Limited edition print
14½ x 20in (35.5 x 51cm)
£70–80 *BuP*

G. H. Barrable
British (active 1873–87)
England-v-Australia at Lords
Sketch in oil on canvas, 1880
25 x 18in (63.5 x 45.5cm)
£1,200–1,400 *MSh*

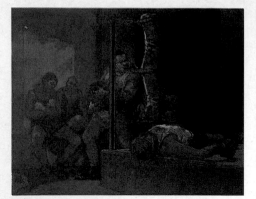

Matthew Burrows
British (20thC)
The Knock Out
Oil on canvas
60 x 72in (152 x 182.5cm)
£2,800–3,000 *Mer*

Bronwen Malcolm
British (b1963)
The Swimming Lesson
Oil on canvas
36 x 26in (91.5 x 66cm)
£1,200–1,400 *TRG*

John Strickland Goodall, R.I., R.B.A.
British (b1908)
Tennis
Watercolour
8½ x 14in (21.5 x 35.5cm)
£1,650–1,750 *SRB*

Kaj Stenvall
British (20thC)
Under the Surface
Oil on canvas
22 x 28in (56 x 71cm)
£1,650–1,750 *JBA*

Frederic Whiting, R.B.A., R.I.
British (1874–1960)
Two Jockeys
Signed, signed and inscribed on reverse, oil on canvas
40 x 30in (101.5 x 76cm)
£11,500–12,500 *C(S)*

Ruskin Spear, R.A.
British (1911–90)
Goal!
Signed, oil on board
31 x 26in (78.5 x 66cm)
£3,500–4,500 *C*

Gabriel von Max
Czechoslovakian (1840–1915)
The Critic
Signed, oil on panel
13¾ x 11½in (35 x 29.5cm)
£1,500–2,000 *C*

Jan van Kessel I
Flemish (1616–70)
A Family of Monkeys with a Goat in a Well
Signed with initials, oil on copper
5¼ x 8in (13.5 x 20cm)
£6,000–7,000 *C*

John Charles Dollman, R.W.S.
British (1851–1934)
The Tiger
Signed, inscribed and numbered '1', pencil
and watercolour and scratching out
19¼ x 29in (49 x 73.5cm)
£4,000–5,000 *C*

Richard Doyle
British (1824–83)
The Pet Bears
Signed with initials, watercolour
6¾ x 7½in (17 x 19.5cm)
£2,000–2,250 *CBL*

Samuel Howitt
British (1756–1822)
A Lioness
Inscribed on mount, watercolour over pencil,
with black border
8¼ x 12¼in (21 x 31cm)
£9,000–9,500 *CW*

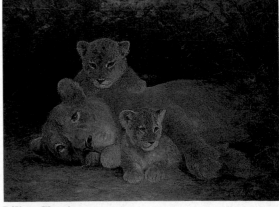

Lilian Cheviot
British (active 1894–1920)
Motherhood
Signed, oil on canvas
30 x 40in (76 x 101.5cm)
£10,000–12,000 *JC*

Isabelle Brent
British (b1961)
Animals Two-by-Two
Gilded watercolour
8 x 6½in (20 x 16cm)
£750–850 *PHG*

Donald Grant
British (20thC)
The Water Hole – Elephants
Signed, oil on canvas
28 x 42in (71 x 106.5cm)
£4,250–4,750 *BuP*

W. R. Waters
British (19thC)
A Tyrolean Peasant Boy with Pet Rodents
Signed and dated '1859', oil on canvas
17¾ x 13½in (45 x 34cm)
£400–500 *WL*

Spencer Roberts
British (20thC)
Otters
Gouache
20 x 30in (50.5 x 76cm)
£1,400–1,600 *RGFA*

Charles Newington
British (b1950)
Stag
Pastel and sfumato
22 x 33in (55.5 x 83.5cm)
£475–525 *RGFA*

Donald Roller Wilson
American (20thC)
Full Moon
Signed, titled and dated '1976', oil on canvas
40 x 32in (101.5 x 81cm)
£11,000–13,000 *S(NY)*

RELIGIOUS & MYTHOLOGICAL

Many of the pictures in the following Religious and Mythological sections fall into the categories of Old Master paintings and drawings. With the disappointing Modern and Impressionist sales held by the major auction houses this spring, art experts are predicting a possible price rise in the Old Master market, which has been undervalued for some years.

If your finances do not stretch to a painting by an Old Master, there are plenty of drawings on offer, with prices starting in the low hundreds. According to Crispian Riley-Smith of Phillips, the Old Master Drawing market is more stable than the Impressionist and Modern, with a strong group of collectors concentrated in Europe and North America. Last year turnover increased by three times and the sale ratio of Old Master drawings improved, a sign that the recession is abating. Riley-Smith stresses that important drawings, fresh to the market, are fetching outstanding prices. Sotheby's agree that the market is buoyant with many people looking to buy, and told us that it is particularly the rare and unusual drawings that are selling well at auction.

Quality and condition are crucial in this field, and provenance can also be important. Many of the great artists of the past collected Old Master drawings as a means of studying the work of their predecessors and contemporaries. These 'domestic museums' were passed down to other artists throughout the centuries: much of Sir Peter Lely's (1818–80) collection of drawings went to the 18thC portrait painter Thomas Hudson, then to his pupil Sir Joshua Reynolds (1723–92), and were subsequently acquired by Sir Thomas Lawrence (1769–1830). Such collectors developed the practice of marking their drawings either by hand or with a stamp, and a good provenance can significantly enhance the value of a work. Today, religious drawings can prove harder to sell than mythological subjects, so this could possibly prove a good area for starting up a reasonably priced collection.

RELIGIOUS
13th–16th Century

Mariotto Albertinelli
Italian (1474–1515)
Madonna and Child
(The Madonna della Melagrana)
Oil on panel transferred to canvas
34¾ x 26¾in (89 x 68cm)
£42,000–52,000 *S*

The pomegranate was a Christian symbol of the Resurrection after its classical association with Proserpine who returned every spring to regenerate the earth. The many seeds enclosed in a tough case made it a symbol of the many under one authority, and it was also an emblem of chastity. The fruit features frequently in religious pictures and in allegorical still life.

Follower of Fra Bartolomeo
Italian (1472–1517)
The Madonna and Child
in a Landscape
Inscribed on reverse 'Plantilla',
oil on panel
18 x 12in (46 x 30.5cm)
£8,500–10,000 *S*

Attributed to Domenico Cresti, called Passignano
Italian (1560–1638)
Ecce Homo
Oil on canvas, laid down on panel
37 x 30¼in (94 x 77cm)
£7,000–9,000 *S*

Agostino Carracci
Italian (1557–1602)
The Holy Family
Pen and brown ink with wash over traces of black chalk, laid down on the corners
13¾ x 9½in (35 x 24cm)
£7,000–9,000 *P*

Locate the Source
The source of each illustration in Miller's can be found by checking the code letters below each caption with the list of contributors.

Florentine School (15thC style)
Saint Thomas Aquinas Kneeling
before the Crucifix at Naples
Oil on panel
13 x 8¾in (33 x 22cm)
£2,000–2,500 *S*

*Christ is shown saying from the
cross, 'Bene scripsisti de me Thoma',
in approval of Thomas's writings.*

Albrecht Dürer
German (1471–1528)
St. Michael Fighting the Dragon
Woodcut, from the Apocalypse
15½ x 11¼in (39 x 29cm)
£13,000–15,000 *S(NY)*

Andrea Mantegna
Italian (1431–1506)
Risen Christ Between Saints Andrew
and Loginus
Engraving
12½ x 9½in (32 x 24cm)
£4,500–5,500 *S(NY)*

Miller's is a price GUIDE
not a price LIST

Bastiano di Bartolo Mainardi
Italian (1466–1513)
The Madonna and Child with Angels
Oil on panel, in carved and giltwood frame
34in (86.5cm) diam.
£30,000–40,000 *S*

*Mainardi was a pupil and assistant of
Domenico Ghirlandaio.*

**Master of the Fiesole Epiphany
(possibly Filippo di Giuliano di Matteo?)**
Italian (late 15thC)
Saint Sebastian and Saint Roch with the
Annunciation above, the left hand wing of
an Altarpiece
Oil on panel
50¼ x 26¼in (128 x 67cm)
£32,000–40,000 *S(NY)*

*Saint Roch was patron saint of plague
victims. In a traditional pose, he lifts his
tunic to show the black spot on his inner
thigh, the part of the body where the plague
typically first manifested itself.
Saint Sebastian was also regarded as a
protector against the plague and the pair are
frequently portrayed together.*

The Master of the Holy Kinship the Younger
Unknown (active in Cologne c1480–1520)
Two exterior wings from an Altarpiece, both oil on panel, framed together
53 x 74in (134.5 x 188cm)
£145,000–170,000 *S*

Attributed to Bonifacio de'Pitati, called Bonifacio Veronese
Italian (c1487–1553)
The Child Moses with the Burning Coals
Oil on canvas
57 x 93¼in (144.5 x 237cm)
£80,000–100,000 *S*

Having discovered the infant Moses in the bullrushes, the Pharaoh's daughter adopted him. One day at court, the Pharaoh jokingly placed his crown on the child's head, and Moses threw it to the ground and trampled on it. The courtiers took this as an omen that Moses would overthrow the Pharaoh. To test him, two dishes were brought, one containing live coals and the other cherries. Moses, guided by an angel, chose the coals and put them in his mouth which was burned. Through this trial by fire, he proved himself innocent of any treasonable intent.

Manner of Andrea del Sarto
Italian (1587–1630)
The Magdalene
Oil on canvas, laid on board
29 x 22¾in (74 x 58cm)
£650–850 *S(S)*

Cosimo Rosselli
Italian (1439–1507)
The Assumption of the Virgin with Saint Thomas receiving her Girdle and Angels, Angels and God the Father on the frame
Tempera on gold ground panel, marouflaged, arched top
33¼ x 22½in (86 x 57cm)
£45,000–60,000 *C*

Spanish School (16thC)
Christ as 'Salvator Mundi'
Inscribed on globe, oil on panel
25 x 21½in (64 x 54.5cm)
£20,000–25,000 *S(NY)*

The globe in the hand of Christ is elaborately inscribed and includes the name of its maker, Caspar Vopell. Vopell, active in Antwerp in the early 16thC, was one of the most highly respected cartographers of his time. Dated 1537, the globe depicts the Christian world coloured differently from the pagan.

Paolo Veronese
Italian (1528–88)
The Rest on the Flight into Egypt
Oil on canvas
17½ x 30in (44.5 x 76cm)
£125,000–150,000 *S*

Venetian School (c1550)
An Illuminated Manuscript Page depicting
a Senator, probably named Nicola Gritti,
being presented by his patron Saint Nicholas,
to the Virgin and Child, in a painted
cartouche decorated with the coat-of-arms of
the Gritti family
Tempera on vellum laid down on paper,
inscribed on backboard
8¾ x 6in (22 x 15cm)
£1,700–2,200 *Bon*

*Such manuscripts, known as giuramenti (oaths),
were produced by holders of public offices in
Venice during the 16thC, in order to commemorate
their advancement, they ordered elaborately
illuminated copies of their commissions and oaths,
of which this would have formed the frontispiece.*

17th Century

Adriaen Backer
Dutch (c1635–84)
The Rape of the Sabine Women
Signed and dated '1671', oil on canvas
42 x 63¾in (106.5 x 161cm)
£16,000–18,000 *C*

Antonio del Castillo
Spanish (c1603–67)
Saint Peter
Inscribed 'J. De Ribera', oil on canvas
69¼ x 43in (176 x 109cm)
£5,600–7,000 *C*

*According to James Hall (see bibliography),
St. Peter's appearance has remained
remarkably constant in art and he is the
most immediately recognisable of the apostles.*

Gioacchino Assereto
Italian (1600–49)
The Saving of Joash by Jehosheba
Signed, oil on canvas
79 x 71¾in (200.5 x 182cm)
£33,000–43,000 *S*

This biblical scene is from Kings 2, chapter II.

Mateo Cerezo
Spanish (1637–66)
The Mystic Marriage of St. Catherine
Oil on canvas
72 x 91½in (182.5 x 232.5cm)
£30,000–40,000 *S*

*Cerezo was a pupil of Carreño in Madrid
and under his influence developed a style
characterised by a van Dyckian handling of
paint and a use of colour that owed much to
Titian and the Venetian School. His
promising career was cut short by his early
death when he was aged twenty nine.*

Attributed to Jan van Kessel the Younger
Flemish (1654–1708)
Landscape with the Animals entering
Noah's Ark
Oil on panel
21¾ x 35½in (55 x 90.5cm)
£60,000–70,000 *S*

*Derived from an original composition by
Jan Brueghel the Elder of 1613.*

Giuseppe Passeri
Italian (1654–1714)
A Study for Susannah and the Elders, and
four further studies of female figures
Inscribed, red chalk, traces of a watermark
9 x 12¼in (22.5 x 31.5cm)
£2,800–3,800 *P*

Christoffel Jegher
German (died c1660)
Susannah Surprised by the Elders
Woodcut, after Rubens, c1632–40
17½ x 22½in (44.5 x 57cm)
£1,300–1,800 *S(NY)*

Rembrandt Harmensz. van Rijn
Dutch (1606–69)
Abraham's Sacrifice
Etching and drypoint, 1655
6 x 5in (15 x 12.5cm)
£30,000–35,000 *S(NY)*

Nicolas Régnier
Flemish (1591–1667)
Saint John the Evangelist
Oil on walnut panel
19¼in (49cm) diam
£30,000–40,000 *S*

Jusepe de Ribera
Spanish (1588–1656)
St. Jerome Reading
Etching, c1624
7½ x 10in (19 x 25cm)
£2,500–3,500 *S(NY)*

*Jusepe de Ribera was born in Spain and is
generally regarded as one of the most
important Neapolitan artists in the 17thC.
He spent his early years in Parma and Rome,
where he was greatly struck by the paintings
of Caravaggio and his circle, and did not
arrive in Naples until 1616. Ribera's etchings
date mainly from 1620–26, when he was most
strongly influenced by Caravaggio's treatment
of light and his naturalistic style.*

Follower of Giovan Gioseffe dal Sole
Italian (1645–1719)
The Penitent Magdalene
Oil on canvas
36 x 28in (91.5 x 71cm)
£2,000–2,500 *CSK*

Spanish Colonial School (c1680)
A painted Memorial to a Saint lying before
an Altar with miracles in painted cartouches
with a commentary displayed by Putti
Oil on canvas
57½ x 43¾in (146 x 111cm)
£4,000–5,000 *CSK*

Cornelis de Wael
Flemish (1592–1667)
The Adoration of the Golden Calf
Oil on canvas
28¼ x 50in (72 x 127cm)
£9,000–11,000 *S*

After David Teniers II
Flemish (1610–90)
The Denial of Saint Peter
Oil on panel
14½ x 20½in (37 x 52cm)
£2,500–3,500 *C*

18th Century

Louis de Boulogne the Younger
French (1654–1733)
Christ as Salvator Mundi
Oil on canvas
24⅛ x 20in (62 x 51cm)
£2,500–3,000 *S*

Placido Costanzi
Italian (1701–59)
The Triumph of Saint Peter over Paganism
Oil on canvas
41 x 21in (104 x 53cm)
£13,000–15,000 *S*

Anonymous, early 18thC Mexican School
Virgen de Guadalupe
Oil and mother-of-pearl on panel
12½ x 9½in (31 x 24cm)
£55,000–65,000 *S(NY)*

*Paintings on mother-of-pearl inlaid into
lacquer are among the most typically Mexican
art forms of the colonial period. Developed out
of techniques found in Oriental inlaid
furniture brought to Mexico and Peru via
the Manila galleons, as well as indigenous
lacquer work and possibly New World jade
and mother-of-pearl work, enconchados (also
called 'pinturas con incrustaciones de concha
nácar') quickly became an early export ware,
avidly collected by European connoisseurs.*

Corrado Giaquinto
Italian (1703–66)
Saint Nicholas of Bari Saving the Victims
of a Shipwreck
Oil on canvas
28¾ x 23¾in (73 x 61cm)
£57,000–70,000 *C*

Joseph Stephan
German (c1709–86)
A View of Bethlehem with the Journey of the
Magi, the Trinity above and the Nativity in a
painted cartouche below
Signed, extensively inscribed with a key
and dated '1752', oil on canvas
34 x 48in (86 x 122cm)
£21,000–30,000 *C*

19th Century

Ule see him come, and know him ours
Ulho with his sunshine and his showers
Curns all the patient ground to flowers.

Daphne Allen
British (19th/20thC)
Angel with Trees and Birds
Signed, watercolour
12 x 16in (30.5 x 41cm)
£150–200 *LF*

After R. Westall
British (1765–1836)
St. Cecilia
Coloured stipple engraving, engraved
by H. R. Cook, published Jan 1st 1802
20 x 14½in (51 x 37cm)
£140–160 *SRAB*

St Cecilia was the patron saint of music.

Sir Edward Coley Burne-Jones, A.R.A.
British (1833–98)
The Star of Bethlehem
Watercolour and bodycolour heightened
with gold
25½ x 38¾in (65 x 98.5cm)
£125,000–150,000 *S*

*This watercolour was painted in 1887 as
a preparatory study for a tapestry to be made
at the works set up by William Morris at
Merton Abbey in 1881. It follows the
iconography of the late Western tradition that
three kings - Melchior, from Nubia, Balthasar
from Godolia and Caspar from Tharsis -
watched for a heavenly star which had been
prophesied. When they saw it, they travelled
from their kingdoms in Asia and Africa to
worship the Christ child. Their bodies were
later found in Constantinople, and
subsequently moved to Cologne, where the
cathedral was built to commemorate them.*

Philippe Haecke
German (b1847)
The Finding of Moses
Signed, oil on canvas
29½ x 39in (75 x 99cm)
£900–1,200 *C*

Gertrude E. Demain Hammond
British (1862–1953)
Five of them were Wise, and Five Foolish
Signed and dated '1888', inscribed with the
artist's address, '33 Lansdowne Gardens,
Clapham, S.W.', on a label on reverse, pencil
and watercolour heightened with white and
gold, shaped, in the original frame and mount.
11 x 31in (28 x 79cm)
£5,500–6,500 *C*

George H. Hay, R.S.A.
British (1831–1913)
The Vesper Prayer
Signed with monogram, oil on canvas
19 x 21¾in (48 x 55cm)
£5,000–6,000 *C*

José Jiménez y Aranda
Spanish (1837–1903)
Venerdi Santo, Far Penitenza
Signed and dated '1874', oil on canvas,
laid down on masonite
20¼ x 30¾in (51.5 x 78cm)
£40,000–50,000 *S(NY)*

Fernand Khnopff
Belgian (1858–1921)
Requiem
Signed and inscribed, pencil, charcoal and
watercolour on paper, 1907
31½in (80cm) square
£145,000–170,000 *C*

Sir Joseph Noel Paton, R.S.A.
British (1821–1901)
Lead Kindly Light ...
Signed with nonogram and dated '1894',
oil on board
12in (30.5cm) diam.
£3,300–4,300 *C*

Piotr Stachiewicz
Polish (1858–1938)
The Crowned Madonna
Signed, pencil and red chalk on paper
18 x 24½in (46 x 62cm)
£1,800–2,200 *C*

Carlos Schwabe
Swiss (1866–1926)
La Vierge aux Lys
Signed and dated '99', watercolour
over pencil and white bodycolour
38 x 18½in (96.5 x 47cm)
£100,000–120,000 *S*

*Schwabe was born in Altona and
settled in Geneva. His greatest
success, however, was found in Paris
where he became known as a
decorative painter and his style
became increasingly Symbolist. His
work there included illustrations for
publications by Zola, Baudelaire and
Maeterlinck. He won numerous
prizes in France, including the
Légion d'Honneur in 1901.*

Frederick James Shield, A.R.W.S.
British (1833–1911)
Patience
Oil on canvas, c1890
74 x 24½in (188 x 62.5cm)
£5,000–6,000 *P*

> **Miller's is a price GUIDE
> not a price LIST**

Simeon Solomon
British (1840–1905)
Shadrach, Meshach and
Abednego in the Fiery Furnace
Signed with monogram and
dated '10/63', watercolour
heightened with white and
gum arabic
13 x 9in (33 x 23cm)
£16,500–18,500 *C*

*Like so much of Solomon's early
work, the picture is inspired by
the Old Testament, taking as its
subject the well known story in
the third chapter of the Book of
Daniel which describes how the
three young Jews were cast into
a furnace for refusing to
worship a golden image set up
by Nebuchadnezzar. To the
King's astonishment, they escape
unharmed, being protected by
an angel.*

Hans Zatzka
Austrian (b1859)
The Virgin Mary and the Infant Jesus
Signed, oil on canvas
30 x 39in (76 x 99cm)
£4,500–5,500 *S*

20th Century

Jessie Bayes
British (active 1901–39)
The Madonna of the Flocks
Signed and dated '1909', tempera and gold
paint on panel
9 x 6½in (23 x 16.5cm)
£6,000–7,000 *S*

Sean Keating, P.R.H.A.
Irish (1889–1977)
The Feast of Bridget
Signed, oil on canvas
37¾ x 46in (96 x 117cm)
£14,000–16,000 *P*

*Saint Bridget of Ireland was a late 5thC saint whose
cult has at times been second only to that of Saint
Patrick. Believed to have been baptised by Patrick and
later to have become Abbess of Kildare, her miracle
stories, often with a theme of multiplication of food,
are repeated in numerous medieval and later Lives,
with translations into both Old French and German.
She is the patron saint of poets, blacksmiths and
healers and her principal feast is held on 1st February.*

Kirill Sokolov
Russian (b1930)
The Miracle of Jairus's Daughter
Signed, silkscreen, 1981
18½ x 14in (47 x 36cm)
£300–350 *VCG*

Edvard Munch
Norwegian (1863–1944)
Madonna (Eva Mudocci)
Signed in pencil and inscribed,
lithograph, 1903
27 x 18¼in (69 x 46cm)
£45,000–55,000 *S*

Rockwell Kent
American (1882–1971)
Wayside Madonna
Signed with initials and inscribed, colour
wood engraving, 1927
10¼ x 5½in (25.5 x 14cm)
£150–200 *SLN*

Tom Wood
British (b1955)
Angel I 1993
Oil on paper and board
23½ x 37in (60 x 94cm)
£1,800–2,000 *HaG*

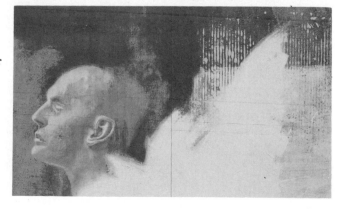

MYTHOLOGICAL
16th–17th Century

Attributed to Johann van Boeckhorst
German (1661–1724)
Janus with the Four Seasons
Signed, oil on canvas
6¾ x 9in (17 x 23cm)
£10,000–11,000 *S(Am)*

Circle of Frencesco Allegrini
Italian (1587–1663)
The Judgement of Paris
Oil on canvas
36 x 43½in (91.5 x 110.5cm)
£7,000–8,000 *C*

Attributed to Pieter Brueghel the Younger
Flemish (1564–c1637)
A Man Pissing on the Moon
Oil on panel
6¾ x 7¾in (17 x 19.5cm)
£35,000–45,000 *S*

*This subject illustrates the old Flemish proverb
'Whatever I try to do, I never succeed: (I am always
pissing at the moon). It derives from the last of a series
of twelve circular paintings by the elder Brueghel, set
together in a single panel, signed and dated 1558.*

Attributed to Giacinto Calandrucci
Italian (1646–1707)
Coronation of an Allegorical Figure
Pen and brown ink over black chalk,
heightened with white
14¼ x 21¼in (36.5 x 54cm)
£2,000–2,500 *P*

**Giusseppe Cesari,
called il Cavalier d'Arpino**
Italian (1568–1640)
Venus Reclining
Oil on panel
16½ x 24¼in (42 x 62cm)
£65,000–80,000 *S*

Dutch School (17thC)
Aeneas rescues his Father from burning Troy
Oil on copper
10½ x 14½in (26.5 x 36.5cm)
£1,500–2,000 *CSK*

Circle of Frans Francken the Younger
Flemish (1581–1642)
Death Playing a Fiddle before a Merchant
Oil on panel
9¾ x 7½in (24 x 19cm)
£4,500–5,500 *S(Am)*

Follower of Johann Carl Loth
German (1632–98)
Venus and Adonis
Oil on canvas
31½ x 38½in (80 x 98cm)
£3,500–4,500 *S(S)*

English Provincial School (16thC)
Coming out of the Little end of the Horn
Inscribed 'This horn embleme here doth
shew of svertishipp what harme doth growe',
oil on panel
18½ x 21¼in (47 x 54cm)
£3,000–4,000 *S*

*This work went way over its £500–700
estimate at Sotheby's. The inscription warns
of the dangers of standing surety, i.e. acting
as guarantor for some third party. Brewer's
Dictionary of Phrase and Fable records an old
English saying 'To be squeezed out at the little
end of the horn' - to come off badly in some
affair, and a number of medieval and early
proverbs stressed the risks of surety.*

Johann Heiss
German (1640–1704)
Diana and Actaeon
Signed and dated '1701', oil on canvas
51¾ x 39¼in (131.5 x 100cm)
£20,000–24,000 *S*

*Diana and Actaeon were particularly
favoured mythological subjects for painting,
because it allowed for the portrayal of nudity.
Diana and her nymphs were bathing in a
stream, Prince Actaeon accidentally stumbled
upon them, and for the crime of seeing their
nakedness was turned into a stag and torn
apart by his own hounds.*

**Giovanni de Niccolò de Lutero,
called Dosso Dossi**
Italian (c1475–1542)
A Personification of Geometry
Oil on canvas
55¼ x 59⅝in (140 x 151.5cm)
£150,000–170,000 *C*

Jan Mytens
Dutch (1614–70)
Portrait of a Young Lady as Diana
Signed, oil on canvas
44½ x 35¾in (113 x 91cm)
£9,500–10,500 *S*

Giuseppe Nicola Nasina
Italian (1657–1736)
Pan
Signed with initials, pen and brown
ink over red chalk
10½ x 15⅞in (26 x 40.5cm)
£800–1,000 *P*

Attributed to Giovanni Antonio Pellegrini
Italian (1675–1741)
Berenice
Oil on canvas
37 x 28½in (93.5 x 73cm)
£9,500–10,500 *S*

*Not a manic hairdresser, but a classical
heroine - Berenice was born in 273 BC and
married Ptolemy III. When her husband went
off to war in Syria, she dedicated a lock of her
hair against his safe return. The lock
disappeared but was rediscovered as a group
of stars by the royal astronomer - the
constellation Coma Berenices (near the tail of
Leo). Callimachus celibrated the story in a
poem which was translated by Catallus.*

Giulio Pippi, il Romano, and Studio
Italian (1499–1546)
The Flight of the Meriones
Black chalk, pen and brown ink, brown wash
heightened with white, on blue paper
10¼ x 14¾in (25.5 x 37.4cm)
£3,500–4,500 *C*

Guido Reni
Italian (1575–1642)
Andromeda (?), her hands tied behind
her back
Pen and brown ink heightened with white,
on grey paper
8 x 6¼in (20 x 15.5cm)
£3,500–4,500 *C*

Sebastiano Ricci
Italian (1659–1734)
Castor and Pollux
Oil on canvas
100¾in (256cm) square
£78,000–88,000 *S*

*According to Homeric tradition, Castor and
Pollux were each born from an egg, the sons
of a union between Zeus and Leda.*

Sir Peter Paul Rubens
Flemish (1577–1640)
An Allegory of Prudence
Oil on panel
25½ x 17¾in (64.5 x 45cm)
£215,000–240,000 *C*

*This picture forms part of a group of four
allegories representing the four Virtues which
are first recorded in an inventory of 1727.
In a manner characteristic of Rubens, several
iconographic elements have been combined in
this composition. The walled crown on
Prudence's head is broadly symbolic of the
body politic which provides the framework
within which the other individual symbolical
elements function. The finger which she
points to her head indicates the need for
intelligent action. Well established as the
attribute of wisdom 'Be wise as serpents',
Matthew, 10.15), the serpent may also carry
a reference to good health.*

**Attributed to Giovanni Battista Trotti,
called Il Malosso**
Italian (1555–1619)
A Putto in Flight
Inscribed, pen and brown ink with wash
over black chalk
6½ x 13in (16.5 x 33cm)
£200–300 *P*

18th Century

Louis de Boulogne the Younger
French (1654–1733)
Galatea Observed by Polyphemus
Oil on canvas
30 x 40in (76 x 102cm)
£24,000–28,000 *S*

Follower of François Boucher
French (1703–70)
Cupid playing with a Bow and Arrow
Oil on canvas
36 x 29½in (91.5 x 75cm)
£1,900–2,400 *C*

French School (18thC)
Portrait of a Lady as Pomona
Oil on canvas
58¼ x 45¼in (147.5 x 115cm)
£12,000–14,000 *S*

Antoine Dubost
French (1769–1825)
Le Retour d'Hélène
Signed in Greek, oil on canvas
51½ x 75¾in (130.5 x 192cm)
£55,000–65,000 *S(NY)*

*Helen, daughter of Zeus and Leda and wife of
Menelaus, was seduced by Paris and carried
away to Troy. Thus began the Trojan War
which endured for ten years. At the end of the
war she is reconciled with Menelaus and
together they return to Sparta, as depicted by
Dubost in this composition.*

**Circle of Sebastian Jacques Leclerc,
called Leclerc des Gobelins**
French (1734–85)
Diana reveals Callisto's pregnancy to the
Nymphs before transforming her into a bear
Oil on canvas
19¾ x 29in (50 x 73.5cm)
£3,000–4,000 *P*

*Diana's nymphs were expected to be as chaste
as the Goddess herself. One of them, Callisto,
was raped by Jupiter who had first disguised
himself as Diana in order to meet her. When
Calisto's pregnancy was discovered Diana,
somewhat unsympathetically, punished the
nymph by changing her into a bear and setting
the dogs on her. Jupiter rescued Callisto just
in time and carried her up to heaven.*

19th Century

Jules Louis Machard
French (1839–1900)
La Rêve d'Eros
Signed, oil on canvas
47¼ x 75in (120 x 190.5cm)
£16,000–18,000 *S(NY)*

Jacques Laurent Agasse
Swiss (1767–1849)
Ondine
Signed, inscribed and dated '1843',
oil on canvas
23¾ x 19⅝in (60 x 50cm)
£70,000–80,000 *S*

*The original title for this striking and
atmospheric subject was 'A Personified
Fountain'. However, it is clear from Agasse's
own inscription that he got inspiration for it
from Undine, the celebrated romance written
in 1811 by the colourful German officer and
writer Friedrich Baron de la Motte Fouqué
(1777–1843). The chilling tale tells of the
water nymph Undine who is brought up by a
humble fisherman and married a knight
called Huldebrand, who subsequently neglects
her for another woman, Bertalda. The couple
quarrel in a boat on the Danube and Undine
is snatched back into the water. She returns
for her husband's wedding to his new bride
and kills him with a kiss. Agasse was clearly
fascinated by the subject and his Record Book
lists four versions of the subject.*

Daniel Maclise, R.A.
British (1806–70)
The Choice of Hercules
Signed and inscribed, oil on canvas
40¾ x 50⅞in (103.5 x 129cm)
£50,000–60,000 *C*

Evelyn de Morgan
British (1855–1919)
Hero holding the Beacon for Leander
Signed with monogram and dated
'1885', gouache on paper laid on panel
22¾ x 11½in (58 x 29cm)
£9,000–11,000 *C*

*Hero was a priestess of Venus at Sestos,
a Thracian town on the shores of the
Hellespont, exactly opposite Abydos on
the Asiatic side. She was loved by
Leander, a youth of Abydos, and by
night he would swim the Hellespont to
join her, Hero directing his course by
holding a beacon. One night Leander
was drowned in a storm, and in despair
Hero threw herself into the sea
and perished.*

Percy Anderson
British (1850–1928)
Paris and Helen
Signed with monogram and dated '1884',
watercolour and bodycolour heightened
with scratching out
84 x 31½in (213.5 x 80cm)
£3,300–4,000 *S*

20th Century

D. Drey
British (b1962)
The Choice of Paris
Oil on board
28in (71cm) diam
£700–800 *FT*

Dame Elizabeth Frink, R.A.
British (1930–93)
Hades and Persophone
Signed, inscribed and
dated '83',pencil
22½ x 15in (57 x 38cm)
£1,000–1,400 *C*

Amanda Rabey
British (20thC)
Seasonal Wishes
Signed and dated '1993', oil on canvas
36 x 27in (91.5 x 69cm)
£350–400 *VCG*

Brigid Marlin
British (20thC)
Cupid and Psyche
Mische technique
25 x 36in (64 x 92cm)
£4,000–4,500 *JBA*

Murray Robertson
British (b1916)
Song of the Siren
Etching, 1992
13½ x 17¾in (34 x 45cm)
£175–200 *GPS*

Reginald Marsh
American (1898–1954)
Dali's Dream of Venus
Signed and dated '1939', watercolour on paper
26½ x 39½in (67.5 x 100.5cm)
£35,000–45,000 *S(NY)*

STILL LIFE

The importation of the tulip from Turkey to
the Netherlands in the late 1500s sowed the
seed for a remarkable period of floral still life
in 17thC Europe. The principal clients for
such works were the wealthy merchants who
imported and collected the plants themselves.
'Tulipomania' was the great vice of the age,
bulbs were auctioned for atonishing sums,
and many collectors bankrupted themselves
with their lust for rare examples. The loving
exactitude with which artists portrayed these
precious flowers has perhaps never been
equalled. A floral still life could take two years
or more to complete. Often, each flower was
painted from life as it came into bloom and
bouquets combined spring, summer and
autumn flowers as artists worked through the
seasons on the same canvas. Many pictures
also contained allegorical elements, for
instance, ears of corn symbolised redemption;
a butterfly, the human soul; birds' eggs,
resurrection. 'The inspiration of the early
flower pieces was the rarity value of the
flowers themselves,' notes garden historian
Diana Baskervyle-Glegg. 'When they ceased to
be rare, flowers were painted primarily for
their decorative value.' The great tradition of
Netherlandish flower painting began to
decline in the mid-18thC and although later
works might have been more technically
accomplished, they lack the sense of wonder
and excitement experienced and reproduced
by the early masters of the floral still life.

16th–17th Century

Follower of Juan de Arellano
Spanish (1614–76)
Flowers in a Basket with a Butterfly
on a Stone Ledge
Oil on canvas
32½ x 40½in (82 x 102.5cm)
£7,000–8,000   C

Evert Collier
Dutch (c1640–after 1706)
A Trompe l'Oeil of a Letter Rack with a print
of a Woman, a Parliamentary speech of 1704,
and other items
Signed, oil on canvas
21¼ x 26½in (54 x 67cm)
£25,000–30,000   C

*This fascinating picture went almost five
times over its £3,000–5,000 estimate.
Trompe l'oeil painting was highly prized in
the 17thC, and clearly remains so today.*

Follower of Osias Beert I
Flemish (c1570–1624)
A Rose, Tulips and Cornflowers
in a Roemer
Oil on panel
13 x 10in (33 x 25.5cm)
£8,000–10,000   CSK

Attributed to Isaac Van Duynen
Dutch (c1630–c1690)
A Still Life of salt water Fish on a Ledge
Oil on canvas
36 x 44½in (91.5 x 112.5cm)
£3,500–4,500   S(Am)

Follower of William Gowe Ferguson
British (1632–95)
A Partridge hanging from a nail with other
Birds on a Ledge
Oil on panel
15¼ x 11½in (38.5 x 29cm)
£600–800 *CSK*

*Still life paintings of dead game, although
they can be beautifully painted, tend to
attract a lower premium than those of
flowers and fruit.*

Follower of Jan Davidsz. de Heem
Dutch (1601–84)
A garland of flowers suspended by
blue ribbons
Signed, oil on panel
11½ x 18in (29 x 45.5cm)
£21,000–26,000 *S*

Henry Howell
British (active 1660–1720)
Trompe l'Oeil of a Letter Rack with a quill
pen, letters, sealing wax and miniature
portrait of King Charles I
Signed, inscribed and dated '1702'
24 x 29in (61 x 73.5cm)
£12.000–14.000 *S(NY)*

Nicolas de Largillière
French (1656–1746)
A Still Life of Flowers in a Gilt Vase with
Fruit, and A Still Life of Fruit on a Table
A pair, oil on canvas
37¾ x 52in (95.5 x 132cm)
£50,000–65,000 *S*

Circle of Jan Van Kessel I
Flemish (1626–79)
Sweetmeats in a Bowl, a Vase of Flowers
and Cherries, Grapes in a Tazza, and Fruit
in a Tazza
4 paintings, oil on copper
2¼ x 5⅜in (2.5 x 14cm) and
one 2½ x 8in (6 x 20cm)
£11,000–14,000 *C*

Attributed to Cornelis Mahu
Flemish (1613–89)
A Pewter Salver with Oysters, a Roemer,
Jug and Salt Cellar
Signed, oil on canvas
20 x 26in (50.5 x 66cm)
£9,500–11,000 *CSK*

Follower of Simon Luttichuys
Dutch (1610–62)
A Vanitas Still Life with a Skull, Books and
a Candle on a Table
Oil on canvas
30¼ x 25½in (76.5 x 64.5cm)
£1,000–1,500 *S(S)*

*This painting includes all the elements of
the traditional 'Vanitas' - a still life which
conveyed the vanity or emptiness of earthly
possessions. The skull is a momento mori
reminding us of the inevitability of death,
the hourglass and the snuffed out candle
signify the passing of time, the empty box,
the ultimate hollowness of earthly possessions.*

Manner of Jean-Baptiste Monnoyer
French (1636–99)
Tulips, Peonies and other Flowers in a
Basket with a Parrot and Landscape beyond
Oil on canvas
25 x 30in (63.5 x 76cm)
£3,500–4,500 *CSK*

Follower of Cornelis Saftleven
Dutch (1607–81)
A Still Life of Cooking Utensils, Baskets
and other items in a Barn interior
Oil on panel
14¾ x 20in (37.5 x 50.5cm)
£2,500–3,500 *CSK*

Attributed to Ludger tom Ring II
German (1522–84)
A Still Life of Wild Flowers in a façon de
Venise filigrana glass vase
Oil on inset panel
23 x 14in (58.5 x 35.5cm)
£170,000–200,000 *C*

Follower of Floris van Schooten
Dutch (1605–55)
A Still Life of fruit in Wanli kraak porselein
Bowls, butter in a Tazza, on a draped table
oil on panel
22¼ x 38⅛in (56.5 x 97cm)
£19,000–24,000 *C*

18th Century

Follower of Andrea Belvedere
Italian (1642–1732)
Flowers in an Urn, and Flowers in
a Porcelain Vase
A pair, oil on canvas
35½ x 15¼in (90 x 38.5cm)
£9,500–11,000 *C*

Michel-Bruno Bellengé
French (1726–93)
A Still Life of Flowers in a Crystal Vase
Oil on canvas
10½ x 8½in (26.5 x 21.5cm)
£15,000–18,000 *S(NY)*

Circle of Felice Boselli
Italian (1650–1732)
Funghi on a Bank
Oil on canvas
16 x 20¾in (41 x 55.5cm)
£3,300–4,000 *C*

Pieter Casteels
Flemish (1684–1749)
A Still Life of Flowers in a Vase
Signed and dated '1733', oil on canvas
29 x 24in (73.5 x 61cm)
£23,000–30,000 *S(NY)*

Jean Coustou
French (1719–91)
A Still Life Trompe l'Oeil of a sculpted
portrait in bas relief, a framed print of
a landscape, volumes of 'Cabinet de Croisat'
and 'Vues de Rome'
Indistinctly signed, oil on canvas
24½ x 50¼in (62 x 127.5cm)
£5,500–6,500 C

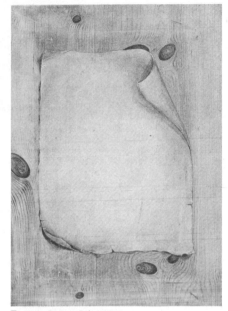

Johann Hendrick Fredricks
Dutch (1751–1817)
A Still Life of Fruit, a Wine Cooler and a Roemer, and a Still
Life of Fruit, with a Hare and Goldfish in a Glass Bowl
A pair, signed and dated '1788', oil on canvas
40 x 32¼in (101 x 82cm)
£25,000–35,000 S

Dutch School (c1750)
A Trompe l'Oeil of Parchment
on a Pine Board
Oil on canvas
21 x 15½in (53 x 39cm)
£1,800–2,200 P

William Jones of Bath
British (active 1764–77)
A Still Life of Fruit with a Squirrel
and a Butterfly on a Ledge
Signed, oil on canvas
19 x 25in (48 x 63.5cm)
£5,500–6,000 WWG

Elias Megel
Unknown (18thC)
A Vanitas Still Life
Signed, oil on copper
8 x 10½in (20 x 27cm)
£4,000–5,000 C

Follower of Willem van Leen
Dutch (1753–1825)
A Still Life of Peonies and
Cornflowers in an Urn with a
Landscape beyond
Oil on canvas
32½ x 27½in (82.5 x 70cm)
£2,500–3,500 CSK

Jan van Os
Dutch (1744–1808)
A Still Life of Flowers and Fruit before a Stone Urn,
and a Still Life with Flowers and a Bird's Nest
A pair, signed, oil on panel
31 x 23in (78.5 x 58.5cm)
£420,000–450,000   *S(NY)*

Follower of Candido Vitali
Italian (1680–1753)
A Still Life of a dead Hare and Birds
on a Bank with a Gun
Oil on canvas
29¼ x 24½in (74.5 x 62cm)
£1,700–2,300   *C*

19th Century

American School (19thC)
A Still Life of Fruit and Squash
in a blue and yellow striped Basket
Watercolour on white velvet, c1830
13 x 20in (33 x 51cm)
£550–750   *S(NY)*

Alfrida Baadsgaard
Danish (b1839)
A Still Life of Flowers
Signed with initials, oil on canvas
27 x 21in (68.5 x 53cm)
£14,000–14,800   *HFA*

Locate the Source

*The source of each
illustration in Miller's
can be found by checking
the code letters below
each caption with the list
of contributors.*

Charles Thomas Bale
British (19thC)
A Still Life of Mallard, Wood Pigeons,
Fruit and a Stoneware Jug on a Ledge
Signed with monogram, oil on canvas
19½ x 29¼in (49.5 x 74cm)
£1,300–1,600   *CSK*

Jacques-Emile Blanche
French (1861–1942)
Roses in a Vase
Signed, oil on canvas
31½ x 23½in (80 x 60cm)
£7,500–8,500 *C*

George Clare
British (active 1860–1900)
Still Lifes with Apples, Plums, Raspberries
and a mossy background
A pair, signed, oil on canvas
6 x 9in (15 x 22.5cm)
£1,500–2,000 *GH*

Gaston Derval
French (19thC)
A Still Life of Fruit with a Glass of Wine
A pair, signed and one dated '1887',
oil on panel
12¾ x 9½in (32.5 x 24cm)
£5,000–6,000   *S*

Oreste Costa
Italian (b1851)
A Still Life of Game, a Hunter's Horn, and
a Basket of Fruit on a Wooden Table
Signed and inscribed, oil on canvas
44 x 32½in (111.5 x 82.5cm)
£5,000–6,000   *CNY*

William Duffield
British (1816–63)
The Day's Bag
Signed and dated '1863',
oil on canvas
12 x 21in (30.5 x 53.5cm)
£900–1,200   *C*

Henri Fantin-Latour
French (1836–1904)
Carafe de Vin et Assiette de Fruits
sur une Nappe Blanche
Signed and dated '1865',
oil on canvas
18½ x 15½in (47 x 39.5cm)
£300,000–350,000   *S(NY)*

Alexander Fraser
British (19thC)
A Still Life of Mackerel, a Lobster, a
Glass and Porcelain on a Table
Signed and dated '1849', oil on board
10¼ x 8in (26 x 20cm)
£800–1,000   *CSK*

Locate the Source
*The source of each
illustration in Miller's
can be found by checking
the code letters below
each caption with the list
of contributors.*

Camilla von Malheim Friedländer
Austrian (1856–1928)
A Tankard, a Wine Cooler, Books and
a Violin on a Table
Signed, oil on panel
8 x 10¼in (20 x 26cm)
£2,000–3,000   *C*

Emmanuel Fries
French (1778–1852)
A Still Life with Grapes and
Peaches on a marble relief in
an Italianate landscape
Signed and dated '1839',
oil on canvas
56¼ x 43¾in (143 x 111cm)
£24,000–30,000 *S*

Jessica Hayllar
British (1858–1940)
Chrysanthemums
Signed, inscribed and dated '1903',
oil on panel
11½ x 7⅜in (29 x 19.5cm)
£3,300–4,000 *C*

Martin Johnson Heade
American (1819–1904)
A Still Life with Apple Blossoms
in a Nautilus Shell
Signed and dated '1870',
oil on canvas
21 x 17in (53 x 43cm)
£85,000–100,000 *S(NY)*

*In the ten year period from
1865–75, Heade produced a
limited number of elaborate
table top still lifes. This is one
of only two known compositions
which incorporate the
nautilus shell.*

Abel Hold
British (19thC)
The Bird's Nest
Signed and dated '1881', oil on canvas
9½ x 11½in (24 x 29cm)
£800–1,000 *CSK*

William Hough
British (active 1857–94)
A Still Life with Plums, a Peach
and Rosehips
Signed, pencil and watercolour heightened
with bodycolour
9½ x 12½in (23.5 x 31.5cm)
£1,700–2,000 *C*

r. George Lance
British (1802–64)
A Grape Vine with
a Stately Home in
the distance
Signed and dated
'1855', watercolour
on paper
21½ x 17¼in
(54.5 x 44cm)
£1,300–1,600 *CNY*

l. Andreas Lach
Austrian (1817–82)
Roses and Grapes
Signed, oil on canvas
24¾ x 19¾in (63 x 50cm)
£7,500–8,500 *C*

Désiré-Alfred Magne
French (1855–1936)
A Lobster, Shrimps and a Crab by an Urn
Signed, oil on canvas
35 x 45¾in (89 x 116cm)
£6,800–8,000 *C*

Edward Ladell
British (1821–86)
Still Life with Fruit, Flowers and
a Bird's Nest
Signed with monogram, oil on canvas
20½ x 17¼in (52 x 44cm)
£45,000–55,000 *S*

Georgius Jacobus Johannes van Os
Dutch (1782–1861)
A Still Life of Flowers in a Vase
Signed, oil on panel
24¼ x 18¾in (62 x 48cm)
£47,000–57,000 *C*

Jules Larcher
French (b1849)
A Tazza of Peaches, Fruit in a Bowl and
Bottles on a draped Table, and
Bottles of Champagne, Bread, Biscuits and
Cakes on a draped table
A pair, signed, one dated '1888', the other
'1889', oil on canvas
28¾ x 26¼in (92 x 73cm)
£65,000–80,000 *C*

> **Miller's is a price GUIDE
> not a price LIST**

David Emile Joseph de Noter
Belgian (1818–92)
Nature Morte aux Poissons et Oranges
Signed, oil on canvas
21¼ x 17½in (53.5 x 44.5cm)
£2,400–2,800 *S(NY)*

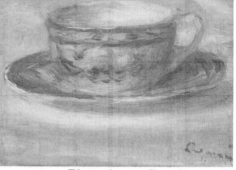

Circle of Alfred Provis
British (active 1843–86)
A Still Life of a Mackerel, Lobster and Monk
Fish on a Ledge
Oil on board
12 x 16½in (30.5 x 42cm)
£500–700 *CSK*

Pierre-August Renoir
French (1841–1919)
Nature Morte, Tasse et Soucoupe
Signed, oil on canvas, 1914
6¼ x 7½in (15.5 x 19cm)
£16,000–18,000 *S*

Dominique-Hubert Rozier
French (1840–1901)
Roses in a Vase
Signed, oil on canvas
21¾ x 18½in (55 x 47cm)
£4,800–5,800 *C*

Friedrich August Schlegel
Austrian (b1828)
Still Life with Mask
and Artefacts
Signed and dated '1846',
oil on canvas
20½ x 17¾in (52 x 45cm)
£5,000–6,000 *S*

John Falconar Slater
British (1857–1937)
Begonias
Signed, oil on board
24 x 18in (61 x 40.5cm)
£700–800 *MSW*

Benjamin Walter Spiers
British (1860–c1910)
Still Life with a Jug, a Plate, a Goblet
and Apples
Signed and dated '1876', pencil and
watercolour heightened with white and
gum arabic
8½ x 8¾in (21 x 22cm)
£800–1,000 *C*

Eloise Harriet Stannard
British (active 1852–93)
Black Grapes with a Wicker Basket,
Butterfly and Secateurs
Signed and dated '1884', oil on canvas
14 x 17in (35.5 x 43cm)
£13,500–14,500 *BuP*

20th Century

Still life is as popular a subject with the painters of the 20thC as it was with the old masters of the 1600s. Every year we receive a large number of still life pictures by living painters. Miller's believe that it is an important function of the *Picture Price Guide* to display works by contemporary artists. Many of these are British and their work is currently available from the galleries listed. The prices of such pictures are often far lower than those of 'older' artists. No one can ever predict if they are buying a future old master, but that is part of the excitement of buying pictures by a living painter.

The cover of this year's Guide includes a still life painted in 1993 by Gail Lilley, wife of the Rt. Hon. Peter Lilley, M.P. The price range of this picture is £300–500. When an exhibition of Lilley's work was shown at the Roy Miles Gallery in London the show was an instant success and sell out.

Francisco Borès
Spanish (1898–1972)
Nature Morte à la Bouteille
Signed, inscribed and dated '38',
oil on canvas
23½ x 28½in (60 x 72.5cm)
£12,000–14,000 *CSK*

John G. Boyd
British (20thC)
Many Happy Returns
Oil on canvas, 1990
36 x 40in (91.5 x 101.5cm)
£3,500–3,750 *VCG*

Carey Clarke, P.H.R.A.
Irish (20thC)
A Still Life with Donatello Angel
Oil on canvas
28 x 36in (71 x 91.5cm)
£4,500–5,000 *SOL*

Mary Dipnall
British (b1936)
Untitled
Oil on canvas
20 x 16in (50.5 x 41cm)
£1,150–1,350 *FGL*

Miller's is a price GUIDE not a price LIST

Ivan Dmitriev
Russian (b1958)
Lilies of the Valley
Signed, oil on canvas
19¾ x 23½in (50 x 60cm)
£700–800 *Ch*

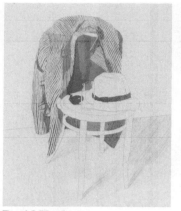

Charles Tattershall Dodd, Jnr.
British (19th/20thC)
Azalea Mollis
Signed, inscribed and dated '1904',
oil on canvas
30 x 22½in (76 x 57cm)
£2,500–2,750 *BuP*

David Hockney
British (b1937)
Panama Hat
Numbered, signed and dated '1972',
etching with aquatint
16¼ x 13¼in (41 x 33.5cm)
£6,000–7,000 *S*

Marjorie M. Incledon
British (1891–1973)
A Still Life with Fruit
Signed with monogram,
oil on canvas
24 x 21in (61 x 53cm
£3,000–3,500 *NZ*

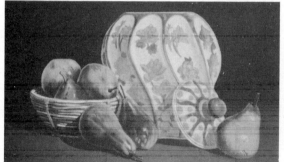

Michael Gill
British (20thC)
A Still Life with Pears
Oil on canvas
13 x 16in (33 x 40.5cm)
£500–600 *LA*

Robert Kelsey
Scottish (b1949)
A Still Life with Fan
Oil on canvas
40in (101.5cm) square
£1,600–1,800 *Tho*

Cecil Kennedy
British (b 1905)
A Silver Urn of mixed Flowers
Signed, oil on canvas
40 x 30in (101.5 x 76cm)
£30,000–40,000 *C(S)*

James McDonald
Scottish (b1956)
Corona
Oil on panel
14in (35.5cm) square
£1,000–1,200 *RB*

*'James McDonald's vision of the
everyday world around us is
unique,' dealer Roger Billecliffe
told Miller's. 'His fascination with
the discarded machinery of an
earlier age and with the
crumbling volumes of the
antiquarian book collector is
reflected in his finely detailed
studies of old typewriters,
lawnmowers, blow lamps and the
decaying books found in the attic
of his grandfather's house. He is
fascinated by texture, whether it
be the well oiled metallic surfaces
of old machines, a bloom on a
petal or the soft and yielding
qualities of silks and knitted
textiles.' 'I love replicating
surfaces,' explains McDonald,
adding, 'Never start to collect
inanimate objects, or they'll start
to collect you.'*

Leo McDowell, R.I.
British (20thC)
Cat with Flowers
Mixed Media
8 x 11in (20 x 28cm)
£450–550 *AdG*

Paul Morgan
British (20thC)
Untitled
Oil on canvas
16 x 12in (40.5 x 30.5cm)
£500–600 *FGL*

Hermione Owen
British (b1951)
A Still Life with Flowers
Signed, pastel
30 x 44in (76 x 115.5cm)
£300–400 *SHF*

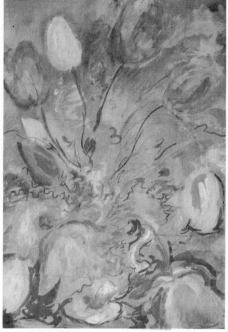

Lélia Pissarro
French (b1960)
Les Fleurs de Lyora
Signed, oil on canvas
21¼ x 25¼in (54 x 65cm)
£2,300–2,600 *STD*

John Piper
British (1903–92)
Tulips
Signed, watercolour, ink and bodycolour
24 x 21in (61 к 53cm)
£5,000–5,500 *NZ*

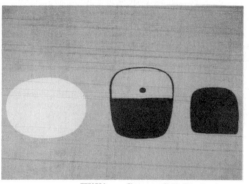

William Scott, C.B.E., R.A.
British (1913–89)
Green Still Life
Signed, and dated '1976', original
lithograph in colours
22 x 33in (56 x 84cm)
£1,000–1,250 *WO*

John Riddle
British (active 1903–34)
Wash Stand
Signed, oil on canvas
29 x 36in (74 x 92cm)
£900–1,100 *SAV*

Derrick Sayer
British (1917–92)
A Still Life
Oil on paper
24 x 32in (61 x 81cm)
£550–650 *HI*

Henry Silk
British (20thC)
A Still Life
Signed, oil on canvas
18 x 22in (46 x 56cm)
£400–450 *JD*

Miller's is a price GUIDE
not a price LIST

Liam Spencer
British (20thC)
Cadmium Window
Oil on paper
12 x 16in (31 x 41cm)
£200–250 *KHG*

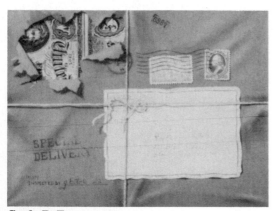

Gayle B. Tate
American (b1944)
Special Delivery, a Trompe l'Oeil Object
Signed with monogram, oil on panel
7½ x 10in (18.5 x 25cm)
£375–500 *SK*

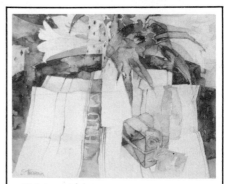

Shirley Trevena
British (20thC)
Lilies and Anemones on a Glass Cloth
Watercolour
14 x 19in (36 x 48cm)
£750–850 *NBO*

Leon Underwood
British (b1890)
Mexican Fruits 1929
Signed and numbered
5¼ x 7½in (13 x 18.5cm)
£250–300 *BLD*

Gwen Whicker
British (active 1935–65)
Distant View of Falmouth
Signed, oil on canvas
20 x 28in (51 x 71cm)
£1,800–2,200 *NZ*

NATURAL & BOTANICAL STUDIES

The most important event in the area of natural and botanical studies was the sale of the Farquhar Collection of Natural History Drawings of Malacca, sold by The Royal Asiatic Society at Sotheby's in October 1993. Dating from c1800, the collection, including both albums and folios, comprised of beautifully detailed and brilliantly coloured drawings of the flora and fauna of Malacca. It had been gathered together by Major General William Farquhar (c1771–1839), nicknamed 'the Rajah of Malacca', where he lived between 1803–18, becoming the most important English patron of the local Chinese artists. Divided into eight lots, but finally sold as a single group, the collection more than doubled its £600,000 upper estimate to sell to a Malaysian lady bidder.

Chinese School (c1800)
The Farquhar Collection of Albums and Folios of Natural History drawings and watercolours of Malacca, comprising:
An album of 61 drawings of Animals, Insects and Reptiles
An album of 59 drawings of Birds
15 x 21½in (38 x 54.5cm) each album
£1,350,000–1,500,000 *S*

Augusta Innes Withers
British (active 1829–65)
An Auricula in a basket cachepot, with Painted Lady and Orange Tip Butterflies
Signed, pencil and watercolour heightened with bodycolour and gum arabic
21 x 17in (53.5 x 43cm)
£17,500–20,000 *S*

Epilobium hirsutum
Great hairy Willow-herb

English School (19thC)
An album of 200 watercolour sketches of wild flowers, most inscribed
8 x 11in (20 x 28cm) each
£2,500–3,500 *DN*

Locate the Source
The source of each illustration in Miller's can be found by checking the code letters below each caption with the list of contributors.

Richard Tratt
British (b1953)
The Painted Lady Butterfly
Oil on canvas
20 x 26in (51 x 66cm)
£750–850 *PHG*

BIRDS

Bird pictures remain high fliers in the marketplace. Christie's have been holding an annual sale of bird pictures since 1989, when the market was at its peak, and their 1994 auction was the most successful since that date. The saleroom was packed with both arty and sporty types in bow ties or Barbour's - everyone was keen to bid and 82% of the 218 lots were sold. As usual, the ever popular Archibald Thorburn ruled the roost, with a number of his works making healthy five figure sums, whilst John Cyril Harrison's pictures nearly all went above their auction estimates. As the following section shows, their mantle has been taken up by a number of contemporary specialists in bird pictures, some of whom are beginning to fetch high prices in the salerooms.

Attributed to Pieter Casteels III
Flemish (1684–1749)
A Collection of Fowl with a Pond beyond
Oil on canvas
56¾ x 78¼in (144 x 198.5cm)
£33,000–40,000   *C*

Marmaduke Cradock
British (1660–1717)
A Landscape with Domestic Fowl and a Pigeon in flight
Oil on canvas
15½ x 9½in (39 x 23.5cm)
£3,000–3,600   *WWG*

Harry Bright
British (active 1867–97)
A Robin, Bullfinch, Greenfinch and Blue Tits in Winter
Signed and dated '1883', pencil, watercolour and bodycolour
16¾ x 12in (42.5 x 30.5cm)
£700–900   *C*

r. **William Foster**
British (1853–1924)
The Peacock
Signed, watercolour
4 x 2½in (10 x 6.5cm)
£650–750   *BCG*

German School (18thC)
Bullfinches, a Flycatcher and a Sparrow, a Swallow and a Finch, a Lark and a Wryneck
A set of 6, inscribed, pencil and watercolour
8¼ x 13in (21 x 33cm)
£900–1,200   *C*

Attributed to Henry Stacey Marks, R.A., R.W.S.
British (1829–98)
A Heron in Flight
Oil on canvas
31¾ x 48in (80.5 x 122cm)
£3,000–4,000 *C*

Archibald Thorburn
British (1860–1935)
European Mallard and Teal in Winter
Signed and dated '1900', pencil and
watercolour heightened with white
17½ x 30¼in (44.5 x 77cm)
£25,000–30,000 *C*

Archibald Thorburn
British (1860–1935)
Goldfinches among Thistles
Signed and dated '1919', pencil
and watercolour with touches of
white heightening
10¾ x 7⅛in (27.5 x 18cm)
£10,000–12,000 *C*

Winifred Marie Louise Austen
British (1876–1964)
Pheasants
Signed, etching
7¼ x 10½in (18.5 x 26cm)
£350–450 *CG*

Neil Cox
British (b1955)
Golden Eagle after Ptarmigan
Signed, watercolour
13 x 19in (33 x 48cm)
£550–600 *PBG*

Barry Castle
Irish (b1935)
Boy and Two Birds
Watercolour
32 x 24in (81 x 61cm)
£1,200–1,400 *SOL*

John Gardiner Crawford
Scottish (b1941)
Sea Storm
Signed, acrylic on masonite, 1989
9½ x 15½in (24 x 39.5cm)
£3,500–3,800 *WH*

Emma Faull
British (b1956)
A Golden Eagle
Signed and dated '981',
pencil, pen and ink
and watercolour
47 x 34¾in (119 x 88cm)
£2,500–3,500 *C*

Alison Guest
British (20thC)
The Other Side of the Coin
Signed, watercolour
14 x 11in (35.5 x 28cm)
£450–500 *RGFA*

John Harwood
British (20thC)
Mallard and Teal
Signed, pencil and watercolour and
bodycolour on blue paper
11 x 14¾in (28 x 37.5cm)
£600–800 *C*

Eliot Hodgkin
British (1905–87)
Eight Eggs and an Eggshell
Signed and dated '60', tempera on card
3 x 10in (7.5 x 24.5cm)
£5,000–6,000 *CSK*

John Cyril Harrison
British (1898–85)
Black Eagles at the Eyrie
Signed, pencil and watercolour
14¼ x 10¾in (36.5 x 27.5cm)
£2,000–2,500 *C*

*Although Harrison worked largely in England,
particularly his native Norfolk, he was fascinated by
all birds of prey. Studying the Golden Eagles took
him to Scotland with the writer and naturalist Seton
Gordon in the late 1920s, and in later life he became
a regular visitor to Africa. He also produced many
landscapes featuring both birds of prey and wildlife.*

Edgar Hunt
British (1876–1953)
Pigeons in the Barn
Oil on canvas
10 x 14in (25 x 35.5cm)
£11,000–12,000 *HFA*

Edwin Penny
British (b1930)
Long-tailed Tits on a Branch
Signed, pencil and watercolour heightened
with white, on blue grey paper
14½ x 10in (36.5 x 25.5cm)
£3,000–4,000 *C*

*Penny was born in Bristol, and studied at
Bath College of Art and the Royal West of
England Academy. Having worked as an
engraver to a printing firm he then went to
study with a Chinese artist in Hong Kong.*

Geroge Edward Lodge
British (1860–1954)
A Cock and Hen Pheasant at the
Edge of a Wood
Signed, pencil and watercolour heightened
with bodycolour
9¼ x 11¾in (23 x 30cm)
£4,000–5,000 *C*

Sir Peter Scott
British (1909–89)
Pinkfeet over an Estuary
Signed and dated '1954', oil on canvas
19½ x 23¾in (49.5 x 60.5cm)
£4,000–5,000 *C*

Richard Robjent
British (b1937)
Pair of Grey Partridges
Signed, watercolour heightened
with bodycolour
21 x 17in (53.5 x 43.5cm)
£4,000–6,000 *S*

*Robjent was fascinated by nature as a child.
He maintained his interest during a 20 year
stint in the army, which he left to become
a bird painter. The painters John Cyril
Harrison and Philip Rickman both
influenced Robjent's work.
From Rickman he learned in particular
how to achieve intense lustrous highlights
on plumage. However, Robjent also developed
his own talent for capturing the muted,
camouflaged colouring of game birds amid
surrounding vegetation, employing an
extremely 'wet' watercolour technique. This
is perfectly suited to portraying the soft tones
of cool British light, weather and water.
In assocation with Colin McKelvie, Robjent
has illustrated and published four monographs
on game birds, and he is regarded as one of
Britain's leading ornithological painters.*

Charles Frederick Tunnicliffe, R.A.
British (1901–79)
Great Crested Grebes with their Young
Signed, pencil and watercolour
13¾ x 19½in (35 x 49cm)
£2,500–3,500 *C*

Julian Waterman
British (b1969)
Great Pied Hornbill
Signed, inscribed and dated '1993',
watercolour with bodycolour
9¾ x 9½in (24.5 x 24cm)
£400–450 *CBL*

Charles Frederick Tunnicliffe, R.A.
British (1901–79)
Herring Gull and Sea Pinks
Signed, oil on canvas
18 x 24in (46 x 61cm)
£3,500–4,000 *MWe*

CATS & DOGS

Cat and dog pictures are always popular in the salerooms, and nothing tugs more on heart and purse strings than a portrait of a favourite pet. The 19thC was the great period of dog painting. Before that, animals tended to be secondary to the main action, shown looking lovingly at their master or master's children in portraits or gambolling around in figure scenes. Among the few dogs judged worthy of an individual portrait were sporting dogs which, like racehorses, often came with a lengthy pedigree that would not have disgraced a member of the royal family. In the Victorian era, as the middle class expanded, so did the custom of keeping pets and the demand for pictures of them. Many artists specialised in dog and cat pictures, both in portraits and genre painting, in which puppies and kittens were rendered even more cute by an anthropomorphic approach. Demand for such pictures remains irresistible today, although it is becoming increasingly hard to find a significant quantity of good quality works. Bonham's annual sale of dog pictures, timed to coincide with Cruft's, was one of their strongest in this field for several years.

Attributed to Agostino Carracci
Italian (1557–1602)
A Boy holding a Crayfish and a Young Girl playing with a Ginger Cat
Oil on canvas
26 x 35in (66 x 89cm)
£235,000–270,000 *S*

The motif of a boy and girl playing with a cat derives from Cremonese prototypes and was taken up in Bologna by Carracci who made a speciality of such intimate genre scenes. Estimated at only £60,000–80,000, this work shot way over expectation at Sotheby's, selling to the Metropolitan Museum of Art in New York.

Philip Reinagle, R.A.
British (1749–1833)
Major, a celebrated Greyhound
Oil on canvas
14½ x 19½in (37 x 49.5cm)
£18,000–20,000 *S*

Charles Burton Barber
British (1845–94)
Sweethearts
Signed and dated '1890', oil on canvas
56½ x 44in (143 x 112cm)
£75,000–85,000 *C*

Barber enjoyed tremendous popularity in his day. He specialised in the winning combination of painting children with dogs and cats. His works were much loved by his clients and gained widespread currency through chromolithographic reproductions. The artist, however, came to resent being chained to such charming themes by his dealers and publishers, talking bitterly about 'manufacturing pictures for the market.' He worked for Queen Victoria for over 20 years, succeeding Landseer as her painter of animals. Whereas Landseer, Barber's great hero, had painted the Queen, Prince Albert and their children, Barber was commissioned to portray the royal grandchildren and their pets.

I. Clark, after Henry Alken Snr.
British (1785–1851)
Stag Hounds
Aquatint, original hand colouring, 1820
7¾ x 11½in (19.5 x 29.5cm)
£350–450 *CG*

Henry Bernard Chalon
British (1770–1849)
A Blenheim Cavalier King Charles Spaniel
on a River Bank
Oil on canvas
17 x 21in (43 x 53cm)
£2,800–3,500 *C*

Horatio Henry Couldery
British (1832–93)
The Captive Audience
Signed with monogram, oil on canvas
12 x 15in (30.5 x 38cm)
£8,000–10,000 *C*

E. M. Fox
British (mid-19thC)
A Maltese Terrier, a White English Terrier,
two English Toy Terriers and an African
Grey Parrot in an Interior
Signed and dated '1868', oil on canvas
15¾ x 20in (40 x 50.5cm)
£4,500–5,500 *C*

*This delightfully naïve account of a corner of
a Victorian drawing room or study, evidently
in a house belonging to an animal lover in
the country or surburbs, is eloquent testimony
to the popularity of Sir Edwin Landseer's
'Scene in Braemar', the engraving of which is
seen on the far wall. The print by the artist's
brother Thomas, was published in 1859, nine
years before this picture was painted.*

Frances C. Fairman
British (1836–1923)
An English Toy Terrier and an Affenpincher
Signed and dated '1903', oil on canvas
24 x 20in (61 x 50.5cm)
£4,800–5,800 *C*

Samuel Fulton
British (1855–1941)
Sentry Duty
Signed, oil on canvas
24 x 20in (61 x 50.5cm)
£9,000–11,000 *C*

Valentine Thomas Garland
British (active 1884–1903)
A Life on the Road
Signed, oil on canvas
19½ x 29½in (49.5 x 75cm)
£12,000–14,000 *Bon*

Joshua J. Gibson
British (late 19thC)
Bulldogs
Signed and dated '1874', oil on canvas
27¾ x 39in (70.5 x 99cm)
£9,000–11,000 *C*

John Frederick Herring, Snr.
British (1792–1867)
Barrister, a hound from Sir Tatton
Sykes' Pack
Signed and inscribed, oil on canvas
10½ x 13¼in (27 x 33.5cm)
£6,500–8,500 *S*

James Hardy, Jnr.
British (1832–89)
Young Man with Dogs and Dead Game
Signed and dated '1876', watercolour
13 x 19in (33 x 48cm)
£4,500–5,500 *LT*

H. Harris
British (active 1910–46)
The Good Companions
Signed, oil on canvas
22 x 32in (56 x 81.5cm)
£1,800–2,500 *C*

John Hayes
British (late 19thC)
A Basket of Mischief
Signed, oil on canvas
28 x 36in (71 x 91.5cm)
£10,000–11,000 *C*

Wilson Hepple
British (1854–1937)
Kittens Playing in the Artist's Studio
Signed and dated '1900', oil on canvas
18 x 12in (45.5 x 30.5cm)
£3,000–4,000 *C*

Gwen John
British (1876–1939)
Tortoiseshell Cat curled up
Stamped with the artist's signature, pencil
and watercolour, c1907–15
4¾ x 6⅜in (12 x 16cm)
£10,500–12,500 *S*

Sir Edwin Henry Landseer, R.A.
British (1802–73)
The Ptarmigan Hill
Oil on canvas, 1869
52 x 88¼in (132 x 224cm)
£215,000–240,000 *S(NY)*

Henry Frederick Lucas-Lucas
British (c1848–1943)
Mickey, a Pekinese
Signed, inscribed and dated '1916',
oil on canvas
9 x 12in (23 x 30.5cm)
£1,500–2,000 *C*

Daniel Merlin
French (1861–1933)
A Proud Mother
Signed, oil on canvas
17¾ x 21¼in (45 x 54cm)
£5,000–6,000 *Bon*

Fannie Moody
British (active 1885–97)
The Best of Friends
Signed, oil on board
14½ x 20¾in (37.5 x 53cm)
£3,000–4,000 *C*

Alfred Arthur Brunel de Neuville
French (19thC)
The Proud Mother
Signed, oil on panel
10 x 12in (25 x 30.5cm)
£4,000–5,000 *JN*

Robert Morley
British (1857–1941)
By the Fireside
Signed, oil on canvas
25 x 31in (63.5 x 78.5cm)
£12,000–14,000 *S(NY)*

Henriette Ronner-Knip
Dutch (1821–1909)
Playful Kittens
Signed, oil on panel
9¾ x 12¾in (24.5 x 32.5cm)
£9,000–11,000 *P*

The reigning queen of cat painters, Henriette Ronner-Knip had a list of wealthy clients throughout Europe and America. Her playful kittens gambolling in decorative, bourgeois interiors spawned a host of immitators, many of them female artists.

Philip E. Stretton
British (active 1884–1919)
Fireside Companions
Signed, oil on board
30 x 25in (76 x 62.5cm)
£8,000–9,000 *C*

Carl Suhrlandt
German (1828–1919)
Foxhounds in a Landscape
Signed, oil on canvas
31½ x 43½in (80 x 110.5cm)
£4,000–5,000 *P*

William Henry Hamilton Trood
British (1860–99)
Friend or Foe?
Signed and dated '1891', oil on canvas
12 x 18in (30.5 x 45.5cm)
£5,000–7,000 *Bon*

Circle of Vincent de Vos
Belgian (1829–75)
A Basket of Mischief
Oil on canvas
24½ x 31in (62.5 x 79cm)
£1,300–1,800 *CSK*

Miller's is a price GUIDE
not a price LIST

William Weekes
British (active 1864–1904)
A Visitor
Signed, inscribed, oil on board
9½ x 13in (24 x 33cm)
£5,000–7,000 *Bon*

Adam Birtwistle
British (20thC)
Toby
Gouache and tempera on paper
30 x 20in (76 x 51cm)
£1,400–1,600 *PN*

Mick Cawston
British (20thC)
Bedlington Lurchers
Oil on canvas
20 x 30in (50.5 x 76cm)
£1,000–1,200 *SMi*

Frederick Bromfield
British (20thC)
Incantation
Signed, watercolour
18 x 14in (45.5 x35.5cm)
£600–800 *GK*

Betty Swanwick
British (1915–89)
Hedge Trimming
Watercolour over pencil
20 x 30in (51 x 76cm)
£800–1,000 *P*

Martin Leman
British (b1934)
R is for Rex - They Make a Fine Pair
Signed, bodycolour
14 x 9in (35.5 x 22.5cm)
£750–850 *CBL*

Lesley Anne Ivory
British (20thC)
Teddy Bears on Patchwork
Signed, watercolour
8½ x 10½in (21.5 x 26.5cm)
£2,550–2,750 *CBL*

FARMYARD ANIMALS

Philip Peter Roos, called Rosa da Tivoli
German (1657–1706)
A Shepherd Resting with his Flock
Oil on canvas
57 x 86½in (144.5 x 219.5cm)
£16,000–18,000 *S*

Attributed to Jacques Laurent Agasse
Swiss (1767–1849)
The Barn Scene
Oil on canvas
20 x 30in (50.5 x 76cm)
£17,000–17,500 *HLG*

Johnann Wenzel Peter
German (1745–1829)
Billy Goats
Signed, oil on canvas
38½ x 53in (97.5 x 134.5cm)
£10,000–12,000 *C*

Jacques Raymond Brascassat
French (1804–67)
Cows in a Landscape
Signed and dated '1846', oil on panel
24 x 30in (61 x 76cm)
£3,000–4,000 *S(Am)*

Charles Collins, R.B.A.
British (active 1867–d1921)
Cattle Watering in a Summer Landscape
Signed, oil on canvas
14 x 30in (35.5 x 76cm)
£2,500–3,500 *JC*

*Charles Collins painted in both oil and
watercolour and specialised in landscapes,
rustic genre and animal subjects, especially
farm scenes with cattle. He was the father
of George Edward Collins who became an
etcher and illustrator.*

Edgar Bundy
British (1862–1922)
Obstructionists
Signed and dated '1888', oil on canvas
19½ x 26½in (49 x 67cm)
£2,800–3,200 *FWA*

Thomas Sydney Cooper, R.A.
British (1803–1902)
Ewe and Two Lambs at Rest
Signed and dated '1874', pencil sketch
4½ x 7in (11 x 17.5cm)
£750–950 *CAG*

Thomas Sidney Cooper, R.A.
British (1803–1902)
In Stour Meadows, Curfew Hour
Signed and dated '1892', stamped with
artist's stamp on the stretcher, oil on canvas
48 x 72¾in (122 x 184.5cm)
£19,000–21,000 *C*

*Demand for Cooper's finest works resulted in
the practice, common to many contemporary
artists, of producing duplicate versions. This
composition, previously confused with the
original exhibit, is another version, identical
in size, of 'In the Meadows at Curfew Hour',
No. 301 in the Royal Academy exhibition of
1892. Cooper generally modified the detail
slightly in the commissioned versions,
sometimes on the client's specific instructions.*

William Sidney Cooper
British (active 1871–1923)
Sunlight and Shadow
Signed and dated '1925', watercolour
6¾ x 9¾in (17 x 25cm)
£750–850 *JC*

Thomas Sidney Cooper, R.A.
British (1803–1902)
On the Stour
Oil on canvas
24 x 36in (61 x 91.5cm)
£19,000–20,000 *WHP*

Henry Garland
British (active 1854–1900)
Drove in Glen Dochart
Signed, inscribed and dated '1900',
oil on canvas
24 x 36in (61 x 91.5cm)
£4,800–5,800 *C(S)*

John Frederick Herring, Jnr.
British (1815–1907)
A Winter Farmyard Scene
Signed and dated '1857', oil on canvas
24 x 36in (61 x 91.5cm)
£70,000–80,000 *C*

G. W. Horlor
British (active 1849–91)
Cattle Grazing
Signed, oil on canvas, 1880
17 x 19in (43 x 48cm)
£5,250–5,750 *HLG*

Joseph Horlor
British (active 1834–66)
Cattle Watering
Oil on canvas
24 x 45in (61 x 114cm)
£3,000–3,500 *FdeL*

Louis Bosworth Hurt
British (1856–1929)
Highland Cattle in a Mountainous Landscape
Signed and dated '1888', oil on canvas
24 x 36in (61 x 91.5cm)
£15,000–16,000 *HFA*

Jean-Baptiste Huet
French (1745–1811)
A Cow and her Calf in a Barn
Signed and dated 'IX', oil on canvas
42 x 50¼in (106.5 x 127.5cm)
£14,000–16,000 *S(NY)*

Cornelis Van Leemputten (1841–1902) and
Theodore Gerard (1829–95)
Belgian
Shepherdess with Sheep in a Landscape
Signed by both artists, inscribed by
Leemputten, oil on canvas
30 x 43¾in (76 x 111cm)
£5,500–6,500 *P*

William Luker, Snr.
British (active 1851–89)
The Outskirts of Burnham
Signed and dated '1880', oil on canvas
20 x 32in (51 x 81cm)
£5,500–6,000 *EG*

William Mellor
British (1851–1931)
Cattle Watering on the Glaslynn
Signed, oil on canvas
16 x 24in (40.5 x 61cm)
£4,800–5,200 *HFA*

Attributed to Thomas Mogford of Exeter
British (1800–68)
Shorthorn Bull, and Shorthorn Cow
A pair, one indistinctly signed and dated
'1839', oil on canvas
20½ x 25¾in (52 x 65.5cm)
£4,800–5,800 *S(S)*

Frank Paton
British (1856–1909)
More Free than Welcome
Signed, inscribed and dated '1884',
oil on panel
30½ x 50in (77 x 127cm)
£7,000–9,000 *C*

Eugène Joseph Verboeckhoven
Belgian (1798–1881)
Sheep and Poultry in a Landscape
Signed and dated '1849', oil on panel
23¾ x 30¼in (60.5 x 77cm)
£9,500–11,000 *C*

Sidney Watson
British (19thC)
Near Loch Awe, and Overlooking Loch Tay
A pair, signed and inscribed, oil on canvas
13 x 19in (33 x 48cm)
£5,500–6,500 *C(S)*

Frederick Williamson
British (active 1856–1900)
Sheep Resting
Signed and dated '1892', watercolour
17 x 26¾in (43 x 68cm)
£1,200–1,500 *S*

Lois Sykes
American (20thC)
Orchard Pig
Oil on board
12 x 11½in (30.5 x 29cm)
£400–500 *LA*

William Weekes
British (active 1864–1904)
The Sleeping Beauties
Signed, oil on canvas
15½ x 11½in (40 x 29.5cm)
£5,500–6,500 *S(S)*

James Walker Tucker
British (1898–1972)
Milking time - A Cotswold Farm
Signed, inscribed and dated '1962',
egg tempera on masonite board
20 x 24in (50.5 x 61cm)
£650–850 *CSK*

FISH

Fish pictures attract a premium because of
their scarcity. Only a handful of 19thC
artists, predominantly British, painted fish
as sporting trophies, showing them either
laid out on the bank or in the process of being
caught. Fish still lifes were popular in 17thC
Netherlands, and came to prominence again
in the 19thC. Fishing prints are always in
demand because of their comparative rarity
compared to hunting prints, and due to the
continuing popularity of the sport today.

I. Clark, after Henry Alken, Snr.
British (1785–1851)
National Sports of Great Britain -
Fishing in a Punt
A set of 3 hand coloured aquatints, 1820
7¾ x 11⅜in (19.7 x 29.5cm)
£575–675 *CG*

Robert Cleminson
British (active 1865–68)
Perch on a Riverbank
A pair, signed, oil on canvas
11½ x 15½in (29 x 39.5cm)
£900–1,200 *S(S)*

Thomas Danby, R.W.S.
British (1817–86)
Landscape with Anglers
Signed and dated '1850', oil on canvas
9 x 13in (22.5 x 33cm)
£1,800–2,000 *HLG*

Alfred Egerton Cooper
British (1883–1974)
An Angler with his Catch, and
Salmon Fishing
A pair, both signed with initials,
one inscribed and dated '45', watercolour
and bodycolour
18 x 14in (45 x 35.5cm)
£300–500 *CSK*

Victor Dartiquenave
French (19thC)
Portrait of a Scotch Fisherman
Signed and inscribed, coloured chalks
31 x 23in (79 x 58.5cm)
£2,500–3,500 *S*

William Geddes
British (19thC)
Salmon on a Riverbank
Signed and indistinctly dated, oil on canvas
28 x 43in (71 x 109cm)
£8,000–10,000 *S*

A. Roland Knight
British (19thC)
Coarse Fish
A pair, signed, oil on panel
6¼ x 8¼in (16 x 21cm)
£1,000–1,200 *S(S)*

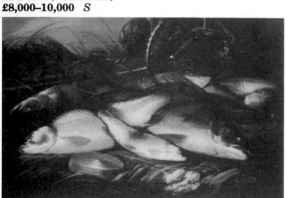

Henry Leonidas Rolfe
English (active 1847–81)
A Still Life with Fish
Signed, oil on canvas
16 x 23⅜in (40.5 x 61cm)
£2,500–2,800 *CGa*

John C. Spencer
American (19th/20thC)
The Finest Catch, a Fishing Still Life
Signed and dated '1897', oil on canvas
16 x 26in (40.6 x 66cm)
£550–750 *SK*

Choo Keng Kwang
Chinese (b1931)
Golden Carp Bring Good Fortune
Signed and dated '93', oil on canvas
32 x 48in (81 x 122cm)
£17,000–18,000 *RMG*

Edwin Julius Detmold
British (1883–1957)
Two Goldfish
Signed, initialled and inscribed, 1926,
etching with aquatint in colours
4½ x 5¼in (11.4 x 13cm)
£250–400 *Bon*

Cyril Mann
British (1911–80)
Upsidedown Lobster
Signed and dated '1969', oil on canvas
17 x 22in (43 x 55.5cm)
£5,500–6,000 *PN*

*The artist chose to paint his lobster living,
rather than depict the unnatural colouration
when cooked. He was well aware that you can
'judge the quality of a painter by his greys.'*

HORSES

'What do we, as a nation, care about books?' bemoaned John Ruskin. 'How much do you think we spend altogether on our libraries, public or private, as compared with what we spend on our horses?' It was not only horses themselves that the English were prepared to spend money on, but equestrian pictures. Britain was the great centre of sporting painting and no gentleman's country home was complete without its horse pictures, equine portraits, hunting scenes and racing pictures.

James Seymour
British (1702–52)
A Racehorse with Jockey up on Newmarket Heath
Signed with initials and dated '1752',
oil on canvas
28¾ x 35⅜in (73 x 91cm)
£47,000–57,000 *S(NY)*

The son of a banker who was a friend of Lely and Wren, Seymour gained contemporary fame as a painter of horses and of racing and hunting scenes. His popularity came from his genius for expressing on canvas the individual characteristics and 'personality' of his horse subjects. Although often 'primitive' in technique, his pictures have vitality and great accuracy of detail.

David Morier
Swiss (c1705–70)
A Prancing Chestnut in the Georgian Riding House, and A Grey led by a Groom
A pair, oil on canvas
20½ x 16½in (52 x 42cm)
£20,000–30,000 *S*

These pictures were probably painted in 1766, and show James Montagu in the Georgian Riding House. James Montagu was appointed Yeoman Rider to George III, Clerk to the King's Mews and, 1790–1812, Equerry to His Majesty's Crown Stable. He was also Clerk of the Stables from 1778 until 1787 to the Prince of Wales, who retained an affection for him and granted him an annual pension. He was still alive in 1804.

George Stubbs, A.R.A.
British (1724–1806)
Ballerina, a Bay Mare belonging to the Earl of Clarendon, in a Landscape
Signed, inscribed and dated '1801',
oil on canvas
25 x 30in (63.5 x 76cm)
£80,000–100,000 *S*

Thomas Villiers, 2nd Earl of Clarendon (1753–1824) of The Grove, Watford, Herefordshire, was Stubbs' most important patron during the last years of his life. He was an M.P. for twelve years (1774–86) until he succeeded his father as Earl. He was a keen hunter, being a founder member of the Hertfordshire Hunt.

Peter Tillemans
Belgian (1684–1734)
A Young Squire on Horseback with a
Dog at heel
Signed, oil on canvas
41½ x 50½in (105.4 x 128.5cm)
£25,000–35,000 *S(NY)*

Tillemans, son of an Antwerp diamond cutter,
was one of the first talented Flemish painters
discovered and brought to England in order
to satisfy the growing demands of the English
aristocracy for equestrian portraits.

Charles Towne
British (1763–1840)
Stallions in a Wooded Landscape
Signed with initials and dated '1808',
oil on board
10¾ x 13in (27.5 x 33cm)
£11,000–12,000 *S(NY)*

I. Clark, after Henry Alken Snr.
British (1785–1851)
The Hunter
Hand coloured aquatint, 1820
6½ x 8¾in (15 x 21.5cm)
£300–400 *CG*

E. G. Hester, after H. Alken, Snr.
British (1785–1851)
Four in Hand, and Tandem
A pair, hand coloured aquatints, c1845
12 x 10in (30.5 x 25cm)
£650–750 *Bur*

Samuel Henry Alken
British (1810–94)
The Finish of the Derby, 1867
Inscribed and dated '1867', oil on canvas
19½ x 32in (49.5 x 81.5cm)
£55,000–65,000 *S*

Henry Barraud
British (1811–74)
Portrait of Thormanby, Winner of the
1860 Epsom Stakes, Epsom with a
Groom in a Stable
Signed, inscribed and dated '1860',
oil on canvas
28 x 36in (71 x 91.5cm)
£8,000–10,000   *S(NY)*

James Barenger
British (1780–1831)
A Chestnut Hunter in a Landscape
Signed, oil on canvas
24½ x 29½in (62.5 x 75cm)
£6,500–7,500   *S(S)*

Circle of John E. Ferneley, Snr.
British (1782–1860)
A pair of horses
Oil of canvas
20 x 26in (51 x 66cm)
£3,500–3,750   *FdeL*

Johannes Hubertus Leonardus de Haas
Flemish (1832–1908)
Donkeys on the Beach at Scheveningen
Signed, oil on panel
13 x 19in (33 x 48cm)
£4,000–5,000 *WG*

Chas. G. Lewis, after Sir Edwin Landseer, R.A.
British (1802–73)
Hunters at Grass
Engraving, 1866
18¼ x 27in (46.5 x 70cm)
£575–675 *CG*

Havell, after J. Pollard
British (1792–1867)
Stage Coach with the News of Peace
Hand coloured aquatint, 1815
12¼ x 17½in (31 x 44cm)
£625–725 *Bur*

George Soper, R.E.
British (1870–1942)
Building the Rick
Watercolour
14½ x 20⅛in (36.5 x 52cm)
£3,250–3,500 *CSG*

William Barns Wollen
British (1857–1936)
The Passing Salute
Signed, oil on canvas
15 x 28in (38 x 71cm)
£5,500–6,000 *HLG*

Keith Bowen
British (20thC)
Training
Signed, pen and ink, 1993
11 x 15in (28 x 38cm)
£200–225 *EAG*

Clare Eva Burton
British (20thC)
Coronation Cup
Tryptich, signed, pastel
11½ x 15in (29 x 38cm)
£1,400–1,500 *RGFA*

Ninetta Butterworth
British (b1922)
The Favourite
Signed and dated '1949', watercolour
9¾ x 13¾in (25 x 35cm)
£350–450 *JC*

Arthur Henry Knighton Hammond
British (1875–1970)
David Copperfield arriving at the
Inn at Yarmouth
Signed, watercolour
17½ x 23½in (45 x 60cm)
£2,650–2,850 *CGa*

Jay Kirkman
British (20thC)
Skewbald Pony in Harness
Signed, conté and pastel on board
31 x 16in (78.5 x 40.5cm)
£4,000–4,500 *CSG*

Stephen Park
British (born c1950)
Lazy Days
Oil on canvas
19½ x 23½in (49.5 x 60cm)
£700–800 *LIO*

Kiddel Monroe
British (20thC)
The original cover design for *'Long Ears'*
by Patricia Lynch
Watercolour
12 x 10in (30.5 x 25cm)
£300–350 *STA*

Harold Septimus Power
New Zealander (1878–1951)
A Pair of Carthorses
Signed, watercolour
13½ x 19½in (33.5 x 49cm)
£2,000–2,250 *CG*

HUNTING

In spite of the growing lobby against hunting, both inside and outside Parliament, there is still a market for hunting prints and pictures, and the finest works are themselves chased by collectors. 'Naturally I wouldn't put a plate of the kill all by itself in the gallery window,' says Nick Potter of Burlington Gallery, 'but I would display it as part of a set in its proper context.'

Sporting prints were generally issued in sets of four, six, eight or even as many as twelve. Though each plate has its individual value, a full set attracts the highest premium, and the quality examples are becoming increasingly rare. 'Bearing in mind earliness of impression, condition and all the relevant qualifying factors,' notes Potter, 'it is jolly hard to find a very good set of sporting prints.'

Henry Calvert
British (1798–1869)
The Meet of the Buck Hounds
Oil on canvas
46 x 80in (117 x 203cm)
£30,000–40,000 *S*

Major Godfrey Douglas Giles
British (1857–1923)
Disappointment, and Anticipation
A pair, oil on canvas
12 x 14in (30.5 x 35.5cm)
£5,500–6,500 *JN*

George Wright
British (1860–1942)
The Meet at Avebury Manor
Signed, oil on canvas
9½ x 14¼in (24 x 36.5cm)
£4,000–5,000 *C*

William Webb
British (19thC)
Charles III, Baron of Southampton,
Master of the Grafton Hunt
Signed, oil on canvas
36½ x 51in (92.5 x 51cm)
£25,000–30,000 *S(NY)*

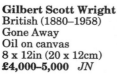

Gilbert Scott Wright
British (1880–1958)
Gone Away
Oil on canvas
8 x 12in (20 x 12cm)
£4,000–5,000 *JN*

SPORTS & GAMES

Golfing pictures are always extremely in demand. The sport is internationally popular, and many of those who play are likely to have the money to collect pictures, although early portrayals of the game are extremely rare. 'You can only reckon on two or three reasonably important pictures coming on to the market in any year,' notes Nick Potter of Burlington Gallery in London, specialist in sporting prints and pictures. As Potter explains, golf only expanded in Britain with the development of the railway system, which enabled players, as well as artists, to get to the courses. 19thC golfing pictures command a large premium and landscape painters, whose works generally achieve only modest sums in the salerooms, can make record prices if the landscape depicted happens to be a golf course. The scarcity of good quality,

early works has inspired many contemporary artists to turn to the subject of golf. 'Ability varies enormously,' warns Potter, who also deals in 20thC golfing prints and pictures. 'You have to sort through a lot of driftwood to find the best pictures.'

Excluding horse and hunting subjects, the general problem for collectors of sporting pictures is that because many sports developed too late to be portrayed by the great generation of sporting painters and print makers, supply easily outstrips demand. 'Rugby ...' sighs Nick Potter, sadly, 'we could easily sell 150 times the number of pictures that we can get our hands on. Tennis is the same. The first lawn tennis club in England didn't open till the 1870s, and apart from real tennis and rackets prints, there are very few early portrayals of the game.'

Adriaen Pietersz. van de Venne
Dutch (1589–1662)
Elck sijn tijt-verdrijff - To each
his own pastime
Signed, red chalk, partially traced verso
in red-brown chalk and wash
14 x 17¾in (35 x 45cm)
£85,000–100,000 *S(Am)*

This remarkable composition works on several levels. On the one hand it is a fascinating early portrayal of the game of shuttlecock. As the title suggests, however, the work also carries an allegorical message, and this is supplemented by the addition of traditional vanitas elements: the skeleton (figure of death), the discarded playing cards and the overturned drinking glasses, all signify the emptiness of earthly pleasures.

Isaac Cullin
British (19thC)
Jockeys weighing in prior to the Waterloo,
Sandown Park
Signed, oil on canvas
30 x 40½in (76 x 103cm)
£20,000–30,000 *S(NY)*

Roberto Domingo y Fallola
Spanish (b1867)
In the Bullring
Signed and dated '1913', oil on canvas
29 x 41in (74 x 104cm)
£6,000–7,000 *S*

Raoul Dufy
French (1877–1953)
Les Turfistes à Ascot
Signed and titled, watercolour, 1938
19¼ x 25¼in (49 x 64cm)
£55,000–65,000 *C*

Frank Elim
British (early 20thC)
The Polo Match
Signed and dated '1914', watercolour and
bodycolour on brown paper
30½ x 21½in (77.5 x 55cm)
£2,500–3,500 *C*

John Strickland Goodall, R.I., R.B.A.
British (b1908)
Henley
Signed, watercolour
5½ x 14in (14 x 35.5cm)
£1,350–1,450 *SRB*

*Goodall started his career as a portrait and
landscape painter and later turned his hand
to Edwardian scenes, for which he is now
famous. His subjects include beach scenes,
tennis, cricket, country walks, nannies and
regattas. He has been illustrating books
for some fifteen years, and many of his
works have been made into greetings cards
and puzzles.*

Irving Levow
American (b1902)
Handball Players
Signed and dated '1939', oil on canvas
16¼ x 24¼in (41 x 61.5cm)
£900–1,100 *CNY*

Marguerite Rousseau
Belgian (1888–1948)
Jeu de Tennis
Signed 'C. Minot', oil on board
15 x 21¾in (38.5 x 55cm)
£4,200–5,000 *C*
*Marguerite Rousseau used 'C. Minot' as
a pseudonym.*

British School (20thC)
Golfer in a Tricorn Hat
Signed 'Thos. Wolfe', oil on canvas
40 x 30in (101.5 x 76cm)
£900–1,100 *SK*

Bill Waugh
British (20thC)
The Old Bridge, St Andrew's
Signed and remarqued print
12½ x 20in (32 x 51cm)
£100–135 *Bur*

Cricket

Whereas golf has an international market, the demand for cricket is largely British based, but nonetheless enthusiastic for that. 'We have probably more collectors for cricketing pictures than for any other subject,' claims Nick Potter of Burlington Gallery.

F. Hayman
British (1708–76)
Cricket
Copperline engraving, c1745
9½ x 13½in (24 x 34.5cm)
£1,000–1,200 *Bur*

Henry Edridge, A.R.A.
British (1769–1821)
Portrait of Edward William Barnard
Signed and dated 1802, grey wash over pencil
11¼ x 8in (28.5 x 20cm)
£1,400–1,800 *S*

Archibald S. Wortley
British (1849–1905)
W.G. Grace at the Wicket
Photogravure, 1890
22½ x 15¼in (56 x 39cm)
£750–850 *Bur*

Not only the archetypal portait of W.G. Grace but also one of the classic images of the game. The original oil painting hangs at Lord's.

After Rev. Tatton Winter
British (19thC)
Cricket Match
Tinted lithograph
11½ x 14¼in (29.5 x 36cm)
£300–375 *Bur*

David Gentleman
British (20thC)
Lord's Pavilion, England v. Rest of the World, 1987, Bicentenary Year
Limited edition print, signed by all players concerned
11½ x 15¾in (29 x 40cm)
£1,300–1,600 *HC*

WILDLIFE & ANIMALS

In a society increasingly conscious of 'green' issues, there appears to be a growing demand for wildlife pictures. June 1994 saw Christie's first ever sale devoted to wildlife pictures, and an auction record of £100,000 for 'African Children', a David Shepherd painting of two zebras. In general, throughout the sale, it was the quality works that performed best, with private collectors prominent among the bidders. The auction was held in conjunction with a number of wildlife charities and a proportion of the proceeds were donated to conservation and education projects. Christie's were pleased with the overall result and plan to repeat the sale next year.

Richard Ansdell, R.A.
British (1815–85)
Dik Dik on a Cliff Top
Signed and dated '1840', oil on canvas
48 x 72in (122 x 183cm)
£19,000–25,000 *C*

Carl Borromäus Andreas Ruthart
German (c1630–c1703)
Studies of a Red Deer yearling, and other animals and birds
Oil on canvas
19 x 30in (48.5 x 76.5cm)
£60,000–80,000 *C*

John Woodhouse Audubon
American (1812–62)
Mountain Brook Minks
Inscribed, oil on canvas
21¾ x 26⅜in (55 x 68cm)
£28,000–35,000 *S(NY)*

Rosa Bonheur
French (1822–99)
Tête de Lion (King of the Desert)
Signed, oil on canvas
39 x 37in (99 x 94cm)
£95,000–115,000 *S(NY)*

Charles Edward Brittan
British (1837–88)
Two Elephants
Signed and dated '1866', watercolour heightened with gum arabic
9½ x 16in (24 x 40.5cm)
£300–500 *C*

Lilian Cheviot
British (active 1894–1902)
Tigers stalking their Prey
Signed, oil on canvas
30 x 50in (76 x 127cm)
£14,000–16,000 *C*

Eric Pape
American (1837–1915)
Camel Resting, Pyramids at Giza beyond
Stamped on reverse, oil on canvas
12¼ x 21⅛in (31 x 53.5cm)
£1,800–2,200 *SK*

Carl Rungius
American/German (1869–1959)
The Last of the Herd
Signed and titled, oil on canvas, 1900
30 x 40in (76 x 101.5cm)
£24,000–30,000 *S(NY)*

This picture was painted near Cosa, Wyoming, west of Fremont Peak.

Frank Paton
British (1856–1909)
A Leveret
Signed and dated '1905', watercolour
8 x 6½in (20 x 16.5cm)
£450–550 *HOLL*

Ferdinand Schebek
Austrian (1875–1949)
A Lioness with her Cubs
Signed and dated '1913', oil on canvas
28 x 39¼in (71 x 100cm)
£7,000–9,000 *C*

August Ternes
German (1872–1938)
Tigers in a Jungle Clearing
Signed, oil on canvas
39½ x 46¼in (100 x 117.5cm)
£14,000–16,000 *C*

Géza Vastagh
Hungarian (b1868)
Lions Stalking
Signed, oil on canvas
53 x 47¼in (135 x 120cm)
£11,000–13,000 *C*

P. J. Crook
British (20thC)
The Lion
Signed, oil on board
16in (40.5cm) square
£800–1,500 *GK*

Andrew Christian
British (20thC)
Mouseterpiece
Signed, watercolour
19 x 14in (48 x 35.5cm)
£550–650 *GK*

Mick Cawston
British (20thC)
Foxes
Signed, oil on canvas
12 x 10in (30 x 25cm)
£1,000–1,200 *SMi*

Charles Newington
British (b1950)
Beast II
Pastel and sfumato
22 x 33in (56 x 84cm)
£500–575 *RGFA*

*The earliest known paintings and carvings
of wild animals appear on the walls and
ceilings of caves once occupied by prehistoric
man. Variously interpreted, these images
appear to be concerned with hunting rituals.
Charles Newington's work is a tribute to these
painters, and a record of his response to his
first encounter with prehistoric cave paintings
in the Dordogne.*

Henry Moore
British (1898–1986)
Leopard
Signed, etching with aquatint and
roulette, 1981
10 x 7½in (25 x 19cm)
£900–975 *WO*

Spencer Roberts
British (20thC)
Kopje
Signed, gouache
21 x 29in (53 x 73.5cm)
£1,500–1,600 *RGFA*

David Shepherd
British (b1931)
African Children
Signed and dated '1967',
oil on canvas
27 x 49¼in (68.5 x 125cm)
£120,000–140,000 *CSK*

the origins of phrases:

to be caught on the horns of a Dalai Lama

Simon Drew
British (b1952)
The Origins of Phrases
Signed and inscribed, pen, ink and pencil
8 x 12in (20 x 30.5cm)
£400–450 *CBL*

John Davis
British (b1928)
The Chief Leaps to his Feet
Watercolour
6½ x 6in (16.5 x 15cm)
£225–275 *CBL*

Peter Firmin
British (20thC)
Ivor the Engine
Watercolour
8in (20cm) square
£225–250 *RGFA*

Isaac Cruikshank
British (1756–1811)
The Old Commodore
Watercolour with pen, ink and pencil
6¼ x 9¾in (16 x 24cm)
£1,250–1,450 *CBL*

r. **Raymond Briggs**
British (1934)
Light from the Freezer
Celluloid
7½ x 9½in (18.5 x 24cm)
£550–650 *CBL*

Paul Cox
British (b1957)
His Excited Friend Shook Out the Table Cloth...
Inscribed with title, pen, ink and watercolour
18 x 14in (45.5 x 36cm)
£750–850 *CBL*

Erté
Russian (1892–1990)
The Alphabet
Signed, 26 designs, gouache on paper
22 x 14½in (56 x 37cm)
£1,000,000–1,125,000 *GRO*

Harry Rountree
British (1878–1950)
The Picnic
Signed, watercolour with pencil
14½ x 10½in (37 x 26.5cm)
£750–850 *CBL*

Joan Hickson
British (20thC)
Pat Began to feel Muddled. He made notes on the
back of an envelope
Watercolour and bodycolour with pen and ink
8 x 9in (20 x 22.5cm)
£300–350 *CBL*

Betty Swanwick, R.A., R.W.S.
British (1915–89)
The Lost Wilderness
Signed and dated '74', watercolour
19 x 14½in (48 x 37cm)
£3,500–3,750 *CBL*

l. **Shaun Magher**
British (20thC)
Biggleswade Flushpenney
Watercolour, c1989
18 x 27in (46 x 69cm)
£1,500–2,000 *LIO*

Kay Nielsen
Danish (b1868)
Stop Prince! You Cannot Run Away
Signed and dated '1930', inscribed on a label on back
panel, watercolour
11 x 8in (28 x 20cm)
£5,500–6,500 *Bea*

Kate Cameron, R.S.W., A.R.E., F.R.S.A.
British (1874–1965)
Rock-a-Bye Baby
Signed, watercolour with pen and ink
7½ x 11in (19 x 28cm)
£2,500–2,750 *CBL*

Susan Beatrice Pearse
British (active 1910–37)
The Water Babies
Watercolour
13 x 9in (33 x 22.5cm)
£350–400 *HI*

Sydney Seymour Lucas
British (1888–1954)
Little People of the Moon
Signed, watercolour with bodycolour
1'6¾ x 13⅛in (42.5 x 34.5cm)
£3,250–3,500 *CBL*

Henry Meynell Rheam
British (1859–1920)
The Princess and the Elf
Signed with monogram, dated '1903', watercolour
10 x 14in (25.5 x 35.5cm)
£1,200–1,400 *GG*

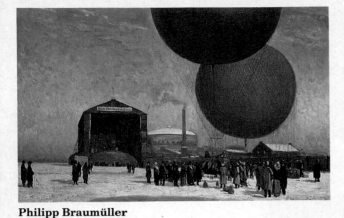

Philipp Braumüller
German? (early 20thC)
Ballooning at the Berliner Verein für Luftfahrt
Signed, oil on canvas
29⅛ x 44¼in (75 x 112.5cm)
£13,000–15,000 *C*

Lionel Edwards
British (1878–1966)
The British Olympic Equestrian Team
Signed, dated '1952', oil on canvas
24 x 36in (61 x 91.5cm)
£10,500–12,000 *C*

Robert Nixon
British (b1955)
Duchess of Gloucester at Speed
Oil on canvas
20 x 16in (51 x 41cm)
£200–300 *WOT*

Roger Brown
American (b1941)
Trailer Park, Truck Stop
Oil on canvas
47 x 59in (119 x 149.5cm)
£6,000–7,000 *S(NY)*

l. **Michael Coulter**
British (20thC)
Leaving Corfe Castle
Watercolour
13½ x 18in
(34.5 x 45.5cm)
£600–675 *PHG*

Cyril Power
British (1872–1951)
The Tube Train
Signed, titled in pencil, linocut, c1934
12½in (32cm) square
£5,500–6,500 *P*

l. **Peter Hearsey**
British (20thC)
Targa Florio
Gouache
24 x 16in (61 x 41cm)
£650–750 *JAR*

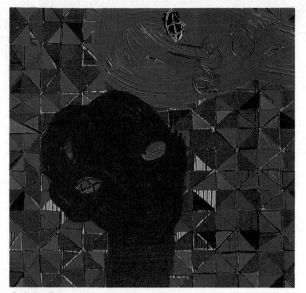

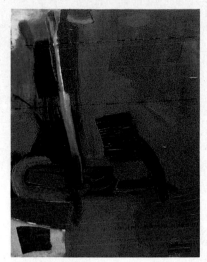

Osi Audu
Nigerian/British (20thC)
The Maiden and Her Suitor
Oil and acrylic on canvas, 1992
40½in (102cm) square
£1,750–2,000 *SG*

John Bischoff
British (b1963)
Untitled
Oil on canvas
60½ x 46½in (153 x 117cm)
£1,600–1,800 *FT*

r. **Shona Barr**
Scottish (b1965)
In The Shade
Oil on Canvas
36in (91.5cm) square
£1,750–2,000 *FCG*

Peter Armstrong
British (20thC)
Peeling Off
Oil on canvas
28 x 34in (71 x 86cm)
£450–550 *VCG*

Karel Appel
Dutch (b1921)
Face
Signed and dated, oil and
gouache on paper laid down on
canvas, 14 x 11in (36 x 28cm)
£3,500–4,500 *CSK*

David Blackburn
British (b1939)
Red Landscape
Pastel on paper
19 x 24in (48 x 61cm)
£1,500–1,600 *HaG*

Alan Cox
British (b1941)
Kiss Whiskey
Lithograph, one of an edition of 12, 1989
20 x 28in (51 x 71cm)
£150–200 *GPS*

Sandro Chia
Italian (b1943)
Untitled
Signed and dated '89', gouache, charcoal and white chalk
65½ x 43½in (166 x 110cm)
£12,000–14,000 *CNY*

l. **Peter Coviello**
British (20thC)
Untitled
Mixed media on paper
20 x 30in (51 x 76.5cm)
£500–600 *FT*

Liza Gough Daniels
British (b1962)
Untitled
Egg tempera on gesso, on panel, 1993
17¾ x 21¾in (45 x 55cm)
£700–800 *FT*

Alexander Calder
American (1898–1976)
La Vague Rouge
Woven signature and Pinton tapestry
mark, aubusson tapestry,
61½ x 41¼in (156 x 105cm)
£5,000–6,000 *C*

Dasto
Swiss (20thC)
The Refuge
Signed, oil on board, 1988
24 x 18in (61.5 x 46cm)
£700–800 *MTG*

Kenneth Draper
British (b1944)
Interior
Pastel on paper
20 x 18in (51 x 46cm)
£1,600–1,800 *HaG*

Dan Flavin
American (b1933)
Untitled
Blue and red fluorescent lights, c1970
7¼ x 48 x 2½in (18 x 122 x 6.5cm)
£15,000–17,000 *(CNY)*

D. Drey
British (b1962)
Madness of the Squatter
Oil on hardboard
24½ x 34½in (62 x 87.5cm)
£800–900 *FT*

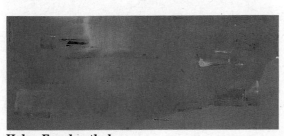

Helen Frankenthaler
American (b1928)
Sea Green
Signed, titled and dated '1977', acrylic on canvas
45 x 107¾in (114 x 274cm)
£30,000–35,000 *CNY*

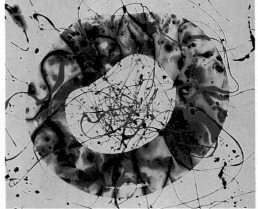

Sam Francis
American (b1923)
Untitled
Signed and dated '73', acrylic and oil on canvas
34 x 42in (86 x 106.5cm)
£28,000–32,000 *S(NY)*

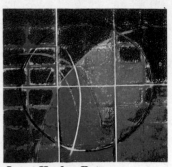

Jonet Harley-Peters
British (20thC)
Deeply Blue with Red
Pastel on constructed paper
39½ x 44⅛in (101 x 112cm)
£750–850 *FT*

Philip Guston
American (1913–80)
As It Goes
Oil on canvas, 1978
76 x 102in (193 x 259cm)
£300,000–350,000 *S(NY)*

r. **Martin Gayford**
British (20thC)
Rapture
Acrylic and paper
on canvas
67½ x 56in (172 x 142cm)
£1,300–1,500 *FT*

David Hockney
British (b1937)
Piscine
Initialled and dated '78', liquid dyes and coloured
pulp applied to pressed coloured paper pulp
72 x 85⅛in (182.5 x 217cm)
£220,000–240,000 *S(NY)*

Paul Hawdon
British (b1953)
The Ladder
Signed and dated '1991', oil on canvas
45 x 60in (114 x 152cm)
£1,750–2,000 *Mer*

Friedrich Stowasser Hundertwasser
Austrian (b1928)
La Picandière
Signed and dated four times '1960', oil, gouache and
gold paint on paper mounted on burlap
51¼ x 38in (130 x 96.5cm)
£70,000–85,000 *C*

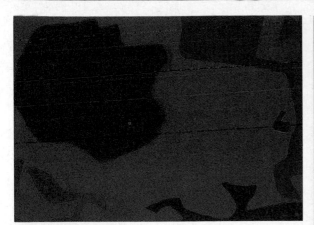

Patrick Heron
British (b1920)
November V: 1972
Signed, titled and inscribed on reverse, gouache
22¾ x 31½in (58 x 80cm)
£1,800–2,200 *P*

Paul Klee
Swiss (1879–1940)
Komposition mit Dreiecken
Signed, dated and numbered '1918.8',
watercolour on joined paper laid down
12 x 8½in (30.5 x 21cm)
£135,000–150,000 *C*

Roy Lichtenstein
American (b1923)
Sunrise
Signed and dated '65' on
reverse, enamel on steel, one
of an edition of 5
22½ x 36in (57 x 92cm)
£25,000–35,000 *S(NY)*

Paul Jenkins
American (b1923)
Phenomena Kanari
Signed, titled and dated
'1979', acrylic on canvas
35 x 28in (89 x 71cm)
£2,750–3,500 *C*

Fernand Léger
French (1881–1955)
Trois Personnages (Esquisse Pour Les Quatre Personnages)
Signed and dated '20', oil on canvas
21½ x 25½in (54.5 x 65cm)
£790,000–850,000 *S(NY)*

El Loko
West African (20thC)
Evolution
Mixed media on canvas
67 x 65in (170 x 165cm)
£3,750–4,000 *SG*

Piet Mondrian
Dutch (1872–1944)
Composition with Yellow, Red and Blue
Oil on canvas
19¾ x 14in (50 x 36cm)
£600,000–650,000 *S(NY)*

Bruce McLean
Scottish (b1944)
Thin Red Pipe Smoker
Etching, on Atlantis paper, 1985
46 x 34½in (116 x 88cm)
£550–650 *GPS*

Matta
Chilean (b1911)
Untitled
Oil on canvas, 1957
32 x 39½in (81 x 100cm)
£48,000–52,000 *S*

l. **Joan Miró**
Spanish (1893–1983)
La Guerre: Ubu Roi X
Signed, gouache and watercolour over
lithography on paper
16¼ x 24½in (41 x 62.5cm)
£30,000–40,000 *S(NY)*

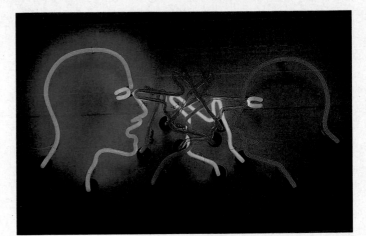

Carey Mortimer
British (1962)
Pot
Fresco and gesso
18 x 8in (46 x 20cm)
£175–200 *FT*

Bruce Nauman
American (b1941)
Double Poke in the Eye II
Aluminium box and neon light
24 x 36 x 11in (61.5 x 91.5 x 28cm)
£18,000–20,000 *CNY*

Executed in 1985. This is from an edition of 40 with eight artist's proofs.

Margaret O'Hagan
Irish (b1957)
Surface Plane
Acrylic on canvas
48in (122cm) square
£1,200–1,400 *SOL*

Walter Nessler
German (b1963)
Assemblage
Collage
31½ x 28in (80 x 71cm)
£1,000–1,200 *JDG*

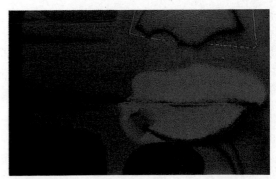

Stephen Powell
British (20thC)
Untitled
Oil on canvas
16 x 22in (41 x 56cm)
£350–400 *OLG*

Ed Paschke
American (b1939)
Coquette
Signed and dated '89', oil on linen
24 x 38in (61 x 96.5cm)
£6,500–7,500 *CNY*

Francis Picabia
French (1879–1953)
Composition
Signed, gouache on paper laid down on
board, 1939
21 x 17¼in (53 x 44cm)
£30,000–35,000 *S(NY)*

Jim Pattison
Scottish (b1955)
Screens
Screenprint, on Somerset texture paper, 1989
43½ x 28¾in (109.5 x 73cm)
£190–215 *GPS*

Serge Poliakoff
Russian (1900–69)
Composition Abstraite Rouge, Jaune et Gris
Signed, oil on board
31 x 25in (79 x 63.5cm)
£35,000–40,000 *S*

l. **Christopher Reed**
British (b1962)
Blue Teapot
Oil on canvas
22 x 26in (56 x 66cm)
£700–800 *FT*

Mark Rothko
Black Stripe
American (1903–70)
Signed and dated '57', oil and magna on canvas
68 x 38½in (172.5 x 97cm)
£600,000–650,000 *S(NY)*

Kenny Scharf
American (b1958)
Save the Jungle
Signed, titled and dated 'Kenny Scharf 1987 Brazil Save the Jungle', oil and acrylic on canvas
90½ x 86½in (229 x 220cm)
£5,000–7,000 *CNY*

Edwina Sandys
English/American (20thC)
Head on Chest
Signed, dated '1990', oil on canvas
40 x 30in (101.5 x 76cm)
£800–1,000 *BRG*

Sean Scully
American (b1946)
Sound
Signed, dated '87', oil on linen, in four panels
96in (243.5cm) square
£50,000–60,000 *S(NY)*

Varvara Shavrova
Russian (b1968)
Two on the Bench, Spring
Oil on canvas
32 x 40in (81 x 101.5cm)
£800–1,000 *FT*

Gérard Schneider
Swiss (1896–1986)
Composition
Signed and dated '70', acrylic
41¾ x 28¾in (106 x 73cm)
£5,000–6,000 *C*

Duncan Shanks, R.S.A., R.S.W., R.G.I.
Scottish (20thC)
Fragments of Memory
Mixed media
38½ x 51in (97 x 129.5cm)
£3,000–3,500 *RB*

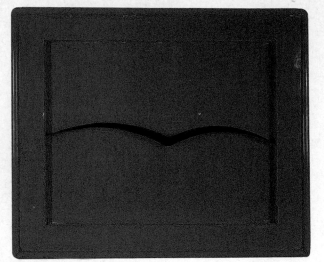

Robert Therrien
American (b1947)
Yellow Seagull
Initialled on reverse, enamel on steel, 1990
98 x 114 x 8in (249 x 289.5 x 20cm)
£9,000–11,000 *CNY*

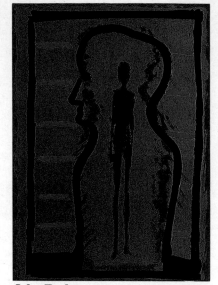

John Taylor
Scottish (b1936)
Within
Screenprint, on Arches paper, 1992
29⅓ x 22¼in (74.5 x 56.5cm)
£125–150 *GPS*

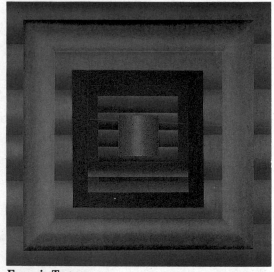

Francis Tansey
Irish (b1959)
Lighting Tubular
Acrylic on canvas
44in (111.5cm) square
£2,000–2,200 *SOL*

William Wilson
West African (20thC)
Le Potentat
Pastel on paper, 1993
25½ x 19¾in (65 x 50cm)
£750–850 *SG*

l. **Joaquín Torres-Garcia**
Uruguayan (1874–1949)
Constructivo con Reloj
Initialled and dated '36', oil on canvas
12 x 14in (30.5 x 36cm)
£45,000–55,000 *S(NY)*

Arderne Clarence
British (active 1908–37)
Fishing Boats Off a Jetty
Signed, watercolour
5 x 9in (12.5 x 23cm)
£90–100 *JA*

Published by Sir Samuel Rush
British (19thC)
For his '*A Critical Inquiry into
Ancient Armour*', 1824, a hand
coloured aquatint heightened in
gold, 'A Knight Armed for the Bond',
12½ x 9½in (31.5 x 24cm)
£8–12 *SRAB*

W. E. Whitty
British (19thC)
Naïve Marine Scenes
A pair, signed, watercolour
10¾ x 7¾ and 9 x 5in (27 x 19.5 and 23 x 12.5cm)
£75–90 *MBA*

Edward Orme
British (18th/19thC)
Drunkeness
Copper plate engraving with original hand
colouring, published June 1810, London
6½ x 8½in (16 x 21cm)
£50–60 *SRAB*

S. Holden
British (19thC)
For *Paxton's Magazine of Botany*, 1846
Ornithogalum aureum
Lithograph with original hand colour
9 x 6in (23 x 15cm)
£35–40 *SRAB*

Diane C. Parkinson
Irish (born c1870)
Country Lane with Sheep
Watercolour
6½ x 9in (16 x 23cm)
£30–35 *STA*

Pamela Davis
British (20thC)
Anemones
Acrylic/ivorine
3 x 4in (7.5 x 10cm)
£95–110 *TLB*

Trevor Price
British (20thC)
The Owl and the Pussycat
Etching in five colours
7¼ x 9½in (18.5 x 24cm)
£50–60 *CCA*

Roger Harris
British (20thC)
Dusk
Signed, mezzotint
8 x 9in (20 x 23cm)
£50–60 *TFA*

M. Gauss-Keown
British (20thC)
Welsh Landscape
Watercolour
10 x 7in (25 x 17.5cm)
£70–80 *MGK*

Jacob Drew
British (20thC)
Suggestion for Stage Set
Signed and dated 'April 23. 32', ink, pencil
and gouache
7 x 9in (17.5 x 23cm)
£85–95 *MBA*

Jenny Webb
British (20thC)
Tulips and Persian Rug
Watercolour and gouache
16 x 20in (41 x 51cm)
£70–80 *LS*

TRANSPORT

Thomas Musgrave Joy
British (1812–66)
The Charing Cross to Bank Omnibus
Signed with monogram, oil on canvas
30 x 25in (76 x 64cm)
£12,000–14,000 *S(NY)*

English School (19thC)
Ascent of Mr Green from the Beach between
Brighton and Shoreham
Inscribed as title and dated 'Augt 17./1843',
pencil and watercolour heightened
with white
5 x 6¾in (12.5 x 17cm)
Together with seven more drawings of views
on the South Coast
£750–950 *CSK*

Marcus Stone, R.A. (1840–1921) **after William Powell Frith, R.A.** (1819–1909)
British
The Railway Station
Signed and dated '1862', oil on canvas
28¼ x 60¼in (72 x 153cm)
£135,000–160,000 *C*

This is a version of Frith's famous painting 'The Railway Station' (Royal Holloway College). The third of the artist's great panoramas of modern life, succeeding 'Ramsgate Sands' (Royal Collection) and 'Derby Day' (Tate Gallery), the original picture was commissioned by the London art dealer Louis Victor Flatow in 1860 for the considerable sum of £4,500, including copyright. The scene is set on Paddington station, the terminus of the Great Western Railway built a decade earlier by Isambard Kingdom Brunel and Matthew Digby Wyatt; and the crowd of over 60 figures includes a number of the anecdotal groups for which Frith was renowned. The picture took two years to paint, its progress being much reported in the press for a public whose interest had been aroused by Frith's earlier successes. Frith waived his right to exhibit it at the Royal Academy for a further £750, and it was shown from April to September 1862 at Flatow's Gallery in the Haymarket, where it was seen by over 21,000 people. The art critic Tom Taylor produced a pamphlet explaining it in detail. It was also exhibited at Hayward and Leggatt's premises in Cornhill before being taken on a tour of provincial towns.
Not surprisingly for such a popular picture, 'The Railway Station' exists in several versions. In 1980, the present example caused some scandal when it was offered by Sotheby's as an autograph version by Frith himself. Two weeks before the sale, Victorian art expert Jeremy Maas issued a memorandum, expressing the opinion, backed up by considerable evidence, that the replica was by Marcus Stone. Offered by Christie's in a recent sale, the work was attributed to Stone.

Rowland Emmett
British (1906–90)
One of Those Magnificent Men in Their
Flying Machines
Signed, oil on canvas
28¾ x 36in (73 x 91.5cm)
£2,200–2,700 *P*

*Rowland Emmett's father was an amateur
inventor, a talent that the artist himself
inherited, registering his first patent for an
invention at the age of 13. Combining his
artistic and scientific talents, Emmett worked
as an industrial draughtsman whilst at the
same time contributing to Punch. He
specialised in creating fantastical machines,
parodies of the technical age, which in the
1950s were turned into 3-dimensional objects.
In 1967, Emmett produced the designs for the
film 'Chitty Chitty Bang Bang'.*

Richard Estes
American (20thC)
Urban Landscapes III: Subway Car
Silkscreen printed in colours, 1981,
signed in pencil
19¾ x 27½in (50 x 70cm)
£700–900 *S*

Peter Hopkins
American (b1911)
Bus Depot
Signed, oil on canvas
20 x 24in (51 x 61cm)
£4,500–5,500 *S(NY)*

Lyonel Feininger
German (1871–1956)
Wartende Lokomotive mit Schlepptender
Signed and dated '08', Indian ink on
paper, 1908
6 x 9½in (15 x 24cm)
£4,000–5,000 *S(NY)*

Edward KcKnight Kauffer
British (1890–1954)
See Britain First on Winter Shell -
The New Forest
Lithograph, in colours, 1931
30 x 45in (76 x 114cm)
£300–500 *P*

**Lynton Lamb, L.G., S.W.E., S.L.L.P.,
F.R.S.A., R.D.**
British (1907–77)
'Stand firm,' said Peter, 'and wave like mad!...
Pen and ink illustration in E. Nesbit's
The Railway Children'
6¾ x 4½in (17 x 11.5cm)
£300–350 *CBL*

Cedric Morris
British (1889–1982)
Gardeners Prefer Shell
Lithograph, in colours
30 x 45in (76 x 114cm)
£180–300 *P*

J. Neave
British (20thC)
BP Shell Domestic Fuel Service
Van Making a Home Delivery
Signed and dated '61', gouache
over pencil
14 x 22in (36 x 56cm)
£150–250 *P*

*Many of the pictures from the BP
collection auctioned at Phillips
were under £1,000. Prices realised
were for the most part extremely
modest with many lots either
falling below or just making their
low estimates.*

Robert Nixon
British (b1965)
Leeds 1950s - Childhood Memories
Oil on canvas
16 x 20in (41 x 51cm)
£200–300 *WOT*

> **Miller's is a price GUIDE
> not a price LIST**

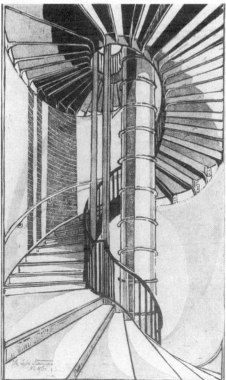

Kirill Sokolov
Russian (b1930)
Goswick Beach with Tractors
Signed, oil on board, 1991
25 x 34in (64 x 86cm)
£1,400–1,500 *VCG*

Cyril Power
British (1872–1951)
The Tube Staircase
Linocut printed in colours, c1929,
signed and titled in pencil
20¼ x 13in (51.5 x 33cm)
£1,800–2,500 *S*

THEATRE & FASHION DESIGNS

Charles de Sousy Ricketts, R.A.
British (1866–1931)
Design for the Drop Curtain of a Play
Black chalk, watercolour heightened with
touches of bodycolour
8 x 10½in (20 x 26cm)
£1,500–2,500 *C*

*Stage design occupied a large proportion of
Ricketts' time from the mid-1900s, when he
produced his first designs for plays by Yeats,
Binyon and Sturge Moore. The present
drawing is for a drop curtain and symbolises
'The Triumph of Faith.' The play has not been
identified, but John Masefield's* Philip the
King, *directed by Harley Granville-Barker
at Covent Garden as a charity matinée in
November 1914, seems a possibility. Ricketts
designed the sets and costumes, as well as
painting 'two pictures by El Greco for Philip
to pray to.'*

Sir Cecil Beaton
British (1904–80)
Set Design - Madame at Rest
Signed, watercolour, bodycolour,
wash, pen and ink
18½ x 11¾in (47 x 30cm)
£750–950 *CSK*

Alexandre Nikolaevich Benois
Russian (1870–1960)
Costume Design for Marguerite in La
Dame aux Camélias
Signed, dated '1923', and inscribed '1er
acte'; watercolour and pencil on paper
18¾ x 12½in (48 x 32cm)
£650–850 *S(NY)*

Christian Bérard
French (1902–49)
(1) Tenue de Plage, Schiaparelli
Stamped with the Atelier mark, watercolour,
gouache, Indian ink and wash, together with
three other fashion designs
14 x 12¼in (36 x 31cm)
£2,500–4,000 *S*

Eugène Berman
Russian (1899–1972)
Décor design for 'Don Giovanni'
Signed and dated '1957', watercolour and
Indian ink on paper heightened with white
6 x 8in (15 x 20cm)
£1,300–1,600 *S(NY)*

*Designed for the production of Giuseppe
Verdi's* Don Giovanni *at the Metropolitan
Opera, New York in 1957.*

Jean Cocteau
French (1889–1963)
Lady Macbeth
Signed on small piece of attached paper
'Jean', brush, pen and black ink on paper
13¼ x 10½in (34 x 26cm)
£550–750 *C*

Erté
Russian (1892–1990)
Symphony in Black
Signed, gouache on paper
14½ x 10½in (37 x 26.5cm)
£27,000–28,000 *GRO*

*The Russian born fashion designer's real
name was Romain de Tirtoff. The pseudonym
Erté was composed from his two initials 'R T',
pronounced in the French and Russian
manner. He adopted this name to protect his
family who thought fashion an undignified
career for a member of a naval family. In
spite of early setbacks - the first Paris
dressmaker who employed the young emigre,
dismissed him after only a month informing
him that he had no gift for costume
whatsoever - Erté rose to become one of the
great fashion and theatrical designers of the
20thC. His name is now synonymous with 20s
and 30s style.*
*Erté loved the idea of being able to design
opulent and fantastic clothes for men as well
as women. 'What is there more saddening
than to see a wordly gathering where all the
women are beautifully dressed and
shimmering with jewels and colour - and the
men all in black looking like an army of head
waiters', he wrote in the early 1970s. 'Since
the 1920s I have been preaching for a radical
change in men's attire... my patience and
efforts are now being rewarded. At last men
have again come to understand that they have
as much right to be handsome as have women
to be beautiful.'*

Erté
Russian (1892–1990)
Perspective
Signed, stamped and inscribed,
gouache and pencil on paper
15¼ x 11in (39 x 28cm)
£3,500–4,500 *S(NY)*

Ronald William Fordham Searle
British (b1920)
Set Design for Wild Thyme, St. Pandora Cross, Act I
Signed, inscribed with title and dated '1955', pen, ink,
watercolour and bodycolour
17 x 24½in (43 x 62cm)
£1,000–1,250 *CBL*

Constantin Alexeievitch Korovine
Russian (1861–1939)
Four Costume Designs for Prince Igor
Three signed, each titled and variously
inscribed with names of characters and with
instructions to the dressmaker, watercolour,
ink, pencil, silver and gold paint on paper
15 x 10½in (38 x 26.5cm)
£700–900 *S(NY)*

Fernand Léger
French (1881–1955)
Etude pour une Décor
Gouache on paper laid down on paper
4in (10cm) square
£4,500–5,500 *CNY*

Anatol' Petritskyi
Ukranian (20thC)
Costume Design for a Persian Slave Girl
Indistinctly annotated 'silk... silk... satin' in
Cyrillic, collage, watercolour, gouache, brush
and Indian ink, gold paint, cloth and pencil
on paper laid down on card
25 x 17¾in (63.5 x 45cm)
£1,800–2,200 *S*

Pavel Tchelitchew
American/Russian (1898–1957)
Savonarola - Decor Design
Signed on reverse, gouache, watercolour
and pencil, c1922
8¼ x 13in (21 x 33cm)
£1,700–2,200 *S*

DECORATIVE DESIGNS

Albrecht Dürer
German (1471–1528)
Coat-of-Arms with a Skull
Engraving, 1503
8¾ x 6¼in (22 x 16cm)
£4,500–5,500 *S(NY)*

Circle of Claude Gillot
French (1673–1722)
Design for a Ewer
Inscribed 'Gillot teacher of Watteau' verso,
pen and black ink with grey wash
12½ x 5½in (32 x 14cm)
£400–600 *P*

Edmé Bouchardon
French (1698–1762)
Design for an Urn
Red chalk, laid down
10¾ x 10¼in (27.5 x 26cm)
£700–900 *P*

After Jaques Gabriel Huquier
French (1725–1805)
Six Rococo Decorative Designs, by
Peyrotte, etchings on laid paper
19 x 13in (48 x 33cm)
£800–1,000 *CSK*

French School (20thC)
A Trumpet of Flowers and Fruit
decorated with Garlands of Flowers
Oil on canvas
77 x 39in (195.5 x 99cm)
£6,000–7,000 *C*

Charles Mozley
British (20thC)
Coronation Design
Signed, poster paint
21 x 28in (53 x 71cm)
£200–300 *P*

Commissioned by Shell and BP in 1953.

CARTOONS & ILLUSTRATIONS

This year the British Patent Office chose to publicise its services in the press with an elaborately framed portrait of one of Roger Hargreaves' Mr Men cartoons. 'No wonder he's Mr Happy,' ran the caption. 'He's worth more than a Mr Holbein.' As the advertisement explained, although a Holbein portrait had recently been sold for just under £1.5m, this was a piffling sum compared with the profits raised by Mr Happy and Co. who, since 1973, have appeared on everything from yoghurt pots to bubble bath, to say nothing of the TV series or the 60 million books sold to date.

It is not only contemporary illustrators who can be worth big money. At the 1994 London Antiquarian Book Fair, the first printed edition of Lewis Carroll's *Alice in Wonderland*, illustrated by Tenniel, was being offered by New York dealer Justin Schiller for almost as much as the Holbein price of £1.2m. 'This is the third most frequently quoted work in English after *The Bible* and Shakespeare,' claimed the dealer, justifying himself to the *Daily Telegraph*. 'This is the best book for children I can conceive ever handling.'

Illustration has traditionally been regarded as a minor art form, but is now attracting more and more attention from collectors and dealers. Foremost among the latter is London gallery owner Chris Beetles, whose annual winter shows of British illustrators, accompanied by wonderfully well-researched catalogues, have become one of the most enjoyable features of the Christmas art season. With works that range from the 18thC to the present day, Beetles' catalogues show the range and richness of illustrators' work throughout the centuries. It is a field in which Britain has reigned supreme and where the fine artists of the past are equalled by the illustrators of the present, many of whom are from modern-day children's books and familiar to parents. In the general market place, prices for cartoons and illustrations can easily begin at under £100, and it is a field that offers something for every taste and pocket.

George Dance the Younger, R.A. (1741–1825) and **Sir Nathaniel Dance-Holland, R.A.** (1735–1811)
British
'Alas I spent all I had in the world to buy this wig',
'No hope remains for such a set of scoundrels,'
Three male figures and Grotesques, Three Figures Four, one monogrammed 'GD', one inscribed 'Sir N.D.', two inscribed with title, pen and grey or brown ink and wash, two on laid paper
3¼ x 5½in (8 x 14cm)
£450–650 *S*

Thomas Rowlandson
British (1756–1827)
Oh You Pretty Creature
Inscribed, pen and ink and wash over pencil
9 x 7⅝in (23 x 19.5cm)
£1,200–1,600 *S*

Henry Fuseli
Swiss (active in Britain) (1741–1825)
Titania's Dream
Signed, pencil with grey and pink wash
5 x 8in (12.5 x 20cm)
£5,000–8,000 *Bon*

Isaac Cruikshank
British (1756–1811)
The Mail Coach
Signed below mount, watercolour with pen and ink
6¼ x 9in (16 x 23cm)
£1,350–1,450 *CBL*

Robert Anning Bell, R.A., R.W.S., N.E.A.C.
British (1863–1933)
Helena *(All's Well that Ends Well)*
Inscribed with book title on reverse,
pen and black and red ink
7¾ x 5¼in (19.5 x 13cm)
£450–550 *CBL*

NADAR. élevant la Photographie à la hauteur de l'Art

Honoré Daumier
French (1808–79)
Nadar élevant la Photographie à la Hauteur
de l'Art, from Souvenirs d'Artistes
Lithograph, 1862, on Chine appliqué, a fine
impression of the first state (of two), before
the words 'Souvenirs d'Artistes' and the
number 367
10½ x 8¾in (27 x 22cm)
£10,000–12,000 *C*

Will Dyson
Australian (1883–1938)
History, Lying Jade, Owning Up to Mr Belloc
Ink and watercolour
17 x 13in (43 x 33cm)
£850–950 *CBL*

*Hilaire Belloc (1870–1953), essayist, poet,
novelist, travel writer and critic is perhaps
best remembered today for his humorous
verses for children, most notably the
'Cautionary Tales.' These included the tale
of little Jim, whose special foible was running
away from his nurse and being eaten by a
lion; Rebecca 'Who Slammed Doors for Fun
and Perished Miserably', Matilda who told
'such Dreadful Lies / It made one Gasp and
Stretch one's Eyes' and was burnt to a crisp
and Henry King 'who chewed bits of String,
and was early cut off in Dreadful Agonies.'
Belloc's verses have inspired many children's
illustrators, and continue to do so today, new
editions of his poems having been recently
illustrated by Tony Ross.*

Charles Keene
British (1823–91)
Two Gentlemen in a Street
An illustration from a *Punch Almanack,* 1883,
Signed with monogram, pen and ink
7¼ x 5⅜in (18 x 14cm)
£650–750 *CBL*

Phil May
British (1864–1903)
The Stage Door Demon
Initialled and inscribed with title,
monochrome watercolour on
tinted paper
10¼ x 7¼in (25.5 x 18cm)
£300–350 *CBL*

Margaret W. Tarrant
British (1888–1959)
Boy and Girl Fairies
Climbing Aquilegia
Signed, watercolour
13 x 7in (33 x 17.5cm)
£3,500–4,500 *GAK*

Edward Ardizzone
British (1900–78)
Front cover of *'Stig of the Dump'*
Pen and ink drawing
7¼ x 11¼in (18 x 29cm)
£1,150–1,250 *CBL*

Arthur Rackham
British (1867–1939)
Peter Pan
Pen, ink and watercolour, an illustration for the title page of
J.M. Barrie's book, published by Hodder & Stoughton, 1906
6 x 13½in (15 x 34.5cm)
£12,000–12,500 *CBL*

*Arthur Rackham was the most famous illustrator of fairy stories and
gift books of his generation and his illustrations are known
throughout the world. With his fine linear style, muted tones, and
evocative imagination, he created an archetypal image of fairyland
that was to influence the generations of artists and children who
succeeded him.*

Sir John Tenniel
British (1820–1914)
A Scene from *'The Miller and His Men'*
A study of perspective after the manner of 'Skelt's Popular
Characters', inscribed with title and 'dramatic' on reverse
6 x 9in (15 x 23cm)
£550–650 *CBL*

*Despite being partially blinded by his father in a fencing incident in
1840, Tenniel became a highly successful artist, working as a
cartoonist for Punch and illustrating books, most notably Lewis Carroll's
'Alice's Adventures in Wonderland' (1865) and 'Alice Through The
Looking-Glass' (1872). In June 1994, the Antiquarian Book Fair in
London included the first printed text of 'Alice in Wonderland',
complete with marginal notes and corrections by Carroll and Tenniel,
and 15 original Tenniel illustrations, priced at an astonishing £1.2m
('Oh my fur and whiskers!'). More modestly priced, 'The Miller and His
Men', comes from earlier in Tenniel's career, when he was producing
comic illustrations with theatrical sources for 'The Book of Beauty'
(c1846), a collaboration with fellow artist Charles Keene.*

STIG OF THE DUMP by Clive King

Illustrated by Edward Ardizzone

Edward Ardizzone
British (1900–78)
The City Walls, York
Initialled, pen and ink and coloured washes
13½ x 17¾in (34.5 x 45cm)
£1,000–1,500 *P*

Henry Mayo Bateman
British (1887–1970)
Some Social Virtues: Tact
Signed and dated '16', inscribed with
title below mount, pen and ink with
monochrome watercolour
9¾ x 4in (24.5 x 10cm)
£4,250–4,500 *CBL*

Tracey Boyd
British (b1961)
U Always Woke Up at the Very Last Minute,
Put Up His Umbrella and Fell Asleep in it
Signed with monogram and dated '90',
watercolour with pen and ink
7 x 6½in (17.5 x 16cm)
£350–400 *CBL*

Peter Brookes
British (b1943)
Thames Barrier
Signed and inscribed, pen and ink
6 x 14¼in (15 x 36.5cm)
£200–250 *CBL*

Lang Campbell
American (20thC)
Five sheets of illustrations for *'Uncle Wiggily'*,
1926, each signed within image and
annotated in the margins, ink on paper
7½ x 9½in (19 x 24cm)
£450–550 *SK*

Hilda Cowham
British (20thC)
Childhood
Signed, pencil, pen and black ink and
watercolour heightened with white
11 x 7½in (28 x 19cm)
£200–300 *CSK*

Frank Dickens
British (b1933)
I Like It When the Wind is in This Direction
Signed, pen and ink
3¾ x 18in (9 x 46cm)
£175–200 *CBL*

Carl Ronald Giles
British (b1916)
Magic Chemical Set, cover design for the
Sunday and Daily Express 6th Series, 1952
Signed with title, watercolour and bodycolour
10 x 26½in (25 x 67cm)
£5,000–5,500 *CBL*

Peter Firmin
British (20thC)
Ivor the Engine
Watercolour
8in (20cm) square
£225–250 *RGFA*

*There is hardly a child of whatever age in
Britain who does not remember the locomotive
of the Merioneth and Llantisilly Rail Traction
Company Limited, Ivor The Engine, and his
many friends, Jones the Steam, Dai Station,
Evans the Song and, of course, Idris the
Welsh Dragon.*
*Ivor the Engine was the first series created
by Peter Firmin and Oliver Postgate for
children's TV, and many others followed:
Noggin the Nog, Bagpuss, The Clangers,
Pinny's House, Tottie and Pogle's Wood, all
conceived, created and filmed in Firmin's
barn near Canterbury. Books based on the
TV characters followed.*

John Harrold
British (20thC)
Rupert Investigates the Village
Signed on overlay, pen ink and watercolour,
an illustration from *Daily Express Rupert
Annual, 1988*
9 x 8⅝in (23 x 22cm)
£750–850 *CBL*

" I'M FROM THE MASSACHUSETTS INSTITUTE OF ADVANCED TECHNOLOGY — WHAT
ARE YOUR PLANS AFTER THE 11- PLUS ? "

Jak (Raymond Allen Jackson)
British (b1927)
'I'm From The Massachusetts Institute of
Advanced Technology - What Are Your Plans
After The 11-Plus?'
Signed, inscribed with title below the mount,
pen, ink, pastel and watercolour
19 x 24in (48 x 61cm)
£300–350 *CBL*

> **Miller's is a price GUIDE
> not a price LIST**

Kay Rasmus Nielsen
Danish (1886–1967)
He Had to Take to his Bed for a Week
Signed and dated '1913', watercolour with
pen, ink and pencil
13½ x 12in (34.5 x 30.5cm)
£6,000–6,500 *CBL*

*Kay Nielsen was born in Copenhagen, son of
the Director of the Royal Danish Theatre. He
studied in Paris, then moved to London,
where he won a contract with publishers
Hodder and Stoughton, for whom this work
was produced. 'Influenced by Beardsley and
the art of the Orient and the Middle East,
Nielsen drew in pen and ink, often with
brilliant watercolour washes,' writes dealer
Chris Beetles.*
*Nielsen's illustration shows his talent for
theatrical design. He created spectacular sets
and costumes for the Royal Danish Theatre
and, after moving to America in 1926, worked
with Walt Disney on Fantasia, one of the most
innovative of all animated feature films.*

William Heath Robinson
British (1872–1944)
The Winkle Squirt. A New Patent for
Blowing the Heads off Winkles
Signed and inscribed with title below
mount, pen, ink and monochrome
watercolour with bodycolour
15 x 10½in (38 x 26.5cm)
£2,250–2,450 *CBL*

*It was during WWI that Heath Robinson
began to emerge as one of the greatest comic
illustrators of his generation. 'To the popular
press,' notes dealer Chris Beetles, 'he was
known as the Gadget King, the inventor of
perfectly logical contraptions that gently
mocked the products of the industrial age
and so endeared society to its own rapid rate
of change.'*

Ronald Searle
British (b1920)
Will it be a Super Summer, Daddy?
Signed with initials, pen and ink, together
with three others by Ronald Searle
21 x 14¼in (53 x 36.5cm)
£450–650 *P*

George Studdy
British (20thC)
Trying to get you on the Long Wave
Signed, watercolour
12½ x 9½in (31.5 x 23.5cm)
£650–850 *BWe*

ANIMATION CELS

An animation cel is a painting on a clear sheet of acetate, usually 10½ x 12½in (26 x 32cm) or larger. These are laid over the backgrounds in sequence to give the illusion of movement. According to the Catto Gallery, specialists in this field, 'a "production cel" is an example which actually appears in the film. A "limited edition cel" has been recreated from the original production cel or a hand tailored cel depicting a favourite character in a special scene.'

Walt Disney Studios
American (20thC)
The Jungle Book (1967)
Hand painted limited edition cel,
King Louie feeds Mogli
£1,000–1,100 *CAT*
© *The Walt Disney Company*

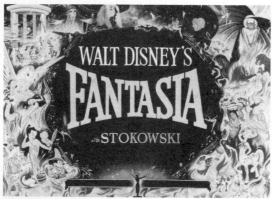

John Coates
British (20thC)
The Snowman (1989)
Original production cel from the 30min. film
£1,000–1,200 *CAT*

Walt Disney Studios
American (20thC)
Sleeping Beauty (1959)
Production cel artwork, Maleficent
transformed into a terrifying dragon
£1,800–2,000 *CAT*
© *The Walt Disney Company*

Walt Disney Studios
American (20thC)
Fantasia (1946)
Opening Sequence
Poster artwork, watercolour on board and
title on celluloid
15½ x 21¼in (39 x 55cm)
£2,500–3,500 *CSK*
© *The Walt Disney Company*

Walt Disney Studios
American (20thC)
Bashful and Dopey (1937)
Original production cel of Bashful
and Dopey with a Courvoisier
background
£3,800–4,000 *CAT*
© *The Walt Disney Company*

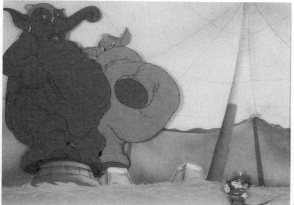

Walt Disney Studios
American (20thC)
Dumbo (1941)
A two-cel set up on a Disney art background,
Timothy mouse, the ring master, scaring the
elephants at the circus
£3,200–3,400 *CAT*
© *The Walt Disney Company*

Bob Godfrey
British (b1921)
Hog Asleep in an Alleyway
Production cel
11 x 16in (28 x 40.5cm)
£600–650 *CBL*

Warner Brothers
American (20thC)
Got Him
Limited edition cel by director Friz Freleng,
signed and with studio seal
£450–520 *CAT*

*A classic moment of Warner Bros. animation is captured
in this limited edition cel from famed director Friz
Freleng. Instead of a tasty snack, Sylvester discovers his
nemesis Spike in a bird cage, as Tweety and Granny look
on and laugh. In 1982 legendary Friz Freleng began
creating a special collection of Limited Edition animation
cels. He personally develops and draws the original
master art of each of his Limited Editions. The cel image
is hand-inked on an original master cel. Silkscreened ink
lines are then created from the master for each of the
Limited Edition pieces. In traditional animation style,
the cels are turned over and hand painted on the back
using animation cel paint. The hand painted background
image is lithography printed on acid free paper. Each
piece has a studio seal and is signed by Friz Freleng.*

Warner Brothers
American (20thC)
Bugs Bunny
Signed by Mel Blanc, a set up from the 1950s
with corresponding pencil drawing
£1,100–1,250 *CAT*

ABSTRACT & MODERN

The beginning of 1994 saw the modern art world plunged into some turbulence. Perhaps one of the most shocking events was the theft of Edvard Munch's 'The Scream' from the National Art Gallery in Oslo, Norway, where the work was being exhibited for the winter Olympics. Though painted in the 1890s as part of Munch's Frieze of Life series, 'The Scream' has become synonymous with 20thC malaise, often used to illustrate the horrors of the Holocaust. Gallery director Alf Boe described the theft as the 'equivalent of stealing the 'Mona Lisa.' The work was recovered later in the year in somewhat mysterious circumstances.

In London in January, 35 artists, gallery owners and critics banded together to write an open letter to *London's Evening Standard,* attacking the paper's celebrated art reviewer, Brian Sewell. Sewell is famed for his remarkable voice, (one journalist described him as sounding like Lady Bracknell on acid), and for his trenchant and relentless exortation of most contemporary art. In print and in interviews, the letter-writers branded him as homophobic, reactionary and mysogenistic; accusing him of ignoring the debates central to modern art, unjust and personalised attacks on painters and neglecting the proper language of art criticsm. Sewell had claimed, for example, that a rather poor Nude by Vanessa Bell, in an all-woman art show, could not even have appealed to a 'purblind lesbian', a phrase that particularly annoyed his more pompous critics and one that is surely destined for future dictionary quotations. Sewell defended himself with wit, energy and habitual cattiness. The dispute mushroomed into a national debate between the modernists - or 'Brickies' as they became labelled after the famous Tate bricks - and the traditionalists - those in favour of artists who are trained to paint pictures rather than produce concepts. Whatever the rights and wrongs of the argument, it brought into focus the fact that many people clearly feel alienated and, more dangerously, bored by the extremes of contemporary abstract and conceptual art.

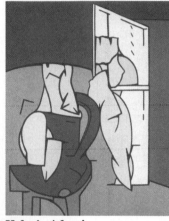

Valerio Adami
Italian (b1935)
Interno con Figure e Specchio
Signed, titled and dated '66'
on the reverse, oil on canvas
38¼ x 30¾in (97 x 78cm)
£8,800–11,000 *S*

Pierre Alechinsky
Belgian (b1927)
Le Nid
Signed, oil on canvas
50 x 36in (130 x 91cm)
£46,000–56,000 *C*

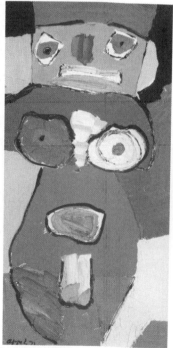

Karel Appel
Dutch (b1921)
Impatient Lady
Signed and dated '71', oil on canvas
36 x 18½in (91.5 x 47cm)
£18,000–22,000 *S(NY)*

Karel Appel
Dutch (b1921)
Untitled
Signed and dated '80', brush and black
ink on paper
35½ x 47in (90 x 119.5cm)
£2,500–3,000 *CNY*

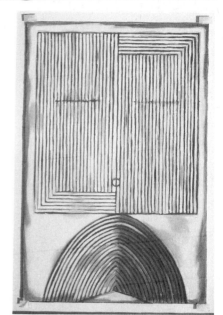

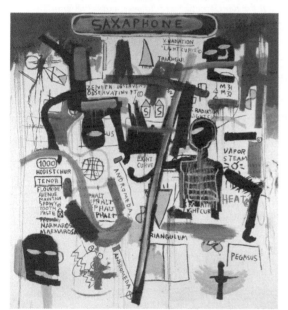

Hans Arp
French (1887–1966)
Set of 7 lithographs, consisting of cover with collage, title and
list of contents, on silver coloured thin wove paper, 1923
18 x 14½in (46 x 36.5cm)
£11,000–15,000 *C*

*Hans Arp, also known as Jean, was born in Strasbourg. He
was associated with several famous 20thC artistic movements,
first exhibiting with the Blaue Reiter group in Munich in 1912.
He then worked with Modigliani and Picasso in Paris, and
was a founder member of the Dada movement.*

Osi Audu
Nigerian (b1955)
The Patriarch
Signed and dated '1992', pastel on paper
42 x 26in (106 x 66cm)
£650–750 *SG*

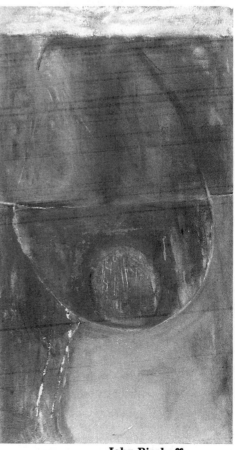

Jean Michel Basquiat
American (1960–86)
Saxaphone
Signed, inscribed and dated '86', oil on
canvas
66 x 60in (167.5 x 142cm)
£60,000–70,000 *C*

Max Bill
Swiss (b1908)
Transcolouration
Signed, titled and dated '1972–73',
oil on canvas
22½in (57cm) diagonal
£10,500–12,500 *S*

John Bischoff
British (20thC)
Abstract
Mixed media
60 x 36in (152 x 91.5cm)
£1,400–1,600 *FT*

Elizabeth Blackadder, R.A.
Scottish (b1931)
Indian Still Life
Etching
11¾ x 9¼in (30 x 23cm)
£175–200 *GPS*

David Blackburn
British (b1939)
Japanese Tree II
Pastel
25 x 21in (64 x 53cm)
£1,500–1,600 *HaG*

Victor Brauner
French (1903–66)
Homme surréaliste
Signed and dated '29.8.1945', brush,
pen and black ink and encaustic on paper
9¾ x 6¾in (25 x 17cm)
£6,000–7,000 *C*

Elizabeth Blackadder, R.A.
Scottish (b1931)
Indian Still Life
Etching
11¾ x 9¼in (30 x 23cm)
£175–200 *GPS*

*Elizabeth Blackadder, born in Falkirk, studied at Edinburgh
University and Edinburgh College of Art between 1949–54. She
travelled extensively in Europe in the early 1950s, and as a result
was much influence by Byzantine architecture and mosaics.
She is well known for her depictions of flowers, cats and small
objects, often placed vertically across paper on canvas.
Watercolour is generally her favoured medium. Her work is
represented in the Tate Gallery and main public collections
in Scotland.*

Les Brown
British (b1930)
Winter Harvest
Signed, oil on canvas
22 x 18in (55.5 x 45.5cm)
£400–450 *TAB*

Pol Bury
French (b1922)
Plans Mobiles
Signed, inscribed and dated '1953',
oil and masonite relief
31½ x 21¾ x 4½in (80 x 55.5 x 11.5cm)
£25,000–35,000 *C*

Mohamed Bushara
Sudanese (b1946)
Untitled
Pen and ink, 1975
7¼ x 10in (18 x 25cm)
£350–400 *SG*

Marc Chagall
French/Russian (1887–1985)
Homage à Marc Chagall
Lithograph, 1969
12½ x 9⅓in (31.5 x 23.5cm)
£290–320 *WO*

Alexander Calder
American (1898–1976)
Two Fish Tails
Signed with initials and dated '75', mobile
of painted sheet metal and rod
Approximate span 98 x 60in (259 x 152.5cm)
£100,000–125,000 *C*

*The word 'mobile' was coined in 1932 by Marcel Duchamp, to
describe the abstract moving constructions created by Alexander
Calder from this period. Calder had studied mechanical
engineering as well as painting, and the mobiles, which constitute
his most famous work, provided a perfect fusion of his interests and
talents. The lightness of touch and joyous movement that
characterise these sculptures run throughout Calder's work whether
two, three or even four dimensional.*

Marc Chagall
French/Russian (1887–1985)
Le Cheval Bleu
Signed, gouache, watercolour and coloured
pencil on paper, c1938–41
23 x 19½in (58.5 x 49cm)
£250,000–280,000 *S(NY)*

*Franz Meyer characterizes the artist's work
from this period as possessing an
unmistakable new fairytale tone. 'The
fantastic motifs recall familiar things and
modes of life in childish harmony with
nature and the world. Fairytale traits are
not uncommon in Chagall's earlier works,
but the fairytale mood was never so simple
and plastically insistent. It gives the pictures
he painted during the last years before the
war and during the war itself their peculiar
character.'*

Iakov Chernikov
Russian (1881–1951)
Composition from the series 'Factory',
late 1920s
Pen and Indian ink and watercolour
11¾ x 9½in (30 x 24cm)
£3,750–4,750 *S*

*Iakov Chernikhov has been described 'the best
of the Constructivists'. A pupil of Alexander
Bois' brother, Leontii, at the Leningrad
Academy, he was himself one of the leading
teachers of the Russian avant-garde. His
work united the principles of Suprematism
and Constructivism with a rich understanding
of construction and the machine. The
extraordinary power of his imagined fantasies
made his work perhaps the richest source of
architectural imagery produced in Russia.*

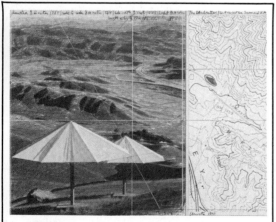

Christo
Rumanian (b1935)
The Umbrellas
Signed, titled and dated '1990', left panel,
coloured crayons, charcoal and fabric collage
on board, right panel, map, enamel and
coloured crayons on board
30½ x 38¾in (78 x 98.5cm)
£24,000–28,000 *CNY*

Phillippa Clayden
British (b1955)
Mythic Hike
Mixed media and collage on board
78 x 60in (198 x 152cm)
£10,000–11,000 *BOU*

Jean Cocteau
French (1889–1963)
Visage
Signed, coloured chalks on blue paper
25 x 19in (63.5 x 48cm)
£1,200–1,600   *CNY*

*Jean Cocteau was well known as poet,
dramatist, film director and critic. He was
a leading figure in European modernism,
working with Picasso, Stravinsky and others.
This chalk drawing is reminiscent of some of
Picasso's drawings. He wrote poetry, several
plays and ballet, whilst his novel 'Les
Enfants Terribles' (1929) was made into a
film in 1950. Again, like Picasso, Cocteau
was interested in ceramics and the present
abstracted face is similar to many of the
images he placed on his pots and plates.*

P. J. Crook
British (20thC)
Karey Karey
Signed, oil on canvas
20 x 16in (50.5 x 40.5cm)
£600–800   *GK*

Locate the Source

*The source of each
illustration in Miller's
can be found by checking
the code letters below
each caption with the list
of contributors.*

Georges Csato
Hungarian (born 1910)
Composition Abstraite
Signed, oil on canvas
40 x 30in (101.5 x 76cm)
£700–1,000   *CSK*

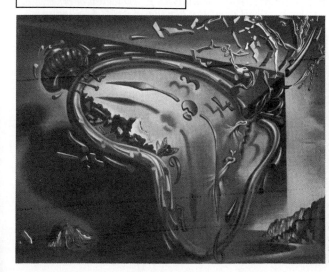

Salvador Dalí
Spanish (1904–89)
La Montre Molle
Signed and dated '49', oil on canvas
8¼ x 10in (21 x 25.5cm)
£460,000–500,000   *S(NY)*

*With reference to Dalí's use of the watch in
his paintings, Dawn Ades has noted 'it is
interesting to compare this famous image of
soft watches with the other images in his post
war pictures, because it does have a greater
and unforced hold on the imagination, partly
because it is less obviously and consciously
determined. The soft watches are an
unconscious symbol of the relativity of space
and time (Camembert of time and space,
Dalí described them), a Surrealist meditation
on the collapse of our notions of a fixed
cosmic order.'*

Michael Davis
British (20thC)
Found at Kilve
Charcoal, conté and eraser
31½ x 45¾in (90 x 116cm)
£1,000–1,200 *CSKe*

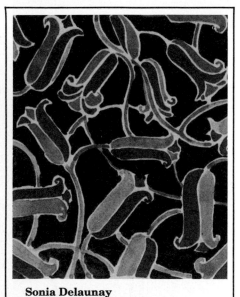

Sonia Delaunay
French (1885–1979)
Fabric design for Robert Perrier
Signed by Charles Delaunay verso,
stamped and dated 'entre 1925 et 1933',
gouache on paper
3¾ x 3¼in (9.5 x 8cm)
£600–800 *S(NY)*

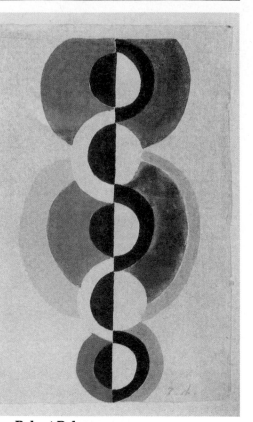

Robert Delaunay
French (1885–1941)
Rythme
Signed with initials, gouache and black ink
on japan paper
7½ x 4½in (19 x 11.5cm)
£5,500–6,500 *C*

*The Delaunay's were a famous husband and
wife painting team, Robert born in France
and Sonia in the Ukraine. Early in his
career, Robert experimented with Neo-
Impressionism and Fauvism but c1909 he
began to develop his own original style,
eventually liberating his works from any
descriptive subject matter to explore the
abstract relationships of colour. 'Colour alone
is form and subject,' he wrote. 'So long as art
does not free itself from the subject, it
remains descriptive ... dooming itself to
servitude and imitation ...(colour) is the sole
theme that develops, transforms itself apart
from all analysis, psychological or otherwise.
Colour is a function of itself.' Apollinaire
coined the term 'Orphism' to describe the
lyrical colour abstractions created by
Delauney and his wife. Sonia worked closely
with Robert and introduced their colour
principles into the field of fabric design and
the applied arts. She had an important
influence on the world of fashion, designing
creations for such famous women as Nancy
Cunard and Gloria Swanson.*

Rashid Diab
Sudanese (b1957)
My Royal Family
Signed and dated '1988'. etching
22½ x 18½in (57 x 47cm)
£200–250 *SG*

Arthur G. Dove
American (1880–1946)
Landscape Formation
Watercolour on paper, 1941
5 x 7in (12.5 x 17.5cm)
£8,000–10,000 *S(NY)*

Kenneth Draper
British (born 1944)
Nile Temple
Pastel on paper
18 x 20in (45.5 x 50.5cm)
£1,600–1,800 *HaG*

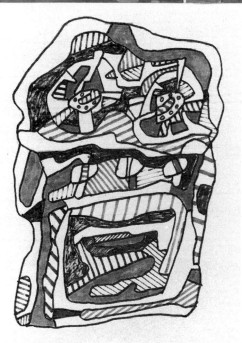

D. Drey
British (b1962)
Melancholy of the Squatter
Oil on hardboard
18 x 50in (45.5 x 127cm)
£700–800 *FT*

Maurice Estève
French (b1904)
Carrière Blanche
Signed, titled and dated '59', oil on canvas
10¾ x 13⅜in (27 x 35cm)
£12,000–14,000 *S*

Jean Dubuffet
French (1901–85)
Rechaud-Four a Gaz II
Signed with initials, dated '66', titled on
reverse, pencil on paper
11½ x 8½in (29 x 21.5cm)
£7,000–8,000 *S(NY)*

Rainer Fetting
German (b1949)
Tanser III
Signed and dated '1982', dry
dispersion on linen
82½ x 110¼in (209.5 x 280cm)
£16,000–18,000 *S(NY)*

Terry Frost
British (b1915)
Trewellard Sun
Signed and numbered, linocut
with handcolouring
25¼in (64cm) square
£290–310 *WO*

Terry Frost
British (b1915)
Black and White Spiral
Signed, inscribed and dated twice
'Nov 88' and 'Jan 89', oil on canvas
74¾ x 55in (190 x 139.5cm)
£5,500–7,000 *C*

Sam Francis
American (b1923)
Untitled
Signed on the reverse, gouache on
paper, c1960
71 x 37in (180 x 94cm)
£55,000–65,000 *S(NY)*

Brian Graham
British (b1945)
Sacred Site
Acrylic on canvas
32 x 40in (81 x 101.5cm)
£1,300–1,500 *OLG*

Keith Haring
American (1958–90)
Untitled
Signed, copyright mark and dated
'April 12 1985', acrylic on particle board
24½ x 13½in (62.5 x 34cm)
£3,200–4,000 *S(NY)*

Keith Haring
American (1958–90)
Untitled
Signed, inscribed and dated 'April 9 1985',
acrylic on canvas
60in (152.5cm) square
£40,000–50,000 *S(NY)*

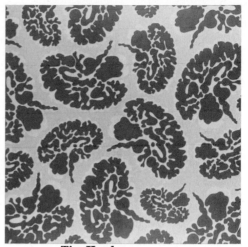

Tim Head
British (b1946)
Living Dead I
Signed, titled and dated '87', acrylic
on canvas
48in (122cm) square
£1,000–1,500 *Bon*

Jonet Harley-Peters
British (20thC)
Red Linear Ellipse
Pastel on constructed paper
62in (157cm) square
£400–450 *FT*

Hans Hartung
French (1904–86)
T61-H6
Signed and dated '61', oil and
crayon on canvas
24 x 63¾in (61 x 162cm)
£40,000–50,000 *C*

Patrick Heron
British (b1920)
Recomplication Round Yellow,
September 1967
Gouache
22¼ x 30⅜in (56.5 x 78cm)
£3,200–4,000 *C*

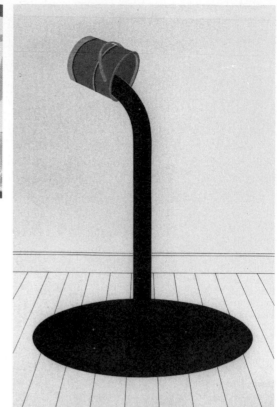

Patrick Hughes
British (born 1939)
Realistic Paint
Signed, inscribed and dated '77', gloss
paint on cut board
48 x 36in (122 x 91.5cm)
£1,500–2,000 *C*

Philippe Jean
French (20thC)
The Captive
Signed and dated '66', collage, pen and ink
and heightened with white on paper
9¼ x 6¾in (23 x 17cm)
Time Flies
Signed, collage, pen and black ink on
paper, 1966
11¾ x 8½in (29 x 21.5cm)
£450–550 *C*

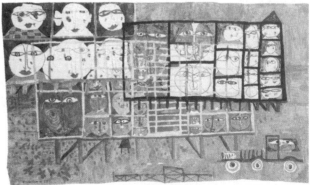

Friedensreich Hundertwasser
Austrian (b1928)
Sommerhaus
Signed, inscribed, numbered '141' and dated
'1952', watercolour and acrylic on paper
15¼ x 27½in (38.5 x 70cm)
£28,000–35,000 *S(NY)*

Alfred Jensen
American (1903–81)
Sixty-five Squares
Signed and dated '1957', oil and paper
collage on board
23in (58.5cm) square
£5,000–6,000 *CNY*

Mike Kelley
American (b1954)
Garbage Drawing No. 33
Numbered, acrylic on paper
24 x 41in (71 x 104cm)
£2,000–3,000   *CNY*

Wassily Kandinsky
Russian (1866–1944)
Standhaftes Grün
Signed with monogram initial and dated '25',
oil on board laid down on panel
27½ x 19¾in (69.5 x 50cm)
£830,000–880,000   *C*

*Kandinsky, who in 1896 left a promising
legal career in Moscow to study painting in
Munich, taught at the Bauhaus between
1922–23. Although its primary function was
as a school of architecture, it was an
important place in the development of
abstract art. Formerly the Schools of Fine
Arts and of Crafts at Weimar, the famous
architect Gropius (1883–1969) renamed it
Bauhaus (the house of building).
'Standhaftes Grün' was painted in April
1925, just as the Bauhaus was closed by the
Nazi régime. He settled in France in 1933.*

Paul Kelpe
American (1902–85)
Composition #353:
A Double-Sided Watercolour
Signed, inscribed, dedicated and dated '32',
watercolour on paper
Another untitled composition verso
11¼ x 7⅜in (28.5 x 20cm)
£12,000–14,000   *S(NY)*

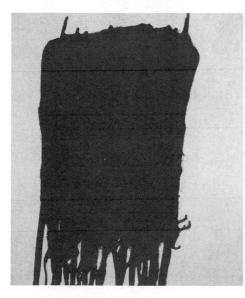

Yves Klein
French (1928–62)
La Coulée Blue
Pigment and synthetic resin on paper
mounted on canvas
25¾ x 19¾in (65 x 50cm)
£25,000–35,000   *C*

Franz Kline
American (1910–62)
Untitled (Study for 'Leda')
Signed, ink on paper, 1950
30¼ x 25¼in (24 x 18cm)
£32,000–40,000 *S(NY)*

*Kline was one of the leading American
Abstract Expressionists. His black and white
paintings are generally considered his most
significant works.*

Willem de Kooning
American/Dutch (b1904)
Untitled (Black and White Abstraction)
Signed, sapolin enamel on paper,
double sided, c1949–50
22 x 30in (56 x 76cm)
£675,000–750,000 *S(NY)*

*'Untitled (Black and White Abstraction)' is
one in a group of works on paper done in
sapolin enamel which followed the 1946–49
paintings in black and white by de Kooning.
He had eliminated other colours from his
palette in the late 1940s in order to focus on
line, form and imagery. The result was the
development of a self assured and energetic
synthesis of abstraction, biomorphic forms
and gestural 'action painting', evident in such
masterpieces as 'Light in August', c1946.*

Paul Klee
Swiss (1879–1940)
Winterbild
Signed, titled, numbered and dated '1930',
gouache, watercolour and silver paint on
gessoed paper, mounted on board
12½ x 19¼in (31.5 x 49cm)
£380,000–450,000 *S(NY)*

*The Swiss born Klee was trained in Munich,
beginning work as a graphic artist and was
influenced by Blake, Goya and Toulouse
Lautrec. He was associated with the Blaue
Reiter group from 1911, and his early
reputation was based on his use of black and
white. He began to use colour from 1914,
having met Robert Delauney. He taught at
the Bauhaus from 1920–33 when he returned
to his native Switzerland.
'Winterbild' is a highly simplified work - the
lower third of the composition is made up of
brilliant white gouache over gesso, the upper
portion is a soft grey blue. A leafless tree to
the right grows above a series of abstract
shapes of red, green, ochre and violet sky.
These shapes represent earth, water and air -
basic elements in painting, as Klee explained
to his students in his lecture notes. Two trees
to the left balance the composition, a tiny tree
in the foreground adds a harmonious footnote.
A large black inverted teardrop floats down
from the sky. This we surmise to be the
element of movement which Klee describes in
his notes, 'The swimmer in the air (flyer or
glider) must become part of the machine and
give himself up to a new kind of movement'.*

Wosene Kosrof
Ethiopian (b1950)
The Rising Sun
Signed, acrylic on canvas, 1993
44 x 36in (111.5 x 91.5cm)
£450–500 *SG*

Charles Lapique
French (1898–1988)
Croiseur au Mouillage de St. Marc, La Nuit
Signed, titled and dated '55', oil on canvas
21¼ x 32in (54 x 81cm)
£16,000–18,000 *S*

George Large, R.I.
British (20thC)
Trap Six
Watercolour
27 x 20in (68.5 x 50.5cm)
£950–1,050 *GL*

Fernand Léger
French (1881–1955)
Fragments
Signed with initials, gouache
on paper
12 x 9in (30.5 x 22.5cm)
£11,000–13,000 *C*

Percy Wyndham Lewis
British (1882–1957)
Futuristic Figure, 1912
Pen and black ink and coloured washes
over pencil
10¼ x 67¼in (26 x 18.5cm)
£6,500–7,500 *S*

*Wyndham Lewis was the founder of the
Vorticist Movement, the British interpretation
of Cubism and Futurism, which flourished
briefly but explosively in 1914. In the aptly
named Blast, the Vorticist journal, Lewis
defined the movement as 'a) ACTIVITY as
opposed to the tasteful PASSIVITY of Picasso,
b) SIGNIFICANCE as opposed the dull or
anecdotal character to which the Naturalist
is condemned, c) ESSENTIAL MOVEMENT
and ACTIVITY (such as the energy of a mind)
as opposed to the imitative cinematography,
the fuss and hysterics of the Futurists'.
It was typical of Lewis to conceive Vorticism
as an aggressive reaction to other movements.
The artist was famous for his disputatious
character, and his vitriolic, witty attacks on
everything and everybody who displeased
him. Unsurprisingly, he earned himself many
enemies. 'I do not think I have ever seen a
nastier looking man', wrote Ernest
Hemingway. 'Under the black hat, when I
had first seen them the eyes were those of an
unsuccessful rapist'.*

Emma Leschallas
British (b1967)
Breakfast Ducks
Watercolour
24in (61cm)
£125–150 *HALC*

Roy Lichtenstein
American (b1923)
Modern Painting with Yellow Arc
Signed and dated '67, oil and magna
on canvas
18 x 24in (46 x 61cm)
£70,000–80,000 *S(NY)*

Adam Gopnik, in the New Yorker Magazine, praised the major retrospective of Roy Lichtenstein's work at the Guggenheim Museum in New York, for 'its almost unalloyed glad hearted delight ... The happiness that radiates from his art .. is based on its faith in reconciliation of cartoons and art, of cliché style and real feeling ... He looks today like the last modern artist in the old role as the mysteriously happy man'.

Ed Loko
Togo (b1950)
Birdman
Mixed media on nettle, 1993
6¾ x 6½in (17 x 16.5cm)
£3,800–4,000 *SG*

Lolly Lonergan
British (20thC)
The Dresser
Oil on board
13 x 11in (33 x 28cm)
£200–250 *DrG*

Man Ray
American (1890–1976)
Mask
Stamped and numbered, silver metal plaque
7 x 5¼in (17.5 x 13cm)
£1,000–1,400 *C*

René Magritte
Belgian (1898–1967)
Scheherazade
Signed, gouache on paper, laid down
on board, 1947
6½ x 6¾in (15.5 x 17cm)
£50,000–60,000 *S(NY)*

*Scheherazade is the mouthpiece of the tales
related in the Arabian Nights. The story goes
that the Sultan, having discovered the
infidelity of his Sultana, resolved to have a
fresh wife every night and have her strangled
at daybreak. Scheherazade, daughter of the
Grand Vizir, married the Sultan but saved
herself from the usual fate by telling him
the fantastical stories that compose the
Arabian Nights. She stopped each evening
at a crucial point in the tale, keeping the
Sultan entranced and entrapped for 1001
nights after which he revoked his cruel
decree. Rimsky Korsakof and Ravel were both
inspired by the same subject, and the present
work is Magritte's surreal tribute to
Scheherazade.*

Marino Marini
Italian (1901–80)
Groso Acrobatico
Signed and titled, gouache and collage
on paper, c1972
15¼ x 20½in (39 x 52cm)
£9,000–11,000 *C*

*Executed c1972, this work is a study for the
lighograph* Chevaux et Cavaliers, VIII, *one of
a series of eight lithographs on the subject of
a horse and rider published in Paris in 1972
(Giorgio e Guido Guastalla, Marino Marini,
Livorno, 1990.)*

Grosvenor Gallery
Modern Masters

Grosvenor Gallery Fine Arts Ltd
18 Albemarle Street, London W1X 3HA
Telephone 071-629 0891
Facsimile 071-491 4391

Mario Sironi
Metaphysical Figure
gouache and tempera
34.3 x 26.2cm. Circa 1917

David Burliuk
"Sibirskaya Flotilla", 1911
signed and dated
oil on canvas, 45 x 38cm

Joan Miró
Spanish (1893–1983)
Untitled
Original lighograph, 1966
10 x 7½in (25 x 18.5cm)
£225–250   *WO*

Joan Miró
Spanish (1893–1983)
Cahiers d'Art
Signed, numbered and dated 1934,
pochoir printed on wove paper
15 x 11in (38 x 28cm)
£19,000–24,000   *S(NY)*

*In modern prints, as in every area of the art
market, the collector should always beware
the faker and, unless you know what you are
doing, it is best to buy from a reputable
dealer. In the past year, Hilda Amiel, a
grandmother in her 70s, along with her two
daughters and granddaughter, were found
responsible for counterfeiting tens of thousands
of limited edition prints by artists such as
Dalí, Chagall, Miró, and Picasso. The family
business 'Artworks' was claimed to be the
largest counterfeiting ring in the world worth
a staggering, if ill-gotten, £325 million. Hilda
Amiel died before the trial commenced but
the rest of the family were all found guilty of
fraud and conspiracy charges.*

Sabina Mirri
Italian (b1957)
Roma
Signed, titled and dated '1984', coloured
chalks on paper
18¾ x 14in (48 x 35.5cm)
£400–600   *CNY*

Duncan Mosley
British (b1966)
Watersporting
Signed and dated '1994', oil on canvas
48 x 35in (122 x 89cm)
£1,350–1,450   *Tr*

*Only in his 20s, the young British artist
Duncan Mosley has already received several
awards. His work has a distinctly humourous
touch, as the artist explains. '...the object of
the exercise is to entertain in a way. Emotions
are important to capture. I am attracted to
the seaside (hence the addition of the
paddling pool and divers). I find it very
charming and warm and real ... the fact that
at sometime in our lives we force ourselves to
have fun ...the work is all about people and
all about me.'*

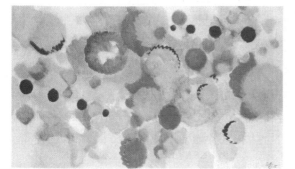

Ernest Wilhelm Nay
German (1902–68)
Gelbe Sphäre
Signed, titled and dated '55', oil on canvas
39½ x 63½in (100 x 160.5cm)
£140,000–160,000 *C*

Otto Nebel
German (1892–1975)
In Warmen Geborgen
Signed, titled, numbered and dated '1955',
oil on panel
7½ x 15¾in (19 x 40cm)
£1,200–1,600 *S(NY)*

Louise Nevelson
American (1899–1988)
Untitled
A pair, signed, pencil on paper
8¼ x 4½in (21 x 11.5cm)
£1,000–1,500 *S(NY)*

Ben Nicholson, O.M.
British (1894–1982)
Little L: 1940–42
Signed and dated '1940–42', oil
on canvasboard
8¾ x 7⅛in (22 x 18cm)
£30,000–40,000 *C*

Walter Nessler
German/British (b1952)
Still Life with Bridge
Signed, oil on canvas
44 x 56in (111.5 x 142cm)
£1,750–1,850 *JDG*

Kenneth Noland and Gloria F. Ross
American (b1924 and 1923)
Mood Indigo II, 1985
Signed, titled and numbered, Navajo
weaving, handspun wool tapestry
66in (167.5cm) square
£1,300–1,600 *C*

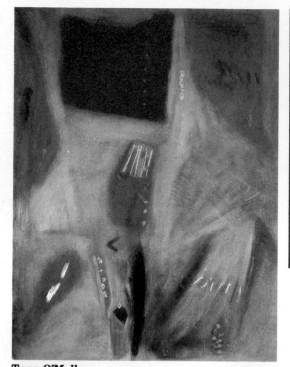

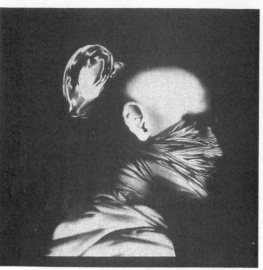

Mauricio Ortiz
El Salvadorian (b1963)
Untitled
Oil on linen
14½in (37cm) square
£400–450 *Mer*

Tony O'Malley
Irish (b1913)
Pedro Barba - Isla de Graciosa
Oil on board, 1993
48 x 36in (122 x 91.5cm)
£5,500–6,500 *TAG*

Victor Pasmore, C.H., R.A.
British (born 1908)
Square Motif: Green and Lilac
Signed with initials, inscribed, oil on
board, 1948
9¼ x 13in (23.5 x 33cm)
£14,000–16,000 *P*

Victor Pasmore, C.H., R.A.
British (b1908)
Blue Movements and Green
Signed and dated '1980', original
screenprint
29½ x 23½in (75 x 59.5cm)
£475–500 *WO*

Mimmo Rotella
Italian (born 1918)
Theatre
Signed, titled and dated '66',
silkscreen on canvas
12½ x 17½in (32 x 44cm)
£1,200–1,600 *CSK*

David Salle
American (b1952)
Unexpectedly, I missed my cousin Jasper
Signed, titled and dated '1980', acrylic on
canvas, in 2 panels
48 x 72in (122 x 183cm)
£75,000–90,000 *S(NY)*

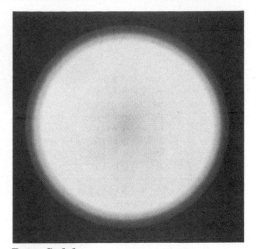

Peter Sedgley
British (b1930)
Mirage
Signed, titled and dated '1966',
acrylic on canvas
60in (152.5cm) square
£2,700–3,300 *C*

Varvara Shavrova
Russian (b1968)
Propped - 2
Oil on canvas
32in (31cm) square
£800–900 *FT*

Daniel Spoerri
Swiss (born 1930)
Tableau Piège
Signed and dated '1972', various objects
on painted wood in Plexiglass box
27½ x 27½ x 13in (70 x 70 x 33cm)
£9,000–11,000 *C*

Frank Stella
American (b1936)
Cato Manor
Signed, titled and dated '1965',
alkyd on canvas
23¼in (59cm) square
£65,000–75,000 *S(NY)*

Kumi Sugai
Japanese (b1919)
Fenêtre Verte
Signed, inscribed and
dated '1970',
oil on canvas
64 x 51½in (162.5 x 130cm)
£19,000–24,000 *C*

Graham Sutherland, O.M.
British (1903–80)
Lane Opening
Signed and dated '44–45', oil on board
36¾ x 28½in (93.5 x 72.5cm)
£70,000–80,000 *C*

*Graham Sutherland is described by the
Penguin Dictionary of Art and Artists as
'The leading British romantic painter of the
20thC. His early works were almost all
etchings and engravings, and he first used
oils in the mid-1930s. He was an official war
artist in WWII and, as a Catholic convert, he
painted many religious works. 'Christ in
Glory (1962)', perhaps the largest tapestry
ever woven, and certainly his largest religious
work, now hangs in Coventry Cathedral.
Sutherland subsequently became a very
successful portrait painter, painting Somerset
Maugham in 1949, Lord Beaverbrook in
1951, and Helena Rubenstein in 1957. His
most notorious portrait, that of Winston
Churchill, was commissioned by Parliament
in 1954 as an 80th birthday present for the
wartime Prime Minister, who was far from
delighted. 'It makes me look half witted,
which I ain't,' was one of his more printable
comments. The portrait was subsequently
burnt by Clementine Churchill.*

Professor Nguyen Thu
Vietnamese (b1930)
Ready for Action
Signed, watercolour on paper, 1965
14 x 11in (35.5 x 28cm)
£400–500 *RMG*

William Wilson
West African (Togo) (b1952)
Les Jumeaux
Pastel on paper, 1993
22 x 30in (56 x 76cm)
£750–850 *SG*

John Wells
British (born 1907)
Composition Variation, No. 13
Signed, inscribed and dated '1963–64',
oil on board
24½ x 20in (62 x 51cm)
£2,800–3,500 *C*

*According to dealer John Noott, many of the
so called 'Modern British Painters' are
comparatively underpriced in the current
market. 'There has been an over-reaction
pricewise as far as the Modern British area is
concerned,' he explains. 'The higher that
prices went in the 80s, the further they fell in
the 90s. Many works now seem very low in
price, affordable to the more modest collector.
There is some very good quality work around
from a period when artists were really taught
how to draw.'*

PICTURES UNDER £100

The following section is devoted to pictures and prints under or close to £100 that Miller's has received from auction houses and galleries over the past year. Looking at many of the prices throughout the Guide, it is easy to assume that you need to have a small fortune to even contemplate becoming an art collector. It is, however, possible to buy pictures without either breaking the bank or at least robbing it. Charity shops, car boot sales and market stalls can all yield treasure to the lucky and dedicated hunter. Local antique shops and galleries can be a good source for lower priced pictures, as can the smaller auction houses. Buying from an artist direct cuts out commission fees, although since the 1980s, and now that the big dealers regularly patronise art student degree shows, there are undoubtedly fewer chances of acquiring bargains from future art world stars. Everyone dreams of stumbling upon a £5 Rembrandt, or some other lost work of art at a local bring-and-buy sale. Although the chances of this are sadly remote, there are certainly opportunities, if one only looks hard enough, to buy attractive pictures for very little money, and hunting them down can be half the pleasure.

W. H. Fuge, after Titian
British (b1849)
Bacchus and Ariadne
Oil on board
14 x 16in (35.5 x 40.5cm)
£30–50 *LF*

Dadley, after Pu-Quà of Canton
Chinese Cobbler
Hand coloured aquatint, published
4 May 1799, by W. Miller, Old
Bond Street, London
12½ x 10in (31.5 x 25cm)
£15–20 *SRAB*

Dutch School (17thC style)
Portrait of a Gentleman
Oil on canvas
22 x 17in (55.5 x 43cm)
£30–45 *LF*

European School (18thC)
Wery Gond of Night Cap
Black and white steel engraving
8 x 6in (20 x 15cm)
£30–40 *LF*

European School (undated)
Portrait of a Gentleman
in Armour
Stipple engraving with original
hand colouring
10½ x 9in (26.5 x 22.5cm)
£50–60 *LF*

Ackermann's (Publisher)
British (early 19thC)
Flowers
Stipple engraving with original
hand colour, July 1819
8 x 6in (20 x 15cm)
£35–40 *SRAB*

George Baxter
British (1804–1967)
Assembly Scene
Black and white print
9 x 10½in (22.5 x 26.5cm)
£35–45 *LF*

British School (19thC)
Fishing Smack in Heavy Seas off Whitby
Watercolour
18 x 12in (45.5 x 30.5cm)
£90–110 *LF*

*Many of the works one comes across within
this price range are either unsigned, or by
unrecorded artists.*

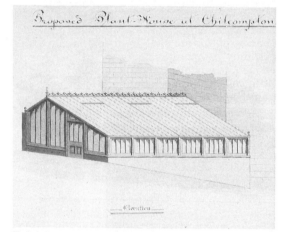

British School (19thC)
Bridge over Stream, and Country Cottage
A pair, signed with monogram
'E.L.', watercolour
11 x 13½in (28 x 34cm)
£80–90 *LF*

British School (19thC)
Proposed Plant House at Chilcompton
Watercolour
9¾ x 12in (24.5 x 30.5cm)
£50–60 *MBA*

British School (19thC)
The Aerial Steam Carriage
Steel engraving
5½ x 7½in (13.5 x 18.5cm)
£60–80 *LF*

British School (19thC)
Girl at Fireside, and 2 others
Coloured prints
13½ x 9½in (34 x 23.5cm)
£35–40 *LF*

British School (19thC)
Monkey and Cat
A pair, steel engravings
12 x 15½in (30.5 x 39cm)
£100–125 *LF*

D. G. Cooper
British (19th/20thC)
Watercolour and drawing
Eastern Youth
10 x 12in (25 x 30.5cm)
£15–30 *LF*

Berenice Fairfax
British (19thC)
Landscape with Church and Canal
Signed and dated '1890', oil on panel
11 x 7in (28 x 17.5cm)
£15–30 *LF*

S. Holden
British (19thC)
Cymbidium Giganteum
Hand coloured lithograph for
Paxton's *Magazine of Botany*, 1846
9 x 6in (22.5 x 15cm)
£35–40 *SRAB*

European School (19thC)
Rome
Watercolour
11½ x 14in (29 x 35.5cm)
£25–40 *LF*

Irish School (19thC)
Pilot Boat Beating up to a Sloop of War
Pencil drawing
4 x 6in (10 x 15cm)
£30–40 *STA*

Diane C. Parkinson
Irish (19thC)
Landscape with Cottage
Watercolour, c1870
4½ x 7½in (11 x 18.5cm)
£25–30 *STA*

Dorothy Black
British (b1963)
Redhead
Lithograph, 1990
38½ x 29in (97 x 74cm)
£95–110 *GPS*

Sir Samuel Rush (Publisher)
British (early 19thC)
Charles the Seventh, the King
of France, and Joan of Arc,
Maid of Orleans
Hand coloured aquatint
heightened with gold, 1824
12½ x 9½in (31.5 x 23.5cm)
£8–10 *SRAB*

Miller's is a price GUIDE
not a price LIST

Elise Allan
Scottish (b1957)
The Perilous Dream Lover
Silkscreen on paper, 1989
43½ x 30½in (110 x 77cm)
£95–105 *GPS*

Mick Cawston
British (20thC)
Greyhound
Signed and numbered, print
11¼ x 15½in (29 x 39cm)
£25–35 *SMi*

Roy Cross
British (20thC)
A Nord - Noratlas
Signed, gouache
10¼ x 13in (26 x 33cm)
£40–60 *P*

British School (20thC)
Hunting Scene
Signed with monogram 'TH', watercolour
10¾ x 12in (27 x 30.5cm)
£58–68 *MBA*

J. M. Elliott
British (20thC)
Crowther's
Signed, watercolour and gouache
9½ x 7½in (23.5 x 18.5cm)
£48–58 *MBA*

M. Gauss Keown
British (20thC)
Nude
Charcoal
33 x 23in (84 x 59cm)
£85–95 *MGK*

Jenny Webb
British (20thC)
Wye College Garden
Pastel
12 x 10in (30.5 x 25cm)
£35–40 *LS*

Harold Speed
British (1872–1957)
The Actress, Lilian Braithwaite
Signed, oil on canvas
25 x 20in (63.5 x 50.5cm)
£100–150 *PCh*

Roger Harris
British (20thC)
Tree of Life
Signed, mezzotint
11 x 6in (28 x 15cm)
£68–78 *TFA*

Annette Johnson
British (20thC)
Jo's Pot
Etching
11½ x 10in (29.5 x 25cm)
£75–85 *CCA*

Hugh Taylor
British (b1958)
The Open Champions, 1860–86
A set of 12 prints, dated '1992–93'
16½ x 11¾in (42 x 30cm) each
£25–30 each *JGA*

BIBLIOGRAPHY

Ades, Dawn; Dalí and Surrealism, New York, 1982.

Archibald, E.H.H.; Dictionary of Sea Painters, Antique Collectors' Club, 1980.

Arts Council of Great Britain; British Sporting Painting, 1650–1850, 1974.

Arts Council of Great Britain; The Modern Spirit: American Painting 1908–1935, 1977.

Baron, Wendy; The Camden Town Group, Scholar Press, 1979.

Baudelaire, Charles; Art in Paris 1845–1862, Phaidon, Oxford, 1981.

Beetles, Chris, Ltd; The Illustrators, London, 1992.

Benezit, E.; Dictionnaire des Peintres, Sculpteurs, Dessinateurs et Graveurs – 10 vols. Paris, 1976.

Bernard, Denvir; The Impressionists at First Hand, Thames and Hudson, 1987.

Bryan, Michael; Dictionary of Painters and Engravers – 2 vols. George Bell & Sons, 1889.

Clifton, Claire; The Art of Food, Windward, 1988.

Crofton, Ian; A Dictionary of Art Quotations, Routledge, 1988.

de Goncourt, Edmond and Jules; French Eighteenth Century Painters, Phaidon, Oxford, 1981.

Farmer, David Hugh; The Oxford Dictionary of Saints, Oxford University Press, 1987.

Griego, Allen J.; The Meal, Scala Books, 1992.

Hall, Donald; and Corrington Wykes, Pat; Anecdotes of Modern Art, Oxford University Press, 1990.

Hall, James; Dictionary of Subjects and Symbols in Art, John Murray, 1979.

Hardie, Martin; Watercolour Painting in Britain, B.T. Batsford Ltd, 3 vols. 1966/67/68.

Heller, Nancy G.; Women Artists, An Illustrated History, Virago, 1987.

Hemming, Charles; British Painters of the Coast and Sea, Victor Gollancz Ltd, 1988.

Hibbert, Christopher; The English Social History 1066–1945, Paladin Books, London, 1988.

Hinde, Thomas; Courtiers, Victor Gollancz, London, 1986.

Holdsworth, Sarah; and Crossley, Joan; Innocence and Experience, Images of Children in British Art from 1600 to the Present, Manchester City Art Galleries, 1992.

Hook, Philip and Poltimore, Mark; Popular 19th Century Painting, Antique Collectors' Club, 1986.

Lucie-Smith, Edward; Faber Book of Art Anecdotes, 1992.

Lucie-Smith, Edward; The Thames and Hudson Dictionary of Art Terms, 1988.

Maas, Jeremy; Victorian Painters, Barrie & Jenkins, 1988.

Mackenzie, Ian; British Prints, Antique Collectors' Club, 1987.

Mallalieu, H.L.; Understanding Watercolours, Antique Collectors' Club, 1985.

Mallalieu, H.L.; British Watercolour Artists up to 1920, Antique Collectors' Club, 1976.

Mallalieu, Huon; How to Buy Pictures, Phaidon-Christie's, 1984.

Mallalieu, Huon; The Popular Antiques Yearbook, Phaidon-Christie's, 3 vols. 1985/87/88.

Marsh, Madeleine; Art Detective, Pelham Books, 1993.

Meyer, Franz; Marc Chagall, New York, 1963.

Mitchell, Sally; The Dictionary of British Equestrian Artists, Antique Collectors' Club, 1985.

Osborne, Harold; The Oxford Companion to Twentieth Century Art, Oxford University Press, 1988.

Ottley, H.; Dictionary of Recent and Living Painters and Engravers, Henry G. Bohn, 1866.

Oxford University Press; Dictionary of National Biography, 1975/81/86/90.

Payne, Andrew Clayton; Victorian Flower Gardens, Weidenfeld & Nicholson, London, 1988.

Radice, Betty; Who's Who in the Ancient World, Penguin Books, 1984.

Redgrave, Richard and Samuel; A Century of British Painters, Phaidon, Oxford, 1981.

Rosenberg, Jakob; Slive, Seymour; and ter Kuile, E. H.; Dutch Art and Architecture 1600–1800, Penguin Books, 1982.

Rothenstein, John; Modern English Painters, Macdonald, 1984.

Spalding, Frances; 20th Century Painters and Sculptors, Antique Collectors' Club, 1990.

Strong, Roy; The British Portrait 1660–1960, Antique Collectors' Club, 1990.

Waterhouse, Ellis; Painting in Britain 1530–1790, Penguin Books, 1978.

Waterhouse, Ellis; The Dictionary of 16th and 17th Century British Painters, Antique Collectors' Club, 1988.

Waterhouse, Ellis; The Dictionary of British 18th Century Painters, Antique Collectors' Club, 1981.

Wilton, Andrew; The Swagger Portrait, Tate Gallery, 1992.

Wood, Christopher; The Dictionary of Victorian Painters, Antique Collectors' Club, 1978.

GENERAL CATALOGUING TERMS

For every picture, *Miller's Picture Price Guide* has followed the basic description provided by the auction house or dealer. As all the auction houses stress in their catalogues, while full care is taken to ensure that any statement as to attribution, origin, date, age, provenance and condition is reliable and accurate, all such statements are opinion only and not to be taken as fact. The conventional cataloguing system used by the auction houses has been maintained.

A work catalogued with the name(s) of an artist, without any qualification, is in their opinion, a work by the artist.
The following meanings are also used:
'Attributed to...' In their opinion probably a work by the artist, but less certainly than in the preceding category.
'Studio of...' 'Workshop of...' In their opinion a work by an unknown hand in the studio of the artist which may or may not have been executed under the artist's direction.
'Circle of...' In their opinion a work by an as yet unidentified but distinct hand, closely associated with the named artist, but not necessarily his pupil.

'Follower of...' 'Style of...' In their opinion a work by a painter working in the artist's style, contemporary or nearly contemporary, but not necessarily his pupil.
'Manner of...' In their opinion, a work in the artist's style, but of a later date.
'After...' In their opinion, a copy of a known work by the artist.
'Signed...'/ 'Dated...'/ 'Inscribed...' In their opinion signature/date/inscription are from the hand of the artist.
'Bears signature, date, or inscription...' In their opinion, signature/date/description have been added by another hand.
Measurements: Dimensions are given height before width.

SELECT GLOSSARY

Acrylic: A synthetic emulsion paint.
Airbrush: A small mechanical paint sprayer permitting fine control and a smooth finish, and similar in appearance to a fountain pen.
Allegory: A work of art conveying an abstract subject, under the guise of another subject.
Aquatint: Etching technique in which a metal plate is sprinkled with resin and then bathed in acid which bites into any uncovered areas. According to the amount of acid used and the density of the particles, darker or lighter shading is obtained.
Bistre: A brown pigment made from charred wood, often used as a wash on pen and ink drawings.
Bodycolour: Opaque pigment.
Cartoon: A full size early design for a painting.
Casein: Protein of milk, the basis of cheese.
Collage: A work of art in which pieces of paper, photographs and other materials are pasted to the surface of the picture.
Conversation piece: A group portrait with the sitters placed informally as in conversation.
Drawing: Representation with line.
Dry-point: The process of making a print by engraving directly on to a copper plate with a steel or diamond point.
Edition: The run of a print published at any one time.
Engraving: The process of cutting a design into a hard surface (metal or wood) so that the lines will retain the ink.
Etching: A technique of print making developed in the 16thC, in which a metal plate is covered with an acid-resistant substance and the design scratched on it with a needle revealing the metal beneath. The plate is then immersed in acid, which bites into the lines, which will hold the ink.
Fête Champêtre: A rustic festival or peasant celebration – also known as a Kermesse in Dutch and Flemish works.
Fête Galante: Ladies and gentlemen at play, often in a parkland setting.
Fresco: Painting in watercolour laid on a wall or ceiling before plaster is dry.
Genre: Art showing scenes from daily life.
Gouache: Opaque watercolour paint.
Grisaille: Painting in grey or greyish monochrome.
Gum arabic: Gum from acacia trees, used in the manufacture of ink.
Icon: A religious painting on panel usually by a Greek or Russian Orthodox artist, its subject and representation conforming to established traditions.
Impression: An individual copy of a print or engraving.
Lithograph: A print made by drawing with a wax crayon on a porous prepared stone which is then soaked in water. A grease-based ink is applied to the stone which adheres only to the design. Dampened paper is applied to the the the stone and is rubbed over with a special press to produce the print.
Medium: The materials used in a painting, i.e. oil, tempera, watercolour, etc.
Mezzotint: The reverse of the usual printing process - the artist begins with a black ground, a metal plate that is completely roughened, and the design is polished or burnished into it, thus the image remains white while the background takes all the ink.

Mixed Media: Art combining different types of material.

Oil: Pigment bound with oil.

Panel Painting: Painting on wood.

Pastel: A dry pigment bound with gum into stick-form and used for drawing.

Pendant: One of a pair of pictures.

Plein-air: A landscape painted outdoors and on the spot.

Plate: The piece of metal etched or engraved with the design used to produce prints.

Print: An image which exists in multiple copies, taken from an engraved plate, woodblock, etc.

Provenance: The record of previous owners and locations of a work of art.

Recto: The front of a picture.

Sanguine: Red chalk containing ferric oxide used in drawing.

Silkscreen: A print-making process using a finely meshed screen, often of silk, and stencils to apply the image to paper.

State: A term applied to prints – to the different stages at which the artist has corrected or changed a plate – and the prints produced from these various 'states', which are numbered first state, second state, third state, etc.

Still Life: A composition of inanimate objects.

Tempera: A medium for pigment mostly made up of egg yolk and water, commonly used before the invention of oil painting.

Tondo: A circular painting.

Topographical painting: A landscape in which the predominant concern is geographical accuracy rather than imaginative content.

Triptych: A set of three pictures, usually in oils, with hinges allowing the outer panels to be folded over the central one – often used as an altarpiece.

Vanitas: An elaborate still life including various elements such as a skull, symbolising the transcience of earthly life.

Verso: The back of a picture.

Wash: A thin transparent tint applied over the surface of a work.

Watercolour: Transparent, water soluble paint, usually applied on paper.

Woodcut: Print made from a design cut into a block of wood.

DIRECTORY OF SPECIALISTS

If you wish to be included in next year's directory or if you have a change of address or telephone number, please advise Miller's Advertising Department by July 1st 1995. Entries will be repeated in subsequent editions unless we are requested otherwise. Finally we would advise readers to make contact by telephone before a visit, therefore avoiding a wasted journey, which is both time consuming and expensive.

GALLERIES

London

Abbey Mills Gallery,
Merton Abbey Mills,
Riverside Craft Village,
Meranton Way, SW19
Tel: 0181 542 5035

Ackerman & Johnson Ltd,
Lowndes Lodge Gallery,
27 Lowndes Street, SW1
Tel: 0171 235 6464

L'Acquaforte,
49a Ledbury Road, W11
Tel: 0171 221 3388

Alberti Gallery,
114 Albert Street,
Camden Town, NW1
Tel: 0171 629 1052

Alpine Gallery,
74 South Audley Street, W1
Tel: 0171 491 2948

Alton Gallery,
72 Church Road,
Barnes, SW13
Tel: 0181 748 0606

Michael Appleby,
7 St James's Chambers,
2-10 Ryder Street, SW1
Tel: 0171 839 7635

Argile Gallery,
7 Blenheim Crescent, W11
Tel: 0171 792 0888

Art Collection,
3-5 Elyston Street, SW3
Tel: 0171 584 4664

Art of Africa,
158 Walton Street, SW3
Tel: 0171 584 2326

Art Space Gallery,
84 St. Peter's Street, N1
Tel: 0171-359 7002

Bankside Gallery,
48 Hopton Street, SE1
Tel: 0171 928 7521

Stephen Bartley Gallery,
62 Old Church Street, SW3
Tel: 0171 352 8686

Baumkotter Gallery,
63a Kensington Church
Street, W8
Tel: 071 937 5171

Beardsmore Gallery,
22-24 Prince of Wales Road,
Kentish Town, NW5
Tel: 0171 485 0923

Chris Beetles Ltd,
10 Ryder Street,
St James's, SW1
Tel: 0171 839 7551

Blason Gallery,
351 Kennington Lane, SE11
Tel: 0171 735 5280

Blond Fine Art,
Unit 10, Canalside Studios,
2-4 Orsman Road, N1
Tel: 0171 739 4383

John Bonham & Murray
Feely,
46 Porchester Road, W2
Tel: 0171 221 7208

Anna Bornholt Gallery,
3-5 Weighhouse Street, W1
Tel: 0171 499 6114

Boundary Gallery,
98 Boundary Road, NW8
Tel: 0171 624 1126

Browse & Darby Gallery,
19 Cork Street, W1
Tel: 0171 734 7984

Bruton Street Gallery,
28 Bruton Street, W1
Tel: 0171 499 9747

Burlington Paintings,
12 Burlington Gardens, W1
Tel: 0171 734 9984

Cadogan Contemporary,
108 Draycott Avenue, SW3
Tel: 0171 581 5451

Caelt Gallery,
182 Westbourne Grove,
W11
Tel: 0171 229 9309

Duncan Campbell Fine Art,
15 Thackeray Street, W8
Tel: 0171 937 8665

Lucy B. Campbell Gallery,
123 Kensington Church
Street, W8
Tel: 0171 727 2205

Catto Animation,
41 Heath Street, NW3
Tel: 0171 431 2892

Catto Gallery,
100 Heath Street, NW3
Tel: 0171 435 6660

Century Gallery,
Westley Richards & Sons,
100/102 Fulham Road,
Chelsea,SW3
Tel: 0171 581 1589

Anna-Mei Chadwick,
64 New King's Road,
Parsons Green, SW6
Tel: 0171 736 1928

Churzee Studio Gallery,
17 Bellevue Road,
Wandsworth Common,SW17
Tel: 0181 767 8113

Connaught Brown Gallery,
2 Albemarle Street, W1
Tel: 0171 408 0362

Cooling Gallery,
2-4 Cork Street, W1
Tel: 0171 409 3500

Cooper Fine Arts Ltd,
768 Fulham Road, SW6
Tel: 0171 731 3421

Cox & Co,
37 Duke Street,
St. James's, SW1
Tel: 0171 930 1987

Crane Kalman Gallery
178 Brompton Road
London SW3
Tel: 0171 584 7566

Curwen Gallery,
4 Windmill Street, W1
Tel: 0171 636 1459

Charles Daggett Gallery
28 Beauchamp Place, SW3
Tel: 0171 584 2969

Sara Davenport Gallery
206 Walton Street, SW3
Tel: 0171 225 2224

John Denham Gallery,
50 Mill Lane.
West Hampstead, NW6
Tel: 0171 794 2635

Colin Denny Ltd,
18 Cale Street, SW3
Tel: 0171 584 0240

Vanessa Devereux Gallery,
11 Blenheim Crescent, W11
Tel: 0171 221 6836

Sebastian D'Orsai Ltd,
39 Theobalds Road, WC1
Tel: 0171 609 1275

Dover Street Gallery,
13 Dover Street, W1
Tel: 0171 409 1540

William Drummond
8 St James Chambers,
Ryder St, SW1
Tel: 0171 930 9696

Durini Gallery,
150 Walton Street, SW3
Tel: 0171 581 1237

Eagle Gallery,
159 Farringdon Road, EC1
Tel: 0171 833 2674

Ealing Gallery,
78 St Mary's Road,
Ealing, W5
Tel: 0181 840 7883

East West,
8 Blenheim Crescent, W11
Tel: 0171 229 7981

Eaton Gallery,
34 Duke Street,
St James's SW1
Tel: 0171 930 5950

Entwistle Gallery,
37 Old Bond Street, W1
Tel: 0171 409 3484

Fleur de Lys Gallery,
227a Westbourne Grove,
W11
Tel: 0171 727 8595

The Florence Trust,
St Saviour's Church,
Aberdeen Park,
Highbury, N5
Tel: 0171 354 0460

Flowers East,
199 Richmond Road, E8
Tel: 0181 985 3333

Frith Street Gallery,
60 Frith Street, W1
Tel: 0171 494 1550

Gagliardi Design &
Contemporary Art,
507-509 Kings Road, SW10.
Tel: 0171 352 3663

Gallery K,
101-103 Heath Street,
Hampstead, NW3
Tel: 0171 794 4949

Gallery Kaleidoscope
64/66 Willesden Lane
NW6 7SX
Tel: 0171 328 5833

The Gallery on Church
Street,
12 Church Street, NW8
Tel: 0171 723 3389

Jill George Gallery,
38 Lexington Street, W1
Tel: 0171 439 7343

Martyn Gregory Gallery,
34 Bury Street, St James's,
SW1
Tel: 0171 839 3731

Grosvenor Gallery,
18 Albemarle Street, W1
Tel: 0171 629 0891

Grosvenor Prints,
28/32 Shelton Street,
Covent Garden, WC2
Tel: 0171 836 1979

Gruzelier Modern &
Contemporary Art,
16 Maclise Road,
West Kensington, W14
Tel: 0171 603 4540

Laurence Hallett
Tel: 0171 798 8977

Hamilton Fine Arts,
186 Willifield Way,
Hampstead, NW11
Tel: 0181 455 7410

Hardware Gallery,
277 Hornsey Road,
Islington, N7
Tel: 0171 272 9651

Marina Henderson Gallery,
11 Langton Street, SW10
Tel: 0171 352 1667

Hicks Gallery,
2 & 4 Leopold Road,
Wimbledon, SW19
Tel: 0181 944 7171

Hildegard Fritz-Denneville
Fine Arts Ltd,
31 New Bond Street, W1
Tel: 0171 629 2466

Holland Gallery,
129 Portland Road, W11
Tel: 0171 727 7198

Holland & Holland Gallery,
31 Bruton Street, W1
Tel: 0171 499 9383

Dennis Hotz Fine Art Ltd,
9 Cork Street, W1
Tel: 0171 287 8324

Houldsworth Fine Art,
4-6 Bassett Road, W10
Tel: 0181 969 8197

Hyde Park Gallery,
16 Craven Terrace, W2
Tel: 0171 402 2904

Malcolm Innes Gallery,
172 Walton Street, SW3
Tel: 0171 584 0575/5559

JPL Fine Arts,
26 Davies Street, W1
Tel: 0171 493 2630

Gillian Jason Gallery,
42 Inverness Street, NW1
Tel: 0171 267 4835

Annely Juda Fine Art,
23 Dering Street, W1
Tel: 0171 629 7578

King Street Galleries,
17 King Street,
St James's, SW1
Tel: 0171 930 3993

Essex

Pearlita Frames Ltd,
30 North Street,
Romford
Tel: 01708 760342

Gloucestershire

Cleeve Picture Framing,
Coach House Workshops,
Stoke Road,
Bishops Cleve,
Cheltenham
Tel: 01242 672785

Surrey

Boathouse Gallery,
The Towpath, Manor Road,
Walton-on-Thames
Tel: 01932 242718

Limpsfield Watercolours,
High Street,
Limpsfield
Tel: 01883 717010

Scotland

Inverbeg Galleries,
Nr Luss, Loch Lomond
Tel: 01436 86277

LIGHTING

London

Chatsworth Commercial
Lighting,
6 Highbury Corner, N5
Tel: 0171 609 9829

Kent

St John A. Burch,
Myrtle House,
Headcorn Road,
Grafty Green
Tel: 01622 850381

Surrey

Acorn Lighting Products,
21a Kings Road, Shalford,
Guildford
Tel: 01483 64180

INSURANCE

London

Burke Fine Art &
Jewellery Ltd,
136 Sloan Street, SW1
Tel: 0171 824 8224

Crowley Colosso Ltd,
Ibex House, Minories, EC3
Tel: 0171 782 9782

Miller Art Insurance,
Dawson House,
5 Jewry Street, EC3
Tel: 0171 488 2345

J. H. Minet,
Minet House,
100 Leman Street, E1
Tel: 0171 481 0707

Dorset

Gibbs Hartley Cooper,
Beech House,
28-30 Wimborne Road, Poole
Tel: 01202 660866

Oxfordshire

Penrose Forbes,
29-30 Horsefair, Banbury
Tel: 01295 259892

West Sussex

Bain Clarkson Ltd,
Harlands Road,
Haywards Heath
Tel: 01444 414141

ART CONSULTANTS

London

Art Image,
1/5 The Garden Market,
Chelsea Harbour, SW10
Tel: 0171 352 8181

Arts Direction,
60 Albert Court,
Prince Consort Road,
Knightsbridge, SW7
Tel: 0171 823 8800

PHOTOGRAPHERS

London

Prudence Cuming
Associates Ltd,
28/29 Dover Street, W1
Tel: 0171 629 6430

Flashlight,
Unit 15, 7 Chalcot Road,
London NW1
Tel: 0171 586 4024

PICTURE PLAQUES

London

A C Cooper Ltd,
10 Pollen St, W1
Tel: 0171 629 7585

Picture Plaques,
142 Lambton Road, SW20
Tel: 0181 879 7841

Somerset

Berkeley Studio,
The Old Vicarage,
Castle Cary
Tel: 01963 50748

SHIPPERS

London

Featherston Shipping,
24 Hampton House,
15-17 Ingate Place, SW8
Tel: 0171 720 0422

Hedleys Humpers Ltd,
Units 3 & 4,
97 Victoria Road, NW10
Tel: 0181 965 8733

Middlesex

Burlington Fine Art &
Specialised Forwarding,
Vulcan International
Services Group,
Unit 8, Ascot Road,
Clockhouse Lane, Feltham
Tel: 01784 244152

GLASS

London

Rankins (Glass) Company,
The London Glass Centre,
24-34 Pearson Street,
London E2
Tel: 0171 729 4200

SECURITY

London

Ambassador Security
Group plc,
4 Blake House,
Admirals Way,
Docklands, E14
Tel: 0171 538 1327

Simba Security Systems
Ltd, Security House,
Occupation Road,
Walworth, SE17
Tel: 0171 703 0485

SERVICES

London

The Antiques Trade
Gazette,
Metropress Ltd,
17 Whitcomb Street,
London WC2
Tel: 0171 930 7195

Art Loss Register,
The Hogg Group,
1 Portsoken Street,
London E1
Tel: 0171 480 4000

Devon

Trace Magazine,
Trace Publications Ltd,
163 Citadel Road,
The Hoe Plymouth
Tel: 01572 228 727

AUCTIONEERS

628

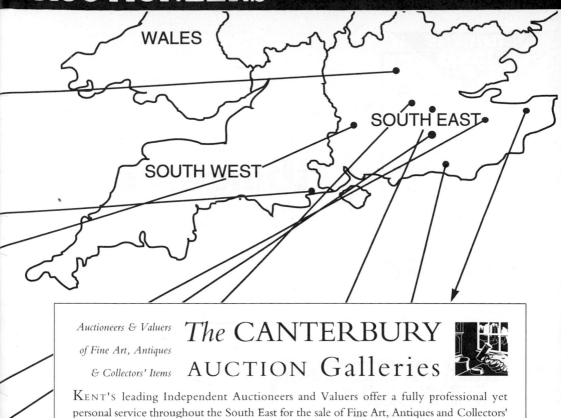

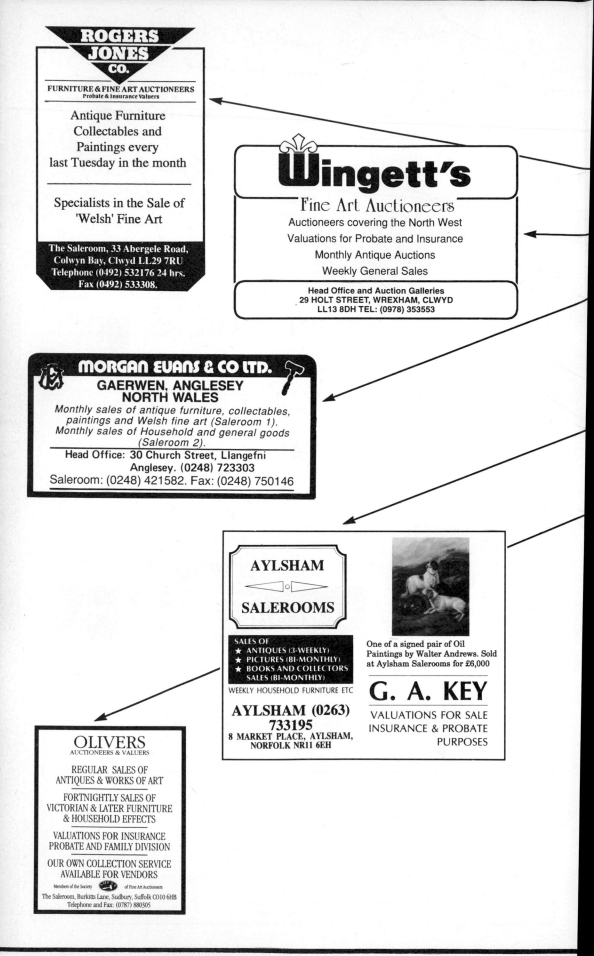

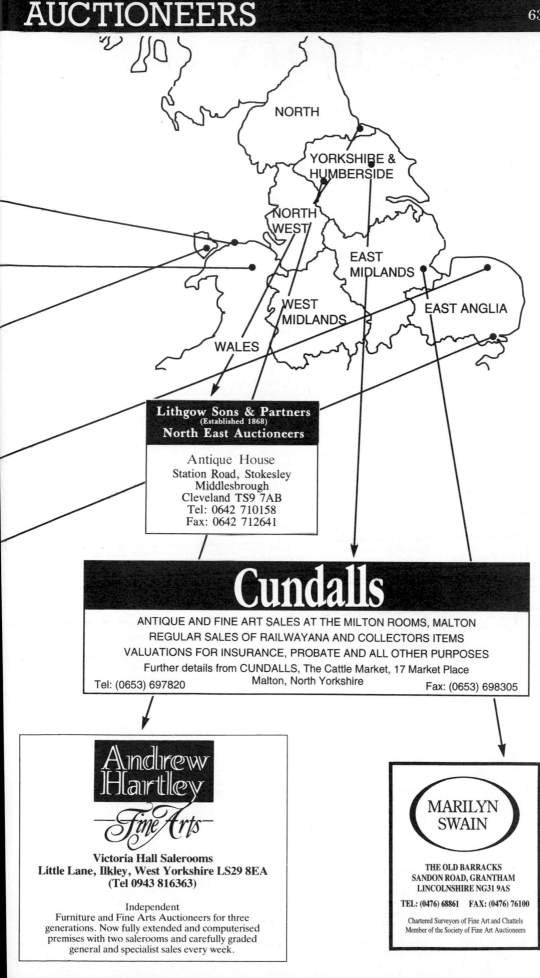

NORTH

YORKSHIRE &
HUMBERSIDE

NORTH
WEST

EAST
MIDLANDS

WEST
MIDLANDS

WALES

EAST ANGLIA

Lithgow Sons & Partners
(Established 1868)
North East Auctioneers

Antique House
Station Road, Stokesley
Middlesbrough
Cleveland TS9 7AB
Tel: 0642 710158
Fax: 0642 712641

Cundalls

ANTIQUE AND FINE ART SALES AT THE MILTON ROOMS, MALTON
REGULAR SALES OF RAILWAYANA AND COLLECTORS ITEMS
VALUATIONS FOR INSURANCE, PROBATE AND ALL OTHER PURPOSES
Further details from CUNDALLS, The Cattle Market, 17 Market Place
Malton, North Yorkshire

Tel: (0653) 697820

Fax: (0653) 698305

Andrew Hartley
Fine Arts

Victoria Hall Salerooms
Little Lane, Ilkley, West Yorkshire LS29 8EA
(Tel 0943 816363)

Independent
Furniture and Fine Arts Auctioneers for three
generations. Now fully extended and computerised
premises with two salerooms and carefully graded
general and specialist sales every week.

MARILYN SWAIN

THE OLD BARRACKS
SANDON ROAD, GRANTHAM
LINCOLNSHIRE NG31 9AS

TEL: (0476) 68861   FAX: (0476) 76100

Chartered Surveyors of Fine Art and Chattels
Member of the Society of Fine Art Auctioneers

INDEX

INDEX TO ADVERTISERS

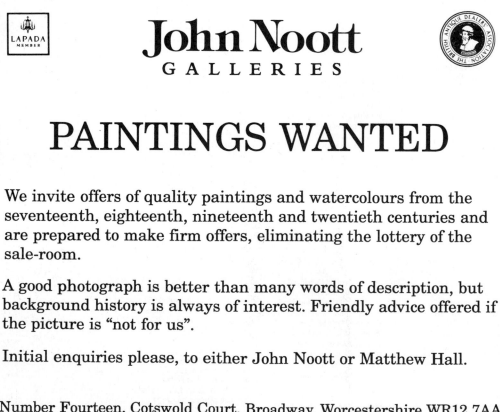

28th September - 2nd October 1994

The Business Design Centre
Islington Green, London

OVER ONE HUNDRED LEADING DEALERS DISPLAYING AN OUTSTANDING RANGE OF HIGH QUALITY ANTIQUES & FINE ART IN THE SUPERB SETTING OF LONDONS MOST EXCITING EXHIBITION CENTRE.

Including 'Antiques for Interiors' a designed presentation by selected exhibitors of period antiques within magnificent room sets.

All exhibits Vetted & Datelined

For more information please contact
Sarah Marris on 071-359 3535